ARCTIC OCEAN

Greenland Sea

Norwegian
Sea

ICELAND

SVALBARD
(NORWAY)

RUSSIA

Sea
of
Okhotsk

SWEDEN
FINLAND

Gulf of Bothnia

NORTHERN
IRELAND (UK)

North
Sea

NORWAY

ESTONIA
LATVIA
LITHUANIA

Baltic Sea

DENMARK

Sea of
Japan

UNITED
KINGDOM

BELARUS

IRELAND

NETH.

GERMANY

POLAND

BELGIUM

LUX.

CZECH REP.

English Channel

Bay of
Biscay

FRANCE

SWITZ.

AUSTRIA

SLOVAKIA

SLOVENIA

HUNGARY

CROATIA

BOS. &
HER.

ITALY

SERB.

MONT.

ROMANIA

MOLDOVA

UKRAINE

KAZAKHSTAN

MONGOLIA

NORTH
KOREA

Sea
of
Japan

East
China
Sea

SOUTH
KOREA

JAPAN

KOSOVO

MAC.

ALBANIA

BULGARIA

Black Sea

GEORGIA
ARMENIA

AZERBAIJAN

Caspian Sea

UZBEKISTAN

KYRGYZSTAN

TAJIKISTAN

CHINA

PORTUGAL

SPAIN

GREECE

TURKEY

TURKMENISTAN

KASHMIR
(INDIA)

TAIWAN

MADEIRA (PORT)

CYPRUS (T)
CYPRUS (G)

Mediterranean
Sea

TUNISIA

SYRIA

LEBANON
ISRAEL

IRAQ

IRAN

AFGHANISTAN

CANARY ISLANDS
(SP)

MOROCCO

JORDAN

PAKISTAN

NORTHERN
MARIANAS
(US)

WESTERN
SAHARA
(MOR)

ALGERIA

LIBYA

EGYPT

KUWAIT

SAUDI
ARABIA

Persian Gulf

NEPAL

BHUTAN

GUAM (US)

INDIA

BAHRAIN

U.A.E.

Gulf of Oman

BANGLADESH

MYANMAR

LAOS

MARSHALL
ISLANDS

MAURITANIA

MALI

NIGER

CHAD

QATAR

OMAN

South
China
Sea

Philippine
Sea

PHILIPPINES

SENEGAL

BURKINA
FASO

NOUTH
SUDAN

ERITREA

YEMEN

Arabian
Sea

Bay of
Bengal

THAILAND

VIETNAM

CAMBODIA

GAMBIA

GUINEA-
BISSAU

GUINEA

CÔTE
D'IVOIRE

BENIN

NIGERIA

Gulf of

Andaman Sea

MALDIVES

SRI LANKA

BRUNEI

PALAU

MICRONESIA

SIERRA
LEONE

GHANA

TOGO

CENTRAL AFRICAN
REPUBLIC

SOUTH
SUDAN

ETHIOPIA

DJIBOUTI

MALAYSIA

LIBERIA

SÃO TOMÉ
& PRÍNCIPE

CAMEROON

SINGAPORE

SEYCHELLES

INDONESIA

EQUATORIAL GUINEA

GABON

UGANDA

KENYA

Equator

PAPUA
NEW GUINEA

0°

ASCENCION (UK)

REPUBLIC
OF THE CONGO

DEMOCRATIC
REPUBLIC
OF THE CONGO

RWANDA

BURUNDI

SOMALIA

INDIAN OCEAN

COCOS
(KEELING ISLANDS)
(AUSTRALIA)

CHRISTMAS ISLAND
(AUSTRALIA)

Timor Sea

TIMOR-
LESTE

TANZANIA

Coral
Sea

ST. HELENA AND
DEPENDENCIES (UK)

ANGOLA

ZAMBIA

COMOROS

MAYOTTE
(FR)

SOUTH
ATLANTIC
OCEAN

ZIMBABWE

MALAWI

MOZAMBIQUE

MADAGASCAR

RÉUNION (FR)

MAURITIUS

AUSTRALIA

NAMIBIA

BOTSWANA

SWAZILAND

SOUTH
AFRICA

LESOTHO

Tasman
Sea

TRISTAN DA CUNHA (UK)

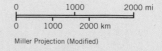

0   1000   2000 mi

0   1000   2000 km

Miller Projection (Modified)

SAGE | **50** YEARS

SAGE was founded in 1965 by Sara Miller McCune to support the dissemination of usable knowledge by publishing innovative and high-quality research and teaching content. Today, we publish more than 850 journals, including those of more than 300 learned societies, more than 800 new books per year, and a growing range of library products including archives, data, case studies, reports, and video. SAGE remains majority-owned by our founder, and after Sara's lifetime will become owned by a charitable trust that secures our continued independence.

Los Angeles | London | New Delhi | Singapore | Washington DC

U.S. FOREIGN POLICY

CQ Press, an imprint of SAGE, is the leading publisher of books, periodicals, and electronic products on American government and international affairs. CQ Press consistently ranks among the top commercial publishers in terms of quality, as evidenced by the numerous awards its products have won over the years. CQ Press owes its existence to Nelson Poynter, former publisher of the *St. Petersburg Times*, and his wife Henrietta, with whom he founded *Congressional Quarterly* in 1945. Poynter established CQ with the mission of promoting democracy through education and in 1975 founded the Modern Media Institute, renamed The Poynter Institute for Media Studies after his death. The Poynter Institute (*www.poynter.org*) is a nonprofit organization dedicated to training journalists and media leaders.

In 2008, CQ Press was acquired by SAGE, a leading international publisher of journals, books, and electronic media for academic, educational, and professional markets. Since 1965, SAGE has helped inform and educate a global community of scholars, practitioners, researchers, and students spanning a wide range of subject areas, including business, humanities, social sciences, and science, technology, and medicine. A privately owned corporation, SAGE has offices in Los Angeles, London, New Delhi, and Singapore, in addition to the Washington DC office of CQ Press.

FIFTH EDITION

U.S.

FOREIGN
POLICY

THE PARADOX OF WORLD POWER

STEVEN W. HOOK

Kent State University

Los Angeles | London | New Delhi
Singapore | Washington DC

Los Angeles | London | New Delhi
Singapore | Washington DC

FOR INFORMATION:

CQ Press
An Imprint of SAGE Publications, Inc.
2455 Teller Road
Thousand Oaks, California 91320
E-mail: order@sagepub.com

SAGE Publications Ltd.
1 Oliver's Yard
55 City Road
London EC1Y 1SP
United Kingdom

SAGE Publications India Pvt. Ltd.
B 1/I 1 Mohan Cooperative Industrial Area
Mathura Road, New Delhi 110 044
India

SAGE Publications Asia-Pacific Pte. Ltd.
3 Church Street
#10-04 Samsung Hub
Singapore 049483

Acquisitions Editor: Sarah Calabi
Developmental Editor: Nancy Matuszak
eLearning Editor: Allison Hughes
Editorial Assistant: Raquel Christie
Production Editor: Libby Larson
Copy Editor: Diane DiMura
Typesetter: C&M Digitals (P) Ltd.
Proofreader: Scott Oney
Indexer: Karen Wiley
Cover Designer: Gail Buschman
Marketing Manager: Amy Whitaker

Printed in the United States of America

Library of Congress Cataloging-in-Publication Data

Names: Hook, Steven W., 1959- author.
Title: U.S. foreign policy : the paradox of world power / Steven W. Hook, Kent State University.
Other titles: United States foreign policy

Description: Fifth edition. | Washington DC : CQ Press, 2016. | Includes bibliographical references and index.

Identifiers: LCCN 2015037801 | ISBN 978-1-5063-2158-5 (pbk. : alk. paper)

Subjects: LCSH: United States—Foreign relations. | United States—Foreign relations—21st century. | United States—Foreign relations—Decision making. | Balance of power.
Classification: LCC E183.7 .H66 2016 | DDC 327.73—dc23 LC record available at http://lccn.loc.gov/2015037801

This book is printed on acid-free paper.

SUSTAINABLE FORESTRY INITIATIVE   Certified Sourcing
www.sfiprogram.org
SFI-00993
This Label Applies to Text Stock Only

QGT 15 16 17 18 19 10 9 8 7 6 5 4 3 2 1

BRIEF CONTENTS

■ FIGURES, TABLES, MAPS, AND BOXES

■ FIGURES

■ TABLES

■ MAPS

■ BOXES

In Their Own Words

Point/Counterpoint

The United States today remains the world's preeminent world power. It is also an embattled and increasingly exhausted power, confronting both the limits of its domestic resources and its capacity to manage rapidly changing conditions overseas. How U.S. foreign policy makers respond to the many challenges facing them will dictate the course of the twenty-first century—not just for the United States but for all states and societies.

The first decade of the twenty-first century proved withering for American leaders, who endured the terrorist attacks of September 11, 2001; launched protracted wars in Afghanistan and Iraq; suffered natural and man-made catastrophes in the Gulf of Mexico; and ended the decade reeling from the worst financial crisis since the Great Depression. By the time President Barack Obama took office in January 2009, the United States faced four crises at once: (1) a financial crisis, with banks and mortgage houses in disarray; (2) a fiscal crisis, with spiraling budget deficits and foreign debts; (3) a political crisis, with partisan gridlock at levels unseen in decades; and (4) a strategic crisis, with U.S. military capacity drained by the wars in Afghanistan and Iraq and by repeated setbacks in fighting asymmetric wars.

The Bush-Obama years also produced a credibility crisis, with many nations overseas upset over U.S. actions such as the torture of suspected terrorists; the "targeted killings" of enemies using aerial drones; and the covert surveillance of U.S. citizens and foreign leaders, including NATO allies. Under these conditions, sustaining the nation's global primacy, the centerpiece of the post–Cold War grand strategy, can no longer be assumed. In sum, the United States lost its way at the very historic moment when its self-proclaimed mission to re-create the global order in its image seemed within its reach.

These developments reveal a paradox in the U.S. experience as a world power: the very sources of strength for the United States during its steady growth—a deeply ingrained sense of national exceptionalism, the diffusion and limitations of political powers, the free rein granted to civil society, and the promotion of free markets domestically and globally—have increasingly become sources of vulnerability. The decentralized federal government, largely unchanged for more than two centuries, seems unable to manage the rapid changes taking place overseas. Meanwhile, nonstate actors such as multinational corporations, powerful ethnic and religious groups, Internet outlets such as WikiLeaks, and transnational agents of global governance, all of which are viewed as vital to American-style democracy, limit the options and actions of U.S. foreign policy makers. Thus, the United States may be considered a victim as well as a beneficiary of its own success.

This lesson is clearly evident in recent events. The near collapse of the U.S. financial system could be seen as a logical extension of the nation's laissez-faire economic system that discouraged regulation while encouraging (and rewarding) reckless speculation and lending practices. The deep recession that greeted President Obama upon his election forced him to focus on domestic recovery—an effort that overshadowed his stature as a global leader and stymied his ability to clear a new path for U.S. foreign policy. More recently, the so-called Islamic State terrorist group gained attention and recruits through the creative use of social media, a technology pioneered in the United States.

The paradox also applies to fateful decisions on war and peace. American leaders have maintained a "separate peace" with other industrialized democracies, while engaging in recurring conflicts against authoritarian regimes and failed states. As international relations theorist Michael Doyle (1983) observed more than a quarter of a century ago, "The very constitutional restraint, shared commercial interests, and international respect for individual rights that promote peace among liberal societies can exacerbate conflicts in relations between liberal and nonliberal societies" (324–325).[1] This problem is compounded by the double standards commonly adopted by U.S. leaders, who preach the gospel of democratic freedoms while tolerating repression in strategically vital countries such as Saudi Arabia and China.

Obama's second term brought a variety of new challenges to U.S. primacy. The Islamic State's occupation of large swaths of Syria and Iraq raised fundamental questions about the Mideast's future political map. Russia's 2014 seizure of the Crimean Peninsula, a region that was part of neighboring Ukraine, renewed tensions between Moscow and NATO. China's government, another aspirant for great-power status, flexed its muscles by claiming off-shore islands also claimed by other states in the South and East China Seas. Taken together, this turbulence suggests a world order out of sync. To Richard N. Haass, president of the Council on Foreign Relations, "The question is not whether the world will continue to unravel but how fast and how far."[2]

As noted earlier, the paradox outlined in this book is ultimately based on the attributes that enabled the United States to expand steadily and serve so often as a catalyst for constructive change beyond its shores. These same strengths, however, contain the seeds of possible peril and threats to U.S. primacy. How have American citizens responded to these tectonic shifts? A 2014 survey by the Chicago Council on Global Affairs found that 40 percent of Americans believed that "the U.S. should stay out of world affairs,"[3] the highest level of isolationism recorded in the council's forty-year history. As the nation muddles its way through its fractious domestic politics and growing foreign policy concerns, a central question confronts students and practitioners of foreign policy: Can America endure as the foremost world power, despite itself?

■ OBJECTIVES AND STRUCTURE OF THE BOOK

My primary objective in writing this book is to explore this paradox, identify its key sources and manifestations, and consider its future implications. Because of the sheer magnitude of U.S. military might, economic wealth, and political and cultural influence, the choices of U.S. foreign policy makers resonate in all corners of the world. Those choices, however, are made within a domestic institutional setting that is purposefully conflicted. The coherence of U.S. policy choices is impaired further by transnational civil society—including corporations, nonprofit interest groups, the news media, and global public opinion—that are integral components of the U.S. foreign policy process.

Because the contradictions and dilemmas inherent to U.S. foreign policy are woven into the nation's culture and institutional structure, they

---

1. Michael Doyle, "Kant, Liberal Legacies, and Foreign Affairs: Part 2," Philosophy and Public Affairs 12, no. 3 (1983): 324–325 (emphasis in original).

2. Richard N. Haass, "The Unraveling: How to Respond to a Disordered World," Foreign Affairs 93, no. 6 (2014). https://www .foreignaffairs.com/articles/united-states/2014-10-20/unraveling.

3. Chicago Council on Global Affairs, Foreign Policy in the New Millennium: Results of the 2012 Chicago Council Survey of American Public Opinion and U.S. Foreign Policy (Chicago: Chicago Council on Global Affairs, 2012). http://www.thechicagocouncil .org/UserFiles/File/Task%20Force%20 Reports/2012_CCS_ Report.pdf.

are unlikely to be overcome anytime soon. The stakes in the policy process for all American citizens, however, will remain enormous. If this book helps readers make sense of these cascading developments, and if the link between the process and the conduct of U.S. foreign policy can be more fully grasped, then the book will have achieved its main purpose.

My secondary goal for this book is to present a clear and concise, yet comprehensive, overview of the U.S. foreign policy process to students at all levels. Instructors deserve a text that meets their pedagogical needs. Their students, meanwhile, deserve a text that is tightly organized, limited in its use of jargon, visually appealing, and even pleasurable to read. No account of U.S. foreign policy will have its intended effect if its readers are lost in translation.

To this end, the twelve chapters that follow are organized into four parts—each with three chapters and each of roughly equal length—that cover distinct aspects of U.S. foreign policy. Part I introduces the book's theme, reviews key historical developments and milestones, and identifies theories of foreign policy analysis that shed light on the decision-making process. This latter material, found in Chapter 3, forms the analytic core of the book. Part II examines the roles of government actors and their institutional structures. Clashes between the executive and legislative branches, which occur alongside bureaucratic rivalries, are of particular interest. In Part III, external pressures from civil society—including public opinion, the news media, and interest groups—take center stage. Finally, Part IV highlights the three primary domains of U.S. foreign policy: national security, foreign economic relations, and transnational concerns such as climate change. All the chapters have been updated thoroughly in terms of both the scholarly literature and coverage of recent developments in U.S. foreign policy. The narrative, including references and key terms, has been tightened in order to encourage more focused reading.

This analytic framework was designed to facilitate instruction in several ways. The symmetrical structure of the volume lends itself to break points and examinations at regular intervals. The boxed features—Point/Counterpoint and In Their Own Words—summarize ongoing debates and provide insightful perspectives on the policy process. The references direct readers to the vast supporting literature on U.S. foreign policy that informs research papers and subsequent study. The selected Internet references (links) that appear at the end of each chapter are another useful resource for students. Finally, a detailed glossary defines the key concepts introduced in bold type throughout the text. It is preceded by two appendixes that list U.S. administrations since World War II and presents the text of the War Powers Resolution of 1973.

This edition features new learning objectives that offer students measurable takeaways for each chapter and engages students in close, focused reading. The revisions highlight both global and domestic shifts in the balance of power that affect U.S. foreign policy. Globally, this edition addresses topics such as rapid developments in the global economy, the revival of great-power rivalry, and ongoing political violence in the Middle East. Domestic coverage includes trends in the U.S. economy, political polarization, domestic intelligence, and the effects of social media as a primary venue for news and opinion. Throughout, the fifth edition continues to ask the most pressing question of whether U.S. foreign policy makers can manage these dynamics in a manner that preserves U.S. values at home and primacy abroad.

■ ANCILLARIES

http://edge.sagepub.com/hook5e

SAGE edge offers a robust online environment featuring an impressive array of tools and resources for review, study, and further exploration, keeping both instructors and students on the cutting edge of teaching and learning. SAGE edge content is open access and available on demand. Learning and teaching has never been easier!

SAGE edge for Students provides a personalized approach to help students accomplish their coursework goals in an easy-to-use learning environment.

- Mobile-friendly eFlashcards strengthen understanding of key terms and concepts.
- Mobile-friendly practice quizzes allow for independent assessment by students of their mastery of course material.
- A customized online action plan includes tips and feedback on progress through the course and materials, which allows students to individualize their learning experience.
- Chapter summaries with learning objectives reinforce the most important material.
- Video and meaningful web links facilitate student use of Internet resources, further exploration of topics, and responses to critical thinking questions.
- EXCLUSIVE! Access to full-text SAGE journal articles that have been carefully selected to support and expand on the concepts presented in each chapter.

SAGE edge for Instructors supports teaching by making it easy to integrate quality content and create a rich learning environment for students.

- Test banks provide a diverse range of prewritten options as well as the opportunity to edit any question and/or insert personalized questions to effectively assess students' progress and understanding.
- Sample course syllabi for semester and quarter courses provide suggested models for structuring one's course.

- Editable, chapter-specific PowerPoint® slides offer complete flexibility for creating a multimedia presentation for the course.
- Video and multimedia content is selected to appeal to students with different learning styles.
- Lecture notes summarize key concepts by chapter to ease preparation for lectures and class discussions.
- A course cartridge provides easy LMS integration.

■ ACKNOWLEDGMENTS

This fifth edition, like the first four, drew on the talents and hard work of a large supporting cast. I am grateful to the entire editorial team at CQ Press and SAGE for making this revision not only manageable but also highly enjoyable. As always, Charisse Kiino, director for the college division of CQ Press and SAGE, fully supported the project. Acquisitions editor Sarah Calabi provided early guidance, and senior development editor Nancy Matuszak kept the project and its many moving parts on schedule. Allison Hughes was instrumental in getting the book's ancillary content to the finish line. Libby Larson skillfully guided the manuscript through production, and Diane DiMura, my copy editor, made sense of my often tortured prose and called out contradictions and ambiguities. Raquel Christie also provided superb editorial support from the CQ Press offices in Washington, D.C. In Kent, Ohio, my research assistants, Eli C. Kaul and Jason Adkins, guided my literature reviews, gathered data, proofread early chapter drafts, and generally helped me "tame The Beast"—our affectionate term for this ambitious and challenging project.

Many reviewers provided much-needed criticism at various stages of the project. They include Linda Adams, Baylor University; Leslie Baker, Mississippi State University; Brian Bow, Dalhousie University; Michael G. Huelshoff, University of

New Orleans; Ivan Dinev Ivanov, University of Cincinnati; Choong-Nam Kang, Murray State University; Steven Green Livingston, Middle Tennessee State University; Peter H. Loedel, West Chester University; David Bell Mislan, American University; Seana Sugrue, Ave Maria University; and one anonymous reviewer. Their suggestions were consistently on target and very useful in guiding this revision. I am also grateful to my students, near and far, who have freely offered their comments about the text either in the classroom or via shook@kent.edu. Any deficiencies in the volume stem from my own inability to heed their collective guidance.

U.S. FOREIGN POLICY

CHAPTER 1

THE UNITED STATES IN A TURBULENT WORLD

Iraqi Army soldiers rally in June 2014 as they prepare to fight against the Islamic State of Iraq and Syria (ISIS), which had captured major cities in the country's northern region. Iraq's military, however, virtually collapsed as ISIS broadened its reign of terror across the region. This conflict quickly became a major concern of U.S. foreign policy.

AP Photo/Karim Kadim

1.1   Discuss the basic indicators of world power and where the United States stands.

1.2   Summarize four categories of challenges facing U.S. world power.

1.3   Explain how culture, institutions, and civil society create the paradox of U.S. world power.

Not long ago, the United States stood tall as the predominant world power. Its victories in the world wars, and then in the Cold War, left the nation widely respected and secure. This status has changed, however, in the face of multiple upheavals that today threaten global stability. The decisions made by the architects of U.S. foreign policy will have long-lasting consequences for all states and societies. In the words of Chuck Hagel (quoted in Graham 2014), the U.S. secretary of defense between 2013 and 2014, "I think we are living through one of those historic, defining times. . . . We are seeing a new world order—post–World War II, post-Soviet implosion—being built." Five factors drive these seismic shifts in the global security environment:

- **Escalating terrorism.** The number of reported attacks soared from 1,500 in 2004 to 13,500 in 2014 (Global Terrorism Database 2015). The majority of these terrorist attacks occurred in the Middle East, where the 2011 Arab Spring sparked civil wars and other forms of political violence. Most worrying, a new and powerful terrorist group, the Islamic State of Iraq and Syria (ISIS), laid claim to vast territories of Iraq and Syria in order to create a regional order based strictly on Islamic law. The group used public beheadings "to instill in us a state of terror" (Stern and Berger 2015, 3). Nigeria's Boko Haram, using similar tactics, forbade all Muslims to engage either politically or socially with Western society (see Chothia 2015).

- **Revival of great-power competition.** The superpower rivalry between the United States and the Soviet Union was a hallmark of the Cold War, which lasted from World War II until the Soviet collapse in 1991. In 2014, Russian president Vladimir Putin revived these tensions by seizing the Crimean Peninsula in neighboring Ukraine. China's government, meanwhile, made a similar power play when its leader, Xi Jinping, annexed off-shore islands in the East and South China Seas that were considered the sovereign territories of Vietnam, the Philippines, Japan, and other coastal states. Rather than launching full-scale wars, both potential U.S. rivals engaged in "ambiguous warfare" based on coercion and intimidation (O'Rourke 2015).

- **Threats to American hegemony.** The United States is often known as a **hegemon**, or a nation-state that exerts a sphere of influence over other states and societies.[1] This stature, however, has succumbed to widespread perceptions of national decline. According to the U.S. Intelligence Council, China is likely to surpass the United States in key categories of national strength by 2040 (see Figure 1.1). Chinese officials have created an Asian Infrastructure Investment Bank designed to rival the U.S.-based World Bank.[2] Other rising powers have taken advantage of massive U.S. foreign debts, political gridlock, and national war fatigue following its protracted conflicts in Afghanistan and Iraq.

- **Advances in military technology.** The growing density of Internet networks allowed hackers to penetrate private files, including U.S. government offices. According to the U.S. Office of Management and Budget (2014), more than 60,000 cyberattacks took place in 2014.[3] Of these attacks, which failed in most cases, more than 8,000 targeted the Defense, State, and Homeland Security departments. This new face of war was matched by Washington's growing reliance on unmanned aerial drones. Originally used for surveillance, the drones became a primary instrument for bombardments of enemy bases and suspected hideouts. Several other governments, including China and Russia, moved quickly to develop their own drone arsenals.

- **Strains in the "global commons."** Demographic and ecological trends pose long-term threats to global security. Total world population, which topped 7.3 billion in 2015, is projected to reach 11 billion by 2100 (Gao 2015). "Competition for

GET THE EDGE ON YOUR STUDIES

edge.sagepub.com/hook5e

- Take a quiz to find out what you've learned.
- Review key terms with eFlashcards.
- Watch videos that enhance chapter content.

1. Hegemony is different from colonization, which denies its subjects statehood. The sovereign governments of Latin America, for example, have been U.S. spheres of influence since the Monroe Doctrine pledged to defend the entire region against external threats early in the 1800s.

2. An informal alliance of BRICS (Brazil, Russia, India, China, and South Africa) took its own steps in marginalizing U.S. world power by creating a New Development Bank that would be funded primarily by China.

3. Aside from the cyberattacks on U.S. government sites, nearly 160,000 attacks targeted commercial enterprises and state, local, and tribal governments.

scarce resources, such as food, water, or energy, will likely increase tensions within and between states and could lead to more localized or regional conflicts" (U.S. Office of the Director of National Intelligence 2014, 5). Recent years have witnessed an unprecedented exodus of 60 million refugees who have been forced from their homes in the midst of civil unrest and political repression (Sengupta 2015). Growing dangers of global warming and climate change further threaten the global commons.

Washington's struggles in the new millennium began on September 11, 2001, when al Qaeda terrorists attacked the United States in New York City and Washington, D.C.[4] President George W. Bush responded forcefully by launching the war against Afghanistan, home base of the attackers. The U.S. overthrow of the Afghan government left the United States responsible for the nation. For American forces, this meant

Figure 1.1 ■ The World in 2030: The Global Power Index Forecast

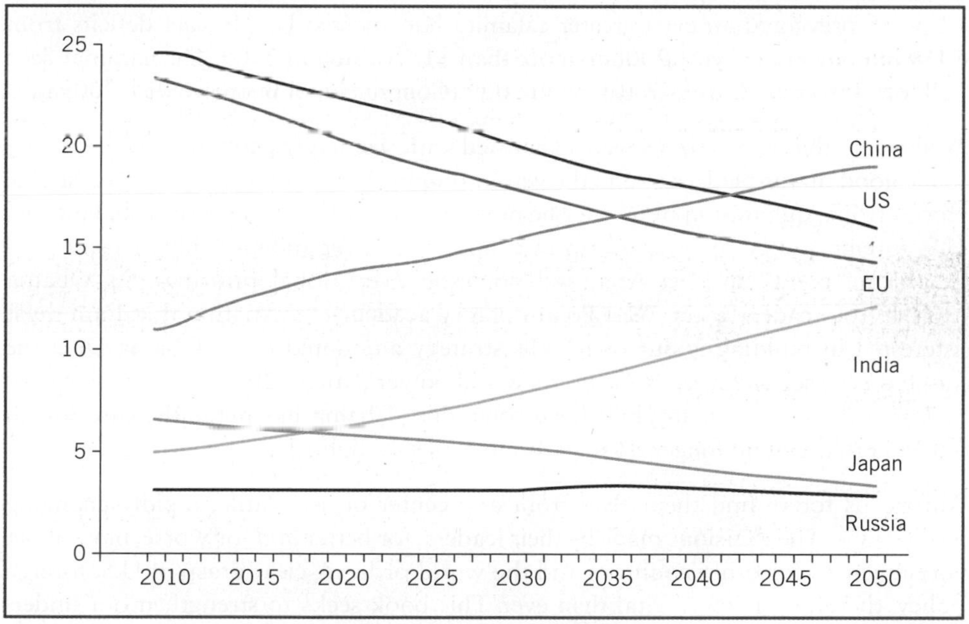

Source: National Intelligence Council, *Global Trends 2030: Alternative Worlds.* December 2012.

---

4. Al Qaeda terrorists hijacked four U.S. commercial jets and flew three of them into highly visible, well-known symbols of American power—the World Trade Center in New York City and the Pentagon near Washington, D.C. The fourth jet, apparently headed for the U.S. Capitol, crashed in rural Pennsylvania after several passengers struggled with the hijackers for control of the cockpit.

a long-term effort to destroy terrorist cells and, even more difficult, to create a stable and democratic government in a remote and tribal nation that had never had such a political system. In 2003, Bush took his "war on terror" to Iraq, whose leader, Saddam Hussein, was suspected of harboring weapons of mass destruction and collaborating with al Qaeda. The president's decision to strike first, a central element of what became known as the **Bush Doctrine**, lacked support from the UN Security Council and forced Washington to proceed with few allies. When both causes of the war proved unfounded, Bush changed the military mission to "nation building" along the lines of the Afghan effort. The combined costs of the two wars exceeded $1.6 trillion by 2014 (Belasco 2014).

Once President Barack Obama took office in January 2009, he devoted much of his energy to reviving the U.S. economy, which virtually collapsed the year before as the result of reckless lending practices by major banks and mortgage brokers. The most serious economic downfall since the Great Depression sent stock markets tumbling around the world. Both Bush and Obama responded by spending massively on bail-outs for paralyzed financial firms and on public projects to jump-start the economy. These actions, including the temporary government takeover of General Motors and Chrysler, prevented an even greater calamity but boosted U.S. budget deficits from $459 billion in fiscal year 2008 to more than $1.5 trillion in 2009. The national debt ballooned from $5.8 to $7.6 trillion in 2009 (Congressional Budget Office 2009a).

Well aware that U.S. citizens were exhausted with seemingly permanent war, Obama made good on his pledges to end the war in Iraq by 2011 and to withdraw most U.S. troops from Afghanistan by 2014. The president adopted a strategy of "rebalancing" U.S. foreign policy in several respects: diplomatic over military initiatives, a geographical "pivot" to East Asia, and domestic over global priorities. As Obama (2009a) told cadets at the West Point military academy, "the nation that I am most interested in building is our own." His strategy amounted to an **Obama Doctrine** based on the selective use of America's world power (Sanger 2012, xv): "In an age of reckonings, when so many bills have come due, Obama has made the case for an America that can no longer do it all. It must pick its fights."

Americans today find themselves front and center on a volatile, rapidly changing world stage. The decisions made by their leaders, for better *and* for worse, have direct consequences for other countries and the world order. A clear grasp of U.S. foreign policy, therefore, is more vital than ever. This book seeks to strengthen our understanding by exploring the process by which U.S. leaders, faced with unending pressures at home and overseas, devise and implement foreign policies. As we will find, the United States maintains an unprecedented degree of world power while confronting many obstacles—many of which are "made in the USA"—that make the coherent use of this power exceedingly difficult. Coming to grips with this paradox of U.S. world power is the primary task of this book.

U.S. Decline vs. Continued Primacy

Recent developments have produced widespread perceptions that the United States is a declining world power. Such fears are not unique to the current period, according to analyst Josef Joffe. During the Cold War, Americans were alarmed by a "missile gap" between the United States and the Soviet Union. The 1980s featured numerous predictions of impending U.S. demise that soon proved unfounded when the Soviet Union, Washington's rival in the Cold War, collapsed in 1991. The September 2001 terrorist attacks on the United States raised new doubts about the government's ability to protect its citizens.

To the current generation of declinists, President Obama's reluctance to deploy U.S. armed forces in regional hot spots is often attributed to national decline. Popular analysts such as Thomas L. Friedman and Michael Mandelbaum believe the nation's polarized politics have become so entrenched that solving domestic problems—and conducting foreign policy with a united front—have become impossible. Other declinists emphasize the sorry state of the U.S. government's finances, which left the United States with a national debt of $13 trillion in 2015—almost three-quarters of the U.S. gross national product. Journalist James Risen believes that war profiteering in the "war on terror" has cost billions of wasted dollars. Elbridge Colby and Paul Lettow predicted that this mounting debt "will limit U.S. competitiveness and freedom of action with a severity not remotely appreciated in today's foreign policy debates."

In contrast, U.S. foreign policy optimists believe the United States will maintain its predominance for many more years. They believe that emerging powers will continue to **bandwagon** with Washington rather than form rival alliances. As for the widely feared rise of China, Andrew J. Nathan and Andrew Scobell argue that "the main tasks of Chinese foreign policy are defensive and have not changed much since the Cold War era." To John Mueller and Mark G. Stewart, U.S. officials have exaggerated terrorist threats since the 9/11 attacks on New York City and Washington. Finally, Joseph S. Nye Jr. presented evidence that the United States still leads the world in education, technological innovation, entrepreneurship, cultural influence, and other forms of "soft power." In his view, "we are not entering a post-American world."

Sources: Thomas L. Friedman and Michael Mandelbaum. 2011. *That Used to Be Us.* New York: Farrar, Straus, and Giroux; James Risen. 2014. *Pay Any Price: Greed, Power, and Endless War.* Boston: Houghton Mifflin Harcourt; Elbridge Colby and Paul Lettow. 2014. "Have We Hit Peak America?" *Foreign Policy* 207 (July–August): 54–63; Nathan and Andrew Scobell, 2012. "How China Sees America: The Sum of Beijing's Fears," *Foreign Affairs* 91 (September–October): 32–47; John Mueller and Mark G. Stewart. 2012. "The Terrorism Delusion." *International Security* 37 (1): 81–110; Joseph S. Nye Jr. 2015. *Is the American Century Over?* Cambridge: Polity Press, 14.

■ SNAPSHOT: AMERICA'S WORLD POWER

We begin this inquiry by reviewing some basic indicators of world power. Taken together, these indicators reveal a **unipolar** balance of power in which one country—at present, the United States—maintains a predominant share of the world's economic, military, and other resources that a country needs to project power beyond its borders. This power balance differs from that of the eighteenth century, when several European states created a **multipolar** world order, and from that during most of the Cold War, which featured a **bipolar** power balance dominated by the United States and the Soviet Union.

Since the end of the Cold War, most foreign policy debates have accepted the reality of U.S. **primacy** as a starting point and focused instead on the extent, consequences, and likely future of the unipolar world power. The concentration of America's world power detailed in this section is notable given that the United States is home to less than 5 percent of the world's population. Much of the nation's advantage derives from the scale of its economy, which produced $17.4 trillion worth of goods and services in 2014, or 22 percent of the world's total output (see Figure 1.2). The value of America's gross domestic product (GDP) was nearly twice that of China—a wide gap even after Beijing had averaged growth rates of 10 percent over the previous two decades. The GDP of the United States in 2014 roughly equaled that of the European Union, whose economy has been battered by budget deficits, external debts, and the growing pains accompanying the creation of its monetary union. Russia, not so long ago the primary U.S. rival in a bipolar balance of power, recorded about one-tenth the U.S. level of economic production.

The United States holds the additional distinction of being the world's foremost trading state, exporting more than all other nations since World War II while displaying a voracious appetite for overseas goods and services. In 2014, American firms exported a record $2.35 trillion in merchandise and services (U.S. Department of Commerce 2015). The volume of U.S. imports was even larger ($2.85 trillion in 2014), leaving the U.S. economy a trade deficit of $505 billion. The nation's imports were even larger in absolute terms (more than $2.9 trillion in 2014) and as a share of world imports. The United States has also served as the world's leading source and destination of foreign direct investment in recent years. In 2014, U.S. firms spent $358 billion on foreign operations, more than one-quarter of the global total. Foreign firms, meanwhile, invested more in the United States ($64 billion) than in all other countries by mid-2014 (OECD 2014).

The degree of U.S. predominance is even greater in the military realm. The United States, the only country that has divided the world into regional military commands, also maintains "command of the commons—command of the sea, space, and air" (Posen 2003, 7). This is a major factor in an age when holding physical territory, while vital, no longer ensures national security. In 2014, the U.S. government spent about $610 billion on its military, or about one-third of the global total (see Figure 1.3).

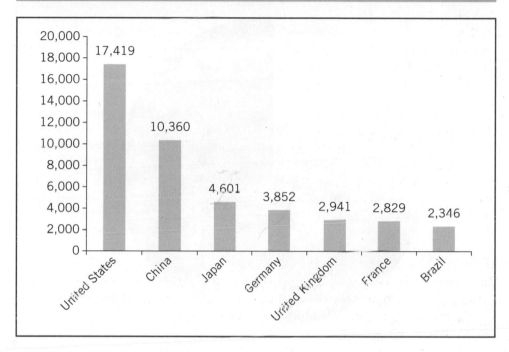

Figure 1.2 ■ World Economic Output, Seven Largest Producers by GDP, 2014

Source: World Bank, World Development Indicators, July 1, 2015, http://data.worldbank.org/.

Note: Figures are current U.S. dollars in billions.

If formal military allies of the United States are taken into account as elements of U.S. world power, the nation's military potency is even greater. The United States also provides the largest volume of weaponry to other countries. In 2014, American arms merchants exported $10 billion in weaponry, or 34 percent of all weapons sales worldwide (SIPRI Arms Transfers Database 2015). At the same time, the United States provided more than 100 foreign governments with military training and education, further solidifying its projection of world power (U.S. Department of State 2015c). All of these military programs fortify U.S. strength.

American primacy also derives from its **soft power,** the expression of its political values and cultural dynamism in ways that other societies and governments may find appealing (see Nye 2004). As noted in Chapter 2, the United States is often regarded as an "idea" rather than an ordinary nation-state, traditionally defined by physical boundaries, common ethnic or religious identities, and material interests. The soft power of the United States enhances U.S. security by highlighting shared rather than

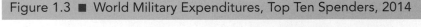
Figure 1.3 ■ World Military Expenditures, Top Ten Spenders, 2014

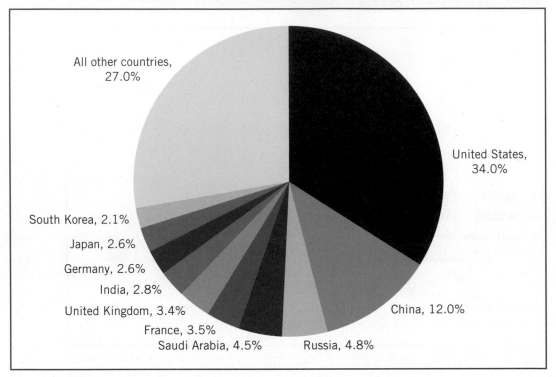

Source: Stockholm International Peace Research Institute, Military Spending and Armament, Recent trends in military expenditure, www.sipri.org/research/armaments/milex/recent-trends.

opposing interests and values. A recent study found that eight of the world's top ten universities—ideal centers for the sharing of ideas, knowledge, and culture—are located in the United States (see Table 1.1). American fashions, popular music, movies, and television programs are so pervasive overseas that they provoke charges of "cultural imperialism." These charges aside, U.S. inventors are widely credited for bringing the world personal computers, the Internet, Facebook, instant messaging, and Twitter.

Maintaining this "predominance of power" (Leffler 1992) has been a central goal of U.S. foreign policy since World War II (see Hook and Spanier 2016). The Cold War strategy of communist containment advanced this overriding goal of sustained primacy (see Chapter 2). The same motivations prompted U.S. leaders to ensure that newly created multilateral bodies—such as the United Nations (UN) and World Bank—consolidated U.S. advantages after World War II while providing tangible benefits for less powerful countries (Ikenberry 2001; Skidmore 2005).

Table 1.1 ■ Top Ten Universities in the World, 2015

Rank	University	Country
1	Harvard University	United States
2	Massachusetts Institute of Technology	United States
3	University of California–Berkeley	United States
4	Stanford University	United States
5	University of Oxford	United Kingdom
6	University of Cambridge	United Kingdom
7	California Institute of Technology	United States
8	University of California–Los Angeles	United States
9	University of Chicago	United States
10	Columbia University	United States

Source: Best Global Universities Rankings, *U.S. News & World Report*, 2015, www.usnews.com/education/best-global-universities/rankings.

Following the Cold War, the George H. W. Bush administration devised a strategy to convince "potential competitors that they need not aspire to a greater role" (Tyler 1992). To Bill Clinton, who served as president from 1993 to 2001, the United States had to remain the "indispensable nation." His successor, George W. Bush, vowed after the September 11 terrorist attacks that U.S. military forces "will be strong enough to dissuade potential adversaries from pursuing a military build-up in hopes of surpassing, or equaling, the power of the United States" (White House 2002, 30). Most recently, while recognizing the domestic limitations of America's world power, the Obama administration proclaimed that the nation "will continue to underwrite global security" (White House 2010, 1).

■ CHALLENGES TO U.S. PRIMACY

Despite its strength, the United States confronts a variety of challenges to its global primacy. Its economic and military strength may be robust on an absolute level, but the nation's power, *relative to that of many other major powers*, is eroding. As the National Intelligence Council (2012, x), an arm of the U.S. federal government, concluded,

> The U.S. most likely will remain "first among equals" among the other great powers in 2030 because of its preeminence across a range of power dimensions and legacies of its leadership role. More important than just its economic weight, the United States' dominant role in international politics has derived from its

predominance across the board in both hard and soft power. Nevertheless, with the rapid rise of other countries, the 'unipolar moment' is over and Pax Americana—the era of American ascendancy in international politics that began in 1945—is fast winding down.

The challenges facing U.S. world power can be grouped into four categories. The first relates to the experience of past great powers and the difficulties they faced in preserving their advantages. The second group of challenges stems from the U.S. government's own historical experience and past foreign policy actions, many of which violated its proclaimed moral principles and created widespread animosity toward Washington. The third set of challenges to U.S. primacy arises from the nation's close association with economic globalization, which "aggravates anti-Americanism and appears to further isolate the United States in the world" (Kohut and Stokes 2006, 143). Finally, the United States faces unfamiliar challenges from international terrorism, a threat the United States largely avoided until September 11, 2001.

Cycles in the Balance of Power

Some political analysts see a U.S.-dominated world order as advantageous not only for the United States but also for the international system as a whole. A benign hegemon maintains stability in the international system, discouraging conflicts among regional powers and covering most of the costs of military security and global economic development. Under these circumstances, less powerful states have incentives to align with the dominant power rather than challenge it by forming rival blocs. This favorable view, however, is hardly universal. Others fear the concentration of power in one country and believe that "unbalanced power, whoever wields it, is a potential danger to others" (Waltz 1997, 915). Historian Timothy Garton Ash (2002) found that "the problem with American power is not that it is American. The problem is simply the power. It would be dangerous even for an archangel to wield so much power."

A related argument identifies historical cycles in the global balance of power. Historian Paul Kennedy traced *The Rise and Fall of the Great Powers* (1987) to a pattern of **imperial overstretch** by which the Roman, Dutch, Ottoman, Spanish, British, and Russian empires bit off more than they could chew and then succumbed to uprisings in their far-flung provinces and to political infighting at home. World history has revealed the "increasing costs of dominance" that accompany global primacy (Gilpin 1981). According to **long cycle theory** (Modelski 1987), the dominant power's strength in relation to others inevitably peaks and then erodes as smaller powers benefit from the leader's technological advances, economic aid, and military protection. This cycle of hegemonic boom and bust prompts major wars and restructurings of the global power balance.

Equally ominous lessons can be drawn from the tendency of major powers to develop inflated perceptions of their capabilities and minimize the costs and risks of militarism. "Napoleon and Hitler marched to Moscow, only to be engulfed in the Russian winter," Jack Snyder (2003, 30) recalled. "Imperial Japan, facing a quagmire in China and a U.S. oil embargo, tried to break what it saw as impending encirclement by seizing the Indonesian oil fields and preemptively attacking Pearl Harbor. All sought security through expansion, and all ended in imperial collapse." Sustained American primacy, in this view, is likely to give way to a new balance of world power (Walton 2007). To journalist Fareed Zakaria (2008), this marks the third fundamental shift in world power in five centuries. The first, around 1500, featured the rise of Europe. The second shift, in the early 1900s, produced the era of U.S. primacy. Today's power shift, he concluded, could be labeled "the rise of the rest."

How Hwee Young/Getty Images

In recent years, several world leaders have sought to challenge the United States and its unprecedented world power. Most prominent among these challengers were Vladimir Putin, the president of Russia, and Chinese president Xi Jinping. These two leaders shared a desire for more influence in world politics. In their frequent meetings, they looked for ways to gain an upper hand in their relations with the United States.

The Shadow of the Past

The foreign policy record of the United States is known intimately to foreign governments, many of which have been engaged, as either allies or adversaries, in the expansion of U.S. power (see Chapter 2). This record, which features burgeoning territorial growth and trade alongside the extension of domestic political rights and a vibrant, multinational civil society, is admired widely overseas. At the same time, many past actions of U.S. foreign policy makers provoked anger and resentment that linger today and inspire anti-American social movements, hostile regimes, and potential threats to the nation's citizens or government (Sweig 2006).

Three episodes in early U.S. foreign policy—the importation of slaves before the Civil War, the wars against Native American tribes during the period of westward expansion, and frequent interventions in Latin America—revealed that for all its rhetoric about freedom and justice, the U.S. government often observed a Darwinian logic favoring survival of the fittest. Slavery has long been condemned as an ultimate denial of human rights, and the U.S. treatment of Native Americans fits the commonly accepted definition of *genocide*.[5] As for Latin America, U.S. forces seized northern Mexico in the late 1840s and then intervened more than sixty times in the Latin America–Caribbean region prior to World War II (Grimmett 2004).[6] This pattern continued during the Cold War, when U.S. leaders turned to the Central Intelligence Agency (CIA) to overthrow elected regimes in Guatemala (1954) and Chile (1973).

Elsewhere, the United States supported dictators such as Ferdinand Marcos of the Philippines and Mobutu Sese Seko of Zaire. American leaders aligned with Saddam Hussein's Iraq during its war against Iran in the 1980s even after Saddam used chemical weapons to massacre Iranian forces and ethnic minorities in his own country. These actions, including the catastrophic Vietnam War that spanned more than a decade, cast doubts on the virtues of U.S. foreign policy even as the nation fought successfully against fascism and communism in the twentieth century. During George W. Bush's **war on terror**, the morality gap appeared in the prisoner abuses by U.S. guards at Iraq's Abu Ghraib prison and in the February 2012 burning of Korans, the religious text of Islam, at an Afghan detention facility. Claims of U.S. double standards also extended to other areas, as critics questioned how the world's foremost nuclear power could demand nonproliferation elsewhere and how a primary source of greenhouse gases could call for "sustainable development" in the world's poorest regions.

The shadow of past actions not only damages U.S. credibility abroad but also has provoked direct challenges to its world power. Iran's 1979 revolution, for example, was fueled by popular antagonism toward the United States, which had propped up its despotic shah for more than twenty-five years. In this context, the theocratic regime that still rules Iran can be seen as an antagonistic response to U.S. policies, or **blowback** (C. Johnson 2000). The same can be said for Nicaragua's revolution in the same year, which toppled a former military general, Anastasio Somoza, who maintained his rule largely on the basis of his close ties to Washington. The terrorists who struck the United States in September 2001 explicitly cited U.S. support for the repressive monarchy in Saudi Arabia as a justification for their attacks. While such a rationale is hardly a defense for committing mass killings, one cannot deny that U.S. actions that violate a foreign country's proclaimed moral and ethical principles commonly spark anti-American movements and acts of vengeance.

Resistance to Globalization

Yet another challenge to the United States stems from the process of **globalization**, or the linking of national and regional markets into a single world economy (see Stiglitz 2002).

---

5. Genocide constitutes acts that are "committed with intent to destroy, in whole or in part, a national, ethnic, racial, or religious group," according to Article II of the 1948 Convention on the Prevention and Punishment of Genocide, to which the United States is a signatory.

6. These military interventions, which protected U.S. economic interests in Central America and the Caribbean, led to long-term occupations in Panama (1903–1914), Nicaragua (1912–1933), Haiti (1915–1934), the Dominican Republic (1916–1924), and Cuba (1917–1922).

Advances in transportation and communications technology, intellectual developments, and public policy shifts in the eighteenth century first spurred this historic trend. The Internet revolution late in the twentieth century accelerated the pace of globalization. In today's world economy, goods, services, and financial investments cross national borders at a record pace. This commerce is increasingly conducted by multinational corporations (MNCs) with headquarters, research centers, production facilities, stockholders, and customers in many countries.

Although Great Britain was at the forefront of the economic globalization through the nineteenth century, the primary catalyst since then has been the United States. Globalization conforms to a national consensus that private enterprise, unfettered by government interference, provides the surest path to prosperity as well as to individual liberty. According to this consensus, a prosperous world economy resembles that of the United States, with few internal barriers to the movement of goods, services, labor, and capital. Trade, not political or military competition, is the primary arena of foreign policy. Furthermore, "trading states" have strong interests in a stable international system and are reluctant to wage wars against each other. Globalization, according to this view, is a harbinger of world peace.

The quickening pace of economic globalization brought improved living standards to many nations, but others fell behind, unable to attract foreign investment or find new markets for their goods. The growing gap between the world's rich and poor placed new strains on the international system. Critics believed that globalization produced a variety of other problems as well: the triumph of consumerism over cultural diversity, heightened pollution and deforestation, and the exploitation of sweatshop laborers by MNCs. Because many MNCs were based in the United States and its government had played such a vital role in the globalization boom, the United States bore the brunt of antiglobalization protests. The most dramatic example of this backlash occurred at the 1999 annual meeting of the World Trade Organization in Seattle, Washington, when protesters blocked streets, smashed storefronts, and distracted the delegates from their focus of expanding free trade. Further complicating matters, the U.S. model of political economy has come under greater scrutiny as China and other rising powers have boosted economic growth while suppressing the political rights of their citizens. "In the final analysis the global population does not see itself as having benefited meaningfully from an era of American-led globalization," Steven Weber and Bruce Jentleson (2010, 178) observed. "Those winners outside the West who have in some degree benefited largely attribute their good fortune not to liberal internationalism or American ideals, but rather to state-directed capitalism run by illiberal governments."

Terrorism and Asymmetric Warfare

The fourth challenge facing the United States comes from the ongoing threat of **terrorism**, a tactic of unconventional warfare that uses threats and acts of violence to raise mass fear as a means of achieving political objectives. Among other motives for the September 11 attacks, the pervasive influence of the United States in the Middle East served as a primary grievance of al Qaeda. The region and its vast oil fields have long been considered a vital interest of the U.S. government, which has used whatever means necessary to gain and retain access to them. Because the Middle East lies in the heart of Islam, many Muslims view encroachments by the United States and its Western allies as desecrations of holy lands. These dissidents, who also dislike Western cultural norms and condemn U.S. interference in their internal affairs and support for Israel, generally lack political power or substantial economic resources. As a result, they frequently turn to terrorism to force political change.

Terrorism has a long history that precedes the rise of militant Islam (see Laqueur 1977, ch. 1). Terrorists do not seek to overpower the enemy in one swift blow—an approach that is not feasible because of their small numbers and lack of resources—but to gain attention and political concessions by instilling mass fear in their enemy. In this regard, terrorism is a form of **asymmetric warfare** that "exploits vulnerabilities . . . by using weapons and tactics that are unplanned or unexpected" (de Wijk 2002, 79). Terrorists choose the time and place of their attacks, leaving an adversary perpetually on the defensive. They operate in secret, often beyond the reach of government forces or surveillance, and meld into civilian communities from which they may receive moral and material support. Terrorists' use of unconventional tactics (for example, car bombings, kidnappings, and airplane hijackings) further confounds their enemies.[7]

© Nameer Galal/Demotix/Corbis

Egyptian protesters in Cairo gather outside the U.S. embassy in September 2012 to denounce the United States and a low-budget American-made film that ridiculed Islam and its spiritual leader, the prophet Muhammad. Similar protests erupted in several Islamic countries, damaging the Obama administration's efforts to establish friendly relations in the region.

The United States faces four problems in confronting terrorism, which was deemed the primary threat to its national security after the September 11 attacks. First, the United States is seen widely as the primary target of global terrorist groups

7. Problems involving asymmetric warfare are not limited to fighting terrorism. The United States confronted the same tactics in the Vietnamese "guerrilla war" of the 1960s and 1970s. American leaders face similar challenges today in trying to ease civil and regional conflicts whose antagonists comprise ethnic or political groups rather than sovereign nation-states (see R. Smith 2005).

because of its visible role in the Middle East and its more general association with economic globalization. Second, U.S. military strategy has historically been based on fighting conventional wars, defeating foreign enemies on the battlefield through the use of overwhelming force, rather than confronting small groups of enemies who operate in secrecy. Third, the United States has traditionally viewed warfare as an exception to the general rule of peaceful coexistence among countries. Finally, the enemy is not typically a nation-state, such as Nazi Germany or even Saddam Hussein's Iraq, but an invisible foe often impossible to engage through diplomacy.

■ THE PARADOX OF AMERICA'S WORLD POWER

These challenges to the United States raise profound questions about the nation's capacity to sustain its dominant position in a unipolar world. As noted earlier, this objective has long been pursued by American leaders. Maintaining this unique position, however, will not be easy given many aspects of the U.S. foreign policy process. A central paradox of America's world power is that, in seeking to sustain its global primacy, the United States is increasingly constrained by the very forces that propelled its rise to global predominance. These strengths—a culturally embedded sense of national exceptionalism, the diffusion of domestic foreign policy powers, an abiding faith in open markets, and the free rein granted to civil society in the policy process—also create vulnerabilities. Derived from an eighteenth century model, the nation's governing structures remain remarkably unchanged in the twenty-first century. Yet the world order that the United States played a lead role in creating has changed in profound ways, along with the country's role in that order.

This book explores this paradox by examining its presence in the process of making U.S. foreign policy. Of particular interest are the institutions of power inside and outside the U.S. government that define the roles of public and private actors; create and reinforce common values, norms, and codes of conduct; and define what is possible among contending foreign policy choices. These institutions of power have become more complex as the scope of U.S. foreign policy broadens, as the lines between domestic and foreign policy concerns are increasingly blurred, as the number and magnitude of problems crossing national borders increase, and as more individuals and groups become stakeholders and participants in the foreign policy process. This paradox is visible in several recent examples:

- Domestic divisions over grand foreign policy strategy early in the 1990s prevented the United States from adopting a coherent world role, despite its resounding victory in the Cold War and unprecedented global power. Instead, the Clinton administration pursued four contradictory strategies, often all at once: retrenchment, primacy, liberal internationalism, and selective engagement (Posen and Ross 1996/1997). This ambivalence was shared by the general public.

When participants in a national survey were asked in 1999 to identify the biggest foreign policy problem facing the United States, they most often replied, "Don't know" (Rielly 1999, 98).

- Several members of Congress sued President Bill Clinton in 1999, without success, to force a withdrawal of U.S. forces from Kosovo, then part of Yugoslavia. Legislators later charged that Clinton intervened in the renegade Yugoslav province to divert the public's attention from his impeachment by the House of Representatives for lying about an affair with a White House intern. Well aware of domestic opposition to the Kosovo intervention, Clinton limited U.S. military action to high-altitude bombing raids, many of which missed their targets and produced large-scale civilian casualties.

- President George W. Bush's intelligence brief on August 6, 2001, featured the headline "Bin Laden Determined to Strike in U.S." and warned the White House of "suspicious activity in this country consistent with preparations for hijackings or other types of attacks, including recent surveillance of federal buildings in New York." No one acted on the warning, however, because of the many conflicting reports by the more than a dozen U.S. intelligence agencies that "lacked the incentives to cooperate, collaborate, and share information" (National Commission on Terrorist Attacks upon the United States 2004, 12).

- The U.S. government, historically a champion for press freedoms, found itself powerless in November 2010 when the *New York Times*, and five foreign newspapers, began publishing the first of more than 250,000 secret U.S. diplomatic cables and military documents gathered by WikiLeaks, an online advocacy group committed to open government (see Chapter 8). Four years later, the *Washington Post* and two other papers published classified information regarding the National Security Agency's "sweeps" of Americans' private information, including their telephone calls, e-mails, bank records, and posts on Facebook. The Obama administration begged the papers not to reveal the program, to no avail.

- Entrepreneurs in the United States have led the way in the development of social media, Internet-based telecommunications that allow for instantaneous messaging around the world. This technology, however, has enabled adversaries of the United States to advance their political and military agendas. Actions by U.S. government officials as well as members of civil society have drawn the wrath of anti-American groups. In September 2012, for example, a low-budget U.S. film that ridiculed the Prophet Muhammad was circulated on YouTube—another American invention—sparking anti-American protests in many Islamic nations.

The costs of this paradox—in the loss of America's world power and prestige—can be enormous. They are amplified by the openness, or transparency, of the U.S. political system and civil society, both of which are closely watched by friends and foes alike. In these and countless other cases, internal dynamics within the U.S. government and society have produced negative consequences for U.S. foreign policy. The failure of the United States to steer a coherent course as the world's preeminent nation-state, a failure that flows from the virtues as well as shortcomings of the American political system, reinforces the nation's image as a potent but dysfunctional superpower.

Cultural Roots of the Paradox

The roots of this paradox can be found in the U.S. **national style**—that is, the cultural influences that historically have shaped the country's approach to international relations (Dallek 1989). Although national style is an ambiguous concept and cultural influences are difficult to identify with precision, the conduct of every country's foreign policy reflects its distinctive sense of place within the international system. This sense of place, in turn, is shaped by tangible factors such as geographic location, the availability of natural resources, and the size and characteristics of the population. Other factors, such as a country's historical experience, also influence its national style.

When it became the first independent country in the Western Hemisphere, the United States was geographically far removed from the great powers of the time. This distance, combined with the ample territory and natural resources available within the thirteen original colonies, enabled the new nation to develop its political and economic systems with little outside assistance. The United States was distinctive in that its civil society, compared with those of most other countries, did not feature sharp divisions between a small but powerful aristocracy and a large but powerless feudal peasantry. As the French political thinker Alexis de Tocqueville ([1835] 1988, 56) observed after his tour of the young United States, "One finds a vast multitude of people with roughly the same ideas about religion, history, science, political economy, legislation, and government."

This consensus encouraged a sense of national exceptionalism, by which citizens felt the United States was destined not simply to survive as a nation-state but also to achieve the status of a superior world power. Long before the nation's independence, the first European settlers to North America proclaimed the founding of a "city upon a hill" that would inspire societies far from its shores. Colonial leaders later believed that independence from Great Britain would create "a more perfect union" based on limited, representative government.

Americans' sense of moral righteousness, reducing world politics to a contest between good and evil, has persisted as a defining trait of U.S. foreign policy. In the early 1980s, President Ronald Reagan condemned the Soviet Union as an "evil empire." Bill Clinton adapted this view to the post–Cold War world by identifying "rogue states" as the principal threat to the United States. After the terrorist attacks of September 2001, George W. Bush described the struggle in starkly biblical terms: "Freedom and fear, justice and cruelty, have always been at war, and we know that God is not neutral between them." A few months later, Bush declared the nation's enemies to be part of an "axis of evil" that must be destroyed for the United States to be truly secure (see Phillips 2006).

Such views have profound, but contradictory, implications for the conduct of U.S. foreign policy (see H. W. Brands 1998; Monten 2005). One school of thought, fearing that an activist foreign policy would only dirty the hands of U.S. leaders in "power politics," believes the United States should lead primarily by example. A second school of thought contends that U.S. leaders should engage in a global crusade against injustice, aggression, and war itself. Lacking consensus between "exemplarists" and "vindicators" in times of peace, the United States has pursued both strategies, detaching itself from the outside world during certain periods and immersing itself in foreign affairs during others. Most often, U.S. foreign policy exhibits the two tendencies at once, confounding observers at home and abroad (see Hook and Spanier 2016).

The public's ambivalent approach toward foreign affairs is most acute when the United States is at peace. Americans tend to focus on more immediate domestic concerns during these times, and elected officials respond in kind. Only when foreign problems reach crisis proportions do they spark the public's interest. As a result, the public hastily demands action by the government, which responds impulsively, with little deep background or understanding of the underlying problems that provoked the crisis. George Kennan (1951, 59), the architect of U.S. Cold War strategy, found this aspect of democratic foreign policy making particularly troublesome:

> I sometimes wonder whether in this respect a democracy is not uncomfortably similar to one of those prehistoric monsters with a body as long as this room and a brain the size of a pin. He lies there in his comfortable primeval mud and pays little attention to his environment; he is slow to wrath—in fact, you practically have to whack his tail off to make him aware that his interests are being disturbed. But, once he grasps this, he lays about with such blind determination that he not only destroys his adversary but largely wrecks his native habitat.

Institutional Branches

Every nation's political culture has a direct impact on the structures of governance that regulate public affairs, define the relationships between the rulers and the ruled, and carry out public policies. The prevalent ideas about the proper role of the government at home and abroad express themselves in the creation of legislatures, courts, and government agencies. These institutional branches of a nation's political culture determine what is possible in the policy-making process, constraining the options of policy makers. In addition, political institutions commonly multiply and produce new agencies and governing structures that further shape the policy process.

The links among prevalent cultural norms, political institutions, and government behavior can be clearly seen in the United States, which was born during the

Enlightenment era. Under the prevailing theory of that time, governments often do not simply regulate society but also deny or suppress basic freedoms and, in the economic sphere, threaten private property and the profitability of firms through excessive taxes and regulations. Thus, governments must be actively restrained to protect individual liberties.

The architects of the U.S. government restrained its power in several ways. First, they established political liberties in the Bill of Rights that limited the sphere of governmental authority. Second, they dispersed power among the federal, state, and local governments. Finally, they provided for the sharing of federal powers among Congress, the president, and the judiciary. This institutional blueprint, devised more than two centuries ago, endures today. "The central feature of American politics is the fragmentation and dispersion of power and authority," Stephen Krasner (1978, 61–62) observed. "It is not clear in the United States where sovereignty rests, if indeed it rests anywhere at all."

Yet for all its virtues in restraining centralized power, this fragmentation creates problems in the conduct of U.S. foreign policy, which requires a unified statement of national purpose, clear chains of command, consistency, and timely presidential action. Democratic norms "undermine and weaken the power and authority of government and detract, at times seriously, from its ability to compete internationally" (Huntington 1982, 18). This problem was illustrated during Obama's presidency, as he could not overcome bitter conflicts between the two political parties. Foreign powers can exploit such internal divisions and try to divide and conquer their more fragmented rivals. At home, a weak state is likely to be "captured" by interest groups that cater to their own needs rather than national interests. In this respect, de Tocqueville considered democracies "decidedly inferior" to other governments (see In Their Own Words box).

In dispersing foreign policy powers across the legislative and executive branches, the architects of the U.S. government extended an "invitation to struggle for the privilege of directing American foreign policy" (Corwin 1957, 171). The institutional reality of divided powers leads to chronic friction between Congress and the White House over the ends and means of foreign policy. Unless the nation faces an unambiguous foreign challenge, the federal government rarely speaks with one voice. As a result, much of U.S. foreign policy is made, in the words of Supreme Court justice Robert Jackson in his concurring opinion in *Youngstown Sheet and Tube Co. v. Sawyer*, 343 U.S. 579 (1952), in a "zone of twilight in which [the president] and Congress may have concurrent authority, or in which its distribution is uncertain."

In wartime, however, presidents are generally granted far more power and freedom of action. As commander in chief, President George W. Bush seized on this heightened authority after the September 2001 terrorist attacks. His decision to declare an open-ended war on terror and to redefine the laws of war in this conflict stemmed directly from this constitutional power. The terrorist attacks in September silenced any differences between the White House and Congress, which gave Bush full discretion in pursuing and punishing the attackers (see Margulies 2006 and J. Mayer 2008). Thus, the pendulum swung radically in the U.S. political system from legislative-executive gridlock to a virtual blank check for the president to prosecute the war on terror.

Still, Bush's efforts raised concerns heard earlier during the Vietnam War, when historian Arthur Schlesinger Jr. (1973) argued that an **imperial presidency** had taken hold in the United States (see Rudalevige 2005). John Yoo, a legal adviser to the president, instructed Bush that Congress cannot "place any limits on the president's determinations as to any terrorist threat, the amount of military force to be used in response, or the method, timing, and nature of the response" (quoted in Shane 2005). This view was rejected strongly by constitutional scholar Louis Fisher (2007, 59), who observed that "the rule of law, the Constitution, and the 'sharing of power' cannot coexist with one-branch government."

An imperial presidency in the United States is of particular concern because of the lack of foreign policy experience most recent presidents have brought to the White House. Only three presidents since World War II—Dwight Eisenhower, Richard Nixon, and George H. W. Bush—had substantial backgrounds in foreign policy. Post–Cold War presidents Clinton and George W. Bush had served only as governors, and Obama's previous experience in national politics was limited to an unfinished term in the U.S. Senate. Also revealing was Secretary of State Hillary Clinton's lack of formal experience in foreign policy. Such a lack of on-the-job training may seem paradoxical in view of the White House's immense world power. Yet it is entirely consistent with the nation's ambivalent view of the "outside world"—a cultural perspective that looks at foreign peoples, places, and events with a mixture of intrigue and indifference, fascination and suspicion.

Institutional struggles within the U.S. government are not limited to legislative-executive relations. The executive branch itself is highly fragmented and prone to fierce internal competition over foreign policy. Officials in the Defense and State Departments routinely disagree over policy issues and compete for White House attention, budgetary resources, and authority. These officials must also share power with their counterparts on the National Security Council (NSC), the intelligence community, and other government agencies.[8] Understandably, presidents often become frustrated by their inability to rein in the bureaucratic actors presumably under their control. President Harry Truman famously expressed this feeling in 1952 when he warned his successor, Dwight Eisenhower, not to expect the kind of discipline he enjoyed as commander of U.S. armed forces during World War II. "He'll sit here and he'll say 'Do this! Do that!' And nothing will happen. Poor Ike—it won't be a bit like the Army. He'll find it very frustrating" (quoted in Neustadt 1960, 9).

....

8. The NSC had such control over the White House's decision to restore diplomatic relations with Cuba that top State Department officials "found out only as (the NSC) neared completion" (DeYoung 2015).

Alexis de Tocqueville *Alexis de Tocqueville, an aristocratic Frenchman, traveled through the United States in 1831–1832 to chronicle the social, political, public, religious, and intellectual life of the emerging democratic nation. His account of these travels,* Democracy in America, *long considered one of the most astute observations of American life ever written, is still widely read and studied by historians and political scientists alike.*

I have no hesitation in saying that in the control of society's foreign affairs democratic governments do appear decidedly inferior to others. . . . Foreign policy does not require the use of any of the good qualities peculiar to democracy but does demand the cultivation of almost all those which it lacks. . . .

Democracy favors the growth of the state's internal resources; it extends comfort and develops public spirit, strengthens respect for law in the various classes of society, all of which things have no more than an indirect influence on the standing of one nation in respect to another. But a democracy finds it difficult to coordinate the details of a great undertaking and to fix on some plan and carry it through with determination in spite of obstacles. It has little capacity for combining measures in secret and waiting patiently for the result.

Source: Alexis de Tocqueville, *Democracy in America,* edited by J. P. Mayer (New York: Perennial Library, 1988), 228–230. First published in 1835.

Pervasive Civil Society

In addition to these domestic political institutions, forces outside the government and, increasingly, beyond the United States altogether further complicate the American foreign policy process. These external forces, which include public opinion, the news media, interest groups, and intergovernmental organizations, collectively form a transnational civil society. Private groups, including business interests, religious institutions, and think tanks, exert pressure continually on the United States to accommodate their policy preferences. Because U.S. elected officials must also heed domestic public opinion for electoral reasons, they must be sensitive to public opinion overseas, particularly in democratic countries whose support for American foreign policy is needed. In addition, the financial ownership of major news outlets has become increasingly transnational, and the impact of their news coverage is felt immediately in the White House.

Presidents choose which private groups, as well as government agencies, they will invite into the foreign policy process. A primary source of input for all recent administrations has been the multinational corporations that share close connections with many top foreign policy officials. These firms actively seek benefits from the U.S.

government in the form of contracts, tax breaks, favorable regulations, and access to foreign markets.[9] The greater influence wielded by multinational corporations than by nonprofit groups such as Amnesty International and Greenpeace demonstrates clearly that not all interest groups are created equal. "If there is government intervention in the corporate economy, so there is corporate intervention in the governmental process," sociologist C. Wright Mills (1956, 8) observed. This pattern, to be expected in any society that emphasizes market-driven economic growth, raises questions about the "democratic" conduct of foreign policy.

Public opinion plays an important role in the policy process of any democratic nation. The first scientific polling, conducted shortly after World War II, found Americans to be largely ignorant of events taking place overseas (Bailey 1948; Almond 1950). Although more recent surveys suggest greater coherence in public preferences (see Jentleson 1992), surveys and nationwide tests of U.S. students reveal a lack of in-depth knowledge of world history, geography, and international problems. Several examples demonstrate this "knowledge gap":

- In 2009, high school sophomores in the United States ranked below the average among 34 member states of the Organization for Economic Cooperation and Development (OECD) in a cross-national test of reading, mathematics, and science skills (OECD 2010, 8).

- In a 2011 survey of 1,000 U.S. adults, 73 percent could not state the reason that the United States fought the Cold War (Romano 2011).

- Nearly two-thirds of U.S. adults in 2014 were unable to identify the three branches of U.S. government. In the same survey, only 38 percent of respondents knew which political party had a majority in the U.S. Senate (Annenberg Public Policy Center 2014).

- Results of the 2014 "Nation's Report Card" revealed that about one-quarter of eighth graders were either proficient or advanced in U.S. history, geography, and civics, all of which are vital to future understanding of domestic and world politics (see Table 1.2).

Trends in public knowledge and public opinion are closely related to coverage of international affairs by the news media. Such coverage decreased dramatically after the Cold War as news organizations closed overseas bureaus and reduced the proportion of international news to about 10 percent of total news coverage in the print and broadcast media (Graber and Dunaway 2015). National surveys consistently reveal that U.S. newspaper readers find foreign news of the least interest (see, for example, Rielly 2003). But this indifference changes when the United States

---

9. A useful guide to these corporate contracts is provided by the Center for Responsive Politics, a nonprofit nongovernmental organization (www.opensecrets.org).

Table 1.2 ■ Young Americans and Educational Attainment, 8th Grade

Subject	Percentage of Proficiency			
	Below Basic	Basic	Proficient	Advanced
U.S. History	29%	53%	17%	1%
Geography	25	48	24	3
Civics	26	51	22	2

Source: U.S. Department of Education, "Nation's Report Card, 2014," www.nationsreportcard.gov/hgc_2014/.

faces an international crisis. At that point, media outlets shift to saturation coverage, "parachuting" into war zones correspondents who have little knowledge of the regions or conflicts they will be covering (see M. A. Baum 2002; A. S. Jones 2009). In keeping with this pattern, extensive coverage of the 2011 U.S. military intervention in Libya, which led to the overthrow of its repressive leader, Muammar Qaddafi, was followed by virtually no attention being paid to Libya's descent into civil war.

■ CONCLUSION

A central question examined in this book is how well the United States can provide the international leadership it espouses in the face of the domestic and global constraints that are essential features of its political and social system. Of particular concern is whether a political culture that is largely indifferent to foreign affairs is compatible with a dominant world role. The institutions of power raise further concerns about the U.S. government's ability to overcome domestic divisions as well as pressures from transnational civil society, particularly economic pressures. How the government manages the paradox of its world power will determine how long U.S. primacy endures in the turbulent new millennium.

This paradox, which can be seen throughout the nation's history, has direct consequences for the course of U.S. foreign policy, which has vacillated for more than two centuries between policies of engagement with and detachment from the "outside world." Most recently, this pendulum has swung from the administration of Bill Clinton (engagement) to that of George W. Bush (detachment from global governance) and then back to Obama's venture in global engagement. These divergent courses, reflecting an endemic ambivalence in America's political culture, make the United States a curious and unpredictable world power (Hook and Spanier 2016).

While this may be frustrating for leaders overseas, they have little choice but to manage the ongoing identity crisis in U.S. foreign policy.

The mutual love-hate relationship between the United States and the world beyond its borders may be inevitable given the nation's unprecedented primacy. There is little doubt, however, that the country's successes and failures also stem from the peculiarities of U.S. government and social structures and the growing pressures imposed by transnational civil society. Historical patterns suggest that the U.S. political system is self-correcting. Previous bursts of "creedal passion" have been followed by restraint and moderation (Huntington 1981). In this context, it remains to be seen how effectively the U.S. government will adapt to vital changes in the strategic environment and global balance of power. That said, many respected observers still make the case for continued U.S. primacy. "The United States' globe-girdling grand strategy is the devil we know," wrote Stephen G. Brooks, G. John Ikenberry, and William C. Wohlforth (2012/2013, 10). "A world with a disengaged United States is the devil we don't know. . . . Retrenchment would in essence entail a massive experiment: How would the world work without an engaged liberal leading power?"

These enduring questions and debates make the study of U.S. foreign policy a challenging yet rewarding enterprise at this critical period in the history of the nation and the world. The chapters ahead examine more closely the impact of domestic and transnational forces on the formulation of U.S. foreign policy. The book's second and third sections analyze these state and non-state actors, respectively, and the final section illustrates their role in the primary domains of foreign policy: security and defense; economic affairs; and global problems such as population growth, climate change, and weapons proliferation. First, however, Chapter 2 reviews the origins and evolution of U.S. foreign policy, and Chapter 3 introduces the contending theories and concepts of foreign policy decision making.

INTERNET REFERENCES

The **American Foreign Policy Council** (http://www.afpc.org) is a nonprofit organization whose research is devoted to democratization and bilateral and regional relationships between the United States and other countries. The organization's programs in Russia, China, and Asia address trade, defense, and other policy issues.

The **Brookings Institution** (http://www.brookings.edu) is a nonprofit, nonpartisan think tank in Washington, D.C. Its scholars, fellows, and academics produce policy reports, briefs, and books related to U.S. foreign policy. Areas of interest are trade, defense, diplomacy, international institutions, and bilateral relations with foreign countries.

The **Carnegie Council for Ethics in International Affairs** (http://www.cceia.org) focuses on human rights, conflict, environmental issues, economic disparities, and political reconciliation around the world. Scholars produce research briefs and books on current topics that analyze the ethics of international relations with a specific focus on the U.S. role in these policy issues. Carnegie Council publications include the journal *Ethics and International Affairs,* much of which is available online via the "publications" link on the council's home page.

The **Carnegie Endowment for International Peace** (http://www.carnegieendowment.org) is a nonprofit, nonpartisan organization that concentrates on global change by examining international organizations, bilateral relations, and political-economic forces in the world. Special attention is devoted to the U.S.-Russia relationship as well as geopolitics involving the United States and other countries. The organization publishes *Foreign Policy,* one of the leading magazines on world politics and foreign policy with an emphasis on the United States (www.foreignpolicy.com).

The **Center for Strategic and International Studies** (http://www.csis.org) is a nonprofit, nonpartisan organization that addresses international defense and security issues with an emphasis on policy analysis, policy recommendations, and geographic analysis. The center publishes the *Washington Quarterly,* which analyzes global changes and foreign policies, looking especially at the U.S. role in the world, defense procurement, terrorism and counterterrorism, and regional issues (www.twq.com).

The **Council on Foreign Relations** (www.cfr.org) studies international affairs, foreign policy, and the role of the United States in the world. The council examines an array of issues as they pertain to the United States, such as trade, defense, security, globalization, terrorism, specific regions, energy resources and the environment, and political systems. The council also publishes *Foreign Affairs,* a leading journal that features scholarly analysis of these issues (www.foreignaffairs.org).

The **Foreign Policy Association** (www.fpa.org) is a nonprofit organization dedicated to educating legislators and the American public on U.S. foreign policy issues. Its mission includes all aspects of U.S. foreign policy, especially current events and global issues. The association produces reports, videos, and books on regional and specific policy issues.

Foreign Policy in Focus (www.fpif.org) is a think tank that produces policy reports on the United States and its role in the world. Specific policy briefs and reports include, but are not limited to, the topics of human rights, regional relationships, bilateral relationships, defense funding and procurement, terrorism, trade, energy, and environmental issues.

Part of Johns Hopkins University, the **Foreign Policy Institute** (http://www.fpi.sais-jhu.edu) provides training and research on the global role of the United States. The institute brings together all disciplines interested in U.S. foreign policy. It also publishes *The SAIS Review of International Affairs,* which analyzes current international policies (www.saisreview.org).

The **Foreign Policy Research Institute** (www.fpri.org) studies U.S. national interests, the war on terror, security relationships, and long-term policy planning. Its research is based on a multidisciplinary approach that includes scholars and advisers from economics, politics, law, the media, and history. *Orbis,* a quarterly journal published by the institute, consists of reports from conferences and scholars on U.S. and world national interests (www.fpri.org/orbis/).

The **Hoover Institution** (www.hoover.org) is devoted to policy analysis and both domestic and international affairs research within the ideological framework of an emphasis on a free society. The Hoover Institution researches trade, markets, postcommunist transition, international law, and democratic growth. Fellows at the Hoover Institution produce policy briefs, the *Hoover Digest* (www.hoover.org/publications/digest/), and books through the Hoover Press.

The **Institute for Foreign Policy Analysis** (www.ifpa.org) provides briefings for foreign policy students who are interested in the costs, benefits, and planning of U.S. foreign policy. The institute covers a variety of issues but focuses on globalization, missile defense, international institutions, and grand strategies.

The **RAND Corporation** (www.rand.org) is a private research group that concentrates on international affairs, homeland security, terrorism, and U.S. national security issues. It also produces reports on individual countries that have close ties to the United States and the *RAND Review,* a magazine about current security and defense issues (www.rand.org/publications/randreview.html).

The **U.S. Department of State** (www.state.gov) manages many aspects of U.S. diplomacy and the U.S. foreign policy process, including foreign aid, peace building, democratization, and disease and poverty prevention. The website provides speeches, policy descriptions, and issue explanations for those studying American foreign policy.

CHAPTER 2

THE EXPANSION OF U.S. POWER

U.S. president Theodore Roosevelt tests a steam shovel during construction of the Panama Canal in November 1906. Roosevelt had supported earlier efforts by Panamanian rebels to seize control of the future canal zone, declare independence from Colombia, and seek diplomatic recognition by the United States. Congress promptly approved a treaty with the new government that granted the United States "power and authority" over the canal "in perpetuity." Under President Jimmy Carter, the U.S. government agreed in 1977 to turn control of the canal over to Panama in 2000.

CHAPTER OBJECTIVES

2.1 Discuss U.S. policies of economic and territorial expansion in the nineteenth and early twentieth centuries.

2.2 Explain how major shifts in the global balance of power led to two world wars and the subsequent rise of U.S. primacy on the world stage.

2.3 Describe the institutional foundations and ideals representing U.S. foreign policy in thepostwar period.

2.4 Identify the foreign policy challenges the United States faced immediately after the Cold War.

The central goal of this book is to help readers understand U.S. foreign policy today. This understanding is impossible, however, without reference to the nation's past, first as a regional power and then as the predominant world power. This chapter reviews these experiences, evaluating their relevance to the current policy process. A single chapter cannot provide an exhaustive survey of U.S. diplomatic history, but it can highlight the pivotal events that shaped the nation's relations with the world beyond its shores.[1]

Such a historical perspective reveals the origins and development of the paradox of America's world power. As the United States grew from a regional power to the holder of global primacy, it continued to maintain the political arrangements, along with the social and cultural traditions, that prevailed in a time of diplomatic detachment. Early American leaders advanced claims of moral, political, and social **exceptionalism,** or a widely held sense of distinctiveness or superiority. Living up to these values, however, proved difficult as American leaders frequently contradicted their righteous claims, placing self-interests above all other goals and opening themselves to charges of hypocrisy. Still, American leaders and their citizens created a nation-state that steadily gained power and ultimately reached a level of global prominence that has no peer in the modern history of world politics.

This historical review covers two distinct time periods. The first involves the gradual expansion of U.S. territory, wealth, and influence from the nation's founding to the First World War. As we will find, early American leaders charted a course of unilateral action, avoiding diplomatic ties to the great powers of Europe while

---

1. For a more comprehensive history of U.S. foreign policy, see Robert J. McMahon and Thomas W. Zeiler, *CQ Press Guide to U.S. Foreign Policy*, 2 vols. (Thousand Oaks, CA: CQ Press, 2012).

building an industrial economy that would make the United States a major force in global trade markets. As for territorial expansion, the western frontier offered a seemingly limitless opportunity to create, in the words of Thomas Jefferson, an "**empire** of liberty" from the Atlantic to the Pacific oceans. Jefferson and his successors acquired vast territories through a variety of means, from negotiated agreements and sales to forced relocations of indigenous peoples and outright military conquest. This pattern of territorial expansion, typical of past imperial powers, was viewed widely as evidence of national exceptionalism. "Such claims are dangerous," observed Godfrey Hodgson (2009, 16), "because they are the soil in which unreal and hubristic assumptions of American destiny have grown." (For a similar critique, see T. Smith 2007.)

The second period covers the conduct of U.S. foreign policy once the country became a great power in the twentieth century. The United States began the century in the midst of a struggle to colonize the Philippines and then asserted hegemonic control over Central America. Emerging from the world wars with unprecedented military strength and economic clout, U.S. leaders became engulfed in a struggle against the Soviet Union and other communist states. The Soviet Union's collapse in 1991 left the United States in a position of unprecedented global primacy. But maintaining this status proved more difficult than expected as regional conflicts and civil wars ignited in many parts of the world. The terrorist attacks on the United States in September 2001 literally brought these conflicts home, shattering the nation's historic sense of invulnerability and ushering in a "war on terrorism" that continues to this day. As journalist Michael Hirsh (2003, 25) observed, "We are in this world with both feet now. We have achieved our Founding Fathers' fondest dream, and, at the same time, their worst nightmare. We are a shining success, the supreme power on earth. And we are entangled everywhere." Recent developments reinforce this view, with the United States being drawn into armed conflicts across the Middle

East and in Russia, whose takeover of Ukraine's Crimean Peninsula has sparked fears of a new rivalry between Washington and Moscow.

In sum, reviewing the history of U.S. foreign policy provides for a stronger grasp of America's role in today's turbulent world. Part of this learning experience includes dispelling widely held historical myths, including the notion that early foreign policy makers adopted a posture of isolationism (Braumoeller 2010). This may be true in the narrow sense of avoiding multilateral commitments until the mid-twentieth century, but the relentless expansion of U.S. territory and trade is hardly a record of isolation. Historical evidence also helps us evaluate theories of world politics, as in the case of structural realism, which claims that domestic politics are marginally important to foreign policy behavior. As this book demonstrates, American politics has never stopped "at the water's edge." In modern times especially, "partisan rancor, political maneuvering, legislative-executive fighting, and electoral politics have had a significant effect on the making of national security policy" (Leffler 2011, 564; see also R. A. Kennedy 2009 and Zelizer 2010).

■ ECONOMIC AND TERRITORIAL EXPANSION

America's earliest leaders were concerned first and foremost with building political institutions that could preserve the nation's independence. The Articles of Confederation, which in 1781 established the framework of the first American political system, featured a very weak central government. Under the articles, the original thirteen states conducted their own trade policies while the cash-starved Congress largely dismantled the nation's military forces, thereby making the United States vulnerable to intimidation by more unified powers overseas. The country cried out for a stronger national government. Under the U.S. Constitution, drafted in 1787 and ratified in 1788, states maintained primary control over their internal affairs while ceding sovereignty to the federal government. The president and Congress shared responsibilities for American foreign policy (see Chapters 4 and 5). James Madison, the primary architect of the Constitution, recognized that such power sharing was crucial for the democratic control of government. On the one hand, the president, who would serve as commander in chief of U.S. armed forces while conducting the day-to-day business of foreign policy, would be able to act more quickly and decisively than Congress. On the other hand, Congress, with powers to declare war and control spending, among others, would restrain the president. Together, they would provide a unified front for the advancement of the nation's foreign policy goals.

The new framework was not meant to encourage U.S. activism in diplomacy, which many Americans saw as an artifact of the Old World, long dominated by monarchs, church leaders, and feudal despots. Thomas Jefferson, the first secretary of state and third president, observed in a note to his personal secretary, William Short, that diplomacy was "the pest of the peace of the world, as the workshop in which nearly all the wars of Europe are manufactured." Although the State Department was the first federal agency created under the Constitution, it received few resources, and for more than a century it maintained only a tiny staff.[2]

Architects of U.S. foreign policy institutions made an exception, however, for foreign *economic* relations, which they considered more suitable than diplomacy for advancing the nation's interests. Early in the nineteenth century, the government hired hundreds of consular officers to secure markets overseas and ensure the protection of U.S. merchant ships and crews. By 1820, the United States had become the fourth-richest country in the world as measured by per capita income (Prestowitz 2003, 84). A leading exporter of agricultural products, especially cotton and tobacco, the nation would soon become a major producer of industrial goods as well. Although early American leaders disagreed about the means for attaining foreign policy goals, they shared an expansive view of the nation's future. Alexander Hamilton, the first Treasury secretary, believed the country should "erect one great American system superior to the control of all trans-Atlantic force or influence and able to dictate the terms of the connection between the old and the new world" (quoted in Wright 2004, 142). Jefferson, too, envisioned U.S. dominance extending beyond the nation's borders. He foresaw a hemispheric order in which "our rapid multiplication will . . . cover the

....

2. The State Department had just eight employees in 1790, twenty-three in 1830, and forty-two in 1860. The U.S. government did not create a full-scale foreign service until 1924, long after the United States had emerged as a major world power (see www.state.gov for a chronology of the department's budget and personnel).

whole northern if not southern continent, with a people speaking the same language, governed in similar forms, and by similar laws" (quoted in McDougall 1997, 78).

Contrary to conventional wisdom, the United States was hardly an isolationist country in its formative years (see Table 2.1). The government pursued an expansionist foreign policy, westward and *away* from the great powers of Europe, while also aggressively seeking foreign trade. The nation's growing territory, detailed below, served as both a blessing and a curse. "Attaining even minimal security," Robert Kagan (2006, 12) observed, "required an ever-enlarging sphere of control and dominance, for whenever one boundary was established, other threats always existed beyond it."

The expansion of American power featured a consistent pattern of **unilateralism**. Rather than collaborating and pooling resources with like-minded states, leaders adopted a unilateral foreign policy favoring autonomy and self-sufficiency. For President George Washington, who severed an alliance with France in 1793 despite that nation's earlier role in securing U.S. independence, the benefits of going it alone were paramount. In his view, peacetime alliances presented unacceptable risks of surrendering the nation's control over its overseas commitments.[3] Upon leaving office three years later, Washington (1796) summarized his view in his Farewell Address:

> The great rule of conduct for us in regard to foreign nations is in extending our commercial relations, to have with them as little political connection as possible. . . . Europe has a set of primary interests which to us have none; or a very remote relation. Hence she must be engaged in frequent controversies, the causes of which are essentially foreign to our concerns. . . . Our detached and distant situation invites and enables us to pursue a different course. . . . It is our true policy to steer clear of permanent alliances with any portion of the foreign world.

Manifest Destiny on the Western Frontier

The United States, driven by a "cult of nationalism" that provided a moral basis for expansion, came to dominate the Western Hemisphere by default (Van Alstyne 1965). The nation's emergence as a regional power coincided with the demise of the British, French, Russian, and Spanish outposts in North America. Globally, a multipolar balance of power existed that was anchored by the European powers, which maintained relatively peaceful relations with each other in the century separating the Napoleonic and world wars. The United States, which along with Japan emerged as formidable "offshore powers" in the nineteenth century (see Figure 2.1), filled this geopolitical

---

3. The ill-fated pact between the United States and France was the last peacetime alliance signed by the U.S. government until the mid-twentieth century. See Gaddis (2005) for a detailed review of unilateralism as a centerpiece of U.S. foreign policy before the world wars.

Table 2.1 ■ U.S. Foreign Policy Chronology, 1783–1945

1783	United States gains independence from Great Britain.
1788	Constitution establishes stronger American government.
1793	United States proclaims neutrality in European wars.
1803	France sells Louisiana Territory to United States.
1812	Territorial and trade disputes provoke U.S. war with Great Britain.
1823	Monroe Doctrine proclaims U.S. sphere of influence throughout Western Hemisphere.
1845	United States annexes Texas.
1846	The Mexican-American War begins.
1853	United States forcefully opens Japan to American trade.
1867	Russia sells Alaska to the United States.
1898	United States annexes Hawaii.
1898	Spanish-American War begins.
1899	United States calls for "Open Door policy" toward China.
1902	U.S. troops, after three years of guerrilla war, colonize the Philippines.
1903	United States signs treaty to build Panama Canal.
1904	Roosevelt Corollary to Monroe Doctrine grants United States "international police power."
1914	World War I begins in Europe.
1917	United States declares war against Germany.
1918	German surrender ends World War I.
1919	U.S. Senate rejects Treaty of Versailles and League of Nations.
1928	Kellogg-Briand Pact renounces war as an "instrument of national policy."
1935	Congress passes Neutrality Acts barring U.S. intervention in Europe.
1939	German territorial conquests lead to World War II.
1941	Japanese attack on Pearl Harbor naval base in Hawaii provokes U.S. entry into World War II.
1944	Bretton Woods system, including World Bank and International Monetary Fund, is created.
1945	Defeat of Axis powers ends World War II. United Nations is established.

Figure 2.1 ■ Multipolar Balance of World Power (mid-nineteenth century)

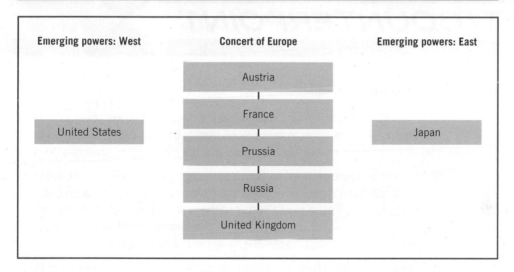

vacuum in a variety of ways: by buying vast territories at bargain prices, negotiating settlements, and forcibly seizing territories when other measures failed. Through these actions, the United States became the hemisphere's economic and military giant, a global superpower in the making.

In expanding westward, settlers and government forces violently subdued the American Indian population, whose relatively small numbers and lack of unity and modern weaponry left them incapable of successfully resisting encroachments on their lands. Early government leaders sought to assimilate the American Indians into the general population and society (Steele 1994), but their successors abandoned such notions and made the displacement or elimination of Native Americans an object of government policy. Although this aspect of U.S. expansion falls outside the conventional bounds of foreign policy, it is nevertheless "a central theme of American diplomatic history" (LaFeber 1989, 10).

The first major territorial gain occurred in 1803, when Jefferson acquired the vast Louisiana Territory, which stretched westward from the Mississippi River to the Rocky Mountains and northward from the Gulf of Mexico to the Oregon Territory. French ruler Napoleon Bonaparte, who had regained the territory from Spain two years earlier, was unable to govern, let alone defend, such a massive amount of land in North America while pursuing his ambitions in Europe. He made the most of the situation by offering Louisiana to the United States for $15 million (or about three cents an acre). Jefferson, though suspecting that his role in the Louisiana Purchase was "an act beyond the Constitution," eagerly accepted the offer (see Kukla 2003).

Hamilton vs. Jefferson

Differences over the direction U.S. foreign policy should take were epitomized in the nation's early years by Alexander Hamilton and Thomas Jefferson. Although both political leaders believed the United States was destined to join the ranks of the great powers, they disagreed about how this feat should be accomplished.

An admirer of Great Britain's political and economic system, Hamilton thought the United States should establish itself as a major industrial power with a strong navy and close financial ties to foreign capitals, including London. Jefferson believed the United States should adopt a more modest course, refining its democracy at home and creating a nation of small farmers rather than industrialists. He worried that building the stronger national government favored by Hamilton would inevitably lead to a standing military force and a tyrannical head of state.

The two men never resolved their ideological differences. However, after taking office in 1801, Jefferson, in the types of actions he undertook, displayed much of Hamilton's penchant for wielding power. The new president moderated his staunch support for France, where he had previously served as ambassador. As France became embroiled in the Napoleonic Wars, Jefferson proclaimed in his 1801 inaugural address that U.S. security should be maintained by "peace, commerce, and honest friendship with all nations—entangling alliances with none." Jefferson also exploited his presidential powers in negotiating the Louisiana Purchase and pursuing other measures that would enhance the nation's territorial and military strength.

The acquisition of the Louisiana Territory, followed by the displacement of Spain from Florida, left the United States free to focus on state building, economic development, and further continental expansion (see Map 2.1, Nineteenth-Century European Empires and U.S. Continental Expansion). After the War of 1812, in which they struggled over unresolved trade and territorial differences, the United States and Great Britain established close economic ties. The demise of the Spanish empire in Latin America, which led to the liberation of its colonies, paved the way for U.S. regional hegemony. In 1823, President James Monroe, seeking to discourage renewed European intrusions into Latin America as well as Russian ambitions along the Pacific coast, proclaimed the **Monroe Doctrine,** which further separated the United States from the European powers:

> In the wars of the European powers in matters relating to themselves we have never taken any part, nor does it comport with our policy to do so. . . . With the movements in this hemisphere we are of necessity more immediately

connected. . . . The political system of the [European] powers is essentially different in this respect from that of America. . . . [W]e should consider any attempt on their part to extend their system to any portion of this hemisphere as dangerous to our peace and safety.

Mexico's independence from Spain in 1821 paved the way for the next significant act of U.S. expansion. Many Americans had purchased land in the northern Mexican province of Texas, and in 1835, this growing population launched an independence movement of its own. Within a year, Texan rebels had defeated the Mexican army and declared Texas an independent country. The U.S. government's annexation of Texas in 1845 was viewed by many Americans as further evidence that the United States had God's blessing to continue its westward expansion. In the *Democratic Review*, editor John O'Sullivan proclaimed the **manifest destiny** of the United States "to overspread the continent allotted by Providence for the free development of our yearly multiplying millions" (quoted in Pratt 1927, 797–798). Such claims were applied to the weakly defended Mexican territories west and north of Texas, for which President James K. Polk initiated a series of border skirmishes that escalated into a full-scale war. The United States quickly defeated the Mexican army and then signed a peace treaty in 1848 requiring Mexico to cede nearly 1 million square miles of land.

Opening the Door to Asia

The conquest of northern Mexico, along with the acquisition of the Oregon Territory from Great Britain in 1846, effectively closed the western frontier, which had been a symbol of virtually endless opportunity for American expansion. Advocates of continued expansion turned to the Pacific Ocean as the new frontier. "He would be a rash prophet who should assert that the expansive character of America has now entirely ceased," wrote historian Frederick Jackson Turner in 1920 (37). "Movement has been its dominant fact, and, unless this training has no effect upon a people, the American energy will continually demand a wider field for its exercise."

The United States had much to gain economically by tapping into the enormous markets of East Asia. Expansionists downplayed this economic rationale while emphasizing nobler motivations instead. An appeal to economic interests would cast the country in the same light as the traditional great powers, which supposedly lacked the "manifest destiny" uniquely bestowed upon the Americans. Even as it fought the Mexican army for control of the western frontier, the United States was making overtures to Japan for commercial relations. When these efforts failed, President Millard Fillmore, in 1853, deployed naval vessels to Tokyo. Faced with this early example of **gunboat diplomacy,** Japan's emperor accepted a "treaty of friendship" in 1854 that provided for U.S. access to the Japanese market.

Map 2.1 ■ Nineteenth-Century European Empires and U.S. Continental Expansion

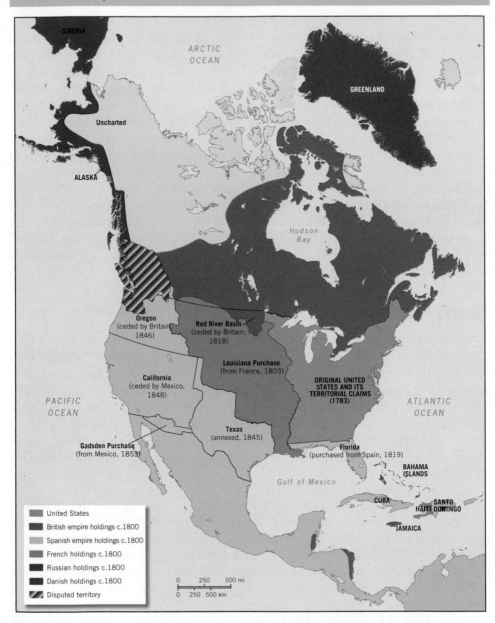

SIBERIA

ARCTIC OCEAN

GREENLAND

Uncharted

ALASKA

Hudson Bay

Oregon
(ceded by Britain, 1846)

Red River Basin
(ceded by Britain, 1818)

Louisiana Purchase
(from France, 1803)

California
(ceded by Mexico, 1848)

ORIGINAL UNITED STATES AND ITS TERRITORIAL CLAIMS (1783)

PACIFIC OCEAN

ATLANTIC OCEAN

Texas
(annexed, 1845)

Gadsden Purchase
(from Mexico, 1853)

Florida
(purchased from Spain, 1819)

BAHAMA ISLANDS

Gulf of Mexico

CUBA

SANTO DOMINGO

HAITI

JAMAICA

Legend:
- United States
- British empire holdings c.1800
- Spanish empire holdings c.1800
- French holdings c.1800
- Russian holdings c.1800
- Danish holdings c.1800
- Disputed territory

0   250   500 mi
0   250   500 km

Source: Thomas M. Magstadt, *An Empire If You Can Keep It: Power and Principle in American Foreign Policy* (Washington, DC: CQ Press, 2004), xviii, xix. Reprinted by permission of CQ press, an imprint of SAGE Publications Inc.

American interests in the Pacific Ocean extended well beyond Japan. In addition to the several islands it occupied to serve as coaling stations for U.S. ships and to prevent other countries from taking the islands, the United States was especially interested in the Hawaiian Islands, located midway between North America and Asia. American officials first sought favorable commercial treatment from the Hawaiian monarchy. Unable to achieve a treaty on its own terms, the U.S. government, in 1893, recruited a rebel army that staged a successful coup against the monarchy. Within days, the new government of Hawaii signed a treaty of annexation with the United States. The United States also gained control of Alaska during this period, purchasing the remote territory from Russia's czar for $7 million.[4]

Critics accused the United States of behaving like the European empires it had long condemned. But such protests proved futile, as illustrated by the Spanish-American War in which the United States clashed with Spain over its colony in Cuba. As American forces were ousting Spain from Cuba, a U.S. fleet on the other side of the world was defeating Spanish forces in the Philippines, another Spanish colony. The United States gained control of the Philippines only after waging a lengthy war that left thousands of casualties, largely Filipino, in its wake. While President William McKinley chose not to annex Cuba, preferring to control the island indirectly, he adopted a different approach to the Philippines. The United States recognized the commercial potential of the Southeast Asian islands, particularly because of their proximity to the rapidly expanding markets of China. Advocates of American occupation seized on the prospect of bringing Christianity and "civilization" to the Philippines. These factors contributed to McKinley's decision in 1902 to rule the Philippines as a U.S. colony, marking an exception to the U.S. government's general rule of opposing colonization.

The United States entered the twentieth century as an emerging superpower with worldwide political, economic, and military interests. The nation's territory extended across North America and the Pacific Ocean; its population doubled between 1865 and 1890 to 71 million, in large part from European immigration. Meanwhile, U.S. economic output matched, and then exceeded, that of the major European powers. More Americans lived in cities than in rural areas, and industrial production contributed more than agriculture to national output. Securing overseas markets, therefore, became a national priority. In 1899, the United States proclaimed an **Open Door policy** that was designed to prevent China from being carved up among European trading interests. Historian William Appleman Williams (1959, 43), a critic of the policy, found it to be "derived from the proposition that America's overwhelming economic power would cast the economy and the politics of the weaker, under-developed countries in a pro-American mold."

----

4. Alaska and Hawaii remained U.S. territories until 1959, when they became the forty-ninth and fiftieth states of the Union, respectively.

A Big Stick in Latin America

President Theodore Roosevelt, a former naval officer and a veteran of the Spanish-American War, and also a strong advocate of U.S. expansion, proved to be the central American figure in foreign policy as the new century began (see E. Morris 2001). He eagerly sought to become a world leader. In 1905, Roosevelt received the Nobel Peace Prize for negotiating the end of the Russo-Japanese War. Two years later, Roosevelt deployed a U.S. naval armada around the world, a symbol of the nation's arrival as a global power. The president believed in a version of social Darwinism that viewed wars as both inevitable and noble, with the victors assigned a "mandate from civilization" to look after less powerful nations. Citing a favorite aphorism from his safaris in Africa, Roosevelt pledged that the United States would "speak softly, but carry a big stick."

The Roosevelt administration concerned itself in particular with Latin America, a U.S. sphere of influence since the proclamation of the Monroe Doctrine. The president engineered a domestic uprising in northern Colombia in 1903, after which the United States recognized the new Republic of Panama and signed a treaty to build and lease the Panama Canal. Concerned now not only with European meddling in the region but also with internal power struggles that threatened friendly governments, the president issued the **Roosevelt Corollary** to the Monroe Doctrine. Such unrest, it stated, "may . . . ultimately require intervention by some civilized nation" and "may force the United States, however reluctantly . . . to the exercise of an international police power" (Roosevelt 1904). Following this logic, Roosevelt ordered U.S. military interventions in the Dominican Republic (1904), Honduras (1905), Cuba (1906), and Panama (1908). This practice continued after his departure from office in 1909 as his successors deployed troops to other countries in the region when internal unrest threatened U.S. foreign investments.

■ FIGHTING TWO WORLD WARS

The Roosevelt Corollary may have affirmed U.S. dominance of the Western Hemisphere, but developments elsewhere created new challenges for the United States. In Europe, a century of relative calm was quickly coming to an end. The creation of a unified German state in 1871 started this downward spiral. Germany's rise coincided with the decline of the Ottoman, Russian, and Austro-Hungarian empires, all of which had contributed to a crude, but durable, stability in Europe. Major shifts in the global balance of power, which included the rise in stature of the United States and Japan, would lead to two world wars in the first half of the twentieth century.

The First World War

For Americans, Europe's plunge into war in 1914 affirmed the prudence of their country's historic aversion to foreign entanglements (see Tuchman 1962). Austria-Hungary's war declaration against Serbia, for example, was made possible by

Germany's support for the Austro-Hungarian Empire. Alliance commitments also came into play as Germany went to war against Russia, an ally of Serbia, and against France, an ally of Russia. Great Britain justified its entry into the war with its security guarantees to Belgium, through which German troops passed on their way to France.

As order unraveled in Europe, President Woodrow Wilson sought to keep the United States "neutral in fact as well as name." But the country could not maintain its detached posture once the conflict in Europe extended into the Atlantic Ocean. The German navy began attacking merchant ships, many of them owned and operated by Americans. Any hopes for U.S. noninvolvement ended in May 1915, when a German submarine destroyed the British ocean liner *Lusitania,* whose passengers had included 128 American citizens. Although the United States managed to stay out of combat for another two years, Germany's prosecution of submarine warfare had angered the American public, inclining it toward war. Russia's withdrawal from the conflict in November 1917 secured Germany's position in the east and allowed its forces to concentrate along the western front. The prospect of German control over all Europe and its implications for U.S. security prompted Congress to declare war against Germany in 1917.

The United States contributed to the war effort in two ways. First, Wilson drew on the nation's immense industrial capacity by shipping massive volumes of weapons, munitions, and medical supplies to its allies, who were mired in a defensive stalemate against Germany. Troops on both sides were dug into long lines of mud-filled trenches, unable to advance against the new generation of armored tanks, long-range artillery, and automatic weapons. Second, Wilson deployed U.S. troops to the western front to reinforce exhausted French and British forces and begin a slow counteroffensive. The strength of the U.S. forces ultimately tipped the balance, leading to Germany's surrender in November 1918.

Failed Efforts to Keep the Peace

As noted earlier, neither the U.S. government nor the general public was eager for the United States to become engaged in the First World War. The "entangling alliances" of the European powers, which transformed a regional crisis into a world war, were precisely what U.S. diplomats had long avoided. However, Germany's early success in the war raised the prospect of an even greater threat: the emergence of a single European state that would upend the balance of power. Such a scenario had struck fear into American leaders at least since 1814, when Thomas Jefferson declared in a letter to Thomas Leiper, "It cannot be to our interest that all Europe should be reduced to a single monarchy" (quoted in Graebner 1964, 122).

The U.S. government, however, was also uncomfortable with a security policy based entirely on geopolitics, the distribution of global power. For Wilson, who was the son of a Presbyterian minister and had a strong sense of moral mission, the nation had to have a moral rationale for intervention (see George and George 1956). In his view, the United States should not fight simply for its survival or that of its allies. The nation should defend a more general principle: the right of citizens of any country to determine their own destinies. World War I, then, became a war to "make the world safe for democracy." When the war ended, Wilson felt duty bound to seek a world order that would put these principles into practice and ensure that the recent conflict had been "the war to end all wars."

Wilson believed that a long-term solution was needed to overcome the anarchic world order, whose lack of global governance had allowed the horror of the Great War to take place. His proposed solution was a new system based on the concept of **collective security.** In such a system, leaders would renounce war as an instrument of statecraft and then pledge to defend each other in the event of outside aggression. If every government agreed to such a scheme and backed up its words with concrete action, any aggression would be doomed. Expansionist states would be deterred, and world peace would be assured. Wilson outlined his plan to Congress in early 1918, when he identified "fourteen points" that all countries should respect. In addition to self-government, an essential right in Wilson's view (Throntveit 2011), the other points included worldwide disarmament, freedom of the seas, open markets, and the prohibition of secret diplomacy. Most famously, the president proposed the formation of a League of Nations that would provide the institutional foundation for collective security. Through the League, conflicting states would have a forum in which to discuss and resolve their differences peacefully. If any government violated the rules and invaded another country, League members would collectively repel the aggression.

Wilson's proposal, which presumably would deter nations from foreign aggression in the first place, was generally well received by other governments. In seeking to transform world politics, however, Wilson forgot about U.S. politics. Specifically, he neglected the constitutional sharing of powers that provided Congress with a vital role in foreign, as well as domestic, policy. Legislators resented their exclusion from the peace conference held in Paris in 1919 to conclude the war and complained that the Treaty of Versailles, by requiring military interventions when necessary to uphold collective security, deprived Congress of its authority to declare war. This combination of animosity toward Wilson and constitutional concerns led Congress to exercise another of its foreign policy powers by voting down the treaty. Thus, the United States, whose leader had been the primary architect of the organization, never joined the League of Nations.

Wilson also underestimated the powerful grip that national sovereignty held on the calculations of political leaders. In seeking to remake the interstate system, the League sought to weaken national sovereignty in its most vital area: military self-defense. The enduring obstacle of sovereignty to collective security was revealed in 1931, when Japanese troops invaded the province of Manchuria in northern China.

This clear case of aggression presumably should have triggered the League's collective security mechanism, yet most members displayed no interest in deploying their troops to a remote region of little concern to them. League members denounced the Japanese invasion and voted to impose economic sanctions, but they took no military action. Italy's 1935 invasion of Ethiopia, in the horn of Africa, brought the same responses. In both instances, the League revealed itself to be a paper tiger that, far from rendering war obsolete, seemed to encourage and reward aggression by creating a false sense of security among nations that did not have aggressive designs.

Its nonparticipation in the League of Nations did not deter the United States from seeking ways to prevent another world war. To the contrary, during the 1920s, the government actively pursued this goal in two ways. First, President Warren G. Harding called for disarmament among the major powers. Many people at this time believed the military buildups that had preceded World War I were driven by arms manufacturers, or "merchants of death," and that the proliferation of weapons fueled distrust among the major powers and brought on a more destructive and protracted war than would otherwise have been possible.[5] At the Washington Naval Conference in 1921 and 1922, the foreign ministers of Great Britain, France, Italy, and Japan agreed on a balance of naval power maintained by strictly regulating the size of the five navies.

Second, the United States cosponsored an international treaty to "outlaw" war. Two assumptions underlay the Pact of Paris, also known as the **Kellogg-Briand Pact** (named for the U.S. and French foreign ministers). First, military force was an unacceptable tool of statecraft. Second, the destructive power of modern military weapons, clearly demonstrated in the First World War, made the future use of such weapons suicidal to all parties. In 1928, representatives from fifteen countries signed the pact, which condemned "recourse to war for the solution of international controversies, and . . . as an instrument of national policy." Eventually, sixty-two governments, including those of Germany, Italy, Japan, and the Soviet Union, signed the agreement.

These heralded reforms, however, did not prevent the major powers from playing the same old game of power politics. After Japan seized control of Manchuria in 1931, Prime Minister Tojo Hideki ordered his forces to gain control of the entire Chinese coastline. Two years later, Adolf Hitler became chancellor of Germany and repudiated the Treaty of Versailles, vowing to obtain the *lebensraum* (living space) required by the German people. Taking its cue from Hitler, Italy's fascist government, led by Benito Mussolini, launched an invasion of Ethiopia in 1935. In the United States, foreign policy makers reverted to their traditional posture of detachment.

----

5. Fears of foreign entanglements after World War I were fueled by the publication of a best-selling book, *Merchants of Death* (Engelbrecht & Hanighen 1934), which charged that the U.S. entry into World War I had been the result of political pressure imposed by profit-hungry arms manufacturers.

The Second World War

Once again, however, events in Europe made the U.S. hands-off policy impossible to maintain. After repudiating the Versailles treaty and rebuilding his armed forces, Hitler annexed Austria and eastern Czechoslovakia. He assured other European leaders afterward that these actions had satisfied his territorial needs, but his pledges soon proved empty. In 1939, Germany invaded Poland and then divided the defeated country with the Soviet Union, with whom Hitler earlier had signed a nonaggression pact. That pact, though, proved just as worthless as the German leader's earlier promises. In 1941, Hitler launched a massive blitzkrieg against the Soviet Union and thrust the world into a bloodbath unmatched in world history (Beevor 2012). Having "neutralized" the eastern front, German forces overran most of Western Europe. Only Great Britain remained free of German domination.

By this time, American leaders generally favored U.S. intervention, but the public remained unconvinced that the escalating conflict in Europe threatened the United States. President Franklin Roosevelt bowed to the popular view. During the 1940 presidential campaign, he declared, "I have said this before and I shall say it again and again and again: Your boys are not going to be sent into any foreign wars" (quoted in Schulzinger 1994, 172). Nevertheless, Roosevelt brought the nation's considerable resources to bear in support of its allies. As German forces advanced toward the English Channel, the president, through the **lend-lease program,** provided Great Britain with U.S. military hardware and ships in exchange for American access to British bases in the Caribbean.

The first direct assault on the United States occurred half a world away. With French and Dutch colonies in East Asia up for grabs, Japanese leaders knew that only the United States stood in the way of their plan to create a Japanese-led "Greater East Asia Co-Prosperity Sphere" throughout the region. On December 7, 1941, Japanese warplanes attacked the large American naval base at Pearl Harbor, Hawaii. The raid killed some 2,500 Americans and devastated the U.S. fleet. Roosevelt declared December 7 a "date which will live in infamy." Three days later, Germany, which had formed an "axis" with Japan and Italy, declared war against the United States. Domestic debates on American intervention ended.

Roosevelt chose to avoid the moralistic rationales that Wilson had employed in World War I. Instead, he identified clear threats to national security and focused on military measures to overcome them. The United States would be engaged militarily on two fronts, thousands of miles apart. In the Pacific, the United States restored its naval forces and reversed Japan's advances, which by 1943 included the Philippines (still a U.S. colony) as well as Malaya, Singapore, and Vietnam. In the European struggle, U.S. and British forces expelled the Axis powers from North Africa and then drove northward through Italy. In 1944, Allied forces landed on the coast of France and began their eastward push against German troops. These forces joined Soviet troops, who had been equally successful on the eastern front. Germany's surrender, along with Hitler's suicide, came in May 1945. The Japanese emperor, however, remained defiant, despite the retreat of his forces to the mainland.

A month before Germany's surrender, Roosevelt had suffered a fatal stroke, and Vice President Harry Truman had succeeded to the presidency. The new president would face the most fateful decision of the war—and possibly the most ominous decision in human history. Unbeknownst to Truman, U.S. military scientists had been experimenting with nuclear energy, which, if ignited through atomic fission, could yield an explosive force of unprecedented magnitude. The scientists involved in the secret Manhattan Project, based in Los Alamos, New Mexico, detonated the first nuclear bomb there on July 16, 1945. Only then did government officials notify Truman of this awesome new weapon, which could soon be made available for use against Japan. The president understood that defeating Japan through conventional means would require a massive assault on the Japanese mainland, leading to an incalculable loss of life on both sides. With this in mind, he approved the August 6 nuclear bombing of Hiroshima and the August 9 bombing of Nagasaki, which together killed nearly 150,000 Japanese citizens. Faced with the prospect of additional U.S. nuclear attacks, Japan surrendered to the United States and brought World War II to a merciful close.

■ GLOBAL PRIMACY AND THE COLD WAR

Immediately after World War II, the United States entered the third global conflict of the twentieth century. This conflict was labeled the **Cold War** because it never led to direct military combat between its principal antagonists, the United States and the Soviet Union. The basis of this conflict was ideological, pitting the capitalist countries, led by the United States, against the communist countries, led by the Soviet Union. Whereas capitalism respected private property and glorified free enterprise, communism sought to improve living standards by erecting a powerful state that owned and operated the means of economic production. A military showdown between the two superpowers would have produced death and destruction of unknowable proportions. The Cold War, while it avoided such an outcome, produced an endless series of "hot" wars in other parts of the world, mainly among developing countries caught in the crossfire (see Table 2.2).

The United States emerged from World War II as the predominant world power, maintaining a nuclear monopoly for a time and producing as much economic output as the rest of the world combined. However, the Soviet Union, exploiting its considerable resources, both real and potential, soon shifted the global balance of power to a bipolar one, with the United States and the Soviet Union representing the contesting "poles" (see Figure 2.2). With a sphere of influence that spanned from East Germany to the Alaskan border, the Soviet Union possessed the world's largest conventional

Table 2.2 ■ U.S. Foreign Policy Chronology: The Cold War	
1945	Yalta Conference of victorious powers seeks to organize the postwar world.
1946	George Kennan devises containment strategy as the Cold War sets in.
1947	Marshall Plan and Truman Doctrine call for U.S. aid to allies.
1948	The State of Israel is created and immediately recognized by the United States.
1949	NATO is formed by United States and eleven other nations.
1950	North Korea attacks South Korea, prompting UN military intervention.
1953	Korean War ends; CIA aids overthrow of Iran's government.
1954	CIA aids overthrow of Guatemala's government.
1959	The Cuban Revolution produces a communist state close to the U.S. border.
1962	Cuban missile crisis prompts nuclear showdown between the Soviet Union and United States.
1964	Congress authorizes U.S. military intervention in Vietnam.
1968	Tet offensive in Vietnam prompts birth of antiwar movement in United States.
1970	Nixon orders invasion of Cambodia; four student protestors are killed at Kent State University.
1972	Nixon launches détente strategy, visits Soviet Union and China.
1979	Iranian militants seize U.S. embassy in Teheran; Soviet Union invades Afghanistan.
1981	Reagan begins major military buildup as the Cold War heats up.
1986	U.S. covert support for Nicaraguan rebels leads to Iran-*Contra* scandal.
1989	Hungary opens borders with Austria, signaling the Cold War's demise.
1990	Russia and Ukraine declare independence from Soviet Union; Germany is reunified.
1991	Soviet Union dissolves, ending the Cold War.

forces and gradually caught up with the United States in the nuclear arms race. In addition to the arms race, the worldwide competition for allies became a defining element of the Cold War. Each superpower hoped to tip the balance in its favor by recruiting allies beyond its borders.

Strains between the United States and the Soviet Union, allies against the Axis powers in World War II, became insurmountable shortly after the war. Joseph Stalin, the

Figure 2.2 ■ Bipolar Balance of Power in Early Cold War

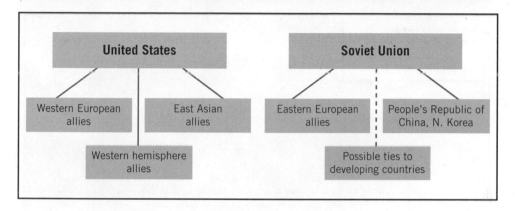

Soviet leader, imposed firm control over the countries of Eastern Europe that his armies had liberated from Nazi Germany. Stalin had no interest in withdrawing from the region that twice in his lifetime had served as a staging area for German invasions. In February 1946, he predicted an inevitable clash between the communist and capitalist countries and the eventual triumph of communism. A month later, Winston Churchill, the former British prime minister who had left office just before the war ended, articulated the division of Europe that would last throughout the Cold War: "An **iron curtain** has descended across the Continent" (see Map 2.2, Cold War Division of Europe).

The task of formulating a Cold War strategy was assigned to George Kennan, a Soviet specialist in the State Department. Kennan first laid out his plan in a February 1946 "long telegram" that circulated within the government. It was reprinted a year later in the journal *Foreign Affairs* (see In Their Own Words box). Kennan's call for the **containment** of communism struck a middle ground between two alternatives: U.S. detachment from the emerging conflict and an all-out invasion and "liberation" of the Soviet Union. Under the containment strategy, the United States would accept the existing sphere of Soviet influence, but it would prevent further Soviet expansion by any means, including military force. In doing so, the United States would wait out the Soviet Union, looking forward to the day when its internal flaws—the denial of individual rights, the lack of a market economy, the high costs of foreign occupation—would cause the communist system to collapse from within.

Beyond waging the Cold War, the United States sought to create a stable world order that reflected its own political and economic principles. The behavior of the fascist governments during World War II had provided a strong case for democratic

Map 2.2 ■ Cold War Division of Europe

Legend:
- Warsaw Pact countries
- Independent communist state
- ( ) Year of communist government control
- •••• Iron curtain to 1989

Sources: Bruce Bueno de Mesquita, *Principles of International Politics: People's Power, Preferences, and Perceptions*, 2nd ed. (Washington, DC: CQ Press, 2003), 197; Steven W. Hook and John Spanier, *American Foreign Policy Since World War II*, 18th ed. (Washington, DC: CQ Press, 2010), 30. Reprinted by permission of CQ Press, an imprint of SAGE Publications Inc.

rule as a means of organizing political life at home and managing foreign relations. Meanwhile, economic prosperity based on private property and free markets would do more than simply prevent communist movements from forming and gaining political power. The U.S. economy would naturally thrive in a market-friendly global trading system that provided outlets for American goods and services. In addition, U.S. banks, multinational corporations, and private investors would benefit enormously if they had free access to foreign markets. In this respect, the American grand strategy during the Cold War pursued objectives that extended well beyond the East-West struggle.

New Structures of Foreign Policy

The challenges and opportunities facing the United States after World War II, combined with the lessons of the interwar years, deterred U.S. foreign policy makers from retreating again into their hemispheric shell. The country had to engage in world politics. Less clear, however, was *how* the United States would engage in politics at

---

IN THEIR OWN WORDS

George Kennan *George Kennan spent years studying the Soviet Union before devising the containment policy that became a pillar of U.S. foreign policy during the Cold War. His knowledge of Russian history and his contact with Soviet leaders during World War II reinforced his sense that, though the coming struggle would be long, the United States would ultimately win it.*

The political personality of Soviet power as we know it today is the product of ideology and circumstances: ideology inherited by the present Soviet leaders from the movement in which they had their political origin, and circumstances of the power which they now have exercised for nearly three decades.

In these circumstances, it is clear that the main element of any United States policy toward the Soviet Union must be that of a long-term, patient but firm and vigilant containment of Russian expansive tendencies . . . Soviet pressure against the free institutions of the Western world is something that can be contained by the adroit and vigilant application of counter-force at a series of constantly shifting geographical and political points, corresponding to the shifts and maneuvers of Soviet policy. . . .

The future of Soviet power may not be by any means as secure as Russian capacity for self-delusion would make it appear. . . . The possibility remains (and in the opinion of this writer it is a strong one) that Soviet power, like the capitalist world of its conception, bears within it the seeds of its own decay, and that the sprouting of these seeds is well advanced.

Source: George F. Kennan, "The Sources of Soviet Conduct," *Foreign Affairs* 25 (July 1947): 566–582. © by the Council on Foreign Relations, Inc. Reprinted by permission.

that level. Would the U.S. government pursue its own interests or those of the international community? Would it choose military or nonmilitary instruments to achieve its goals? Would it act alone or in collaboration with other governments? The answers came in the late 1940s, when President Truman concluded that the nation's interests intimately tied to global stability, political reform, and economic growth. Led by Secretary of State Dean Acheson, the "wise men" of the Truman administration believed that a world of governments and economies resembling those of the United States would be more peaceful, democratic, and prosperous than the present one (see Isaacson and Thomas 1986; McMahon 2008).

A common element of all postwar American foreign policies was the creation of new institutions to put the nation's principles into practice. Global pressures compelled the United States to centralize national security structures and increase the president's direct control over military policy—steps viewed as vital in the nuclear age. The National Security Act of 1947, the most sweeping reorganization of U.S. foreign policy in the nation's history, paved the way for the creation of the Department of Defense (DoD), the National Security Council (NSC), and the Central Intelligence Agency (CIA).

The creation of these agencies produced new tensions within the U.S. government and foreign policy process. Rivalries among the armed services, primarily the Navy and Air Force, turned the DoD into its own kind of battle zone. Struggles over budget resources and, more important, missions in the emerging Cold War led the service chiefs to place their organizational self-interests above those of the nation. Meanwhile, the NSC soon found itself competing against the State Department for control of the foreign policy agenda, and the huge budget outlays required by the DoD left the foreign service chronically shortchanged (see Hook 2003). The CIA proved incapable of serving as a "central" source of intelligence; more than a dozen other intelligence agencies came into being within various federal departments. In preserving and even encouraging internal power struggles, the new system was "flawed by design" (Zegart 1999).

Transnational institutions also took shape during these hectic transition years from World War II to the Cold War. The United States led the way in creating a worldwide intergovernmental organization that adopted many goals sought by the League of Nations while recognizing that organization's limitations. Toward this end, officials from fifty governments came to San Francisco in early 1945 to create the United Nations (UN). Along with the other major powers of the immediate postwar period—China, France, Great Britain, and the Soviet Union—the United States protected its interests by means of a permanent seat and veto power on the UN Security Council. Key votes in the UN General Assembly, in which all countries had one vote, could also be nullified by the Security Council's permanent members. Under Article 51 of the UN Charter, the United States and other countries kept their military options open by reserving "the inherent right of individual or collective self-defense" if they were attacked.[6]

Meanwhile, the U.S. government departed from its traditional practice of avoiding peacetime military alliances. The creation of the North Atlantic Treaty Organization (NATO) in 1949 resulted from several troubling developments in Europe. In 1947, Great Britain had withdrawn its military support for Greece and Turkey, whose governments faced internal revolts by communists and other groups. Under the **Truman Doctrine,** the United States provided military aid to both states and, more broadly, pledged support for "free peoples who are resisting attempted subjugation by armed minorities or by outside pressures." In February 1948, the Soviet Union gained control of Czechoslovakia by supporting a coup against its elected leader and imposing a communist regime in its place. These developments led to the formation of NATO, which comprised the United States, nine Western European countries, Canada, and Iceland. Under the terms of the North Atlantic Treaty, signed in April 1949, an armed attack against one or more of the members "shall be considered an attack against them all." By assuming the lead role in NATO, the United States committed itself to the security of Western Europe for the duration of the Cold War, and long after its conclusion.

On the economic front, the U.S. government also engaged in a flurry of institution building. The nation's economy had grown rapidly in the years before and during the war (see Figure 2.3), and by 1945, U.S. output matched that of the rest of the world combined. In the summer of 1944, officials from forty-four governments met in Bretton Woods, New Hampshire, to discuss postwar financial arrangements. The **Bretton Woods agreements** created a system of fixed currency exchange rates based on the U.S. dollar, which because of American economic clout would be considered "good as gold." The Bretton Woods system included two international financial institutions designed to stabilize the world economy further (see Chapter 6). The World Bank would lend money to member states to rebuild their industries, and the International Monetary Fund (IMF) would manage currency exchanges and provide relief to member states facing short-term currency crises. Another multilateral pact, the General Agreement on Tariffs and Trade (GATT), was signed in 1947 to create rules for keeping national markets open to global commerce.

The **Marshall Plan,** named after Secretary of State George Marshall, paved the way for Western Europe's economic recovery and its eventual political alignment within the European Union (EU). Truman agreed with Marshall that Europe urgently needed U.S. help to revive its slumping economies. Congress then authorized the transfer of $13 billion (about $100 billion in current dollars) in low-interest loans to

---

6. This provision allowed the United States and other governments in the Western Hemisphere to form the Organization of American States in 1947, based in Washington, D.C. Its primary mission was to preserve regional security.

Figure 2.3 ■ U.S. Economic Growth, 1885–1945

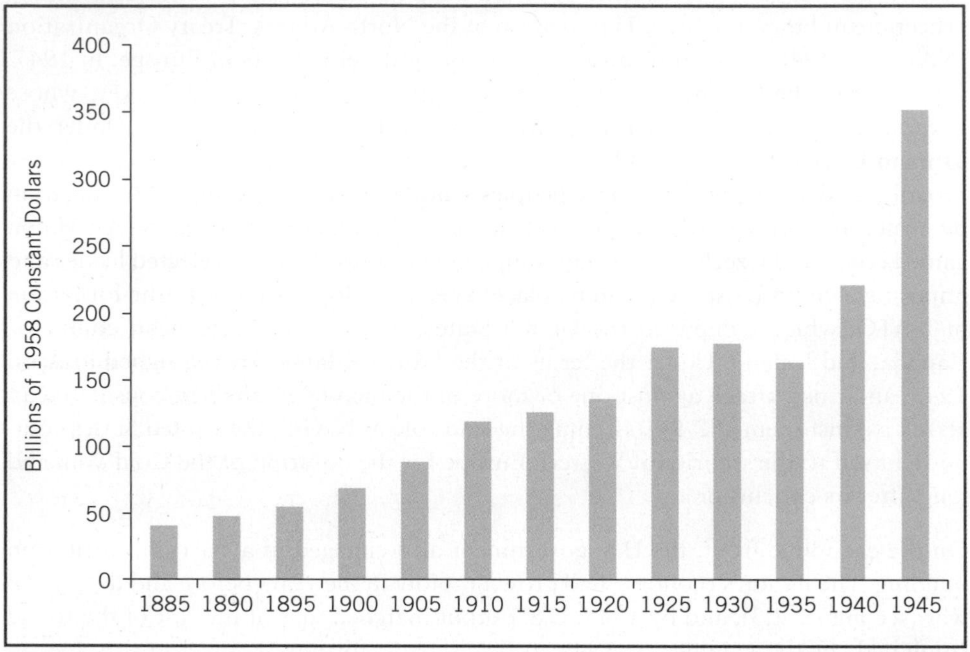

Source: U.S. Bureau of the Census, *The Statistical History of the United States: From Colonial Times to the Present* (New York: Basic Books, 1976).

these countries, which were required to coordinate their plans for recovery. They did so in 1948 by creating the Organization for European Economic Cooperation (OEEC). By 1950, with political stability returning to the region, the Europeans had regained their prewar economic growth. The success of the OEEC led to the creation in 1957 of the European Economic Community (EEC), which later became the European Community (EC) and is now the EU. In this respect, the Soviet Union was instrumental not simply in rallying a unified Western response to a perceived external threat but also in forcing the Western European states to overcome their deep historical animosities toward each other.

Regional Conflicts and the Vietnam Syndrome

These measures laid the institutional foundations for postwar U.S. foreign policy. Such wide-ranging initiatives seemed essential in view of the opportunities available to the United States (the only major power to emerge stronger from the war) for achieving its historic mission of creating a world order in its own image. The new architecture also countered the threat posed by the Soviet Union, which detonated a nuclear device in September 1949 and neutralized the U.S. advantage in this area of military power. Of concern to U.S. leaders as well was the victory of communist forces in China after more than three decades of civil war. The People's Republic of China (PRC) came into being in October 1949 under the leadership of Mao Zedong. Among its first actions, the PRC signed a treaty of cooperation in 1950 with the Soviet Union, which deepened fears in Washington that the balance of global power was shifting against the United States and toward communism.

The PRC was particularly troubling because, unlike the Soviet Union, China represented a potential role model for other developing countries, located largely in the Southern Hemisphere, whose populations greatly outnumbered those in the industrialized nations. Colonial rule was yielding to the creation of new Asian and African countries, which quickly gained a voting majority in the UN General Assembly. The crushing poverty in these new states, and the lack of political institutions in place to satisfy their citizens' rising expectations, raised additional U.S. fears that these countries would turn to communism. The *third world*, a term used to distinguish the region from the *first world* (the capitalist bloc) and the *second world* (the communist bloc), figured prominently in U.S. foreign policy and attracted military intervention by both superpowers in three areas: Korea, Cuba, and Vietnam.

Korea. After World War II, the Soviet Union and the United States were concerned about future control of the Korean peninsula in Northeast Asia, which had been a Japanese colony. The two governments agreed to divide the peninsula along the thirty-eighth parallel—with Moscow controlling the northern and the United States the southern region—until the creation of a unified national government. Such a prospect became unlikely, however, and in 1948 two separate states, North Korea and South Korea (Republic of Korea), were created. Any hopes for reunification vanished in June 1950 when communist forces from North Korea attacked their counterparts in South Korea, prompting Truman to seek relief from the UN Security Council. A multinational force led by the United States pushed North Korean troops back across the thirty-eighth parallel.[7] Then North Korea struck again and seized Seoul, the South Korean capital, and the conflict dragged on. Truman failed to negotiate an end to the war in 1951 and 1952. His successor, Dwight Eisenhower, threatened North Korea with a new offensive if a peace treaty could not be signed. The two sides finally reached an agreement in July 1953 that effectively restored the prewar status quo. With no clear victor, North Korea and South Korea remained divided for the rest of the Cold War and are still separate nations, and a large contingent of U.S. troops continues to patrol the border to keep the peace.

----

7. The Soviet Union, which would have vetoed the resolution, was boycotting the UN at the time to protest its refusal to recognize the new communist regime in China.

The Korean War demonstrated the importance of developing countries to U.S. foreign policy in the Cold War. Recognizing this, Eisenhower turned the CIA into a tool for influencing weaker governments and occasionally toppling regimes disfavored in Washington. In Iran, the CIA backed the 1953 overthrow of Prime Minister Mohammed Mossedegh after he nationalized the country's oil fields. Once he returned to power, Shah (King) Mohammed Reza Pahlavi reopened the oil fields to British and U.S. oil companies. In 1954, the CIA staged another coup in Guatemala, whose elected president, Jacobo Arbenz Guzmán, had launched sweeping land reform and was suspected of being a communist with allegiance to Moscow.[8] Arbenz was replaced by a military general who aligned with the United States and reversed the land reforms.

Nuclear weapons also played an important role in Eisenhower's foreign policy, which he labeled the **New Look**. The president believed nuclear weapons provided more bang for the buck than did conventional forces. The New Look also featured new military alliances that created a "containment belt" around the Soviet Union and China (see Map 2.3, Cold War Alliances with the United States).[9] Each ally found a place under the U.S. "nuclear umbrella," and each became eligible for large amounts of U.S. foreign aid.

Cuba. The gravest challenge to U.S. foreign policy during the Cold War was posed by the nearby island of Cuba, less than a hundred miles from Florida. In 1959, the U.S.-backed military regime of Fulgencio Batista was overthrown and replaced by a Marxist regime led by Fidel Castro, who openly declared the United States to be an enemy of the Cuban people. Eisenhower's successor to the presidency, John Kennedy, turned to the CIA in 1961 to get rid of Castro. But the agency's covert operation failed when the invading force of Cuban exiles was repelled at the Bay of Pigs. Later efforts by the CIA to assassinate Castro, through the use of exploding cigars and other bizarre tactics, served only to elevate the Cuban leader's stature among other developing nations.

The standoff between the United States and Cuba took a perilous turn in November 1962. During routine aerial reconnaissance overflights, American officials discovered that the Cuban government, at the behest of the Soviet Union, had begun installing medium-range nuclear missiles on the island. The missiles had been secretly shipped to Cuba from the Soviet Union, and U.S. cities were their intended targets. Kennedy, well aware of the source of the nuclear missiles, insisted that Castro remove the missiles or face swift military action. After nearly two weeks of tense negotiations between the U.S. and Soviet governments, which came to be called the **Cuban missile crisis,** Soviet

8. At the time, the richest 2 percent of Guatemala's population owned nearly three-fourths of its land. The U.S.-based United Fruit Company was the largest landholder in the country.

9. The United States pledged under the 1945 Inter-American Treaty of Reciprocal Assistance to protect the Western Hemisphere. The alliance wave accelerated with the creation of the ANZUS alliance (with Australia and New Zealand) in 1951, the Southeast Asia Treaty Organization (SEATO) in 1954, and the Central Treaty Organization (CENTO) in 1959. In addition, the United States formed bilateral alliances with Japan, the Philippines, South Korea, and Taiwan (Republic of China).

Map 2.3 ■ Cold War Alliances with the United States

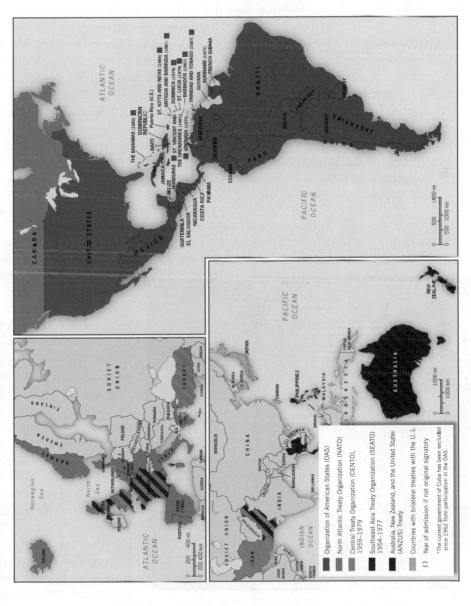

Sources: Organization of American States, www.oas.org; North Atlantic Treaty Organization, www.nato.int; Steven W. Hook and John Spanier, *American Foreign Policy Since World War II*, 19th ed. (Washington, DC: CQ Press, 2013), 69.

leader Nikita Khrushchev ordered the missiles removed. A direct, and possibly apocalyptic, clash between the superpowers was narrowly averted. Castro's Cuba, however, remained a stubborn obstacle to U.S. regional and global interests (Schoultz 2009).

Vietnam. As the events in Cuba unfolded, the United States also was becoming more deeply immersed in a more distant conflict. Its outcome would reveal the limits of U.S. military power, raise doubts about the country's moral posture in the Cold War, and shatter the domestic consensus favoring the containment strategy (Hess 2009). The conflict had erupted after World War II in Indochina, a tropical region in Southeast Asia long dominated by foreign powers. After Japan's defeat in 1945, France had insisted on reclaiming its colony in Vietnam. But the French could not subdue an independence movement in Vietnam and withdrew in 1954. The U.S. government, which feared the rise to power of a communist regime, stepped into the quagmire. Eisenhower viewed Vietnam through the lens of the domino theory, which held that a communist victory in one country would lead to a succession of additional victories in neighboring states.

The U.S. military presence in Vietnam grew slowly in the early 1960s and then soared to half a million soldiers and advisers by 1968. Like Korea, Vietnam was split into northern and southern regions, with the north allied with communism and the south receiving support from the United States and its allies. Despite the superior firepower of the United States, Kennedy and his successor in office, Lyndon Johnson, could not defeat the North's Viet Cong forces, led by Ho Chi Minh. Back in the United States, growing U.S. deployments, followed by ongoing defeats and casualties, prompted the birth of an antiwar movement. As television networks broadcast graphic images of the carnage on a daily basis, the Vietnam War engulfed President Richard Nixon and his administration as he took office in January 1969. Despite Nixon's promises to end the war, the conflict continued into the mid-1970s, when Vietnam at

AFP/Getty Images

North Vietnamese troops celebrate their victory over the United States atop a tank in front of the presidential palace in Saigon on April 30, 1975. Thousands of Vietnamese citizens joined this celebration in Saigon, later renamed Ho Chi Minh City in honor of the leader of the revolutionary movement.

last gained its independence under a communist government. Nearly 59,000 U.S. troops had died in the conflict, and another 153,000 had been wounded. More than 1 million Vietnamese had been killed or wounded.

The Vietnam War proved disastrous for the United States in several ways. For one thing, U.S. leaders had wrongly viewed it as an ideological struggle rather than a war of independence and self-determination. As a result, their goal of winning the hearts and minds of the Vietnamese people had been doomed from the start. Militarily, U.S. forces had failed to adapt to the demands of guerrilla warfare, ground forces had been left without clear orders, and daily aerial assaults by American bombers had merely strengthened the will of the Vietnamese.[10] All of these pitfalls offended the moral sensibilities of many Americans, who had long believed in the righteousness of their country's actions overseas. As the national soul-searching associated with the **Vietnam syndrome** took hold across the country after the war, the moral superiority of the United States could no longer be taken for granted—nor could the virtues and open-ended military commitments of the containment doctrine.

The End of the Cold War

By the early 1970s, the Soviet Union had caught up with the United States in the most potent category of military power, nuclear weapons. At the same time, the U.S. economy was showing serious signs of distress. The costs of the Vietnam War and other burdens had prevented the country from maintaining its role as the "lender of last resort." Domestic unrest and new regional crises, particularly in the Middle East, forced Nixon to change the course of U.S. foreign policy.

Nixon assigned his national security adviser, Henry Kissinger, the task of designing a strategy that recognized these new realities. Kissinger, a Jewish refugee from Nazi Germany and a passionate advocate of U.S. primacy (Keys 2011), soon settled on **détente,** a term borrowed from the French meaning an easing of tensions. Under the détente policy, U.S. and Soviet leaders established a closer working relationship so that regional crises could be resolved without threatening a direct confrontation. In addition, in return for Soviet restraint, the United States offered that country material benefits, including badly needed American agricultural exports. The two governments also negotiated a series of arms control treaties that first limited, and later reduced, the stockpiles of nuclear weapons on both sides.

Nixon also sought improved relations with the People's Republic of China, whose communist government the United States had not yet recognized. The PRC, still ruled by Mao Zedong, was struggling, so it stood to benefit greatly from the economic

---

10. For a reassessment of the Vietnam ordeal by the secretary of defense under Kennedy and Johnson, see McNamara and VanDeMark (1995).

opportunities U.S. recognition would bring. The breakthrough between the countries came in a May 1972 visit by Nixon to China, during which the United States officially recognized the PRC as the legitimate government of China. In return, Mao agreed to cooperate with the United States rather than the Soviet Union. By securing this commitment, Nixon and Kissinger achieved the upper hand in the now triangular superpower rivalry.

Despite these gains, the memories of Vietnam and the Watergate scandal that drove Nixon from office in 1974 compelled Americans to seek yet another shift in U.S. foreign policy. President Jimmy Carter, a former peanut farmer and born-again Christian from Georgia, turned the nation's attention away from the confrontation of the Cold War and toward a more cooperative posture emphasizing human rights, improved living conditions in the developing world, and a stronger role for the United Nations. Carter's policy of **liberal internationalism** offered a new route to global stability, and the president achieved a major foreign policy goal by brokering the 1978 Camp David Accords between Israel and Egypt.

In his final years in office, however, Carter suffered a series of setbacks (see Kaufman 2008). First, a 1979 revolution in Nicaragua brought a Marxist regime to power there. Second, the U.S.-backed shah of Iran was replaced in 1979 by a new government based on Islamic law and harshly critical of the United States. The final blow came in December 1979, when the Soviet Union sent 80,000 troops into Afghanistan to bolster a new puppet government. Carter could not overcome these challenges and lost his 1980 bid for reelection to Ronald Reagan, a Republican "hawk" who launched a more forceful approach to foreign policy (see Mann 2009).

As president, Reagan revived superpower tensions and, in 1983, called the Soviet Union "the focus of evil in the modern world." His rhetorical offensive was accompanied by an expansion of U.S. armed forces, which the president believed had been neglected during the détente and Carter years. The president took action on several occasions, including a 1983 invasion of Grenada amid chaos on the island, and an ongoing effort to overthrow the communist government of Nicaragua. In this case, the White House approved secret shipments of weapons to be sent from Iran to the rebel *Contras*, a maneuver that was later rejected by Congress and criticized by a special commission.[11]

Reagan also raised the stakes of the arms race by proposing a U.S. "missile shield" in outer space that would shoot down Soviet missiles headed for the United States. By the mid-1980s, annual U.S. defense spending had nearly doubled, thanks to a Congress that supported Reagan's proposals. As the buildup continued, many Americans became anxious about an impending nuclear war. Their fears were strengthened by scientific evidence suggesting that even a "limited" nuclear war

---

11. See Lynch (2011) for a recent analysis of the Iran-*Contra* affair.

would produce a "nuclear winter," leading to the extinction of most plant and animal life (C. Sagan 1983/1984).

Amid these fears appeared new signs of hope for improved superpower relations. The deaths of three aged Soviet leaders—Leonid Brezhnev, Yuri Andropov, and Konstantin Chernenko—between 1982 and 1985 brought to power a new generation, most notably Mikhail Gorbachev, who openly acknowledged his nation's problems. The economy had succumbed to centralized control, a demoralized labor force, and a crumbling infrastructure, while the rigid political system discouraged public participation and new ideas. Gorbachev proposed two reforms to rectify these problems: *perestroika*, the restructuring of the Soviet economy to spur innovation and efficiency, and *glasnost*, greater openness in the political system. Soviet citizens and foreign leaders, including Reagan, welcomed both reforms.

By the time George H. W. Bush took office in January 1989, the only question remaining about the Soviet Union was whether its decay was irreversible. Gorbachev sought to ease strains on the Soviet periphery in Eastern Europe by permitting client states to launch their own reforms. Citizens seized on the opportunity—not to restructure their communist systems but to get rid of them altogether. The critical turning point came in September 1989, when Hungary's government opened its borders with Austria, permitting thousands of East Europeans to cross the iron curtain. The Berlin Wall fell two months later, and in quick succession democratic regimes were established across the region.

As the Soviet bloc crumbled around him, Gorbachev confronted independence movements among the fifteen republics that comprised the Soviet Union. The largest of these, Russia, held free elections in May 1990 that brought President Boris Yeltsin to power. Gorbachev's efforts to salvage the Soviet Union proved futile, and on Christmas Day 1991, the nation ceased to exist. The U.S. government's primary role during this period was to support a "soft landing" for the Soviet Union. In the end, the United States won the Cold War in the most favorable manner possible—through the peaceful and orderly dismantling of its longtime rival in Moscow.

■ NEW CHALLENGES AFTER THE COLD WAR

The end of the Cold War caught the world by surprise. The East-West conflict had become a deeply entrenched fact of life on both sides of the iron curtain. The ideological competition between communism and capitalism had seemed to defy resolution. The nuclear doctrine of mutual assured destruction (MAD) had locked the Soviet Union and the United States into a strategic stalemate, and the logic of bipolarity had established a manageable framework for superpower relations while constraining the ambitions of regional powers. Few analysts anticipated the dissolution of the Soviet bloc, an outcome that seemed beyond the realm of possibility because of the firm grip in which the Kremlin held its citizens and the Warsaw Pact states. Moreover, the Kremlin's massive nuclear stockpile appeared to provide Moscow with indefinite status as a military superpower.

Even so, the Soviet monopoly on power could not be sustained amid poor living conditions and drained government budgets. The communications revolution of the early 1990s broke down the walls between the Soviet bloc and the outside world. Advances in satellite technology extended the reach of televised coverage into areas that were previously isolated. The arrival of personal computers in the Soviet bloc, including Internet access and e-mail capabilities, permitted contacts across national borders that could not be controlled by government officials. As a result, citizens gained new exposure to the world around them. What they learned not only contradicted the images and messages they had been fed by the government but also revealed the profound gaps between their living standards and those of their Western neighbors.

Elements of the New World Order

The victory of the United States in the Cold War represented more than the defeat of one international coalition by another. The Soviet Union's collapse marked the triumph of liberalism over the two competing ideologies of the twentieth century: fascism and communism. The challenge of fascism was subdued with the military defeat of Germany, Italy, and Japan during World War II. Communism died a slower death with the demise of the Soviet bloc and the transition of Chinese communism into an economic system based largely on market forces. The United States, now the centerpiece of a unipolar balance of power, had achieved its two-century objective of transforming world politics (see Figure 2.4). In his 1989 article "The End of History," Francis Fukuyama captured the exuberant spirit of the time: "What we may be witnessing is not just the end of the Cold War, or the passing of a particular

Figure 2.4 ■ Unipolar Balance of World Power, 2010

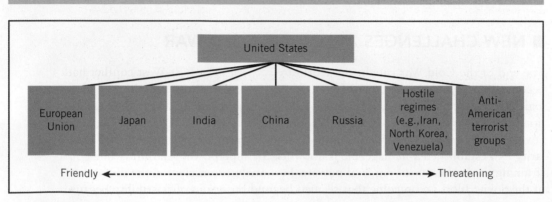

period of history, but the end of history as such, that is, the end point of mankind's ideological evolution and the universalization of Western liberal democracy as the final form of government" (4).

Nine months before the collapse of the Soviet Union, President George H. W. Bush (1991) had expressed this sense of triumphalism in an address to a joint session of Congress: "We can see a new world coming into view, a world in which there is the very real prospect of a **new world order,** a world where the United States—freed from Cold War stalemate—is poised to fulfill the historic vision of its founders; a world in which freedom and respect for human rights finds a home among all nations" (see Table 2.3). The president did not fully detail what this order would look like, but in his public statements, he repeatedly emphasized three overlapping elements: democratization, economic globalization, and multilateral cooperation.

Democratization. The dismantling of communist regimes advanced the trend toward global democratization that had been under way since the 1970s. During that decade, many Latin American countries overcame long histories of military rule and installed new political systems based on constitutionalism, free multiparty elections, and the protection of basic civil and political rights. Many African and Asian countries adopted similar reforms in the 1980s, as did the postcommunist countries in Europe in the early 1990s. Democratic freedoms and human rights, Americans widely believed, should be adopted and protected on a universal basis.

Economic globalization. Another central aspect of the new world order was a trend toward market-based economic commerce both within and among states, a trend that gained momentum in the latter stages of the Cold War. In short, international commerce in the world economy would resemble interstate commerce within the U.S. economy, which occurs with limited government intervention. Free trade in this model would be accompanied by foreign investments on a massive scale, enriching multinational corporations and effectively creating a single global economy.

Multilateral cooperation. Economic globalization was also fueled by multilateral institutions such as the World Bank and the IMF, which undertook new missions after the Cold War. Meanwhile, the World Trade Organization, created in 1995, enforced the market-friendly trade reforms written into the most recent global trade pact. Multilateralism extended further to environmental efforts, culminating in the 1992 Earth Summit in Brazil. On the security front, the U.S. government welcomed greater cooperation and expected the UN to assume the stronger peacekeeping role unattainable during the Cold War. The United States also led the effort to maintain and expand NATO, even though its adversary, the Soviet Union, had disappeared.

President Bill Clinton embraced all three elements of this new world order when he took office in January 1993. Clinton, whose primary interest was domestic rather than foreign policy, believed the United States would be more secure and prosperous in a more tightly knit world whose nations shared common values, interests, and political institutions. His national security policy of "engagement and enlargement" presumed that closer interactions between countries, primarily on economic matters, would provide collective benefits to them while discouraging defections from, or challenges to, the status quo. Along these lines, Anthony Lake (1993, 659), Clinton's national security adviser, observed that "the successor to a doctrine of containment must be a strategy of enlargement of the world's free community."

Overseas Unrest and Domestic Unease

Despite their great expectations for the new world order, U.S. leaders confronted a variety of armed conflicts overseas, which revealed that history had not "ended" with the demise of the Soviet Union. Instead, regional conflicts and internal power struggles suppressed during the Cold War resurfaced, producing large-scale violence and attracting the attention and military intervention of outside forces, including the United States. Conflicts in three regions—the Persian Gulf, Northeast Africa, and Yugoslavia—dampened the enthusiasm of American leaders for "engagement" and provoked a turn away from multilateral cooperation, which would intensify in the new millennium under Clinton's successor, George W. Bush.

The first regional conflict erupted in the Persian Gulf before the Soviet Union collapsed. Iraq's invasion of neighboring Kuwait on August 2, 1990, directly challenged the new world order and prompted the United States to deploy a military force to protect Saudi Arabia and, later, to oust Iraq from Kuwait. The international response to the invasion included a series of UN resolutions demanding Iraq's withdrawal. When Iraqi leader Saddam Hussein ignored these resolutions, the UN authorized a military assault (**Operation Desert Storm**) on Iraqi troops in the Kuwaiti desert. The U.S.-led assault quickly crushed the Iraqi military. Saddam remained in power, however, and defied resolutions that he comply with UN inspectors in ridding his country of weapons of mass destruction. The imposition of economic sanctions and a "no-fly zone" across much of the country did not produce compliance from Saddam, whose control over Iraq only deepened in the years to come.

The UN also struggled to resolve upheavals in **failed states**—those countries incapable of maintaining order or providing even minimal services to their citizens (see Map 2.4, Post–Cold War U.S. Military Operations). Primary among these failed states was Somalia, where nearly 50,000 citizens died in a civil war before a UN-sponsored cease-fire could be arranged in March 1992. By this time, a drought had led to widespread famine, and no government was in place to provide relief to the starving population. The humanitarian crisis compelled the United States to intervene militarily and provide relief to the Somalis. Meanwhile, a more ambitious UN effort to find a long-term solution failed, leading to more unrest and American casualties, which prompted Clinton to withdraw from Somalia. When a much bloodier ethnic conflict broke out in nearby Rwanda and Burundi in 1994, leaving nearly 1 million dead in

Table 2.3 ■ U.S. Foreign Policy Chronology: Post–Cold War

1991	Iraq is forced out of Kuwait by a UN coalition led by the United States.
1992	Civil war escalates across former Yugoslavia.
1993	U.S. forces killed in Somalia, forcing U.S. withdrawal; Congress ratifies North American Free Trade Agreement (NAFTA).
1994	Plan for World Trade Organization is approved.
1994	Ethnic Hutus in Rwanda and Burundi commit genocide of more than 800,000 ethnic Tutsis.
1995	United States brokers Dayton Peace Accords, ending ethnic warfare in Bosnia-Herzegovina.
1996	Clinton signs Comprehensive Test Ban Treaty (CTBT).
1997	Czech Republic, Hungary, and Poland are invited to join NATO.
1998	Al Qaeda terrorists bomb U.S. embassies in Kenya and Tanzania.
1999	NATO forces intervene in Kosovo to stop ethnic cleansing by Yugoslav government.
2000	Terrorist bombing of USS *Cole* kills seventeen and injures thirty-seven Americans.
2001	Islamic terrorists crash commercial airplanes into World Trade Center and Pentagon, United States invades Afghanistan and overthrows regime linked to 9/11 attacks.
2002	President Bush threatens preemptive strikes against U.S. enemies.
2003	The United States invades Iraq and overthrows Saddam Hussein's regime; U.S. occupation fails to uncover weapons of mass destruction that prompted invasion.
2004	First democratic elections are held in Afghanistan; insurgency spreads across Iraq.
2005	Iraqi voters elect parliament and approve a constitution amid political violence.
2007	Bush announces surge of U.S. troops in Iraq to suppress sectarian violence.
2008	Financial crisis, based in the United States, is worst since the Great Depression.
2009	President Obama's surge in Afghanistan reverses gains by Taliban insurgents.
2010	United States leads relief effort following devastating earthquake in Haiti.
2011	Mass democratic uprisings occur across North Africa and the Middle East in the "Arab Spring."
2012	Terrorists invade U.S. consulate in Benghazi, Libya, killing Ambassador Christopher Stevens.
2013	Three people are killed and nearly 300 injured in a terrorist attack on the Boston Marathon.
2014	Russian government seizes the Crimean Peninsula and fuels pro-Russian uprisings in Ukraine; Islamic State of Iraq and Syria (ISIS) captures large territories across the two countries.

Map 2.4 ■ Post-Cold War U.S. Military Operations

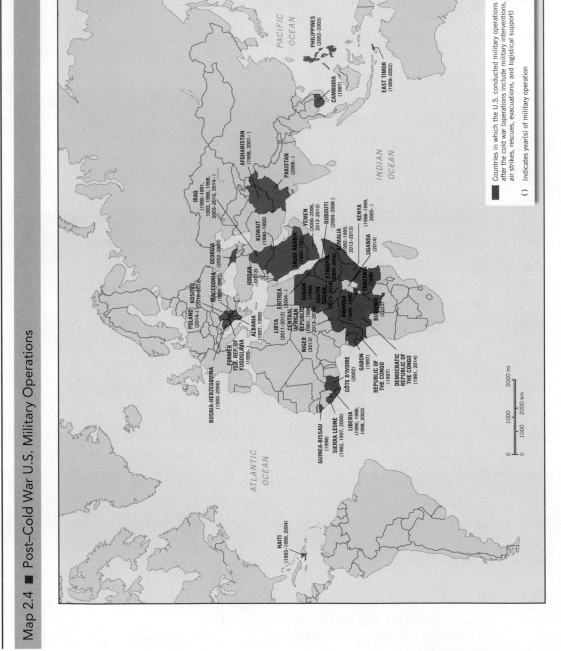

Source: Barbara Salazar Torreon, *Instances of Use of United States Armed Forces Abroad, 1798–2014,* CRS Report RL 42738 (Washington, DC: Congressional Research Service, September 15, 2014).

a matter of months, the United States, fearing a repeat of the Somalia disaster, let the carnage run its course. With no other major powers willing to step in, the UN stood by as the genocide unfolded.

The end of the Cold War also revived hostilities in the crumbling European state of Yugoslavia. Religious differences among Catholics, Orthodox Christians, and Muslims had been suppressed for decades by a communist government led by Marshal Josip Tito. But the end of the Cold War quickly unearthed these differences, producing a new cycle of violence, territorial conquest, and foreign intervention. Neither the UN nor the European Union could organize an effective response to the "ethnic cleansing" in Yugoslavia. In response, the United States finally ended the bloodshed in the provinces of Bosnia-Herzegovina (in 1995) and Kosovo (in 1999). By the end of the decade, Yugoslavia had broken up into several republics.

These foreign entanglements occurred as the United States was experiencing unprecedented economic growth and prosperity. As stock markets reached record highs, inflation and unemployment fell to negligible levels. Enjoying a heyday in the first post–Cold War decade, Americans had little patience for conflicts overseas. This domestic focus, and a move away from multilateral foreign policy, gained further momentum in November 1994, when the Republican Party won control of both houses of Congress for the first time in four decades. The Senate's refusal to sign the Comprehensive Test Ban Treaty (CTBT) in October 1999 epitomized the unilateral turn in U.S. foreign policy. Upon taking office in January 2001, President George W. Bush renounced the Kyoto Protocol on Climate Change, the International Criminal Court, and the Anti-Ballistic Missile Treaty with the Soviet Union. His approach ran counter to that of Bill Clinton and his successor, Barack Obama, revealing deep divisions over foreign policy among the post–Cold War presidents (see Onea 2013).

On September 11, 2001, al Qaeda terrorists attacked the United States by flying two commercial jets into the World Trade Center, bringing down the twin towers and killing nearly 3,000 people. A third hijacked airliner crashed into the Pentagon, and a fourth crash landed in Pennsylvania on its way to another target in the nation's capital.

September 11 and the War on Terrorism

As the United States entered the new millennium, it seemed secure from foreign threats, and most Americans agreed with President Bush's emphasis on domestic problems. But all this changed on the morning of September 11, 2001, when al Qaeda terrorists hijacked four U.S. commercial jets and flew three of them into highly visible, well-known symbols of American power—the World Trade Center in New York City and the Pentagon near Washington, D.C. The fourth jet, apparently headed for the U.S. Capitol, crashed in rural Pennsylvania after several passengers struggled with the hijackers for control of the cockpit.

The attacks forced the grounding of all air traffic in the United States and the indefinite closing of the New York Stock Exchange and many public attractions, including Disney World in Florida and the arch in Saint Louis, Missouri. After returning to the White House from Florida and conferring with his advisers, the president made two decisions that formed the core of the Bush Doctrine. First, the U.S. government would treat the attacks not as crimes but as acts of war. Second, the U.S. response would target not only the terrorist groups but also the countries that harbored them. The subsequent "global war on terrorism" then became the centerpiece of U.S. foreign policy and the defining feature of Bush's presidency.

American officials immediately traced the terrorists to Afghanistan, whose Taliban government had provided Osama bin Laden, al Qaeda's leader, with political cover and sites for training camps on the country's remote mountainsides.[12] U.S. retaliation, which began in late September, unfolded in two stages. First, American forces would help antigovernment Afghan militias overthrow the Taliban and round up the al Qaeda terrorists responsible for the attacks. Second, the United States would create a new, democratic regime that would not threaten its neighbors or serve as a sanctuary for Islamic terrorists. Although the first phase of the plan met with initial success (the capital of Kabul fell on November 12), bin Laden evaded his would-be captors and remained at large in the rugged terrain along Afghanistan's 1,500-mile border with Pakistan. But even without bin Laden's capture, the effort to replace the Taliban regime proceeded on schedule; Afghans elected a new leader, Hamid Karzai, in 2004 and a new parliament in 2005.

After routing the Taliban from power in Afghanistan, Bush made the fateful decision to make Iraq the second front in the war on terrorism. Saddam Hussein's cat-and-mouse game with UN weapons inspectors had outlasted the Clinton administration, and many of Bush's top advisers—who had been labeled neoconservatives or "Vulcans"—had long argued that Saddam must be removed from power. It remained

---

12. This was not the first time bin Laden had supervised paramilitary forces in Afghanistan. He had also served during the 1980s in the Afghan *mujahidin,* or resistance fighters, against the occupying Soviet army. The *mujahidin* had generous support from the CIA (see Coll 2004).

unclear whether Iraq possessed weapons of mass destruction, and the White House feared that Saddam's shared hatred of the United States with Islamic terrorists might tempt him to supply terrorists from his stockpiles. Information provided by Iraqi exiles became part of the National Intelligence Estimate issued in October 2002, whose opening line summarized the case against Saddam: "Baghdad has chemical and biological weapons as well as missiles with ranges in excess of UN restrictions; if left unchecked, it probably will have a nuclear weapon during this decade."

This report convinced Bush that the time was right to settle matters with Saddam. Although the president faced a skeptical UN Security Council, he secured support from Congress in October 2002 to organize a "coalition of the willing" for an invasion. The invasion, code-named **Operation Iraqi Freedom,** began on March 20, 2003. As in the Afghanistan campaign, the initial "shock and awe" bombing campaign allowed coalition forces to advance rapidly and seize control of the capital and government. Although Saddam initially evaded capture, he was apprehended in December 2003 and placed on trial before an Iraqi war crimes tribunal.

Despite their initial military victory, U.S.-led occupying forces faced unexpected resistance as they sought to bring Iraq under control. Far from being "greeted as liberators," as Vice President Dick Cheney had predicted before the invasion, coalition forces were subjected to daily attacks, which intensified after Pentagon officials dissolved Iraq's police and security forces. Secretary of Defense Donald Rumsfeld's decision to limit the size of the invading force to fewer than 200,000 troops left Iraq's border open to other insurgents. But the chaos in Iraq extended far beyond attacks on the coalition forces. Iraqi militias, representing rival Sunni and Shiite Islamic groups, also turned their guns and missiles on each other in an effort to gain control of postwar Iraq. A third group, the ethnic Kurds in the north, saw an opportunity to realize their historic goal of seceding from Iraq and forming their own government.

The Bush administration found that its stymied mission in Iraq was imperiling its war on terrorism (see Gordon and Trainor 2006; Ricks 2006). The United States was spending an estimated $8 billion a month on the war while receiving little in return. Yet the president remained determined to convert Iraq, whose citizens had now participated in unprecedented national elections, into a democratic and peaceful state. The nation's slide toward civil war not only threatened this transition but also raised the prospect that regional sectarian struggles would extend into neighboring Iran and across the Muslim world. At home, Bush faced turmoil within his own national security team. Colin Powell, his secretary of state, left the administration after Bush was reelected in November 2004, and Defense Secretary Donald Rumsfeld resigned late in 2006 amid continuing failures in Iraq (see Woodward 2008).

Bush approved a **surge strategy** in January 2007 that added five military brigades to conflict zones in Baghdad and other cities. The strategy included a heightened effort to train Iraqi security forces and to reassure Iraqi citizens that the United States supported their aspirations for peace and freedom. Although the level of violence eased along with the pace of American casualties after the surge, Bush left office in January 2009 with the U.S. mission in Iraq—and his global war on terrorism—far from over.

Even as the violence in Iraq subsided, insurgents and Taliban forces regained control of much of Afghanistan, leaving Bush's successor, Barack Obama, with the difficult choice of withdrawing from the war-torn nation or escalating U.S. military activities there. In December 2009, Obama chose to replicate Bush's surge strategy by ordering the deployment of 30,000 additional troops to Afghanistan. He assured Americans that this would be a temporary measure to regain the upper hand in the power struggle, which had spread into neighboring Pakistan and threatened to become a regional conflagration. Obama pledged to remove U.S. forces from Afghanistan beginning in 2011, when that country's government security forces would presumably be self-sufficient.

In 2009, Obama came into office facing the nation's most severe economic crisis since the Great Recession. By then, the U.S. real estate bubble had burst as millions of Americans forfeited the over-priced homes offered to them by reckless mortgage brokers and investment banks (see Chapter 11 for details). The U.S. Treasury, faced with an imminent collapse of the nation's financial system, lent $700 billion to these banks, along with teetering economic sectors such as the automobile industry, to stay in business. The financial crisis quickly spread worldwide, as foreign firms had close financial links to major U.S. banks and had adopted many of their failed practices. In sum, the losses to U.S. banks amounted to nearly $4 trillion. Lost assets worldwide were estimated at $27 trillion, or about one-half of global economic output in 2008 (Drezner 2014, 123).

Although forced to focus on domestic problems, Obama succeeded in removing U.S. troops from Iraq in 2011, and his effort to "kill or capture" leading al Qaeda terrorists, including Osama bin Laden, proved effective (Klaidman 2012). The president cautiously navigated the **Arab Spring** of 2011, a democratic revolution that spread from North Africa across the Middle East. Tunisia's democratic revolution, which sparked the Arab Spring, produced a peaceful regime change. Other uprisings were less successful. Syria's government succumbed to a civil war that continued into 2013.[13] A military coalition led by the United States overthrew the Libyan regime led by Muammar Qaddafi, ridding the nation of a brutal autocrat but leaving the nation in the hands of rival militias. And in Egypt, mass demonstrations led to the ouster of its entrenched leader, Hosni Mubarak, and to an election won by Mohamed Morsi,

---

13. More than 200,000 Syrians were killed in the civil war by the end of 2014. Another 10 million had fled their homes by that time, nearly half of whom were forced to live as refugees in bordering states. (New York: United Nations High Commissioner for Refugees, "UNHCR Country Operations Profile—Syrian Arab Republic," accessed March 23, 2015.)

a leader of the Muslim Brotherhood who promised to treat all citizens fairly and equally. When he failed to uphold these promises, he was overthrown and replaced by a military general who quickly restricted political rights.

Of greatest concern was the breakdown of order in Iraq after the U.S. troops had withdrawn. The power vacuum that resulted, along with a similar breakdown in war-torn Syria, opened the doors for a powerful terrorist group known as the Islamic State of Iraq and Syria (ISIS). Resorting to extreme violence that included mass killings and televised beheadings, ISIS captured and occupied a region in both countries the size of Great Britain. Obama, caught off guard by the ISIS juggernaut, organized a coalition of nations to repel the terrorists. He refused, however, to commit American "boots on the ground" beyond military trainers to assist Iraq and other regional allies. While frequent air strikes disrupted its operations, ISIS made steady progress in creating an Islamist caliphate, to be governed by a strict version of *sharia* (Islamic) law.

A New Era of Power Politics

Among the many changes in the current strategic environment is the revival of **power politics,** an aggressive form of statecraft that relies on threats of aggression and shows of force based on the military strength of rivals (see Wight 1946). Power politics, deeply founded in realism, adopts an amoral approach to world politics in which "might makes right." It was widely associated with great-power conflicts through the seventeenth century, and later in the two world wars. While the Cold War featured a perpetual competition over nuclear supremacy, the two superpowers chose to maintain strategic parity and peaceful coexistence. The "new world order" declared after the Cold War presumed the continued absence of power politics, with multilateral cooperation and global governance guiding conflict resolutions.

These assumptions were challenged early in 2014, when Russia's military took over Ukraine's Crimean Peninsula, restoring Moscow's control over a major naval base that was reverted to Ukraine after the Soviet Union collapsed in 1991. Sensing a lack of resolve in the United States, Vladimir Putin also fomented uprisings in eastern Ukraine, where mobs of Russian nationalists demanded secession and membership into Russia. The violence escalated when a Malaysian jetliner, filled with 298 passengers and crew members, was shot down over eastern Ukraine. Putin denied Russian involvement in the attack, a claim that was widely rejected in the midst of recent surface-to-air attacks against Ukrainian aircraft that relied upon missiles that were plainly made in Moscow.

The election of Xi Jinping as Chinese president in 2012 fueled the latest return of power politics. Since the Cold War, the People's Republic of China (PRC) and Russia joined together in calling for the end of U.S. primacy and its replacement with a multilateral balance of power. Such a call was hardly new. At the United Nations in 1997, the two governments signed a Joint Russian-Chinese Declaration about a Multipolar

World and the Formation of a New World Order. More recently, state visits between Jinping and Putin went further by suggesting that, in the face of apparent U.S. decline, a new multilateral order had already arrived. Jinping signaled a more aggressive policy by claiming control over an expansive range of islands near the Chinese coast that were considered the domain of Japan, the Philippines, Vietnam, and other maritime nations.[14]

China and Russia sought to strengthen their move toward multipolarity by forming a bloc of developing states that reflected their growing economic clout. The countries of Brazil, Russia, India, China, and South Africa (BRICS) held annual summit meetings that paved the way for closer ties and partnerships. In 2014, the BRICS created a New Development Bank that would offer $50 billion in aid to other developing countries. This action was meant to offset the dominance of the U.S.-led World Bank and International Monetary Fund, which since World War II had assumed responsibility for a stable global economy. While not an overt act of power politics, the creation of the New Development Bank showcased the growing influence of these governments, whose leaders presided over roughly 40 percent of the global population.

■ CONCLUSION

As described in this chapter, U.S. foreign policy historically stems from an uneasy combination of normative values and self-interested quests for greater power in the interstate system. A cultural sense of exceptionalism has provided both a moral rationale and an explanation for the nation's steadily growing strength and influence. Wielding a potent combination of hard and soft power, American leaders first gained control of a sweeping landmass stretching from the Atlantic to the Pacific Oceans, and then established the nation's place as a global trading state. The world wars ended with the United States gaining a stature of primacy in the balance of power that has endured to the present time. Such a record of national growth and longevity, which encompasses unmatched political, economic, military, and cultural assets, has no precedent in modern history.

Along the way, U.S. leaders faced a paradox of their nation's own world power. The same values and norms that fueled its rise to primacy also created problems for its management of foreign policy. While the U.S. system of diffused political authority enhanced democracy at home, its fragmented structure hindered coherent and consistent decision making while exposing challenges to national unity. The government's transparency also furthered its democratic mission while revealing internal schisms, policy bottlenecks, and plans for national security that were useful to potential or active enemies. America's dynamic civil society, another check on government,

---

14. For an informative visual analysis, see Council on Foreign Relations (2013), *China's Maritime Disputes*, http://www.cfr.org/asia-and-pacific/chinas-maritime-disputes/p31345#!/.

also offered pathways for powerful interest groups to skew foreign policies in ways that benefitted them while running counter to stated national priorities.

The paradox of America's world power gradually went global with the spread of modern technologies, the advent of transnational civil societies, and the growing interconnectedness of globalized trade and financial networks. Social media, for example, was founded on U.S. technology but also empowered anti-American groups and movements. Steps toward global governance, most of which were backed by the U.S. government, frequently turned against U.S. foreign policies and actions, and new institutions such as the World Trade Organization routinely sanctioned U.S. policies. The nation's function as a locomotive of market-driven economic growth affirmed another of its founding ambitions but also fueled the rise of economic competitors, particularly China in recent years. As noted above, gaps between America's values and actions—such as the torture of suspected terrorists in Iraq and Afghanistan—drew charges of hypocrisy from foreign governments and ruptured the nation's vital soft power. In these and other respects, American world power was a role model for countless states and societies while also suffering as a victim of its own success.

The United States today must make the most of a world order it had a large hand in creating. The "shadow of the past" has left the United States with many adversaries—but many more friends— in the nation-state system. The future of American primacy will depend on its success in balancing its commitments and capabilities, standing up to foreign threats, reconciling domestic divisions, and, most of all, aligning the nation's power and principles. The alternative—a vacuum in the balance of power—is far more likely to rupture the global trend toward democratic governance, economic progress, and receding conflicts among states that was a defining feature of the late twenty-first century. Achieving this goal will ultimately depend on the decisions made by American leaders. Their roles and relationships, which play out daily in the foreign policy process, are the primary concerns of this book.

KEY TERMS

Arab Spring, p. 70

Bretton Woods agreements, p. 53

Cold War, p. 47

collective security, p. 44

containment, p. 49

Cuban missile crisis, p. 56

détente, p. 59

exceptionalism, p. 31

failed states, p. 64

gunboat diplomacy, p. 39

iron curtain, p. 49

Kellogg-Briand Pact, p. 45

lend-lease program, p. 46

liberal internationalism, p. 60

manifest destiny, p. 39

Marshall Plan, p. 53

Monroe Doctrine, p. 38

New Look, p. 56

new world order, p. 63

Open Door policy, p. 41

Operation Desert Storm, p. 64

Operation Iraqi Freedom, p. 69

power politics, p. 71

Roosevelt Corollary, p. 42

surge strategy, p. 69

Truman Doctrine, p. 53

unilateralism, p. 35

Vietnam syndrome, p. 59

INTERNET REFERENCES

The **BBC's history section** (http://www.bbc.co.uk/history/) is "dedicated to bringing history to life" by providing animations, movies, and virtual tours, as well as a collection of articles by noted writers on historical subjects, figures, wars, and time periods.

The **Best of History Websites** (http://besthistorysites.net) provides more than 1,000 links to American and world history sites. American sites are categorized further by historical period and topic, including Native Americans, African Americans, women, government, and immigration.

This site, informally called **a chronology of U.S. historical documents** (http://www.law.ou.edu/hist/), is maintained and updated by the University of Oklahoma–College of Law. The college provides links to the full text and printable versions of U.S. historical documents, such as speeches, charters, major laws, and agreements, from the precolonial era through the twenty-first century.

CNN Special Coverage and Hot Topics (http://www.cnn.com/specials/) provides in-depth articles, reports, maps, and interviews on U.S. current events and foreign relations. Reports on topics such as WikiLeaks and ways to "Impact Your World" are of interest. Interactive media features include moving maps, live coverage of the events, and photographs.

In conjunction with the Smithsonian Institution, the **Cold War Museum** (http://www.coldwar.org) chronicles the half-century struggle between the United States and the Soviet Union, from early developments in the 1940s to the demise of the Soviet Union in the early 1990s. The site includes links to specific texts, chronologies, videos, congressional testimony, and relevant books and websites to illuminate specific aspects of the Cold War, and it highlights presidential doctrines, strategies, and military conflicts.

The Government Printing Office's **Core Documents of U.S. Democracy** site (http://www.gpo.gov/libraries/core_docs.htm) provides full-text links to the documents considered most relevant to educating citizens on U.S. democracy. Categories range from early presidential addresses to bills and laws from all congressional sessions. In addition to these documents, this site provides access to demographic and economic indicators and statistics.

Developed and maintained by the University of Houston, the **Digital History** project (http://www.digitalhistory.uh.edu) uses web technology to present chronologies, images, and sound bites from U.S. history. A full U.S. history and development textbook is included on the site, as well as suggested readings on specific time periods relevant to U.S. foreign relations, such as colonial expansion, military history, and relations with Europe.

Organized, researched, and published by the U.S. Department of State, the **Foreign Relations Series** (https://history.state.gov/historicaldocuments/about-frus) covers U.S. diplomacy and foreign policy decisions from the early 1800s through 1980. Included are presidential documents, treaties, intelligence reports, government conversations, and other relevant activities.

History Matters (http://historymatters.gmu.edu) is developed and maintained by the City University of New York (CUNY) and George Mason University. This site provides links and sources to help students and researchers understand crucial events in U.S history. The site also provides advice and discusses methods for analyzing historical works.

The **History News Network** (http://historynewsnetwork.org) is a nonprofit, independent group of historians and journalists sponsored by George Mason University who post articles and editorial writings on U.S. foreign relations. Critical reactions to historical events, quotes, polls, and multimedia links for understanding history are included.

The **Library of Congress** (http://www.loc.gov) provides up-to-date access to legislation, historical documents, memorials, maps, and virtual and digital collections of historic time periods. For researchers with a specific focus, the library provides bibliographic and citation lists for topics such as the Cuban missile crisis or the war on terrorism. The library also has an interactive feature for communicating with a researcher or a librarian to get answers to questions and help with research activities.

PBS (http://www.pbs.org) provides detailed access to historical events and biographies of leaders relevant to U.S. foreign relations. In addition to original Web text, PBS incorporates its television programs by posting interviews and the full text of its programs (with video clips) on this site. Photos, maps, chronologies, and links to relevant sources are part of each series. *American Experience* (http://www.pbs.org/wgbh/americanexperience/), *Frontline* (http://www.pbs.org/wgbh/pages/frontline/), and *People's Century* (http://www.pbs.org/wgbh/peoplescentury/) are the three primary programs relevant to U.S. foreign relations. *Frontline* features in-depth coverage of the Bush Doctrine and the ongoing war on terrorism.

The **Smithsonian Institution** (http://www.si.edu) is committed to helping researchers and citizens understand American identity, history, and culture. Exhibitions (http://www.si.edu/exhibitions/) such as "The Mexican Revolution! American Legacy" and "The Price of Freedom: Americans at War" as well as biographies of key leaders are useful to those wishing to understand the development of American foreign policy.

CHAPTER 3

DYNAMICS OF DECISION MAKING

© Brooks Kraft/Corbis

Secretary of State Colin Powell (left) engages in a heated exchange with Donald Rumsfeld, the secretary of defense, prior to a White House cabinet meeting in January 2003. Despite Powell's popularity and stature, Rumsfeld's closer relationship with the president and vice president gave him greater influence over U.S. foreign policy.

3.1   Summarize the three theories with assumptions about the international system that inform U.S. foreign policy decision making.

3.2   Describe the three spheres of political activity and their importance in foreign policy making.

3.3   Identify the ways in which U.S. civil society participates in foreign policy making.

3.4   Explain the role of bureaucratic politics in shaping U.S. foreign policy.

3.5   Discuss the influence of political psychology on the making of U.S. foreign policy.

The paradox of America's world power, which is woven into the nation's social and political fabric, became more consequential as the United States emerged victorious in World War II and became embroiled in the Cold War. The creation of new power centers in the executive branch invited bureaucratic rivalries, sparked miscommunications, and tested the limits of congressional oversight. The arrival of television, which brought the Vietnam War into millions of living rooms, and the mobilization of antiwar activists further debunked the conventional wisdom that "politics stops at the water's edge." Domestic upheavals had reached such an extent by the Reagan years that U.S. foreign policy makers suffered "a systematic breakdown when attempting to fashion a coherent and consistent approach to the world" (Destler, Gelb, and Lake 1984, 11).

The Cold War's demise in 1991 settled a score that defined world politics for nearly half a century. It did not, however, simplify the task of making U.S. foreign policy. To the contrary, the following years witnessed the rise of diverse transnational forces that produced ethnic warfare in some countries and democratic revolutions in others. Distinguishing friends from foes became a daily challenge for diplomats as old security pacts gave way to regional trading blocs. Connected by the Internet and later mobilized by Facebook, Twitter, and other social networking sites, thousands of nongovernmental organizations (NGOs) placed new pressures on U.S. leaders to support their agendas on such issues as human rights, climate change, and global poverty. Paradoxically, this non-state activism has been encouraged by the United States, the architect of the "constitutional" world order that emerged after World War II (see Ikenberry 2001).

This chapter explores America's exercise of world power by considering theories of international relations and foreign policy decision making. Theories are useful in

identifying the causes of foreign policy behavior in order to anticipate, explain, and possibly influence government action. As we will find, theories make very different claims regarding the international system, the role of states and societies within that system, and the capacity of human beings—the vital but often "irrational" policy makers—to formulate and conduct coherent foreign policies. A theoretical perspective goes beyond questions of what happens in the foreign policy process, who makes key decisions, and when or where decisions are made. It also offers insight into *why* policy makers act the way they do. According to the authors of a classic study of foreign policy, "We would go so far as to say *that the 'why' questions cannot be answered without analysis of decision-making*" (R. Snyder, Bruck, and Sapin 2002, 35).

Many Americans in 2015, for example, asked why President Obama was determined to strike a deal with Iran over its nuclear program. Was this a rational decision based on cost-benefit analysis, or a sure sign that Obama was hopelessly naïve? Was the president forced to reconcile the conflicting demands of the foreign policy bureaucracy and find a middle ground that would appease Congress? Or was Obama swayed by pressure from multinational corporations that sought trade with Iran? More broadly, what did this episode reveal about the larger forces that propel U.S. foreign policy? Definitive answers to such questions are elusive due to the ambiguities of political behavior. By basing their explanations of specific events on theories of international relations and decision making, analysts can discern more general lessons about U.S. foreign policy.

■ THE GLOBAL CONTEXT: RIVAL PERSPECTIVES

Analysts and practitioners of U.S. foreign policy see the world in very different ways. To some, the nation-state system is a treacherous jungle in which states must respect the "survival of the fittest." To others, the system is far more benign than this bleak image conveys, rewarding cooperation rather than conflict in most areas of foreign policy. Still others believe the international system—whether anarchic or orderly—is "constructed" in the minds of political leaders along with their sense of national identity and perception of friends and enemies. For each of these primary theoretical traditions, assumptions about the international system drive the values, goals, and strategies of U.S. foreign policy makers.

Assumptions of Structural Realism

Our point of departure is the theory of **structural realism**, a modern variant of the traditional realist theory that has dominated world politics for centuries (see Morgenthau 1967). It emphasizes the lack of a world government to regulate and moderate the behavior of countries, a condition commonly referred to as **anarchy**.[1] Structural realism offers a bleak vision of chronic power struggles that are inevitable given the absence of binding global governance (Waltz 1979). A common reference point is the **Treaty of Westphalia** of 1648, which ended the Thirty Years' War in Europe and created the nation-state system based on **sovereignty** that exists today. Although the treaty provided a basis for an orderly, durable state system to govern nations, in terms of international relations, it left the anarchic world order intact. Upholding the **national interest**, or *raison d'état*, became the overriding moral obligation of all governments. Only a **balance of power** among the great powers would produce stability in a world dominated by national self-interest (Mandelbaum 2010).

Another offshoot of realist theory, **geopolitics**, examines the impact of a nation's geographic position and resources relative to those of other powers, a perspective that is useful in understanding the historic conduct of U.S. foreign policy (see Brzezinski 1997; Turchin 2003).[2] From this perspective, U.S. territorial expansion in the nineteenth century can be explained by the nation's favorable position in North America and the fading presence of other great powers in the Western Hemisphere (Sicker 2002). American leaders later concluded that the nation would be threatened only if either Europe or Asia became controlled by a single state, a concern that spurred U.S. action against Germany and Japan in the Second World War and the Soviet Union in the Cold War.

From the standpoint of structural realism, political leaders must confront a **security dilemma** that results from uncertainty about the motives of potential rivals. For President Obama, the growing prominence of China created a classic security dilemma. While he could interpret Beijing's military modernization as a defensive move, such an assumption could also leave the United States unprepared for offensive

---

1. The view that international conflict is rooted in the flaws or passions of human nature, which dates back to ancient times, later became a central assumption of traditional realism. Structural realists, on the other hand, chose to focus on the systemic rather than individual level of analysis. For an elaboration of all three theories covered in this chapter, see Mingst and Arreguín-Toft (2011, ch. 3).

2. See Spykman (1942) and Mackinder (1942) for earlier analyses of geopolitics that emphasized the importance of Europe (the "rimland") to the global balance of power—and to U.S. security.

military action by China. The safest course for the president, therefore, was to "pivot" the geopolitical focus of U.S. foreign policy from Europe and the Middle East toward East Asia, even if such a shift sparked an arms race between the two countries regardless of their stated intentions.

A central assumption of structural realism—that weaker powers are destined to "balance" against a unipolar power—is challenged by the lack of balancing behavior targeted at the United States (see Nexon 2009). As noted earlier, most governments have chosen to align with Washington, either directly or informally, rather than seek to neutralize its overwhelming strength on their own or by forming rival blocs. This absence of balancing may be due to the enormous gap between the United States and secondary world powers (Wohlforth 2012) or to fears that taking on the United States would eventually lead to a catastrophic nuclear war (Craig 2009). Secondary powers have, however, resorted to **soft balancing**, a strategy that "accepts the current balance of power but seeks to obtain better outcomes within it" (Walt 2005). Several governments, including U.S. allies France and Germany, adopted this strategy in opposing the 2003 U.S. invasion of Iraq in the UN Security Council.

Liberal Theory and Global Governance

Like realists, liberals also acknowledge the anarchic structure of the interstate system, but unlike realists, they believe the absence of a world government does not inevitably lead to conflict (see M. W. Doyle 2008). To the contrary, problems such as global warming and nuclear proliferation, which do not respect national boundaries, create a growing sense of **interdependence** that rewards cooperation among governments out of "enlightened" self-interest (see Keohane and Nye 2001).

Because many global problems do not respect state sovereignty, they must be solved beyond the narrow bounds of the nation-state system. In this view, the UN, World Trade Organization (WTO), and other intergovernmental organizations manage collective problems that individual states cannot resolve alone. Non-state groups such as Greenpeace and Amnesty International also play a crucial role in pressuring governments on such issues. These actors have created a network of **global governance** that fills the "sovereignty gap" in world politics (see Slaughter 2004; D. A. Lake 2010).

Liberal theorists also believe that representative governments maintain a **democratic peace** with each other (Dafoe, Oneal, and Russett 2013). This presumed connection has a long history. Immanuel Kant ([1795] 1914), an Enlightenment philosopher, argued that only joint efforts by democratic governments could maintain a "perpetual peace." This concept was refined during the Cold War with the emergence of a **security community** in North America and Western Europe, an informal system of economic, political, and military cooperation that rendered war among the member countries unthinkable (Deutsch et al. 1957). In recent years, George W. Bush implicitly applied this theory when he justified the U.S. invasion of Iraq as an effort to bring democracy—and peace—to the Middle East.

Liberal theorists have their own explanation for the endurance of U.S. primacy in the global balance of power. As described in Chapter 1, the nature of America's world power must be taken into account. Specifically, since World War II, the U.S. government has sought to reassure, rather than frighten, other states by espousing liberal values, restraining its own power, and promoting multiple avenues of global governance (Finnemore 2009). As a "liberal Leviathan," the United States has led the creation of a liberal

Rogers Photo Archive/Getty Images

world order based upon "notions of cooperative security, democratic community, collective problem solving, and shared sovereignty" (Ikenberry 2011, 19).

Liberal theory has another variation, **neoliberal institutionalism,** which sees interstate cooperation as deriving from repeated interactions between governments. Friendly gestures, in short, are reciprocated by gestures of trust and goodwill, which in turn promote future cooperation. These personal interactions, however, are not sufficient. Transnational institutions such as the United Nations adopt standards of behavior for governments to follow. Nations' failure to heed such standards—by violating human rights, for example—reduces mutual trust and often disqualifies the offending states from benefiting from other areas of cooperation. In some areas of foreign policy, this institutionalized cooperation takes the form of issue-based **regimes.** The development aid regime, for example, has rendered economic assistance from rich to poor countries as a moral obligation (Hook and Lebo 2010).

Foreign Policy in a "Constructed" World

Still another theory of world politics with clear applications to U.S. foreign policy hails from the more contemporary tradition of social **constructivism** (see Onuf 1989; Katzenstein 1996; Checkel 2008). Advocates of this approach argue that world politics, along with domestic politics and other aspects of public life, do not have fixed properties; they are instead "socially constructed" by people, primarily through public discourse. Conflicts, therefore, are only possible if political leaders *create* threats by making arbitrary distinctions between friends and foes. Anarchy, in short, is "what states make of it" (Wendt 1992; see also Flanik 2011).

A central aspect of constructivist theory relates to **identity**, or the definition of an individual or a group as considered apart from others. Political identities, which have no objective material basis, define relations among governments. From this perspective, the shared identities of the United States and Western Europe after World War II had as much to do with the creation of NATO as with the threat posed by the Soviet Union. "If material capabilities are all that count in world politics, one would have expected Western Europe to align with the Soviet Union rather than with the United States" (Risse-Kappen 1996, 359). Constructivists view the nineteenth-century discourse of "manifest destiny" in the United States as a moral justification for westward expansion and territorial conquest. The same can be said for President Theodore Roosevelt's 1903 "corollary" to the Monroe Doctrine that granted the United States "international police power" over the Western Hemisphere. More recent historical cases further illustrate the impact of discourse in "creating" the world of U.S. foreign policy:

- In rallying the public during World War II, the U.S. government and major media outlets bolstered national morale by spreading stereotyped images of German soldiers as monsters and Japanese soldiers as rats, insects, and apes (Dower 1986; Hunt 1987).

- Harry Truman's 1947 call for U.S. action to protect the Greek and Turkish governments from communist takeovers failed to name communism as the target of the Truman Doctrine (see Chapter 2) but instead cast the first major escalation of the Cold War as a struggle between global "liberty" and "tyranny" (Sjöstedt 2007).

- In vilifying nations such as Fidel Castro's Cuba at the height of the Cold War, American leaders fomented global tensions that brought the world close to nuclear holocaust (Weldes 1999).

- Bill Clinton's concerns about "rogue states" after the Cold War served the purpose of constructing a perilous world that required aggressive action by Washington to maintain primacy (O'Reilly 2013).

- President George W. Bush "constructed" the terrorist attacks of September 2001 as the beginning of a "war on terror" rather than, for example, a mass homicide that should be investigated by law enforcement agencies and punished by courts (Nabers 2009).

These examples demonstrate how U.S. foreign policy makers characterize problems overseas in ways that advance their priorities in global politics (see Widmaier 2007). Even in the absence of this manipulative use of discourse, however, studies of political psychology, described later in this chapter, reveal that the "construction" of reality is a natural process by which individuals—private citizens as well as public figures—make sense of the complex world around them. Foreign policy analysts, therefore, have much to offer by examining the manner in which state actions

POINT / COUNTERPOINT

Realists vs. Liberals on Causes of War

A central question posed by theorists of world politics is, What causes war? Classical realists believe wars break out whenever there is no central power to restrain human passions or competition for limited resources. "During the time men live without a common Power to keep them all in awe, they are in that condition which is called war, and such a war as is of every man against every man," wrote English philosopher Thomas Hobbes. Contemporary neorealists believe this linkage between anarchy and war, which Hobbes applied to civil conflicts, also applies to foreign affairs. "Among states the state of nature is a state of war," wrote political analyst Kenneth Waltz. "Among men as among states, anarchy, or the absence of government, is associated with the occurrence of violence."

Theodore Roosevelt adopted another realist rationale for war: the advancement of national character. As assistant secretary of the Navy, he observed in 1097, "A rich nation which is slothful, timid, or unwieldy is an easy prey for any people which still retains those most valuable of all qualities, the soldierly virtues. . . . There are higher things in this life than the soft and easy enjoyment of material comfort." As a senior naval officer and later as president, Roosevelt pursued this vision by advocating U.S. military expansion in Asia and Latin America; in 1898, America went to war with Spain.

Liberals reject these rationales for war. For John Locke, an English theorist of the Enlightenment era, state tyranny over individual freedoms was a more common cause of war than anarchy in a "state of nature." Immanuel Kant, a like-minded German philosopher, argued that wars squander private liberty as well as public energies. As a result, "the full development of the predispositions of [human] nature is impeded in its progress."

The U.S. leader most closely associated with liberal theory, Woodrow Wilson, rejected the "martial virtues" highlighted by Roosevelt and sought instead to direct U.S. foreign policy toward the transnational cause of peace. "I am proposing that all nations henceforth avoid entangling alliances which would draw them into competitions of power, catch them in a net of intrigue and selfish rivalry, and disturb their own affairs with influences intruded from without. There is no entangling alliance in a concert of power." Wilson's failure to achieve his goals through the League of Nations has not prevented contemporary liberals from promoting world peace through the Wilsonian means of international law, cooperation through the UN, and democratic governments that protect individual rights.

Sources: Thomas Hobbes, *Leviathan* (Indianapolis: Bobbs-Merrill, [1651] 1983), 64; Kenneth N. Waltz, *Theory of International Politics* (Reading, Mass.: Addison-Wesley, 1979), 83; Theodore Roosevelt, "Washington's Forgotten Maxim" (address, Naval War College, June 1897), in *The Works of Theodore Roosevelt*, vol. 1, *American Ideals and Administration—Civil Service* (New York: P. F. Collier and Son, 1897), 266, 287; Immanuel Kant, "An Idea of an Universal History in a Cosmopolitical View," 1784, in *Essays and Treatises on Moral, Political, and Various Philosophical Subjects* (London: William Richardson, 1798), 1: 424; Woodrow Wilson, "A World League for Peace" (message to the U.S. Senate, January 22, 1917), in *Why We Are at War: Messages to the Congress, January to April 1917* (New York: Harper & Brothers, 1917), 16.

originate within the minds of individuals rather than from the objective or brute "facts" of world politics (see Houghton 2007).

In sum, the theories of structural realism, liberalism, and constructivism maintain very different conceptions of the global context. In so doing, these theories offer divergent guidance for the formulation and conduct of U.S. foreign policy. This may be illustrated by applying the three theories to the emergence of China as a major world power (see Table 3.1). This comparison reveals the link among theories and their related foreign policy prescriptions.

■ OPENING THE "BLACK BOX" OF DOMESTIC POLITICS

Given that systemic theories have such a foothold in the field of international relations, it may seem surprising that they are widely dismissed by foreign policy analysts who focus on domestic politics—that is, the internal competition and bargaining among government agencies, interest groups, and individual policy makers with a stake in foreign policy outcomes (see Neack 2013).[3] Opening this black box is a daunting task. Press reports that the United States "made" a particular decision may be easy to digest, but lurking behind such a decision are multiple

Table 3.1 ■ Theory in Practice: U.S. Foreign Policy toward People's Republic of China (PRC)

Theory	U.S. Perception	U.S. Response
Structural realism	Challenge to unipolar balance of power and U.S. primacy	Strengthen military forces with emphasis on Asia-Pacific region and alliances; resist Chinese military expansion and economic nationalism; shame PRC for domestic repression and human rights abuses
Liberalism	Arrival of PRC into globalized, interdependent, and "constitutional" world order	Engage PRC through diplomacy and networks of global governance; reach out to Chinese citizens through soft power and NGOs; highlight win-win nature of trade and cultural ties
Constructivism	China is "the other" with an alien identity and a clashing value system	Through discourse, persuade the PRC to become a "responsible citizen" and join the "community of nations"

3. Research concerning the actors in systemic theories figures prominently in the specialized academic journal *Foreign Policy Analysis*, which began publishing in 2005.

power centers. Decisions about each foreign policy issue produce winners and losers in the policy process; the resulting outcomes for U.S. world power follow directly from the compromises and bargains government officials make at home.

As we will find in this chapter, several dynamics shape the decision-making process in U.S. foreign policy (see Redd and Mintz 2013). The interstate system provides the setting of U.S. foreign relations, imposing a variety of *external* demands on the United States. Policy makers must also accommodate *internal* factors—rooted in civil society and the foreign policy bureaucracy—that further complicate decision making. Finally, presidents and their top advisers are also guided by psychological forces—preexisting beliefs, cognitive limitations, and diverse personality traits, among others—that are unique to each individual. Group behavior also reveals the cognitive and behavioral traits of policy makers.

The dynamics of decision making in U.S. foreign policy are best understood by examining policy behavior at various **levels of analysis**: the interstate system, civil society, government institutions, and political psychology (see Figure 3.1). Each of these levels focuses on different actors in the policy process and the anticipated behaviors that occur in the day-to-day world of foreign affairs (see Table 3.2). Most often, pressures are at play on multiple levels, creating a chaotic decision-making environment (Yetiv 2011).

Structural realism provides a common point of departure for considering the domestic sources of U.S. foreign policy. Structural realists assume political leaders are **rational actors** who weigh their options based upon objective national interests, tangible measures of power, and external threats. In this view, foreign policy goals are self-evident, as are the relative merits of alternative means to achieve those goals. Structural

Figure 3.1 ■ Converging Factors in the Foreign Policy Process

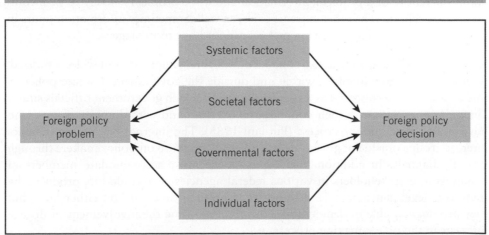

Table 3.2 ■ Levels of Analysis: Actors and Actions

Level	Key Actors	Anticipated State Behavior
Systemic	Nation-states, intergovernmental organizations	Pursuit of national interests
Society	Interest groups, social movements, multinational corporations, news and social media, citizens expressing preferences in public opinion surveys	Bargaining between U.S. government and private groups; government efforts to satisfy groups and public opinion
Governmental	White House, federal agencies, Congress, courts, state governments	Conflict between executive and legislative branches, bureaucratic competition, judicial intervention
Individuals and groups	Policy makers acting alone and in groups	Reliance on cognitive shortcuts to ease decision making, groupthink

realists also see governments as **unitary actors**, speaking with one voice in confronting global problems. Based on these assumptions, structural realists believe it is possible to understand foreign policy without reference to the internal debates or trade-offs that led to those policies. In this sense, these assumptions support the view that foreign policies result from **rational choice** (see Bueno de Mesquita 2009).

Many foreign policy analysts take issue with this approach, which falsely reduces decision making to objective calculations of costs and benefits. Opening the black box reveals fragmented centers of decision making in contradiction to the notion of rational action (see Table 3.3). In practice, decision makers routinely disagree about the content of national interests, severity of threats to those interests, and implications of both for the day-to-day conduct of foreign policy. Even if all decision makers agree about the nature of a problem, information about the problem is likely to be incomplete or inaccurate. The other extreme exists as well: Sometimes information pours in at such high volumes that decision makers cannot hope to manage it.

As for "unitary" action, the actual conduct of U.S. foreign policy is highly decentralized, with multiple actors involved within and outside the government. Foreign policy in this view can be represented as a **two-level game** in which government officials simultaneously negotiate with their counterparts overseas and with domestic actors who have stakes in the policy process (Putnam 1988). The internal bargaining includes interest groups outside of government who apply pressure on policy makers through several channels. In addition, the White House must accommodate members of Congress and stakeholders in various federal agencies. The trade-offs produced by these two-level games may lead to less-than-optimal outcomes on either level, but they are unavoidable in democratic states that welcome the involvement of diverse interests in the policy-making process.

Table 3.3 ■ Rational Action versus the Real World

Policy Area	Rational Action	The Real World
Key actors in foreign policy process	Small groups of like-minded decision makers	Multiple and conflicting centers of power in the White House, federal agencies, and Congress; constant pressure from private groups
State preferences	Determined objectively by national interests	Disputed by rival government and societal actors
Nature of decision-making environment	Centralized, consensual	Fragmented, chaotic
Degree of certainty regarding foreign policy problems	High	Low
Magnitude of varying foreign policy problems and merits of possible solutions	Discernible by objective cost-benefit analysis	Impossible to calculate given personal and institutional biases
Implementation of new policies	Efficient	Prone to bureaucratic delays, procedural conflicts, and communication breakdowns
Outcome for U.S. foreign policy	Optimal	Suboptimal; often ineffective and self-defeating

For our purposes, it is useful to view the arena of U.S. foreign policy as being located at the intersection of three spheres of political activity: transnational civil society, the interstate system, and domestic governing institutions (see Figure 3.2). The degree to which different actors engage in the foreign policy process varies across issue areas, as is demonstrated throughout this book. Nevertheless, the effective management of foreign policy requires that the needs and policy preferences of actors in all three spheres be taken into account, if not ultimately reconciled. Although external problems and opportunities create the contextual basis for making foreign policy decisions, one must recognize that, ultimately, the policy process begins at home.

This central reality requires that we explore domestic sources of U.S. foreign policy in greater detail. The following sections review the dynamics of decision making at the societal, governmental, and individual/group levels of analysis, respectively. Although understanding all three levels is a vital analytic task, one must avoid the temptation to view the levels as mutually exclusive. In fact, the success or failure of U.S. foreign policy often involves all three domestic forces. Analysis of President Bush's decision to invade Iraq in 2003, for example, finds that the influence exerted by interest groups,

Figure 3.2 ■ The Matrix of U.S. Foreign Policy

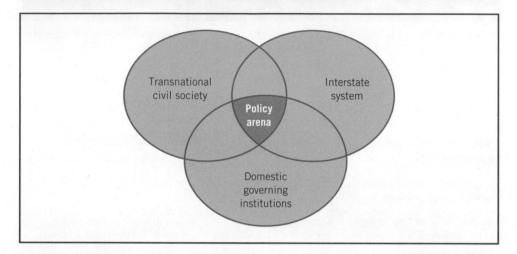

defects in the administration's foreign policy bureaucracy, efforts to manipulate public opinion and news media coverage, and unique features of the president's worldview and management style collectively paved the way for the problems encountered by U.S. troops as they conducted their mission (see Mitchell and Massoud 2009).

■ THE IMPACT OF CIVIL SOCIETY

Like other democracies, the U.S. government provides many opportunities for citizens and groups to influence the nation's foreign policy. Early U.S. leaders saw civil society as a hedge against future government repression. Modern-day societal groups, public opinion surveys, and news media coverage continue to serve this vital function. Along the way, such forces enhance the openness of government and empower ordinary citizens in public life. Foreign policy makers often find this input difficult to manage, but they cannot ignore the citizens who represent the ultimate power base in American politics. Such is to be expected in a government "by the people," despite the difficulties such external pressures raise for the orderly formulation and conduct of foreign policy. The paradox of America's world power owes much to this interplay between state and society.

Foreign Policy in a "Small State"

The United States is said to feature a "small state" that is overshadowed by a "large society" (Krasner 1978). This is a common characteristic of democracies, in contrast to authoritarian polities in which the state dominates public life and represses many forms of civic expression (see Figure 3.3). The U.S. government, which employs millions of people in a variety of civilian and military agencies, is by no means small on an absolute level. Still, the ability of politicians and government bureaucrats to shape foreign policy is commonly dwarfed by the impact of societal actors just as potent as "the branches of government formally established by law or constitution" (Truman 1951, 502).

Private citizens and interest groups advance their policy agendas by providing campaign donations to political candidates, publishing reports on pressing policy issues, organizing mass e-mail campaigns, and staging high-profile media events (Bloodgood 2011). Ethnic minority groups, such as Cuban-Americans in Florida, frequently have an impact on congressional elections that far exceeds their small numbers (Rubenzer and Redd 2010). Well-organized business groups also get Washington's attention, as in the case of grain exporters who benefit from the government's Food for Peace aid program (Diven 2006). The same can be said for religious groups that appeal to widely shared spiritual values rather than economic self-interests (Warner and Walker 2011). For example, a critical study of the "Israel lobby" argued that pressure from the group has jeopardized U.S. security interests in the Middle East (Mearsheimer and Walt 2007).

The impact of civil society has increasingly assumed a global dimension with the emergence of **transnational civil society**. While elected officials must heed domestic public opinion for electoral reasons, they must also be sensitive to global public opinion, particularly in democratic states whose support for U.S. foreign policy is needed (B. E. Goldsmith and Horiuchi 2012). Political leaders must also pay attention to global news coverage, whose impact is felt immediately in the White House. Nongovernmental organizations have influenced foreign policy throughout U.S. history, but never before have they been so connected with their counterparts overseas (Mathews 1997). In this sense, transnational civil society serves as an extension of

Figure 3.3 ■ Policy Influence and Control: Two Models of State-Society Relations

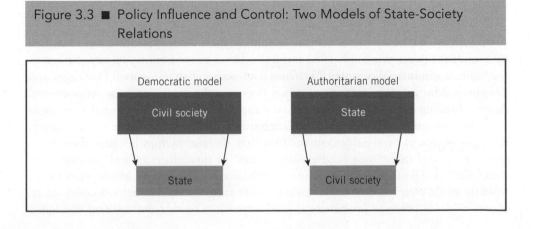

America's own civil society, which values public opinion and a free press while providing interest groups with access to the government through many channels—congressional committees, executive agencies, the White House, and political campaigns. Such openness comes at a price, however, as societal actors frequently oppose U.S. foreign policies. Indeed, their challenges to U.S. sovereignty on such issues as global warming, human rights, and military interventions prompted the Bush administration's turn away from the international community (Daalder and Lindsay 2003).

The U.S. political system lends itself to such challenges in several ways. Legislative debates are documented in the *Congressional Record*, and other government records, including the federal budget, are freely available on the Internet. Major news outlets, along with blogs and think tank reports, benefit from this transparency even as they criticize the U.S. foreign policies. Public opinion surveys, meanwhile, provide U.S. citizens "voice opportunities" that are often highly critical. A June 2012 survey by the Chicago Council on Global Affairs, for example, found more than two-thirds of those surveyed believed that the decade-long U.S. war in Afghanistan "has not been worth fighting." In these and other ways, agents of civil society effectively "shrink" the power of the state.

Iron Triangles and Issue Networks

The fragmentation of the U.S. political system and the nature of foreign policy allow government decision makers to maintain a high degree of autonomy from the public and even the president, who cannot possibly rein in the far-flung bureaucratic and societal forces that find niches in the political system. Powerful interest groups, for example, pursue their policy preferences by forming alliances with supportive government agencies and officials. Some aspects of the foreign policy process can thus be viewed as an **iron triangle** linking influential interest groups, congressional committees, and the corresponding executive branch agencies that carry out policies of mutual concern. At the same time, an iron triangle effectively excludes other members of Congress, the White House, and the general public from affecting key foreign policy decisions (see Figure 3.4).

A commonly cited example of an iron triangle is the U.S. defense industry, identified by President Eisenhower in his 1961 farewell address to the nation as a key element of the "**military-industrial complex.**" Defense contractors such as General Dynamics and Lockheed Martin exert strong influence over members of Congress who control defense funding and the fate of individual weapons programs. These legislators, most of whom are on the Armed Services Committees of either the House or the Senate, have political and personal incentives to satisfy the contractors because these businesses represent many jobs (and possible votes) in their districts and provide large campaign contributions. The Pentagon's incessant desire to maintain or increase its funding levels, coupled with the lobbying efforts of self-interested defense contractors, places ongoing pressure on congressional committees to increase military spending.

Figure 3.4 ■ The Iron Triangle

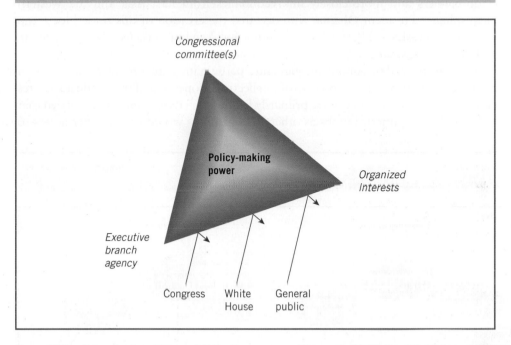

Congressional
committee(s)

Policy-making
power

Organized
Interests

Executive
branch
agency

Congress   White   General
            House   public

Source: William T. Gormley Jr. and Steven J. Balla, *Bureaucracy and Democracy* (Washington, DC: CQ Press, 2004). Reprinted by permission. Reprinted by permission of CQ Press, an imprint of SAGE Publications Inc.

Other iron triangles in the foreign policy process are in the areas of energy policy, foreign investment, veterans' affairs, and arms exports (see Hook and Rothstein 2005).

Decision making in other areas involves more actors and is more open to competing viewpoints. Here **issue networks** bring together interested government and private actors with shared knowledge and expertise, if not similar policy preferences (Heclo 1978). At times, the groups that come together in ad hoc issue networks bitterly oppose one another, leading to a process of competition rather than collusion, which is the essence of iron triangles. The growth of issue networks in the 1970s followed structural reforms by Congress, which created more subcommittees and expanded the federal bureaucracy in response to public demands for more services and greater access to the decision-making process.

"Politics makes strange bedfellows," a popular axiom in the study of government, has been affirmed repeatedly in U.S. foreign policy. The antiglobalization protests during the 1999 WTO conference in Seattle, Washington, for example, involved anarchists, trade unions, environmentalists, feminists, and human rights activists. Much more recently, a similar issue network formed around the issue of the proposed Trans-Pacific Partnership (TPP), a multilateral trade agreement that would reduce trade barriers and more closely link economies from East Asia and the Western Hemisphere.[4] President Obama, who declared the creation of this trade bloc a top goal of his presidency, was among its most vocal champions. As often happens in such initiatives, stakeholders within and outside governments mobilized in favor and against the proposal. Among proponents, participating governments joined with multinational corporations, owners of intellectual property, and free-trade advocates (see Figure 3.5). Opponents were primarily led by U.S. labor unions that worried that they would lose American jobs as other TPP members would have greater access to

Figure 3.5 ■ Trans-Pacific Partnership Issue Network

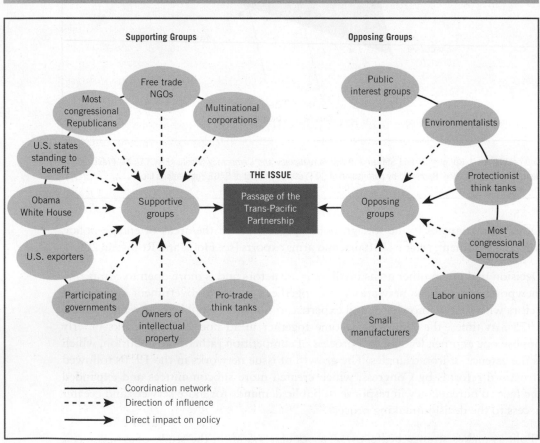

-----

4. As of August 2015, the twelve member states of the proposed TPP included the United States along with Australia, Brunei, Canada, Chile, Japan, Malaysia, Mexico, New Zealand, Peru, Singapore, and Vietnam.

the nation's import markets. Small-scale manufacturers, meanwhile, feared for their livelihoods in the face of intensified competition, and public interest groups argued that new measures regarding labor and environmental standards did not go far enough.

■ COPING WITH BUREAUCRATIC POLITICS

The decentralized structure of the U.S. government produces a high level of tension within the executive branch. The manner in which bureaucrats do their work plays a crucial, though often dysfunctional, role in shaping U.S. foreign policy. "The bureaucracy arises out of politics," political scientist Terry Moe (1989, 267) observed, "and its design reflects the interests, strategies, and compromises of those who exercise political power." This reality, which afflicts other governments to varying degrees, is clear in the historical record. As societies modernized throughout nineteenth-century Europe, bureaucrats took on an ever-widening array of tasks and became powerful political actors as well. Their greater expertise, longevity in government, and direct access to the instruments of policy gave them significant advantages over elected leaders. These civil servants and political appointees were thrust into competition against other agencies over important missions, access to the White House, and perhaps most important, steady if not growing financial support.

Two models of policy decision making shed light on the foreign policy process. The first model, **bureaucratic politics**, highlights the competition among rival agencies (Allison and Zelikow 1999). These conflicts, driven by bureaucratic self-interests rather than national interests, can shape the future direction of policy. Graham Allison (1971, 144), the first scholar to apply bureaucratic politics to U.S. foreign policy, viewed bureaucrats as "players who act in terms of no consistent set of strategic objectives but rather according to various conceptions of national, organizational, and personal goals; players who make government decisions not by a single, rational choice but by the pulling and hauling that is politics."

The positions held by decision makers are of utmost importance, as "where you stand depends on where you sit." The Defense Department, for example, was strongly in favor of escalating the Vietnam War while many in the State Department argued against deeper involvement in the war. The same pattern appeared in 2009, when bureaucratic turf determined the advice offered President Obama regarding a possible surge of troops in Afghanistan. Whereas all the military advisers, including Defense Secretary Robert Gates, supported the surge, nearly all of those from the civilian side, including Vice President Joe Biden, opposed the operation.[5] For weeks, the two sides "engaged in political combat with one another" (Marsh 2014, 284). Obama finally approved the surge, though on a smaller scale than recommended by

---

5. The exception to this rule involved Secretary of State Hillary Clinton, who stood alone among civilian advisers in supporting the surge.

the Pentagon.[6] Such policy battles were commonly won by the Defense Department, whose enormous budget and security focus gave it an advantage over other agencies, including the State Department (Glain 2011). As noted earlier, the State Department also fought an uphill battle against the National Security Council (NSC), whose staff of advisers had greater access to the White House than the diplomatic corps, which grew from 25 in the 1970s to more than 400 by 2015 (DeYoung 2015).

The second model, **organizational process**, refers to the **standard operating procedures** (SOPs) that bureaucratic managers routinely follow in performing their tasks. In contrast to bureaucratic politics, which refers to interagency bargaining, the organizational process occurs *within* agencies. The focus here is on efficiency and tightly followed routines. While SOPs may be rational in terms of the internal functioning of each agency, a lack of interagency coordination prevents the central government from seeing the big picture. The September 2001 terrorist attacks, for example, combined domestic and international elements, including suspicious visa requests for flight training in the United States (FBI concerns), and heightened "chatter" among al Qaeda operatives in Europe and Asia (a CIA concern). Compounding this overlap in jurisdiction was reluctance by CIA and FBI counterterrorism units to share intelligence with each other. "Everybody who does national security in this town knows the FBI and CIA don't talk," observed former senator Bob Kerrey (quoted in *New York Times* 2004, 25), a member of the 9-11 Commission. In sum, both models of decision making operate on separate tracks, skewing foreign policy outcomes for better or worse.

Bureaucratic behavior in U.S. foreign policy also reflects differences in **organizational culture,** or the shared values, goals, and functional priorities of the members of a government agency. According to James Q. Wilson (1989, 91), an expert on bureaucracy, "Culture is to an organization what personality is to an individual. Like human culture generally, it is passed from one generation to the next. It changes slowly, if at all." The presence of so many foreign policy agencies in the U.S. government inevitably leads to clashes of organizational cultures. The tendency of diplomats to favor negotiated settlements over military coercion contributes to the State Department's reputation for excessive caution and timidity. Similarly, the inherent secrecy of intelligence gathering creates a highly insular organizational culture within the CIA and other intelligence agencies. Within the Pentagon, each of the armed services maintains a distinct organizational culture—and sense of superiority over other services. Such differences energize the morale of each unit and serve as valuable recruiting tools, but they can create problems by sparking public disputes over funding allocations and the assignment of operational missions.

....

6. In other cases, such struggles are literally built into daily routines. In the U.S. embassy of Mexico City, for instance, the presence of many federal agencies housed produced bureaucratic politics "so complex, so multilayered, so conflicting, that it hamstrings, frustrates, and often paralyzes policy, making it virtually impossible for the United States to carry out a successful foreign policy there" (Wiarda 2000, 175).

Robert M. Gates *Past leaders of U.S. foreign policy have frequently written memoirs that shed light on their experience in office. The same could be said for Robert M. Gates, who served both George W. Bush and Barack Obama as secretary of defense. In his career, which also included a term as CIA director, Gates worked closely across the U.S. foreign policy bureaucracy. As the excerpt below reveals, the retired defense secretary likened bureaucratic politics to a constant "war" for policy influence.*

My policies were clear: to continue taking care of the troops and their families; to achieve greater balance between preparing for future large-scale conflicts and supporting the fights we were already in . . . , to tackle the military acquisition process . . . , and to do all I could to enhance our prospects for success in Afghanistan.

The first three priorities meant continuing my war on the Pentagon itself, the second and third meant more war with Congress, and the fourth would involve war with the White House. It was clear that every day of my entire tenure as secretary would involve multifront conflict.

Source: Robert M. Gates, *Duty: Memoirs of a Secretary at War* (New York: Knopf, 2014, 304).

Patterns of Organizational Behavior

Bureaucracies in the United States and other industrialized societies exhibit similar characteristics. Their structures and day-to-day patterns of behavior also pertain to domestic policies as well as those that involve foreign affairs. Among the most important of these characteristics for understanding of U.S. foreign policy are resilience, autonomy, self-interest, conservatism, and inefficiency.

Resilience. "Once it is fully established," German sociologist Max Weber (1946, 228) once observed, "bureaucracy is among those social structures which are the hardest to destroy." The creation of U.S. federal agencies is a time-consuming task requiring public support, consensus within Congress, and presidential approval. Once formed, an agency becomes part of the institutional landscape, welcoming new missions and clients that have a stake in its future activities (Mabee 2011). The Agency for International Development (USAID), for example, has successfully fended off multiple attempts by Congress to dissolve the foreign aid agency and place it under the strict control of the State Department.

Autonomy. Bureaucracies enjoy a high level of freedom from outside interference. Agency managers have more expertise than elected leaders and thus have the upper hand in shaping policy. They also tend to last longer in their jobs and become masters of the political system. "Agencies can ignore presidential directives, delay implementation of presidential programs, and limit presidential options when it suits their needs to do so because presidents do not have the time or resources to watch them" (Zegart 1999, 47). Such autonomy led to the 1986 Iran-Contra scandal, in which the NSC conducted secret military operations in Central America with little or no oversight by President Reagan.

Self-interest. Agency managers are often more concerned with their bureaucratic needs than serving national interests. They routinely compete for material resources and for influence over policy. During the Cuban missile crisis, for example, the advice of military leaders reflected their parochial biases rather than objective judgments of the most effective means for preventing a nuclear war between the United States and the Soviet Union (see Allison and Zelikow 1999, 340). While Secretary of State Dean Rusk argued for a diplomatic solution, for example, the Joint Chiefs of Staff favored a military invasion of Cuba. In George W. Bush's first term, tensions between Secretary of State Colin Powell and Secretary of Defense Donald Rumsfeld over Iraq had as much to do with built-in bureaucratic rivalries as with substantive policy differences (Woodward 2006).

Conservatism. Agencies' reliance on SOPs stresses continuity over change and a high level of internal order. Organizational cultures, though unique to each agency, consistently discourage innovation or changes of course (see Drezner 2000). These problems plagued Rumsfeld in 2003 as he sought to "transform" the U.S. military. His frustration became so great that he fired Tom White, the Army secretary, in part because of White's refusal to support the cancellation of a pet project, the outmoded $11 billion Crusader artillery system. Attempts to reform agencies, though occasionally successful, generally lead to frustration and failure (Abramson and Lawrence 2001).

Inefficiency. The fragmentation of bureaucracies leads to breakdowns in communication and coordination. This problem was illustrated during the 1983 U.S. invasion of the tiny Caribbean island of Grenada, launched by the Reagan administration to prevent a pro-Soviet regime from taking power. Despite their overwhelming force, the U.S. troops needed three days to subdue a small brigade of enemy fighters. Eighteen Americans died in battle, partly as the result of an invasion plan that guaranteed each of the armed services a role. There were also communication problems. One Marine, unable to contact his superiors by radio, used a pay telephone to contact the Pentagon and provide the location of enemy forces.

These aspects of bureaucratic behavior suggest, to many observers, a U.S. government controlled by bureaucrats who are driven by institutional self-interests. It is important to note, however, that this bureaucratic politics model is not universally accepted and is challenged by two other models of decision making. The **presidential control model** views presidents as "caretakers of the national interest" who can rise above domestic politics, particularly when U.S. security interests are at stake (Bendor and Hammond 1992; see also Krasner 1972 and Art 1973). The **congressional dominance model** holds that legislators make their preferences clear to agency managers, who then have a material incentive—in the form of future budget support—to ensure that those preferences are realized (see Weingast 1984). Students can find evidence that supports all three models in different areas of U.S. foreign policy, as revealed in the chapters that follow.

State and Local Governments

The pluralistic nature of U.S. foreign policy extends to the state and local levels as well. As described in Chapter 2, the original blueprint for American government—the Articles of Confederation—granted state governments control over most aspects of foreign policy. Placed in a system of domestic anarchy, the thirteen original states engaged in trade wars among themselves, pursued separate relations with foreign governments, and conducted their own military expeditions on the western frontier. As a result, the founders designed the Constitution in part to shift key foreign policy powers to the federal government, a system that remains in place today.

Under this system, however, state and local governments can still pass resolutions on foreign policy issues, pursue foreign investments, organize cultural exchanges, and manage the intermestic problems—those that concern both international and domestic affairs, such as pollution—that affect them. "As decisions are made and events transpire outside the boundaries of the nation-state that may have an immediate and profound effect on citizens at the grassroots level, these citizens demand that their interests be protected and enhanced not only by their national governments, but also by the subnational governments closest to where they live" (Fry 1998, 15). Likewise, Jessica Mathews (1997, 65–66), president of the Carnegie Endowment for International Peace, has observed, "Nation-states may simply no longer be the natural problem-solving unit."

Public activism in U.S. foreign policy frequently takes place at the state and local levels. It is there that Americans learn about problems overseas, discuss possible solutions to those problems, and take action to influence national policy makers (see McMillan 2008). With more direct access to the political process at these levels, citizens frequently mobilize around the slogan "Think globally, act locally." State governments often respond to these pressures by speaking out or taking action on foreign policy issues, as in these prominent examples:

- Nearly 1,000 localities called for a nuclear freeze by the time the Cold War ended in 1991, nearly 200 had demanded a halt to nuclear testing, and 120 had refused to comply with federal civil defense guidelines in the event of nuclear war (Shuman 1992).
- Twenty-eight state governments imposed trade and other commercial restrictions on U.S. and foreign businesses operating in South Africa by the time that country's government, in 1994, abolished its system of apartheid that denied political rights to the majority nonwhite population (Fry 1998).

- Thirty governors visited Iraq in the first three years of the Iraq war (O'Connor 2006). All fifty governors signed a letter in 2007 asking that President Bush provide additional federal funds to resupply their "depleted National Guards" (Scharnberg 2007).

- Sixteen state governments filed briefs in 2012 supporting Arizona's effort to impose aggressive measures against illegal immigration. The Supreme Court, which struck down most of the measures as a usurpation of federal law, may have been swayed by the forty U.S. cities and counties that, along with eleven states, filed their own briefs opposing the Arizona crackdown (Winograd 2012).

- Lawmakers in 45 states and the District of Columbia passed 184 laws and 234 resolutions in 2013 that involved immigration. Most measures called for greater support for unauthorized residents. Eight states extended driver's licenses and four states expanded in-state tuition for this vulnerable population (National Council of State Legislators 2014).

To an extent previously unseen, the war on terror declared in 2001 brought local governments directly into the foreign policy process. These governments serve on the front lines of the homeland security effort in three ways. First, they must protect their citizens with enhanced police forces. Second, they must be prepared to respond immediately and effectively to terrorist attacks, a task managed with courage on September 11 by the New York City Fire Department and other first responders. Third, local governments and agencies must play an intelligence-gathering role in looking out for possible terrorist "cells" or suspicious activities in their jurisdictions. In all three areas, local governments must work closely with federal officials and, when necessary, secure additional resources from Washington.

In the economic realm, the annual output of many U.S. states exceeds that of most foreign countries. The exports of U.S. manufacturing firms grew rapidly in recent decades. As a result, most states now operate overseas offices in foreign countries and promote joint ventures, sponsor trade conferences, and subsidize export promotion at home. Governors compete intensely to attract foreign industries to locate in their states, offering a variety of economic incentives, such as tax breaks, highway improvements, and regulatory relief. Members of Congress commonly support these efforts and provide federal resources where possible to attract industries. In addition, military bases provide a substantial boost to employment, tax revenue, and spin-off economic activity at the state and local levels. State governments also may pursue environmental policies that have impacts far beyond their borders.

In California, for example, a measure was placed on the November 2006 ballot to raise $4 billion in tax revenues from oil producers to fund research and development of alternative energy. The proposed Clean Alternative Energy Act, or Proposition 87 on the ballot, sought to reduce oil consumption by 25 percent in California, the nation's leading oil consumer. An array of politicians, including former President Bill

Clinton, joined Hollywood celebrities and tycoons from Silicon Valley in supporting the measure, which was opposed largely by the oil companies that would have to pay the new taxes. The act would have filled the gap left in federal energy policy, which had yet to include stringent measures for energy conservation and reduced emissions of greenhouse gases (see Chapter 12). Though the measure was defeated, similar actions were proposed elsewhere as the threat of global warming increased.

Local governments are even more likely than states to voice their opinions on general foreign policy issues, attracting attention by approving resolutions on these matters. For example, more than 160 cities and counties approved resolutions opposing President Bush's preventive invasion of Iraq early in 2003. "Military action in Iraq will divert attention from economic issues and challenges confronting the American people and American cities," the city of Cleveland's resolution stated ("Cleveland City Council" 2003). Although this plea went unheeded by national policy makers—as such resolutions often do—the opposition of Cleveland, along with that of Chicago, Philadelphia, San Francisco, and other major cities, was made clear to a global audience.

■ THE HUMAN FACTOR

Foreign policy is made by people, not by inanimate entities such as nation-states or bureaucracies. Despite efforts to understand world politics by focusing on such abstractions, the simple fact remains that individuals respond in different ways to similar problems. Individual actions are more likely to have significant consequences "when leaders have an inordinate amount of power" (Mintz and DeRouen 2010, 19), but individuals can have impacts even in complex democratic polities such as the United States. Presidents who are risk averse, for example, have been shown to be less likely to resort to military force than presidents who take risky chances in U.S. foreign policy (Gallagher and Allen, 2014). The human factor, therefore, can never be eliminated from the policy-making equation (see Hill 2003, chs. 4–5). The field of **political psychology** recognizes this central fact "by asserting the importance of individual psychological processes to political outcomes" (McDermott 2004, 3).

In this world of **bounded rationality**, foreign policy makers cope as best they can with the personal as well as the institutional limitations facing them (Simon 1957). The characteristics of individual actors are vital to decision making. This link between psychology and political behavior, as demonstrated in recent studies of American presidents (see Table 3.4), shapes the U.S. foreign policy process in important ways. It is therefore critical that the political psychology of foreign policy be examined in four areas: the beliefs and perceptions of key decision makers, their personalities and styles of leadership, the dynamics of decision making in groups, and the dynamics of decision making during crises.

Beliefs and Cognitive "Shortcuts"

According to political psychologists, decision makers come to their positions of authority with distinctive **belief systems** that directly influence their foreign policy goals and strategies as well as their responses to specific problems (O. R. Holsti 1962). Belief systems, which are formed early in life and are stubbornly resistant to change, link the fragmented impressions people have of the outside world into a coherent whole (see Mowle 2003).[7] These beliefs shape the manner in which leaders identify the nature of each problem that arises in foreign policy, a vital step in determining a nation's response (Knecht 2009).[8]

Two types of beliefs guide the judgment of policy makers (see Goldstein and Keohane 1993, ch. 1). Every individual maintains **principled beliefs** regarding the virtues and limitations of human nature, the proper roles of governments, and the national and global problems that are of greatest concern. Each person also maintains **causal beliefs** about the best means available for solving these problems. President Obama, for example, maintained the principled belief that the United States should provide moral leadership in conducting U.S. foreign policy. His causal beliefs led him to revive diplomatic cooperation, affirm U.S. support for international law, and call for nuclear disarmament.

Principled and causal beliefs combine to form an **operational code**, "a political leader's beliefs about the nature of politics and political conflict, his views regarding the extent to which historical developments can be shaped, and his notions of correct strategy and tactics" (George 1989, 486; see also Schafer and Walker 2006). Foreign policy decisions are guided by their operational code. Woodrow Wilson's moralistic approach to world politics, for instance, was shaped profoundly by his childhood as the son of a Presbyterian minister (George and George 1956). Early in the Cold War, Christian beliefs led Secretary of State John Foster Dulles to assume the worst about the "atheistic" regime of the Soviet Union (Holsti 1962). As for Secretary of State Henry Kissinger, his conception of world politics as an arena of great-power manipulation dictated his approach to the Vietnam War (Walker 1977), just as the "black-and-white" thinking of Ronald Reagan shaped that president's confrontational approach toward the Soviet Union (Glad 1983).

Such links between operational codes and foreign policy behavior continued to shape the course of U.S. foreign policy during the Clinton years (Walker, Schafer, and Young

---

7. According to role theory, policy makers form rigid conceptions of their national identity and the related foreign policy priorities and obligations of their government (K. J. Holsti 1970). These role conceptions, which reflect personal values and extend to perceptions of foreign governments, may not be shared by others in the bureaucracy, fueling internal conflicts (Thies and Breuning 2012; Cantir and Kaarbo 2012).

8. The belief systems of private citizens directly influence whether they adopt realist or liberal views of world politics (Kertzer and McGraw 2012). Those who are less trustful of other citizens or foreign governments, for example, are more likely to adopt the more pessimistic views of realism.

2003) and could be seen in George W. Bush's forceful response to the September 2001 terrorist attacks (S. Renshon and Larson 2003). Most recently, Barack Obama's operational code led him to favor "pragmatic cooperation" in world politics (Walker 2011). Although he was pessimistic about realizing all of his foreign policy goals, he believed diplomacy was more likely to achieve U.S. goals than conflictual strategies. This cautious aspect of the president's world views, which preceded his coming to power, explained his patience in negotiations with China, Russia, Iran, and other foreign governments that posed challenges to U.S. national security.

Decision makers' perceptions are critical to the ways they define and respond to foreign policy problems. This assertion, borne out by historical research, leads to consideration of **cognitive psychology**, the process by which individuals obtain and process information about the world around them (see Jervis 1976; Vertzberger 1990). Studies show that these highly personal factors can have a direct impact on decision making. For example, leaders found to have "low conceptual complexity," seeing the world in black and white rather than in shades of gray, are more likely than other policy makers to favor military rather than cooperative solutions to foreign policy problems (Foster and Keller 2014). Due to the sheer volume of information available, individuals can absorb less than a tiny fraction of it. They must, therefore, constantly make choices about what information they will expose themselves to and how they will act on what they have learned. These "shortcuts," described below, help policy makers function in a highly complex environment that would otherwise be overwhelming.

Table 3.4 ■ The Political Psychologies of Presidents Bill Clinton and George W. Bush

Bill Clinton	George W. Bush
Favorable view of policy-making environment	Moralistic worldview
Optimism regarding political goals	Need to control or dominate others
Cooperative approach to problem solving	Sensitivity to criticism
Reliance on rewards rather than punishments	Tendency to take impulsive action
Aversion to taking risks	Willingness to take risks

Sources: Stephen G. Walker, Mark Schafer, and Michael Young, "William Jefferson Clinton: Operational Code Beliefs and Object Appraisal," in *The Psychological Assessment of Political Leaders,* ed. Jerrold M. Post (Ann Arbor: University of Michigan Press, 2003), 324–328; Aubrey Immelman, "The Political Personality of U.S. President George W. Bush," in *Political Leadership for the New Century: Personality and Behavior Among American Leaders,* ed. Linda O. Valenty and Ofer Feldman (Westport, CT: Praeger, 2002), 81–103.

Selective perception. Once their belief systems have formed during the socialization process, people tend to seek out information that reinforces their views while ignoring information that contradicts them. In making foreign policy, this selective use of information discourages presidents from weighing information evenly or considering contrary evidence. Senior officials in the Bush administration appear to have engaged in selective perception as they prepared for war against Iraq early in 2003, relying primarily on those reports that claimed Saddam Hussein had weapons of mass destruction and posed an imminent danger to the United States (Rieff 2003).

Use of analogies. Decision makers often search familiar historical precedents that allow them to "match new pieces of information against their stored memories" (Yetiv 2004, 59). Cold War presidents frequently drew on the analogy of the U.S. "appeasement" of Adolf Hitler in justifying U.S. intervention in Korea and Vietnam (Khong 1992). The same analogy was revived prior to the Gulf War in 1991 by President George H. W. Bush, who repeatedly compared Saddam Hussein to Hitler. In still another case, Bill Clinton's memories of his failed 1993 military intervention in Somalia clearly biased his judgment against taking action during the genocides in Rwanda and Burundi the following year (Brunk 2008).

Cognitive closure. Policy makers may find the process of decision making stressful, particularly when the information they receive is incomplete and contradictory. Their desire to make a decision quickly leads them to adopt a given solution to a problem before the available information has been fully examined and alternative strategies have been considered. For example, President Lyndon Johnson's strategy in the Vietnam War became increasingly rigid despite mounting problems on the battlefield and the intensification of domestic opposition to the war.

Bolstering. Once a decision is made, policy makers often use the decision to bolster their claims regarding the problem at hand. As Deborah Larson (1985) discovered, Truman's anti-Soviet beliefs became more pronounced *after* he had settled on the containment policy and was compelled to sell the strategy to Congress and the public. A similar pattern was evident after the September 2001 terrorist attacks as President Bush demanded quick action. "Once on a course, he directed his energy at forging on, rarely looking back, scoffing—even ridiculing—doubt and anything less than 100-percent commitment. He seemed to harbor few, if any, regrets" (Woodward 2002, 256).

In summary, how government leaders see the world directly affects their conduct of U.S. foreign policy. Their perceptions of the external environment, which are ingrained at an early age and then reinforced through selective perception, bolstering, and other cognitive shortcuts, can predict how they will respond to the most serious problems facing the United States overseas (Hermann 1984). Because such perceptions are highly personal and vary widely, foreign policy choices cannot be predicted reliably on the basis of purely rational calculations. This is a central claim of **prospect theory**, which argues that astute decision makers don't expect optimal outcomes but intuitively gauge the risks and rewards of policy choices relative to the imperfect status quo (for an elaboration, see McDermott 1998 and Below 2008).

The Power of Personality

A second general area of political psychology involves the outward, observable behavior of policy makers, which serves as an expression of their beliefs and perceptions of the outside world. Most analysts assume that the personality of a president, or that of an organizational leader in any setting, plays an important role in the decision-making process (Hermann 1984; Howell 2003). In short, it matters whether a leader is aggressive or passive, gregarious or withdrawn, competitive or cooperative, and emotionally stable or temperamental. A recent personality study of presidents made it clear that "some are better at channeling their emotions to help shape foreign policy than others" (McDermott 2014). These and other personality traits directly, if subtly, shape the social environment in which decisions are made.

More specifically, the personality traits and leadership styles of top policy makers often determine the roles played by secondary members of the decision-making team. A study of President George W. Bush, for example, found that his high need for power, sense of control over events, and lack of trust toward others contributed directly to his decision to invade Iraq in 2003 (Shannon and Keller 2007). The quality of Bush's decision making was also problematic because, compared with other political leaders, he exhibited a lack of self-confidence in making key decisions, which may have explained his reliance on key advisers such as Vice President Cheney after the 9/11 attacks. Bush also exhibited a lack of curiosity about the details of important foreign policies (see Schafer and Crichlow 2010). The same psychological factors can also afflict cabinet officials. Donald Rumsfeld, Bush's defense secretary, shared the president's need to control his subordinates and favor some over others (Dyson 2009).

One prominent study divided U.S. presidents into four categories based on where they fit along two dimensions (Barber 1992). The first dimension addresses whether presidents take an "active" or "passive" approach to their jobs. Of particular interest is how much energy presidents invest in their work and how strongly they assert themselves in decision making. The second dimension addresses whether presidents maintain a "positive" or "negative" view of their working environment. Is their work "a burden to be endured or an opportunity for personal enjoyment"? The study found that the personalities of "active-positive" presidents such as Franklin Roosevelt and John Kennedy were best suited to their tasks. By contrast, those presidents who fell into the "active-negative" category, including Woodrow Wilson, Lyndon Johnson, and Richard Nixon, often met with personal frustration and professional failure. The impact of personality on foreign policy is certainly not confined to the United States. Indeed, a measurable link can be found between the personality traits and foreign policy decisions of leaders in a wide range of countries (see Hermann 1984, 1993).

One might ask what impact presidential personality has on U.S. foreign policy, especially in light of the president's broad powers in times of national crisis and war. Also of concern is whether the U.S. political system attracts "high-dominance individuals with a greater personal disposition to use force" (Etheridge 1978, 451). In his own study, foreign policy scholar John Stoessinger (1985, xiii) divided U.S. presidents into two general categories: crusaders and pragmatists. *Crusaders* demonstrate a "missionary zeal to make the world better" and "tend to make decisions based on a preconceived idea rather than on the basis of experience." Among the twentieth-century presidents examined by Stoessinger (1985), those fitting the crusader profile were Woodrow Wilson, Lyndon Johnson, Jimmy Carter, and Ronald Reagan. *Pragmatists,* by contrast, confront foreign policy problems more flexibly. They try to make decisions based on the available evidence, weigh the pros and cons of alternative policies, and are quick to reverse themselves if those policies prove unsuccessful. Franklin Roosevelt fit this category, and Richard Nixon's foreign policy was driven by the pragmatism of national security adviser Henry Kissinger. From this historical review, Stoessinger concluded that pragmatists are better equipped to manage foreign relations, which demand that presidents adapt quickly to rapidly changing circumstances.

The Dangers of "Groupthink"

The third dimension of political psychology is group behavior—an important object of scrutiny because much of the day-to-day formulation of U.S. foreign policy occurs in group settings. Often, the pressures imposed by collective decision making prevent individuals from simply demanding that their policy preferences be followed. Some sort of collaboration and compromise among several individuals, whose beliefs and personalities meld or clash with those of other participants in the decision process, are usually involved. Although cohesion rather than discord is generally preferred, dangers arise when group pressures force individuals to reach and support a consensus before they are prepared to do so.

In the 1970s, psychologist Irving Janis introduced the concept of **groupthink** and the policy problems it presents. In his view, major U.S. foreign policy "fiascoes," such as the failure to anticipate Japan's attack on Pearl Harbor and the poor prosecution of the Vietnam War, could be attributed to the dysfunctions of collective decision making. Specifically, Janis (1982, 174–175) identified three characteristics of groupthink:

- Overestimation of the group's power and morality, "inclining members to ignore the ethical or moral consequences of their decisions"

- Closed-mindedness, or a collective reluctance to question basic assumptions about the problems at hand

- Pressures toward uniformity, or "a shared illusion of unanimity," combined with "direct pressure on any member who expresses strong sentiment against any of the group's stereotypes, illusions, or commitments"

Later studies reinforced and refined the concept of groupthink. For example, one study found that "structural deficiencies" in group deliberations hindered the outcome of major U.S. foreign policy decisions from 1975 to 1993 (Schafer and Crichlow 2002). Another study discovered that newly formed groups appear most vulnerable to reaching premature consensus (Hart, Stern, and Sundelius 1997). And yet another pointed out that the dangers of groupthink are not limited to foreign policy crises; they apply to routine decision making as well (P. Hart 1994). Indeed, the problems associated with groupthink may be observed within government bodies at all levels and in private organizations.

Reports on the Bush administration's deliberations before the March 2003 invasion of Iraq offer additional evidence of the persistent problems associated with groupthink. Of particular interest are reports claiming that, shortly after taking power, senior administration officials reached a consensus that Saddam Hussein should be overthrown and then searched for an appropriate pretext to make this happen (Woodward 2004, 2006; Badie 2010). As Greg Cashman and Leonard Robinson (2007, 355) observed, "The net effect of the bureaucratic struggle was something that looked like groupthink. The moderates in the State Department had been allowed to play in the game, but they were driven into self-censorship and into confining their criticism to tactical issues in order to stay on the playing field. Thus a small group of decision makers were able to control the agenda and the options and ensure that nothing stood in the way of the president's predisposition for a preventive war against Iraq."

Crisis Decision Making

A final dimension of political psychology is the behavior of presidents and other key decision makers in times of heightened stress or crisis. International crises are crucial because they occur at a midpoint "between peace and war" (Lebow 1981). The actions taken by political leaders in such crises often determine whether longstanding differences will be resolved peacefully or through violent conflict. Legal constraints and institutional structures play an important, but relatively indirect, role in such stressful circumstances. Of greater consequence are the psychological and behavioral orientations of the decision makers. To political psychologists Jonathan and Stanley Renshon (2008, 511), "no crisis or war is understandable without direct reference to the decision making of individual leaders."

Three factors converge in a crisis to shape the response of foreign policy makers (Hermann 1993): (1) the element of surprise, (2) a perceived threat to vital national values and interests, and (3) a compressed time frame that demands quick action. Each of these circumstances hinders a rational policy response. Information on the nature and cause of the crisis is limited, as are relative calculations about the costs and benefits of possible responses. Emotions run high, further impairing the process. Normal decision-making routines are often suspended, and presidents are likely to consult only members of their inner circle of advisers. Leaders must make the final decisions,

Members of the National Security Council consider U.S. options during the October 1962 Cuban missile crisis. In carefully weighing advice from multiple advisers, and then adopting a forceful, but flexible posture in his negotiations with Soviet leaders over their nuclear missiles in Cuba, President John Kennedy (facing forward, third from left) avoided a catastrophic clash between the world's two superpowers.

however, and they often do so by relying on their existing beliefs about the foreign governments and leaders involved, by focusing on short- rather than long-term goals, and by adopting a rigid stance that discourages dissent or a protracted search for alternative actions (George 1980; Holsti 1984).

All these conditions and policy responses were evident in the Bush administration's response to the September 11, 2001, terrorist attacks. Although government officials had long been aware that terrorism posed a danger to the nation, the attacks took the Bush administration by surprise and shattered the sense of national security felt by government leaders and the general public. The prospects of additional attacks, affirmed by a series of anthrax poisonings in the weeks that followed, compelled Bush to respond quickly by ordering an invasion of Afghanistan and the overthrow of its government. As Bush's advisers acknowledged, the ordeal strained the emotional capacities of all government officials, who had to respond immediately and forcefully with only limited information about the proposed invasion and the viability of other responses.

International crises pose the most acute challenge to rational foreign policy making (see Monten and Bennett 2010). In some cases, presidents have managed crises in a way that produced a favorable outcome. Most notable among these cases were John F. Kennedy's patience and careful attention to conflicting advice during the 1962 Cuban missile crisis and his selection of a "measured" U.S. response that offered the Soviet Union a peaceful way out of the crisis. Even the best efforts of leaders, however, cannot prevent the pressures of time, combined with the dynamics of individual and group psychology, from hindering the rational conduct of U.S. foreign policy.

■ CONCLUSION

As this chapter suggests, the conduct of U.S. foreign policy derives from pressures that arise not only from overseas but also from within the country's borders. Events in key areas—the start of the Korean War in 1950, the terrorist attacks of September 2001, and Russia's seizure of Ukrainian territory in 2014—focus the attention of foreign policy makers. How they respond, however, depends on the outcome of a complex deliberation process that engages powerful figures in civil society, multiple federal agencies, and individual decision makers who draw upon their own belief systems and personal experiences. These dynamics of decision making occur within the "black box" of U.S. foreign policy, which is a primary concern of this chapter and those that follow.

In analyzing these dynamics of decision making, it is worth recalling that each foreign policy decision is made in a unique time and place, the contextual features of which define the problems facing the United States, establish alternative solutions, and determine final choices (Farnham 2004). The range of choices is restricted not only by their anticipated outcomes but also by whether a given course of action will be acceptable politically to important domestic stakeholders within and outside the federal government (George 1980). These *political* factors have a logic of their own and may be related indirectly, or not at all, to accepted *policy* goals. Although such political pressures vary widely and are difficult to discern in specific cases, they are keenly familiar to the players in the two-level game of U.S. foreign policy.

Consideration of the president's vital role, outlined in Chapter 4, demonstrates further the power of the human factor in the White House. Yet the institutional constraints on this power, based in Congress and in the various federal agencies engaged in foreign policy, guarantee that other agendas will be represented in the policy determination process as well. Moreover, these agendas may be either shared or resisted by external actors whose affiliations and agendas are increasingly transnational in their scope. One thing is certain, however. Making rational decisions, always a difficult task in view of the limitations of human nature and political psychology, proves especially difficult in the complex institutional environment in which U.S. foreign policy is made.

3

anarchy, p. 79

balance of power, p. 79

belief systems, p. 100

bounded rationality, p. 99

bureaucratic politics, p. 93

causal beliefs, p. 100

cognitive psychology, p. 101

congressional dominance model, p. 96

constructivism, p. 81

democratic peace, p. 80

geopolitics, p. 79

global governance, p. 80

groupthink, p. 104

identity, p. 82

interdependence, p. 80

iron triangle, p. 90

issue networks, p. 91

levels of analysis, p. 85

military-industrial complex, p. 90

national interest, p. 79

neoliberal institutionalism, p. 81

neorealism, p. 83

operational code, p. 100

organizational culture, p. 94

organizational process, p. 94

political psychology, p. 99

presidential control model, p. 96

principled beliefs, p. 100

prospect theory, p. 103

rational actors, p. 85

rational choice, p. 86

regimes, p. 81

security community, p. 80

security dilemma, p. 79

soft balancing, p. 80

sovereignty, p. 79

standard operating procedures (SOPs), p. 94

structural realism, p. 79

transnational civil society, p. 89

Treaty of Westphalia, p. 79

two-level game, p. 86

unitary actors, p. 86

INTERNET REFERENCES

The **Center on Budget and Policy Priorities** (http://www.cbpp.org) focuses on federal and state budget priorities, including research on taxes and spending. Subjects of interest include trends in military spending and the budgets of other foreign policy programs. Hosted by Dalhousie University, the **Centre for Foreign Policy Studies** (http://www.dal.ca/dept/cfps.html) provides useful information on conferences, seminars, and publication series, as well as specific links to policy, government, and international institutions. The center's recent research seminars and publications analyze unilateralism and multilateralism decisions after the Cold War.

The **Congressional Research Service (CRS) Reports and Issue Briefs** (http://digital.library.unt.edu/explore/collections/CRSR/), produced by the research arm of Congress, provide briefings on specific policy issues that include background information, chronologies, bibliographic references, and budget statistics. Two of the larger policy domains within the CRS are "Foreign Affairs" and "Defense and Trade." *CRS Reports* on particular topics are often updated each year. Current examples of such topics are terrorism, international and free trade, foreign aid, global finance, arms trade and control, missile defense, energy policy, and U.S.-Russia and U.S.-Israel relations.

The **International Action Center** (http://www.iacenter.org) critically considers international labor, poverty, militarization, and multinational corporations. This site lists dozens of links to books, journals, and web resources on antiwar and antiglobalization activities and efforts to improve the standard of living in poverty-stricken countries.

The **International Studies Association** (http://www.isanet.org) provides conference papers, journal articles, and relevant links to timely and scholarly research on empirical testing and analysis of issues in foreign policy and international politics in general. Included are syllabi collections, which contain additional readings and links from various professors around the globe. The Foreign Policy Analysis Section of the association publishes *Foreign Policy Analysis,* a multidisciplinary, peer-reviewed journal on the process, outputs, and empirical testing of foreign policy (http://www.isanet.org/pubs/fpa.html).

The **National Center for Policy Analysis** (http://www.ncpa.org) is a nonprofit, nonpartisan public policy research center that promotes market-based solutions to public problems. Areas of concern to U.S. foreign policy include immigration, energy, trade, and environmental issues.

The **National Center for Public Policy Research** (http://www.nationalcenter.org) is a conservative foundation that researches current international and national events with a free-market and individual liberty orientation. Topics of interest for foreign policy researchers are environmental and energy policy, national security, national sovereignty, and defense procurement.

The **Policy Section, American Political Science Association** (http://www.apsanet.org/RESOURCES/For-the-Public/Related-Cognate-Associations/Policy-Studies-Organization-), designed by a group of scholars in that field, provides useful links to journals, think tanks, and centers for those interested in studying public policy. The site also provides links to recent conferences where papers and roundtables on public policy issues were presented; full-text downloading capabilities are available.

The **Woodrow Wilson International Center for Scholars** (https://www.wilsoncenter.org) provides a research hub for scholars and students to review current events and how they relate to relevant theories of policy. In addition to specific regional coverage and research, the center engages in ongoing projects on security and peace strategies along with research on conflict prevention and international trade and finance. The center publishes books in each area of research and the *Wilson Quarterly* (http://www.wilsonquarterly.com).

CHAPTER 4

PRESIDENTIAL POWER

AP Photo/Jacquelyn Martin

As commander in chief, President Obama relied on top cabinet officials to help him make his most important decisions regarding U.S. foreign policy. Among these advisers, Secretary of State John Kerry also played a direct role in negotiating with Iran, Syria, Russia, and other nations of concern to the United States.

4.1   Discuss how the powers and constraints of the Constitution influence the president's role in foreign policy.

4.2   Identify the ways that presidential prerogative is evident in three areas of U.S. foreign policy.

4.3   Describe the White House–centered structure of foreign policy decision making and how it has changed over time.

4.4   Explain the role of the judicial branch in U.S. foreign policy.

The president of the United States maintains a position of power that is unequaled in the world. No other person has a greater capacity to mobilize the nation's vast political, economic, and military resources or to affect the tenor of global politics. The extent of presidential power is greater in foreign policy than in domestic policy because presidents are regarded, at home and overseas, as living symbols of the United States. The White House's control over foreign policy, which has grown steadily since World War II, led one scholar to conclude that **two presidencies** operate simultaneously: a constrained president on domestic issues and a president who reigns supreme in foreign affairs (Wildavsky 1966).

Like the leaders of other countries, U.S. presidents know that foreign affairs can be a safe haven from their troubles at home. Status as head of state carries with it unmatched prestige and provides an opportunity to "rise above politics" in the pursuit of national interests. State visits abroad, as well as high-profile visits by foreign dignitaries, boost the president's approval ratings. For this reason, presidents "have a natural inclination to escape the frustrations and controversies of domestic policy making by seeking opportunities to strut their stuff in the realm of foreign and national security policy" (Rockman 1997, 26).

Presidential power has grown steadily since World War II. In the late 1940s, Cold War pressures led to the centralization of foreign policy making in the White House. The National Security Council (NSC), created in 1947, effectively replaced the State Department as the primary source of foreign policy advice to the president. Since then, presidents have relied on their national security advisers, whose offices located close to the Oval Office make them available on a moment's notice. In the Obama years, "if your office is not in the complex at 1600 Pennsylvania Avenue, regardless of your title, you are often out of the loop" (Rothkopf 2014b, 49). Members of

Congress, despite their own constitutional authorities in foreign policy, are more likely than in the past to yield to the executive branch. Presidents, therefore, have freely utilized a variety of unilateral tools at their disposal that strengthen their ability to control U.S. foreign policy (see Howell and Kriner 2008). Recent examples include the following:

- President Bill Clinton signed an executive order on June 25, 1994, that outlined measures for implementing the Chemical Weapons Convention. Five years later, Clinton cited his role as commander in chief in authorizing U.S. air strikes, in conjunction with NATO forces, against Serbia without seeking or gaining the approval of Congress.

- On October 25, 2001, President George W. Bush issued a national security directive that outlined plans for the U.S. invasion of Afghanistan in retaliation for that government's role in sponsoring the September 11 terrorist attacks. Bush later signed a military order creating military tribunals for the prosecution of suspected terrorists, and he lifted an executive order signed by President Gerald R. Ford that banned CIA-backed political assassinations.

- President Obama used a UN Security Council resolution rather than the consent of Congress to justify sending U.S. military forces to Libya, which was on the brink of civil war in March 2011. Obama also issued a presidential "finding" that authorized covert CIA action to help rebels overthrow the nation's despotic ruler, Muammar Qaddafi.

Even with these broad powers, presidents face multiple obstacles in conducting foreign policy. On Capitol Hill, Democratic control of Congress under the Republican administrations of Dwight Eisenhower, Richard Nixon, Ronald Reagan, George H.W. Bush, and George W. Bush led to frequent clashes over foreign policy. The Republican-led Congress of 1995–2001 waged a vigorous campaign to blunt the "neo-Wilsonian" aspects of Clinton's foreign policy. Under

GET THE EDGE ON YOUR STUDIES

edge.sagepub.com/hook5e

- Take a quiz to find out what you've learned.
- Review key terms with eFlashcards.
- Watch videos that enhance chapter content.

President Obama, legislators from both parties frequently criticized the White House on vital foreign policy issues. Presidents must also navigate their way through multiple power centers within the executive branch whose interests routinely conflict with one another (see Figure 4.1). The judicial branch can also impose limits on presidential power, although the courts are generally "content to function as an arm of the executive branch on matters concerning foreign affairs and national security" (Fisher 2007, 59). Finally, presidents are engaged daily with foreign leaders along with hundreds of domestic and global interest groups that have their own stakes in the conduct of U.S. foreign policy.

Presidents have much to win or lose with each decision they make, but they retain considerable freedom to make such choices as they see fit. Successful presidents exploit their status and authority by effectively persuading subordinates in the executive branch, along with members of Congress, to support their policy preferences. According to Richard Neustadt (1960, 34), who became an adviser to President John Kennedy, "The essence of a president's persuasive task is to convince [others] that what the White House wants is what they ought to do for their own sake and on their own authority."

Figure 4.1 ■ Influences on the President in Foreign Policy

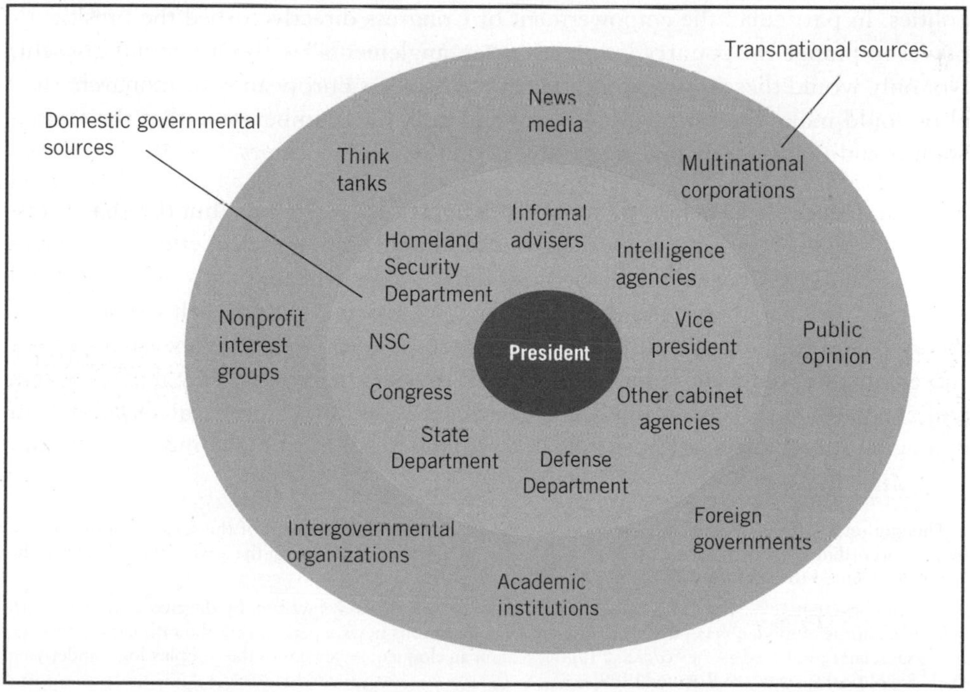

Transnational sources

Domestic governmental sources

News media

Think tanks

Multinational corporations

Informal advisers

Homeland Security Department

Intelligence agencies

Nonprofit interest groups

NSC

President

Vice president

Public opinion

Congress

Other cabinet agencies

State Department

Defense Department

Intergovernmental organizations

Foreign governments

Academic institutions

■ THE CONSTITUTION'S MIXED BLESSING

Understanding the president's role in foreign policy begins with the U.S. Constitution, which calls for the sharing of powers between the executive and legislative branches of government and for legal questions to be resolved by the judicial branch.[1] This central principle of **codetermination** reflects the twin fears of tyranny at home and adventurism abroad that preoccupied the founders of the United States (see Chapter 2).

Much of the Constitution has less to do with the scope of federal authority than with its distribution among the branches of government. On this point, the founders were deeply divided. Alexander Hamilton believed a strong president was needed to guide the United States in the unpredictable and often perilous realm of world politics. Hamilton's nemesis in this debate was James Madison, the primary author of the Constitution, who believed a legislature must be empowered to prevent the emergence of a tyrannical head of state.[2] Madison, taking his cue from the French political philosopher Baron de Montesquieu, insisted that national powers be shared by the executive and legislative branches of government and that an independent judiciary be established to ensure that government action, as well as private behavior, complied with the rule of law.

Although the Constitution did not emphasize foreign policy, these checks and balances were intended in large part as restraints on the U.S. government in world politics. In particular, the empowerment of Congress directly curbed the president's power to plunge the country into foreign "entanglements" without popular consent. Not only would these restrictions prevent the rise of a European-style monarch: they also would make the formulation of foreign policy so cumbersome that the United States would only rarely take aggressive action in foreign affairs.

Modern presidents have not questioned this constitutional design, but they have consistently resisted efforts by Congress to tie their hands. Among twentieth-century presidents, Theodore Roosevelt was the most outspoken advocate of strong presidential power in war and peace (see In Their Own Words box). Roosevelt's **stewardship theory** called for a dominant president in domestic and foreign policy. Although his successors adopted a more balanced view of presidential power, they have asserted, and generally have been granted, considerable discretion, or **prerogative powers,** in managing foreign affairs (Silverstein 1997). This freedom to make independent and

---

1. This notion of *sharing* powers is more accurate than the widespread concept of the *separation* of powers, because according to Article II, section 2, of the Constitution, the president, with the advice and consent of the Senate, is required to make joint decisions on vital foreign policy matters.

2. This public debate over the Constitution, which took the form of essays written by the two men along with John Jay, another founder, was published anonymously in various newspapers during the ratification process. The essays, later published as the *Federalist Papers,* remain an eloquent statement of the complex logic underlying the U.S. political system (see Rossiter 1999).

binding judgments extends beyond national emergencies to include day-to-day decisions that do not require the blessing of Congress or the courts. Yet the Constitution still provides the essential framework for the formulation of foreign policy.

The Sharing of Foreign Policy Powers

The powers of Congress and the president are defined in Articles I and II of the Constitution, respectively (see Table 4.1). The language on foreign policy is very brief and sufficiently vague to provoke widely varying interpretations of the framers' intent. References to foreign policy powers do not appear in separate sections of either article but are interspersed among references to powers in domestic policy. The president has formal powers in foreign policy in four key areas: (1) directing the

IN THEIR OWN WORDS

Theodore Roosevelt *Among twentieth-century U.S. leaders, Theodore Roosevelt was one of the strongest advocates of presidential power. He believed that the president, who alone serves the nation as a whole, should be a "steward" of the people. To act as a steward, the president must have broad authority to exercise power without interference from Congress or the courts. According to political scientist Michael Nelson, Roosevelt's stewardship theory rests on the assumption that "the president could do anything that the Constitution or laws did not expressly forbid," a view of presidential power in sharp contrast to that held by many nineteenth-century presidents. Roosevelt explained the theory himself in his autobiography.*

The most important factor in getting the right spirit in my Administration . . . was my insistence upon the theory that the executive power was limited only by specific restrictions and prohibitions appearing in the Constitution or imposed by the Congress under its Constitutional powers. My view was that every executive officer, and above all every executive officer in high position, was a steward of the people bound actively and affirmatively to do all he could for the people, and not to content himself with the negative merit of keeping his talents undamaged in a napkin. I declined to adopt the view that what was imperatively necessary for the Nation could not be done by the President unless he could find some specific authorization to do it. My belief was that it was not only his right but his duty to do anything that the needs of the Nation demanded unless such action was forbidden by the Constitution or by the laws. Under this interpretation of executive power I did and caused to be done many things not previously done by the President and the heads of the departments. I did not usurp power, but I did greatly broaden the use of executive power. In other words, I acted for the public welfare, I acted for the common well-being of all our people, whenever and in whatever manner was necessary, unless prevented by direct constitutional or legislative prohibition.

Sources: Michael Nelson, ed., *Historic Documents on the Presidency: 1776–1989* (Washington, DC: Congressional Quarterly, 1989), 170; *Theodore Roosevelt, An Autobiography* (New York: Macmillan, 1913), also available online at www.bartleby.com/55/ (Bartleby.com, 1998).

Table 4.1 ■ The Constitutional Balance of Power

	Executive	Legislative
Actors	President, cabinet, NSC, bureaucracy, White House advisers	House of Representatives and Senate, committees and subcommittees
Advantages	Coherence, speed, secrecy, national constituency, control of information	Deliberation, compromise, openness
War powers	Commander in chief of the armed forces, authority to repel attacks	Power to declare war, authorize ongoing deployment (per War Powers Resolution of 1973)
Diplomatic powers	Recognize and conduct routine relations with foreign governments	Initiate fact-finding missions
Appointment powers	Nominate ambassadors and cabinet secretaries	Confirm nominees
Treaty powers	Negotiate and sign treaties	Ratify treaties
Administrative powers	Oversight through cabinet, bureaucracy, and staff	Appropriations, oversight of executive branch
Economic powers	Lead economic agencies; adopt fiscal, monetary, and trade policies	Regulate commerce, power of the purse
Special powers	Declare national emergencies, sign executive orders	Impeach president

conduct of warfare, (2) negotiating and signing treaties and international agreements, (3) appointing cabinet secretaries and ambassadors, and (4) conducting diplomacy.

Directing the conduct of warfare. The rationale for the Constitution's division of labor for war powers is clear: sending troops to war, widely considered the most crucial decision any government can make, must be a collective, not an individual, undertaking. A declaration of war, therefore, must follow a reasoned discussion of the alternatives. Furthermore, hostilities must proceed only after most legislators determine war to be the best available option. Once war has been declared, however, the president as commander in chief must be free to direct the conflict. As a result of the need for prompt, unified, and decisive leadership, military conflicts require centralized command rather than legislative deliberation. Thus, once the United States has become engaged in warfare, the government checks and balances deemed so essential by the framers no longer pertain to the actions of the commander in chief.

No area of U.S. foreign policy has been as controversial as the president's war powers. Three factors account for this unending controversy. First, formal declarations of war are no longer standard practice in diplomacy. The United States has declared war in only five conflicts: the War of 1812, the Mexican-American War, the Spanish-American War, World War I, and World War II. Since December 1941, the U.S. government, despite intervening in dozens of armed conflicts—including those in Korea, Vietnam, Panama, the Persian Gulf, the former Yugoslavia, Afghanistan, Iraq, and Libya—has not issued a formal declaration of war. This is possible because presidents can resort to military force with little concern for the preferences of Congress. Even when war declarations were customary, American presidents unilaterally deployed troops overseas when they felt national interests were at stake. For example, Thomas Jefferson dispatched U.S. naval forces, without congressional authorization, to the Mediterranean Sea to repel attacks on shipping.

Second, military interventions provide a fait accompli for presidents. Once troops are deployed, domestic opposition not only appears unpatriotic but also may weaken the mission and threaten the lives of American military personnel. For this reason, members of Congress are reluctant to question presidential uses of force even when they believe their own prerogatives have been blocked. President James Polk established this precedent in 1845 by sending U.S. troops into disputed territory along the U.S.-Mexico border. The deployment quickly provoked skirmishes between U.S. and Mexican forces that led to war between the two countries.

Third, presidents have broad discretion to conduct wars in whatever ways they deem appropriate. Although such discretion is clearly within the authority as commander in chief, critics have frequently assailed presidents whose military actions were seen as immoral or illegal. During the Civil War, for example, Abraham Lincoln suspended many constitutional freedoms for the sake of military necessity. Harry Truman did not seek congressional approval of the use of atomic bombs against Japan. Richard Nixon openly defied Congress during the Vietnam War, withholding vital information about U.S. incursions into Cambodia and Laos. In the war on terror, domestic critics charged the Bush administration with abusing Iraqi prisoners, violating the civil rights of Muslims in the

Truman Presidential Museum and Library

President Harry Truman poses at his desk, which features a sign with the blunt message "The buck stops here!" Although Truman came to power as a result of the death of President Franklin Roosevelt, he quickly emerged as a strong president. He took decisive action in ending World War II, including the atomic bombing of two Japanese cities in August 1945. Truman also laid the foundations for the U.S. campaign against the Soviet Union during the Cold War.

United States, and unjustly restricting the civil liberties of all Americans (see Roth 2004). Obama's frequent use of aerial drones to conduct bombing missions, many of which killed innocent civilians, provoked condemnations from many nations, including U.S. allies (Bergen and Rothenberg 2014).

Negotiating and signing treaties and international agreements. Presidents and Congress share the power to conclude agreements with foreign governments. Whereas the executive branch negotiates treaties, the U.S. Senate must approve them with a "super majority" of two-thirds of its members (or sixty-seven votes). The Senate has complied with the president's wishes in virtually every historical case. The exceptions to this rule—the Senate's rejection of the Treaty of Versailles in 1919 and of the Comprehensive Test Ban Treaty in 1999, for example—illustrate how delicate the constitutional balance between branches can be.[3] In 2013, Obama was forced to retract an authorization to use military force against Syria when it became clear that Congress would not go along.

The framers expected senators to play a role throughout the treaty-making process, and for this reason, the Senate's advice and consent were written into the Constitution. Such collaboration is helpful, and often essential, for a smooth and successful ratification process. A president's failure to consult with Congress can prove disastrous. After World War I, Woodrow Wilson insisted on negotiating the Treaty of Versailles personally and took no members of Congress with him to Paris for the peace conference. The ambitious treaty, which called for the creation of the League of Nations, was rejected by the Senate. More recently, President Clinton in 1996 signed a path-breaking global ban on nuclear weapons testing but paid little attention to the ratification process in the Senate. This proved to be a serious misjudgment, as the Senate later rejected the Comprehensive Test Ban Treaty.

Formal treaties represent only a small fraction of the agreements reached between the United States and foreign governments. Increasingly, presidents submit **executive agreements** that do not require congressional approval (see Figure 4.2). While most of these involve routine matters such as small-scale trade deals, they often address crucial defense and national security issues (see Caruson and Farrar-Myers 2007, 635). These include Franklin Roosevelt's lend-lease agreements with European allies during World War II, the various commitments made by Roosevelt at the Yalta Conference and by Harry Truman at the Potsdam Conference, the agreement between the United States and North Vietnam ending the Vietnam War, and multiple agreements granting U.S. forces access to foreign military bases. In March 2014, Obama signed three executive agreements that imposed economic sanctions against Russia after its annexation of the Crimean Peninsula.

----

3. Many other governments share this foreign policy power and face clashes between heads of state and legislatures over the ratification of treaties (see Lantis 2009).

Figure 4.2 ■ Executive Agreements versus Treaties

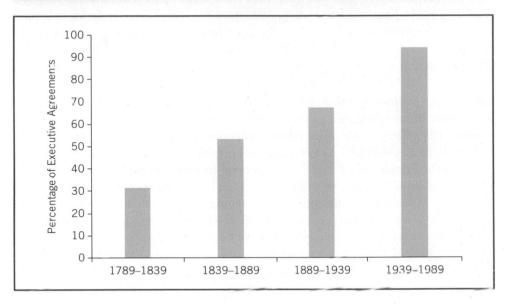

Source: Glen Krutz and Jeffrey S. Peake, *Treaty Politics and the Rise of Executive Agreements: International Commitments in a System of Shared Powers* (Ann Arbor: University of Michigan Press), 42.

Presidents favor executive agreements for three reasons. First, they gain more independence in advancing their foreign policy goals. Second, in the process of negotiating formal treaties, American diplomats and other negotiators have trouble maintaining the trust of foreign partners who cannot be sure if the treaties will be rejected by Congress. Finally, even if the treaties are ratified, the lengthy periods of congressional consideration can delay the taking of action, a serious problem on urgent matters such as humanitarian crises and secret missions by **Special Forces**. Despite its loss of influence in foreign relations, Congress benefits by focusing only on the most vital decisions that will be presented as treaties. Legislators also know that they must approve any measures that require government spending. Critics in Congress can also wait for the next president to take office who can nullify any executive agreements. In this sense, Congress is a willing partner in an "institutional bargain grounded in requirements for efficiency that are demanded by modern realities" (Krutz and Peake 2009, 10).

Although all presidents since George Washington have used executive agreements, the pace of these actions accelerated in the early twentieth century. Franklin Roosevelt was the most prolific, issuing 3,721 of the agreements. The rate has rapidly declined since then, with post–Cold War presidents averaging about forty executive agreements. Still, this practice frequently produces tensions between the White House and Congress. This was the case in 2015, when Obama, along with five other governments, signed the "Framework Agreement" with Iran that would require its government to suspend any attempts to build a nuclear weapon in return for relief from paralyzing economic sanctions. Facing bipartisan demands for input from the Senate, the president bowed to political reality and agreed to provide Congress an opportunity to approve or reject the agreement.

Appointing cabinet secretaries and ambassadors. Under the Constitution, presidents must submit their choices for top positions in the foreign policy bureaucracy to Congress. Senate approval of presidential appointees, like treaties, is granted in virtually every case. Observers widely agree that presidents, upon being elected, deserve to select the people they believe best equipped to promote the presidential agenda in foreign as well as domestic policy. In the rare instance a nomination is rejected, it and the surrounding circumstances capture the public's attention. Although Congress has usually deferred to the president on high-level appointments, confirmation hearings in these uncontroversial cases still serve important functions. Nominees have a chance to outline their goals and strategies and to promote the president's agenda. Committee members relish the opportunity to advance their own ideas about U.S. foreign policy and to enlist a nominee's support for their priorities.

Presidents sidestep the appointment process in several ways, particularly by receiving their primary guidance from the national security adviser, a position that does not require Senate confirmation. George W. Bush's 2005 appointment of John Bolton as the U.S. permanent representative to the United Nations provoked widespread opposition in Congress because of Bolton's previous criticism of multilateral diplomacy in general and the UN in particular. Faced with imminent defeat of the nomination in Congress, Bush placed Bolton in the position through a **recess appointment,** a constitutional measure permitting the temporary installation of political appointees when Congress is not in session. President Obama avoided congressional scrutiny by appointing a special envoy—former senator George Mitchell of Maine—to pursue a resolution of the Arab-Israeli conflict and by dispatching Richard Holbrooke, a longtime foreign policy adviser, to pursue a political settlement of the conflicts in Afghanistan and neighboring Pakistan.

Conducting diplomacy. The Constitution is especially vague about the day-to-day conduct of U.S. foreign policy. There is little doubt, however, that the president, as head of state, represents the United States in foreign relations. With this authority, the president directs the State Department and its worldwide staff of ambassadors and foreign service officers to manage the routine functions of diplomacy. The president personally conducts diplomacy by visiting foreign countries and hosting delegations of government officials in Washington, D.C. Presidents also communicate with foreign leaders on a regular basis, whether from the Oval Office, Air Force One, or other locations. This is particularly true during crises, when personal contacts and bargaining at the highest levels may make the difference between war and peace.

These presidential powers are captured in Article II, section 3, of the Constitution, which declares that the president "shall receive Ambassadors and other public Ministers." This wording is considered significant because, according to international law, "the reception of an ambassador constitutes a formal recognition of the sovereignty of the state or government represented" (Adler 1996b, 133). Such recognition is not automatic, however. George Washington set the precedent for U.S. recognition of newly installed foreign governments in 1793, when he invited the French envoy Edmond Charles Genêt for a state visit to Philadelphia, then the U.S. capital. Washington's invitation represented "tacit recognition" of the new revolutionary regime in Paris (H. Jones 1988, 34).

More recent presidents have taken it upon themselves to recognize foreign governments and to deny recognition to regimes they consider illegitimate. Formal recognition by the United States brings with it a wide array of potential economic, military, cultural, and political arrangements that are part of routine bilateral relationships. Richard Nixon's "opening" to the People's Republic of China in 1972 reversed long-standing U.S. policy that denied the legitimacy of China's communist government. In the early 1990s, Bill Clinton's recognition of the breakaway Yugoslav republics of Croatia, Slovenia, and Bosnia-Herzegovina paved the way for U.S. assistance to all three governments. In contrast, nonrecognition is often accompanied by economic sanctions and other punitive measures. President Clinton refused to recognize the Taliban regime in Afghanistan, a position also taken by his successors. Similarly, in 2014 President Obama rejected Russia's seizure of Ukraine's Crimean Peninsula, a decision that opened the door for sweeping U.S. sanctions against Vladimir Putin's government.

White House Advantages over Congress

Aside from the president's formal powers, the office enjoys a variety of informal powers that Congress lacks. The following six advantages of the presidency have helped the White House to strengthen its hold on the foreign policy process:

- *A national constituency.* The president is the only elected official who represents a national constituency and can claim to speak for "all the people." Senators and House members represent states and congressional districts, respectively, and thus are obliged to promote the relatively narrow self-interests of their constituents in these areas even if they conflict with perceived national interests. Presidents face no such dilemma in their foreign policy choices.

- *Use of the "bully pulpit."* As noted elsewhere, presidents have unparalleled access to the general public in making their case for their chosen foreign policies. The news media follow every word and deed of the president on a daily basis, which gives the

White House an opportunity to communicate directly with citizens through interviews and press briefings (see Chapter 8). The **bully pulpit**, a term coined by President Theodore Roosevelt, can influence public opinion and, consequently, congressional support for the president's foreign policies.

- *Status as the party leader.* As party leader, presidents generally can rely on support from within their own political party, not only in Congress but also among state and local officials. George W. Bush's strong support among congressional Republicans, for example, strengthened his resolve to press forward on his plans to invade Iraq in 2003. Party members who openly oppose presidents from "within the ranks" run the risk of appearing disloyal. As noted above, Democrats in Congress made exceptions to this rule on several foreign policy issues.

- *The perpetual "session."* The presidency, unlike Congress, is always in session. Thus, the president can respond to foreign policy problems at any time and with little notice. Congress lacks this element of expediency. It is often in recess and, except for times of national emergency, operates by means of a legislative calendar that is notoriously slow and rigid.

- *The bureaucracy's CEO.* The president serves as the chief executive officer of the federal bureaucracy and its employees. Presidents can expect that the general principles and policy goals they adopt will be supported by federal employees. "The political machinery will simply not work without effective presidential control over it" (Rodman 2009, 275).

- *Information dominance.* The president's control of information is extensive and closely protected. The intelligence agencies, diplomatic corps, and armed services, all located within the executive branch, collect the vital information on foreign affairs that the president uses in making decisions. In most routine areas of foreign policy, members of Congress are kept out of this loop. Even when Congress is consulted, the White House is able to provide selective intelligence findings that support its policy preferences (Richelson 2008).

Constraints on Presidential Power

Although the framers of the U.S. Constitution set up a complex system of checks and balances for the formulation of U.S. foreign policy, in the modern era this delicate sharing of powers has been overridden frequently. As a global superpower, the United States has found itself in a nearly perpetual state of crisis, faced with two "hot wars" of global proportions, a protracted Cold War, and, more recently, a string of regional conflicts and a two-front war (domestic and overseas) against terrorism. These circumstances have produced major changes in the institutions of U.S. foreign policy, which have, in turn, given the president unprecedented influence in the foreign policy process.

Despite these changes and all the other presidential advantages just noted, the president faces many constraints in managing U.S. foreign policy. In coming to grips with the possibilities for, and limitations of, presidential power, three closely related factors must be considered:

- *Developments overseas.* U.S. foreign policy is often a reactive process. International crises cannot be anticipated with confidence, nor can changes within foreign governments and their consequences for U.S. bilateral relations. In recent years, the al Qaeda terrorist attacks, Russia's invasion of Georgia, and nuclear tests in North Korea have altered the short- and long-term priorities of U.S. foreign policy.

- *Domestic politics.* The ability of presidents to achieve their foreign policy goals depends largely on whether the president's party controls one or both houses of Congress (see Fleisher, Bond, and Wood 2008).

- *Personal limitations.* As described in Chapter 3, presidents cannot be expected to act "rationally" amid the wide array of foreign and domestic problems facing the United States at any given time. Although they benefit from restraining their emotions and being as fully informed as possible, they still must take cognitive "shortcuts" to simplify this bewildering environment.

This framework for analysis highlights the central reality that the president's role in foreign policy cannot be determined without reference to the details of specific policy problems and solutions. In short, one cannot generalize about presidential powers, nor can one predict how these powers will express themselves in given situations with a high degree of certainty. The *context* of foreign policy is crucial in this respect, framing the possibilities as well as the limitations of presidential power.

■ PRESIDENTIAL PREROGATIVE IN THE "ZONE OF TWILIGHT"

The president enjoys a great degree of discretion, or prerogative, in managing U.S. foreign policy (see Genovese 2011). This is important given the high level of mutual distrust between the two branches of government that is woven into the nation's institutional fabric and reinforced by historical experience. Many foreign policy powers of the president and Congress—those not explicitly written into the Constitution—are not clearly apportioned. As Supreme Court Justice Robert Jackson observed in 1952 in his famous concurring opinion in *Youngstown Sheet and Tube Co. v. Sawyer*, 343 U.S. 579, "[T]here is a **zone of twilight** in which [the president] and Congress may have concurrent authority, or in which its distribution is uncertain." Most routine actions by the U.S. government in foreign affairs fall within this twilight zone, and presidents have consistently filled the void by wielding "power without persuasion" (Howell 2003).

American presidents closely guard their prerogatives, which give them broad latitude to conduct U.S. foreign policy. In a one-on-one meeting with Soviet leader Mikhael

Gorbachev, for example, Ronald Reagan nearly agreed in October 1986 to abolish all the nuclear weapons in both countries' arsenals. George W. Bush, who once labeled himself "the decider," chose to declare an open-ended "war on terror" following the 9/11 terrorist attacks. Barack Obama, who as a senator and presidential candidate criticized Bush's use of war powers, later adopted many of his same practices such as indefinite detentions and military tribunals for suspected terrorists. As one legal expert observed during Obama's third year, "it seems clear that Obama has not yielded any grounds in his claims for prerogative power, and in some respects he has gone further in these claims than his predecessor" (Pious 2011, 265).[4]

The vast scope of presidential prerogative is evident in three areas of U.S. foreign policy: setting the agenda, organizing the chain of command, and taking the initiative. Effective presidents exploit all these applications to determine the course of foreign policy.

Setting the Foreign Policy Agenda

The president is uniquely equipped to set the nation's foreign policy agenda. Only the president can approve and articulate the grand strategy of the United States in global affairs, and only the president can make the most critical decisions about the tactics of foreign policy derived from this chosen grand strategy. In setting the agenda, presidents may not gain immediate consensus on what actions should be taken about a particular foreign policy problem. They can, however, use their unrivaled stature to influence what problems will receive the greatest attention in the press and public opinion. Although legislators claim to have a voice in this process, "Congress does not exert leadership on the president's agenda. The evidence points to a reactive Congress" (Rutledge and Larsen-Price 2014, 460). Presidents' public statements related to the ends and means of foreign policy are a core element of this informal power. It is widely accepted that these statements "give authoritative articulation to the nation's foreign policy" (D. L. Robinson 1996, 118). This presidential agenda-setting power—promoted actively through deeds as well as words—was evident throughout the Cold War. Harry Truman launched the containment strategy that guided U.S. foreign policy until the collapse of the Soviet Union in 1991 (see other doctrines in Table 4.2). In the late 1960s, Richard Nixon adopted the "realpolitik" model of statecraft championed by national security adviser Henry Kissinger, and in the 1970s Jimmy Carter revived the moralism of Woodrow Wilson. Carter's successor, Ronald Reagan, placed the revival of Soviet containment at the top of his agenda and, with a supportive Congress and favorable public opinion, enjoyed free rein to manage the superpower conflict at its pivotal moment (see J. M. Scott 1996).

---

4. Obama also exercised his prerogative not to prosecute officials in the Bush administration who may have violated laws regarding the treatment of detainees and chose not to create a special commission to investigate the practices of his predecessor.

Table 4.2 ■ Post–World War II Presidential Doctrines

Year	Presidential Doctrine	Description
1947	Truman Doctrine	Committed U.S. support to foreign governments facing internal or external subversion
1957	Eisenhower Doctrine	Declared the Middle East to be a vital region to the United States
1969	Nixon Doctrine	Shifted U.S. involvement in Asia to a more limited role by encouraging allies to fight communism on their own
1985	Reagan Doctrine	Pledged U.S. support for countries fighting communism through insurgents or "freedom fighters"
1994	Clinton Doctrine	Identified global engagement and "enlargement" of democratic rule as a central goal of U.S. foreign policy
2002	(George W.) Bush Doctrine	Defended preventive attacks on state terrorists; identified U.S. primacy as a key goal of grand strategy
2010	Obama Doctrine	Maintain U.S. primacy through soft power, heightened allied support, and a smaller-scale military "footprint"

Conversely, the lack of presidential vision in foreign policy can be costly. George H. W. Bush acknowledged that his failure to identify a coherent post–Cold War grand strategy contributed to his unsuccessful reelection campaign in 1992. For his part, Bill Clinton remained preoccupied with domestic reforms long after taking office in 1993. He finally decided on the guiding principle of his foreign policy—the "enlargement" of global democracy—but the doctrine never caught on with Congress or the public. By the time the Republican Party captured both houses of Congress in November 1994, Clinton had largely relinquished his ability to set the foreign policy agenda (Dumbrell 2002).

Although presidents have a great deal of discretion over their foreign policy agendas, unforeseen global events "can blow the president's foreign-policy ship into seas the president never planned to enter" (Brenner 1999, 187). The Japanese attack on Pearl Harbor in 1941, for example, shattered Franklin Roosevelt's efforts (and promises) to stay out of World War II. The same can be said for President Carter's foreign policy, which assumed a more aggressive stance after three developments abroad: the takeover of Nicaragua's government by Marxist rebels, the taking of U.S. hostages in Iran, and the Soviet Union's invasion of Afghanistan (Rosati 1987).

This pattern repeated itself with George W. Bush, for whom the terrorist attacks of September 11, 2001, provided the defining focus not only of his foreign policy but also of his presidency.[5] The Bush Doctrine that followed focused on proactive, often unilateral assertion of America's world power. Although Obama's foreign policy agenda was overtaken by the near collapse of the U.S. economy just prior to his election, he remained determined to improve U.S. moral leadership through the use of soft power and to change the course of Bush's war on terror by reducing its scope to a more narrow "war on al Qaeda." This change was not merely rhetorical: Obama fundamentally altered U.S. military strategy, turning away from large-scale troop deployments in favor of special operations designed to capture or kill terrorists while leaving a smaller "footprint" (Sanger 2012).

Organizing the Chain of Command

A second prerogative power of the president in foreign policy is the ability to organize the chain of command. Presidents have a great deal of flexibility in determining the roles played by various government institutions in formulating and conducting U.S. foreign policy. These institutions include the NSC, the Departments of State and Defense, the intelligence agencies, and the many agencies concerned with conducting foreign economic policy (see Chapter 6 for an elaboration).

With the concentration of foreign policy power in the White House after World War II, a new and more complex framework was established for the institutions of national security, which grew in number and in size during the late 1940s and early 1950s. Presidents have since assumed a crucial role in coordinating the activities of these institutions, in mediating their occasional conflicts, and, most important, in deciding which of them will have the greatest influence over specific policy choices. The creation of the NSC after World War II permanently shifted the locus of foreign policy decision making into the White House. The president also controls a large personal staff located within the Executive Office of the President (EOP). The office, created in 1939, resulted from President Franklin Roosevelt's "frank recognition that the sprawling federal bureaucracy, which he had helped create, was beyond his control" (D. E. Lewis 2008, 238).

The chain of command, as noted earlier, includes top foreign policy makers in the cabinet who are appointed by the president with the consent of Congress. Despite the more direct, day-to-day influence of the national security adviser, the secretary of state remains the chief diplomat in U.S. foreign policy. The secretary of defense, meanwhile, stands atop the nation's massive military complex. The relative influence of both cabinet members varies across presidential administrations, and competition between the secretaries of state and defense can be fierce. George W. Bush's reliance on military advice after the September 2001 terrorist attacks "was enormously frustrating to [Secretary of State] Colin Powell, who found himself

---

5. In his February 2004 appearance on NBC's *Meet the Press,* Bush repeatedly said that ever since September 11, 2001, he had considered himself a "war president."

the odd man out" (Gordon and Trainor 2006, 39). Seeking a more harmonious inner circle, Obama in his first term selected a defense secretary, Robert Gates, and a secretary of state, Hillary Clinton, who agreed on most foreign policy issues. Presidential prerogative extends to the day-to-day missions assigned to members of the inner circle. After Susan Rice, the U.S. ambassador to the United Nations, took over as national security adviser in 2013, her abrasive negotiating style frequently offended U.S. allies as well as adversaries. When sensitive meetings approached in 2014 over U.S. surveillance practices in Germany, Obama sent Denis McDonough, his chief of staff, to represent the United States rather than Rice. Such a move was highly unusual, as was his decision to exclude the State Department from the talks (Rothkopf 2014b, 48). Nonetheless, the president acted well within his prerogative as commander in chief.

Taking the Initiative

Finally, presidents can dominate the foreign policy process by taking the initiative, or dictating the flow of events. Presidents wield this power simply by conducting U.S. foreign policy on a day-by-day basis. They are granted considerable discretion in doing so, and they choose from many options in deciding which issues should receive their attention, which foreign countries they should consider friends or foes, and which actions they should take to achieve their goals. Their decisions set the foreign policy process in motion, determining the roles to be played by other government officials and forcing leaders overseas into a reactive posture. Electoral politics also plays a role in this process. Presidents who win their elections by a wide margin are especially prone to favor the use of force over negotiated settlements of disputes (Potter 2013).

This informal power often involves military action. Presidents must constantly manage tensions with foreign adversaries, and, depending on circumstances, they may choose to ease those tensions through diplomacy or escalate them with a show of military force. In the latter case, **saber rattling** is a common technique used to intimidate adversaries through hostile rhetoric, arms buildups, or the deployment of forces into contested territories. Such actions, intended to coerce adversaries into making concessions favorable to the United States, also run the risk of sparking a military conflict, upsetting regional power balances, or raising fears at home that stymie economic growth (Wood 2009). In April 2015, Obama used this tactic by deploying an American aircraft carrier group to the coast of Yemen in order to prevent Iranian vessels from delivering weapons to Shiite rebels who sought greater control of the embattled state. The show of U.S. force convinced the Iranian convoy to reverse course.

As noted earlier, the Constitution permits presidents, as commanders in chief, to deploy forces in response to imminent threats without the consent of Congress. Ronald Reagan took the initiative in 1983 when he invaded the Caribbean nation of Grenada after domestic turmoil had led to the rise of a neo-Marxist government.

Reagan claimed the mission was essential to rescue U.S. medical students stranded on the island. The mission served the larger purpose, however, of demonstrating Reagan's resolve to prevent such regimes from taking power on his watch. In overthrowing the government of Panama in 1989, George H. W. Bush showed that he was serious about the "war on drugs." In 1992, Bush's relief mission to Somalia symbolized the benevolent use of U.S. military force after the Cold War. For his part, Bill Clinton believed he had to act decisively to end the ethnic cleansing of Bosnia (1995) and Kosovo (1999), despite opposition from Congress and the public to both interventions in the former Yugoslavia.

President George W. Bush also seized the initiative to change the course of U.S. foreign policy when he adopted a "forward-leaning" security strategy that included the invasion of Iraq in March 2003 (Gregg 2004). For his part, President Obama expanded the use of unmanned drones in bombing attacks, ordered the risky capture and killing of Osama bin Laden in May 2011, and approved the U.S. military intervention in Libya. Late in 2014, Obama took the initiative by authorizing a larger U.S. military presence in Afghanistan and stepped-up aerial attacks on the Taliban and other militant groups.

The consequences of such assertiveness can be enormous. Taking action alters the strategic landscape and changes the calculus of future foreign policy decisions. Some options open and others close. Lyndon Johnson's decision to force the Vietnam issue through the Tonkin Gulf resolution, for example, started the United States down the slippery slope to war in Southeast Asia. More positively, Ronald Reagan's plans for a "Star Wars" antimissile system pushed the Soviet Union beyond its limits in the arms race, hastening the end of the Cold War.

■ STRUCTURES OF THE "PRESIDENTIAL BRANCH"

The White House serves as the institutional nucleus of the foreign policy process (Hart 1987). This status was codified in the 1930s, when Congress, persuaded that the president required a larger staff to accommodate the nation's arrival as a major global power, created the Executive Office of the President (EOP). This office has expanded steadily since then. More than a dozen units have comprised the EOP in recent years, ten of which have been engaged in foreign policy making (see Figure 4.3). This expansion of White House power, which created a "presidential branch separate from the executive branch" (Polsby 1990), had its greatest impact on U.S. foreign policy with the creation in 1947 of the National Security Council. Presidents have consistently used the council and its staff as an independent policy-making center (Daalder and Destler 2000).

While facilitating decisions and reducing interagency disputes, the White House–centered model has several drawbacks. First, the political appointees in these offices,

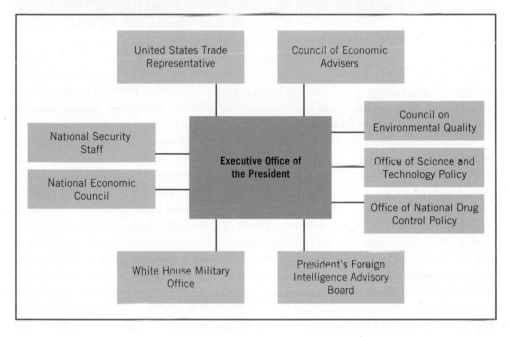

Source: The White House, https://www.whitehouse.gov/administration/eop.

including the national security adviser, are not subject to Senate confirmation, which deprives Congress of a constitutional means of advice and consent. Second, decision making in the White House tends to be highly secretive, with staffers hidden from public view more than their counterparts elsewhere in the federal government. Finally, the creation and expansion of White House agencies has inevitably led to redundancy in the foreign policy process. To many critics, the NSC is merely a "second State Department," without a global network of embassies.

Advisory Systems in the Inner Circle

As described in Chapter 3, the president's organizational skills are vital to sound decision making, and each president adopts a unique system of management. "In the modern era, Dwight Eisenhower applied the skills he mastered as a general, Lyndon B. Johnson horse-traded his way to legislative triumphs, Ronald Reagan managed with a light touch as if he were a congenial 'chairman of the board,' the elder George Bush oversaw what was arguably the most disciplined and inclusive national security process in recent history, and Bill Clinton was able to strike a balance between master politician and wonk in chief" (Rothkopf 2013, 6).

Each president constructs an **advisory system** of trusted aides and confidants who have the most direct impact on the president's final decisions (George 1980; S. Hess and Pfiffner 2002). The structure of these advisory systems may be rigid, with the president listening selectively to like-minded aides, or they may be more open, with conflicting views welcomed. In either case, presidential decisions can often be traced to input from the president's "inner circle," which can take multiple forms and adopt widely varying tactics in influencing foreign policy (Garrison 1999). The president's inner circle often includes advisers outside the cabinet. Woodrow Wilson listened most closely to adviser Edward House, who lacked a formal title but had his own living quarters in the White House. Wilson was later blamed, during the debilitating League of Nations debate, for elevating the counsel of his personal adviser above that of Congress. Karl Rove, George W. Bush's senior policy adviser and deputy chief of staff, similarly enjoyed unequaled access to the Oval Office. His influence was so great that Rove seemed to act as "co-president" on critical policy decisions, including foreign policy choices. The **management style** of presidents shapes the role their advisory systems play—that is, the procedures, working relationships, and standards of behavior among their foreign policy advisers. The working environment within advisory networks plays a key role in shaping policy outcomes in war (Crabb and Mulcahy 1995; Haney 1997) and peace (J. J. Best 1992). A president's management style can have direct consequences for U.S. foreign policy (Rodman 2009). Richard Nixon's selection of Henry Kissinger to be his national security adviser in 1969 made it inevitable that the United States would continue to fight the Vietnam War. A decade later, Jimmy Carter's turn away from his secretary of state, Cyrus Vance, in favor of national security adviser Zbigniew Brzezinski led directly to a more hawkish foreign policy. In the war on terror, George W. Bush turned to a "small, tightly controlled group of loyalists" in making his decision to invade Iraq in 2003 (Haney 2005, 296). Obama was even more guarded, rarely engaging actively with members of Congress and the Pentagon.

Although the management styles of presidents vary widely, three general models have been identified (R. T. Johnson 1974). As depicted in Figure 4.4, the **formalistic model** is orderly and hierarchical, with advisers adhering to narrowly defined roles and channeling their advice through a "gatekeeper" in the White House. President Nixon used this model and relied on Kissinger, his national security adviser, to represent the views of other advisers and present his own perspective. This model was well suited to George W. Bush, who positioned himself at the top of a rigid hierarchy rather than at the center of a "spoke-and-wheel" policy-making system (Walcott and Hult 2004).

Presidents adopting the **competitive model** of management encourage open debate and conflict among advisers. Franklin Roosevelt, an exemplar of this model, found

Figure 4.4 ■ Management Styles in U.S. Foreign Policy

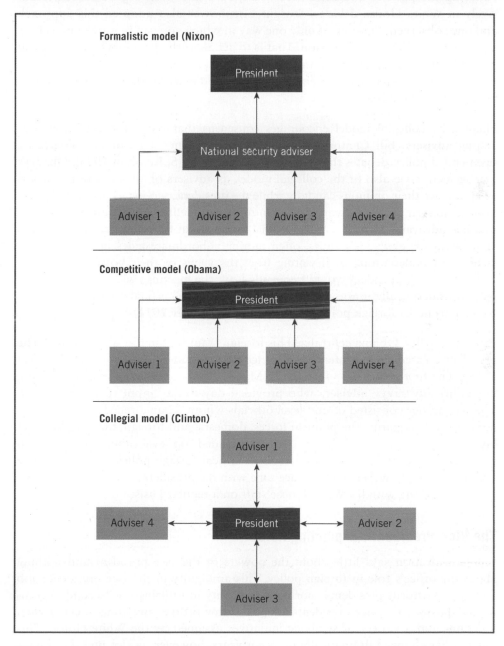

Formalistic model (Nixon)

President

National security adviser

Adviser 1   Adviser 2   Adviser 3   Adviser 4

Competitive model (Obama)

President

Adviser 1   Adviser 2   Adviser 3   Adviser 4

Collegial model (Clinton)

Adviser 1

Adviser 4   President   Adviser 2

Adviser 3

Note: Arrows denote the direction of policy input.

that the best ideas emerged from this unfettered, occasionally chaotic competition among viewpoints. He felt comfortable presiding over such competition and choosing the policies and rationales he believed had been argued most persuasively in White House debates. Dwight Eisenhower also adopted this approach and once observed: "I know of only one way in which you can be sure you've done your best to make a wise decision. That is to get all of the people who have partial and definable responsibility in this particular field, whatever it may be. Get them with their different viewpoints in front of you, and listen to them debate" (quoted in Pfiffner 2005, 220).

Finally, the **collegial model** encourages consensus that reconciles the differences among advisers. Bill Clinton adopted this management style, often encouraging open-ended policy debates that ran long into the night (S. Renshon 1996). Obama's management style also fit the collegial model, as advisers of all ranks were encouraged to voice their opinions candidly while the president, serving as his own "honest broker," looked on (Woodward 2010). In utilizing a deliberative strategy known as **multiple advocacy** (George 1972), Obama "was known for going around the room and asking for everyone's views, often putting subordinate aides in the awkward position of undercutting or deviating from the views of their bosses" (Rothkopf 2014b, 49). The president would frequently leave the meetings without a resolution. After considering all the arguments, he would later make his final decision and expect backing from the foreign policy bureaucracy (see Pfiffner 2011).

As noted earlier, Obama centralized his foreign team within the White House. The president created three centers of influence that extended outward from the Oval Office. The first group of "Obamians" (Mann 2012) consisted of relatively young but politically savvy advisers who provided day-to-day input to the president. The second tier consisted of mid-level officials whom Obama relied upon when he needed help navigating the political forces, domestic and foreign, that would affect his policy options. Finally, the third group included top-level cabinet officials who were called upon to inform Obama's most critical foreign policy decisions. These senior advisers, however, had less face time with the president, who was more comfortable working with his White House staff on a regular basis.

The Vice President's Expanding Roles

The Constitution says little about the powers of the vice president and nothing about the office's role in foreign policy. This ambiguity in the vice president's job description affords presidents enormous flexibility in utilizing the "second in command." Historically, vice presidents adopted a low profile, attending to ceremonial functions and a variety of symbolic initiatives assigned by the White House. This mission has changed dramatically in recent years, however, as vice presidents have played a powerful role in domestic and foreign policy.

POINT/COUNTERPOINT

Clashing Views of Obama's Foreign Policy

As is the case with all presidents, assessments of the Obama presidency have varied widely. These conflicting viewpoints commonly follow the ideological positions of citizens and pundits. They also reflect the success or failure of major foreign policies and related actions. As the end of Obama's second term approached, debates over his performance remained highly polarized.

Critics of the Obama foreign policy voiced two primary concerns: that Obama did not live up to his campaign pledges, and that he was too passive in responding to multiple crises, mostly in the Middle East. Author Robert Singh (2012) was initially pleased with Obama's vow to "transform" U.S. foreign policy, but he was disappointed that many promises, such as closing the Guantánamo Bay prison camp in Cuba and making climate change a top priority, were not fulfilled. Leon Panetta (2014), a former secretary of defense under Obama, described the president as an indecisive commander in chief who too often "avoids the battle, complains, and misses opportunities." Historian Robert Kagan (2014) also warned that Obama's cautious approach, known as "leading from behind," would have grave consequences: "When the United States appears to retrench, allies necessarily become anxious while others look for opportunities." For its part, the *Financial Times* (Luce 2014) feared that the United States was "acting like a declining hegemon: unwilling to share power, yet unable to impose outcomes."

For those pleased with Obama, the president had shown strong leadership in managing the financial crisis that peaked as he took office, in ordering the successful capture of Osama bin Laden, and in imposing harsh economic sanctions on Russia after its seizure of Ukraine's Crimean Peninsula. "Judged by the standard of protecting American interests, Obama's foreign policy so far has worked out quite well" (Indyk, Lieberthal, and O'Hanlon 2012, 31). To Ivan Eland (2014), director of the Center on Peace and Liberty, Obama's cautious approach "was helping the United States avoid the entanglements that the American people have come to hate." Historian Fred Kaplan (2014) also had praise for the president: "Perhaps more than any president since Dwight Eisenhower, Obama defines the national interest narrowly and acts accordingly. And in following this course, he has been much more successful than his critics allow. In fact, his deepest failures have occurred when he has veered off his path."

The makeover began in 1992, when Tennessee Senator. Al Gore accepted the job of Bill Clinton's vice president. Gore, a Vietnam War veteran and long-time member of the Senate Foreign Relations Committee, immediately played a key role in gaining congressional support for the North American Free Trade Agreement (NAFTA). His expertise in national security came into play when Gore assisted the Russian government in managing its nuclear arsenal, which was spread among several Soviet provinces that had become independent nations.[6] On the domestic side, Gore oversaw a project of "reinventing government" that led to billions of dollars in government budget cutbacks.

Dick Cheney, a former House member and defense secretary, became George W. Bush's vice president in January 2001. After the 9/11 attacks, Cheney became "the most empowered vice president in history" (Witkover 2014, 515). After Bush called upon Cheney to manage the U.S. response to the attacks, the vice president assembled his own national security team with direct connections to the Pentagon. Cheney became a strong backer of the U.S. invasion of Iraq in March, and he also waged an intense campaign to protect Bush's war powers (Priest and Wright 2005).[7]

The empowered vice presidency continued under Obama, who turned to Joe Biden, a longtime member and leader of the Senate Foreign Relations Committee. Biden brought two assets to the White House. First, he retained close connections to members of Congress and was among Washington's most knowledgeable experts on legislative politics. Second, Biden retained wide-ranging ties to world leaders, having traveled extensively in the Middle East and other regional trouble spots. Despite his lower-key presence in the White House compared with Cheney, Biden played a forceful role in foreign policy debates. He argued against the surge in Afghanistan, for example. He also urged the president to adopt a strategy of counterterrorism rather than counterinsurgency, an unsuccessful approach that relied on U.S. forces to win the "hearts and minds" of civilians in war zones (Mann 2012).

■ JUDICIAL INTERVENTIONS IN FOREIGN POLICY

Debates over how constitutional powers figure in U.S. foreign policy generally focus on the roles of the president and Congress. But what about the role of the judicial branch in tempering presidential power? The courts have assumed a relatively low profile in foreign affairs, leaving the executive and legislative branches alone so long as they do not directly violate the explicit terms of the Constitution or otherwise deny the rights of American citizens. As Louis Henkin (1996, 148), a leading scholar on the Constitution and foreign policy, has noted: "Overall, the contribution of the courts to foreign policy and their impact on foreign relations are significant but not

6. This initiative, formally known as the Nunn-Lugar Cooperative Threat Reduction Program, remained intact until 2012, when Russian President Vladimir Putin chose to suspend his nation's participation in the program.

7. The vice president survived a scandal in his own office as his chief of staff, Lewis "Scooter" Libby, was convicted in March 2007 of charges related to the "outing" of an undercover CIA agent, Valerie Plame. The leaking of her identity to the press was in apparent revenge for critical remarks by her husband, Joe Wilson, a former ambassador who questioned the White House's evidence of Iraq's nuclear program. Libby was convicted on several counts, including perjury and obstruction of justice. President Bush commuted his prison sentence of two and a half years, calling it excessive, while leaving his fine of $250,000 intact.

large. The Supreme Court in particular intervenes only infrequently and its foreign affairs cases are few and haphazard. The Court does not build and refine steadily case by case, it develops no expertise or experts; the Justices have no matured or clear philosophies; the precedents are flimsy and often reflect the spirit of another day."

Although the Constitution does not make such a claim, courts have consistently dismissed issues relating to U.S. foreign policy as "political questions" and therefore beyond the scope of judicial review. In other words, struggles over the formulation and conduct of U.S. foreign policy are best waged in the political arena and should not be resolved by judges. In the Supreme Court case *Marbury v. Madison*, 5 U.S. 137 (1803), Chief Justice John Marshall defended the process of judicial review but argued that such review should be limited. The Constitution, Marshall wrote, invested the president "with certain important political powers, in the exercise of which he is to use his own discretion, and is accountable only to his country . . . and to his own conscience."

Supreme Court Justice William Brennan restated this position in 1962: "Not only does resolution of such issues frequently turn on standards that defy judicial application, but many such questions uniquely demand a single-voiced statement of the Government's views" (quoted in Henkin 1996, 145). His view was generally shared by lower courts, which felt ill equipped to resolve matters of foreign policy. In this spirit, judges repeatedly refused to consider lawsuits that claimed U.S. presidents were waging an illegal war in Vietnam and, later, in the former Yugoslavia.

Rulings on Executive and Federal Power

Although the judicial branch has generally steered clear of disputes between the president and Congress, its occasional rulings have tended to support the executive branch (see Table 4.3). This tradition is traced to John Marshall, who as a member of Congress in 1800 claimed that "the President is the sole organ of the nation in its external relations. . . . Of consequence, the demand of a foreign nation can only be made on him" (quoted in Adler 1996a, 25–26). Importantly, Marshall was referring to the president's exclusive role as the contact between the United States and foreign governments. His view, however, was construed widely as a rationale for broad presidential authority in foreign affairs. Marshall's language was applied much later in the landmark case of *United States v. Curtiss-Wright Export Corporation*, 299 U.S. 304 (1936), in which the Supreme Court upheld Franklin Roosevelt's authority to enforce an arms embargo previously authorized by Congress.[8] In making this decision, Justice George Sutherland wrote that foreign policy should be considered "the very delicate, plenary, and exclusive power of the president as the sole organ of the federal government in the field of international relations."

....

8. In *Curtiss-Wright*, the Court also affirmed the external sovereignty of the federal government. The delegation of power from Congress to the president was appropriate in this case, the Court ruled, because the issue at hand concerned foreign rather than domestic policy.

Table 4.3 ■ Major Supreme Court Rulings on Foreign Affairs, 1920–2012

Year	Court Case(s)	Importance
1920	*Missouri v. Holland*	Established primacy of federal government over states in approving treaties
1936	*United States v. Curtiss-Wright Export Corporation*	Affirmed the president's foreign policy powers
1937	*United States v. Belmont*	Upheld executive agreements by the president
1942	*United States v. Pink*	
1952	*Youngstown Sheet and Tube Company v. Sawyer*	Restricted the power of the president to seize private assets in the name of national security
1971	*New York Times v. United States* (Pentagon Papers)	Ruled that First Amendment freedoms of the press outweighed presidential claims of national security
1979	*Goldwater et al. v. Carter*	Affirmed the president's power to terminate treaties
1983	*INS v. Chadha*	Ruled the legislative veto was unconstitutional
1983	*Crockett v. Reagan*	Affirmed presidential war powers
1985	*Conyers v. Reagan*	
1987	*Lowry v. Reagan*	
1990	*Dellums v. Bush*	
1993	*Sale v. Haitian Centers Council*	Affirmed the president's power to intercept aliens on the high seas and return them to their homelands
2000	*Crosby v. National Foreign Trade Council*	Affirmed federal primacy over states on international sanctions
2004	*Rasul v. Bush*	Upheld the right of prisoners in the war on terror to appeal their detentions in U.S. courts
2004	*Hamdi v. Rumsfeld*	
2006	*Hamdan v. Rumsfeld*	
2008	*Boumediene v. Bush*	
2012	*Arizona v. United States*	Affirmed federal primacy over states regarding the terms of immigration enforcement

Nevertheless, members of Congress have frequently turned to the courts to restrain presidents in foreign policy. In *Goldwater et al. v. Carter*, 444 U.S. 996 (1979), for example, the Supreme Court supported President Jimmy Carter's right to terminate the U.S. Mutual Defense Treaty with Taiwan. In the Court's view, the case was "political" because no clear violations of the Constitution had occurred. Similarly, in *Crockett v. Reagan*, 232 U.S. App. D.C. 128, 720 F.2d 1355 (1984), and *Lowry v. Reagan*, 676 F.Supp. 333 (1987), the Court again dismissed as "political" congressional claims that the president had overstepped his constitutional bounds by deploying troops into conflicts overseas.

On some occasions, the Supreme Court has acted to curb presidential powers. For example, in *Youngstown Sheet and Tube Co. v. Sawyer* (1952), the Court declared unconstitutional President Truman's seizure of American steel mills to avert a national strike during the Korean War. Such authority, the Court ruled, could be exercised only with the explicit consent of Congress. Then, in 1971, the Supreme Court ruled against the president in the *Pentagon Papers* case (*New York Times Company v. United States*, 403 U.S. 713). The Court rejected Nixon's claim that damaging information possessed by the *New York Times* about U.S. involvement in Vietnam should be barred from publication on the grounds of national security.

Since the Cold War, the Supreme Court has remained an arm's length from foreign policy while intervening on several key issues. The Court, for example, backed the federal government's legal primacy in three foreign policy cases. In 1993, the Supreme Court upheld President Clinton's policy of intercepting Haitian refugees in international waters and returning them to their homeland before they could seek asylum in the United States, a policy that critics viewed as violating international law (Rohter 1993). The Court ruled in 2000 that federal sanctions against the repressive government of Myanmar (formerly Burma) "preempted," or nullified, sanctions later imposed by the Commonwealth of Massachusetts that were seen as obstacles to U.S. enforcement. And in June 2012, the Court upheld Washington's authority to nullify state laws regarding the enforcement of federal immigration statutes (see Chapter 3). As detailed below, the September 2001 terrorist attacks sparked a variety of challenges to the U.S. government's war powers.

Legal Quandaries in the War on Terror

As noted earlier, presidents wield greater foreign policy authority in wartime, a historic pattern that continued with the onset of the war on terror. President Bush seized upon his constitutional role as commander in chief in casting the September 2001 attacks as a casus belli (cause of war) rather than a matter for law enforcement or diplomacy and in declaring a national emergency three days after the attacks. These war powers were affirmed on September 18 by Congress, which granted Bush broad authority "to use all necessary and appropriate force . . . to prevent any future acts of international terrorism against the United States" (U.S. Congress 2001).

The war on terror differed from previous conflicts in many respects. In this war, the United States did not oppose a sovereign nation-state such as Japan or Germany in World War II. Instead, American leaders squared off against a shadowy network of terrorist groups and their spiritual mentors, financial patrons, arms providers, and supporters within sympathetic governments. The judicial branch, beyond working with the executive branch in prosecuting captured terrorist suspects, offered little guidance regarding the laws of fighting terrorism on such a broad scale (Wittes 2008). From the standpoint of domestic and international law, the White House found itself in a legal "netherworld" that proved fertile for the assertion of presidential war powers (Adler 2006).

Among his first responses to this legal void, President Bush issued an executive order in November 2001 that called for treating captured al Qaeda forces in Afghanistan not as prisoners of war, the designation used in conventional interstate conflicts, but as "unlawful enemy combatants." Bush's order also called for such "detainees" to be tried by military commissions, and it prevented them from seeking "any remedy . . . in any court of the United States, or any State thereof" (White House 2001a).

White House lawyers declared that U.S. actions in the conflict fell outside the reach of the Geneva Conventions, the most recent of which, adopted in 1949, prohibited the "cruel treatment and torture" of war prisoners. Attorney General John Ashcroft believed the September 11 attacks constituted a "crime of war and a crime against humanity" that demanded extraordinary measures by Washington. Alleged terrorists were transferred from Afghanistan to a U.S. detention facility at the Guantánamo Bay Naval Station in Cuba. More than 500 "high-value" detainees were regularly held after the facility opened early in 2002, although few were formally charged and none were tried during the first four years of the war. Reports of the mistreatment of these prisoners and of riots and hunger strikes at the facility, followed by revelations of abuses at Iraq's Abu Ghraib prison in 2004, fueled protests and legal challenges.[9] The U.S. government's "coercive interrogations" of suspected terrorists alarmed legal experts as well as many citizens, foreign leaders, and human rights organizations (see Chapter 5).

Contrary to Bush's executive order, prisoners at the Guantánamo facility sought, and gained, support from U.S. courts to challenge the legality of their detention. In two separate cases—*Rasul et al. v. Bush*, 542 U.S. 466 (2004), and *Hamdi v. Rumsfeld*, 542 U.S. 507 (2004)—the Supreme Court ruled that such appeals were permissible and should be heard in civilian courts. A central issue in both cases concerned the prisoners' right of **habeas corpus,** a centuries-old legal principle that prisoners must be able to hear the charges against them in court and challenge the legality of their detention (see C. Doyle 2006). In supporting the majority view on behalf of Yaser Hamdi, an American citizen, Justice Sandra Day O'Connor observed that the Supreme Court "made clear that a state of war is not a blank check for the president when it comes to the rights of the nation's citizens" (*Hamdi v. Rumsfeld*).

....

9. The International Committee of the Red Cross (2004, "Legal Concerns") concluded that the prisoners at Guantánamo were placed "beyond the law . . . [with] no idea about their fate, and no means of recourse through any legal mechanism." A year later, the United Nations Economic and Social Council (2006, 12) claimed that the extended detention of prisoners at the facility without charges or legal counsel marked a "radical departure from established principles of human rights."

The Supreme Court ruled against the White House again in June 2006. In *Hamdan v. Rumsfeld*, 548 U.S 557 (2006), the Court asserted that government plans to place Guantánamo detainees on trial before military commissions were not authorized by federal law as it was currently written and violated international law. Writing for the majority, Justice John Paul Stevens argued that, in its prosecution of Salim Ahmed Hamdan, "the Executive is bound to comply with the Rule of Law that prevails in this jurisdiction." Responding to the Supreme Court's concern that U.S. policies lacked formal authorization from

Among the most controversial aspects of presidential war powers after the 9/11 terrorist attacks involved the treatment of suspected terrorists. In this January 2002 photograph, the first group of "enemy combatant" detainees is confined in a holding area under the watchful eye of U.S. guards. President Obama pledged to close the facility in his first term but could not convince Congress that the "high-value" detainees could be safely held in other U.S. facilities

the legislative branch, the Bush administration implored Congress to provide a legal basis for its use of military commissions and "coercive interrogations" of alleged terrorists. The White House strategy paid off when legislators in both houses approved the Military Commissions Act of 2006. Although the act affirmed the Geneva Conventions as an appropriate international standard, it allowed the president to "interpret the meaning and application" of the conventions. The act also denied detainees habeas corpus rights while permitting coercive interrogations. Finally, the act immunized, or protected from prosecution, U.S. officials who were found to have committed acts of torture prior to 2006.

Once again, in June 2008, the Supreme Court addressed this detention issue in the case of *Boumediene v. Bush*, 553 U.S. 723 (2008). In a five-to-four vote, the Court ruled that the Guantánamo Bay detention center was not a legal vacuum in which detainees had no rights. Instead, they must have the same rights, including habeas corpus, to which defendants in the United States are entitled. Even legislation passed by Congress and signed by the president could not overcome this legal reality.

When Bush left office in January 2009, the conflicts over presidential war powers remained for future presidents—and courts—to resolve. On his second day in office, President Obama issued three executive orders to end the use of coercive interrogations, close the Guantánamo Bay detention center by 2010, and develop alternatives to military tribunals, respectively. Human rights advocates celebrated these measures, but loopholes in the first executive order allowed for flexibility in the "enhanced techniques" used by CIA agents. Congressional concerns over whether the Guantánamo prisoners would be relocated, and how they would be prosecuted, kept the Cuban facility open indefinitely.[10] Strong pressure from Pentagon and CIA lawyers, along with much of Congress, persuaded Obama to maintain the military tribunals. In yielding on military tribunals to try "high-value" suspects, Obama rejected the advice of Attorney General Eric Holder, who argued that deferring to civilian courts in such cases would demonstrate the nation's commitment to the rule of law.

While Obama sought the middle ground on this controversy, he took a hard line when it came to the "targeted killings" of suspected terrorists. Three previous presidents—Gerald Ford, Jimmy Carter, and Ronald Reagan—had signed executive orders that banned political assassinations. To Obama, targeted killings were different since they fended off imminent threats to U.S. security. Such killings were also less destructive than large-scale bombing raids or boots-on-the-ground military deployments. In personally making life-or-death decisions regarding dozens of human targets, the president assumed an operational military role "unprecedented in presidential history" (Becker and Shane 2012). Among those to be killed was Anwar al-Awlaki, an American citizen who had left the United States to serve as an Islamist cleric and prominent media spokesperson for al Qaeda.

■ CONCLUSION

As we have seen, American presidents have assumed unprecedented powers over foreign policy since World War II, particularly in the exercise of war powers. The constitutional checks on the president remained in place, although Congress became more inclined to defer to the White House on most foreign policy issues. Preoccupied by domestic issues and endless runs for reelection, most legislators concluded that frequent engagement on foreign policy was a luxury they could not afford. This did not, however, leave the president without multiple constraints on his ability to conduct foreign policy. Paradoxically, the most powerful figure in world politics was routinely hampered by the pressures of bureaucratic politics, well-endowed interest groups, public opinion, judicial rulings, and occasional demands from Congress to change course.

----

10. The Obama White House, continuing a process begun by Bush, transferred most Guantánamo detainees to more than forty other countries, primarily Afghanistan and Saudi Arabia (Savage, Glaberson, and Lehren 2011). By the end of 2014, all but 132 detainees were freed from the prison. Most of the 600 detainees that were released were never formally charged with any offenses during their confinement. Those remaining faced indefinite detentions, another practice Obama had earlier denounced. See National Religious Campaign Against Torture, Guantánamo Bay Detention Center, *Fact Sheet*, December 22, 2014.

These constraints were wired into the U.S. political system and political culture. Beginning in 2004 and continuing through Bush's second term in office, a series of Supreme Court decisions forced the White House to provide basic legal rights to war prisoners. Congress's passage of the Detainee Treatment Act of 2005, targeted primarily at the CIA, effectively halted the most brutal forms of coercive interrogations. Within the executive branch, internal auditors and legal inspectors demanded greater accountability in the gathering and use of intelligence. Societal checks also came into play as critics denounced Bush's "arrogance of power." While media outlets and bloggers revealed U.S. excesses on and off the battlefield, public-interest groups "swarmed the government with hundreds of reports and lawsuits that challenged every aspect of the president's war powers" (J. Goldsmith 2012, xii). All these forces produced a new, but fragile, equilibrium in the U.S. government's conduct of war.

Despite these ebbs and flows in presidential power, one prediction could be made with confidence. The "invitation to struggle" extended by the U.S. Constitution will remain a permanent and defining aspect of foreign policy making. As when the United States was founded, a fundamental tension exists between two contradictory principles deeply ingrained in American governance: the fear of an overzealous and authoritarian central government and the need for decisive leadership in the face of a menacing international system. Politics, therefore, will never truly stop "at the water's edge" in the United States. Conflicts of interest are embedded in its foreign policy institutions and civil society. In another paradox, the success or failure of the United States in world politics is largely a by-product of the president's use of power at home.

KEY TERMS

advisory system, p. 130

bully pulpit, p. 122

codetermination, p. 114

collegial model, p. 132

competitive model, p. 130

executive agreements, p. 118

INTERNET REFERENCES

The **American Presidency Project** website (http://www.presidency.ucsb.edu), maintained and researched by political scientists at the University of California–Santa Barbara, presents a wealth of data, links, statistics, and multimedia clips on the presidency. Included are presidential speeches, public papers, and statistics on specific policy areas. A variety of documents related to the 2008 election are also on the site.

The website for the **Center for Congressional and Presidential Studies** (http://www.american .edu/spa/ccps/), hosted by American University, provides access to conferences, speeches, and articles on the presidency. Of particular interest to the center is the relationship between the executive and legislative branches, as well as presidential and congressional campaigning. The center publishes books and series on these issues and the peer-reviewed journal *Congress and the Presidency* (the journal's index is available at http://www.american.edu/spa/ccps/journal.cfm).

The **Center for the Study of the Presidency and Congress** (http://www.thepresidency.org) provides useful links to White House documents as well as research opportunities and tips on studying the presidency. In addition to sponsoring internship and fellowship opportunities, the center publishes *Presidential Studies Quarterly,* which investigates all aspects of the institution of the presidency (the contents of each issue are available at http://www.thepresidency.org/publications/presidential-studies-quarterly/).

The University of Virginia's **Miller Center of Public Affairs** (http://millercenter.org) has compiled historical biographies and recordings of the presidents. The center directs much of its research toward study of the media and the presidency. It also produces the Miller Center Papers, a historical collection of documents that describe presidential public policy making; some are available for download at http://millercenter.org/about/publications.

POTUS, on the Internet Public Library (http://www.ipl.org/div/potus/), is hosted by Drexel University. It provides full biographical data on all the presidents, timelines of their administrations, and descriptions of their major actions.

The National Archives hosts a website on the **Presidential Libraries** (http://www.archives.gov/presidential-libraries/) that includes links to thirteen presidential libraries. The websites of most libraries contain speeches, memoirs, and links to research resources on the specific policies of the respective presidents.

Presidents of the United States (http://www.presidentsusa.net), hosted by CB Presidential Research Services, serves as a comprehensive resource, with monthly updates, on presidential speeches, salaries, quotes, military history, and major policies. This site also details each president's vetoes, appointments, and election data.

The website for the **White House** (https://www.whitehouse.gov) lists links to presidential speeches, executive agencies and committees, and issue information released by the president and White House advisers. Of particular interest to foreign policy researchers is the "foreign policy" link (https://www.whitehouse.gov/issues/foreign-policy) to progress updates on U.S. policy endeavors throughout the world.

The **White House Historical Association** (http://www.whitehousehistory.org) is committed to teaching citizens and providing links for scholars studying the presidency. It serves as a "hub" for information on presidential administrations and includes timelines related to the presidency, information about first ladies, and the biographies of each president.

CONGRESS BEYOND THE "WATER'S EDGE"

REUTERS/Lucas Jackson

Members of Congress often travel to overseas war zones in order to get a better sense of the problems facing U.S. armed forces. Sen. John McCain (R-AZ), chairman of the Armed Services Committee, frequently made these visits. In December 2014, he traveled to Afghanistan to celebrate the Christmas holidays with the troops.

CHAPTER OBJECTIVES

5.1 Describe the ebb and flow of legislative-executive relations over foreign policy matters since World War II.

5.2 Explain four constraints on congressional action.

5.3 Summarize the institutional factors that determine the extent to which Congress engages in foreign policy.

5.4 Identify the ways in which Congress has exercised authority regarding war powers and the use of force.

5.5 Discuss Congress's power of the purse and the two key areas of foreign policy in which it comes into play.

On January 21, 2015, plans were announced for a visit by Benjamin Netanyahu, Israel's prime minister, to deliver a speech to a joint session in Congress. Netanyahu, an arch enemy of the Iranian government, would make his case against the multilateral negotiations with the Islamic Republic that had begun years earlier. Instead of more talk, the Israeli leader called for more economic sanctions against Iran and stronger military efforts to weaken Iranian influence throughout the Middle East.

While such events have taken place before, this speech was different. The invitation did not come from the president. Indeed, Barack Obama did not know it would take place until the offer was made. It was Rep. John Boehner, R-Ohio, the Speaker of the House, who made the call to Netanyahu. Boehner knew of Obama's keen interest in the "5+1" talks that were under way among the permanent members of the UN Security Council (China, France, Great Britain, Russia, and the United States), along with Germany. Boehner also knew that Netanyahu's visit would embarrass the commander in chief before a world audience.

In another paradox, the speech that followed both showcased the checks and balances in action while further revealing the ruptures in, and vulnerabilities of, American foreign policy. While presidential power has reached new heights in recent decades, the legislative branch can throw wrenches in the White House's agenda in surprising and often potentially destructive ways. After hearing Netanyahu's hawkish speech, which boosted his prospects in parliamentary elections and sealed his victory on March 18, 2015, U.S. strategic and economic partners were once again reminded that the United States was an unpredictable and unreliable ally.

Alongside the president, Congress plays a vital role in the formulation and conduct of U.S. foreign policy. Despite the long-standing maxim that politics "stop at the water's edge," the legislative branch confronts presidents on a wide variety of international issues, from military interventions to foreign aid and arms control. Even U.S. trade, long shielded from interbranch rivalry, frequently falls prey to domestic politics. Although claims of an "imperial Congress" (G. S. Jones and Marini 1988) are overstated, presidents know their global objectives cannot be realized without the blessing of Capitol Hill. Foreign policy clearly begins at home.

As noted in Chapter 4, early U.S. leaders looked to Congress as a crucial hedge against potential abuses of executive power. Article I of the Constitution assigns "the first branch of government" more explicit grants of authority than Article II does presidents. Among the authorities granted to Congress are the powers to declare war, raise military forces, regulate commerce, and provide "advice and consent" on treaties and key appointments. Congressional activism in foreign policy is therefore expected in a system of "separate institutions sharing power" (Neustadt 1960). Besides curbing presidential power, such activism provides opportunities for the public to be heard, encourages open deliberation, and rewards compromise on foreign policy issues.

Congress is the U.S. government's institutional home for partisan politics, or the competition between the two dominant political parties. Whether Republicans or Democrats hold the most seats in Congress has proved especially crucial since the Vietnam War because *unified government*, with one political party controlling the executive and legislative branches, has been an exception to the general rule of *divided government*. Of the twenty-eight Congressional sessions between 1961 and 2015, in just ten cases presidents and legislators would be fighting on the same side. Otherwise, presidents knew to expect constant pushback from the legislative branch. These electoral ebbs and flows have profound implications for both foreign and domestic policy: "When the two branches are controlled by opposing parties, gridlock increases. When government is divided, presidents are forced to oppose a greater number of foreign policy bills initiated by Congress" (Peake 2002, 80). Unified government, by contrast, encourages legislative activism and tempts the dominant party to cement its advantages in new laws and policies. Partisan support in Congress also affects the gravest decision made by presidents: whether to send military forces into battle (Howell and Pevehouse 2005).

After the Cold War, both houses of Congress turned their primary attention to foreign trade, particularly the rise of China as a major competitor to the United States in world markets. This legislative shift had much to do with economics, but it also had a geostrategic foundation. With the Soviet Union being the U.S. government's primary concern during the Cold War, American leaders favored Beijing as a source of leverage against Moscow. Such a wedge, however, was no longer needed after the Soviet Union collapsed in 1991. Congressional policy makers then became fixated on China's growing economy and corresponding U.S. trade deficits (Gagliano 2015). Congress also called attention to Beijing's repression of political and human rights, concerns that the president needed to avoid in order to maintain close and vital relations with the People's Republic.

Legislative activism has a downside, however. Despite the concerns raised on Capitol Hill over President Bush's abuse of power in foreign policy, legislators have strong self-interests in focusing on domestic issues that relate more directly to the needs of their constituents. As congressional scholar Barbara Hinckley (1994, 13) has observed, "This is a legislative body where time and influence must be carefully expended, where conflict must be kept within tolerable levels, and where many other policies can fulfill the goals of members better than foreign policy programs do. Seen in this light, foreign policy making by Congress should be the exception and not the rule."

As we will find in this chapter, Congress's role has varied over time and across the many domains of foreign policy. Developments overseas—such as civil and interstate wars, regime changes, and economic crises—shape the policy options and opportunities available to congressional legislators in any given period (Henehan 2000). Members of Congress have significant control over the World Bank and International Monetary Fund (IMF), which rely on Washington as their primary source of revenue. In this respect, Congress is the "indispensable legislature" of these global financial institutions (Lavelle 2011, 3).

Domestic factors also come into play. As discussed previously, such pressures have led to foreign policy "mood swings" among legislators, who historically have alternated between global engagement and detachment in reaction to U.S. public sentiment (Klingberg 1952; Holmes 1985). Significant as well is the domestic balance of power between political parties and the related shifts in the population of states and congressional districts (Rohde 1994). For example, the mid-twentieth-century mass migration of Americans from the Rust Belt states of the Northeast to the Sun Belt states of the South and Southwest eventually transformed the partisan balance in Congress, as evidenced by the 1994 Republican takeover of both chambers (Trubowitz 1992).

Foreign policy, in short, cannot be divorced from domestic politics. Although this feature of U.S. foreign policy is a timeless one, the current period has been unusually volatile. The partisan balance of power swerved from unified Republican rule in the first six years of Bush's presidency to divided government after the 2006 midterm elections. Barack Obama's victory in the 2008 national elections revived unified government—this time led by the Democratic Party. Obama lost his legislative majority in 2010, however, and entered his second term with divided government.

Three characteristics of legislative politics have been significant in recent years:

- *Longevity.* Members of Congress are more likely than ever to make careers out of legislative office. Frequently holding "safe seats" with little interparty competition, legislators have been reelected in more than 80 percent of cases since the 1950s (Davidson and Oleszek 2006). Of the 441 House seats in the 2014 elections, 377 were considered "safe," lacking serious competition from other candidates (http://www.270towin.com).Whereas most members of Congress served only one term in the nation's first century, fewer than 10 percent have done so in recent years. Despite calls for an end to "careerism" in Congress, its members spend years gaining seniority on critical committees and are reluctant to give up their heightened stature and political power. This pattern favors the status quo, including legislators clinging to obsolete military bases and unnecessary weapons programs.

- *Polarization and party unity.* In contrast to the public, whose political beliefs cluster near the center of the ideological spectrum, members of Congress are increasingly holding more rigid liberal or conservative views. This "unprecedented disappearance of the political center" has left Congress highly polarized (Binder 1996, 36). Rather than searching for middle ground, legislators have voted along party lines at record levels in recent years. Obama, who looked forward to a "post-partisan" relationship with Congress, found this to be an impossible dream. Instead, "polarized politics have caused the U.S. government to seize up" (Salam 2012, 149).

- *Public discontent.* Highly polarized and unresolved debates on Capitol Hill have left Americans deeply cynical about the legislative branch, whose plummeting public-approval ratings reached a record low of 10 percent in 2012 (see Figure 5.1) This public disregard extended to the executive branch and political parties, suggesting a generalized loss of faith in the U.S. political system. Among other complaints, American citizens in 2014 and 2015 faulted the president and Congress for failing to adopt a united front on critical foreign policy issues such as Iran's nuclear program and the Islamic State's widening acts of terror.

Figure 5.1 ■ Plunging Public Approval of Congress, 2000–2015

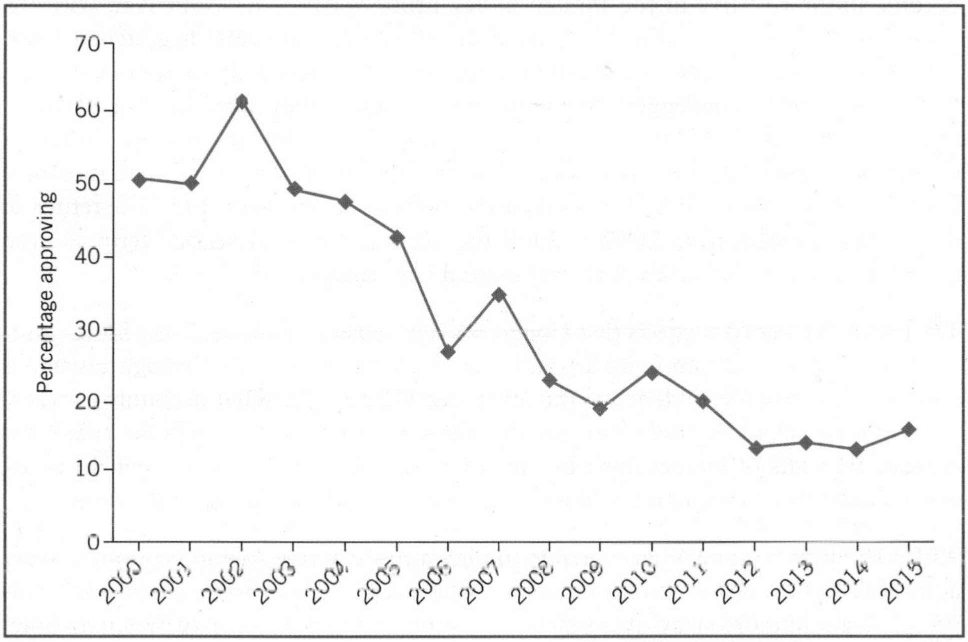

Source: Gallup Polls, Congress and the Public, January ratings, http://www.gallup.com/poll/1600/congress-public.aspx.

Each of these features of recent legislative sessions affects the capacity of Congress to "codetermine" U.S. foreign policy, as the U.S. Constitution requires. Despite calls for consensus from leaders on both sides of the aisle, party loyalty rather than cooperation with the White House is often a safer bet for legislators engaged in constant reelection campaigns. This behavior could be seen in recent years as Republicans and Democrats clashed over immigration and the treatment of illegal aliens along the nation's boundary with Mexico (see Chpter 12). In this case and many others, members of Congress know that foreign policy is no exception to the rule that "all politics is local."

■ TRENDS IN LEGISLATIVE-EXECUTIVE RELATIONS

This section reviews the ebb and flow of legislative-executive relations over foreign policy matters since World War II.[1] The early years of the Cold War featured broad

---

1. Diplomatic histories of U.S. foreign policy rarely focus on Congress but rather on the president or socioeconomic forces outside of government (R. D. Johnson 2001).

cooperation between the White House and Capitol Hill that stemmed from a consensus between the branches on the ends and means of foreign policy. However, the nation's failure in the Vietnam War ruptured this consensus and led Congress to become more assertive in the foreign policy process. After the Cold War, with the United States facing no direct threats from other great powers, heightened inter-branch conflict continued as a Republican majority captured both houses of Congress and subsequently challenged Bill Clinton's foreign policy agenda. The terrorist attacks of September 2001 restored bipartisan cooperation on foreign policy as Congress supported the invasions of Afghanistan and Iraq, approved broad measures for homeland security, and passed major increases in defense spending. The return of divided government from 2007 to 2009 and again in Obama's second term spurred ongoing legislative action to curb presidential war powers.

The historical record suggests that Congress's relationship with the White House runs along the entire spectrum from legislative compliance at one end, through resistance and rejection, to independence at the other (see Figure 5.2). What accounts for these fluctuations? Scholarly studies suggest that the situational context of policy making is critical. Two sets of factors must be taken into account when considering the situational context of foreign policy: the *nature* of issues and the *timing* of decisions.

As for the first factor, Congress tends to play a more active role in economic issues and other issues with a strong domestic component such as immigration, whereas presidents hold more sway over issues pertaining to national security. When it comes to the timing of decisions, presidents generally enjoy freedom of action during the "honeymoon" period shortly after taking office when they have strong public and political support. Taking advantage of this support, they announce their foreign policy agendas and expect Congress to provide the necessary resources to convert these agendas into programs. Presidents also exert more power over foreign policy during crises, such as the Japanese attack on Pearl Harbor in 1941 and the 2001 terrorist attacks on New York City and Washington, D.C. In these cases, members of Congress usually defer to the commander in chief.

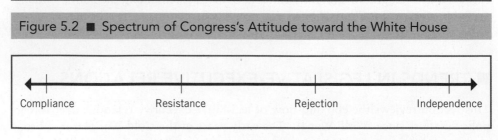

Figure 5.2 ■ Spectrum of Congress's Attitude toward the White House

Compliance   Resistance   Rejection   Independence

Source: James M. Scott and Ralph G. Carter, "Acting on the Hill: Congressional Assertiveness in U.S. Foreign Policy," *Congress and the Presidency* 29, no. 2 (2002), 151–169.

Like the situational context, **congressional diplomacy** plays a critical role in legislative-executive relations in foreign policy matters. Congressional diplomacy concerns the degree of presidential leadership in and attention to the legislative process, a vital aspect of a president's foreign policy goals (LeLoup and Shull 2003). In short, presidents ignore members of Congress at their peril, as Clinton learned the hard way. By lobbying key legislators intensely, he successfully gained ratification of the North American Free Trade Agreement (NAFTA) and of the treaty permitting NATO expansion. However, in 1999, Clinton neglected Congress in the weeks before its vote on the Comprehensive Test Ban Treaty. After discovering that he lacked the necessary votes to ratify the treaty, the president made a last-minute attempt to delay the vote but was blocked by Republican leaders. The treaty, which discouraged nuclear proliferation by outlawing the testing of such weapons, had already been ratified by fifty foreign governments. The rejection, largely across party lines, marked the first time since the 1919 Treaty of Versailles that the Senate had defeated a major multilateral security agreement.

Collaboration and Discord in the Cold War

As described in Chapter 2, the post–World War II threat posed by the Soviet Union led congressional leaders to support President Harry Truman's efforts to put the containment doctrine into practice. Some of the important measures approved by Congress were the Bretton Woods accords, the Marshall Plan, the Truman Doctrine, and the creation of NATO. Of greatest institutional significance was the National Security Act of 1947, which created the Department of Defense, the National Security Council, and the Central Intelligence Agency (CIA). Exploiting this support on Capitol Hill, Truman deployed U.S. troops to South Korea in 1950 without a declaration of war from Congress. He justified this unilateral action on the grounds that the deployment was part of a UN peacemaking mission. His decision to sidestep the legislative branch set a precedent for future U.S. military deployments in Vietnam, Central America, the Middle East, and other areas.

As had his predecessor, President Eisenhower encountered little resistance from Capitol Hill as he created new military alliances, expanded the U.S. nuclear arsenal, and allowed the CIA to organize and sponsor military coups in countries such as Iran and Guatemala. The foreign policy role of Congress during this period was reduced to "the legitimizing of presidential decisions" (Bax 1977, 887–888). Such support not only reflected broad agreement on the containment strategy but also stemmed from the ample benefits flowing to congressional districts in the form of military contracts; the building of military bases; and the construction of a massive interstate highway system, which was justified on national security grounds.

The domestic consensus continued through the presidency of John Kennedy. Congress funded the launch of Kennedy's Alliance for Progress, a development program aimed at strengthening U.S. allies and promoting economic reforms in Latin America, and the Peace Corps, an agency of paid volunteers trained to help developing countries. On the military front, Kennedy made the fateful decision to send U.S. military advisers to Vietnam to help southern forces resist unification under communist leadership. Congress later affirmed the intervention in the 1964 **Gulf of Tonkin Resolution**, which authorized Kennedy's successor, Lyndon Johnson, to "take all necessary measures" to protect U.S. forces supporting the government of South Vietnam.[2] The protracted fighting that followed and the eventual U.S. defeat ruptured legislative-executive consensus on foreign policy.

President Richard Nixon's secret invasions of Cambodia and Laos, and his attempts to spy on domestic opponents, further fueled the challenge by Congress. Sen. J. William Fulbright, D-AR, chair of the Senate Foreign Relations Committee from 1959 to 1974, declared the United States to be under "presidential dictatorship" (Franck and Weisband 1979). The 1970s and 1980s saw the passage of a wide range of legislation designed to enhance the legislative branch's **oversight** role—that is, its ability to monitor the president's conduct of foreign policy. The following measures, among others, provided explicit guidelines for congressional oversight:

- The **Case-Zablocki Act** (1972) required presidents to report all international agreements to Congress within sixty days of their entering into force.

- The **War Powers Resolution** (1973), described shortly, required presidents to inform Congress about U.S. military deployments and authorized Congress to order the troops home after sixty days if a majority of legislators opposed the deployments.

- The **Nelson-Bingham Amendment** to the 1974 Foreign Assistance Act authorized Congress to review foreign arms sales of more than $25 million and to reject such sales through a concurrent resolution of both chambers.

- The **Jackson-Vanik Amendment** to the Trade Act of 1974 prevented presidents from granting most-favored-nation (MFN) trade status to foreign countries that restricted the emigration of their citizens.[3]

- The **Intelligence Oversight Act of 1980** empowered House and Senate committees to oversee U.S. intelligence activities and required presidents to notify Congress about covert (secret) operations in foreign countries.

This antagonism continued after the Nixon years. While President Jimmy Carter tried to usher in a new era of American moral leadership, Congress was more

---

2. The resolution, based on Johnson's claim that two U.S. ships were attacked in the Vietnamese waterway, passed 416–0 in the House and 88–2 in the Senate. Evidence uncovered later raised doubts about the reported attacks (see Karnow 1983, 366–373).

3. The Jackson-Vanik Amendment, which was targeted at the Soviet Union, was repealed by Congress in December 2012. Although new legislation granted stronger trading relations with Russia, it also imposed strong penalties on Russia's widespread abuse of human rights.

concerned about double-digit inflation and unemployment at home. Lawmakers also blamed Carter for Iran's anti-American revolution and the Soviet invasion of Afghanistan in 1979. His successor, Ronald Reagan, struggled with divided government but also clashed with Republicans. Sen. Barry Goldwater, R-AZ, head of the Select Intelligence Committee, was surprised in 1984 that the CIA was secretly mining harbors in Nicaragua, which was in the midst of a socialist revolution. "The president has asked us to back his foreign policy, (but) how can we back his foreign policy when we don't know what the hell is going on? This is an act violating international law. It is an act of war. I don't see how we are going to explain it" (quoted in Maddow 2012, 97). Such public criticism by a member of the president's own party was not unusual then, but is very rare today.

Tensions in the "New World Order"

Paradoxically, as the United States reached its peak in world power upon the collapse of the Soviet Union in 1991, the "new world order" celebrated by President George H. W. Bush only produced more animosity and distrust between the White House and Capitol Hill. Partisan and interbranch debates revealed deep divisions over the nation's post–Cold War grand strategy and how it should balance foreign and domestic priorities. In place of overriding security issues, **intermestic policy** concerns—those such as trade and the environment that merge international and domestic interests—became more prominent in the wake of the Cold War, further complicating legislative-executive relations.

Multiple factors combined to intensify the polarization of Congress in the 1990s. The absence of superpower tensions after the Cold War "removed the ready guide for responding to events that had promoted bipartisanship" (J. M. McCormick, Wittkopf, and Danna 1997, 135). At the same time, a generational shift was rapidly diminishing the number of legislators with military experience in World War II or the Korean or Vietnam Wars (Greenberger 1995/1996). The new members of Congress also had no legislative experience with the politics and struggles of the Cold War. The defining military memory for many of them was the 1992 U.S. intervention in Somalia, a humanitarian aid mission that degenerated the following year into bloody street fighting and attacks by Somali militias against U.S. and UN peacekeepers.

Most of the period's new congressional members came from the Republican Party, which became dominant in the South after more than a century in which Democrats, liberal and conservative, controlled the region's politics.[4] This partisan shift shattered the Democratic coalition of southern conservatives and northern liberals that had produced consensus on U.S. foreign policy during much of the Cold War. The

---

4. This shift resulted in part from racial issues, particularly the passage of the Civil Rights Act (1964) and Voting Rights Act (1965), which, especially in the South, prompted "white flight" from the Democratic Party. See Jacobson (2000) for an elaboration.

Republicans gained control of Congress at a time when national attention had turned from overseas concerns to domestic ones, a pattern typical in the United States after major wars. Republican Dick Armey of Texas, the second most powerful House member, captured the isolationist sentiment on Capitol Hill when he declared, "I've been to Europe once. I don't have to go again" (quoted in Barone and Ujifusa 1999, 1583). In the divisive years that followed, Clinton failed to gain congressional support for a string of U.S. foreign policy initiatives. Congress, led by Sen. Jesse Helms, R-NC, the conservative chair of the Senate Foreign Relations Committee, forced deep cutbacks in foreign aid and refused to pay the United Nations more than $1.5 billion in past dues.

Deference in the War on Terror

George W. Bush came into power in January 2001 with united government and a political agenda that had little to do with foreign policy. To the contrary, Bush had pledged to avoid overseas entanglements such as the humanitarian "wars of choice" in Somalia and Kosovo that preoccupied the Clinton presidency. A Republican-led Congress would surely support Bush's domestic and foreign policies. The narrow Republican advantage dissolved in May 2001, however, when Sen. James Jeffords of Vermont left the Republican Party and became the Senate's lone independent member. The move by Jeffords gave the Democrats majority control of the Senate, and intense partisan conflict promptly returned (M. Nelson 2004).

The 9/11 terrorist attacks on the World Trade Center and Pentagon quickly ended the period of discord between Congress and the White House. A joint resolution of both chambers authorized President Bush to "use all necessary and appropriate force against those nations, organizations, or persons he determines planned, authorized, committed, or aided the terrorist attacks that occurred on September 11, 2001, or harbored such organizations or persons, in order to prevent any future acts of international terrorism against the United States by such nations, organizations or persons."[5] The open-ended resolution did not specify the targets of this military response, an omission "unprecedented in American history" (Grimmett 2001, 46). In addition, Congress passed sweeping legislation, known as the **USA PATRIOT Act** (short for Uniting and Strengthening America by Providing Appropriate Tools Required to Intercept and Obstruct Terrorism), that increased the federal government's ability to investigate suspected terrorists in the United States.

Bush received an equal level of deference from Congress in 2002 when he sought its support to wage war against Iraq. Fearful of being perceived as unpatriotic and hoping to neutralize Iraq as an election issue, most Democrats went along with the war

---

5. 107th Congress, Joint Resolution. "To Authorize the Use of United States Armed Forces against Those Responsible for the Recent Attacks Launched against the United States." Public Law 107-40 [S.J. Res. 23], August 18, 2001.

resolution and gave Bush wide discretion in initiating hostilities. Neutralizing the war issue did not help Democrats, however, as Republicans gained control of both chambers in the 2002 midterm elections. Bush enjoyed continued united government upon his reelection in 2004, which allowed him to pursue his war on terror with Congress's blessing. Bush lost this advantage in 2006, however, when Democrats claimed both houses of Congress. Exit polls revealed deep misgivings over the wars in Iraq and Afghanistan. The 110th Congress that came into power in January 2007 was determined to restore the legislative branch's oversight role, which had "virtually collapsed" during the first six years of George W. Bush's presidency (Ornstein and Mann 2006, 67).

Partisan Pushback in the Obama Years

Obama's victory in 2008, combined with the strengthening of the Democratic Party's majority in Congress, raised expectations for a new direction in U.S. foreign policy. The president had pledged to restore U.S. credibility as a world leader and to end the wars in Iraq and Afghanistan. Upon taking office, however, the president was forced to focus on domestic matters, especially the financial crisis which threatened the global economy. Obama also undertook a major reform of U.S. health care, a policy change that was strongly opposed by Republicans in Congress. Consumed by domestic politics, Obama was unable to exploit his opportunity to assume a leading role on the world stage. The hostility between Obama and his legislative foes intensified after the 2010 midterm elections returned Republicans to a majority in the House. Obama's victory in the 2012 presidential election, which was driven by domestic rather than foreign policy issues, left him with more divided government and political gridlock. "In recent years, the U.S. Congress has been unable to act decisively on foreign policy, or, in many cases, even debate international issues," argued Richard Lugar (2012), a former senator and chairman of the Senate Foreign Relations Committee. "Faced with reflexive partisan roadblocks and the growing number of unresolvable hot-button issues that get attached to foreign policy bills, Congress has retreated from legislation dealing with foreign policy."

Obama's final two years found the president facing Republican control over both houses of Congress. The midterm elections in November 2014, which also focused primarily on domestic issues, further weakened the president's clout on Capitol Hill. To the extent that foreign policy issues were raised, Congressional Republicans criticized Obama for being too passive in the face of a series of challenges to U.S. world power. Led by Sens. John McCain and Lindsay Graham in the Senate, lawmakers faulted Obama for not being prepared for Russia's annexation of Ukraine's Crimean Peninsula earlier in the year and for standing by while Chinese leaders laid claims on islands in the South China Sea that were considered the territory of other nations in the region. By July 2014, Senate Republicans had blocked the appointment of forty-three nominees for positions as ambassadors; another eleven nominees for State Department positions were also left in limbo. The Senate also rejected a measure

IN THEIR OWN WORDS

Members of the U.S. Senate *It is rare for members of Congress to intervene directly in foreign policy negotiations with other countries. In a recent exception to this rule, forty-seven members of the U.S. Senate sent a letter directly to Iranian leaders. They warned these leaders that Congress, not only the president, would have a say in approving a deal with Iran that would bring about a suspension of their programs leading to the development of nuclear weapons.*

An Open Letter to the Leaders of the Islamic Republic of Iran:

It has come to our attention while observing your nuclear negotiations with our government that you may not fully understand our constitutional system. Thus, we are writing to bring to your attention two features of our Constitution—the power to make binding international agreements and the different character of federal offices—which you should seriously consider as negotiations progress.

First, under our Constitution, while the president negotiates international agreements, Congress plays the significant role of ratifying them. In the case of a treaty, the Senate must ratify it by a two-thirds vote. A so-called congressional-executive agreement requires a majority vote in both the House and the Senate (which, because of procedural rules, effectively means a three-fifths vote in the Senate). Anything not approved by Congress is a mere executive agreement.

Second, the offices of our Constitution have different characteristics. For example, the president may serve only two 4-year terms, whereas Senators may serve an unlimited number of six-year terms. As applied today, for instance, President Obama will leave office in January 2017, while most of us will remain in office well beyond then—perhaps decades.

What these two constitutional provisions mean is that we will consider any agreement regarding your nuclear-weapons program that is not approved by the Congress as nothing more than an executive agreement between President Obama and Ayatollah Khamenei. The next president could revoke such an executive agreement with the stroke of a pen and future Congresses could modify the terms of the agreement at any time.

We hope this letter enriches your knowledge of our constitutional system and promotes mutual understanding and clarity as nuclear negotiations progress.

Source: U.S. Senate, Office of Sen. Tom Cotton (R-AR), Open Letter to the Leaders of the Islamic Republic of Iran, March 9, 2015. http://www.cotton.senate.gov/sites/default/files/150309%20Cotton%20Open%20Letter%20to%20Iranian%20Leaders.pdf.

favored by the White House that would have restricted the National Security Agency's ability to collect the telephone records of American citizens.

With the U.S. economy growing in 2015 after years of recession, Obama's detractors in Congress lost a major issue on which to criticize the president. House Speaker Boehner filled the foreign policy void by inviting Netanyahu to address Congress. Forty-eight Senate Republicans followed up by sending a letter to Iranian leaders that the legislative branch would have a say in the outcome of nuclear talks. Taking the offensive in February 2015, Obama vetoed legislation approving the Keystone XL oil pipeline, which would have carried 800,000 barrels of heavy petroleum from Canada to the Gulf of Mexico. Obama ultimately succeeded in gaining the necessary votes to approve the Iran nuclear agreement, and he achieved another foreign policy goal by restoring diplomatic relations with Cuba after more than half a century of isolation. Congress, however, refused to waive U.S. economic sanctions against Havana. As the president's term neared completion, tensions between Congress and the White House reached a high level reminiscent of the Vietnam era. The adage that "foreign policy stops at the water's edge" could not have been further from the truth.

■ CONSTRAINTS ON CONGRESSIONAL ACTION

As we have seen, the role played by Congress in U.S. foreign policy has varied widely since World War II, depending on circumstances in the global environment as well as the partisan balance of power at home. These variations, however, mask a general trend of congressional deference to the executive branch. Several factors deprive Congress of the vital role in foreign policy the founders designed it to play in the U.S. Constitution:

- **Passing the buck**. Legislators know the White House, not Congress, will receive credit for any breakthroughs in foreign policy. By distancing themselves from foreign policy, they protect themselves from blame if the president's actions fail. "Taking a position on a difficult issue leaves a member of Congress politically exposed and complicates his or her next election," noted Lee Hamilton (2009, 9), who served in the House of Representatives from 1965 to 1999. "The far easier route is to delegate the tough decisions to the president."

- **Structural weaknesses**. The sheer size of Congress hinders its efforts to compete with the president, who sits alone atop the executive branch. Unity within Congress has proved to be a rare exception to the rule of partisan division because Democrats and Republicans disagree chronically over the primary goals of U.S. foreign policy and the means to achieve them. The laborious and time-consuming nature of the legislative process further constrains legislators' ability to influence foreign policy. Presidents have greater access than Congress to intelligence on foreign policy issues, and having command of the "bully pulpit" gives presidents an additional advantage in shaping public opinion.

- **Judicial noninterference**. As noted in Chapter 4, Congress has received little help from the judicial branch in foreign policy disputes. Court rulings have consistently acknowledged the president as the "sole organ" of foreign policy or dismissed as political turf battles between the White House and Congress. The Supreme Court's refusal to rule on the constitutionality of the War Powers Resolution (see the next section), despite repeated appeals by Congress that it do so, has encouraged presidents to ignore much of the legislation.

- **Constituent service.** Recognizing their limitations in the foreign policy arena, legislators have strong incentives to meet the material needs of the citizens in their states and districts rather than focus on "abstract" foreign policy concerns (Weissman 1995; Silverstein 1997). Legislators receive more immediate gains by delivering tangible benefits, such as highway projects and defense contracts, to their constituents. Meeting these needs is especially vital to House members, whose two-year terms in office force them into nearly perpetual reelection campaigns.

■ LEGISLATING FOREIGN POLICY

Despite these limitations, Congress has an inescapable role to play in U.S. foreign policy. In any consideration of this role, it is helpful to recall the basic features of the legislative body. In the Senate, two senators, who serve six-year terms, represent each of the fifty states. In the House of Representatives, 435 members, who serve two-year terms, represent congressional districts within each state. The number of House members assigned to each state is based on the state's population. In structuring Congress, the framers chose the bicameral (two-chamber) design to create checks and balances *within* the legislative branch. More broadly, they purposefully made the passage of bills difficult in order to inhibit governmental activism. Legislation comes from many sources and takes many forms, some of which favor Capitol Hill at the expense of the executive branch. Members of Congress must balance a variety of factors in voting on legislation, the primary means by which they influence policy. Finally, the congressional committee system serves as the incubator of legislation and as a vital instrument of presidential oversight.

Dynamics of the Legislative Process

Congressional action on foreign policy originates from many sources. The executive branch, for example, often writes laws on such matters as defense appropriations, the terms of proposed treaties, and new human rights standards and then submits the bills to Congress for consideration. Prominent interest groups and think tanks also take part in drafting legislation that, not surprisingly, advances their own foreign policy goals. In still other cases, **foreign policy entrepreneurs** within Congress "have chosen to lead the way on the foreign policy issues they care about without waiting for the administration to take action" (R. G. Carter and Scott 2009, 221). For example, as Senate majority leader in the late 1950s, Lyndon Johnson filled this role when he proposed creating the National Aeronautics and Space Administration (NASA) in response to the Soviet Union's launching of the Sputnik satellite. Sen. William Fulbright, chair of the Senate Foreign Relations Committee in the 1960s, led the way in organizing congressional opposition to the Vietnam War. After the Cold War, Sens. Sam Nunn (D-GA) and Richard Lugar (R-IN) designed the Cooperative Threat Reduction Program described in the previous chapter.

POINT/COUNTERPOINT

CONGRESS VS. UN AMBASSADOR SUSAN RICE

Confusion over the Benghazi terrorist attack in Libya was fueled by televised comments made on September 16, 2012, by Susan Rice, the U.S. ambassador to the United Nations. Speaking for the U.S. government, Rice told Chris Wallace on *Fox News Sunday* that "the best assessment we have today is that in fact this was not a preplanned, premeditated attack. That what happened initially was that it was a spontaneous reaction to what had just transpired in Cairo. People gathered outside the embassy and then it grew very violent and those with extremist ties joined the fray and came with heavy weapons."

Rice's account, provided to several other news networks on that day, was later proven wrong as the attack was found to be planned in advance by terrorists affiliated with al Qaeda. In response, senior members of the Senate Foreign Relations Committee declared their lack of trust in Rice, who had emerged after the November elections as a candidate to replace Secretary of State Hillary Clinton. "She is so disconnected from reality that I don't trust her," declared Sen. Lindsey Graham (R-SC) on November 14. "I want to make sure that we don't promote anybody that was an essential player in the Benghazi debacle." Alongside Graham, Sen. John McCain (R-AZ) pledged that "we will do whatever is in our power" to prevent Rice from replacing Clinton.

President Obama strongly defended Rice on the same day, saying she had "done exemplary work" on Libya and other foreign policy flashpoints. "If Sen. McCain and Sen. Graham and others want to go after somebody they should go after me. For them to go after the UN ambassador who had nothing to do with Benghazi . . . to besmirch her reputation is outrageous."

On November 27, Rice met with senators from the committee, some of whom suspected that Rice had distorted the record prior to the election in order to protect Obama's public image as "winning" the war on al Qaeda. After her comments failed to reassure her critics on Capitol Hill, on December 13, Rice withdrew her name from consideration as the next secretary of state. Writing in the *Washington Post* on that day, Rice observed that "U.S. leadership abroad is and always has been strengthened when we transcend partisan differences on matters of national security. America is seriously weakened when politics comes first." Ironically, in June 2013, Obama assigned Rice to be his national security adviser, an appointment that did not require confirmation by the Senate.

Sources: Fox News Sunday, September 16, 2012; Barack Obama, "Remarks by the President in a News Conference," November 14, 2012, www.whitehouse.gov; Susan Rice, "Why I Made the Right Call," *Washington Post,* December 13, 2012.

Without congressional action, the creation of federal agencies is impossible. The 2002 birth of the Department of Homeland Security, for example, stemmed from a joint effort by the Bush administration and Congress. Legislators can also modify the structures of—or even abolish—existing agencies. For example, in the 1990s, Congress forced the State Department to absorb two formerly independent agencies, the U.S.

Information Agency and the U.S. Arms Control and Disarmament Agency. During this same period, Sen. Jesse Helms (R-NC) tried to abolish the U.S. Agency for International Development. He finally agreed to allow the foreign aid agency to survive but only under greater State Department scrutiny.

Also, Congress can impose reporting requirements on the executive branch. These reports may include special notifications to Congress on matters such as military deployments and covert operations. The executive branch also may be asked to provide one-time reports on specific issues, such as the likely impact of military base closings on neighboring communities or sectors of the U.S. economy. Periodic reports, too, are required by legislators. Since 1975, for example, the Defense Department has submitted annual reports on the impact of U.S. weapons programs on global arms control. Legislators have frequently imposed such reporting requirements to gain control over federal agencies.

Finally, Congress can enact laws that ensure legislative participation in U.S. foreign relations, as it did with the Trade Act of 1974. The act required that five members each from the Senate Finance Committee and the House Ways and Means Committee serve as official advisers to the executive branch in international trade negotiations. Through such participation, Congress hoped to regain at least part of its constitutional power to regulate commerce, power it had surrendered to the White House decades earlier.

The Calculus of Voting Behavior

A central question of interest to students of Congress is related to the motivations of legislators. Why do they support some policies and programs and oppose others? What factors do they consider when determining their positions on specific issues and deciding how much time and attention to devote to these issues? Four sets of factors converge to shape voting behavior: situational, ideological, electoral, and strategic (see Figure 5.3). Each set affects decisions to varying degrees in different cases.

Situational factors. In lawmaking, legislators must assess the objective details of the problem at hand and the costs and benefits of the proposed legislative solution—that is, the situational factors. According to rational models of decision making, such costs and benefits can be estimated with some confidence and weighed against the status quo. In the months preceding the 2002 midterm elections, for example, President Bush requested authority to use force against Saddam Hussein knowing that a negative vote by legislators would be seen by some as unpatriotic.

Ideological factors. Voting behavior is commonly assumed to reflect the **ideology** of legislators—that is, their general principles and beliefs about human nature, the relationships between states and society, and the nation's roles and responsibilities in world politics (see Chapter 3). From this perspective, the political activity of legislators serves as a natural extension of their deeply held worldviews. Academic studies

Figure 5.3 ■ Sources of Congressional Voting Behavior

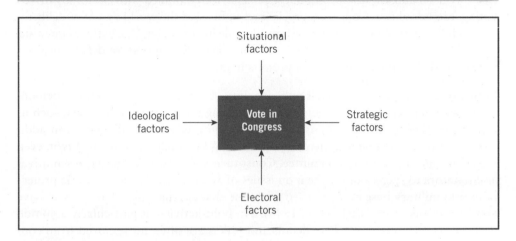

consistently reveal a link between the ideology of legislators and their behavior on such foreign policy issues as U.S.-Israeli relations (Rosenson, Oldmixon, and Wald 2009), Taiwan (Kastner and Grob 2009), and human rights (J. M. McCormick and Mitchell 2007). Such ideological factors may lead legislators to vote in different ways over time. For example, Senate conservatives discouraged foreign policy activism prior to the 1960s but later became the leading advocates of intervention in Vietnam and other frontline states during the Cold War (see Cronin and Fordham 1999). Liberals, who resisted military interventionism during these years, later led the charge for increased U.S. involvement in multilateral peacekeeping operations and relief for "failed" states.

Electoral factors. Viewing legislative action in terms of ideology oversimplifies the equation. Scholars today pay closer attention to the electoral calculations of legislators. An expert on voting behavior, David Mayhew (1974, 5), defined legislators as "single-minded seekers of reelection." Studies of congressional voting on foreign policy issues generally support this electoral connection. Eileen Burgin (1993) interviewed dozens of House members about their foreign policy positions in the early 1980s and found the influence of "supportive constituents" to be the decisive factor in 90 percent of votes. Electoral factors late in the Cold War played a role in legislating a freeze in the nuclear arms race (Overby 1991), proposed defense cutbacks (R. G. Carter 1989), and military base closings (Twight 1989). In 2012, Congress was so paralyzed by out-of-control deficits that it approved *automatic* Pentagon budget cuts if legislators failed to approve an overall strategy to reduce the federal budget.

Strategic factors. In deciding foreign policy positions, congressional members also consider strategic factors, such as the probable consequences of individual votes for the outcome of legislation. Legislators examine the linkage between votes on different bills coming to the floor of the House and the Senate and routinely engage in **logrolling**, a practice in which they "support one measure for later support for another measure" (see Davidson and Oleszek 2004). But such behavior, combined with electorally driven voting, casts doubt on Congress's proclaimed stature as "the world's greatest deliberative body" and its ability to play a responsible role in advancing U.S. national interests. It is not uncommon, for example, for legislators to "trade" support for defense projects in one district for greater funding of projects in others.

Voting on legislation, of course, is only one duty of members of Congress. To demonstrate their service to constituents, members engage in more symbolic acts, such as making speeches, cutting ribbons, and appearing on television talk shows. In addition, legislators please constituents by sponsoring bills that constituents favor, even if the bills never get out of committee. Constituents also expect their representatives and senators to speak out for them on issues of acute concern, such as trade protections and military base closings, even when the chances that this advocacy will have any impact seem slim (see Deering 1996). Symbolic activism is particularly common in foreign policy matters, where details and stakes are often far removed from constituents. "On foreign policy matters, legislators can engage in activities that appeal to constituents without expending much effort, political capital, or time. They can take stands without taking action, and they can make pronouncements, hold hearings, and run investigations without having to produce results" (Zegart 1999, 32).

Foreign Policy by Committee

Majority status within Congress brings with it great advantages, beyond the simple fact that the majority will win votes cast strictly along party lines. The majority party also receives the most seats in congressional committees and chooses chairmen and chairwomen to decide what proposals will be considered and to lead deliberations. All of this makes party control vital, particularly important in foreign as well as domestic policies (see Deering and Smith 1997).

Among the congressional committees with primary concern over foreign policy are the Senate Foreign Relations Committee and the House Committee on Foreign Affairs (see Figure 5.4). The Senate Foreign Relations Committee is especially important because its members consider treaties and presidential appointments before the full Senate votes on them. With its focus on global affairs, the committees offer members public visibility, as well as exposure to foreign leaders, intergovernmental organizations, and transnational interest groups. However, the issues the committees address rarely have material ties to constituent needs, a deficiency that has made membership less attractive to legislators in recent years. In short, approving a treaty is not likely to "bring home the bacon" and thereby enhance legislators' prospects of reelection in their home states or districts. "Foreign Relations has been kind of a wasteland," then-senator Chuck Hagel (R-NE) said in 1998. "It is not a particularly strong committee to fundraise from" (quoted in Pomper 1998, 3203).

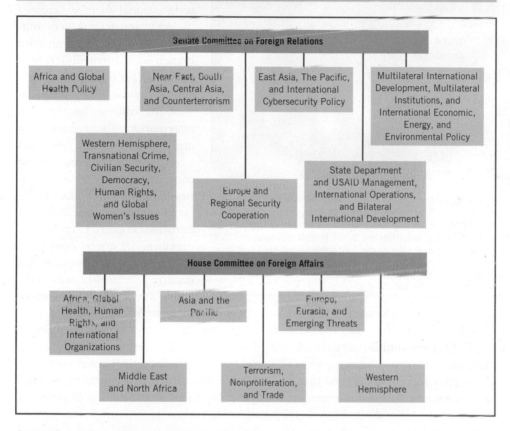

Sources: Senate Foreign Relations Committee, http://www.senate.gov/general/committee_membership/committee_
memberships_SSFR.htm; House Committee on Foreign Affairs, http://foreignaffairs.house.gov/subcommittees.

The Senate and House Armed Services Committees are concerned primarily with Department of Defense matters. Their jurisdictions include the development of weapons systems; structure of the U.S. Armed Forces; benefits for active and retired military personnel; and the Selective Service System. The Armed Services Committees, unlike the Senate Foreign Relations Committee and the House Committee on Foreign Affairs, attract legislators because of the large financial stakes involved in the operations of the Pentagon. Committee members frequently represent states or districts with sizable military bases or defense contracting firms, both of which pressure legislators to maintain or increase the levels of support coming from Washington. On average, legislators on these committees tend to be more conservative than their congressional colleagues,

© Corbis

No member of Congress had more impact on U.S. foreign policy during the Cold War than J. William Fulbright (D-AR), who chaired the Senate Foreign Relations Committee from 1959 until 1974. During his long tenure on the committee, Fulbright led the legislative effort to ensure U.S. entry into the United Nations and supported most presidential measures to implement the containment policy against the Soviet Union. Fulbright later became a harsh critic of U.S. involvement in Vietnam and of the "militarized economy" in the United States.

favoring strong military forces as a primary national goal.

After the Vietnam War, both congressional chambers created "select" intelligence committees, providing the legislative branch with a structural role in an area previously managed almost exclusively by the president. In addition to receiving information about conditions and developments overseas from the executive branch, these committees monitor the activities of the CIA and other intelligence-gathering agencies. Of particular concern to committee members are covert operations by the U.S. government, which occurred frequently during the Cold War without congressional knowledge (see Smist 1990). After September 11, 2001, the Senate committee conducted an investigation into the events leading up to the terrorist attacks (U.S. Senate 2004). They concluded that the CIA and other agencies had failed to act on mounting evidence that Islamist terrorists were planning a major attack on the United States. For their part, CIA officials argued that the torrent of fragmented data regarding possible terrorist attacks worldwide prevented analysts from focusing on the threat posed by Osama bin Laden and his al Qaeda cell based in Afghanistan.

Appropriations Committees in each chamber designate the amount of money to be spent on individual federal programs. In foreign policy, these programs include the operations of the State and Defense Departments and foreign aid. Other congressional committees play roles in specific areas of U.S. foreign policy. Trade policy, for example, is handled primarily by the Senate Finance Committee and the House Ways and Means Committee.[6] Agriculture Committees approve the terms of commodity exports and overseas food aid, and Judiciary Committees consider matters relating to international crime and terrorism. Legislation in the areas of energy and environmental policy, agricultural programs, and military construction is also channeled through the vast network of congressional committees.

6. At least a dozen other congressional committees and subcommittees are concerned with U.S. trade. As in other areas of U.S. foreign policy, the overlapping jurisdiction of committees in trade matters further complicates the policy-making process.

Presidents who resist congressional interference usually prevail in keeping legislators at bay. The practical difficulties of monitoring the executive branch in highly complex and secretive areas further hinder Congress's oversight role. Still, legislators are free to hold hearings on foreign policy issues of interest, and these sessions offer them a chance to criticize the executive branch and demand changes in policy. After Democrats regained majority control of Congress in 2007, for example, members of the Senate Foreign Relations Committee frequently called in Bush administration officials to explain their actions in Iraq and Afghanistan. More recently, congressional hearings focused on Syria, Ukraine, and the spread of the Islamic State as primary topics of discussion (see Table 5.1). Even though the hearings rarely produced changes in policy or further congressional action, they offered legislators important "voice opportunities" in the foreign policy process.

Table 5.1 ■ Selected Congressional Oversight Hearings on U.S. Foreign Policy, Senate Foreign Relations Committee, 113th Congress (2013–2014)

Hearing Date	Subject	Administration Representative
January 23, 2013	Benghazi: The Attacks and the Lessons Learned	Hillary Rodham Clinton, Secretary of State
April 11, 2013	U.S. Policy Toward Syria	Robert Ford, U.S. Ambassador to Syria
May 15, 2013	U.S. Policy Toward Iran	Wendy Sherman, Under Secretary for Political Affairs, Department of State
September 3, 2013	Authorization of Use of Force in Syria	John Kerry, Secretary of State; Chuck Hagel, Secretary of Defense; Gen. Martin Dempsey, Chairman of the Joint Chiefs of Staff, Department of Defense
December 10, 2013	Transition in Afghanistan	James Dobbins, Special Representative for Afghanistan and Pakistan, Department of State
May 6, 2014	Ukraine: Countering Russian Intervention and Supporting a Democratic State	Victoria Nuland, Assistant Secretary of State for European and Eurasian Affairs, Department of State
July 9, 2014	Russia and Developments in Ukraine	Victoria Nuland, Assistant Secretary of State for European and Eurasian Affairs, Department of State
July 29, 2014	Iran: Status of the P5+1	Wendy Sherman, Under Secretary for Political Affairs, Department of State
September 17, 2014	United States Strategy to Defeat the Islamic State	John Kerry, Secretary of State
December 9, 2014	Authorization for the Use of Military Force against the Islamic State	John Kerry, Secretary of State

■ WAR POWERS AND THE USE OF FORCE

The use of U.S. military force is the most vital and controversial area of legislative-executive relations. The stakes are always immense when American troops are called into actions that could kill them or leave them disabled for the rest of their lives. Decisions over war and peace are also critical to the nation's security long into the future. In this area, lawmakers have three sets of concerns: (1) *whether or not* to approve military action; (2) if action is ordered, *what steps* Congress could play to support the use of force; and (3) *how well* the missions have been planned and executed.

The War Powers Act

As noted previously, although the Constitution explicitly bestows on Congress the power to declare war, since World War II presidents have frequently deployed troops without a congressional declaration. This apparent breach of the spirit and the letter of the Constitution led to the passage of the War Powers Resolution (50 U.S.C. 1541–1548) over President Richard Nixon's veto, on November 7, 1973. Congressional leaders at the time were highly critical of Nixon's conduct of the Vietnam War, particularly his secret invasions of Cambodia and Laos, his massive bombing of civilian areas, and his resort to CIA spying on antiwar activists.[7]

The legislators' goal in passing the resolution, as stated in its introductory section, was to "fulfill the intent of the framers of the Constitution of the United States . . . that the collective judgment of both the Congress and the President will apply to the introduction of United States Armed Forces into hostilities." To fulfill this goal, congressional members crafted a resolution with two key requirements: the president must *consult* with Congress before deploying troops into possible armed conflict in other countries and must *report* to Congress "periodically on the status of such hostilities." Upon receiving an initial notification from the president of such a deployment (which may be sent up to forty-eight hours *after* the mission has been launched), Congress, through a majority vote of its members, can order that troops be withdrawn after sixty days. The White House may extend this deadline by up to thirty days.

Presidents have dismissed the War Powers Resolution (WPR) as unconstitutional, claiming that their power as the commander in chief permits them to deploy troops overseas into armed conflicts without a formal declaration of war from Congress. Despite these assertions, between April 1975 and April 2015, presidents chose to comply with the resolution by submitting WPR reports to Congress on 160 military actions. Among post–Cold War presidents, Bill Clinton submitted sixty reports during his two terms, George W. Bush filed thirty-nine, and Barack Obama sent thirty-four WPR reports to Capitol Hill through December 2014 (Weed 2014, 63–86). Most of Obama's early reports detailed ongoing U.S. actions in Iraq, Afghanistan,

---

7. Also important, in 1973, Congress was in the midst of investigating the Watergate scandal, which would lead to Nixon's resignation in August 1974.

and "a number of locations in the Central, Pacific, European, Southern, and African Command areas of operation in support of anti-terrorist and anti-al Qaeda actions" (Grimmett 2012b, 19). Among the more recent hot spots, Obama reported U.S. military actions in Jordan (June 2013), South Sudan (2013), Chad (2014), and Syria (2014).

Since the Cold War, the United States has engaged in seven military conflicts that involved the president's legal authority (see Table 5.2). In three of these cases—the

Karen Kleier/AFP/Getty Images

U.S. Senators Kelly Ayotte (R-NH), Lindsey Graham (R-SC), and John McCain (R-AZ) voice their criticism in November 2012 of Susan Rice, the U.S. ambassador to the United Nations. At the time, Rice was among President Obama's top choices to replace Hillary Clinton as secretary of state. Rice, who later withdrew as a possible nominee, was criticized for not acknowledging early enough that the September attack on the U.S. consulate in Benghazi, Libya, was linked to the al Qaeda terrorist group.

Gulf War, the response to 9/11, and the Iraq War—Congress approved an Authorization for the Use of Military Force (AUMF). In four other cases—Somalia, Bosnia-Herzegovina, Kosovo, and Libya—presidents responded to UN Security Council resolutions that called for military actions in the absence of peaceful cooperation. The pattern demonstrates that Congress is likely to authorize the use of force in "**wars of necessity**" that are based on perceived threats to U.S. vital interests. In "**wars of choice**," which do not pose immediate or vital threats to the United States, presidents have used the UN as their legal authority to use force.

During the 1990s, congressional efforts to retain some measure of codetermination over military deployments failed consistently. In 1993, legislators threatened to cut off funding for the U.S. intervention in Somalia if the mission was not completed by March 31, 1994, but U.S. troops remained in Somalia a year beyond this deadline as part of a UN mission. In 1995, the House and the Senate approved "sense-of-the-Congress" resolutions stating that U.S. combat troops should not be deployed to Bosnia-Herzegovina without congressional approval. But Clinton ignored these resolutions and ordered the deployment of 32,000 troops to the former Yugoslav republic. When Clinton deployed troops to Kosovo in March 1999, several members of Congress filed suit against him to force a withdrawal. Three months later, the U.S. Court of Appeals dismissed the suit, ruling that the legislators lacked "legal standing" to sue the president. The U.S. Supreme Court upheld the ruling in October 2000. These and other legal cases affirmed the authority of presidents to send troops into combat in the absence of a declaration of war from Congress.

Table 5.2 ■ Post–Cold War U.S. Military Actions and Congressional Roles

Conflict (Year)	President	Type of Conflict	Legal Basis
Gulf War (1991)	George H. W. Bush	Reversal of Invasion of Kuwait by Iraq	Authorization by Congress
Somalia (1991–1992)	George H. W. Bush and Clinton	Humanitarian mission caused by failed state	Approval of UN Security Council
Bosnia-Herzegovina (1991)	Clinton	UN peacekeeping	Approval of UN Security Council
Kosovo (1999)	Clinton	Humanitarian mission caused by civil war	Approval of UN Security Council
War on Terror (2001)	George W. Bush	Response to terrorist attacks on United States	Authorization by Congress
Iraq (2003)	George W. Bush	Preventive action to ward off attacks by weapons of mass destruction	Authorization by Congress
Libya (2011)	Obama	Humanitarian mission caused by violent uprising	Approval of UN Security Council

Sources: Matthew C. Weed, "A New Authorization for Use of Military Force against the Islamic State: Issues and Current Proposals in Brief" (2015). Washington, DC: Congressional Research Service, February 20; Jennifer K. Elsea and Matthew C. Weed, "Declarations of War and Authorizations for the Use of Military Force: Historical Background and Legal Implications" (2014). Washington, DC: Congressional Research Service, April 18.

Obama came to power claiming that he would honor the co-determination of foreign policy that is reflected in the U.S. Constitution. On war powers, however, the president followed George W. Bush's claim that, as commander in chief, he had broad authority to deploy forces without the approval of Congress. In this respect, it was "Obama, not Bush, who has proven the master of unilateral war" (Goldsmith and Waxman 2014). In April 2011, Obama did not request an authorization for the use of military force against Libya and its leader, Muammar Qaddafi, who threatened mass killings of his enemies. According to the Justice Department, "Prior congressional approval was not constitutionally required to use military force in the limited operations under consideration."[8]

---

8. Carolyn D. Krass, Principal Deputy Assistant Attorney General, Department of Justice. "Memorandum Open for the Attorney General," April 1, 2011. This approach may have worked against Obama, as history shows that members of Congress, when included in war councils, are more likely to support the president's military strategies in the future (see Kriner 2014).

The president tried, but failed, to gain congressional support for military action against Syria, whose leader, Bashar al-Assad, had unleashed chemical weapons against civilians in 2013, killing thousands of civilians. Defending his war powers, Obama deployed warships to the eastern Mediterranean and readied them for missile attacks. Lacking domestic and international support for this action, Obama backed down on his military option. The president in 2014 claimed that he could take military action against the Islamic State under Congress's 2001 authorization that granted Bush broad powers to retaliate against terrorist groups and their state sponsors. Still, he pushed Congress to pass an AUMF, saying that he "would welcome action by the Congress that would aid the overall effort."[9]

The Oversight of Torture

As noted earlier, members of Congress since the Vietnam War have used their oversight powers as a vital check on the executive branch. By requiring the White House to provide details of its actions in domestic as well as foreign policies, lawmakers can inform their constituents about government initiatives, provide feedback to the executive branch, and hold policy makers accountable for their actions.

After September 11, the Bush administration gained renewed congressional support for covert operations to penetrate and destroy terrorist cells around the world (see Cumming 2006). Controversy soon arose, however, after the CIA was found to be holding suspects in secret overseas prisons, also known as "black sites" (Priest 2005). These prisoners and those held in other detention centers were routinely subjected to "coercive interrogations" that, according to most international standards, amounted to torture. The CIA also engaged in a practice known as **extraordinary rendition** by which suspected terrorists were transported to foreign countries whose interrogation practices did not have to comply with U.S. laws.

In an interview on NBC's *Meet the Press* five days after the 9/11 attacks, Vice President Cheney said U.S. agents would have to work "the dark side, if you will. We've got to spend time in the shadows in the intelligence world. . . . That's the world these folks operate in, and so it's going to be vital for us to use any means at our disposal, basically, to achieve our objective." White House lawyers also declared that U.S. actions in the conflict fell outside the reach of the Geneva Conventions, the most recent of which, adopted in 1949, prohibited the "cruel treatment and torture" of war prisoners. Attorney General John Ashcroft argued the September 11 attacks constituted a "crime of war and a crime against humanity" that demanded extraordinary measures by Washington.

An internal report by the CIA (2004), made public in 2009 under court order, revealed that between September 2001 and October 2003, CIA interrogators had

---

9. Interview with President Obama, *Meet the Press*, September 7, 2014.

beaten a prisoner to death with a metal torch, threatened another with a power drill, staged a fake execution of another prisoner, threatened to rape and kill the families of prisoners, and routinely conducted "waterboarding" exercises in which bound suspects were nearly drowned while being ordered to divulge secret information. Khalid Sheikh Mohammad, the alleged mastermind of the September 2001 terrorist attacks, received the treatment 183 times. These and other interrogation techniques appeared to violate the terms of the *U.S. Army Field Manual,* updated in 2006, which held that no person in custody "shall be subject to torture or cruel, inhuman, or degrading treatment or punishment" (U.S. Department of the Army 2014, 13-9).[10]

Using its oversight powers, the U.S. Senate (2014) conducted a detailed study of the CIA's treatment of detainees during the Bush years. Sen. Dianne Feinstein (D-CA), chair of the Senate Select Committee on Intelligence, led the effort to gather all relevant facts about the CIA's actions between 2001 and 2006. The report concluded that a string of CIA directors—George J. Tenet, Porter J. Goss, and Michael V. Hayden—knew about the torture practices and misled other government agencies along with the press and general public. Among the main findings of the Senate committee's report (Ashkenas et al. 2014) were the following:

- The CIA's interrogation techniques were more brutal and employed more extensively than the agency portrayed.
- The interrogation program was mismanaged and was not subject to adequate oversight.
- Interrogators in the field who tried to stop the brutal techniques were repeatedly overruled by senior CIA officials.
- The CIA misled members of Congress and the White House about the effectiveness and extent of its brutal interrogation techniques.
- The CIA leaked classified information to journalists, exaggerating the success of the interrogation methods in an effort to gain public support.

Although the Senate committee's report was shocking, no figures from the CIA were charged with crimes. To the contrary, former officials from the agency continued to insist that their tactics produced vital information for future counterterrorism missions. For his part, President Obama chose not to criticize the agency and its interrogators, most of whom had left the agency before he took office. The legislative branch's latest use of its oversight powers, however, played a critical role in making the nation and its citizens aware of the high costs of torture and its consequences for American credibility and moral leadership.

---

10. The U.S. actions, since acknowledged by government officials, also violated key elements of the UN Convention against Torture, which was signed by President Reagan in 1988.

■ THE POWER OF THE PURSE

One of Congress's most potent weapons in foreign policy relates to its taxing and spending power. Article I, section 8, of the Constitution explicitly provides Congress with authority to "lay and collect taxes, duties, imposts and excises, to pay debts and provide for the common defense and general welfare of the United States." The framers of the Constitution, whose primary concern was restraining a potentially tyrannical head of state, viewed this control over government spending as a crucial hedge against excessive presidential ambition. As James Madison wrote in *Federalist* No. 58 (A. Hamilton, Madison, and Jay 1787–1788), power over government spending is "the most complete and effectual weapon with which any constitution can arm the representatives of the people."

The power of the purse is not important simply as a matter of checks and balances. Decisions about the amount of money received by the government, and how that money will be spent, dictate what is possible in public policy. In short, those who hold the keys to the treasury establish both the opportunities and the limitations of government action. Indeed, the failure of past world powers to keep their fiscal houses in order precipitated their decline. Economic crises may result from the overwhelming commitments associated with "imperial overstretch" (P. Kennedy 1987). Alternatively, in modern democratic governments, the demands of domestic interest groups may drain public treasuries and deprive military forces and diplomatic services of the funds they need to maintain a strong posture in foreign affairs (Olson 1982).

Government spending has special significance in foreign policy. Foreign leaders closely watch the amount of money the United States directs toward military programs and other operations abroad, viewing it as a sign of the government's priorities and future intentions. "If budget levels are thought to affect the behavior of potential foreign threats, budget totals then become an instrument of foreign policy" (Wildavsky and Caiden 1997, 232). Similarly, the U.S. government's financial commitments to allies, whether in the form of military or development aid, often speak louder than the rhetorical statements of presidents and diplomats.

Conflicts between the legislative and executive branches over foreign policy frequently come down to matters of dollars and cents. In 1907, President Theodore Roosevelt dispatched the Great White Fleet on a symbolic cruise around the world and then dared Congress not to appropriate the funds to bring the fleet home. In the 1970s, Congress forced President Nixon to end the Vietnam War by cutting off funds for further U.S. military action. Republicans in Congress slashed foreign aid budgets in the 1990s, and Democrats later threatened funding cuts for the Iraq War as a means to accelerate a U.S. withdrawal from the conflict. More recently, Republicans, in 2011, called for deep cuts in the U.S. Institute of Peace, a government-funded program alleged by its critics to have pursued a liberal rather than a scholarly agenda.

Congressional spending authority in foreign policy comes into play in two distinct areas. First, Congress approves the *defense* budget, by far the largest single spending category in the federal budget. Second, it approves the *international affairs* budget, which finances the State Department and related agencies. As part of this budget, the legislative branch also decides how much money the United States will spend on assistance to foreign governments and international financial institutions such as the World Bank and IMF.

Managing the Defense Budget

Though the share of the federal budget devoted to defense spending has dropped considerably since the mid-1950s, as has the share of U.S. economic output represented by defense spending, the government still devotes the largest share of its discretionary spending to national defense. Annual spending in this area averaged $282 billion during the first post–Cold War decade (1992–2001). After the September 2001 terrorist attacks, the defense budget increased by $100 billion in the next two years and continued rising steadily to more than $800 billion by fiscal years 2011 and 2012 (see Figure 5.5). Described by Aaron Wildavsky and Naomi Caiden (1997, 219) as the "largest organization in the free world," the Department of Defense in 2015 employed nearly 3 million people, or about three out of every four federal employees. Of this total, 1.3 million service men and women were on active duty, 826,000 served in the National Guard and reserve forces, and 742,000 worked in civilian positions (see Department of Defense 2015).

Defense spending is not only the largest component of the federal budget but also one of its most controversial. Four factors in particular account for this controversy. First, proposed legislation for defense spending routinely provokes **guns-or-butter debates** within Congress and among the general public. In short, critics of higher defense spending argue that domestic needs are being sacrificed in the name of national defense. Generally speaking, Republicans in Congress are more likely than Democrats to support military spending over nonmilitary programs such as Medicare, education, and foreign aid.

Second, presidents and members of Congress nearly always disagree about the amount of money needed for national defense and engage in acrimonious public debates over the issue. In fiscal year 2001, for example, Republicans in Congress charged President Clinton with neglecting both the combat readiness of active U.S. troops and the living standards of veterans. The $291 billion approved for defense in that year included $5 billion in spending beyond the amount proposed by Clinton. Similarly, the U.S. armed services compete with each other over the distribution of military spending. Gen. David Jones found that this "intramural scramble for resources" distracts the armed services from their core mission of promoting national defense (quoted in Wildavsky and Caiden 1997, 224).

Figure 5.5 ■ National Defense Outlays, Fiscal Years 2004–2014

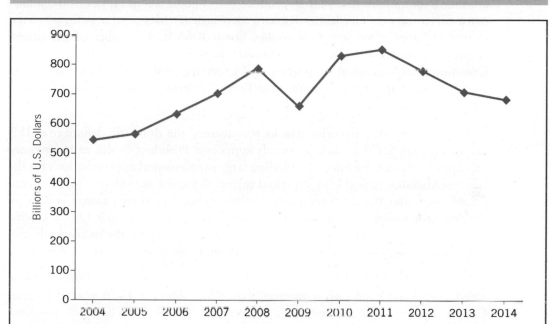

Source: U.S. Office of Management and Budget, *Budget of the U.S. Government: Fiscal Year 2013 Historical Tables*, Table 3.1, "Outlays by Superfunction and Function: 1940–2017," 54–55, http://www.whitehouse.gov/sites/default/files/omb/budget/fy2013/assets/hist.pdf.

Third, government and private studies frequently expose cases of overpriced weapons systems and wasteful spending practices in the Pentagon (see Goodwin 1985; Gregory 1989; W. G. Mayer 1992). As noted in Chapter 3, critics charge that three elements— Congress, the Defense Department, and military contractors—form an "iron triangle" that conspires to increase weapons spending beyond the levels needed to maintain U.S. security. This problem is compounded when former legislators and military officials pass through a "revolving door" and become lobbyists for defense contractors with direct access to Capitol Hill. This issue gained national attention in 2003, a year that otherwise witnessed national consensus over military spending. A subsidiary of Halliburton, a major military subcontractor, admitted to overcharging the federal government for its services in Iraq. Then-vice president Dick Cheney previously ran the oil services firm, which garnered more than $15 billion in contracts to support the U.S. occupation (Jehl 2003).

Finally, influential members of Congress are frequently able to gain spending approval for pet military projects in their states or districts. In 2000, for example,

Senate majority leader Trent Lott (R-MS) won approval for $460 million in spending on a helicopter carrier in Pascagoula, his hometown. Congress appropriated another $400 million that year to produce F-15 fighter jets in St. Louis, the hometown of House minority leader Richard Gephardt (D-MO) and a politically vital source of support for Sen. Christopher Bond (R-MO), a member of the Senate Appropriations Committee. Most observers view members of the Armed Services Committees as "uncritical supporters of the military establishment who receive, in exchange for that support, a continuous flow of defense spending in their districts" (Deering 1993, 175).

The September 2001 terrorist attacks transformed the domestic debate over U.S. defense spending. Congress consistently supported President Bush's calls for sharp increases in the defense budget, including large supplemental appropriations for the wars in Afghanistan and Iraq. As noted earlier, this spike in military spending continued even after the 2006 midterm elections, when Democrats gained control of the Pentagon's budget. As in the past, Democratic legislators avoided being labeled "soft on defense" or unsupportive of U.S. troops by voting for the increases despite their stated misgivings about the progress being made in the war on terror and in the war in Iraq.

The U.S. defense budget grew to more than $800 billion in fiscal year 2010 after Congress approved a 3.4 percent increase in pay for the armed forces. President Obama also gained congressional approval to eliminate funding for weapons systems that the White House did not consider to be vital. Foremost among these was the F-22 fighter jet, the world's costliest aircraft, which was designed in the 1980s to repel the Soviet Union's air force. By cancelling future purchases of the F-22, the Senate in July 2009 supported the president's view that U.S. force should be prepared for the unconventional wars of the future rather than the superpower showdowns that seemed imminent during the Cold War (see O'Hanlon 2009).

By fiscal year 2012, the defense budget fell to $788 billion and future cutbacks appeared inevitable, for two reasons. First, U.S. troop withdrawals from Iraq and Afghanistan permitted much-needed cost savings for the Pentagon. Second, the nation's soaring budget deficits and debts forced Congress to reduce federal spending in most areas, including military spending. The Budget and Control Act of 2012 required Congress to "sequester" (or force) reductions in federal spending by $2.1 trillion over the next decade if legislators failed to achieve the needed savings themselves. A large share of the automatic cuts would come from the defense budget. After the first wave of forced cutbacks occurred early in 2013, projections of Pentagon spending anticipated reductions to less than $700 billion by 2015.

With future cutbacks in defense spending inevitable, Pentagon managers searched in many places for reductions, including by reducing the number of active forces in the Army and Marine Corps and the size of the nuclear arsenal (O'Hanlon 2012).

Defense lobbyists, meanwhile, continued to push for continued funding of weapons systems that the Pentagon deemed obsolete. In 2014, Defense Secretary Chuck Hagel called for the elimination of the Air Force A-10 attack aircraft, the decades-old U-2 spy plane, and an aircraft carrier that was slated for retirement in 2016. Under pressure from lobbyists and legislators from districts that benefited from these programs, the House Armed Services Committee approved all three. The same committee approved continued funding for military bases the Pentagon concluded were not needed. Policy analyst Stewart Patrick had a simple explanation for this behavior: "When you look at the Pentagon and its gargantuan budget, it's likely that every single congressional district in the United States has either a U.S. military installation or a defense contractor" (T. Johnson 2013).

The Price of Diplomacy

The second primary arena of congressional spending power in foreign policy is the budget for international affairs. This budget comprises the costs of running the State Department and other nondefense agencies, as well as U.S. spending on foreign aid and contributions to international organizations. Together, these expenses soared between fiscal years 2001 and 2011, from $20 billion to more than $45 billion, a level that remained through fiscal year 2014 (U.S. Office of Management and Budget 2015). The spike in funding followed appeals from three secretaries of state, Colin Powell, Condoleezza Rice, and Hillary Clinton. Still, these figures represented less than 10 percent of the Pentagon's budget. Foreign aid, one of the most embattled federal spending programs, annually consumed just 1 percent of the federal budget (see Figure 5.6).

The State Department claims only one-quarter of the international affairs budget. These funds cover the department's Washington headquarters and the hundreds of U.S. embassies and consulates scattered throughout the world. In addition, the State Department funds a variety of programs designed to promote economic development, disaster relief, energy conservation, solutions to climate change, and democratic reforms. Finally, the international affairs budget advances U.S. "soft power" through public diplomacy, exchange programs, and organizations such as the Peace Corps and the U.S. Institute of Peace.

Despite the global scope of these activities, the State Department and its related agencies have long faced a skeptical and sometimes hostile Congress during budget deliberations, particularly since the end of the Cold War. Congressional hostility toward the State Department stems from several sources. From legislators' point of view, the department is poorly managed, does not make efficient use of federal resources, and resists a close working relationship with Congress. The State Department's lack of a domestic constituency further reduces its position on the priority list of most members of Congress.

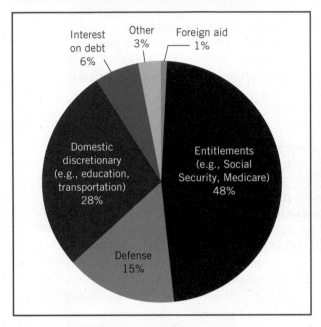

Figure 5.6 ■ Distribution of Federal Spending as a Percentage of Total, Fiscal Year 2013

Source: U.S. Office of Management and Budget, Summary Tables, p. 208 http://www.whitehouse.gov/sites/default/files/omb/budget/fy2013/assets/tables.pdf.

The legislative branch's resistance to State Department funding has deep roots in U.S. history and political culture (see Hook 2003). Public disregard for diplomacy in general, and the State Department in particular, reflects a long-standing skepticism toward traditional statecraft that extends beyond immediate circumstances or individual relations with foreign governments. As a result, the State Department has been routinely neglected in each of its primary areas of responsibility: the development and articulation of foreign policy, the conduct of diplomacy, the pursuit of solutions to transnational problems such as global warming, and the transfer of foreign assistance. According to a study by the Overseas Presence Advisory Panel (1999, 19), at the turn of the century, U.S. embassies, consulates, and specialized missions were found to be "near a state of crisis." The panel reported "shockingly shabby and antiquated building conditions" in overseas missions, which were increasingly being staffed by personnel from other U.S. agencies.

As described in detail in Chapter 11, U.S. foreign aid programs, the objects of deep congressional cuts in the 1990s, rank among the least popular in the federal budget. Public opinion surveys consistently find Americans concerned that nonmilitary programs overseas come at the cost of domestic programs and priorities. Legislators have few electoral incentives to champion the causes and costs of such activities, which are so far removed from the day-to-day lives of average U.S. citizens. In this environment, it came easy in September 2012 for Rep. Kay Granger (R-TX), the chairwoman of a powerful appropriations subcommittee, to block a $450-million relief package to Egypt that had already been promised by the White House.

After the September 2001 terrorist attacks, members of Congress rushed to increase funding for counterterrorism efforts undertaken by the Defense Department and assistance to law enforcement in foreign countries. President George W. Bush, however, became convinced that fighting terrorism should also include efforts to relieve suffering in developing countries where desperate citizens may turn to terrorism out of frustration with their living conditions. Bush, backed by U.S. religious groups, was also persuaded that U.S. foreign aid served an important moral as well as strategic purpose for the United States, and he gained the support from Republicans as well as Democrats in Congress to increase the aid budget (Hook 2008). Under Secretary of State Hillary Clinton, the State Department also received more funds to improve its facilities, computer networks, and working conditions for foreign service officers.

Upon taking office in January 2009, Obama continued this effort to enhance the soft-power elements of U.S. foreign policy. He also looked for chances to rebuild trust among foreign leaders who were upset over Bush's aggressive actions in his war on terror. Secretary of State Clinton and defense secretary Robert Gates shared Obama's view that constructive State Department programs could advance U.S. national security without the costs in money, lives, and ill will around the world that the use of military force may incur. Obama also had substantial support in Congress, which approved nearly $50 billion in funding from fiscal years 2010 through 2014 (U.S. Office of Management and Budget 2015). While diplomats, Foreign Service Officers, and aid specialists welcomed these higher funding levels, they knew the State Department was vulnerable to cutbacks that were needed to rescue the United States from the "fiscal cliff."

■ CONCLUSION

As we have seen, tensions between Congress and the White House are hardwired into the U.S. political system and foreign policy process. If today's national security architecture is a relic of the early Cold War, legislative-executive conflicts are creatures of the American Revolution and the ill-fated Articles of Confederation. Both experiences shaped the political culture of the United States in profound ways, placing individual freedoms above the orderly and efficient exercise of state power. The framers merely codified this arrangement in the U.S. Constitution, providing enough central governance to keep the new republic intact while allowing the dynamism and centrifugal forces of federalism and civil society to be expressed freely. The fragmentation and diffusion of government power, of which legislative-executive relations is but one element, ensure the erratic exercise of world power by the United States.

The climate of perpetual war that has prevailed for most of the past century rewards congressional deference to the executive branch. Presidents have repeatedly claimed the authority to put U.S. forces in harm's way without a congressional declaration of war, and they have done so freely. Yet, whatever the rationale invoked by presidents and whatever the positions taken by legislators, the unilateral exercise of war powers by a U.S. president contradicts the spirit of the U.S. Constitution, which explicitly calls on Congress to make this most fateful decision. According to legal expert Benjamin

Wittes (2008, 132–133), "Only Congress can effectively constrain the executive in its exercise of the powers of presidential preemption and at the same time constrain the courts in their ambitions for a greater role in foreign and military affairs."

Even in the comfort zone of unified government, presidents cannot maintain the support of Capitol Hill indefinitely if their foreign policies fail. "The fact that members of Congress defer to the White House when [the president's] foreign policy takes off does not mean they will be deferential when it crashes" (Lindsay 2003, 545). This insight pertained to the George W. Bush administration, as recurring setbacks in the war on terror encouraged legislative pushback against the commander in chief. Although Obama enjoyed broad support in Congress upon his election, critics later blamed him for neglecting the sectarian violence in Iraq, resurgence of Taliban insurgents in Afghanistan, Russia's power plays in Ukraine, and Iran's refusal to temper its nuclear ambitions. The same adversarial relations continued in Obama's second term, tempting the president to focus on the domestic issues that appealed to voters and had fueled his reelection. While this made sense in terms of domestic politics, such a strategy, if sustained, would prevent Obama from realizing his potential as a major force in global politics, a stature that seemed likely when he first came to office in 2009.

The lesson of history is clear: Mutual accommodation between the White House and Congress is essential for the nation's global ambitions to be realized. Presidents may test the limits of their executive power in today's seemingly permanent state of war (Bacevich 2010), but they inevitably confront resistance from Capitol Hill when legislators are left out of the loop. For its part, Congress may gain politically by challenging the president's foreign policies, despite the message it sends around the world that the United States is anything but united when it comes to solving some of the most critical global problems. Both branches of government, therefore, must continually accept, but ultimately overcome, the Constitution's "invitation to struggle" for the United States to reassure its friends, resist its enemies, and overcome the paradox of its own world power.

KEY TERMS

Case-Zablocki Act, p. 152

congressional diplomacy, p. 151

constituent service, p. 158

extraordinary rendition, p. 169

foreign policy entrepreneurs, p. 158

Gulf of Tonkin Resolution, p. 152

guns-or-butter debates, p. 172

ideology, p. 160

Intelligence Oversight Act of 1980, p. 152

Jackson-Vanik Amendment, p. 152

judicial noninterference, p. 157

logrolling, p. 162

Nelson-Bingham Amendment, p. 152

oversight, p. 152

passing the buck, p. 157

structural weaknesses, p. 157

USA PATRIOT Act, p. 154

War Powers Resolution, p. 152

wars of choice, p. 167

wars of necessity, p. 167

INTERNET REFERENCES

The **Almanac of Policy Issues** (http://www.policyalmanac.org) is an independent public resource that provides background information and web links on a host of U.S. policy issues such as foreign affairs and national security, education, public health and social welfare, and the environment. The website also includes an archive of policy documents from a variety of sources such as the Congressional Research Service and the Congressional Budget Office.

The Capitol.Net (http://www.thecapitol.net) is a nonpartisan firm that provides seminars, workshops, and publications to assist government and business personnel in understanding policy making in Washington, D.C. It focuses on, among other things, congressional operations, media and testifying training, and business etiquette. The site includes links to legislative reports, records, and schedules.

The Center for Congressional and Presidential Studies (http://www.american.edu/spa/ccps/), hosted by American University, provides access to conferences, speeches, and articles on Congress, the presidency, and their interaction. Elections, ethics, and lobbying are just some of the topics addressed in the publications, such as *Congress and the Presidency: A Journal of Capital Studies* (http://www.american.edu/spa/ccps/journal.cfm), that are available through this site.

The Center on Congress (http://congress.indiana.edu) at Indiana University is a nonpartisan organization dedicated to increasing civic engagement by improving public understanding of how Congress works. The articles, e-learning modules, and commentaries available through the website are not highly technical. Rather, they focus on matters such as the impact of Congress on the daily lives of Americans.

The Politics page on CNN's website (http://www.cnn.com/politics/) is a comprehensive source for news on current events and political topics. The interplay between Congress and the presidency is often the subject of discussion.

Congress.org (http://www.congress.org) is a private, nonpartisan company that provides descriptions and analyses of the latest issues and votes on Capitol Hill to improve civic participation. Links enable visitors to search current bills and research congressional voting patterns.

The Congressional Budget Office (https://www.cbo.gov) provides recent and historical data along with economic forecasts of U.S. government spending. It also offers links to testimony, letters, budget reviews, and reports related to government expenditures on a wide range of policy areas, from the war on terror to Medicare.

CQPolitics.com, a product of Washington, D.C.–based publisher *Congressional Quarterly*, fulfills its mission ("Every District. Every State. Every Day.") by complementing staff-written articles on congressional electoral politics with links to Congress and its members and to fund-raising data.

The Library of Congress's THOMAS (http://thomas.loc.gov/home/thomas.php) makes federal legislation freely available to the public by means of links that are helpful for exploring bills, resolutions, the *Congressional Record,* committee information, schedules, and legislative calendars. Links to both houses of Congress, as well as to every committee and subcommittee, are also provided.

Organized and maintained by the Public Broadcasting Service (PBS), the **Weekly Political Wrap** (http://www.pbs.org/newshour/tag/political-wrap/) reports on salient political issues in Congress and in the media more generally. Video and transcriptions of testimony are especially helpful for researchers.

CHAPTER 6

THE FOREIGN POLICY BUREAUCRACY

Official White House Photo by Pete Souza

American leaders frequently meet in the White House's "Situation Room," a secure space where key decisions are made regarding U.S. foreign policy. In September 2013, President Obama consulted with members of the National Security Council regarding his plans to bomb Syria's government in retaliation for its use of chemical weapons against civilians caught in the nation's civil war.

6.1   Summarize two models of foreign policy bureaucracy and how they contribute to dysfunction.

6.2   Describe the conduct of U.S. diplomacy and three criticisms of its practice.

6.3   Discuss the institutions that comprise the U.S. security complex.

6.4   Explain the work of and challenges facing the U.S. intelligence complex.

6.5   Describe the role of key players in the conduct of U.S. foreign economic policy.

America's emergence as a global superpower after World War II gave rise to a large foreign policy bureaucracy that sustained U.S. primacy during and after the Cold War (see Stuart 2008). New global roles and responsibilities prompted leaders to overcome the nation's traditional distaste for standing armies and worldwide diplomatic outposts. The institutions created during the post–World War II period are much larger today and are far more complicated. As described in Chapters 4 and 5, the White House and Congress *formulate* U.S. foreign policy—that is, determine the nation's primary goals and provide the means to achieve them. Once adopted, however, executive branch agencies *implement* (or put into place) these policies, a task that places them on the front lines of U.S. foreign policy.

As described earlier, the institutions of U.S. foreign policy have become more concentrated in the White House since World War II. President Obama took this pattern to new levels when he took office in 2009, seeking most day-to-day advice from staffers in the National Security Council (NSC) who operate in close proximity to the Oval Office. Meanwhile, his secretaries of State and Defense have played a vital but more distant role, advancing their agendas and special missions assigned by the president. The resignation late in 2014 of Defense Secretary Chuck Hagel, who sought a closer advisory role, signaled "the final triumph of a White House–centric approach to national security" (Landler 2014b, A12).

Although bureaucrats behave in similar ways across industrialized countries, the distinctive features of the U.S. political system must be taken into account. The government's authority is disbursed *vertically* among local, state, and federal agencies; *horizontally* across the three branches of government; and *internally* within the bureaucracies themselves. These agencies represent strong and often independent power centers that can determine the success or failure of foreign policy initiatives. As described in Chapter 3, negotiations among bureaucrats over foreign policy powers and missions can be as exhaustive as negotiations with foreign governments. Three factors make bureaucratic managers at the federal level especially powerful:

- *Congressional deference.* While legislators play a central role in creating government agencies, they tend to leave them alone afterward. "Legislators know that presidents take their foreign policy agencies seriously," Amy Zegart (1999, 34) has observed. "Any move to eliminate, reform, or significantly reduce the funding of these organizations without presidential approval is bound to incur executive wrath and invite inter-branch conflict—a fight that presidents almost always win."

- *White House constraints.* The president is hampered by the sheer mass of policy issues and institutions that must be overseen at any given time. This gives bureaucracies substantial autonomy, or freedom of action. In contrast to the regular turnover of presidents, federal agencies are semipermanent structures with deeply entrenched self-interests, preferences, and standard operating procedures. According to a popular aphorism, "Presidents may come and go, but the bureaucracy lives forever."

- *Organizational expertise.* As specialists in their functional areas, often with many years of experience, bureaucrats "become more expert about their policy responsibilities than the elected representatives who created their bureau" (McCubbins, Noll, and Weingast 1987, 247). Elected officials, who stand to gain little by meddling in day-to-day bureaucratic functions, routinely trust agencies to implement foreign policies as they see fit. In most cases, politicians intervene only after policy breakdowns have occurred.

Because bureaucratic structures are easier to build than dismantle, the foreign policy architecture has not changed significantly since the signing of the National Security Act of 1947 (see Chapter 2), which created the National Security Council, the Department of Defense, and the CIA. Since then, the foreign policy bureaucracy has exhibited **path dependency**, a pattern by which past structural choices, informed by their architects' values and goals, push future policies in particular directions. For example, the sheer

GET THE EDGE ON YOUR STUDIES

edge.sagepub.com/hook5e

- Take a quiz to find out what you've learned.
- Review key terms with eFlashcards.
- Watch videos that enhance chapter content.

size and capacity of the Defense Department relative to the State Department may lead foreign policy makers toward military rather than diplomatic solutions. Conversely, advocates for global environmental protection have difficulty gaining traction because of the lack of a formidable federal agency charged with that mission.

The foreign policy bureaucracy is loosely arranged within four complexes, or bureaucratic clusters, which manage diplomatic relations, national security, intelligence, and economic affairs, respectively (see Figure 6.1). Each complex features "a smorgasbord of institutional types," including cabinet-level departments, subordinate agencies, diplomatic posts, military services, and special units within the Executive Office of the President (Seidman and Gilmour 1986, 249). Although the functions of these complexes overlap, their specialized roles give them advantages in their areas of expertise—and a strong basis for maintaining the institutional rivalries that afflict U.S. foreign policy on a regular basis. For many foreign policy makers, the tangled bureaucracy often becomes "our own worst enemy" (Destler, Gelb, and Lake 1984). In this respect, the elaborate system designed to advance U.S. foreign policy goals contributes further to the paradox of America's world power.

■ AGENCY DYSFUNCTIONS AND THE PARADOX OF WORLD POWER

Bureaucracies provide ballast, or stability, to government. They lend "continuity and constancy" to the federal government, which is otherwise prone to recurring changes that stem from shifting political alignments and external demands

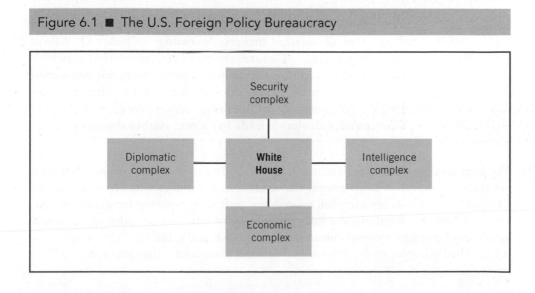

Figure 6.1 ■ The U.S. Foreign Policy Bureaucracy

(Rockman 1997, 21). Yet, as students and practitioners of bureaucratic politics well know (see Chapter 3), such organizations often fall short of the standards of rationality they were designed to achieve. This is especially true for democratic states, with their vibrant civil societies, and for major powers, with their elaborate military forces, intelligence services, and diplomatic networks. Rather than working as partners toward a common vision of the national interest, bureaucrats frequently compete with each other for resources and influence while resisting changes that threaten their institutional turf. Clashing goals, dominant self-interests, and overlapping responsibilities contribute to the fragmentation of bureaucratic authority and reinforce the paradox of world power as exercised by the United States.

These interagency tensions inevitably create long-lasting schisms between policy makers. The rivalry between Secretary of State Colin Powell and Defense Secretary Donald Rumsfeld became legendary. Bush's closer ties to the Pentagon left Powell with such a low profile that *Time* magazine asked on its cover, "Where have you gone, Colin Powell?" Struggles between the State Department and U.S. Agency for International Development (USAID) over their roles in the postwar reconstruction of Iraq created a "disconnect between what each agency is tasked to do and what it is actually oriented toward doing" (Renanah 2013, 500). The Central Intelligence Agency, meanwhile, repeatedly fought with the Defense Intelligence Agency over missions and budgets. These family feuds extended to legislative-executive relations. In his 2014 memoir, Defense Secretary Robert Gates (2014, 580) expressed deep hostility toward Congress: "I was constantly amazed and infuriated at the hypocrisy of those who most stridently attacked the Defense Department for being inefficient and wasteful, but would fight tooth and nail to prevent any reduction in defense activities in their home state or district no matter how inefficient or wasteful."

Bureaucratic behavior reflects differences in **organizational culture**, or the shared values, beliefs, and priorities of decision makers. According to James Q. Wilson (1989, 91), an expert on bureaucracy, "Culture is to an organization what personality is to an individual. Like human culture generally, it is passed from one generation to the next. It changes slowly, if at all." These orientations, in turn, affect management styles and rewards. The presence of so many departments, agencies, and bureaus in the U.S. government inevitably leads to culture clashes that persist over long periods of time.

The U.S. foreign policy bureaucracy is no exception to this rule of organizational behavior. At the State Department, the tendency of diplomats to favor negotiated settlements over military coercion contributes to their reputation for excessive caution and timidity. Similarly, the inherent secrecy of intelligence gathering creates a highly insular organizational culture within the CIA and other intelligence agencies. Within the Pentagon, each of the armed services maintains a distinct organizational

IN THEIR OWN WORDS

Condoleezza Rice *National Security Adviser Condoleezza Rice, along with other Bush adminis-*
tration officials, testified before the 9-11 Commission in April 2004. In her testimony, Rice emphasized the
institutional barriers that had prevented the U.S. government from "connecting the dots"—the numerous
clues that had indicated a large-scale terrorist attack was imminent.

The threat reporting that we received in the spring and summer of 2001 was not specific as to time, nor
place, nor manner of attack. Almost all of the reports focused on al Qaeda activities outside the United
States, especially in the Middle East and in North Africa. In fact, the information that was specific enough
to be actionable referred to terrorist operations overseas. Most often, though, the threat reporting was
frustratingly vague.

Let me read you some of the actual chatter that was picked up in that spring and summer:

"Unbelievable news coming in weeks," said one.

"Big event . . . there will be a very, very, very, very big uproar."

"There will be attacks in the near future."

Troubling, yes. But they don't tell us when; they don't tell us where; they don't tell us who; and they don't
tell us how. . . .

Throughout the period of heightened threat information, we worked hard on multiple fronts to detect, protect against and disrupt any terrorist plans or operations that might lead to an attack. For instance, the
Department of Defense issued at least five urgent warnings to U.S. military forces that al Qaeda might
be planning a near-term attack, and placed our military forces in certain regions on heightened alert. The
State Department issued at least four urgent security advisories and public worldwide cautions on terrorist
threats. . . . The FBI issued at least three nationwide warnings to federal, state and [sic] law enforcement
agencies, and specifically stated that although the vast majority of the information indicated overseas targets,
attacks against the homeland could not be ruled out. . . .

[I]n looking back, I believe that the absence of light, so to speak, on what was going on inside the country, the
inability to connect the dots, was really structural. . . . the legal impediments and the bureaucratic impediments. But I want to emphasize the legal impediments. To keep the FBI and the CIA from functioning really
as one, so that there was no seam between domestic and foreign intelligence, was probably the greatest
[impediment]. . . . [W]hen it came right down to it, this country, for reasons of history and culture, and therefore, law, had an allergy to the notion of domestic intelligence, and we were organized on that basis. And it
just made it very hard to have all of the pieces come together. . . .

Source: Condoleezza Rice, "Hearing of the National Commission on Terrorist Attacks upon the United States" (April 8, 2004),
7–9, 20, http://www.9-11commission.gov/archive/hearing9/9-11Commission_Hearing_2004-04-08.pdf.

culture—and sense of superiority over other services.[1] Such differences energize the morale of each unit and serve as valuable recruiting tools, but they can create problems by sparking public disputes over funding allocations, deployments, and the assignment of operational missions in military conflicts.

Today's foreign policy bureaucracy displays many of the same operational flaws that have hindered the U.S. government's actions in the past. Seven chronic problems, detailed recently by the Congressional Research Service (Dale, Serafino, and Towell 2008), are familiar to foreign policy makers: (1) domination of policy input by the Pentagon, (2) lack of resources for civilian agencies, (3) weak central leadership, (4) poor planning, (5) inadequate reporting across agencies, (6) lack of budget coordination, and (7) poorly structured congressional oversight. Solving all these problems will be difficult, especially as those who must reform the process are entrenched in their bureaucratic bunkers, favoring institutional survival above all else.

Chronic parochialism in the bureaucracy has prompted current foreign policy makers to encourage a "whole-of-government" approach to making foreign policy. Such an approach is considered vital as missions increasingly overlap. The Pentagon, for example, worked closely with State in responding to natural disasters such as the March 2011 earthquake and tsunami in Japan. Intelligence agencies have stepped up pressures on diplomats to share the personal information of foreign dignitaries, pressures that "appear to blur the traditional boundaries between statesmen and spies" (Mazzetti 2010, A1). Agents from the CIA, meanwhile, increasingly conduct missions with military personnel as part of the Joint Special Operations Command. Still, each bureaucracy strongly resists combined efforts that are likely to shrink their budgets, personnel, or political clout (see In Their Own Words box).

■ THE DIPLOMATIC COMPLEX

A central element of U.S. foreign policy is the conduct of **diplomacy**—the interactions among representatives of two or more sovereign states on official matters of mutual or collective concern. In particular, diplomats seek to maintain stable and functional relations with as many foreign governments as possible and to resolve interstate differences without resorting to force. The absence of tensions offers openings for constructive relations, particularly regarding commerce in which the citizens and governments of all parties involved may profit. Diplomats posted overseas also serve as the "eyes and ears" of their governments, providing leaders at home with timely firsthand information about developments in their host countries.

---

1. Long-lasting derogatory nicknames such as grunts (Army), jarheads (Marines), squids (Navy), and flyboys (Air Force) are staples of military life.

In the country's first decades, the post of chief U.S. diplomat, or secretary of state, served as a stepping-stone to the presidency. Thomas Jefferson, James Madison, James Monroe, and John Quincy Adams all became chief executives in this manner. Yet, despite this impressive showing of strong secretaries, early U.S. leaders, including the nation's third president, frowned on the routine practice of diplomacy. Jefferson, the first secretary of state, described eighteenth-century diplomacy as "the workshop in which nearly all the wars of Europe are manufactured" (quoted in R. B. Morris 1966, 43–44). In the popular imagination, the nation's early foreign policy achievements, particularly the rapid pace of continental expansion, resulted from a *rejection*, rather than an embrace, of diplomatic relations.[2]

Largely for this reason, the U.S. government did not create a full-scale foreign service until after World War I. American leaders agreed, reluctantly, that the nation's arrival as a global power required it to "dirty its hands" in diplomatic activity. Even then, State Department budgets and salaries were kept at minimal levels, and the travel and schedules of diplomats were scrutinized closely. Once the United States achieved the status of a great power, other government agencies became enmeshed in the foreign policy process. Since 1947, the U.S. government has maintained "two foreign ministries," in the State Department and the National Security Council, respectively (Rockman 1981). This blurring of foreign policy authority created problems over jurisdiction and access to the president that continue to plague the foreign service today.

Department of State

The State Department, created in 1781 as the Department of Foreign Affairs, is the U.S. government's oldest executive agency. Officials at Foggy Bottom (the State Department's Washington, D.C., headquarters, which got its informal name from the area of the city in which it is located) manage a diplomatic complex that includes foreign policy specialists based abroad and at home. As many as 60,000 federal employees from 30 agencies have been stationed in State Department offices in recent years. Duties of department employees include representing U.S. positions to foreign governments, international organizations, and private citizens while also serving as contacts for representatives of foreign governments who wish to convey their views to the U.S. government. Beyond these diplomatic tasks, the State Department serves the following six functions:

- Advising presidents on the ends and means of U.S. foreign policy
- Gathering and sharing information about recent developments overseas
- Negotiating directly with foreign governments

---

2. Foreign policy analysts from the constructivist perspective (see Chapter 3) reject many U.S. diplomatic practices as "myth." To Walter Hixson (2008, 307), widespread notions of U.S. exceptionalism contributed directly to "the nation's pathological militancy and hostility to multilateral diplomacy."

- Providing representation and services to U.S. citizens abroad

- Regulating and managing foreign travel to the United States

- Investigating solutions to transnational problems such as environmental decay, large-scale poverty, and weapons proliferation (see Chapters 11 and 12)

The secretary of state, who oversees the U.S. diplomatic complex, serves as the ranking member of the president's cabinet and stands fourth in the line of presidential succession. This official serves as the government's chief diplomat while also advising the president and overseeing the State Department bureaucracy. The task of diplomacy, which may make the difference between war and peace, is a delicate one. It requires "patience, persistence, empathy, discretion, boldness, and a willingness to talk to the enemy"—skills that were historically taken for granted but have not come easily to recent U.S. officials (R. Cohen 2013).

Beyond these formal duties, secretaries of state have played widely varying roles in presidential administrations—roles determined by the officeholder's relationship with the president and other top leaders, communications skills, and management style. Further affecting the secretary of state's role is the blurring of foreign policy authority that began after World War II, as presidents chose to rely on a larger group of foreign policy advisers. This fragmentation of authority has made life difficult for the secretary of state, who "has to use a great deal of time and energy to get anything done" (Rubin 1985, 263). Within the Obama administration, Hillary Clinton became a "rock-star diplomat" whose visits overseas commanded worldwide attention (Myers 2012). She was not, however, frequently included in the White House inner circle. Her successor, John Kerry, focused on high-profile negotiations with his foreign counterparts on such issues as climate change and Iran's nuclear program.

The secretary of state oversees an elaborate worldwide bureaucracy organized along regional and functional lines (see Figure 6.2). In 2011, the State Department employed about 72,000 employees in the United States and overseas (U.S. Department of State 2015a). Of these, about 15,000 **foreign service officers** (FSOs) operated in 275 embassies (in foreign capitals) and consulates (in other major cities). In addition to the FSOs, another 15,000 civil service workers managed State Department activities in Washington. Still others worked in related offices, including USAID and the U.S. Permanent Representative to the United Nations. Some State Department offices have a regional focus (for example, African and Near Eastern affairs) and others perform functional tasks, including arms control, economic affairs, and democracy promotion. Still other specialists handle policy planning, counterterrorism efforts, intelligence gathering, and other functions from the State Department headquarters. The State Department also hires foreign nationals who support U.S. programs overseas.

Figure 6.2 ■ U.S. Department of State

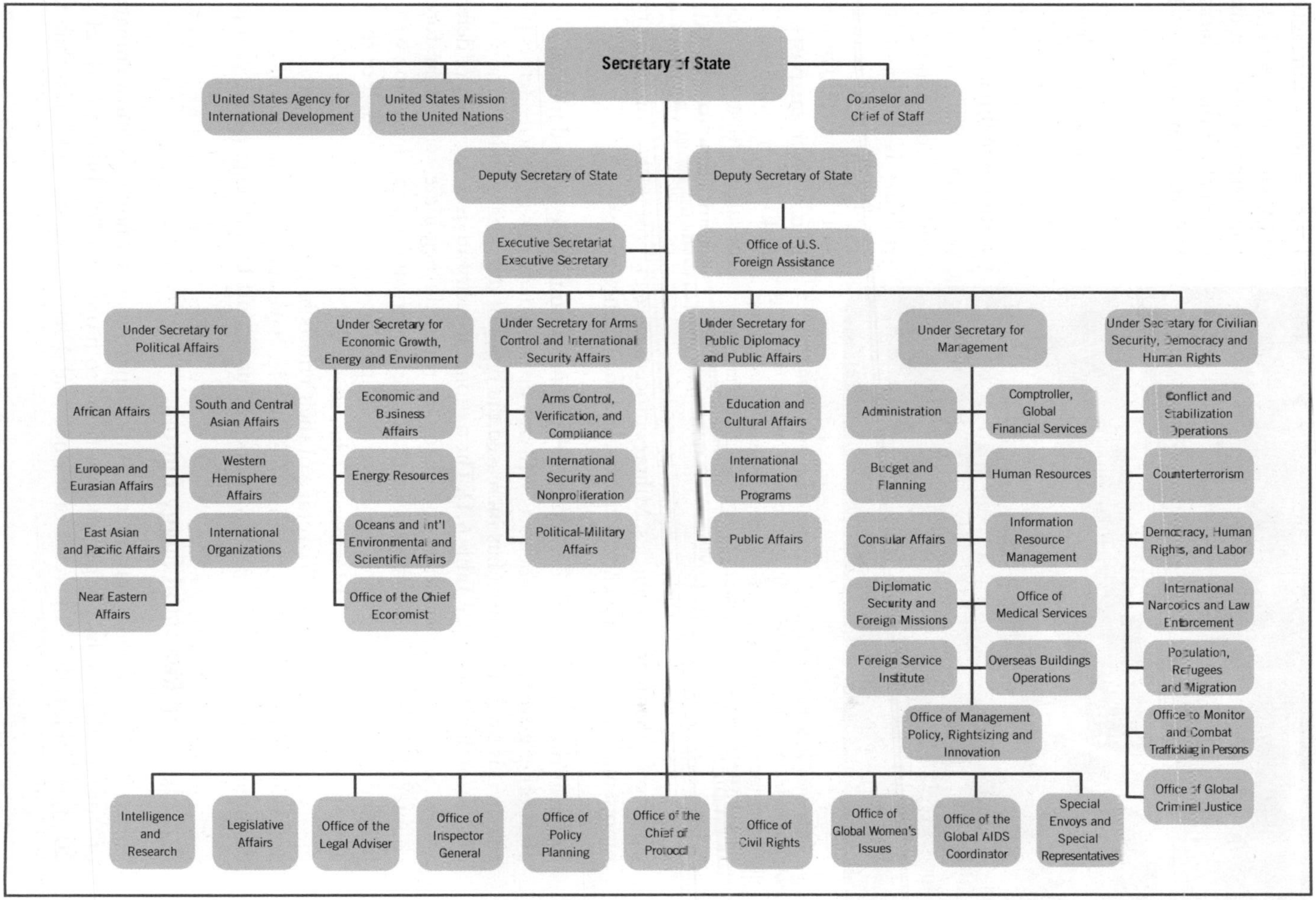

Secretary of State

- United States Agency for International Development
- United States Mission to the United Nations
- Counselor and Chief of Staff

Deputy Secretary of State
- Executive Secretariat Executive Secretary

Deputy Secretary of State
- Office of U.S. Foreign Assistance

Under Secretary for Political Affairs
- African Affairs
- South and Central Asian Affairs
- European and Eurasian Affairs
- Western Hemisphere Affairs
- East Asian and Pacific Affairs
- International Organizations
- Near Eastern Affairs

Under Secretary for Economic Growth, Energy and Environment
- Economic and Business Affairs
- Energy Resources
- Oceans and Int'l Environmental and Scientific Affairs
- Office of the Chief Economist

Under Secretary for Arms Control and International Security Affairs
- Arms Control, Verification, and Compliance
- International Security and Nonproliferation
- Political-Military Affairs

Under Secretary for Public Diplomacy and Public Affairs
- Education and Cultural Affairs
- International Information Programs
- Public Affairs

Under Secretary for Management
- Comptroller, Global Financial Services
- Administration
- Human Resources
- Budget and Planning
- Information Resource Management
- Consular Affairs
- Office of Medical Services
- Diplomatic Security and Foreign Missions
- Overseas Buildings Operations
- Foreign Service Institute
- Office of Management Policy, Rightsizing and Innovation

Under Secretary for Civilian Security, Democracy and Human Rights
- Conflict and Stabilization Operations
- Counterterrorism
- Democracy, Human Rights, and Labor
- International Narcotics and Law Enforcement
- Population, Refugees and Migration
- Office to Monitor and Combat Trafficking in Persons
- Office of Global Criminal Justice

- Intelligence and Research
- Legislative Affairs
- Office of the Legal Adviser
- Office of Inspector General
- Office of Policy Planning
- Office of the Chief of Protocol
- Office of Civil Rights
- Office of Global Women's Issues
- Office of the Global AIDS Coordinator
- Special Envoys and Special Representatives

Source: U.S. Department of State (U.S. Department of State, "Department Organizational Chart: March 2014), http://www.state.gov/documents/organization/187423.pdf.

American celebrities often voice their concerns about problems overseas. Ben Affleck, a popular movie star, has taken several trips in recent years to the Democratic Republic of Congo, a nation embattled by civil war and starvation. Affleck also testified to Congress and other government panels in order to urge greater U.S. humanitarian aid to the region.

Face-to-face interactions between FSOs and their counterparts overseas make up much of the business of U.S. foreign policy.[3] The ambassador serves as the president's official representative and the "leading protagonist, protector, and promoter" of U.S. interests within each foreign country (Kennan 1997, 207). Second in command at an embassy is the deputy chief of mission, who is responsible for the routine operation of overseas posts. This task is an imposing one, because embassies include many functional sections routinely staffed by officials from other federal agencies. Military officers serve in most posts, along with trade representatives, development specialists, and intelligence agents.

Whereas the State Department represents the institutional core of the diplomatic complex, other government agencies as well as a growing network of private actors play a role in this area. This trend has increased the types of diplomacy that are now a part of U.S. foreign policy (see Table 6.1). The national security adviser, secretary of defense, and U.S. trade representative, for example, routinely negotiate with their foreign counterparts. It is not uncommon, furthermore, for private citizens, including wealthy philanthropists like Bill Gates, to undertake diplomatic missions on behalf of the U.S. government. As described further in Chapter 8, U.S. leaders often engage the news media to provide favorable coverage of their efforts in public diplomacy (see Cowan and Cull 2008). Hollywood actors, meanwhile, have furthered the rise of **celebrity diplomacy** (A. F. Cooper 2008) by speaking out against U.S. foreign policy positions.

Criticism and Reform at Foggy Bottom

For all its constitutional stature, the State Department is among the most embattled of federal agencies. Its budget, though rising to more than $45 billion in fiscal year 2014, is still less than 2 percent of the national defense budget and far less than that

---

3. See Kopp and Gillespie (2008) and Dorman (2003) for detailed descriptions of the work of FSOs in the State Department.

for intelligence and homeland security. Though its problems stem in large part from the widespread skepticism of "Old World" diplomacy that is deeply embedded in U.S. political culture, the department faces criticism for a variety of other reasons, all of it further limiting its prestige, influence, and budgetary support. Three criticisms in particular continue to plague the State Department:

- *Elitism.* Political leaders and the general public often see diplomats as "objects of suspicion" because of "their arcane interests as well as their cosmopolitan behavior and manners" (Rubin 1985, 6). A recruitment pattern in which affluent white males from Ivy League universities have disproportionately filled the foreign service and top appointed positions has fueled this perception. In response to this criticism, Colin Powell increased the proportion of women and minorities at the State Department. Hillary Clinton, who followed Condoleezza Rice, Powell, and Madeleine Albright in the secretary of state's office, became the fourth consecutive secretary to personally break these gender and racial barriers.

- *Excessive caution.* Critics often complain that foreign service officers resist making changes or taking chances in diplomatic relations because of their determination to maintain stable relations with foreign governments. Furthermore, critics say, they avoid initiatives that may not be popular among members of Congress whose support may be needed in the future. State Department officials respond that U.S. national interests are served by maintaining congenial and reliable diplomatic relations, a point demonstrated by Clinton when she resisted the ouster of Egyptian president Hosni Mubarak during the Arab Spring of 2011. Clinton also backed the oppressive Saudi Arabian government as the uprisings spread, fearing the loss of a major strategic ally in the Middle East.

- *Clientitis.* Foreign service officers are prone to develop close relationships with governments and citizens overseas that may cloud their judgment about U.S. global priorities. "It's a disease not unique to the Foreign Service," former Secretary of State James Baker (1995, 29) observed. "Some of the worst cases of clientitis I encountered involved politically appointed ambassadors who fell so thoroughly in love with their host country and its government that they sometimes lost sight of what was in the national interest." To help prevent such compromising ties from forming, FSOs rotate every four years among overseas posts and domestic offices.[4]

In view of these criticisms and cross pressures, it is not surprising that State Department morale—long a major problem— slumped to new lows in recent years. This morale problem persisted in George W. Bush's administration despite Powell's success in increasing diversity, improving working conditions, and enhancing employee compensation. As a result, attracting and keeping skilled employees, particularly those with greatly needed language skills, has been difficult for the

---

4. Such rotation has produced its own criticism—that FSOs lack the necessary knowledge about the countries and regions in which they work.

Table 6.1 ■ The Many Faces of U.S. Diplomacy

Type	Description	Example
Celebrity	Highly publicized efforts by celebrities that draw attention to foreign policy issues	Several visits by actor Ben Affleck to the Democratic Republic of the Congo on behalf of victims of the nation's civil war (2012)
Conference	Organized events, often multilateral, that concern specific areas of U.S. foreign policy	United Nations Climate Change Conference in Copenhagen, Denmark (2009)
Digital	Use of modern telecommunications to facilitate U.S. foreign policy goals	State Department Facebook messages that yielded more than one million "likes" in the Obama administration's first seven years
Gunboat	Shows of force that compel foreign governments to support U.S. foreign policy positions	Deployment of U.S. naval forces to the coast of Japan to compel opening of trade relations with United States (1853)
Public	Efforts by U.S. leaders to gain public support for foreign policy goals	Speeches by Secretary of State Hillary Clinton to students, entrepreneurs, and activists overseas promoting U.S. "soft power" (2009–2012)
Shuttle	Direct mediation by U.S. leaders to foster agreements between warring parties	Mediation by Secretary of State Henry Kissinger to end Yom Kippur War between Israel and its Arab neighbors (1973)
Special mission	Assignment of U.S. negotiator, often not in government, to manage a specified foreign policy problem	Appointment of Richard Holbrooke to manage U.S. foreign policy efforts in Afghanistan and Pakistan (2009)
Summit	Role of U.S. presidents to sign treaties already approved by foreign governments	Signing of Intermediate-Range Nuclear Forces (INF) Treaty by President Reagan and Soviet President Mikhail Gorbachev (1987)
Two-track	Coordinated diplomacy conducted by government and private actors	U.S. economic relations with trading partners in Europe and East Asia (ongoing)

department. Recent efforts to rectify this problem have improved morale among State Department officials in Washington as well as foreign service officers. Still, filling vacant "hardship" posts in war-torn locations such as Beirut, Lebanon, and Peshawar, Pakistan, is a constant problem and weakens the State Department's diplomatic readiness (Ford 2009).

As noted in the previous chapter, the dangers faced by American diplomats became starkly clear on September 11, 2012, when J. Christopher Stevens, the U.S. ambassador to Libya, was killed along with three other U.S. officials in an attack on the U.S. mission in Benghazi. The ambassador's death, the first of its kind since 1979, turned other U.S. missions in the region into armed camps, precisely the opposite of the environment in which diplomacy thrives. According to Prudence Bushnell (2012, A29), a former ambassador to Kenya and Guatemala, "You have to get out from behind the walls and engage with people. We know this can put us in harm's way; our people in Benghazi consulate knew it. And they did their jobs anyway."

■ THE SECURITY COMPLEX

In contrast to the agencies of the diplomatic complex, the agencies of the U.S. security complex cast an immense shadow over the entire federal government, consuming much of its discretionary funding and controlling its largest workforce. In the years following World War II, the security complex grew enormously. The framework for national defense had been established early on with passage of the National Security Act of 1947 (see Chapter 2). The legislation and subsequent amendments created the National Security Council (NSC) and the National Military Establishment, which later became the Department of Defense. These institutions, which played a crucial role in waging and ultimately winning the Cold War, remained intact after the collapse of the Soviet Union in 1991. The terrorist attacks on the United States a decade later prompted a new expansion of the security complex—creation of the vast Department of Homeland Security.

National Security Council

The enhanced world role of the United States after World War II, combined with the onset of the Cold War, required a more centralized system of foreign policy making. This need led to the creation of the NSC, which since 1947 has served as the nerve center of the foreign policy process. The council comprises four statutory members, four statutory advisers, top presidential aides, and a variety of other senior government officials who attend meetings involving their areas of expertise (see Table 6.2). Based in the White House, the NSC serves three primary functions:

- *Agent of policy coordination.* The NSC attempts to establish an orderly working relationship among the many federal agencies involved in U.S. foreign policy, particularly the Defense and State Departments along with the intelligence agencies. The special assistant for national security affairs, more commonly known as the **national security adviser**, serves as a gatekeeper in the White House, controlling access to the president. Policy coordination is further promoted through an array of interagency committees that comprise "principals" (cabinet secretaries) and "deputies" (second-tier officials) who meet regularly on foreign policy matters.

- *Source of neutral policy guidance.* The national security adviser meets regularly with the president to review and interpret recent developments in U.S. foreign policy, a role formerly filled by the secretary of state. The president receives additional staff support from NSC policy experts in the White House. Of critical importance is the neutrality, or lack of institutional bias, underlying this guidance, which is an essential alternative to the parochial, self-interested advice of cabinet heads and agency directors (see J. P. Burke 2009).

- *Forum for crisis management.* Finally, the NSC provides an organizational setting for the management of national security crises. The breakout of the Cold War and the ensuing nuclear arms race created a nearly perpetual state of crisis that solidified the NSC's crisis management role. Although recent occupants of the White House have preferred ad hoc meetings of selected advisers to formal NSC meetings, the council remains a useful forum for presidents.

The NSC system has proved highly malleable over the years, assuming different shapes and roles in each presidential administration (see Daalder and Destler 2011, and Inderfurth and Johnson 2004). The rationale is that the council "must be left flexible to be molded by the President in the form most useful to him" (Tower Commission 1987, 4). Presidents Harry Truman and Dwight Eisenhower, for example, viewed the NSC warily, relying instead on their secretaries of state for advice. John F. Kennedy was the first president to use his national security adviser, McGeorge Bundy, as an active policy advocate. The national security adviser's power peaked in the Nixon

Table 6.2 ■ Members of the National Security Council (NSC)

Statutory Members	Statutory Advisers	Nonstatutory Members, Invited to All Meetings	Nonstatutory Members, Attend as Necessary
President (chair) Vice President Secretary of State Secretary of Defense	Director of National Intelligence Chair, Joint Chiefs of Staff	National Security Adviser Deputy National Security Adviser White House Chief of Staff Secretary of the Treasury	Secretary of Energy Attorney General White House Counsel Secretary of Homeland Security U.S. Representative to the United Nations Assistant to the President for Economic Policy Other Government Officials Invited by President

Source: White House, http://www.whitehouse.gov/administration/eop/nsc/.

Note: Attendance can also vary subject to topic. When economic issues are on the agenda, regular attendees also include the secretary of commerce, the U.S. trade representative, and others; when homeland security is on the agenda, the assistant to the president for homeland security and counterterrorism; and so on.

administration, when Henry Kissinger dominated the U.S. foreign policy process as no one else has before or since. Obama made his own mark on the NSC's design when he merged its staff with that of the Homeland Security Council, forming a unified National Security Staff in the White House.

Formal meetings of the NSC, particularly those during a crisis, receive most of the public's attention. The bulk of the council's work, however, involves the day-to-day examination of foreign policy problems and options by the NSC staff. Three aspects of this work have been an object of controversy and criticism.

The first concern relates to the staff's emergence as an independent power center within the security complex and a rival, rather than partner, of other federal agencies, most notably the State Department. Critics allege that NSC staff members have over-stepped their bounds by taking formal policy positions, interacting with foreign governments, and appealing to the public through the news media (Daalder and Destler 2000, 7). For example, even as Secretary of State Clinton maintained cordial relations with Robert Gates and his successor, Leon Panetta, she repeatedly clashed with the NSC over control of key foreign policy issues (Calabresi 2011, 30). The steady growth of NSC staff, from a small cohort at its inception in 1947 to more than 400 in recent years, further frustrates outsiders (Ballasy 2014). In this respect, the NSC tends to fuel rather than subdue the interagency tensions that fester daily among cabinet departments.

A second, related concern is that Congress is left out of the workings of the NSC, negating the checks and balances written into the U.S. Constitution. Unlike cabinet secretaries and other high-level presidential appointees, the national security adviser does not require Senate confirmation. Based in the Executive Office of the President, these foreign policy managers are beyond the reach of congressional oversight. In a pinch, their actions can be kept secret by a presidential claim of executive privilege.

Finally, the secretive nature of the NSC raises concerns about potential abuses from the concentration of power in the presidency. This fear was realized in the 1980s when NSC staffers conducted secret, "off-the-shelf" paramilitary operations in the Middle East and Central America, leading to the Iran-*contra* scandal. Although Ronald Reagan was the last president to permit such an operational role, his successors have consistently turned to the NSC staff knowing that their deliberations would be less likely to be revealed outside the White House.

Department of Defense

As noted earlier, the Department of Defense (DoD) is by far the largest and most expensive organization within the U.S. government. It is also the largest single employer in the United States. The military-industrial complex, which includes the contractors that provide goods and services to the DoD, employs millions of other workers, further compounding the department's economic impact (see Chapter 3). Because of its vast scale, the DoD has a predictably complex structure (see Figure 6.3). At the top of the hierarchy stands the secretary of defense, a civilian appointed by the president and confirmed by the Senate.[5] The secretary and the secretary's deputy oversee the three armed services—the U.S. Army, the U.S. Navy, and the U.S. Air Force—which in 2012 operated out of 5,211 military installations in all 50 U.S. states, seven U.S. territories, and 40 foreign countries (U.S. Department of Defense 2012, 7).[6] The DoD maintains military installations and alliances around the globe that are organized through six regional commands (see Map 6.1, Department of Defense Regional Commands).

The Joint Chiefs of Staff (JCS), composed of the leaders of all the armed services, provides guidance to the secretary of defense on military strategy and operations. This role has heightened as the Pentagon has made several changes to encourage "jointness" in military missions. The Defense Reorganization Act of 1986 (more commonly known as the **Goldwater-Nichols Act** after its congressional sponsors) altered the balance of power within the Pentagon in two distinct ways. First, the act strengthened the power of the JCS chair, who became the primary military adviser to the president and secretary of defense and was thus better able to prevent "end runs" by the individual service chiefs. Second, Goldwater-Nichols increased the power of the regional commanders in chief, who manage forces across the armed services.

The first direct beneficiary of Goldwater-Nichols was Gen. Colin Powell, chair of the JCS under Presidents George H. W. Bush and Bill Clinton. Powell used his clout to devise a blueprint for U.S. military forces after the Cold War that included large-scale cutbacks in military personnel and installations. By the mid-1990s, the U.S. Army had reduced its divisions from eighteen to ten, and the U.S. Navy had reduced its fleet from 551 to fewer than 400 ships. The Pentagon closed about 20 percent of U.S. military bases between 1998 and 2002, saving the government an estimated $30 billion initially and $6 billion a year afterward. By 2012, more than 130 bases in the United States were approved for closure. In 2015, fifteen military bases and facilities in Europe were slated for closing, a move that was estimated to save taxpayers $500 million annually (Wong 2015).

The size and scope of the Pentagon make institutional reform a continuous, but exceedingly difficult, process. In a study titled *America's Military Meltdown* (Wheeler 2008), a team of defense analysts charged that internal turf battles preoccupied policy makers in the Pentagon, preventing the White House from devising a security

---

5. On February 17, 2015, Ashton B. Carter became the nation's twenty-fifth secretary of defense. With his long history of government service and a professorship at Harvard University, Carter was chosen by President Obama to oversee a modernization of defense operations while reducing the size and budgets of the armed services.

6. A fourth armed service, the U.S. Marine Corps, is based within the Department of the Navy but operates its own network of commands and agencies. The U.S. Coast Guard, formerly controlled by the U.S. Navy in wartime, is overseen by the Department of Homeland Security (see www.dhs.gov/organization/).

Map 6.1 ■ Department of Defense Regional Commands

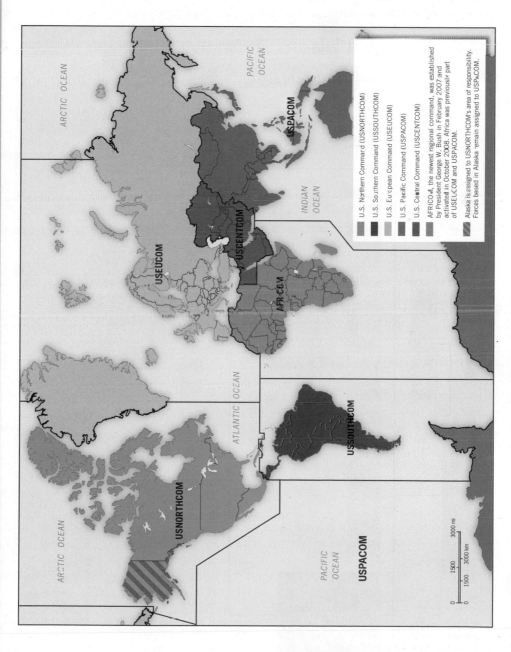

Source: U.S. Department of Defense, http://www.defense.gov/Sites/Unified-Combatant-Commands.

Figure 6.3 ■ U.S. Department of Defense

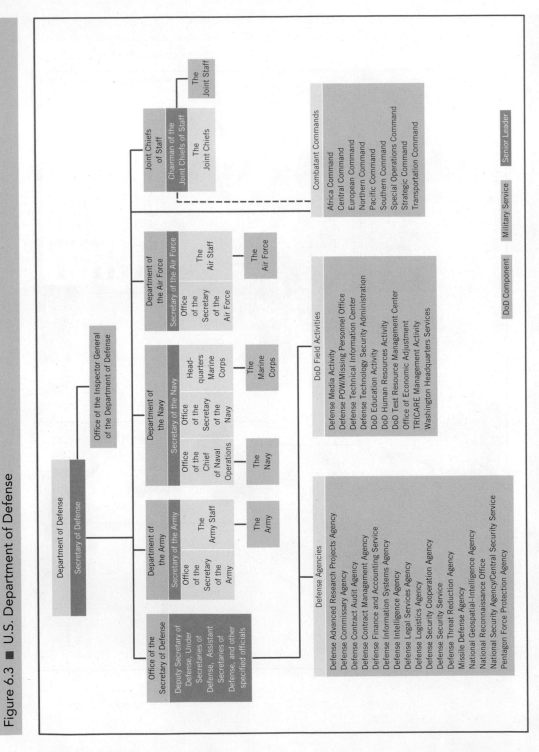

Source: Director of Administration and Management, U.S. Department of Defense, "Organization and Functions Guide," March 2012, http://odam.defense.gov/Portals/43/Documents/Functions/Organizational%20Portfolios/Organizations%20and%20Functions%20Guidebook/DoD_Organization_March_2012.pdf.

strategy that reflected current and future threats to the United States. The "great recession" that began in 2008, which propelled U.S. deficits and foreign debts to record levels, forced the Pentagon to rethink its strategic doctrine. As Mike Mullen, former chair of the Joint Chiefs of Staff, acknowledged in 2011, "Debt is the single biggest threat to our national security." Secretary of Defense Panetta, a former budget director who replaced Gates, accepted this logic by approving budget cuts that would satisfy accountants in Congress while leaving the current force structure largely intact (Jaffe 2012). More ambitious reforms, it seemed, would have to come from civilian agencies.

U.S. Military Alliances

The DoD, with its global military commands, also plays a lead role in a variety of alliances that are extensions of the U.S. security complex. Growing concerns about the Cold War prompted the United States to join forces with its Western European allies in 1949 through the creation of the North Atlantic Treaty Organization (NATO). Lord Hastings Ismay, NATO's first secretary general, succinctly captured the alliance's threefold mission: "NATO was designed to keep the Americans in, the Russians out, and the Germans down" (quoted in Yost 1998, 52). More broadly, NATO advanced the process of **regional integration** in Europe—that is, closer economic and political cooperation that offered a remedy for the chronic wars that had long ravaged the continent.

The persistence of NATO after the Cold War posed a central challenge to alliance theory, which held that alliances naturally dissolve when their stated adversaries are defeated (see Walt 1987, 26–27). NATO has not only endured since 1991: it has steadily grown larger as well (see Asmus 2002). The first round of NATO "enlargement" added the Czech Republic, Hungary, and Poland in 1999 (see Map 6.2, NATO Expansion). Seven other Eastern European countries—Bulgaria, Estonia, Latvia, Lithuania, Romania, Slovakia, and Slovenia—joined the alliance in 2004, bringing the total membership to twenty-six. For these countries, joining NATO affirmed their broader membership in the West, their former nemesis.

The "enlargement" process unfolded as NATO members identified new roles for the alliance long after the accomplishment of its original primary mission. In taking command of the International Security Assistance Force (ISAF) in Afghanistan in August 2003, thousands of NATO troops embarked on the first "out-of-area" mission in the alliance's history. At its peak of 130,000 troops, the ISAF mission grew beyond NATO and consisted of 51 "partner" states. The missions of each country varied, and in some cases NATO governments, facing domestic impatience with the mission, withdrew their forces before their scheduled departures (Auerswald and Saideman 2014). By 2014, Afghan forces assumed full responsibility for the nation's security, and the ISAF mission ended.

The alliance, meanwhile, turned its attention on Eastern Europe, where Russian aggression in Ukraine caused fears among neighboring NATO states. Russian president Vladimir Putin had long complained about the alliance's eastward expansion, which he considered a direct threat to Moscow. His decision in 2014 to escalate military exercises at sea and in the air prompted even greater anxiety for America's allies. In response, NATO leaders created a rapid-reaction force in 2015 that extended from the Baltic to the Black seas. According to NATO's secretary general, Jens Stoltenberg (2015), "We are taking these steps in response to our changed security environment." The DoD also continues to support other alliances. These include the Rio Treaty, formed in 1947 with Latin American states as part of the U.S. effort to contain Soviet communism. The same motives led the United States to create a three-way alliance with Australia and New Zealand in 1951. Finally, the United States maintains formal bilateral alliances with Japan and South Korea, two countries whose strategic importance and security ties to Washington also have endured decades after the end of the Cold War. These alliances, combined with dozens of informal security agreements with allies, reflect past U.S. commitments while foreshadowing potential future military interventions.

Department of Homeland Security

The September 11 terrorist attacks shattered the sense of invulnerability Americans had enjoyed throughout the nation's history. Suddenly, the United States found itself joining dozens of other countries for which the trauma of global terrorism was a fact of life. Seven months before the attacks, the U.S. Commission on National Security/21st Century (2001, 10) had found the U.S. government to be "very poorly organized to design and implement any comprehensive strategy to protect the homeland" [italics deleted]. The onset of the war on terror produced calls for new institutions to bolster the country against its enemies. In this case, the institutions were intended to guard against future catastrophic attacks at home while supporting rapid responses to such attacks should they occur.

One of President George W. Bush's first actions after the events of September 11 was to create the Office of Homeland Security by executive order. Based in the White House, the office was to take a lead role in protecting the United States against future attacks on U.S. territory. Bush appointed Tom Ridge, the former governor of Pennsylvania, to the new position of homeland security adviser. It soon became obvious, however, that the U.S. government needed more than a White House office to assume the formidable burdens of homeland security. This prompted the creation in March 2003 of the Department of Homeland Security (DHS), which brought more than 180,000 employees from 22 federal agencies together under one institutional roof (see Figure 6.4). These agencies included, among others, the U.S. Coast Guard, U.S. Customs and Border Protection, Secret Service, Citizenship and Immigration Services, Transportation Security Administration, and Federal Emergency Management Agency (FEMA).

Map 6.2 ■ NATO Expansion

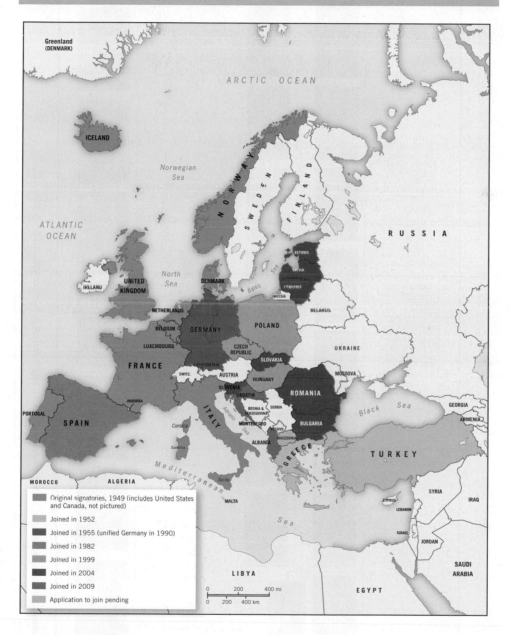

Original signatories, 1949 (includes United States and Canada, not pictured)

Joined in 1952

Joined in 1955 (unified Germany in 1990)

Joined in 1982

Joined in 1999

Joined in 2004

Joined in 2009

Application to join pending

Sources: Various primary and secondary sources, including North Atlantic Treaty Organization, "Enlargement," http://www.nato.int/cps/en/natohq/topics_81136.htm.

Figure 6.4 ■ U.S. Department of Homeland Security

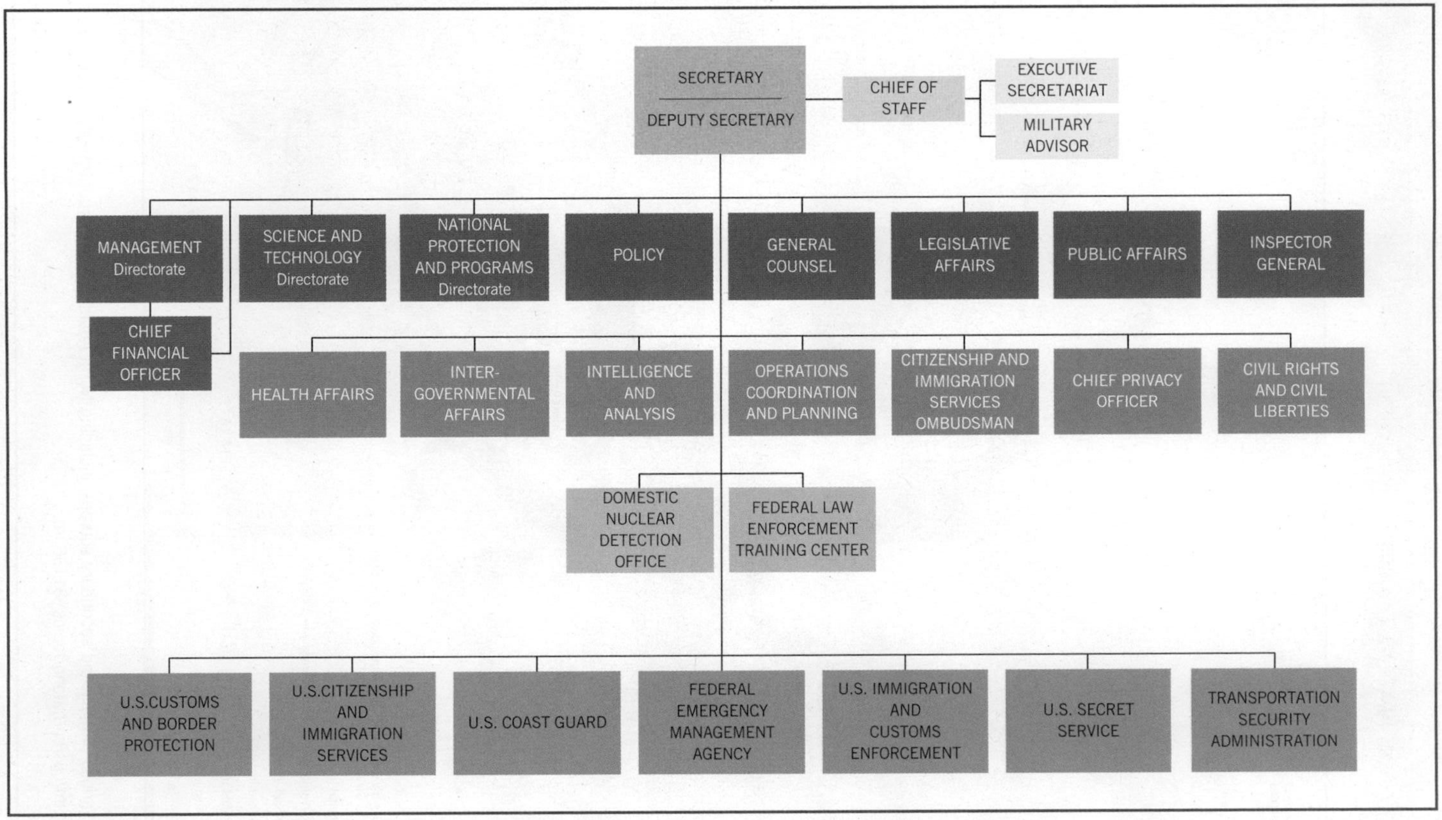

Source: Department of Homeland Security, "Organizational Chart," 2012, http://www.dhs.gov/xlibrary/assets/dhs-orgchart.pdf.

The DHS, which became the third largest among federal agencies in personnel, managed a budget that reached nearly $65 billion by fiscal year 2016 (see Department of Homeland Security 2015). Alongside its primary mission to prevent terrorist attacks in the United States, the agency pursues the following core missions:

- Securing U.S. borders
- Managing immigration
- Responding to natural disasters
- Safeguarding cyberspace

The vast scope of this endeavor guaranteed that the DHS would face serious challenges. As noted throughout this chapter, efforts to merge federal agencies and functions often succumb to clashing organizational cultures, disputes over budgets and missions, and other forms of bureaucratic rivalry. These problems were compounded within the DHS, an unwieldy unit that many agencies did not want to join. Officials and legislative allies of the FBI, for example, made it clear that proposals to add the bureau to the DHS roster would be dead on arrival. "Far from being greater than the sum of its parts," journalist Michael Crowley (2004, 17) observed, "DHS is a bureaucratic Frankenstein, with clumsily stitched together limbs and an inadequate, misfiring brain." Early problems at DHS included a color-coded national alert system that only seemed to confuse Americans and a lethargic response by FEMA to Hurricane Katrina in August 2005.

Having suffered through troublesome growing pains, DHS succeeded in several areas, including improved coordination with the hundreds of state and local agencies that would be thrust onto the front lines of a domestic disaster. The agency's response in October 2012 to Superstorm Sandy, whose destruction affected twenty-four states, was widely praised. Technological advances also allowed DHS officials to monitor travel into and outside the United States. Still, serious internal problems remained at DHS, which in 2014 had the lowest level of morale among all federal agencies (Markon, Nakashima, and Crites 2014). Workers expressed frustration with the chronic overlaps in missions across the bureaucracy. Among other complaints, they pointed to seemingly endless demands for reports from the ninety committees and subcommittees in Congress that were involved with homeland security. The chronic turnover could be seen at the top, with senior officials commonly leaving after one year and gaining more lucrative job offers in the private sector.

■ THE INTELLIGENCE COMPLEX

Foreign policy makers have long relied on the gathering of timely information about conditions and developments in other countries that might affect their national interests. Intelligence gathering, the "first line of defense" in foreign policy, has been especially critical for the United States since its arrival as a global superpower after World War II. The attack on Pearl Harbor in 1941 revealed the tragic consequences of faulty intelligence. By contrast, sound intelligence gathering, as demonstrated during the Cuban missile crisis, has proved to be invaluable. The phrase "knowledge is power" is nowhere more applicable than in the field of intelligence.

The chronic tensions between centralized authority and bureaucratic fragmentation that characterize the federal government are particularly troubling to the intelligence complex, whose member agencies have long demanded strict independence in carrying out their missions. This pattern emerged during World War II and continued into the Cold War. President Harry Truman, more determined to unify the armed services than the intelligence agencies after World War II, made the latter a low priority (Zegart 1999). The National Security Act of 1947 paved the way for the establishment of the CIA but left other intelligence units intact. These agencies maintained their independence to protect their sources and avoid interference from other agencies. While such parochialism was natural for intelligence agents, who pride themselves on secrecy, it impeded the U.S. government's effort to anticipate and respond to overseas threats.

Many government officials and outside experts believed the collapse of the Soviet Union in 1991 would lessen the need for foreign intelligence. The outbreak of regional crises in the early 1990s and the subsequent rise of Islamist terrorism, however, soon revealed that gathering such information must remain a critical element of U.S. security policy (Hilsman 2000). Today's intelligence comes not only from rival governments but from a highly diffuse array of terrorist groups, drug cartels, criminal syndicates, clans, provincial warlords, religious organizations, and transnational banks. In confronting the Soviet Union, Washington's main obstacle was a lack of information. The current challenge is the polar opposite: making sense of an unending tidal wave of intercepted phone conversations, Internet postings, news media reports, financial records, and other sources.

Paradoxically, America's open society makes it an "open book" for its current adversaries, which closely guard information, operate in secret, and are extremely difficult to penetrate. In contrast, these groups and their state sponsors find it relatively easy to learn about developments in the United States. To identify internal divisions within the government or to learn about new foreign policy initiatives, these adversaries need look no further than the twenty-four-hour U.S. news networks or the televised congressional hearings and debates on C-SPAN (see Chapter 8). This **intelligence gap** between open and closed societies contributed directly to al Qaeda's 9/11 attacks.

Although their missions vary, intelligence agencies are involved primarily in the process of converting **raw intelligence**—information collected from various sources usually without their knowledge or permission—into **finished intelligence**—information made useful to policy makers. The information gathered in this process takes three forms: **human intelligence** (or **HUMINT**), which comes from informants and other personal sources; **signal intelligence** (or **SIGINT**), which is derived from intercepted communications; and **image intelligence** (or **IMINT**), which comes from the recorded surveillance from satellites and military aircraft. Each intelligence agency manages an intelligence cycle that includes five stages:

- *Planning and direction*—identifying what information policy makers require
- *Collection*—gathering information from various sources
- *Processing*—transcribing, translating, and decrypting information and processing digital images and other visual data
- *Analysis*—clarifying and interpreting messages to guide policy makers
- *Dissemination*—sending intelligence to the proper authorities, a task undertaken with great care given that policy makers can be overwhelmed by the huge volume of potentially vital information that is collected

In addition to these standard functions, intelligence agencies engage in two other activities. The first, **counterintelligence**, involves safeguarding of classified data within the agency and the "acquisition of information or activity designed to neutralize hostile intelligence services" (Richelson 1985, 3). Although much of this information can be found by intercepting the internal messages of foreign governments, U.S. agents must in many cases penetrate these governments, often by recruiting—and rewarding—informants in their own bureaucracies. The second activity, executing secret or **covert operations**, is designed to change foreign governments by force in ways that are favorable to the United States (Prados 1996). These "covert ops"—involving spies in the field rather than analysts within the Beltway—played a major role in the Cold War and are conducted regularly in U.S. foreign policy today.

Today, the intelligence community consists of seventeen units, including an Office of the Director of National Intelligence (ODNI) that attempts to integrate the findings of the other units (see Figure 6.5). Nine of the agencies are managed by the Department of Defense (R. A. Best and Bazan 2006). Six nondefense agencies are also part of the intelligence complex. The Energy, State, and Treasury Departments manage their own intelligence units, as does the Department of Homeland Security. Within the Justice Department, the FBI and the Drug Enforcement Agency have also expanded their intelligence functions in recent years. As it has since World War II, the CIA plays a key role in gathering intelligence and carrying out covert operations overseas. Although these agencies pursue distinctive missions and specialized roles, they often fall prey to the pattern of bureaucratic competition that became a defining feature of the intelligence complex at its inception. The FBI, which had formerly focused on fighting domestic crimes, adopted counterterrorism as its primary function after the 9/11 terrorist attacks. This shift did not come easily to the Bureau, and legal restrictions limited the extent to which the FBI could meld its intelligence and criminal investigations.

Figure 6.5 ■ Hub and Spokes: The Intelligence Complex

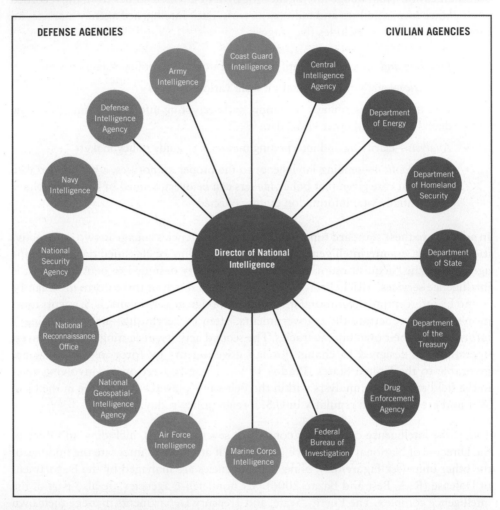

DEFENSE AGENCIES

CIVILIAN AGENCIES

- Coast Guard Intelligence
- Army Intelligence
- Central Intelligence Agency
- Defense Intelligence Agency
- Department of Energy
- Navy Intelligence
- Department of Homeland Security
- National Security Agency
- Director of National Intelligence
- Department of State
- National Reconnaissance Office
- Department of the Treasury
- National Geospatial-Intelligence Agency
- Drug Enforcement Agency
- Air Force Intelligence
- Federal Bureau of Investigation
- Marine Corps Intelligence

Source: Office of the Director of National Intelligence, "Seventeen Agencies and Organizations United under One Goal," 2012.

The 9/11 attacks offered foreign policy makers a golden opportunity to bring order to the government's far-flung intelligence community. Acting on the recommendations of the 9-11 Commission, Congress approved and President Bush signed the Intelligence Reform and Terrorism Prevention Act of 2004. The measure created the ODNI to oversee the activities of each agency and to serve as the primary source of intelligence to the president, military commanders, and Congress. In addition, the act created the National Counterterrorism Center, based in McLean, Virginia, to integrate intelligence findings and anticipate future attacks.

Beyond this important reform, the intelligence complex has retained its complicated Cold War structure (see Figure 6.5), most recently with a combined budget of nearly $70 billion in fiscal year 2014 (Federation of American Scientists 2015). The Pentagon still manages its own Defense Intelligence Agency, separate intelligence units in each of the armed services, and three other agencies that support its intelligence mission:

- The National Security Agency, which provides intercepted electronic communications to foreign policy makers
- The National Reconnaissance Office, which manages the nation's spy satellites
- The National Geospatial-Intelligence Agency, which supplies intelligence used by U.S. leaders for tracking troop deployments, refugee flows, and other information

Since its inception, bureaucratic rivalries have hampered the ODNI's ability to coordinate U.S. intelligence. The CIA has retained much of its authority to recruit spies and to funnel money to friendly governments and pro-American rebel groups. Given their need for secrecy, intelligence agents "have tended to err on the side of maintaining the security of information even at the cost of not sharing information with those having a need to know" (R. A. Best 2011, 4). Attempted reforms have failed to resolve the simmering tensions between the CIA and the FBI, although the two agencies have little choice but to work closely together given the growing overlap between domestic and foreign intelligence. These cross-pressures fall on the ODNI, who is ultimately responsible for the performance of all intelligence agencies. The frequent turnover of ODNIs prompted Obama to describe the ODNI as "the most thankless job in Washington." Clearly, attempts to integrate or even coordinate intelligence functions have not produced harmony within the intelligence complex.

Intelligence Failures and Scandals

The CIA and other intelligence agencies played vital roles in achieving the central goals for which they were created during the Cold War: "containing" communism and contributing to the demise of the Soviet Union. In some instances, including the 1962 Cuban missile crisis, intelligence breakthroughs saved the United States from imminent threats.

Defenders of the intelligence complex claim that the record of U.S. intelligence agencies is stronger than generally believed. According to Robert Gates (1996, 562), who served as the CIA director before becoming secretary of defense, the fact that there were "no significant strategic surprises" in the Cold War owed much to sound intelligence reporting. In the 1980s, CIA-sponsored assistance to anti-Soviet militants in Afghanistan played a significant role in hastening Moscow's withdrawal from that

From 2001 to 2004, a primary target of criticism in the U.S. war on terrorism was George Tenet, the Director of the Central Intelligence Agency. Tenet, who was appointed to the post by President Clinton, fought an uphill battle defending the CIA's record prior to the attacks of September 11 and gathering intelligence about the threat posed by Saddam Hussein's regime in Iraq. Congressional investigators concluded that faulty intelligence contributed to U.S. setbacks in the war on terrorism. Tenet resigned from his post in June 2004, citing "personal reasons."

country a decade after its 1979 invasion (Coll 1992). More recently, the agency in 2010 was successful in rupturing parts of Iran's nuclear program through cyberattacks on the program's computer systems. The CIA was praised for its role in locating Osama bin Laden in a Pakistani residential compound, which led to his capture and killing by U.S. special forces in 2011. Two years later, intelligence agents thwarted plans by al Qaeda in the Arabian Peninsula to attack multiple U.S. diplomatic offices in Yemen (Morell 2015, xv).

Accompanying this success, however, has been a variety of problems that have damaged the intelligence complex's credibility. To defense analyst John Diamond (2008, 15), "The sixty-year history of the CIA is pockmarked with failures, whether botched or illegal covert operations, failures to warn of foreign invasions, or lying by Agency officers in testimony to Congress or to government investigators." Five problems in particular remain acute:

- *Strategic surprises.* U.S. security interests have been damaged repeatedly by events overseas that intelligence agencies were expected to anticipate and, if possible, prevent (see Table 6.3). Japan's 1941 attack on U.S. naval forces at Pearl Harbor, Hawaii, and the al Qaeda attacks on the U.S. homeland in September 2001 remain the most notorious such surprises. Among other prominent examples, U.S. presidents were surprised by North Korea's attack on South Korea in 1950, by the overthrow of the shah of Iran and the Soviet invasion of Afghanistan in 1979, and by the entry of India and Pakistan into the nuclear club in 1998 (Auster and Kaplan 1998). Other, more subtle lapses have also been significant. Estimates of the Soviet Union's military and economic power, for example, were exaggerated repeatedly throughout the Cold War, a pattern that swelled Pentagon budgets and provoked U.S. interventions in regional conflicts that may not have been necessary (see Goodman 2008, ch. 6).

- *Operational failures.* Efforts by intelligence agents to influence political and military developments overseas frequently create additional problems for the United States. When a lightly armed brigade of Cuban "freedom fighters" was crushed by government forces in 1961, for example, it turned out that the CIA had trained and armed the rebels before their tragic assault at the Bay of Pigs. As a result, U.S.

credibility was immensely damaged throughout the world: The failed overthrow of Fidel Castro's regime revealed not only that the U.S. government had been involved but also that it had acted incompetently. Similarly, secret U.S. missions to arm antigovernment rebels in Nicaragua in the 1980s failed to unseat the communist regime while provoking widespread criticism of the United States for meddling in the internal affairs of a sovereign country.

- *Internal security.* The nation's interests are also damaged when agents in the intelligence complex are found to be working on behalf of foreign governments. One of the most troubling cases was the arrest in 1994 of Aldrich Ames, a career CIA officer who sold military secrets to the Soviet Union and Russia for more than $2 million. Ames compromised dozens of CIA missions, and his leaks to Moscow led to the deaths of at least ten Soviet agents secretly working for the United States. The CIA was not alone in failing to maintain internal security. Robert Hanssen, an FBI agent, passed more than 6,000 pages of highly classified documents to the Soviet and Russian governments over a twenty-one-year period in return for payments exceeding $1.4 million.

- *Politicized intelligence.* The deliberate manipulation of findings about conditions overseas to promote an administration's foreign policy preferences creates additional problems for members of the intelligence community. A common complaint during the Cold War was that estimates of Soviet power were exaggerated to generate domestic support for higher levels of U.S. military spending. The same charges were articulated during the Vietnam War, when investigators found that the Nixon administration had encouraged the CIA to inflate reports of communist influence in Southeast Asia. More recently, congressional investigators concluded that the George W. Bush administration distorted intelligence on the presence of weapons of mass destruction in Iraq (U.S. Senate 2004; Jervis 2010). According to a former CIA analyst who served under several presidents, including Bush, the White House first "bullied" the CIA to skew its reports so they would support White House decisions and then blamed the agency for the setbacks that plagued the war effort (Pillar 2011).

- *Domestic surveillance.* The National Security Agency drew criticism during the Bush years when it engaged in domestic surveillance of American citizens, primarily by tapping phone lines and Internet transmissions, without the requisite court orders. These actions violated the Foreign Intelligence Surveillance Act (FISA) of 1978, which sought to ease the fears of many Americans that a "Big Brother" in Washington, D.C., would violate their privacy rights and individual freedoms. Bush circumvented these restrictions, claiming that it would be perilous for the White House to seek court permission to spy on the large number of suspects who posed an imminent danger to the United States. On a far larger scale, the NSA was found in 2014 to be engaged in wholesale data mining of Americans' electronic communications when Edward Snowden, an NSA contractor, leaked thousands of classified files to the news media (see Chapter 8). It was also revealed that the U.S. government was spying on American allies, including Germany's Chancellor Angela Merkel, whose cell phone calls were being tapped.

Table 6.3 ■ Caught by Surprise: Major U.S. Intelligence Failures, 1941–2015

Year	Event
1941	Japanese attack on Pearl Harbor
1950	Outbreak of Korean War
1956	Soviet military crackdown in Hungary Outbreak of Suez Canal crisis
1957	Soviet launch of Sputnik satellite
1962	Soviet nuclear weapons in Cuba
1968	Tet Offensive in Vietnam Soviet military crackdown in Czechoslovakia
1973	Outbreak of Six-Day War in Middle East
1979	Soviet invasion of Afghanistan Iranian revolution; takeover of U.S. embassy
1980	Iraqi invasion of Iran
1982	Terrorist attack on U.S. marines in Lebanon
1990	Iraqi invasion of Kuwait
1991	Collapse of Soviet Union
1994	Genocide in Rwanda and Burundi
1998	Nuclear tests in Pakistan and India
2001	Terrorist attacks on New York City and Washington, D.C.
2003	Absence of weapons of mass destruction in Iraq following U.S. invasion
2009	Attempted destruction of U.S. commercial jet by Nigerian terrorist
2011	Death of Kim Jong-il, North Korea's "supreme leader"
2012	Terrorist attack on U.S. consulate in Benghazi, Libya
2013	Terrorist attack on Boston Marathon
2014	Russian annexation of Crimean Peninsula Rise and expansion of Islamic State
2015	Terrorist attack on California target

Sources: Amy B. Zegart, *Spying Blind: The CIA, the FBI, and the Origins of 9/11* (Princeton, NJ: Princeton University Press, 2009); Melvin A. Goodman, *Failure of Intelligence: The Decline and Fall of the CIA* (Lanham, MD: Rowman & Littlefield, 2008); other sources.

Growing Reliance on Covert Operations

When the CIA was created in 1947, its mission statement identified the gathering of intelligence as its primary role. Little was said about the agency's "operational" role, which began with a large-scale effort (Operation Gladio) to undermine communist movements in Western Europe. The CIA's secret (or covert) operations expanded steadily in the years to come and included the overthrows of elected leaders in Iran (1953), Guatemala (1954), Indonesia (1965), and Chile (1973), among other countries.[7] President John F. Kennedy approved several CIA attempts to assassinate Cuba's leader, Fidel Castro, all of which failed. In 1963, Kennedy supported coups in South Vietnam and the Dominican Republic that led to the murders of their leaders—Ngo Ninh Diem and Rafael Trujillo, respectively. The CIA's covert operations extended internally as well, as the Johnson and Nixon administrations approved domestic spying and censorship of critics of the Vietnam War.

American policy makers justified these covert operations as vital to the nation's effort to "contain" communism. Even so, the tactics employed by CIA agents often contradicted the political values widely promoted by the United States, not to mention violating national and international laws. The uncovering of CIA involvement in these cases proved embarrassing to the agency and provoked anti-American backlash in the countries involved. In response to these spillover effects of covert operations, the Senate and the House of Representatives created select committees in 1976 to oversee the intelligence complex in general and the CIA in particular, which Sen. Frank Church (D-ID) charged had become a "rogue elephant."[8] The **Church Committee,** as the Senate body became known, found many CIA operations to be abuses of presidential power. President Gerald Ford later signed an executive order that prohibited political assassinations by the U.S. government.

The CIA's operational role expanded rapidly after the 9/11 attacks. From its inception, the agency "evolved from an agency devoted to its mission of spying on foreign governments to one whose current priority is tracking and killing individual militants in an increasing number of countries" (Dreazen and Naylor 2015, 38). These "special activities," managed by the CIA's National Clandestine Service, included Osama bin Laden's capture and killing in 2011 (see Mazzetti 2014). The Pentagon, meanwhile, has challenged the CIA's exclusive control over covert operations. Its Joint Special Operations Command has "grown from a rarely used hostage rescue team into America's secret army" (Priest and Arkin 2011). Covert operatives face an uphill battle due to the nature of counterterrorism. The use of HUMINT is generally out of the question given the difficulty and danger of infiltrating terror cells. The most organized groups are widely disbursed, are difficult to locate, and are very careful not to send electronic signals that could be intercepted by U.S. intelligence. Penetrating these groups has become a constant and frustrating challenge.

---

7. The CIA conducted more than 900 major covert operations and thousands of smaller ones between 1961 and 1974 (U.S. Senate 1976, 445).

8. The status of these intelligence committees as "select" rather than "standing" gives the party leadership in each chamber greater power to appoint members—a power deemed necessary because of the sensitive nature of national intelligence.

Military Use of Drones

The use of military drones has spurred an intense debate in the United States and overseas. Public opinion surveys consistently found broad public support for the use of drones against suspected terrorists; about one-half supported attacks on American citizens abroad who were found to be engaged in terrorism. The view from overseas was far more negative. In 2014, a majority of citizens surveyed in 37 of 44 countries opposed the U.S. drone program (see Chapter 7).

President Obama shared his predecessor's enthusiasm for **drone warfare**. "Conventional airpower or missiles are far less precise than drones, and are likely to cause more civilian casualties and more local outrage," the president said. "And invasions of these territories lead us to be viewed as occupying armies, unleash a torrent of unintended consequences, are difficult to contain, result in large numbers of civilian casualties, and ultimately empower those who thrive on violent conflict." The president, along with most members of Congress, favored the use of drones over the deployment of ground forces, particularly in distant hot spots where the deployment of "boots on the ground" would likely produce American casualties. Finally, fiscal conservatives point to the lower cost of drone warfare compared with conventional military tactics. As an influential U.S. think tank concluded, "Unmanned systems have saved American lives, saved noncombatant lives, and imposed high costs on the enemy."

Critics of drone warfare raise four key concerns. First, they question whether the lethal attacks are legal, alleging that the actions violate U.S. and international law. A United Nations report argued that the practice has led to "the displacement of clear legal standards with a vaguely defined licence to kill, and the creation of a major accountability vacuum." A second problem relates to the debilitating effects of drones on the day-to-day lives of civilians in war zones. "Drones hover twenty-four hours a day . . . striking homes, vehicles, and public spaces without warning," an academic study observed. "Their presence terrorizes men, women, and children, giving rise to anxiety and psychological trauma among civilian communities. Those living under drones have to face the constant worry that a deadly strike may be fired at any moment, and the knowledge that they are powerless to protect themselves." Third, drone attacks have repeatedly missed their targets, leading to the deaths of civilians, including American citizens. Fourth, critics believe that U.S. drone attacks set a dangerous precedent for future wars and will invite future blowback, or violent retribution against the United States for resorting to this tactic. Terrorist groups have openly cited drone attacks as a basis for anti-Americanism and their own recruitment efforts.

Sources: Pew Research Center. 2014. *Global Opposition to U.S. Surveillance and Drones, but Limited Harm to America's Image.* Washington, DC: Pew Research Center, July; White House. 2013. *Remarks by the President at the National Defense University.* May 23. Washington, DC: The White House; Samuel Brannan. 2014. *Sustaining the U.S. Lead in Unmanned Systems.* Washington, DC: Center for Security and International Studies; Philip Alston. 2010. *Report of the Special Rapporteur on Extrajudicial, Summary or Arbitrary Executions.* New York: United Nations; Stanford Law School and New York University School of Law. 2012. *Living under Drones: Death, Injury, and Trauma to Civilians from U.S. Drone Practices in Pakistan.* Palo Alto, CA: Stanford Law School, September, *vii.*

Among other responses, the U.S. government turned to a growing fleet of unmanned **aerial drones**, which conducted remote-controlled bombing raids against suspected leaders of al Qaeda, the Taliban, and other hostile groups (see Bergen and Tiedemann 2011). Most of these drones conduct surveillance and reconnaissance missions, but Predator and Reaper drones are equipped with powerful missiles used to kill known terrorists. Whereas 95 percent of U.S. assault aircraft were manned in 2005, more than 40 percent had no pilots (Gertler 2012, 9). Under the system established to conduct drone attacks, the National Counterterrorism Center prepares lists of specific targets, which are then reviewed by the NSC and the CIA director. The president then decides whether or not to launch attacks on recommended targets.

The U.S. government had used primitive surveillance drones beginning in the 1990s during the civil war in the former Yugoslavia and the Gulf War. After 9/11, the first bombing raid targeted terrorists in Afghanistan in October 2001. President Bush approved forty-six **targeted killings** on his watch, most of which were focused on the Afghan-Pakistani border. The Obama administration rapidly expanded the program. By the end of 2012, an estimated 411 drone strikes had killed 3,430 enemies and left 401 civilians dead (Zenko 2013, 13). The bombing attacks, which also struck targets in Afghanistan, Yemen, and Somalia on several occasions, have proven highly controversial (see Point/Counterpoint). A January 2015 drone strike in Pakistan, which accidentally killed two hostages, including the American Warren Weinstein, fueled further concerns. Neither Congress nor the courts have effectively challenged U.S. actions that seem to critics to be "extralegal," and press reports of drone attacks have elicited little concern among the public. Although the select committees on intelligence have enhanced Congress's oversight role, the executive branch's refusal to provide full disclosure has frustrated lawmakers who complained of the "high degree and pervasiveness of secrecy surrounding intelligence policy, information, activities, operations, resources, and personnel" (Halchin and Kaiser 2012, 1, 34).

The use of aerial drones appears to be a permanent feature of modern warfare. More than seventy-five countries, including China, Russia, India, Iran, and Israel have acquired drone technology. The Russian government has moved forward on deploying drones on a defensive basis. In May 2015, Obama amended U.S. regulations for weapons sales that would allow the export of drones to U.S. allies. Meanwhile, the development of drones for dozens of commercial, governmental, and scientific uses further ensures the future of this new airborne technology.

■ THE ECONOMIC COMPLEX

This chapter now turns to the fourth component of the U.S. foreign policy bureaucracy, the economic complex. The end of the Cold War permitted American leaders to broaden their foreign policy agendas from concerns based primarily on military security, or geopolitics, to include concerns regarding the growing interaction of national markets in the world economy, or **geoeconomics**. Among other consequences of the end of the Cold War was the widening support among governments for market-based economies rather than those dominated or strictly controlled by states. The U.S. model of free enterprise and open markets became a role model of sorts for the postcommunist states of Eastern Europe and for many less-developed countries that embraced the "Washington consensus" on free trade in return for economic aid from the United States.

The impact of geoeconomics becomes stronger as national and regional markets give way to a more integrated—and regulated—global economy. Agreements on trade and foreign investment increasingly require a unified set of labor and human rights standards, immigration policies, environmental protections, and provisions for financial record keeping. For the United States, the emergence of China as a peer competitor in the global economy is a primary rationale for predictions of American decline and the end of the unipolar balance of world power (see Friedberg 2011). These pressures have also led Washington to pursue closer trade and investment ties with other "Asian Tigers" in the Pacific region.

Promoting national prosperity is, of course, an intermestic concern, with both international and domestic components. Well-organized groups represent the interests of private actors to the federal government, which provides many points of access within the executive and legislative branches. Congress plays a larger role in economic affairs than in national security. The regulatory powers approved by Congress in areas such as labor practices, environmental standards, and product safety affect business activity in the United States and the commercial relations of U.S. firms with their foreign counterparts. Congress also must approve major trade agreements, although it has largely deferred to the executive branch in this area.

Federalism is another major factor in foreign economic policy. American governors and mayors eagerly pursue foreign markets for the goods and services produced by their constituents. At the same time, states and cities compete with one another for the attention of foreign-owned firms planning to set up shop in the United States. The outcome of this internal competition has long-lasting implications for American political, as well as economic, relations abroad. At the federal level, various agencies such as the Treasury and Commerce Departments have long engaged in different aspects of economic affairs.

The most important structural change in the economic complex occurred after World War II with the creation of the World Bank and the International Monetary Fund (IMF). These bodies, which are based in Washington while relying on financial support from other countries, serve as institutional extensions of the U.S. economic model (T. Carroll 2010). The General Agreement on Tariffs and Trade

(GATT), first signed in 1947 by the United States and other governments, has since taken the form of the World Trade Organization (WTO), which also embodies the free-market principles long espoused by American leaders (see Kim 2010). Paradoxically, the United States is frequently named in cases alleging unfair trade practices, more than twenty of which were brought to the WTO between 2008 and 2013. In another paradox, the IMF concluded that the financial crisis of 2008, which spread outward from the United States, resulted from an unwarranted "adherence to the principles of market discipline and light-touch intervention" long advocated by Washington (Moschella 2010, 137).

Key Players in Economic Policy

Among the array of agencies that play a role in advancing U.S. economic interests overseas (see Table 6.4), four merit special attention: the National Economic Council, the Office of the United States Trade Representative, and the Treasury and Commerce Departments. Taken together, these and other bureaucratic actors aim to improve U.S. competitiveness in world trade, facilitate foreign investments to and from the United States, regulate currency exchanges, and pursue bilateral and multilateral agreements that make the globalized economy more stable.

Table 6.4 ■ Agencies of Foreign Economic Policy

Agency	Function
Council of Economic Advisers	Provides guidance to the White House on foreign economic policy
Department of Agriculture	Supports efforts by farmers and agricultural firms to sell products overseas
Department of Commerce	Promotes and manages interests of firms doing business overseas
Department of State	Manages day-to-day economic relations with foreign countries
Department of the Treasury	Manages U.S. financial issues, such as private investment, monetary policy, and global debt
Federal Reserve Board	Makes decisions about the money supply and "prime rate" of interest offered to major borrowers
National Economic Council	Plays a coordinating role with the White House to align policies of all the agencies in the economic complex
National Security Council	Integrates economic issues into its consideration of national security policy
Office of Management and Budget	Manages fiscal policy for the federal government and develops the president's budget proposals for federal spending
Office of the U.S. Trade Representative	Gains access to foreign markets by negotiating bilateral and multilateral trade agreements

National Economic Council. Among Bill Clinton's first acts as president in 1993 was the creation, through executive order, of the National Economic Council (NEC). The eighteen members of the council include the president and vice president; the chair of the Council of Economic Advisers; the U.S. trade representative (see below); the director of the Office of Management and Budget; and the secretaries of agriculture, commerce, energy, labor, transportation, and the Treasury. An assistant to the president for economic policy serves as the director of the NEC and provides direct guidance to the president on all matters related to economic policy, foreign and domestic. President Clinton's executive order assigned four tasks to the NEC: (1) coordinate policy making on economic issues, (2) coordinate the flow of economic policy advice to the president, (3) ensure that economic policies are consistent with the president's goals, and (4) monitor implementation of economic policies. The NEC director has become more outspoken on policy issues in recent years.

U.S. Trade Representative. Concern about U.S. competitiveness in overseas trade markets has been a constant in the nation's history. This concern became more acute after World War II as the United States sought to preserve its status as the world's predominant economic power. In 1962, Congress created the Office of the United States Trade Representative (USTR), whose primary task is to gain access to foreign markets by negotiating bilateral and multilateral trade agreements. Contrary to the nation's free-market values, the USTR draws much of its political support from advocates of protectionism—that is, the manipulation of trade by governments to serve the interests of domestic stakeholders, including producers and consumers, at the expense of foreign competitors (Dryden 1995). The trade representative, who holds the rank of ambassador and sits on the president's cabinet, promotes the interests of domestic producers who want to see the U.S. market closed to foreign countries that discriminate against their goods.

Treasury and Commerce Departments. Although many federal agencies support U.S. economic growth, two are most directly involved in foreign economic policy. First, the Treasury Department is considered the "steward" of the U.S. financial system. Its core duties, in addition to advising the White House on economic policy, include producing currency, collecting and disbursing federal funds, and borrowing money to cover the government's functions. In the foreign policy process, the Treasury Department imposes sanctions on foreign governments that are seen as threatening U.S. global interests (see Chapter 11). Second, the Commerce Department serves as an ally of U.S. firms, banks, and other private economic actors. Its officials support the USTR by promoting U.S. exports, by seeking new markets for U.S. goods and services, and by opposing tariffs and other barriers to overseas trade. The pro-business orientation of the Commerce Department is clear in the mission statement of its Export.gov program, which "brings together resources from across the U.S. Government to assist American businesses in planning their international sales strategies and succeed in today's global marketplace."

International Financial Institutions

The conduct of U.S. foreign economic policy, like military alliances in the security complex, extends to financial institutions that are based in the United States but that have members, stakeholders, and ongoing programs worldwide. Two international financial institutions—the World Bank and the IMF—arose from the Bretton Woods conference of 1944 (see Chapter 2) and continue to hold a central position within the economic complex.

The World Bank offers low-interest loans, grants, and technical assistance to struggling economies for long-term development projects. Two agencies form the core of the World Bank Group, which has provided nearly $1 trillion in low-interest loans and grants to developing countries since World War II. In 2012 alone, the bank approved nearly $53 billion in assistance for projects involving public health, food and energy production, public administration, and other purposes that are often beyond the means of impoverished governments to afford (World Bank 2012, 1). A primary goal of World Bank assistance is for the recipients of assistance to create the conditions for businesses to start and grow, supported by an educated workforce and elected governments that enforce the rule of law. For the United States and other industrialized countries, these funds build upon their annual transfers of development assistance, which are more closely targeted to advance their political and strategic interests.

The larger of these two agencies is the International Bank for Reconstruction and Development (IBRD), created in 1946 to manage the distribution of Marshall Plan loans to U.S. allies, primarily in Western Europe. The IBRD's focus then moved to developing nations, many newly freed from colonial rule. The second agency, the International Development Association, helps the world's poorest countries to address immediate problems such as malnutrition and the HIV/AIDS epidemic. All World Bank presidents have been U.S. citizens nominated by the federal government, which located the bank's headquarters near the U.S. Treasury for more than symbolic reasons. The U.S. contribution to the bank's budget (about 17 percent) is more than twice that of the second-largest contributor, Japan. Because the weight of member votes is based on their financial contributions, the United States effectively has veto power over loans, which must be supported by at least an 85 percent share of votes cast.

The IMF also plays an important role in the U.S. economic complex. A central lesson of the Great Depression was that governments must have confidence in the currencies and long-term stability of their trading partners. Governments quickly lose this confidence when they see those partners accumulating so much debt and suffering such high inflation that they cannot pay for routine government programs. The economic calamities that follow, including deep cuts in public services, defaults on foreign debts, political disarray, and social unrest, extend far beyond the debtors and creditors directly affected to include the world economy as a whole. In addition to helping the global system of "floating" exchange rates operate smoothly, the IMF serves three other functions: (1) monitoring the fiscal and monetary policies of member states; (2) lending money at "concessional" rates to IMF members in financial distress; and (3) providing technical assistance or advice on matters such as national accounting, tax policies, and strengthening of individual economic sectors.

Both Bretton Woods institutions are widely perceived, first and foremost, as instruments of U.S. economic power. To its critics, the World Bank has unfairly required foreign governments to adopt U.S. free-market policies in return for emergency loans, has repeatedly "subsidized" repressive governments, and has supported numerous development projects that harm the environment. According to Toby Carroll (2010), the World Bank recently has been determined to "embed" the U.S. economic model of unfettered free enterprise in the cultural and political practices of Southeast Asian states. The IMF, labeled by one analyst the "poster child for the evils of globalization" (Willett 2001, 594), is blamed for contributing to a variety of economic calamities, including the collapse of market reforms in Russia, the East Asian economic crisis in the late 1990s, and the near-bankruptcy of Mexico's government in 1995.

The WTO advances a cause long embraced by American leaders: unrestricted cross-border trade in goods and services. As described more fully in Chapter 11, after World War II, the White House favored the creation of such a trade body, but protectionists in Congress rejected this plan. For the managers of the U.S. economic complex, the WTO supports U.S. geoeconomic goals by encouraging the "invisible hand" of market forces, rather than restrictions imposed by self-interested states, to determine trade practices. Although the United States is sanctioned repeatedly by the WTO for its own protectionist policies, U.S. leaders support the system of dispute resolution that holds all countries accountable for their trade practices. More broadly, pressure from the United States to exclude repressive regimes from the WTO has spurred political reforms in some countries while strengthening the political legitimacy of the trade body (Drezner 2006, 92–94).

■ CONCLUSION

In implementing foreign policy, bureaucrats maintain their places on the front lines of the policy process and continue to determine, in large measure, the success or failure of policy initiatives adopted by the president and Congress. And yet, while actively pursuing more personnel and greater influence, agencies have resisted the sweeping changes in their organizational structures and missions long advocated by critics inside and outside the U.S. government. The National Security Council is less of a forum for deliberations among high-level cabinet officials than a shadow State

Department with a large staff and immediate access to the Oval Office. The CIA and related agencies remain highly antagonistic toward one another even after the creation of a director of national intelligence. Despite its moves toward "jointness," the Pentagon continues to struggle with inter-service rivalries that have grown more contentious in the midst of mandated budget cuts across the board. These budget pressures have also prevented the Department of Homeland Security from gaining a sense of united purpose.

The U.S. foreign policy bureaucracy exhibits two entrenched but contradictory patterns: the increasing *centralization* of authority within the White House and the continuing *fragmentation* of control across a far-flung bureaucracy. From managing military crises to negotiating trade deals, presidents and their advisers have sought, and have generally been granted, greater authority to conduct foreign policy. While the executive branch has amassed greater power relative to Congress, its authority has shifted internally from the State Department and other federal agencies to the White House. At the same time, the size, scope, and intricacy of the foreign policy complexes described in this chapter have increased steadily since the current structure was devised after World War II.

To some observers, the sheer mass of the foreign policy bureaucracy makes the United States a "headless monster" that is incapable of acting in a consistent and coherent manner. To others, such a bureaucracy is not only inevitable but also generally effective in advancing the interests of the world's most powerful nation. Either way, the capacity of the United States to maintain its world power depends on the coherence and cohesion of its foreign policy institutions. At once centralized and fragmented, these structures are vital in determining the future of U.S. world power. As we will find in the book's next section, which explores the external or "outside-in" sources of foreign policy, U.S. leaders must also pay heed to pressures from civil society, which impose an additional layer of complexity upon the policy process.

6

INTERNET REFERENCES

The **Center on Budget and Policy Priorities** (http://www.cbpp.org) focuses on federal and state budget priorities, including research on taxes and spending. Projects of interest deal with analysis of military spending, specific foreign policy spending, and tax burdens for national security.

The **Central Intelligence Agency** (https://www.cia.gov) operates a website that provides detailed information on the CIA's mission as well as about global developments. The *CIA World Factbook* (https://www.cia.gov/library/publications/resources/the-world-factbook/index.html) contains comprehensive political, economic, military, and other data on all nation-states.

CRS Reports (http://fpc.state.gov/c18185.htm; http://www.fas.org/sgp/crs/index.html) from the Congressional Research Service, the research arm of Congress, provide briefings on specific policy issues and include background information, chronologies, bibliographic references, and budget statistics.

The website for the **Department of Defense** (http://www.defense.gov) presents reports on defense-related activities and specific programs, along with information on the military and its past operations. In addition, news releases, speeches, and transcripts from defense officials on topics such as casualties, funding, and officer assignments are available. Also included are links to agencies within the Defense Department as well as a list of online publications such as the defense budget, *Defense Almanac,* and reports on capabilities and security measures.

The newest cabinet agency, the **Department of Homeland Security** (http://www.dhs.gov), offers consistent updates on the war on terror as well as missions to contain and combat domestic terrorism. The site also has information on immigration, border control, and policies related to emergency actions. Speeches, documents, and research links are provided as well.

The **Department of State** (http://www.state.gov) is vested with many aspects of diplomacy, including foreign aid, peace building, democratization, and disease and poverty reduction, as well as other aspects of the U.S. foreign policy process. The State Department's website includes speeches, policy descriptions, and issue explanations for those studying U.S. foreign policy.

The **Government Accountability Office** (http://www.gao.gov) evaluates and reports on congressional and presidential decision making, budgets, and policies. Included on its website are audits, evaluations, and policy analysis reports on intergovernmental relations and policy decisions.

The **International Monetary Fund** (http://www.imf.org) promotes a more stable global economy by enhancing monetary cooperation and aiding countries in distress. The IMF's website provides details on its financial programs along with country-by-country economic data and reports on current issues such as globalization, rural poverty, financial regulation, and debt relief.

The website of the **Office of the United States Trade Representative** (https://www.ustr.gov) provides links and access to bilateral and multilateral trade data and events. Researchers will find the information on NAFTA, the WTO, and free trade negotiations particularly helpful. Speeches, testimony, trade legislation, and daily updates on international trade are also posted on this site.

The website for the **U.S. Intelligence Community** (http://www.intelligence.gov) offers information on the organization of all U.S. intelligence agencies and their relationships with each other and the government as a whole. Meetings and special report findings on national and international intelligence are summarized on this site, which is broader in scope than the CIA website.

The **World Bank** (http://www.worldbank.org) is an intergovernmental organization that focuses on economic development and growth. Its website includes speeches, project summaries, regional analyses, and data resources on global trends for all countries.

CHAPTER 7

PUBLIC OPINION AT HOME AND ABROAD

A Filipino surplus vendor watches President Barack Obama's January 2010 State of the Union address from his shop in Manila. Obama sought not only the support of Congress and American citizens in his speech; he also reached out to global public opinion for approval as he began his second year in the White House.

Val Handumon/epa/Corbis

CHAPTER OBJECTIVES

7.1   Discuss the factors at play in the tensions between democratic governance and U.S. foreign policy.

7.2   Identify the shifts in public opinion since World War II.

7.3   Describe the trends in the sources of news and information regarding U.S. foreign policy.

7.4   Discuss the ways in which various interest groups place pressures on foreign policy makers.

The previous section of this book focused on the government actors engaged in the formulation and conduct of U.S. foreign policy. This section shifts to the "outside in" forces—public opinion, the news media, social movements, and interest groups—that seek to influence the foreign policy process from many vantage points, domestic and foreign. Trends in world politics increase the importance of this external dimension, which blurs common distinctions between domestic and foreign policy and between private and public life.

We first explore the impact of public opinion on U.S. foreign policy. This is a critical concern given the central place of private citizens in the governance of a democratic polity. For a nation "of the people, by the people, for the people"—Abraham Lincoln's famous construction in his Gettysburg Address—public opinion provides an essential guide for directing government action. As we will find, however, this role is controversial and has varied significantly over time. Moreover, since the American public is highly fragmented among diverse groups with differing interests, it rarely sends a unified signal to policy makers. Deepening U.S. trade with China, for example, pleases corporate and banking interests while angering labor unions and human rights activists (see Chapter 3). Seeking consensus in such a conflictual environment is often a futile task.

Political leaders do not passively await the public's verdict on their actions. Instead, they actively *gauge* citizens' attitudes in advance and base their decisions, at least in part, on the likely response. In this respect, public opinion plays the productive role envisioned by democratic theorists—that of increasing the likelihood that government policies will reflect public preferences (see Shapiro 2011). Yet leaders also manipulate public opinion in several ways: by focusing on particular issues in speeches and interviews, by strategically timing their actions to gain political advantage, and by creatively interpreting developments overseas. Policy makers, well

aware of the general population's lack of knowledge about most foreign policy problems, can expect their depictions of friends and foes to be accepted readily (Ginsberg 1986).

The manipulation of public opinion is hardly unique to the current period. As Seymour Martin Lipset (1966, 20) noted nearly half a century ago, on many occasions the president "makes opinion, he does not follow it. The polls tell him how good a politician he is." Such efforts have been refined in recent years with the rise of more sophisticated polling techniques; the use of carefully targeted focus groups; and new outlets of mass communication, particularly the Internet. The U.S. government also manipulates news and social media by "spinning" foreign policies in a favorable direction (see Chapter 8). Increasingly, a **public relations presidency** exists in the current political system as presidents "act in deliberate ways to achieve heightened popularity in the polls and in elections" (Brace and Hinckley 1993, 383).

The temptation of presidents to "make" public opinion is especially strong in foreign policy because of their high profile and expansive powers in this area and because of Americans' general preoccupation with domestic affairs. As noted in Chapter 4, most foreign policy issues permit presidents to exercise their prerogatives, or freedom to pursue their objectives, more so than in the realm of domestic policy. Still, policy makers cannot ignore public opinions regarding foreign policy if they wish to maintain domestic support for their actions overseas. They especially cannot ignore the opinions of well-organized societal groups—based on common ethnicities, religious affiliations, economic needs, devotion to human rights, and other shared interests—that follow closely the foreign policies that affect them directly. The same policy makers must also be concerned with global public opinion toward the United States, as unfavorable views from foreign governments and citizens can produce pushback against U.S. foreign policies. Two aspects of public opinion and U.S. foreign policy preoccupy research on the subject. The first involves the *sources* of public opinion, which include a mixture of personal and political values, news media coverage

(Gartner 2011), and perceptions of foreign threats (Merolla and Zechmeister 2009). According to a recent study, domestic support for the use of U.S. military force is much stronger when the United Nations and other multilateral institutions support the action (Grieco et al. 2011).

Conversely, the *effects* of public opinion are also of interest to researchers. The withdrawal of the United States from Iraq in late 2011, for example, was driven by deepening public opposition to the war as reported in surveys. On the other hand, the relative lack of public concern about the war in Afghanistan, which also faced major setbacks, encouraged U.S. leaders to prolong their counterinsurgency effort there (Jacobson 2010b). Public opinion also affects the voting behavior of American citizens, whose views regarding foreign policy directly shape their evaluations of presidential candidates, particularly those in the Republican Party (Gadarian 2010).

■ DEMOCRACY AND THE PARADOX OF WORLD POWER

Since its beginnings, the U.S. government has expected individuals and groups to insert themselves into the policy process by expressing their wishes to policy makers. In the democratic model, elected leaders are servants, rather than masters, of the private citizens who voted those leaders into office. For this reason, recognizing public preferences and providing "constituent service" are viewed as essential responsibilities of elected officials.

Fundamental tensions often exist, however, between democratic governance and foreign policy. Short-term electoral pressures divert the judgment of policy makers and legislators from long-term concerns, including transnational problems that affect the "global commons" (see Chapter 12). Openness, an essential quality of democratic governance, can also be a liability when intelligence secrets are leaked to the press for partisan advantage, or when domestic debates reveal a lack of national unity. These inescapable by-products of modern democracy are confronted by all countries with decentralized governments and robust civil societies, but the costs are magnified in the United States, whose foreign policies profoundly affect other countries and the overall climate of world politics.

At the same time as Americans' influence on government action is important, it is also highly uneven. As one analyst (Schattschneider 1960) observed half a century ago, most American citizens are "semisovereign" given the dominance of powerful interest groups, particularly corporations, in shaping domestic and foreign policies (see Chapter 9). Few observers dispute that the U.S. government maintains procedural democracy in the form of regular elections, but many doubt whether a substantive democracy exists that truly empowers the majority of citizens on a day-to-day basis

(Key 1961). This problem is reflected in studies of public opinion, which find that U.S. citizens, in their impact on foreign policy, can be divided into three categories:

- The **foreign policy elite**, who comprise less than 5 percent of the general public but hold powerful positions in government, business, and interest groups. These elites, also known as opinion leaders, are often engaged directly in issues relating to U.S. foreign policy and are able to guide or manipulate public opinion as they see fit.

- The **attentive public**, about 15 percent of the population, includes policy analysts, government bureaucrats, scholars, journalists, and political activists with substantial knowledge of global issues. This group is "inclined to participate, but still lacks the access or opportunity to do so" (Rosenau 1961, 33).

- The **mass public**, the vast majority of American citizens, who are neither well informed about nor interested in most foreign policy issues. Because these issues generally have little salience, or direct impact on citizens, they open the door for elites and special interests to determine policies.

On key issues such as war and peace, the mass public takes a strong interest but generally defers to the views of elites as covered in the news media (Zaller 1992). Otherwise, foreign policy elites direct most of their efforts at the attentive public, whose concurrence on policy matters may be reflected in favorable news coverage, supportive research findings, and financial contributions to political campaigns. In this respect, the attentive public serves as a courier of elite "signals" to the mass public, a crucial role that renders this group a pivotal source of public opinion (see Figure 7.1). For most Americans, these signals are sufficient to inform their own views on specific issues; they feel that further scrutiny of most matters of foreign policy is best left to the experts.

Rival Views of Political Leadership

Political theorists have long disagreed about the public's ideal role in shaping policy. Two general models of political representation capture the alternative approaches to democratic governance. The **delegate model** holds that elected officials should reflect the general public's preferences on a given issue, making decisions based on the majority view. In short, officials should act as they believe their "constituents should want" (Pitkin 1967, 147) and not allow their personal preferences to enter into the equation. Abraham Lincoln expressed this view to the House of Representatives in July 1848, when he declared as the "primary, the cardinal, the one great living principle of all democratic representative government—the principle that the representative is bound to carry out the known will of his constituents."

By contrast, the **trustee model** prefers that elected officials be granted greater flexibility and autonomy than is envisioned in the more restrictive delegate model. This more

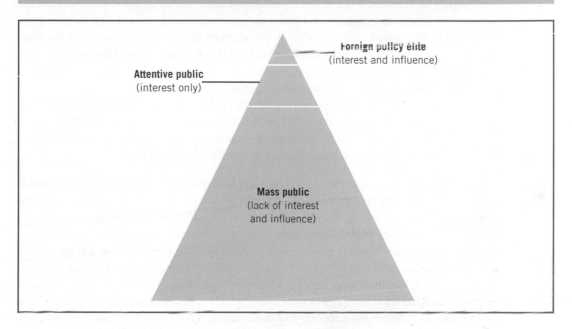

conservative view is most often associated with Edmund Burke, the eighteenth-century British statesman and political theorist who did not consider the mass public qualified to make informed judgments about public policy. Burke, living in an era of widespread illiteracy and ignorance, argued that representatives should follow their own, more "enlightened" beliefs about what is best for the body politic. He believed that "your representative owes you not his industry only, but his judgment; and he betrays, instead of serving you, if he sacrifices it to your opinion" (quoted in Hofman and Levack 1949, 115).

In the late 1970s, Jimmy Carter made it clear that his foreign policy would reflect the public's desire to resist militarism and promote human rights instead. His adoption of the delegate position was shared in 1990 by President George H. W. Bush, whose aggressive response to Iraq's invasion of Kuwait had broad support of the general public. More recently, President Obama frequently made reference to Americans' war fatigue when he oversaw the withdrawal of U.S. troops from Iraq and Afghanistan. In 2014, Obama resisted calls by some members of Congress for military involvement in Syria. Among other reasons for this decision, Obama responded to widespread public doubts that the United States had a responsibility to become involved in the expanding conflict (Pew Research Center for the People and the Press 2012b).

President Clinton assumed the trustee role in 1999 when he ordered U.S. military intervention in Kosovo, a province of the former Yugoslavia, without public or even congressional support. Former vice president Dick Cheney applied this view to the current era when, in response to a press question regarding whether he follows public opinion, he replied, "No. . . . I think you cannot be blown off course by the fluctuations in the public opinion polls" (World Public Opinion 2008). His president also ran against the grain of U.S. public opinion, which favored military action against Iraq only if the Security Council endorsed the invasion. In this case, Bush assumed the role of a trustee, at one point defending his authority as "the decider" on the most important policy issues. For those favoring the delegate model, the problems that subsequently plagued the U.S. occupation of Iraq reinforced their position that the "general will" of American citizens must be heard to be heeded.

This historic debate about the role of political leadership in democratic governance is related directly to the two primary bodies of international relations theory: realism and liberalism (see Chapter 3). Recall that traditional realists have a bleak assessment of human nature, which they believe to be plagued by momentary passions, chronic distrust, ignorance, and hostility toward others. For this reason, realists cast a skeptical eye on public opinion as a reliable guide to foreign policy. "The government is the leader of public opinion, not its slave," observed Hans Morgenthau (1967, 547–548), a prominent realist. Realists believe citizens may be competent to participate in matters of local governance that touch their day-to-day lives, such as education, but they are not competent to do so in foreign policy matters, which are more removed from daily life.

Liberal theories of world politics provide a more positive view of the public's role in foreign policy. During the Enlightenment era, liberal European theorists such as Jeremy Bentham, Immanuel Kant, John Locke, and Jean-Jacques Rousseau had great confidence in the reason and judgment of the mass public, whose views of foreign as well as domestic affairs, they believed, should be followed closely by elected leaders. In modern times, Woodrow Wilson is the president most closely associated with the liberal view and its application to U.S. foreign policy (see In Their Own Words). This debate over the public's role in the governance of democracies continues today. Presidents are prone to make their decisions on a case-by-case basis, and their concerns for public opinion often vary depending on the foreign policy problem facing them. Their frequent adoption of the trustee role, however, rarely extends to members of Congress, whose closer ties to voters naturally compel them to place their constituents' views at the forefront of their political calculations.

Mood Swings or Pragmatism?

The penchant for U.S. citizens to look inward is nothing new. When French sociologist Alexis de Tocqueville toured the United States in the early 1830s, he found Americans to be far less interested in public affairs than their European counterparts. "Intent only on getting rich, they do not notice the close connection between private

IN THEIR OWN WORDS

Woodrow Wilson *Among advocates of the delegate model of representation, President Woodrow Wilson was known to give great weight to the opinions of American citizens. In a September 1918 speech addressing a public meeting in New York, Wilson made it clear that U.S. public opinion regarding World War I should guide the nation's foreign policies during and after the "great war."*

It is the peculiarity of this great war that while statesmen have seemed to cast about for definitions of their purpose and have sometimes seemed to shift their ground and their point of view, the thought of the mass of men, whom statesmen are supposed to instruct and lead, has grown more and more unclouded, more and more certain of what it is that they are fighting for. National purposes have fallen more and more into the background and the common purpose of enlightened mankind has taken their place. The counsels of plain men have become on all hands more simple and straightforward and more unified than the counsels of sophisticated men of affairs, who still retain the impression that they are playing a game of power and playing for high stakes. That is why I have said that this is a peoples' war, not a statesmen's. Statesmen must follow the clarified common thought or be broken.

Source: Woodrow Wilson, "Five Needs of Permanent Peace," in *Selected Addresses and Public Papers of Woodrow Wilson,* ed. Albert B. Hart (New York: Boni and Liveright, 1918), 275–282.

fortunes and the general prosperity. They find it a tiresome inconvenience to exercise political rights which distract them from industry" (de Tocqueville [1835] 1988, 540).

Scholars in the early twentieth century echoed de Tocqueville's concerns about the public's role in U.S. public affairs. Walter Lippmann (1922), a prominent journalist and social commentator, faulted Americans for ignoring German expansionism in Europe until it threatened their own country and forcing U.S. entry into World War I. The same criticism came after World War II, when popular commentators and prominent scholars cited the U.S. public's apathy during the interwar period as a contributing factor to the rise of fascist regimes in Europe and Asia (see Bailey 1948; M. Kriesberg 1949; Almond 1950).

Gabriel Almond's 1950 book, *The American People and Foreign Policy,* provided a bleak view of the connection between public attitudes and U.S. foreign policy. Drawing on survey data provided by the newly founded Gallup Organization, Almond (1950, 71) complained that Americans generally felt so secure at home that "foreign policy, save in moments of grave crisis, has to labor under a handicap; it has to shout loudly to be heard even a little." Making matters worse, he argued, were the "mood swings" in public opinion that led to constantly shifting demands for global activism and withdrawal.[1]

---

1. See Holmes (1985) and Klingberg (1983) for later analyses of "mood swings" in U.S. public opinion.

The similarities between this view and Lippmann's produced what became known as the **Almond-Lippmann consensus,** which is based on three assumptions (O. R. Holsti 1992). First, public opinion is *volatile,* shifting erratically in response to the most recent developments. Mass beliefs early in the twentieth century were "too pacifist in peace and too bellicose in war, too neutralist or appeasing in negotiations or too intransigent" (Lippmann 1955, 20). Second, public opinion is *incoherent,* lacking an organized or a consistent structure to such an extent that the views of U.S. citizens could best be described as "nonattitudes" (Converse 1964). Finally, public opinion is *irrelevant* to the policy-making process. Political leaders ignore public opinion because most Americans can neither "understand nor influence the very events upon which their lives and happiness are known to depend" (Kris and Leites 1947, 393).

In contrast, more recent research challenges this gloomy assessment, detecting greater consistency and coherence in mass attitudes and greater concern among decision makers with public opinion than the early pessimists assumed. Although the mass public tends to be more nationalistic on economic issues than elites, especially regarding the protection of U.S. jobs against foreign competition (Page and Barabas 2000), both groups favor U.S. engagement in the United Nations and other forms of multilateral cooperation. Small segments of the public do consider themselves to be "isolationist," but most favor an internationalist foreign policy. The only question among these citizens is whether the United States should pursue a policy of **militant internationalism** or **cooperative internationalism** (Wittkopf 1990). Whereas realists, embracing a competitive and zero-sum worldview, prefer the former approach, liberals favor active government collaboration and pooling of resources.

At its core, public opinion is reducible to the belief systems of individual citizens, whose normative values and presumptions about human nature, the state, and society shape their judgments about foreign policy (see Chapter 3). In this respect, the dichotomy between militant and cooperative internationalism reflects a more subtle difference in the level of **international trust** felt by individuals. An extension of political trust (Hetherington 1998), which is a generalized faith in government, international trust hinges on the perception that "most foreign countries behave in accordance with normative expectations regarding the conduct of nations" (Brewer et al. 2004, 96). Although many Americans—the cooperative internationalists—see the world as generally benign, the majority "believe the United States is surrounded by untrustworthy nations seeking their own advantage" (105). Such perceptions dictate policy opinions on a broad spectrum of global issues such as UN peacekeeping, foreign aid, and nuclear proliferation.

Other surveys contradict the notion of incoherent public opinion. Even though test scores and survey research find the public to be generally ill informed, citizens seem to approach foreign policy problems with deeply held principles, values, and standards of evaluation (Graber and Dunaway 2015). Public opposition to the Korean and Vietnam Wars, for example, corresponded logically with growing U.S. casualties in each conflict (Mueller 1970, 1973). At other times, citizens responded pragmatically to perceived excesses in presidential behavior. For example, whereas Jimmy Carter's "dovish" foreign policies in the late 1970s prompted public calls for a tougher response to Soviet aggression, Ronald Reagan's "hawkish" approach alarmed many Americans and led to public appeals for moderation (Nincic 1988). Both presidents altered their approaches to foreign policy in part because of public dissatisfaction. Their actions suggested that the public can have a moderating effect on U.S. foreign policies regarding war and peace.

From this perspective, Americans do not suffer from "mood swings" but instead react in a reasoned and predictable manner to problems facing the United States (W. G. Mayer 1992). Unless they are experts in world politics, private citizens evaluate a problem on the basis of their underlying beliefs and values (Page and Shapiro 1992). During the Cold War, Americans evaluated possible military interventions on a case-by-case basis rather than supporting or opposing the use of force across the board (Jentleson 1992; see also Peffley and Hurwitz 1992).

The same can be said of public opinion since the Cold War. One of the public's core beliefs—that U.S. power should be applied only to repel clear threats to vital national interests—produced support for military intervention in some situations (such as the Persian Gulf War and Afghanistan) and calls for restraint in others (such as Rwanda, the former Yugoslavia, and Iraq). Once an intervention is under way, support for its continuation has hinged largely on public assessments of whether the mission would ultimately succeed or fail (Kull and Ramsay 2001). Fluctuations in public opinion thus have more to do with the *context* of foreign policy problems than with the general population's lack of understanding (see E. V. Larson 1996).

The Almond-Lippmann assumption that public opinion is irrelevant in the policy process is contradicted by elected officials' vigorous efforts to gauge that opinion in recent years. All presidents since John F. Kennedy have created elaborate polling operations within the White House to guide their decisions in foreign and domestic policy (see L. R. Jacobs and Shapiro 1995). After the Cold War, Bill Clinton refused to authorize military intervention during the genocide in Rwanda and Burundi due in large part to strong public opposition in the wake of the failed U.S. humanitarian action in Somalia. Similarly, President Obama cited public weariness with the war in Afghanistan as he ordered gradual withdrawals of U.S. troops from the war zone. As his bid for reelection approached, Obama was well aware that voters cared more about domestic problems in the United States than further nation building thousands of miles away.

America's Knowledge Gap

It is commonly understood that American citizens are largely detached from politics, lacking both extensive knowledge of, and interest in, government at any level. Mass

Public Opinion: Master or Pawn?

A primary and enduring debate in the realm of public opinion and U.S. foreign policy is whether the general public is fit to guide political leaders in managing relations with other countries. Skeptics such as political scientist Gabriel Almond find that Americans tend to be well informed only about immediate concerns. "But on questions of a remote nature, such as foreign policy, they tend to react in more undifferentiated ways, with formless and plastic moods which undergo frequent alteration in response to changes in events," Almond wrote in 1950. "The characteristic response to questions of foreign policy is one of indifference. A foreign policy crisis . . . may transform indifference to vague apprehension, to fatalism, to anger; but the reaction is still a mood, a superficial and fluctuating response."

According to political scientist Bruce Jentleson, more recent studies have contradicted "the traditional view of the public as boorish, overreactive, and generally the bane of those who would pursue an effective foreign policy." Citizens are not easily manipulated by presidents, these studies suggest, and citizens are able to distinguish between vital U.S. interests worth defending and nonvital interests that should not be pursued at the cost of American lives. "It is difficult to explain much of the foreign policy behavior of the United States during the mid- to late-1970s," political scientist Eugene R. Wittkopf has observed, "without some sense of the constraining forces of the Vietnam Syndrome that the Ford and Carter administrations must surely have perceived."

Nevertheless, the debate over public opinion continues today. Surveys conducted in 2003–2004 revealed widespread public misperceptions about the U.S. invasion of Iraq, including the view that Saddam Hussein had been an accomplice in the September 11 terrorist attacks. These erroneous views proved remarkably persistent despite a steady stream of evidence to the contrary. As Almond predicted, U.S. leaders continue to exploit gaps in public attentiveness to foreign affairs and pursue their own course in foreign policy, knowing that citizens will follow their lead.

Sources: Gabriel Almond, *The American People and Foreign Policy* (New York: Harcourt, Brace, 1950), 53; Bruce W. Jentleson, "The Pretty Prudent Public: Post Post-Vietnam American Opinion on the Use of Military Force," *International Studies Quarterly* 36 (March 1992): 71; Eugene R. Wittkopf, *Faces of Internationalism: Public Opinion and U.S. Foreign Policy* (Durham, NC: Duke University Press, 1990), 219.

public opinion is often characterized by "non-attitudes" (Converse 1964), with citizens holding unstructured and often inconsistent beliefs regarding public affairs. One of the first studies of American voting behavior revealed "the general impoverishment of political thought in a large proportion of the electorate" (A. Campbell et al. 1960, 543).

Although most Americans believe the nation should play an active role in world politics, they commonly focus their energies on domestic issues unless the United States is directly threatened with or involved in an international crisis (Sobel 2001). For example, as is typical when the country is enjoying peace and prosperity, U.S. public interest in foreign affairs declined in the 1990s, after the Cold War ended. The September 2001 terrorist attacks disrupted this period of complacency, although domestic issues and scandals soon captured unneeded headlines—and public attention.

The U.S. educational system has reinforced rather than remedied this problem (see Figure 7.2). Surveys of public knowledge, combined with a recent finding that the United States ranks sixteenth worldwide in college graduations, suggest that "the U.S. is fast losing its edge" in educational attainment (OECD 2011). Just 1 percent of high school seniors demonstrated advanced science knowledge in 2009, while 40 percent lacked even basic knowledge of the subject (National Assessment for Education Statistics 2011a, 46). In the same year, only 3 and 5 percent of twelfth graders exhibited advanced knowledge of mathematics and reading, respectively (National Assessment for Education Statistics 2011b, 9, 26). The sense of intellectual decline has become so pervasive that popular books with such titles as *Just How Stupid Are We?* (Shenkman 2008), *The Dumbest Generation* (Bauerlein 2008), and *Idiot America* (Pierce 2009) became best sellers in recent years.

Of more immediate concern regarding public knowledge and U.S. foreign policy is the fact that students' grasp of civics declined between 1998 and 2010. While most students took courses that covered subjects related to American government, less than one-half studied foreign governments or global organizations such as the United Nations (National Assessment of Educational Progress 2011a, 39). Less than one-quarter of high school seniors were found to be "proficient or higher" in civics; more than one-third effectively failed the test of civics knowledge. The success level for fourth and eighth graders was 27 and 22 percent, respectively. According to Sandra Day O'Connor (PRNewswire 2011), a former U.S. Supreme Court justice and a strong advocate of primary education, "The scores reveal a very disturbing lack of basic knowledge of our system of government and how and why citizens must be engaged." Cultural detachment from the

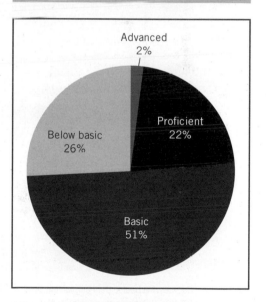

Figure 7.2 ■ Underachieving: Civics Knowledge of U.S. Students, 2014

Source: U.S. Department of Education, "Nation's Report Card, 2014," www.nationsreportcard.gov/hgc_2014/. Total 101, due to rounding.

"outside world" has a long tradition in the United States, reflecting the nation's geographic distance from other major powers as well as an "exceptional" national identity deeply rooted in U.S. political culture (see Chapter 1). This lack of knowledge about global events has held constant throughout the nation's geographic expansion and subsequent emergence as the world's predominant power—and despite the nation's pervasive overseas presence (see Table 7.1).

Table 7.1 ■ U.S. Public Knowledge about World Affairs: Nationwide Survey Results, 1942–2014

Question Topic (survey year)	Percentage Able to Answer
India a British colony (1942)	51
Purposes of U.S. foreign aid (1958)	48
U.S. Secretary of State (2008)	42
Soviet Union not in NATO (1964)	41
Purpose of NATO (1988)	40
Prime Minister of Israel (2014)	38
Name of citizens' U.S. House representatives (1998)	37
President of Russia (2007)	36
President of France (1986)	34
Two signatories of SALT (1979)	30
Reason U.S. fought the Cold War (2011)	27
Location of Persian Gulf (1988)	25
U.S. Secretary of Defense (2007)	21
U.S. National Security Adviser (1977)	17
Location of Common Market (1961)	13
Secretary-General of UN (1953)	10
President of Mexico (1991)	3

Sources: Michael X. Delli Carpini and Scott Keeter, *What Americans Know about Politics and Why It Matters* (New Haven, CT: Yale University Press, 1996), ch. 2; Andrew Romano, "How Dumb Are We?" *Newsweek* (March 28 and April 4, 2011); American National Election Studies, Pew Research Center for the People and Press, various knowledge surveys, 2007–2014.

The lack of public knowledge about foreign affairs has tangible consequences for public opinion. Almost 60 percent of Americans reported having little or no knowledge about Islam (Council on American-Islamic Relations 2006). The same survey respondents reported widespread antagonism toward Muslims, with an average of 25 percent agreeing with the following statements: "Muslims value life less than others," "Muslims teach children to hate," and "Islam teaches violence."

Is this knowledge gap limited to the mass public? Apparently not. In 2006, when journalist Jeff Stein interviewed U.S. counterterrorism officials, his final question was "Do you know the difference between a Sunni and a Shiite?" He expected that his sources would have considerable knowledge of the two Islamic sects that were primary antagonists in Iraq's burgeoning civil war. "But, so far, most American officials I've interviewed don't have a clue," Stein observed in the *New York Times*. "That includes not just intelligence and law enforcement officials, but also members of Congress who have important roles overseeing our spy agencies. How can they do their jobs without knowing the basics?" (Stein 2006).

When ordinary citizens lack knowledge about a particular U.S. foreign policy, they rely on "cues" from opinion leaders that are often misleading or simply false (Zaller and Chiu 1996). For example, surveys conducted in 2003–2004 revealed widespread public misperceptions about the U.S. invasion of Iraq, including the erroneous view that Iraqi leader Saddam Hussein had been an accomplice in the September 11 terrorist attacks. In this respect, the "marketplace of ideas," assumed to reveal the truth in democratic societies through rigorous public scrutiny and debate, broke down in the months preceding the 2003 invasion. The American public, still reeling from the September 2001 terrorist attacks, proved highly susceptible to White House claims that Iraq posed a clear and present danger.

The societal forces expected to impose such scrutiny, including the press and the opposition political party, failed to serve this societal check-and-balance function (Kaufmann 2004). "All of this has contributed to a political and policymaking environment in which political leaders are (compared to previous historical periods) relatively free to ignore or misperceive public opinion on foreign affairs" (Shapiro and Jacobs 2002, 200).

Misperceptions plague U.S. public opinion and foreign policy in other ways as well. Regarding foreign aid, a majority of the public favored cutbacks in aid levels, but this preference was based on a misreading of current spending levels. Whereas the majority of survey respondents believed the U.S. government was spending 15 to 20 percent of the federal budget on foreign aid—and believed this level should be reduced to 5 to 10 percent—the actual level of U.S. aid spending was just 1 percent of the federal budget. These and other findings revealed a foreign policy "disconnect" between mass opinion and U.S. foreign policies (Page and Bouton 2006). Members of Congress, when considering future votes on foreign policy issues, wrongly perceive that the public favors unilateral policies (Todorov and Mandisodza 2004). These problems are magnified when Americans lose interest in political issues, as they have recently. In 2011, for example, just a quarter of U.S. citizens indicated that they "follow what's going on in government and public affairs" (Pew Research Center for the People and the Press 2011b, 9).

■ PUBLIC OPINION SINCE WORLD WAR II

Because public opinion plays a crucial role in democratic nations, whose citizens decide at the polls who will lead them in times of war and peace, politicians clearly recognize that their survival relies on securing and maintaining the public's confidence. Such support provides a variety of secondary benefits as well. Aside from their improved prospects for reelection, popular presidents have generally enjoyed a more favorable partisan balance of power in Congress (Marra and Ostrom 1989). They have also been more successful in achieving the goals of their major policy initiatives (Rivers and Rose 1985).

American foreign policy goals are no exception. Indeed, the success or failure of presidents, who alone represent "all the people," often hinges on how the public reacts to events overseas and how the White House manages those critical situations. For example, the failure of President Woodrow Wilson to enlist public support for his activist agenda after World War I led to his political downfall. Since 1945, the ebbs and flows of public support for U.S. foreign policy have determined not only the political fates of presidents but also their goals and tactics and the outcomes of their policies. Harry Truman and Lyndon Johnson watched their presidencies collapse under the weight of foreign entanglements in Korea and Vietnam, respectively, a lesson apparent to George W. Bush as the war in Iraq spiraled out of control during his second term.

While public opinions may vary over time, they consistently find Americans in favor of an active role for the United States in world politics (see Table 7.2). This consensus has weakened in recent years, however, with a growing share of citizens seeking a more passive world role. In 2014, more than 40 percent believed the United States should "stay out of world affairs," the highest level since World War II. It is helpful, therefore, for students of U.S. foreign policy to understand the ebbs and flows of public opinion during and after the Cold War.

Consensus and Discord during the Cold War

After World War II, President Truman faced a major policy problem: sustaining public support for an assertive foreign policy that matched the nation's military, economic, and political predominance. With peace, Americans had demanded—and received

Table 7.2 ■ Support for Active U.S. Participation in World Affairs, 1974–2014

Year	Take an Active Part (%)	Stay Out of World Affairs (%)
1974	66	24
1978	59	29
1982	54	35
1986	64	27
1990	62	28
1994	65	29
1998	61	28
2002	71	25
2006	69	28
2010	67	31
2014	58	41

Source: *Foreign Policy in the Age of Retrenchment. Results of the 2014 Chicago Council Survey of American Public Opinion and U.S. Foreign Policy*. Chicago Council of Foreign Affairs, 2014, 6.

from Congress—sharp cutbacks in military spending, which dropped from $83 billion in 1945 to less than $10 billion in 1948 (U.S. Office of Management and Budget 2002, 44).[2] Yet, Truman felt the United States should be actively engaged overseas in restoring political stability and economic growth. The onset of the Cold War in the late 1940s gave Truman further impetus to shake the public out of its customary shift toward postwar disengagement. The start of the Korean War solidified the containment consensus that would propel U.S. foreign policy over the next two decades (Yergin 1977).

Public support encouraged presidents Dwight Eisenhower and John Kennedy to continue Truman's military buildup and focus on anticommunism. Along with most members of Congress, the public supported Lyndon Johnson's early deployments of U.S. troops to Vietnam (Bardes 1997). That support continued until the 1968 Tet offensive revealed that the United States would not, as Johnson had promised, soon win the war. Opposition mounted as Richard Nixon instituted a lottery for drafting Americans into the armed services. By May 1970, the month

2. Defense spending between 1945 and 1948 fell from 90 percent of overall federal spending to 31 percent.

in which National Guard troops killed four students at Kent State University during an antiwar demonstration, a majority of the public considered their nation's involvement in Vietnam a mistake. Controversy over U.S. covert operations, revelations of CIA abuses against domestic opponents, and a prolonged economic downturn contributed further to the Vietnam syndrome, a generalized aversion to U.S. military activism coupled with a sense of defeatism (O. R. Holsti and Rosenau 1979).

In this respect, President Jimmy Carter followed, rather than created, the national sentiment that identified human rights as a central pillar of U.S. foreign policy in the late 1970s. By the end of Carter's term, however, a combination of public pressure and overseas developments had forced the president to increase military spending and adopt a more confrontational foreign policy. The revival of Cold War tensions led to the 1980 election of Ronald Reagan, who hailed the Vietnam War as a "noble effort" and promised to rid the public and the government of the Vietnam syndrome. But the spiraling arms race of the early 1980s spawned a new generation of public protests and a "nuclear freeze" movement in the United States and Europe. Failing to generate public or congressional support for U.S. intervention in Central America, the Reagan administration turned to covert operations that ultimately produced the Iran-*contra* scandal.

AP Photo/Nick Ut

Vietnamese children flee in terror from a napalm attack by the United States in June 1972. The nude girl in the center, nine-year-old Kim Phuc, had stripped off her burning clothes after the attack. Her brother, Phan Thanh Tam (left), lost an eye as a result of the napalm, a chemical defoliant used widely by the U.S. Air Force in an attempt to locate military targets. Behind the children are soldiers from the South Vietnamese army. This and other photographs fueled public opposition to the war and eventual U.S. withdrawal from Vietnam.

President George H. W. Bush, who succeeded Reagan in 1989, inherited both the favorable international climate that accompanied the approaching end of the Cold War and the broad public approval that went with it. Bush declared the Vietnam syndrome a thing of the past at the time of the Persian Gulf War, which featured the largest deployment of U.S. troops since Vietnam. Ironically, though, Bush's preoccupation with foreign affairs proved his undoing after the war, when a recession at home prompted challenges in 1992 from former Arkansas governor

Bill Clinton and H. Ross Perot, an independent candidate for president. Perot, who drew most of his votes from disillusioned Republicans, effectively handed the White House to Clinton, who received only 43 percent of the votes cast.

Public Ambivalence in the Clinton Era

The end of the Cold War brought about new patterns in public opinion—ones that reflected the demise of superpower tensions and the birth of U.S. predominance among the great powers. Considerable ambivalence among the public and government leaders about U.S. foreign policy provided the backdrop for these new dynamics. This uncertainty continued throughout the decade because no single foreign policy issue dominated the public's attention or played a decisive role in national elections (see Posen and Ross 1996/1997). Surveys in the early 1990s demonstrated that most Americans wanted their government to pay more attention to domestic problems. By 1998, in the midst of an economic boom at home and no major perceived threats abroad, Americans generally felt little concern about foreign policy. When asked in a prominent survey what was "the biggest foreign policy problem facing the country today," the most common response was "Don't know" (Rielly 2003).

Although public opinion surveys revealed a low regard for his foreign policy performance, Clinton still received the highest approval ratings among the ten postwar presidents, in part because of his high sensitivity to the ebbs and flows of public opinion. Initially committed to completing the U.S. military intervention in Somalia, he quickly pulled the plug on the mission after U.S. troops were killed in October 1993. Similarly, he withdrew U.S. forces from Haiti after they confronted a hostile band of rebels in the nation's capital. From Clinton's perspective, such foreign policy problems could not be allowed to interfere with his primary goal as president—reviving the nation's economic output and competitiveness in markets abroad. Even though Clinton identified "enlargement" of global democracy as a top foreign policy goal, he did not vigorously pursue this goal because of limited public and congressional interest.

Recognizing the lack of public support for military intervention in the former Yugoslavia, Clinton avoided large-scale intervention in Bosnia-Herzegovina despite his stated concerns about "ethnic cleansing" in the region. Public and congressional opposition to U.S. involvement in Kosovo led the president in 1999 to adopt a "zero-tolerance" policy for American casualties, which limited NATO's military role to high-altitude bombings of military targets and the Yugoslav capital of Belgrade. Clinton's refusal to consider deploying ground troops, further motivated by a lack of consensus among the western European allies, angered U.S. military commanders, who sought to keep all options open in order to secure a prompt and overwhelming victory (see Daalder and O'Hanlon 2000; Clark 2001). Although

Americans generally resisted military intervention in the first post–Cold War decade, they still favored active involvement and multilateral cooperation in other areas of foreign policy. This consensus, however, was not reflected in U.S. foreign policies during the 1990s, which took a "unilateral turn" that continued into the new millennium (Kull and Destler 1999).

Rallying around the Flag after 9/11

Domestic issues dominated the 2000 presidential race between George W. Bush and Vice President Al Gore. A September 2000 survey conducted by ABC News and the *Washington Post* found that, of the seventeen election issues of potential concern to voters, "national defense" and "foreign affairs" ranked eleventh and thirteenth on the list, respectively. The four issues of greatest concern to the registered voters surveyed— education, the economy, Social Security, and health care—received the most attention in campaign advertisements and speeches. By contrast, foreign policy issues came up rarely during the presidential debates. Most voters believed the nation was sufficiently secure to make foreign policy a secondary concern.

Fears of terrorism predictably rose to the top of the public's list of concerns after the September 11 attacks, and the ensuing war on terror transformed Bush's presidency. Following a consistent pattern in the history of U.S. public opinion, presidential approval rose sharply as the nation faced a major military conflict overseas. This **rally around the flag effect** is generally attributed to a patriotic sense among citizens that national unity must be maintained in times of crisis (Mueller 1970, 1973). For similar reasons, members of Congress usually avoid criticizing presidents when U.S. troops are in harm's way. The benefits from this rally effect are difficult to gauge, however, and the boost in public approval may be short-lived if the missions falter (see W. D. Baker and Oneal 2001). But there is little doubt that presidents gain politically at the onset of international crises. Some scholars have gone so far as to put forth a **diversionary theory of war**, suggesting that presidents may *provoke* conflicts to boost their approval ratings (see Levy 1989).

Bush clearly benefited from the rally around the flag effect. His public approval ratings before September 11 were lukewarm, averaging 53 percent in eight major surveys.[3] After the terrorist attacks, these ratings soared to an average of 82 percent and peaked at 90 percent, the highest enjoyed by any president. Bush retained his strong reservoir of public support in the months that followed, although his popularity sagged along with the U.S. economy and the military's failure to apprehend al Qaeda leader Osama bin Laden in 2002. Bush experienced a second rally effect in March 2003, when he ordered the invasion of Iraq. A third, but more modest and short-lived rally effect followed the capture of Iraqi leader Saddam Hussein in December

---

3. See http://www.pollingreport.com/BushJob.htm for details of these polls.

2003 (see Figure 7.3). By any measure, the rally effect for Bush was enormous—three times the level experienced by President Franklin Roosevelt after the Japanese attack on Pearl Harbor in 1941.

This period of complacency did not last long. Escalating political violence in Iraq, combined with a deluge of critical reports on the lack of U.S. postwar planning, sent public support for the president's foreign policies into a tailspin. His overall decline in approval, no longer buoyed by rally effects, closely paralleled public dissatisfaction with the war in Iraq and the broader war on terror (see Figure 7.4). By March 2006, Americans had concluded by a two-to-one margin that the war in Iraq was one of choice, not necessity, and that the U.S. position in the conflict was worsening (World Public Opinion 2006).

Figure 7.3 ■ George W. Bush Public Opinion and Rally Effects, February 2, 2001–April 18, 2004

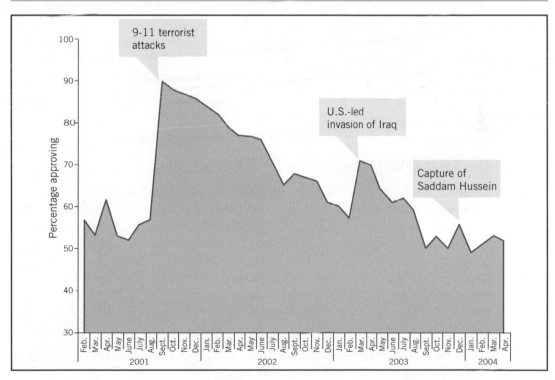

Source: Gallup Organization surveys via the Roper Center for Public Opinion Research, "Presidential Approval Ratings" (2004), http://www.ropercenter.uconn.edu.

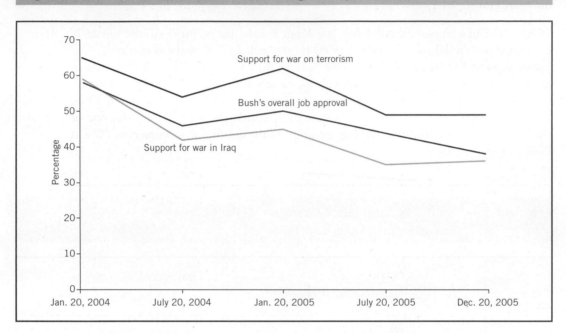

Figure 7.4 ■ Bush's Public Decline: The Foreign Policy Connection

Support for war on terrorism

Bush's overall job approval

Support for war in Iraq

Source: Pew Research Center for the People and the Press, "Iran a Growing Danger, Bush Gaining on Spy Issue" (February 7, 2006), http://www.people-press.org/2006/02/07/iran-a-growing-danger-bush-gaining-on-spy-issue/.

The Onset of War Fatigue

President Bush left office in 2009 with an increasing number of citizens growing wary of the Bush Doctrine and the damage it was doing to U.S. credibility, moral leadership, and overall world power. A July 2008 survey found "improving America's standing in the world" to be the general public's top U.S. foreign policy priority (Chicago Council on Global Affairs 2008). The majority view of U.S. foreign policy aligned with the positions espoused by Barack Obama during his presidential campaign, providing him a clear public mandate to adopt a more liberal approach to foreign affairs. This alignment between public preferences and Obama's foreign policy was visible in four primary areas:

- *Diplomacy.* The United States should negotiate on foreign policy matters with all foreign governments, including those such as Cuba, Iran, and North Korea that are openly hostile to Washington.

- *Multilateral cooperation.* The United States should support global governance and sign global agreements to combat climate change and prohibit the testing of nuclear weapons.

- *International law.* The U.S. government should conduct its foreign policy in accordance with international law, which establishes normative standards of behavior for all governments and a legal basis for sanctions in response to violations.

- *International institutions.* American leaders should support the creation of new global institutions that monitor energy supplies, enforce climate-change agreements, and regulate capital markets.

This alignment of values aside, foreign policy fatigue set in among a majority of citizens by 2012, who believed that U.S. world power was declining and that the Pentagon budget should be cut to help revive the nation's economy. Foreign policy makers, they felt, should be more selective in taking on global problems and should focus their attention on promoting U.S. economic self-interests rather than altruistic goals such as human rights and democratic reforms. In sum, Americans "are seeking a lower profile. They clearly reject the role of the U.S. as a hegemon and want to take a more cooperative stance, even if this means the United States might have to go along with a policy that is not its first choice" (Chicago Council on Global Affairs 2012, 4). These views were starkly reflected in a poll shortly before the 2012 presidential election, when voters placed foreign policy problems dead last on their list of considerations in the race between President Obama and Mitt Romney, the Republican candidate (see Table 7.3).

Developments in Obama's second term fueled the nation's sense of fatigue. The Arab Spring of 2011 unleashed conflicts that appeared beyond Washington's ability to control. Power plays by Russia and China in 2014, combined with the swift rise of the Islamic State terrorist group, further aroused concerns about the future of American primacy. Still, most Americans opposed U.S. intervention in the Middle East. Nor did they favor U.S. intervention on behalf of Ukraine, which suffered from aggression from Russia. Whereas more than 50 percent of Americans in 2002 felt the United States had become more important during the past decade, by 2014 only 21 percent felt this way (Chicago Council on Global Affairs 2014, 10).

As for Obama's overall approval rating, the president followed his predecessors by starting his first term with

Table 7.3 ■ Public Priorities in the 2012 Presidential Election

Question: "Which one of the following is the single most important issue in deciding for whom you will vote?"

The economy	46%
Social issues and values	15%
Social Security and Medicare	12%
Health care	10%
The federal deficit	7%
Foreign policy and the Middle East	6%
Terrorism	1%
Other, not sure	2%

Source: NBC News/Wall Street Journal Survey, September 26–30, 2012, 11, http://msnbcmedia.msn.com/i/MSNBC/Sections/A_Politics/_Today_Stories_Teases/NBCNews-WSJPoll_9-12.pdf.

Note: Total does not equal 100 percent due to rounding.

positive voter ratings and then falling into disfavor by a growing percentage of citizens. Entering office in January 2009 with a positive 67 percent approval rating, the president's approval rating had fallen to 46 percent in May 2015 (Rasmussen Reports 2015). Many surveys found Americans feeling that Obama was not strong enough in response to the many foreign problems facing the United States. A March 2015 survey found that 56 percent of Americans disapproved of the president's response to the threat posed by the Islamic State (Lightman 2015). These critical evaluations contradicted the pattern of voters to oppose U.S. military action in specific cases such as Ukraine, Syria, Iraq, and Yemen. Such inconsistency would not surprise skeptics whose disregard for public opinion led to the Almond-Lippmann consensus.

The View from Overseas

Global public opinion also matters as U.S. political, diplomatic, and military leaders increasingly appeal to foreign citizens for support of their policies and actions. This has been especially true since the end of the Cold War, which, paradoxically, left the United States not only unmatched in power but also highly vulnerable to external scrutiny and criticism by foreign observers. The growing impact of world public opinion stems from several sources: the advance of information technologies, the widespread growth of civil societies in response to democratic reforms, and the greater array of issues and problems that cross national borders. In most countries, foreign citizens in the first post–Cold War decade held favorable views of the United States and its people. Such attitudes toward the United States and American citizens played a key role in advancing U.S. soft power, a far more important asset than its capacity for military coercion (B. E. Goldsmith and Horiuchi 2012). In much of the world, objections to U.S. foreign policies focused on the nation's leaders and their policies, not its people.

Growing domestic doubts about America's wars in the Middle East coincided with a steep rise in global anti-Americanism. Citizens overseas registered deep concerns over many perceived shortcomings of U.S. foreign policy: its penchant for favoring military over diplomatic solutions, its failure to consider or consult with other countries, and its perceived control by multinational corporations.[4] In particular, Bush's decision to launch preventive war against Iraq in 2003 angered much of the global community. By the end of 2006, citizens in thirty-three of thirty-five countries surveyed believed the U.S. war in Iraq had increased the likelihood of terrorist attacks around the world (World Public Opinion 2006). Even in

---

4. Public views of foreign government actions are often linked to personal, cross-cultural impressions. Although foreign citizens associate Americans with several positive traits—"hardworking," "inventive," and "honest"— Americans are also widely perceived as "greedy" and "violent." The negative impressions have been highest in Muslim countries; in those countries that are allied with the United States, including Canada and European nations, "rudeness" is identified as a common negative cultural trait. See Pew Global Attitudes Project (2005).

Table 7.4 ■ Global Public Opinion of U.S. Foreign Policy, 2009

Question: "In our government's relations with the United States, do you think the U.S. more often treats us fairly or abuses its greater power to make us do what the U.S. wants?"

Country	Treats Us Fairly (%)	Abuses Its Great Power (%)
China	14	76
France	26	68
Great Britain	27	68
Indonesia	21	63
Mexico	10	87
Pakistan	6	90
Poland	20	65
Russia	12	75
South Korea	17	81
Turkey	9	86

Source: Steven Kull, Clay Ramsay, Stephen Weber, and Evan Lewis, "America's Global Image in the Obama Era," WorldPublicOpinion.org, July 7, 2009, 3, http://www.worldpublicopinion.org/pipa/pdf/jul09/WPO_USObama_Jul09_packet.pdf.

countries considered close allies, most citizens by 2009 believed the United States "abuses its great power" (see Table 7.4).

Obama's effort to restore U.S. credibility and moral leadership paid off in most surveys of global public opinion. By the spring of 2012, citizens in all European countries surveyed reported more favorable views of the United States and of American citizens than four years earlier (Pew Global Attitudes Project 2012). Perceptions of the United States also rebounded in China, Japan, and Mexico, whose citizens expressed greater respect for American soft power, including its democratic values and "ways of doing business." This favorable trend continued in 2014, when a majority of citizens in countries across Africa, Europe, Asia, and Latin America expressed favorable views of the United States (see Figure 7.5).[5] Reasons for this upward turn in pro-American sentiment varied. Despite his problems at home, President Obama was generally respected

---

5. Among those surveyed, young adults between 18 and 29 were the most enthusiastic about the United States. Citizens older than 50 were most critical, a finding that may be attributed to their longer memory of past problems with U.S. foreign policies.

U.S. foreign policies are frequently criticized at home and overseas. In Multan, Pakistan, protesters gathered in 2012 to express their anger over an attack by U.S. drones that killed eighteen suspected insurgents.

by citizens in most countries surveyed. As for sub-Saharan Africa, its population consistently supported Obama and saw it as a "point of African pride that the leader of the world's most powerful country has roots in their continent" (M. Fisher 2013).

The only negative majorities from the same global surveys came from the Middle East, where only 30 percent of its population had a favorable view of Washington (Pew Research Center 2014a). Only 10 percent of Egyptians approved of the United States, the lowest level among the 42 countries surveyed around the world. Citizens of Turkey, a NATO ally, had only slightly more positive views. Elsewhere, Russian citizens' view of the United States plummeted from 51 percent positive in 2013 to 23 percent in 2014, an outcome directly related to U.S. economic sanctions imposed on Russia following its government's aggressive actions in Ukraine. Finally, the Obama administration's use of aerial drone attacks was widely opposed in global public opinion, including by European citizens who otherwise had warm feelings toward the United States.

Opinions on War and Peace

Public opinion regarding matters of war and peace plays a crucial role for U.S. foreign policy makers whose decisions will have profound consequences for the nation, its allies, and its adversaries. Public sentiments are also vital to politicians seeking to assume or maintain office. In keeping with the trustee model of representation,

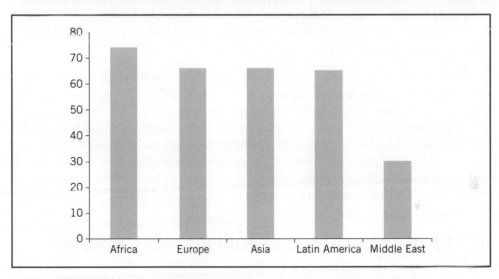

Figure 7.5 ■ U.S. Favorability Ratings from Overseas, 2014

Source: Pew Research Center. *Global Attitudes and Trends.* Washington, DC: Pew Research Center, July 2014.

government elites are presumed to have the necessary background and information at their disposal to make such judgments. Still, the delegate model is also at play because convincing citizens that resorting to war—with all of its uncertainties, hazards, costs, and uncertain consequences—is essential to maintain public support once hostilities have begun. In this section, we review recent studies of public opinion on war and peace.

As noted previously, Americans are generally pragmatic when it comes to the use of force. They have consistently supported military action if the perceived threat is deemed essential to the nation's vital interests, as in the world wars, the Gulf War, and the 2001 invasion of Afghanistan. Most Americans, however, will oppose wars that involve threats that do not seem critical, as in the U.S. interventions in Somalia, the former Yugoslavia, and the more recent attacks on Libya that led to the over-throw of its leader, Muammar Qaddafi. The historical record also suggests that Americans are more likely to support aggression against autocratic and tyrannical governments rather than democracies (Tomz and Weeks 2013).[6]

In fighting terrorism, surveys found a majority of American citizens prepared to defeat this threat aggressively. In a survey conducted by The Pew Research Center (2014b), more than half of citizens supported the use of "coercive interrogations" of

6. In the Afghan war, American citizens who lived in communities where soldiers were killed or injured were more prone to support the war than others (Kriner and Shen 2012).

suspected terrorists. Fifty-six percent believed these measures would reveal vital information needed to prevent future terrorist attacks. To many Americans, harsh treatment of war prisoners served as revenge for their assumed acts against the United States and its allies. Although these views were not shared by foreign policy elites, it is possible that the detention policies of lawmakers could be swayed by pressure from angry constituents demanding retribution (Liberman 2014).

A significant portion of the American electorate also made a "terror exception" regarding civil liberties. In a prominent survey, nearly half of respondents supported measures to compel testimony by suspected terrorists. About one-third believed it was appropriate for government officials to search the homes of suspects without a search warrant and to hold suspected terrorists in detention indefinitely. From this perspective, "principles such as the right against self-incrimination apparently are not cornerstones of the American political system, but rather obstacles to the maintenance of order" (Mondak and Hurwitz 2012).

■ GROUP IDENTITIES AND FOREIGN POLICY VIEWS

Citizens' political viewpoints come from a combination of sources, including their past experience, moral and social values, and exposure to current events. Public opinion is highly personal in this respect, an outcome of factors that are unique to each individual. Still, citizens share many common attributes with others that further define their ideas and interests in U.S. foreign policy. Surveys consistently affirm the strength of **group identity**, or a sense of common cause with other citizens with shared personal traits. According to Donald Kinder and Lynn Sanders (1996, 89), "The interests that enter into the formation of public opinion are collective rather than personal, group-centered rather than self-centered." Citizens are more likely to change their views of U.S. military conflicts when the issues at stake relate to their group identities (Althaus and Coe 2011).

Public opinion regarding U.S. foreign policy tends to cluster in ways that reflect group identities in three primary areas: physical traits, social associations, and political belief systems (see Chapter 3). These group identities, detailed below, are reliable predictors of foreign policy views on a variety of issues. Support for U.S. internationalism is strongest, for example, among affluent Americans with higher levels of education and professional stature. Those with military experience, furthermore, have "systematically different opinions on whether and how to use force" (Feaver and Gelpi 2004, 184). Even the regions in which Americans live provide clues regarding public opinion, as residents of the South and western mountain states tend to favor unilateral and military-based foreign policies more than their Northeastern, Midwestern, and West Coast counterparts (Trubowitz 1992). Understanding the **demographics** of public opinion reminds us that this concept, like that of "national interest," is rarely monolithic and is instead a mosaic of ties that cut across American society.

Physical Identities: Gender, Race, and Generation

Shared physical traits provide a strong foundation for group identities. Men and women, studies show, consistently diverge in their opinions regarding foreign policy. This **gender gap** is clear on the most critical issues of war and peace, as surveys have found men to be more supportive than women of U.S. military involvement in the Korean, Vietnam, and Persian Gulf wars (Mueller 1973, 1994; see also Caprioli 2000). These differences appeared in both *whether* to intervene in a particular conflict and *how* such an intervention should proceed (Nincic and Nincic 2002, 550). "In practically all realms of foreign and domestic policy," Benjamin Page and Robert Shapiro (1992, 295) concluded bluntly, "women are less belligerent than men."[7]

Racial differences, though less often studied by scholars, are also significant in shaping foreign policy views. Compared with whites, African Americans are consistently more inclined to favor U.S. detachment in foreign policy (Holsti 1996) and more skeptical of U.S. military interventions (Mueller 1994). African Americans are also more likely than whites to oppose higher levels of defense spending, a pattern that may be explained by the economic gaps between the two races and the greater desire among African Americans for domestic spending on social programs. To one analyst (Bowser 2003, 19–20), these differences reflect deeper problems in American society that threaten its foreign policy ambitions: "A continued failure to face racial inequality and do something about it means continued isolation and hostility overseas tomorrow." This perspective suggests that African Americans, like women, suffer from political alienation, feeling less empowered in public affairs than white men and therefore less influential in U.S. foreign policy (see Figure 7.6).

Finally, generational differences among Americans have been found to "endow the individual with a common location in the social and historical process" (Mannheim 1952, 291). It is widely assumed, for example, that those who experienced World War II learned distinct "lessons of history" that were not apparent to Americans born and raised after the war. The same can be said for the "Vietnam generation," which expressed greater reluctance about U.S. military interventionism than did those who grew up in the 1950s and 1960s (Roskin 1974). Public opinion polls provide modest support for this generational link, although other demographic attributes tend to have greater impact on foreign policy opinions (O. R. Holsti 1996).

Social Identities: Education, Wealth, and Religion

Unlike physical identities, social and political identities involve shared attributes that derive from personal experience. Two sources of social identity—education and

---

7. There are exceptions to this gender gap on matters of war and peace. Women have been found to be equally or more supportive than men of U.S. military interventions when they are backed by the United Nations or if they are motivated by humanitarian concerns (D. J. Brooks and Valentino 2011).

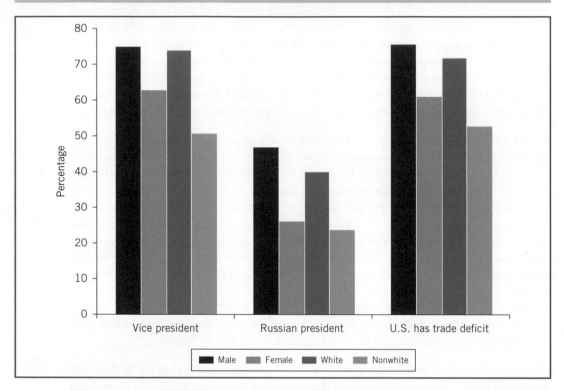

Figure 7.6 ■ Societal Gaps in Public Knowledge: Percentage of Americans Who Could Identify . . .

Source: Pew Research Center for the People and the Press, "What Americans Know: 1989–2007," April 15, 2007, 17–18, http://www.people-press.org/files/legacy-pdf/319.pdf.

wealth—have a clear impact on Americans' foreign policy views. These two attributes are so closely related in statistical studies, however, that they are commonly considered together. Religious affiliation, the other attribute considered in this section, has a different, but equally strong influence on public opinion and U.S. foreign policy.

Relatively high levels of wealth and education are defining features of the foreign policy elite and, to a lesser extent, the attentive public. In short, affluent Americans typically favor "cooperative internationalism" in U.S. foreign policy, a pattern that contrasts with the mass public's greater tendency to support isolationism or "militant internationalism" (Wittkopf 1990, 38). These differences extend to the economic realm, as those with more education and wealth are more likely than other citizens to favor open trade with other countries (Page and Barabas 2000). Taken together, these findings suggest that affluent Americans identify more closely with global issues than does the mass public, which views foreign affairs more skeptically and is more concerned with U.S. national interests. Affluent Americans, furthermore, may have a more personal stake in the global economy that compels them to favor open trade.

Religious beliefs, another source of social identity, also shape public views regarding U.S. foreign policy. This "faith factor" (Wald and Wilcox 2006) contributes to foreign policy views that stand apart from those of citizens who rarely, if ever, attend religious services. Public opinion surveys affirm this **divine divide** in public opinion. During the Bush years, regular churchgoers believed far more than their counterparts that the United States was "doing the right thing" in foreign policy (see Table 7.5). In Christian churches, active members commonly respond to surveys with views that "echo the traditional theme of American exceptionalism: Americans are a people chosen for a special mission in the world and especially blessed by God" (Yankelovich 2005). Not surprisingly, Jewish and Muslim Americans tend to favor Israel and Arab states in the Middle East, respectively, in their positions regarding U.S. foreign policy (Page and Bouton 2006).

Evangelical Protestants formed a cohesive voting bloc that proved critical to Bush's reelection in 2004, demonstrating the importance of social movements in shaping

Table 7.5 ■ The "Divine Divide" in U.S. Foreign Policy (percentage who agree, based on attendance at religious services)

Statement	Frequency of Church Attendance			
	Never	Occasionally	Regularly	Frequently
Believe the U.S. is "generally doing the right thing with plenty to be proud of" in its relations with the rest of the world	28	33	49	52
"Worry a lot" that the war in Iraq is leading to too many casualties	63	60	50	45
Agree that the U.S. can help other countries become democracies	31	35	43	48
Give a high grade to the U.S. on giving the war on terror all the attention it deserves	48	56	64	64

Source: Daniel Yankelovich, "Poll Positions: What Americans Really Think About U.S. Foreign Policy," *Foreign Affairs* 84 (September–October 2005), 2–16.

U.S. foreign policy (see Chapter 9). By 2008, thousands of evangelical "megachurches" served more than 5 million worshippers, a majority of whom were under thirty-five years old, middle class, and not formerly involved in church life (Thumma and Bird 2009). These citizens, primarily white-collar workers living in the suburbs, were also likely to have conservative political beliefs and a preference for Republican candidates in national elections. On national security matters, evangelical Protestants provided the strongest support among religious subgroups for Bush's aggressive response to the September 11 attacks and his decision to invade Iraq in 2003 (Pew Research Center for the People and the Press 2006b). A more recent survey found that "rising death tolls, spiraling financial costs, and negative media reports about the Iraq war [had] the least effect on Evangelicals because of their firm religious beliefs that conflict in the Middle East is part of a divine plan" (Baumgartner, Francia, and Morris 2008).

Political Identities: Ideology and Political Party

A final source of group identity involves the general views citizens hold of politics—their ideology—and the political parties that they regularly support. The "basic attitudes" (Page and Bouton 2006, 238) of citizens, once formed early in life, tend to be highly stable over time and guide their judgments on a variety of specific issues. On foreign policy matters, for example, those who identify themselves as liberals express more concern over human rights, global poverty, and environmental decay than do conservatives, whose primary concerns tend to focus on strengthening U.S. military power, restricting immigration, and promoting U.S. businesses overseas. The results of one prominent study (Wittkopf 1990, 34) "strongly confirm the view that ideology colors perceptions of the appropriate role of the United States in world affairs." Specifically, liberals were most closely identified with *accommodationist* foreign policy positions, whereas conservatives best fit the category of *hard-liners*. For example, Gallup surveys during the 1991 Gulf War found a majority of conservatives favoring U.S. military action and most liberals favoring extended economic sanctions and negotiations (O. R. Holsti 1996, 152).

Citizens' ideological views have a direct impact on their party affiliations, with conservatives overwhelmingly aligning with the Republican Party and liberals supporting candidates from the Democratic Party. Like basic attitudes, these partisan identities are firmly embedded and show little fluctuation over time. For their part, Republican voters tend to favor more unilateral and militaristic U.S. foreign policies (Dueck 2010). These positions have hardened since the 1990s, with those aligned with each party growing less likely to adopt alternative positions on specific foreign policy issues. With regard to the Iraq War, self-identified Republicans were between 50 and 60 percent more supportive of the U.S. invasion than Democrats (O. R. Holsti 2011).

Trends in public opinion reflect the erosion of the political center in U.S. politics (see Chapter 5). The increased polarization of both mass and elite views has, in turn, produced unprecedented partisan conflict over U.S. foreign policy. As noted elsewhere, the Republican-led Congress in the late 1990s effectively overrode President Clinton's national security strategy of global "engagement" and democratic "enlargement." Congress also approved deep cuts in several areas of U.S. foreign policy that aligned with goals of engagement, including multilateral peacekeeping, financial support of the United Nations, and foreign aid. Although a majority of Americans supported these programs, most Republicans did not, a well-researched statistical finding that fueled legislative opposition to Clinton's foreign policies. With a Republican majority in both houses of Congress, George W. Bush claimed that he was fulfilling a national mandate to adopt a "muscular" response to the September 2001 attacks. Still, most Democrats in the general public were critical of the Bush Doctrine, particularly the invasion of Iraq. This lack of consensus, which continued into the Obama administration, casts further doubt on the once-popular proposition that "politics stops at the water's edge."

■ CONCLUSION

Political and technological trends have converged in the past fifty years to magnify the public's impact on U.S. foreign policy. American citizens expect the government to take their views and policy preferences into account (World Public Opinion 2008). For their part, political and military leaders routinely gauge public sentiments and likely responses to their foreign policy choices. Overseas, technological developments and the spread of democratic rule empower private groups and expand press freedoms, adding a potent transnational dimension to the pressures already imposed by domestic civil society.

As this chapter has described, public support for U.S. foreign policy has shifted from general acceptance during the early Cold War to greater skepticism since the Vietnam War. The views of citizens have also shifted from consensus to widespread contention over the ends and means of U.S. foreign policy. This polarization, which mirrors the general political climate in Congress, virtually ensures that any foreign policy will face substantial and outspoken dissent within the public and on Capitol Hill. These debates, which are fueled by activists within the attentive public (Abramowitz 2010), deprive the United States of a united front on the most urgent problems in world politics.

The impact of U.S. public opinion will continue to be hampered by a political culture that remains stubbornly ignorant of world history, geography, and current events. Such aloofness breeds misperceptions of world politics and makes citizens susceptible to manipulation by political leaders. The lack of public scrutiny also gives elites considerable leeway to provide favors to special interests, particularly corporate leaders (see Jacobs and Page 2005). The insular character of U.S. public opinion, a throwback to the nation's "splendid isolation" at its founding, runs counter to its primacy and pervasive global presence today.

The paradox of America's world power stems in part from a disconnect between public opinion and government behavior. As political scientist I. M. Destler (2001b, 75) described that disconnect, "We seem to have a rational public and an ideological ruling class. Average Americans are basically centrist, prone to balance, compromise, fair shares, and reasonable resolutions." This argument is strengthened by several U.S. foreign policy decisions in the past two decades that ran counter to prevailing public preferences. These actions included the government's refusal to pay past UN dues, its rejection of the Comprehensive Test Ban Treaty, and the invasion of Iraq in the absence of UN authorization. The mass public's general inattention to foreign affairs—reflected in test scores and public opinion surveys—surely made the government's decisions to defy the popular will easier and safer politically.

WANT A BETTER GRADE?

Get the tools you need to sharpen your study skills.
Access practice quizzes, eFlashcards, video, and multimedia at
edge.sagepub.com/hook5e.

KEY TERMS

Almond-Lippmann consensus, p. 232

attentive public, p. 228

cooperative internationalism, p. 232

delegate model, p. 228

demographics, p. 250

diversionary theory of war, p. 242

divine divide, p. 253

foreign policy elite, p. 228

gender gap, p. 251

group identity, p. 250

international trust, p. 232

mass public, p. 228

militant internationalism, p. 232

public relations presidency, p. 226

rally around the flag effect, p. 242

trustee model, p. 228

INTERNET REFERENCES

The **Chicago Council on Global Affairs** (http://www.thechicagocouncil.org) is one of the world's largest groups organized for studying and informing the public about world affairs. The council publishes regular studies of public opinion and U.S. foreign policy that are closely followed by scholars and policy makers.

Gallup (http://www.gallup.com) has studied public opinion and behavior for more than half a century and continues to conduct nationwide and international surveys on political and social issues.

The **Inter-University Consortium for Political and Social Research** (http://www.icpsr.umich .edu) provides the world's largest archive of digital and social science data, which are compatible with a variety of statistical software programs.

The **National Opinion Research Center** (**NORC**; http://www.norc.org), at the University of Chicago, specializes in public opinion data and analysis.

The **Pew Research Center for the People and the Press** (http://people-press.org) is an independent research center that studies public opinion, news media coverage, and political issues. The Pew Center conducts a wide range of surveys in the United States and overseas, focusing in recent years on global public attitudes toward U.S. foreign policy.

Polling Report (http://www.pollingreport.com) is an independent, nonpartisan group that offers public opinion data from a variety of sources. Of particular interest to foreign policy researchers are topics such as national security, presidential elections, and the role of the United Nations.

The **Program on International Policy Attitudes** (http://www.pipa.org), part of the School of Public Affairs at the University of Maryland, focuses on public opinion and media coverage related to U.S. foreign policy and international issues.

The **Roper Center for Public Opinion Research** (http://www.ropercenter.uconn.edu) at the University of Connecticut offers access to public opinion and polling data through a historical and current archive. Reports include the General Social Survey, National Election Survey, and a variety of other polls.

8

THE IMPACT OF MASS COMMUNICATIONS

William B. Plowman/NBC/NBC NewsWire via Getty Images

Much of the televised discourse on U.S. foreign policy takes place on cable networks. Among the most popular hosts of such programming in recent years has been Rachel Maddow, whose nightly talk show became a fixture on MSNBC. While Maddow and her guests offer viewers a liberal viewpoint on a nightly basis, conservatives have turned for many years to *The O'Reilly Factor* and its host Bill O'Reilly on Fox News. Maddow took on U.S. foreign policy with her book titled *Drift: The Unmooring of American Military Power* (2012).

CHAPTER OBJECTIVES

8.1   Identify the functions of the news media in a democracy.

8.2   Discuss three different factors that influence foreign news coverage in the United States.

8.3   Explain the ways the U.S. government tries to control media coverage.

8.4   Summarize the ways that government has used or been impacted by social media.

8.5   Describe the role of foreign media sources to U.S. news consumers.

The Arab world erupted in political violence in September 2012 after a low-budget American film, *The Innocence of Muslims*, went viral on YouTube. Contrary to its title, the film slandered the Prophet Mohammed by depicting him as irresponsible and depraved. Connected by Facebook and Twitter, an angry crowd gathered in Cairo, Egypt, to denounce the United States. The protest soon turned violent, as many in the crowd burned American flags and tried to overrun the U.S. Embassy. The chaos, which left hundreds injured and many more arrested, quickly drew media attention as al Jazeera and other regional networks provided vivid footage of the clashes, which spread to more than twenty countries. "The vehemence and volatile nature of the protests in capital after capital—images of which were broadcast around the globe almost instantly via blogs, social media networks, and cable news stations—were unmistakable" (Birnbaum and DeYoung 2012).

The U.S. government, whose negative image in the region improved after the election of President Obama in 2008, was again vilified in the Arab world. More generally, the episode demonstrated the powerful foreign policy role played by mass communications, which include both traditional news media and a burgeoning array of social media linked to the Internet. Social media, driven by technological advances, provide vital platforms for the voices of civil societies. It did not take long, however, for other advocates of social media to foment civil wars and political violence across the Middle East. Terrorist groups such as the Islamic State became skillful in exploiting social media as valuable recruiting tools.

This chapter explores the impact of mass communications on U.S. foreign policy. It first examines the roles and behaviors of the news media in covering the relations and actions of the United States beyond its borders. The chapter then describes how social media have complicated the flow of information between American citizens and their government, which is engaged in "real-time diplomacy" (Seib 2012) through

a perpetual dialogue. The convergence of news coverage and social media further complicate U.S. foreign policy by disseminating messages—good, bad, and often ugly—to a global audience. As Obama (2012) noted in an address to the United Nations, "At a time when anyone with a cell phone can spread offensive views with the click of a button, the notion that we can control the flow of information is obsolete. The question, then, is how do we respond?"

The United States serves as a primary source of world news, as well as a common subject—and target—of foreign-based news coverage. The capacity of other governments and societies to make judgments about U.S. foreign policies will continue to increase as mass communications give a voice to more private citizens who were previously excluded from public affairs. With growing scrutiny of Washington, political scandals, fissures in U.S. public opinion, and missteps in foreign policy become subjects of daily conversations worldwide. In this respect, the enhanced freedoms of speech and press coverage in many countries, while fulfilling a long-standing goal of U.S. foreign policy, heighten U.S. vulnerabilities and compound the paradox of America's world power.

For most Americans, news reports and Internet contacts are their primary sources of information about the "outside world." As discussed in Chapter 7, Americans have limited knowledge of world history and geography and are generally uninterested in foreign affairs unless the United States is facing a clear and present danger to its security (see Table 8.1). Local and national news consistently draw interest from Americans. By contrast, most respondents in a survey indicated that they follow world news only "when something important is happening" (Pew Research Center for the People and the Press 2008, 111). In terms of ratings, the biggest U.S. news story in the early 1990s was not the collapse of communism or the genocide in Rwanda but rather the murder trial of former football player O. J. Simpson. Between June 1 and June 3, 2015, the three major U.S. broadcast networks allotted more than forty-eight minutes to the gender-change operation of former Olympic champion

Table 8.1 ■ Public (In)Attention to World News

Americans Who Follow . . .	Local News (%)	National News (%)	World News (%)
Most of the time	57	54	39
Only when important	39	44	56
Don't know	4	3	5

Source: Pew Research Center for the People and the Press, "In Changing News Landscape, Even Television Is Vulnerable: Trends in News Consumption, 1991–2012," September 27, 2012, 31, http://www.people-press.org/2012/09/27/section-3-news-attitudes-and-habits-2/.

Bruce Jenner (now Caitlyn Jenner). None of these networks, however, offered coverage of the sudden drop in U.S. economic output, a spike in health care costs, or the falling approval ratings of President Obama (J. Meyer 2015).

The managers of U.S. news coverage respond to public interests by focusing primarily on domestic issues. This strategy, based on a desire for greater appeal to a mass audience, was clearly on display in 2014 and 2015 when far more articles written by the Associated Press covered education and health care than those covering the rise and spread of the Islamic State (see Figure 8.1). Of the most popular news-related topics appearing on Facebook in 2013, users placed international news close to the bottom among topics they commonly discussed (Anderson and Caumont 2014, 5).[1] In view of this weak appetite for world news, even the most cursory press reports give many citizens all the information they seek. Their lack of direct international exposure, through travel or personal contacts abroad, leaves Americans further dependent on the news and social media for information and ideas about U.S. foreign policy.

Commercial and technological changes in the news industry compound the public's superficial understanding of global developments. The contraction of the newspaper industry in recent years has deprived Americans of detailed coverage of foreign affairs, which is rarely offered by television networks and most Internet sources.[2] The major broadcast networks, meanwhile, have reduced coverage of world news, which has higher costs, more logistical complications, and less appeal to most viewers. For their part, cable news networks and political blogs are prone more to polemics than to serious efforts to find common solutions to foreign policy problems.

1. The most popular Facebook topic: entertainment.

2. Foreign news in a representative sample of U.S. newspapers fell by 53 percent between 1980 and 2010 (Kumar 2011). In recent years, leading newspapers such as the *Chicago Tribune*, the *Philadelphia Inquirer*, and the *Boston Globe* closed all of their overseas news bureaus.

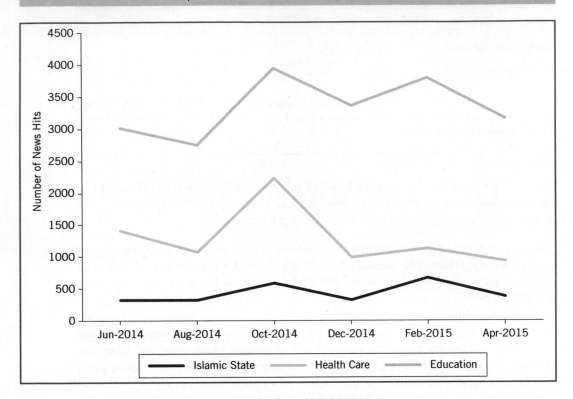

Figure 8.1 ■ Home Sweet Home: News Coverage of Foreign and Domestic Issues, June 2014–April 2015

Source: Compiled by the author, based on Associated Press Online, Westlaw Next database.

■ FUNCTIONS OF THE NEWS MEDIA

A free press stands as a pillar of democratic governance, providing civil society with a crucial check on government authority. The U.S. Constitution reflects this belief in its First Amendment, which explicitly protects freedom of the press. As Thomas Jefferson (1787) once mused, "Were it left to me to decide whether we should have a government without newspapers, or newspapers without a government, I should not hesitate a moment to prefer the latter."

The news media play an even more vital role in modern, mass-based democracies. Because of the large scale of these political systems, most people do not participate directly in the political process. Instead, they learn what their government is doing primarily by following news reports in the electronic and print media. The public is even more dependent on the news media for learning about foreign policy issues that involve faraway and seldom-seen people and places. Their judgments regarding U.S. foreign policy, therefore, are often driven by journalists who simply pass along presidential declarations (Eshbaugh-Soha and Linebarger 2014).

Print and broadcast news outlets, as well as a rapidly widening array of Internet sources, fill three primary roles in the U.S. foreign policy process:

- *Source of information and opinions.* The most vital role played by the news media is to keep the public informed about developments at home and abroad. Throughout U.S. history, foreign correspondents have provided firsthand accounts of events overseas, including the many wars fought by the United States. Print and broadcast outlets also supplement news reports with commentaries on such foreign policy issues as the war on terror, U.S. relations with China, and global trade. Newspapers have long filled their editorial pages with such commentaries, whether written by staff editors or guest columnists. In recent years, debates over foreign policy have also become the staple of cable television news channels, such as CNN, Fox News, and MSNBC. In addition, millions of Americans tune in daily to radio commentators like Rush Limbaugh, whose conservative arguments and attacks on liberals appeal to millions of Americans.

- *Agenda setter.* Studies of the news media have consistently established a link between news coverage and the perceived importance by the public and governments of the issues covered. In short, media coverage of a political problem, whether in domestic or foreign policy, increases the importance attached to that problem by citizens and foreign policy makers. The same relationship holds for the U.S. public's perception of foreign countries. Extensive media coverage of Russian aggression in 2014 led to steep declines in Vladimir Putin's approval ratings, which fell from 51 percent to 15 percent between 2013 and 2015 (Pew Research Center for the People and the Press 2015a). Similarly, extensive press coverage of foreign policy issues such as foreign aid tends to stimulate the U.S. government to pay greater attention to those issues (Van Belle and Hook 2000).

- *Government watchdog.* A third and crucial role of a free press is to scrutinize government actions and to reveal wrongdoings when they occur. The CBS newsmagazine *60 Minutes II* served this function on April 29, 2004, when it featured horrifying photographs of Iraqi detainees at Abu Ghraib prison, which was once the site of brutal acts of torture under Saddam Hussein. Subsequent investigative reports disclosed that U.S. military officials had known for months about the abuses in Iraq as well as others in Afghanistan, some of which led to the deaths of detainees (see Hersh 2004). News stories on other problems related to U.S. military operations also provided the public with vital information that was withheld by government sources. A November 2014 article in the *New Yorker* revealed that U.S. drone strikes in Pakistan led to many more civilian casualties than were acknowledged by the Obama administration (Coll 2014).

The functional role of the news media in the U.S. foreign policy process is a dynamic one in which influence runs in both directions between the news media and their partners in the information chain—the public and the government (see Figure 8.2). For government officials, the news media serve as means for explaining government policies, disseminating propaganda, and "leaking" confidential information officials want the public to know about. As Theodore White observed, "No major act of the U.S. Congress, no foreign adventure, no act of diplomacy, no great social reform can succeed in the United States unless the press prepares the public mind" (quoted in Graber and Dunaway 2015, 14). For the public, as noted earlier, news organizations serve as vital sources of information and opinions and instruments of governmental oversight. Citizens are also granted voice opportunities, or ways to express their viewpoints, through letters to the editor, op-ed articles, and other means. They also convey feedback to the commercial news media by purchasing the goods and services companies pay the media to advertise.

The relationship between journalists and the government agencies they cover is inherently fraught with tension. By their very nature, reporters want to learn all they can about what the government is doing, and they stand to benefit greatly when they uncover evidence that government officials have acted improperly, illegally, or incompetently. Government officials are therefore understandably hesitant to open their doors to the news media. In the foreign policy arena, because of the secrecy that routinely surrounds diplomatic negotiations, military maneuvers, and other aspects of policy making, government officials are especially eager to keep journalists at arm's length.

Figure 8.2 ■ The News Media's Bidirectional Impact

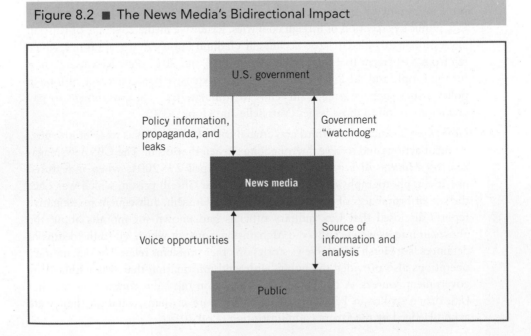

■ PATTERNS OF FOREIGN NEWS COVERAGE

The field of journalism, always in flux, has undergone seismic change in recent years. Within the past generation, a few open-air television networks have given way to hundreds of cable channels, satellite radio has ended the dominance of local AM and FM stations, local newspapers are an endangered species, and social media have assumed a central role in everyday life. Many journalists have enhanced their stature by creating their own blogs and interacting directly with their followers. American news outlets no longer compete just against each other but also vie with foreign news operations and postings on Politico, the Monkey Cage, the Huffington Post, the Daily Beast, and other digital outlets.

News consumers seek out and habitually follow "media outlets that match their beliefs and dispositions" (Stroud 2008, 342).[3] This pattern of **selective exposure** is important given the changing roles and forms of the news media. Although news consumers pay close attention to the messages of like-minded media figures and thus may be better informed, they tend to adopt more rigid political beliefs that make national consensus less likely. In this way, today's more diverse media contribute to the recent polarization of public opinion—and to the ideologically charged politics that have become a fact of life in Washington.

As noted earlier, the U.S. media rarely cover international news unless the United States is facing a major crisis. After the Cold War, the major broadcast and print outlets curtailed their foreign coverage in response to viewer preferences for domestic news and increased competition from cable networks. With a shrinking number of foreign correspondents covering global events, major newspapers rely on wire services such as the Associated Press and Reuters. Even the most prestigious newspapers like the *Washington Post* frequently turn to freelance writers and photographers to assume the often-dangerous work of foreign news coverage. Among the top twenty-five magazines sold in the United States in 2014, only one—*Time* (ranked eleventh)—provided detailed coverage of international news (BurrellesLuce 2015).

These trends reflect the intensifying market pressures imposed on U.S. news outlets, which must respond to audience preferences to maximize market share and advertising revenue. For a decade before the war on terror, news consumers sent the media the clear message that they had limited interest in foreign news. Newspaper readers consistently ranked their interest in news coverage as (1) state and local news, (2) national news, (3) foreign news involving the United States, and (4) foreign news not involving the United States (Rielly 2003). As in the case of Facebook noted earlier, news consumers consistently rank international affairs near the bottom of topics they follow regularly in the news (Pew Research Center for the People and the Press 2012a, 30).

----

3. This cognitive trait is linked closely to that of selective perception (see Chapter 3), by which citizens generally seek out information and "cues" that reinforce their existing belief systems.

The majority of Americans find only the most urgent news about events abroad worthy of their attention. Indeed, surveys find that the huge audiences that tuned into the evening news broadcasts in the pre-cable era were not actually interested in current events and public affairs. Instead, most viewers were habitually drawn to the medium of television itself, which in the 1950s was a novel source of relaxation after the workday, and the evening news on ABC, CBS, and NBC was all the local stations carried at this time of day. Once given opportunities to watch reruns of *The Office*, *South Park*, and other entertainment shows on cable television, most viewers abandoned the evening news on the open-air networks, which today serve a small fraction of their former audiences. "In a high-choice environment, lack of motivation, not lack of skills or resources, poses the main obstacle to a widely informed electorate" (Prior 2005, 577).

Opinion leaders and the attentive public, while relying on commercial news to a limited degree, are more prone than the mass public to seek the thorough news coverage available from the Public Broadcasting Service (PBS) and National Public Radio (NPR), which are not owned by corporations focused on making profits. These networks, which air programs such as, respectively, the *Frontline* documentary series and *All Things Considered*, win prestigious news awards every year but have far smaller audiences than for-profit outlets. Highly educated and affluent Americans are also drawn disproportionately to foreign news networks and Internet sites. Although the explosion of media options has reduced the knowledge gap within this small share of the national population, it has widened the overall gap between wealthy and well-educated Americans and those at the other end of the socioeconomic spectrum.

Evolving Technologies and Media Coverage

Linkages among technological advances, news coverage, and public opinion appear throughout U.S. history. The invention of the telegraph in the nineteenth century permitted newspapers to provide immediate coverage of the Civil War. In the months preceding the Spanish-American War, newspaper publishers learned to rally public opinion and thereby greatly expand their sales. Radio became an essential source of public information during World War II. Meanwhile, the newsreels shown at movie theaters and the photographs featured in popular magazines provided visual images of the fighting in Europe and Asia.

The Vietnam War became the first **living-room war,** bringing footage of U.S. military actions into American homes on a daily basis (Mandelbaum 1983). Graphic scenes of carnage in Vietnamese villages incited citizens already skeptical of the war. Such coverage also provided daily reminders that a U.S. victory in Vietnam was not "at hand," as had been stated repeatedly by the Johnson and Nixon administrations. The war also marked a turning point in the news media's coverage of U.S. foreign policy. Before the war, reporters and editors generally had supported the government's stated goals and had not subjected its tactics to close scrutiny. Vietnam, along with the

Watergate scandal, produced a generation of skeptical journalists who openly questioned the motives and judgments of national leaders.

The advent of cable television in the early 1980s expanded the range of news providers. The Atlanta-based Cable News Network (CNN) was the first to provide around-the-clock coverage of breaking news in the United States and abroad. Its coverage of the 1984 famine in Ethiopia generated widespread sympathy for the victims and prompted a series of benefit rock concerts, Live Aid, that were televised worldwide and raised tens of millions of dollars for emergency relief. Five years later, CNN transmitted live footage of the pro-democracy uprising in China that culminated in the government slaughter of protesters in Tiananmen Square. This use of force against unarmed students outraged global public opinion and led to condemnations and sanctions by most industrialized states against the Chinese government.

The end of the Cold War created a "new global optic" that included the absence of U.S.-Soviet ideological competition, the rise of regional conflicts, and accelerated economic globalization (Grunwald 1993, 14). The 1991 Persian Gulf War gave television networks their first opportunity to broadcast a major military conflict in "real time" (W. L. Bennett and Paletz 1994). The instigator of the war, Iraq's Saddam Hussein, reportedly tuned in to CNN throughout the conflict, while U.S. officials relied on the same broadcasts for battlefield information. **Rooftop journalism** became a staple of televised war coverage, with flak-jacketed CNN reporters gaining celebrity status by narrating U.S. attacks on downtown Baghdad. CNN's audience increased tenfold during the war, and on some days it exceeded the sizes of the broadcast networks' audiences. Meanwhile, twenty of the twenty-five largest U.S. newspapers experienced sharp gains in circulation during the war (Hallin and Gitlin 1994).

The rapidity with which globalized news coverage prompts government action is often referred to as the **CNN effect**. Among the most vivid examples are Somalia's 1992 civil war and the resulting famine, which were covered extensively by CNN and other networks. President George H. W. Bush said the images of starving Somalis so disturbed him that he felt compelled to order a humanitarian intervention. Many analysts (e.g., Strobel 1997; P. Robinson 2001) have found a reciprocal relationship between press coverage and U.S. foreign policy: U.S. responses to problems overseas, provoked in part by media reports, increase future coverage and public interest in the areas in question.

In the 1990s, the media repeatedly cut back coverage of international affairs despite the fact that the United States had emerged from the Cold War as the undisputed world leader in terms of military power, economic wealth, and political influence. Print and broadcast news organizations closed foreign bureaus and paid more attention to developments at home. Foreign news predictably regained its hold on media attention after the terrorist attacks of September 2001. In early 2003, news outlets provided saturation coverage of the invasion of Iraq, aided by the nearly 3,000 journalists armed with

Table 8.2 ■ Cable Networks and the Iraq War, Spring 2003		
Network	Average Viewership	Change of Ciewership since War Sarted
Fox News	3.3 million	+ 236%
CNN	2.7 million	+ 313%
MSNBC	1.4 million	+ 360%

Source: Nielsen Media Research, www.nielsenmedia.com.

videophones and laptop computers who received press credentials. While the "big three" broadcast networks recorded higher ratings, the cable networks such as CNN and Fox News enjoyed explosive growth in viewership (see Table 8.2).

Advances in interactive media technology have allowed citizens to take action in response to global events. This included an unprecedented global response to the January 2010 earthquake in Haiti, which killed more than 200,000 people and nearly leveled the capital city of Port-au-Prince. Within weeks of the disaster, nonprofit groups received more than $500 million in donations, most of which were transmitted electronically via the Internet. A similar digital outpouring followed the March 2011 earthquake and tsunami in Japan, which killed nearly 16,000 people and crippled the Fukushima Daiichi nuclear power plant.

News consumers, who previously were loyal to a small number of news outlets, are now free agents who receive their political news from an ever-widening range of sources. A survey conducted by the Project for Excellence in Journalism (2013) found that nearly one-third of news consumers had abandoned at least one of their traditional news sources. According to a recent survey (American Press Institute 2014), the average American uses four devices for news, and half of them have signed up for news alerts. A majority of those surveyed also said the new technologies increase their interest in politics, including world news. Finally, most said they continue to depend on established news organizations for facts while following social media for opinions.

Characteristics of World News

Technological developments thus play a critical role in shaping the form and content of news coverage, but a closely related factor is the growing concentration of media outlets (see Compaine and Gomery 2000). This trend has been hastened in recent years by media deregulation in the United States. In the name of free enterprise, government officials abolished a variety of rules designed to foster competition and diversity. By 2014, six conglomerates were dominating the U.S. news and entertainment industry.[4] Their holdings extended far beyond news providers to include movie studios, radio stations, music studios, local television stations, book and magazine

---

4. These major conglomerates were General Electric, News Corp, Disney, Viacom, Time Warner, and CBS (Snyder 2014).

publishers, and makers of consumer electronics. These and related links to banks and other financial institutions threaten the editorial independence of each news outlet, whose reporting is presumed to be free from economic pressure. The potential conflicts of interest in these cases are obvious.

News coverage of U.S. foreign policy features six common trends and characteristics:

From print to video. The emergence of CNN in the 1980s coincided with a long-term contraction in the newspaper industry, whose advertising revenues fell from nearly half of the national total to just 22 percent in 1998 (Compaine and Gomery 2000, 3). By 2009, fewer than thirty U.S. newspapers managed bureaus in Washington, D.C., in contrast to the more than seventy bureaus in the 1980s (Project for Excellence in Journalism 2009).[5] Most Americans still rely on television as their primary source of news (see Figure 8.3). This type of coverage favors events with strong visual appeal. News executives allocate less time to less telegenic, but equally important problems such as nuclear proliferation. News consumers are also attracted to the visually stimulating content they find on their home computers, tablets, and smart phones.

The rise of niche media. Not long ago, most Americans relied on their local newspapers; mass-circulation magazines such as *Time* and *Newsweek;* and three television networks—ABC, CBS, and NBC—for their daily news. These media outlets provided millions of citizens with news of general interest and avoided controversies and debates. All this has changed in recent years. Whereas the circulation of local newspapers has plummeted since the 1980s, the number of specialty publications and newsletters (most delivered electronically) has increased dramatically (Project for Excellence in Journalism 2009). As can be seen on most cable news networks, news consumers interested in domestic and international politics seek "niche" media outlets that reinforce their ideological positions (Stroud 2011). While the proliferation of blogs and other social media outlets provides an essential venue for specialized news content, they also discourage a collective search for shared values and frames of reference that lead to social consensus.

U.S.-centrism. News organizations have learned that foreign news, to interest most Americans, must have a "peg" to the United States, such as a possible deployment of U.S. forces or an impact on trade or immigration. Because general news about political developments overseas usually does not concern Americans, news managers avoid stories that do not relate directly to this audience (Golan 2010). This bias in news budgets produces coverage that may exaggerate the importance of the United States in global affairs, while prompting readers and viewers to disregard important problems that affect much of the world's population but not U.S. citizens.

----

5. Leading newspapers such as the *Chicago Tribune, Baltimore Sun,* and *Los Angeles Times* had closed their Washington bureaus by the end of 2008.

By contrast, major foreign outlets such as the BBC provide more coverage of foreign news, including a substantial volume of news about U.S. foreign policy.

Conflict orientation. Coverage of all news, foreign and domestic, tends to emphasize conflict rather than cooperation, chaos rather than order. "If it bleeds, it leads" is a popular standard used widely by local and national news editors in deciding what is worth covering. In foreign policy, such a standard leads to an emphasis on civil wars and international conflicts, whose dramatic images have the strongest impact on viewers and readers. Of secondary importance are nonviolent political conflicts, such as closely contested elections and struggles for power. This bias in news management distorts public understanding by subjecting citizens to the misperception that the "outside world" is plagued by unrest and disorder.

Superficiality. The preoccupation with visual images, conflict, and late-breaking news prevents reporters from providing in-depth coverage of their stories or paying attention to long-range problems such as global warming, economic inequalities, population growth, and weapons proliferation. News consumers thus have little context in which to understand day-to-day crises elsewhere and U.S. options in responding to them. Coverage of the Persian Gulf War, for example, rarely moved beyond breaking news to explore the underlying cultural and economic problems in the region that had fueled the conflict (Iyengar and Simon 1994). Such coverage has given rise to **parachute journalism,** a pattern in which reporters descend on a trouble spot and then move on, never gaining the deep understanding of the problems in the area that would have given their reporting greater substance.

Arbitrariness. Foreign news coverage in the United States tends to be guided by immediate developments rather than long-term priorities and principles. The news media's attention to a foreign country generally lasts only as long as the crisis of interest, after which journalists flock en masse to other trouble spots. This was clearly the case when Israeli forces fought a short but devastating war against Palestinians in the Gaza Strip. Only a moderate amount of media attention was paid to the simmering tensions in Gaza in the early months of 2014. This coverage spiked dramatically during the intense hostilities in July and August, and then gradually disappeared from the radar screens of U.S.-based news editors (see Figure 8.4). The arbitrary nature of U.S. news coverage can have direct consequences for U.S. foreign policy, as the lack of public attention to the sources and aftermaths of war zones can tempt policy makers to ignore ongoing problems that can spark violence at any time.

As noted earlier, the U.S. military intervention in Somalia was prompted in large part by media coverage of the war-induced famine in the African nation. A similar crisis in nearby Sudan received little press or government attention. Even in areas that attract the media spotlight, however, the effects on government policy are skewed. "If you look at how humanitarian aid is delivered in Bosnia you see that those areas where the TV cameras are most present are the ones that are best fed, the ones that

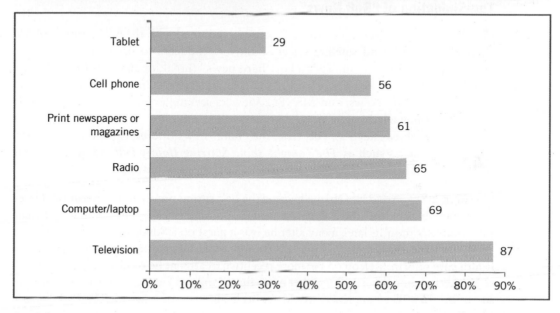

Figure 8.3 ■ Reliance on Sources of News, 2014 (percentage of Americans using various media)

Source: American Press Institute, "The Personal News Cycle: How Americans Choose to Get their News," 2014. Arlington, VA: American Press Institute.

receive the most medicine," observed Mohamed Sacirbey, Bosnia's ambassador to the United Nations. "While on the other hand, many of our people have starved or died of disease and shelling where there are no TV cameras" (quoted in Seib 1997, 90).

The ability of global news coverage to shape the agenda of U.S. foreign policy raises troubling questions, ones that Thomas Jefferson and other early advocates of a free press could not have anticipated. First, public and government attention is drawn only to trouble spots abroad that are readily accessible to camera crews. In other war-torn areas, such as the Democratic Republic of the Congo in the 1990s, the absence of news coverage prevented public awareness of the bloodshed and discouraged engagement by the U.S. government. Second, the media's focus on regional hot spots tempts foreign policy makers to neglect long-term problems (Van Belle and Hook 2000).

Most important, media-driven foreign policy erodes the capacity of diplomats and other public officials to pursue a clear, consistent, and coherent national strategy. As George Kennan (1996, 297) observed, "If American policy from here on out, particularly policy involving the uses of our armed forces abroad, is to be controlled by popular impulses . . . provoked by the commercial television industry, then there is no place—not only for myself, but for the responsible deliberative organs of government."

The Seduction of "Soft News"

The dominance of television as a news source, combined with the proliferation of TV channels on cable and satellite systems, allows producers to offer many forms of news suited to different audiences. For "hard news" (breaking news stories), viewers turn to the major U.S. networks—ABC, CBS, and NBC—and the cable networks such as CNN, Fox News, and MSNBC. Viewers seeking entertainment turn to **soft news**. Newsmagazines such as *60 Minutes,* video tabloids such as *Entertainment Tonight,* talk shows such as *The View,* the "fake" news offered by *The Daily Show,* and variety shows such as *The Tonight Show Starring Jimmy Fallon* have attracted comparable, if not larger, audiences than the purveyors of hard news.

In March 2009, President Obama became the first sitting president to appear on a late-night comedy program, the *Tonight Show.* He appeared on *The Late Show with David Letterman* six months later, a day after he was a guest on a Sunday morning hard news program, *This Week with George Stephanopoulos.* Obama, actively promoting his health care reform, welcomed the more receptive treatment he received on Letterman's show. At the same time, he knew that more than 7 million viewers, more than twice the size of his *This Week* audience, would get his health care message on *The Late Show.*

Soft news producers commonly rely on celebrity stories—the 2000 marriage of Jennifer Aniston and Brad Pitt, the death of Michael Jackson in 2009, and the divorce of Kim Kardashian in 2011—for the huge audiences (and advertising revenues) they attract, but they also frequently address pressing issues of the day. In contrast to traditional news programs, which provide basic facts and details about the crises, soft news outlets emphasize personal stories that highlight the role of the people caught up in the events. Soft news productions also "frame" foreign policy conflicts in moralistic terms to make the stories understandable and compelling to an audience that ordinarily avoids political news.

Packaged this way, such **infotainment** highlights specific foreign policy issues without burdening its audience with their multifaceted origins and political complexities. Critics of soft news fear that this casual approach to news merely makes citizens cynical rather than sharpening their sense of civic-mindedness (Clawson and Oxley 2013). Soft news advocates, however, see it as a "gateway" that can stimulate greater attention to public affairs in the future (M. A. Baum and Jamison 2011). They also point to evidence that consumers of soft news learn more from its presentation of political issues than they do from hard news presentations.

The sources of soft news also include popular magazines, books, and Internet sites that examine U.S. military conflicts, the political travails of other countries, and

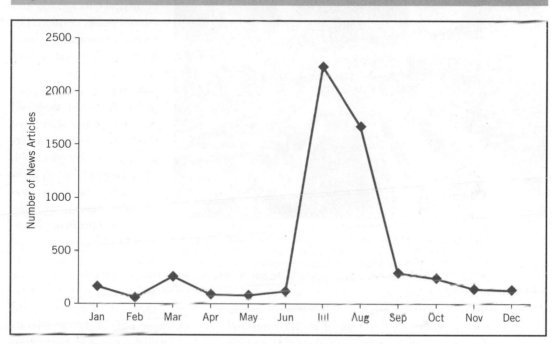

Figure 8.4 ■ News Articles about Gaza before and after Its 2014 War with Israel

Source: Compiled June 2015 by the author, based on Associated Press Online, Westlaw Next database.

other foreign policy issues. War movies such as *Apocalypse Now* (1979), *Black Hawk Down* (2001), *The Hurt Locker* (2008), *Zero Dark Thirty* (2012), and *American Sniper* (2014) may produce greater knowledge of world events, which in turn may elicit more public concern for peaceful conflict resolutions. Studies show that citizens who are unfamiliar with policy issues are often receptive to new information and political causes (see Iyengar 1991; Zaller 1992). The news media, therefore, can lower the nation's knowledge gap even when moviegoers, readers of fiction, and Internet surfers are less interested in learning than in being entertained.

■ GOVERNMENT EFFORTS TO CONTROL THE MESSAGE

When it comes to the news media's coverage of its actions, the U.S. government is not a simple bystander. On the contrary, government officials work actively to shape that coverage in ways that show them in the best possible light. **Spin control**, or the elaborate efforts by government leaders to improve their public approval by influencing media reports, has become an art form in recent years (see Kurtz 1998).

The remains of U.S. casualties from the recent military conflicts in Afghanistan and Iraq are delivered to Delaware's Dover Air Force Base for subsequent release to families and burial. The Pentagon had earlier resisted the release of this and other photographs to the news media, fearing that such images would weaken public support for the ongoing conflicts linked to the global war on terror.

By manipulating information, the government seeks to advance its agenda and control public opinion. The media historically have been a primary instrument of **propaganda**—that is, false and misleading public information designed to enhance the stature of the government or its policies. Jody Powell (1984, 223), Jimmy Carter's press secretary, believed the government "has not only the right but a positive obligation to lie" when national interests are at stake. Early in the war on terror, White House press secretary Ari Fleischer carried out an elaborate "system of disinformation—blunter, more aggressive, and in its own way, more impressive than spin" (Chait 2002, 20). Alarmist government warnings of possible terrorist threats had two primary effects: heightening public concerns about terrorism and boosting President Bush's approval ratings (Nacos, Bloch-Elkon, and Shapiro 2011).

The most common means by which the U.S. government controls information is *keeping secrets*. Secrets are especially common in foreign policy, which relies to a large extent on classified information and on necessarily private lines of communication between Washington and foreign governments. Most news outlets accept the need for secrecy, and they may even withhold from the public information they receive "off the record" from government officials. Journalists and government officials view this practice as essential, both to maintain national security and to preserve their mutually beneficial ties.

"Framing" U.S. Foreign Policy

News organizations generally support government attempts at **framing** foreign policy problems—that is, structuring and simplifying these problems so that they are understood by U.S. citizens in ways that favor the government's position. Political leaders know that policy problems are viewed from several perspectives, so they work to devise news frames that serve their interests. Opponents of regulations to slow global warming, for example, frame the issue as an economic barrier rather than an environmental problem (McCombs et al. 2011, 30). The United States, with its two-party system, has a more narrow range of policy debate than most other democracies, which makes the government's framing of domestic and foreign policy relatively easy.

As noted in Chapter 3, government officials routinely "construct" a particular image of allies and adversaries to garner support for their foreign policies, knowing that the vast majority of Americans with little knowledge of or interest in foreign affairs "can be routinely manipulated by alternative framings of a problem" (Chong and Druckman 2007, 103). Ronald Reagan's depiction of *contra* rebels in Nicaragua as "freedom fighters" in the 1980s served this purpose, as did George H. W. Bush's portrayal of Saddam Hussein as "Hitler" before the United States ousted Iraq from Kuwait in 1991 (Norris, Kern, and Just 2003). In 2008, George W. Bush framed the war between Russia and Georgia as a move back to the Cold War.

The process by which government frames penetrate the news media and public opinion is complex (see Habel 2012). As conceived by the White House, news frames "cascade" through the federal government and are adopted by the lower-level officials who maintain regular contact with the press. Only when internal divisions among U.S. officials are exposed do the news media depart from the government's frame and create their own images of the foreign policy problem (D. A. Lewis and Rose 2002; Entman 2004). Otherwise, news organizations freely grant government leaders access to audiences and adopt the government's ideology and viewpoints (see Hunt 1987).

All governments have a keen interest in the content of news coverage because of its critical role in the formulation of public opinion. A country's government and its media outlets tend to frame foreign policy coverage in ways that adhere to that country's distinctive customs and political systems. For example, in 2001, a U.S. surveillance plane and a Chinese jet fighter collided off the coast of China, killing the fighter pilot and forcing the damaged U.S. plane to land on Chinese territory and the crew to suffer a prolonged period of detention and interrogation. Whereas U.S. media focused mainly on the diplomatic standoff over the stranded crew, the government-controlled Chinese press framed the incident as an example of U.S. hegemony and imperialism (Hook and Pu 2006).

The White House demonstrated its skill in "manufacturing consent" (E. Herman and Chomsky 1988) during the U.S. invasion of Iraq. Despite their expressed reservations about the invasion, the editorial boards of major U.S. newspapers "conditioned themselves to treat Bush's national security argument with deference" (Mooney 2004, 29). As the invasion began, the government "embedded" reporters within military units to provide firsthand accounts of the overthrow of Saddam Hussein's government. The White House correctly anticipated that the **embeds** would identify with the troops and thus produce favorable reports of the missions (see Katovsky and Carlson 2003). Still, Americans commonly draw their own conclusions on such matters based on their worldviews, partisan loyalties, and other personal factors (Baum and Groeling 2010).

Public Diplomacy and Strategic Communications

Although foreign policy makers customarily conduct their statecraft through conventional diplomatic channels, they also resort to **public diplomacy** to achieve their objectives. In effect, public diplomacy goes over the heads of foreign leaders by appealing directly to the citizenry of other countries. The messengers of public diplomacy, whose ranks have included diplomats as well as scholars, artists, and journalists, are uniquely positioned to project the nation's cultural values and demonstrate the vitality of its civil society. In doing so, they may strengthen international support for the United States in ways beyond the reach of conventional diplomats and political leaders.

The U.S. government has sponsored programs of public diplomacy for many years. The Fulbright Program, for example, provides for the international exchange of scholars, teachers, and students in many fields of study. Another program is the Voice of America, a worldwide international radio service, which has been joined in recent years by regional broadcasters Radio Martí and TV Martí (to Cuba), Radio Free Europe/Radio Liberty, Radio Free Asia, and Radio Sawa (to Arab countries). As part of its public diplomacy mission, the State Department also operates press centers in the United States and funds democracy programs in foreign countries. Overseeing these efforts is the department's Office of International Information Programs, an agency created in 1999 to replace the U.S. Information Agency.

Although President Obama attained instant popularity upon taking office in January 2009, lingering anti-Americanism and ongoing security threats to the United States frustrated his effort to revive public diplomacy. Led by Hillary Clinton, the State Department turned to social media as a vehicle for public diplomacy during the 2011 Arab Spring. While this outreach in support of democratic freedoms enhanced goodwill in some countries, ongoing U.S. drone strikes and targeted killings in the Middle East had the opposite effect.

The State Department is not alone in trying to create a stronger image for the United States overseas. The same goal is pursued regularly by the Pentagon in the form of **strategic communications**, defined by the Defense Science Board (2004, 97) as "the U.S. Government's ability to communicate with foreign audiences and thereby shape understanding of and support for U.S. national security policies." Civilian and military officials around the world conduct **influence operations** directed toward "opinion leaders whose credibility and trustworthiness [are] judged to be high" (E. V. Larson et al. 2009, 6). These contacts include private briefings with foreign governments and media owners, press releases, and other tools of public relations that are, in this case, designed to advance the interests of U.S. world power.

Controlling the message requires unity of purpose and getting the facts straight. Both of these, however, are often difficult in a complex organization such as the U.S. government. The costs of mixed signals can be severe. For example, in September 2012, after Muslim citizens began protesting the U.S. film *The Innocence of Muslims,* the U.S. embassy in Cairo released a statement that rejected "the actions by those who abuse the universal right of free speech to hurt the religious beliefs of others." To some, this statement amounted to a justification for the anti-American demonstrations that spread across the Arab world. Efforts by the White House to disavow the embassy's statement failed to subdue the protests while revealing policy and tactical differences within the U.S. government.

Leaking Foreign Policy: For Better and Worse

Government officials frequently reveal secrets by way of **press leaks** to journalists. Some leaks, such as those used by Bill Clinton regarding a new trade pact with China, may serve as trial balloons to gauge public support for a possible policy change. Other leaks are used to punish dissenters by secretly providing embarrassing information about them to reporters. The Bush administration resorted to this tactic in 2003 by revealing to columnist Robert Novak that Joseph Wilson, a former ambassador and career foreign service officer, was married to a clandestine CIA agent. The leak, intended to discredit Wilson (2004) after he wrote a *New York Times* op-ed disputing Bush's claims about Iraq's pursuit of nuclear materials in Africa, ended his wife Valerie Plame's intelligence career and placed her life in jeopardy.

Unofficial leaks, by contrast, are supplied by anonymous critics who hope to reform government behavior by revealing potentially harmful or illegal practices. Government whistleblowers, for example, frequently alert reporters to cost overruns in the defense industry and failed weapons systems tests that would otherwise be unknown to the public. Government employees who find press leaks a useful way to affect policy from behind the scenes may apply the same tactics.

The U.S. government is more often the target than the source of leaks. In 1971, for example, the *New York Times* published a series of leaked documents that revealed the White House's misinformation campaigns in the Vietnam War. The Nixon administration tried, but failed, to suppress the documents. Such attempts to prosecute the sources of leaks were rare until the Obama administration filed six such complaints between 2009 and 2012 (Savage 2012, A14). The leaked information involved an array of topics and media outlets, from classified information about North Korea (Fox News) to mismanagement of the National Security Agency (the *Baltimore Sun*) and U.S. efforts to sabotage Iranian nuclear research (a 2006 book titled *State of War* written by James Risen).

The tidal wave of press leaks in recent years merely amplified a long-standing practice of government agencies and news outlets to reveal sensitive political information when it suits their needs. For advocates of government transparency, the costs of press leaks are outweighed by their benefits. "Everyone leaks in this town—the White House, members of Congress, their staffs, the Pentagon, the CIA, the State Department—everyone," claimed Patrick B. Pexton (2012), ombudsman

IN THEIR OWN WORDS

Edward Snowden *Press leaks have long played a role in the relationship between U.S. government and the news media. When Edward Snowden, a former NSA officer, chose to release evidence of a secret NSA program that gathered personal information on millions of American citizens, he knew he would likely never step foot again in the United States. In several interviews, Snowden explained why he made this momentous decision.*

The NSA specifically targets the communications of everyone. It ingests them by default. It collects them in its system and it filters them and it analyzes them and it measures them and it stores them for periods of time simply because that's the easiest, most efficient, and most valuable way to achieve these ends. So while they may be intending to target someone associated with a foreign government or someone they suspect of terrorism, they're collecting your communications to do so.

Any analyst at any time can target anyone, any sector, anywhere. Where those communications will be picked up depends on the range of the sensor networks and the authorities that analyst is empowered with. Not all analysts have the ability to target everything. But I sitting at my desk certainly had the authorities to wiretap anyone from you or your accountant to a Federal judge to even the President if I had a personal e-mail. . . . I think that the public is owed an explanation of the motivations behind the people who make these disclosures that are outside of the democratic model.

The greatest fear that I have regarding the outcome for America of these disclosures is that nothing will change. People will see in the media all of these disclosures. They'll know the lengths that the government is going to grant themselves powers unilaterally to create greater control over American society and global society. But they won't be willing to take the risks necessary to stand up and fight to change things to force their representatives to actually take a stand in their interests.

Source: Laura Poitras and Glenn Greenwald, "NSA Whistleblower Edward Snowden: 'I Don't Want to Live in a Society That Does These Sorts of Things.'" *The Guardian*, June 9, 2013. Video.

of the *Washington Post.* "Leaks lubricate the gears of foreign and defense policy. Leaks are part of the dialogue over policy."

In comparison to the sheer volume of previous press leaks, nothing equaled the mountain of secret documents compiled by **WikiLeaks,** an Internet site founded in 2006 by Julian Assange, an Australian journalist and political activist (see Domscheit-Berg 2011). Millions of leaks have since been released by the website, including about 750,000 military and diplomatic documents involving the U.S. wars in Iraq and Afghanistan. Assange was aided in the effort by Bradley Manning, a private first class in the U.S. Army. Manning, who served as an intelligence analyst with a top secret security clearance, volunteered to search out secret documents relating to U.S. foreign policy. In 2013, he was convicted of violating the Espionage Act and sentenced to thirty-five years in prison.

Much of the leaked information was published by major newspapers, including the *New York Times.* Secretary of State Clinton, otherwise a strong advocate for press freedoms, condemned "in the strongest terms the unauthorized disclosure of classified documents and sensitive national security information." To the *New York Times,* publishing the leaks was justified given their importance as a "secret chronicle of the United States' relations with the world in an age of war and terrorism" (Shane and Lehren 2010, A1). The leaks "provide an unprecedented look at backroom bargaining by embassies around the world, brutally candid views of foreign leaders, and frank assessments of nuclear and terrorist threats." The *Times,* which was joined by several foreign newspapers in circulating material from WikiLeaks, pledged to withhold publications of documents labeled "top secret."

© Andres Pantoja/Demotix/Corbis (Assange)/
The Guardian via Getty Images (Snowden)

The U.S. government is often stung by media press leaks that reveal undisclosed information about its foreign policies. Two figures, Julian Assange (left) and Edward Snowden, engineered the most damaging press leaks. Assange posted thousands of WikiLeaks between 2006 and 2009 that revealed previously unknown actions of U.S. leaders. In 2014, Snowden used his security clearance in the National Security Agency to reveal its program of domestic surveillance.

Most of the WikiLeaks were trivial in nature, reflecting the personal rifts among politicians and government officials that commonly occur out of public view. Other revelations in the first wave of WikiLeaks had more weight (Elliot 2010), providing information such as the following:

- Secretary of State Clinton asked U.S. diplomats stationed overseas to collect personal information about the foreign officials with whom they worked on a regular basis.

- In 2010, the United States conducted multiple drone strikes in Yemen with the approval of that country's president, Ali Abdullah Saleh, who privately told Gen. David Petraeus, commander of U.S. forces in the region, that "We'll continue saying the bombs are ours, not yours."

- The leaders of Saudi Arabia urged the United States to attack Iran in response to its apparent nuclear weapons program. King Abdullah personally advised U.S. military leaders to "cut off the head of the snake."

A second and more damaging array of classified government documents was leaked to journalists by Edward Snowden, a twenty-nine-year-old contractor working with the NSA. Snowden, who previously worked for the CIA, was hired by both agencies due to his highly advanced computer skills, without having earned a college degree.

He became deeply concerned in 2013 when he discovered the depth of an NSA program that gathered much of the U.S. population's telephone calls, e-mails, financial transactions, and other personal information. This practice, which ran against the agency's long-standing ban on domestic surveillance without a warrant, transformed the NSA into a wholesale collector of private communications wherever they could be found.

The Snowden leaks began on June 5, 2013, with an article written by journalist Glenn Greenwald (2013) of the London-based *Guardian* newspaper. Greenwald revealed that in April, the Justice Department issued a secret court order that required the telecom giant Verizon to turn over its database of electronic communications. All customers' records were opened to the U.S. government, not just persons suspected of committing crimes or acts against the United States. A day later, Greenwald and his co-author Ewen MacAskill reported that the NSA had previously tapped into the electronic files of Microsoft, Facebook, Yahoo!, Google, YouTube, Skype, and other online sources (see Figure 8.5). In addition to phone calls and e-mails, the NSA gained direct access to citizens' videos, photographs, file transfers, and online social network details. The program, known as PRISM, "allows the agency to directly and unilaterally seize the communications off the companies' servers" (Greenwald and MacAskill 2013).

This was not the first time the U.S. government adopted these measures. During the Vietnam War, the *New York Times* revealed that the CIA was spying on American

Figure 8.5 ■ The NSA's PRISM Program

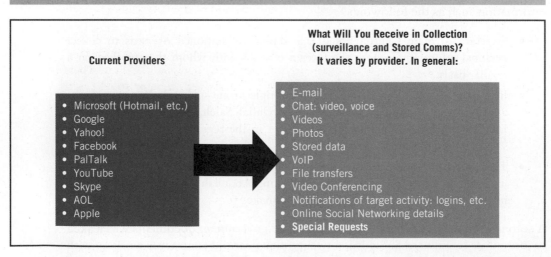

Current Providers

- Microsoft (Hotmail, etc.)
- Google
- Yahoo!
- Facebook
- PalTalk
- YouTube
- Skype
- AOL
- Apple

What Will You Receive in Collection (surveillance and Stored Comms)? It varies by provider. In general:

- E-mail
- Chat: video, voice
- Videos
- Photos
- Stored data
- VoIP
- File transfers
- Video Conferencing
- Notifications of target activity: logins, etc.
- Online Social Networking details
- **Special Requests**

Source: U.S. National Security Agency via www.extremetech.com.

antiwar activists and other private citizens whose actions, in the view of the Nixon administration, posed a threat to U.S. security. According to Seymour Hersh (1974, 1), the actions of about 7,000 individuals and 1,000 organizations were actively monitored by the agency. The revelations of tapped phones and other forms of domestic surveillance prompted Congress to pass legislation that barred the practice. Sen. Frank Church (D-ID), who led this effort, warned that the CIA's domestic spying "could be turned around on the American people, and no American would have any privacy left" (quoted in Greenwald 2013).

More recently, the *New York Times* revealed that, shortly after the 9/11 terrorist attacks, President Bush issued a presidential order that approved the monitoring of "the international telephone calls and international e-mail messages of hundreds, perhaps thousands, of people inside the United States without warrants" (Risen and Lichtblau 2005). In 2006, *USA Today* reported that the U.S. government had contracted with AT&T, Verizon, and BellSouth to collect telephone records of tens of millions of Americans. "For the customers of these companies, it means that the government has detailed records of calls they made—across town or across the country—to family members, co-workers, business contacts and others" (Cauley 2006).

Snowden's news leaks were most noteworthy as they provided media outlets with a vast range of classified documents regarding domestic surveillance that circulated within the intelligence community. Snowden said he knew the risks he was taking. Shortly after the leaks were made public, the U.S. government charged him with illegally releasing classified information, a violation of the 1917 Espionage Act. Fearing an imminent arrest, Snowden left Hong Kong and flew to Russia, one of the few governments that would allow him to land on its territory. He sought asylum in several other countries, but was unable to leave Moscow after the State Department revoked his passport.

This controversy raised vital questions regarding the balance between personal privacy and national security. Government officials defended their actions as necessary given the sheer mass of potential terrorists operating in the United States. They claimed that processing so many arrest warrants had slowed, and in some cases thwarted, potential captures or kills of known terrorists. In a variety of public opinion polls, a majority of citizens seemed prepared to accept sacrifices in their privacy in order to maintain the nation's security. The public was more equally divided as to whether Snowden, by leaking the details of the NSA's secret surveillance program, was a well-intended whistleblower or a criminal worthy of life in prison.

With the support of Congress in June 2015, Obama approved new restrictions on the NSA's ability to collect and store citizens' telephone records. The Freedom Act, however, still permitted the agency to request these records from telecoms with a court order, and it left open the status of e-mail and other forms of expression. It remained to be seen whether the NSA's expanded mission would end at some point or become a permanent fixture of American life.

■ THE SOCIAL MEDIA REVOLUTION

As described earlier, technological advances have historically propelled changes in relations between citizens and states, in the role and impact of the press, and in the day-to-day conduct of foreign policy. This pattern certainly applies to social media, defined as "the collection of websites and web-based systems that allow for mass interaction, conversation, and sharing among members of a network" (Murphy, Hill, and Dean 2013). This technology, barely utilized before the new millennium, provides new outlets for government and private expression along with a nearly limitless range of information for students, observers, and practitioners of world politics.

Web-based news providers such as Yahoo!/ABC News, CNN, and NBC News Digital are now primary sources of world news for millions of Americans (see Table 8.3). As of fall 2015, Facebook served more than 1.4 billion users worldwide, and the number of Twitter users approached 300 million (Statista 2015). Nearly 60 percent of American adults were Facebook users, and 71 percent of adult Internet users had Facebook accounts (Pew Research Center 2015b). At the same time, one-half of Internet users used Twitter, and more than a quarter of users were tied in to Instagram (photographs), Pinterest (photographs), and LinkedIn (business connections).

Mohammed Al-Shaikh/AFP/Getty Images

The paradox of world power is demonstrated in many ways. In 2014, Shiite Muslims in Bahrain take a selfie during a religious ceremony. Their use of social media, which was invented and developed by the United States, was also used widely to coordinate attacks on American targets in the Mideast and other parts of the world.

As the centerpiece of the new media, the Internet has altered the landscape of U.S. foreign policy. The U.S. military's swift overthrows of the governments of Afghanistan (2001) and Iraq (2003) owed much to improvements in web-based communications—a central element of the revolution in military affairs (see Chapter 6).[6] Meanwhile, managers of U.S. foreign economic policy have used the nation's technological edge to capture a greater market share of overseas investments and exports. The Internet

6. The Defense Department was the primary sponsor of the development of the Internet during the 1960s and 1970s (Margolis and Resnick 2000, 25–51).

also has accelerated the pace of diplomatic communications within the foreign service and between the United States and foreign governments. This shift toward **digital diplomacy** marks "the most important innovation affecting diplomatic practices since the fifteenth century" (Dizard 2001, 1).

The Internet combines the immediacy and visual impact of television with the substantive depth of the print media, offering its users a vast range of information at little or no cost. According to Netcraft, a British Internet service company, the number of websites increased to more than 861 million by January 2014, a 28 percent increase over the previous year (Netcraft 2014). This global network is congested further by cell phones, text-messaging systems, and portable tablets that convey and transmit information. American troops now communicate instantaneously with their families at home, exchanging messages that used to take days or weeks to deliver.

For the United States, the Internet has become a powerful source of cultural influence. According to Don Heath, president of the Internet Society, "If the United States government had tried to come up with a scheme to spread its brand of capitalism and its emphasis on political liberalism around the world, it couldn't have invented a better model than the Internet" (quoted in Lohr 2000, WK-1). English is the dominant language of the web, and most web "visits" are to sites based in the United States. According to Internet World Stats (2014), while the United States has among the highest rates of Internet penetration (87 percent of U.S. population), Chinahas more than 600 million Internet users, nearly twice the entire U.S. population (see Table 8.4).

As part of its public diplomacy campaign, the State Department in 2010 launched a project titled *21st Century Statecraft* that placed the Internet and social media at the service of U.S. foreign policy. Among other initiatives, the department created a Facebook page that drew 13 million "friends" and a Twitter feed that attracted 2 million followers by 2012 (Tomei 2012). Common themes of these transmissions

Table 8.3 ■ Top Ten Online News Sites, January 2015

News Site	Monthly, Unique Visitors (in millions)
Yahoo!/ABC News	128
CNN	102
NBC News Digital	101
Huffington Post	100
CBS News	84
USA Today	79
BuzzFeed	78
New York Times	58
Fox News	57
Daily Mail	51

Source: Pew Research Center, *State of the News Media* 2015c, 11.

Table 8.4 ■ Global Online Populations, 2014	
Country	Number of Internet Users (millions)
China	642
United States	277
India	243
Japan	110
Brazil	110
Russia	87
Indonesia	71
Germany	71
Nigeria	70
Mexico	59
United Kingdom	57
France	55
Egypt	46
South Korea	45
Iran	45

Source: Internet World Stats, www.internetworldstats.com/.

included the importance of Internet freedoms, which were depicted as "universal" political rights. Foreign policy makers have used this technology in many ways. For example:

- During her term as secretary of state, Hillary Clinton oversaw an Internet project that "connected millions of Afghans equipped with cellphones and other mobile devices, allowing an exchange of ideas that has never been possible in Afghanistan outside Kabul, the capital" (Nixon 2014, A8).

- American officials relied on a variety of social media, including smartphone photographs and posts on YouTube, Instagram, and Twitter, to refute Russian President Putin's assertions that his armed forces were engaged in destabilizing the eastern region of Ukraine (Gordon 2015).

- Secretary of State John Kerry became an avid Twitter user beginning in 2014, and among his first tweets was a blunt condemnation of Syria's government for its bombing of apartment buildings and a mosque in Aleppo (Landler 2014a).

- The U.S. ambassador to Japan, Carolyn Kennedy, launched a social media campaign to pressure Tokyo about its approval of large-scale dolphin slaughter, an effort that also drew media-based criticism from celebrities such as Ricky Gervais and Bryan Adams (B. Powell 2014).

The Foreign Policy Blogosphere

The Internet is often considered a more "democratic" news source than established media outlets because it allows individuals and groups an opportunity to engage actively in policy discussions and debates. Indeed, Internet content can be viewed more as a dialogue than a one-way stream of information from media or government elites to the general population. In this respect, the proliferation of Internet blogs represents a breakthrough in mass communications. This trend, which in the United States began in the mid-1990s with the online *Drudge Report*, has since spread to specialized areas of interest, including U.S. foreign policy. Andrew Sullivan (2008), a well-known author, magazine writer, and editor, launched his own blog, *The Daily Dish,* which received nearly 40 million visits in 2007. His description of blogging captures the unique nature of this new media form:

> This form of instant and global self-publishing . . . is the spontaneous expression of instant thought—impermanent beyond even the ephemera of daily journalism. . . . Every writer since the printing press has longed for a means to publish himself and reach—instantly—any reader on Earth. Every professional writer has paid some dues waiting for an editor's nod, or enduring a publisher's incompetence, or being ground to literary dust by a legion of fact-checkers and copy editors. If you added up the time a writer once had to spend finding an outlet, impressing editors, sucking up to proprietors, and proofreading edits, you'd find another lifetime buried in the interstices. But with one click of the "Publish Now" button, all these troubles evaporated.

Not surprisingly, *blogs,* a term derived from *Web log,* have entered the realm of U.S. foreign policy. These sites generally extend beyond the host's personal views and provide links to a variety of supporting materials: newspaper and magazine articles, government reports, videos, and other foreign policy blogs. Those interested in current actions by the White House and underlying tensions in the foreign policy process—many of which are not covered by mainstream media outlets—can gain vital insights from a variety of these blogs, including the following:

- *Democracy Arsenal* (www.democracyarsenal.org), sponsored by the National Security Network, provides ongoing commentary on U.S. foreign policy issues written by a team of experts plus useful links to other blogs.

- The *Foreign Policy Association* (www.fpa.org/blogs/) offers timely and in-depth analyses of such issues as U.S.-China relations, global crime, and the Persian Gulf as part of the association's Great Decisions Global Affairs Education Program.

- *Monkey Cage* (themonkeycage.org) offers news consumers timely *Washington Post* articles on U.S. foreign policy and analyses of policy problems originating from political science researchers. Its goal is to make complex issues more understandable to a wide audience.

- *FP Voices* (www.foreignpolicy.com/category/voice), a widely read blog sponsored by the magazine *Foreign Policy,* offers news updates and commentaries by leading experts. Well-respected foreign policy experts such as Thomas E. Ricks, Lauren Wolfe, and Stephen M. Walt maintain blogs that contribute to public awareness.

- *Real Clear World* (www.realclearworld.com) provides daily links to newspaper and magazine articles from around the world on all aspects of global politics. A related blog, *Real Clear Defense* (http://realcleardefense.com), manages a data bank of articles, reports, and government documents regarding U.S. security policy.

- *Global Voices* (http://globalvoicesonline.org) provides reports from more than 700 authors whose coverage extends beyond the range of mainstream news media. Most of the content comes directly from journalists as well as reformers and victims of poverty and political repression in the developing world.

As in the case of print and broadcast outlets, regular visitors to the blogosphere are highly selective. They tend to be dissatisfied with mainstream news sources run by corporations or governments, and they seek viewpoints that generally conform to their existing beliefs. "Few would deny that blogs are inherently subjective, in line with their authors' perspectives or predispositions; indeed, for many bloggers, a non-biased blog would be pointless, even if it was possible to achieve" (Allan 2006, 85). In this respect, blogs reinforce rather than challenge existing opinions, a pattern that reduces further the prospects for national consensus on key foreign policy issues. Still, by actively engaging in Internet chat rooms and other interactive venues, many people seize the opportunity to express their own ideas and concerns about foreign policy and make contacts, however "virtual," with like-minded citizens around the country and world.

Social Media's Call to Arms

The interactive nature of social media provides citizens a golden opportunity to make their voices heard in new and meaningful ways. Among these, social media outlets have proven to be vital for antigovernment activists who seek political reforms or wholesale regime changes. Their ability to communicate with each other while also voicing their grievances and demands has radically altered the balance of power between states and societies.

The first demonstration of social media's power to influence the direction of political violence came in Iran, when, in 2009, pro-democracy activists turned to social media in order to gain global support for their protests over the outcome of national political elections. The Green Revolution, as it became known, was "the first major world event broadcast worldwide almost entirely via social media" (Keller 2010). American media outlets received an avalanche of text messages, e-mails, blog posts, and video feeds that described the clashes between activists and the Iranian government. According to the *Washington Times* (2009), "Well-developed Twitter lists showed a constant stream of situation updates and links to photos and videos, all of which painted a portrait of the developing turmoil." Although the uprising was ultimately suppressed by Iran's armed forces, the capacity of social media to support mass movements became clear.

These developments were closely followed by citizens in Tunisia, where antigovernment protesters organized in 2000 to demand the ouster of its president, Ben Ali. When word spread early in 2011 of a street vendor who killed himself in order to publicize government harassment, activists used social media to organize mass demonstrations against the state (Delany 2011). Their photographs of police brutality fueled more unrest, as did government statements that were revealed by social media to be false.

POINT / COUNTERPOINT

The Iraq War: Hawks vs. Doves in the Blogosphere

Many foreign policy debates today are waged on the Internet, in blogs hosted by well-known experts that invite comments from readers. Thomas E. Ricks, a senior fellow at the Center for a New American Century, spurred such a debate on February 24, 2010, when he argued on his blog, *The Best Defense*, that the United States should not withdraw all its forces from Iraq—a central goal of President Obama. His blog posting, "OK, Time to Think about Staying in Iraq," excerpted below, elicited dozens of rebuttals within hours, including those also featured below. Note the rapid pace of this debate, which continued for many days:

> (3:20 P.M.) *Thomas E. Ricks:* I have a piece in the *New York Times* today that contends that we need to think about keeping at least 30,000 troops in Iraq for many years to come, instead of getting them all out at the end of next year. . . . Do you know anyone who thinks that Iraqi forces will be able to stand on their own at the end of next year? Uh-huh, me neither.

As I note in the article, it doesn't make me happy to say it, because I think that invading Iraq was a huge mistake, perhaps the biggest error in the history of American foreign policy. I mean, invading a country pre-emptively on the basis of false information? That would get you thrown out of night court. But I think that staying beats the hell out of the alternatives. We've had too much rushing to failure in the Iraq war.

Rebuttals

(4:25 P.M.) From *Rubber Duckey:* In all, it's one hell of a price to pay to protect our lost investment in the imperialism of the last Administration. If it feels bad, quit doing it. Put the money to work at home or send it back to the taxpayers. Fix the United States of America, not Bush's Iraq brainfart.

(5:38 P.M.) From *Tyrtiaos:* Keeping such a conventional force in place has its pluses, but also has its minuses. One negative consequence of such an American force, besides seen as an occupier, is being directed to pick sides and thus alienating other competing factions. At that point all neutrality is given-up and the force becomes an enemy to some.

(5:40 P.M.) From *Kieselguhr Kid:* I read the article this morning and was really irritated by one thing: you just barely tipped your hat to the fact that the troop drawdown is, well, something binding that was negotiated with the Iraqis.

(6:19 P.M.) From *Hunter:* Some of us who have done a tour in Iraq or two don't want to go back there again after it dissolves into civil war (again) or is annexed by Iran. Some of us know good people in Iraq who we don't want to see lost in the quagmire (like when we abandoned many nominal allies in Vietnam). We're there now, let's do it right.

(Continued)

(6:34 P.M.) From *NNELGL:* Tom: Your advocacy of maintaining a sizable American troop presence in Iraq for years to come is cut from the same cloth as the original arguments for the Iraq war: Play up fears about not following your policy prescription, trump up the benefits of following your advice and talk little—if at all—about the costs.

(8:30 P.M.) From *Zathras:* Ricks ignores the question of opportunity cost. The resources we devote to Iraq can't be used to do other things. I can imagine that some of those other things might be more important to the United States than the evolving politics of one, mid-sized Arab country. Ricks cannot. Ricks ignores the possibility of an Iraqi civil war engulfing the much-reduced, less capable American force he proposes to leave as a deterrent to civil war.

Source: Thomas E. Ricks, "OK, Time to Think about Staying in Iraq," *The Best Defense,* February 24, 2010, http://ricks .foreignpolicy.com/posts/2010/02/24/ok_time_to_think_about_staying_in_iraq/. Reproduced with permission from ForeignPolicy.com.

The protesters' widely circulated posts played a key role in the success of the "Jasmine Revolution" and sparked the Arab Spring across the Arab world. A similar outpouring of social media served as a catalyst for mass protests against Egypt's government, which was overthrown later in 2011 (Vargas 2012). Two years later, citizens in Ukraine, along with the U.S. and other governments, relied on social media to reveal the falsehoods spread by Russian officials as they wreaked havoc in the nation's eastern provinces.

These events demonstrate how social media can play important roles in fomenting political unrest and gaining moral and sometimes material support from faraway citizens, groups, and governments. As we have also discovered, such pressure cannot ensure the outcomes sought by political reformers—as was the case with Iran, Egypt, and other counties such as Syria which retained oppressive regimes. The path toward true transformation requires more than mass movements and protests. Underlying cultural, social, and economic practices must be in place that will open the doors to political change and democracy (Reddy 2013).

■ ONLINE NEWS AND VIEWS FROM OVERSEAS

For the relatively small segment of the American public that follows news of U.S. foreign policy on a regular basis, the Internet provides ready access to news coverage generated by journalists overseas. Approximately one-quarter of regular Internet users turn to these sources, which include online newspapers, magazines, blogs, and broadcast outlets.[7] This trend accelerated as the United States responded to the

7. The number of accredited foreign correspondents working in Washington, D.C., has increased from 160 in 1968 to more than 1,500 in 2010 (Castle 2010).

September 2001 terrorist attacks by invading Afghanistan in 2001 and Iraq in 2003 and then became mired in a series of military setbacks, scandals, and internal controversies over the use (and misuse) of intelligence. The Internet, and the innumerable foreign-based websites it hosts, provided a primary vehicle for the expression of anti-American sentiment, which became commonplace during this period.

News from foreign sources, once beyond the reach of American consumers, provides a valuable alternative to the dominant news frames generated by the White House and adopted by most domestic media sources (see Table 8.5). Whereas most Americans accept the media's uncritical coverage of U.S. foreign policy (Zaller and Chiu 1996), those with doubts about Washington's motivations or tactics are more likely to pursue these doubts on foreign news sites. "Never before has it been possible to gauge so many views—not only in the United States but from Europe and the Middle East" (S. J. Best, Chmielewski, and Krueger 2005, 52).

Some foreign news outlets, including the BBC, rarely challenge Washington's foreign policies and media frames. More commonly, foreign media adopt a more skeptical view of the United States (Lehman 2005). These include al Jazeera ("the island" in Arabic), a news network based in Qatar whose video streams and online articles rejected the assumptions and policy choices of Bush's war on terror. The network provided extensive coverage of U.S. mistreatment of Iraqi prisoners and deadly terrorist attacks on U.S. forces while providing Arab and Islamic leaders daily opportunities to criticize the United States.

In 2006, the network launched an English-language network, al Jazeera English, which made these broadcasts accessible to an American audience. Although its coverage

Table 8.5 ■ Selected English-Language Foreign News Outlets

Newspapers	Television Networks
My Afghan News (Afghanistan)	CNC (China)
Sydney Morning Herald (Australia)	BBC World News (Great Britain)
Globe and Mail (Canada)	I24news (Israel)
Munich Eye (Germany)	JibTV (Japan)
The Hindu (India)	ETC (Philippines)
Daily Nation (Kenya)	RT (Russia)
Today's Zaman (Turkey)	SABC (South Africa)
El Universal (Venezuela)	al Jazeera English (Qatar)

Sources: English Online International Newspapers, www.inkdrop.net/news; World Press Links, www.geotrees.com/wpp.html; other sources.

remained generally critical of U.S. policies in the Middle East, the network provided detailed coverage of social and economic problems in the region that were otherwise neglected by American broadcast and cable networks. In this sense, al Jazeera English provided its audience, which included English speakers in Europe and other areas, "a more truly global perspective" (Seib 2012, 196).[8] It is very likely that other foreign news networks will emerge and find their place among the hundreds now available on cable television, creating risks as well as rewards for U.S. foreign policy.

■ CONCLUSION

Like public opinion, mass communications play a vital role in U.S. foreign policy in keeping with the underlying virtues of democratic governance. News organizations, whether print, broadcast, or digital media, link events overseas and citizens at home. Their coverage shapes the agenda of foreign policy makers and, occasionally, brings attention to scandals and policy miscalculations that are otherwise unknown to the public. Although journalists may at times reveal internal dissension among foreign policy elites or gaping holes in the nation's intelligence or defense capabilities, such revelations are viewed widely as a reasonable price to pay for a free press.

The news media's role, however, is fraught with complications. Even in the midst of the world's latest "information revolution," the mass public remains focused on concerns close to home. The news media reinforce this pattern by alternately ignoring foreign news and providing saturation coverage of crises overseas. Such inattention to serious global issues, including the status of U.S. primacy in a shifting balance of power, is paradoxical given the nation's historical reliance on the role of a free press in shaping and empowering an informed citizenry.

The preoccupation of media conglomerates with profitability, combined with the growing concentration of media ownership, discourages news outlets from funding major news investigations that may offend audiences. The conglomerates' top officers also fear alienating the U.S. government officials, whether in the White House or Congress, on whom they rely for regulatory concessions or tax relief. This influence reaches down to the newsroom. "Journalists and editors not only sympathetically report on the activities of political elites, but are, for all intents and purposes, a part of the elite themselves" (Dimaggio 2009, 16). In these ways, the news media fail to advance the *public interest,* a term cited widely in the past as the primary mission of a free press.

Amid the creative destruction of mass communications, three aspects of the media's future can be assured. First, the pace of change in news gathering and dissemination will accelerate ever more swiftly. Second, news consumers will play an

8. Early in 2013, al Jazeera sought to increase its U.S. media presence by purchasing Current TV, a cable network cofounded by former vice president Al Gore.

even more interactive role in responding to news and social media messages. Finally, the United States will no longer have a preponderant influence on global narratives that were devised during the "American century." Rival narratives will persuasively challenge basic assumptions of American culture, economics, government, and foreign policy.

The news and social media often frustrate rather than enhance the coherent conduct of U.S. foreign policy. This confusion is heightened by the growing overlaps of news and social media, national and world news, objective information and advocacy, and news and entertainment. In the absence of greater mass participation, public action will continue to take place within narrow interest groups whose members have direct stakes in the outcomes of U.S. foreign policy choices and present their demands daily to the federal government. This third "outside-in" influence on the foreign policy process is the subject of Chapter 9.

WANT A BETTER GRADE?

Get the tools you need to sharpen your study skills.
Access practice quizzes, eFlashcards, video, and multimedia at
edge.sagepub.com/hook5e.

$SAGE edge™
for CQ Press

KEY TERMS

INTERNET REFERENCES

al Jazeera (http://america.aljazeera.com/) provides in-depth coverage of issues and events relevant to the Islamic world. Included on this website, which is an offshoot of the group's television network, are news reports about world events, survey results, and other information related to Islamic countries.

Based in England, the **BBC** (http://news.bbc.co.uk) is a media hub for worldwide news coverage. The BBC's website features detailed reports on all regions of the world and links to its television and radio broadcasts.

The **Center for Media and Democracy's PR Watch** (http://www.prwatch.org) examines the role of public relations advocacy and spin control in the dissemination of news coverage. Its website includes links to features such as the wiki "Sourcewatch" that chronicle the impact of propaganda in news reports.

CNN (http://www.cnn.com) provides an Internet-based supplement to the global cable television news network's coverage. Its website includes print versions of broadcast reports as well as links to the network's broadcast outlets.

The **Freedom Forum** (http://www.newseuminstitute.org/freedom-forum/) is a nonpartisan research center that promotes the cause of press freedom in the United States and overseas. Based in Arlington, Virginia, the group's website features reports and essays on issues related to the First Amendment, the creation of independent media outlets overseas, and newsroom diversity.

The **Media Research Center** (http://www.mrc.org), a self-proclaimed "media watchdog," promotes the dissemination of conservative opinions and policy analyses that seek to counter the "liberal bias" in U.S. news coverage. The group's website features reports on media coverage and links to articles and broadcasts of programs that support its policy agenda.

Netcraft (http://news.netcraft.com), a British Internet services company, offers detailed reports on the Internet itself, including survey results that document the rapid proliferation of websites. The firm also assists its clients, located throughout the world, in protecting their sites against piracy and fraudulent use.

Russia's largest news and media source, **Pravda** (http://english.pravda.ru), provides articles and news coverage of world affairs and Russia's relations with the United States and other countries. Its website features current and archived articles and feature stories, most of which are concerned with Russian domestic and foreign policies.

The **Pew Research Center's Journalism Project** (http://www.journalism.org) is a rapidly growing "fact tank" that focuses on trends in the American news media. Previously affiliated with Columbia University and now part of the Pew Research Center, the project maintains its focus on media coverage and industry trends.

9

SOCIAL MOVEMENTS AND INTEREST GROUPS

EPA/Michael Reynolds

Foreign policy makers are constantly pressured by interest groups that want to shape the nation's actions. Among these groups, the American Israel Public Affairs Committee is known to have the most clout. Vice President Joe Biden, for example, was sure in March 2013 to attend the group's conference in Washington, D.C.

CHAPTER OBJECTIVES

9.1 Identify features in U.S. society that favor the development of private groups and their role in politics.

9.2 Discuss three different social movements that concern domestic or foreign public policy.

9.3 Summarize different types of foreign policy nongovernmental organizations (NGOs).

9.4 Define four types of group strategies and tactics that can influence U.S. foreign policy.

9.5 Explain the role of multinational corporations in U.S. foreign policy making.

Chapters 7 and 8 described how public opinion and the news media impose external pressure on the U.S. foreign policy process. As expressions of the nation's civil society, both shed light on public preferences and are watched closely by reelection-minded political leaders. At the same time, national surveys consistently reveal a mass public that is largely disengaged from foreign policy issues. Only a small elite and the attentive public have significant knowledge of world history, geography, and current events. Similarly, most Americans pay little attention to foreign news coverage on a regular basis, preferring instead entertainment programs, video games, and interactions on social media. Public interest and media coverage spike only during times of crisis and then quickly return to their usual tepid levels.

This seeming indifference of the American public, paradoxical for the dominant and most pervasive global power, leaves the field open for a relatively small segment of the population—social movements and interest groups—to influence U.S. foreign policy. These groups, which promote a vast array of causes, are highly diverse but share a common objective: to steer government action in directions favorable to their members, participants, and other possible stakeholders. American leaders may choose to ignore survey results or critical news coverage, but they cannot ignore the constant pressure exerted by vocal and well-endowed groups.

Group action fills a vacuum created by the neglect or inadequate resources of governments. Private charities provide food and shelter to those in need, while grassroots environmental groups demand and initiate conservation measures that would otherwise be ignored. Government "demand" for interest groups was also evident after the 9/11 terrorist attacks, when the Department of Homeland Security's creation led to an outpouring of interest groups that offered services and products

not provided by the government (LaPira 2014). Interest groups focusing on U.S. intelligence frequently reveal practices that contradict U.S. laws or social values. When private groups provide such vital information, "they help reconfigure the relation between government institutions and U.S. citizens" (Puyvelde 2012, 155).

The need for public action is even greater at the global level due to the absence of a centralized, authoritative body to ensure that collective problems such as nuclear proliferation are being addressed. This **sovereignty gap** leaves critical transnational problems without governmental stewards. The issue of land mines, which are designed to maim civilians in war zones and continue to ruin lives long after the conflicts are over, is a case in point. The problem barely registered on government radar screens until the mid-1990s, when a coalition of groups, the International Campaign to Ban Landmines, called for a global ban on the mines. By December 1997, 123 countries had signed a comprehensive ban on land mines.[1] When it took effect in March 1999, the ban became the most rapidly adopted international agreement of its kind in history. The campaign and its coordinator, the American activist Jody Williams, received the 1997 Nobel Peace Prize "in part for helping create a fresh form of diplomacy" (Rutherford 2000, 75).

While social movements are generally antagonistic toward government policies they oppose, many interest groups support U.S. foreign policies. Their members have an easier time getting their voices heard when they are "pushing on an open door." This was the case of Cuban and Iraqi exiles who teamed up with like-minded U.S. leaders in promoting foreign policies that affected their countries of origin (Vanderbush 2009). In such cases, "the goals of interest groups and policy makers are closely aligned and it is often not clear who is serving whom" (Lieberman 2009, 251). Private

---

1. The full name of the agreement is the Ottawa Convention on the Prohibition of the Use, Stockpiling, Production and Transfer of Anti-Personnel Mines and on Their Destruction. By June 2015, 162 countries had ratified the accord. The U.S. government was among thirty-two other governments, including those of China and Russia, that had not joined the convention.

citizens frequently engage in **Track II diplomacy** by communicating with fellow advocates overseas, increasingly through social media, and devise solutions to shared problems that are often considered by governments.

The activism of diverse and often competing interest groups complicates the U.S. foreign policy process beyond the political rivalries that fester among agencies and branches of government (Diven 2006). In some cases, interest groups become so strong that they are able to "capture" government policies, a problem known as **hyperpluralism**. As noted below, in 1961 President Eisenhower warned against a "military-industrial complex" that threatened to leave defense contractors effectively driving U.S. national security policy. Similarly, policy analysts have argued that the American Israeli Public Affairs Committee, a powerful interest group in Washington, skewed its analyses of U.S. Middle East policy options in its favor (Mearsheimer and Walt 2009).

Social movements and interest groups commonly form **transnational advocacy networks** that place pressure on multiple governments at once. Policy advocates have learned that such problems as climate change require cooperation by leaders worldwide. Gaining support from one country creates momentum for further agreements, particularly when reluctant leaders are chastised by their peers. Transnational advocacy networks use the same tools—support for like-minded political parties and candidates, public information campaigns, and mass mobilization—used by domestic interest groups (Bloodgood 2011). Their efforts are also expedited through contacts established through social media.

■ GROUP ACTION AND THE PARADOX

Private organizations have always served as the backbone of the U.S. democratic system. As do public opinion and the news media, these groups represent alternative centers of power that can counteract government abuses while offering outlets for the expression of societal needs. As in economic markets, the demand for favorable government policies determines the supply of groups promoting them. "The public is not only represented in the formal political sense by a variety of elected officials," political scientist Gabriel Almond (1950, 231) noted long ago, "but there are few groups of any size in the United States today which do not have their interests represented."

Several features of U.S. society and its political system favor the development and persistence of private groups (see Risse-Kappen 1994):

- Fragmented *governmental structures* offer many points of access to the legislative and executive branches through which private groups can affect foreign policy.

- Robust *societal structures*, a result of the constitutional restraints on state power and the broad political and social freedoms granted to individuals and groups, provide a fertile environment for NGOs to recruit new members and affect policy.

- Numerous *policy networks* allow NGOs to join with issue-related government agencies that share a basic consensus on the merits of U.S. government and society.

As noted earlier, the membership of NGOs has increasingly crossed national boundaries, mobilizing like-minded citizens from multiple countries. The activism of transnational groups, though associated most often with liberal theories of world politics (see Chapter 3), is better understood as "an arena of struggle" among political actors than as a stepping-stone to world government (Keck and Sikkink 1998, 33). In this respect, the empowerment of NGOs is compatible with realist theories, whose emphasis on chronic conflicts of interest may be extended beyond the anarchic system of nation-states.

As members of transnational civil society, these groups have widely varying relationships with the U.S. government. President Bill Clinton, for example, reached out to public interest NGOs but soon faced their wrath when antiglobalization protesters disrupted the 1999 meetings of the World Trade Organization (WTO) in Seattle, Washington. The relationship between Washington and these NGOs became more adversarial with the coming to power in 2001 of George W. Bush, who feared the agents of "global governance" as a threat to U.S. sovereignty. Yet at the same time, Bush reached out to a different set of NGOs: evangelical Christian churches whose members had funded his 2000 campaign and shared his policy priorities. For his part, President Obama favored the organized groups that had formed his electoral base in 2008, including minority and women's groups, labor unions, and NGOs concerned with renewable energy and climate change.

The U.S. government naturally attracts so much NGO attention given its predominant stature and openness to citizen engagement. Although constraints on state power were precisely what the Constitution's framers had in mind when they fostered a vigorous civil society at home, they could not have anticipated the challenges posed by organized citizens and groups from around the world. Their challenges to state authority affect all democratic countries that open themselves to group pressures, including the United States.

■ DYNAMICS OF SOCIAL MOVEMENTS

When citizens determined to change government policies join together in pressure groups and coalitions, their collective action often takes the form of a **social movement**. Frequently, the issue of concern—whether it be war, human rights, globalization, the environment, or something else—involves foreign policy. The goals of these movements vary widely, but they can be divided into two broad categories: those that seek to change bad policies already in place (such as ill-conceived military interventions) and those that seek to create good new policies (such as sanctions to halt human rights abuses). Unlike the self-interested campaigns of economically oriented groups, the motivations of social movements are not solely reducible to the material welfare of their members. Their goals' focus commonly extends to the public as a whole.

The term *social movement* is notoriously vague and stubbornly resistant to a simple definition. Here, social movements are viewed as broad-based collective actions undertaken by citizens and groups to solve perceived societal problems through the reform of domestic or foreign public policy. This definition suggests a causal chain that begins with the perceived problem, which then stimulates the mobilization of concerned citizens through organized interest groups (see Diani 2012). The solutions sought by activists may involve the policy itself or the decision-making process used to make and enforce the unpopular policy. If governments resist or reject such pressure, the groups commonly employ additional tactics to achieve their policy goals (see Figure 9.1).

Aside from their concrete policy goals, social movements are driven by norms that represent their underlying values and visions of how the state and society *should* function. Norms on human rights and other transnational issues gain enduring value when they are codified in international law (Donno 2011). As such, transnational norms provide social movements with significant moral authority that often compensates for their lack of political support.

Antiwar Protests from Vietnam to Iraq

One of the most familiar expressions of social movements is the antiwar demonstration in which protesters seek en masse to force governments to avoid military confrontations. As noted in Chapter 2, antiwar protests erupted frequently on college campuses during the Vietnam War, sometimes with tragic results. A weekend of protests in May 1970 at Kent State University in Ohio prompted government officials to impose martial law and deploy the National Guard to Kent. When protesters gathered again on the following Monday, confronting the armed forces in a bitter standoff, the National

Figure 9.1 ■ The Cycle of Public Pressure and Political Change

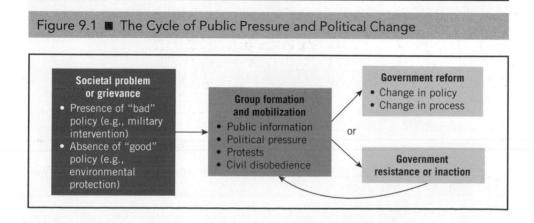

Guard opened fire on the protesters, killing four students and wounding nine others. The tragedy at Kent State literally "brought home" the war in Vietnam and hardened public opposition to the U.S. intervention there. President Richard Nixon never regained public support for the Vietnam War after the Kent State shootings.

No comparable antiwar movement has emerged in the United States since the Vietnam War, despite nearly constant U.S. military interventions. The small scale of these conflicts restricted mass opposition, and for many—such as those in Grenada, Panama, and Somalia—the abrupt timing and short duration of the interventions did not allow opponents time to mobilize. By contrast, the 1991 Persian Gulf War was much larger in scope and was preceded by months of sanctions, diplomatic negotiations, and legislative debates. Still, the creation of a thirty-six-country coalition, combined with a UN Security Council resolution to eject Iraqi forces from Kuwait, gave the impending conflict a legitimacy that tempered antiwar sentiments.

The opposite conditions surrounded the U.S.-led invasion of Iraq in early 2003. The lack of regional and UN support for preventive war left the United States largely isolated in pressing for a military solution. These circumstances, combined with the profound implications and uncertain consequences of major war in the Middle East, sparked a surge of peace activism in the United States and overseas. More than 1 million protesters took to the streets of London, Madrid, Rome, and other European cities on February 15. An estimated 500,000 demonstrated against the impending war in Washington, D.C., and dozens of city councils formally registered their opposition to the war. These actions, organized and carried out by a coalition of more than forty NGOs, constituted a discernible antiwar movement as the diplomatic struggle wore on (see Table 9.1). All this pressure, however, failed to discourage the White House from carrying out its threat to overthrow Saddam Hussein's regime.

Table 9.1 ■ The Iraq War Protest Coalition

Group Type	Number of Groups	Example
Antiwar	11	Peace Action
Religious	11	United Church of Christ
Identity (e.g., racial, ethnic)	8	NAACP
Social justice	8	MoveOn
International politics	5	Global Exchange
Environmental	2	Greenpeace

Source: David S. Meyer and Catherine Corrigall-Brown, "Coalition and Political Context: U.S. Movements against Wars in Iraq," *Mobilization* 10 (2005), 327–344.

What accounted for the different outcomes of the movements against the wars in Vietnam and Iraq? A prominent factor was the much higher death toll in Vietnam, which exceeded 50,000 Americans by the early 1970s, in contrast to the approximately 3,200 Americans killed during the first four years of the Iraq war. Other factors were the larger troop deployments to Vietnam—nearly 500,000 at the height of the conflict—and the military draft that forced many Americans to fight in the unpopular war. Above all, the inability of transnational peace activists to prevent the U.S. invasion of Iraq demoralized the coalition and prompted many groups to disband or shift their energies to other issues (Meyer and Corrigall-Brown 2005).

Still, small-scale efforts to oppose the war continued. After U.S. Army Specialist Casey Sheehan was killed in Iraq in March 2004, his mother, Cindy Sheehan, emerged as an outspoken war critic. Her protracted vigil outside President Bush's Texas ranch in the summer of 2005 drew worldwide attention. Similarly, filmmaker Michael Moore produced a documentary, *Fahrenheit 9/11*, that depicted the Bush administration's war on terror as a misguided campaign driven by economic and military elites. After its release in June 2004, the documentary earned a record $200 million, nearly half of which came from foreign audiences. Meanwhile, more than 1,200 local and national peace groups organized efforts to stop the war in Iraq and resist the calls for war against neighboring Iran.

The Christian Conversion on Foreign Aid

Long before the Iraq war, a very different social movement helped to change the course of U.S. foreign policy. The 1990s witnessed a surge in foreign policy activism among American religious, or faith-based, groups, whose interest in public policy

Although no large-scale, organized antiwar movement emerged in the early years of the war on terrorism, several high-profile figures rallied opponents of the conflict to maintain pressure on the U.S. government. Two such figures, Cindy Sheehan (left), the mother of a slain U.S. soldier, and documentary filmmaker Michael Moore (right), led this opposition through public appearances that drew large audiences and extensive coverage in the news media.

had previously centered only on domestic social issues such as abortion, gay rights, and capital punishment (see Martin 1999). Debates over such issues reflected deeply held religious beliefs that offered "ultimate perspectives, broad criteria, motives, inspirations, sensitivities, warnings, and moral limits" (Bennett 1966, 36). The passage of the International Religious Freedom Act of 1998, which identified freedom of religion and conscience as a "core objective" of U.S. foreign policy, was driven by church groups. The same groups compelled Congress to pass the Sudan Peace Act of 2002 and the North Korea Human Rights Act of 2004.[2]

In shifting their focus to foreign policy, Christian groups were inspired further by deeply held concerns about the declining state of "family values" and lobbied aggressively to exclude abortion services from U.S.-funded family-planning programs overseas. Elsewhere, their heightened concern for human rights and the end of religious persecution prompted such groups to embrace the promotion of democratic rule worldwide, a central foreign policy goal of the Clinton and Bush administrations.

Evangelical Christians proved highly effective in applying pressure on Washington to adopt the role of "good Samaritan" in poverty and HIV/AIDS relief (Hook 2008). Once staunchly opposed to foreign aid, this powerful constituency detached itself from other conservatives, who considered aid spending a form of global welfare. Two initiatives demonstrated the impact of this social movement on U.S. aid policy. The first, a worldwide campaign for debt relief, Jubilee 2000, prompted industrialized states to forgive loans to countries in extreme poverty. The U.S. government had resisted calls for large-scale debt relief, but its views changed when faith groups united around the idea that crippling debt obligations amounted to a moral crisis that could no longer be ignored. The mobilization of these groups, combined with personal pleas to government officials by celebrities such as Bono, the leader of the rock band U2, convinced U.S. leaders to commit $435 million in debt relief in 2001.

The second aid initiative was aimed at economic support for victims of HIV/AIDS in the developing world. Christian conservatives again mobilized and aligned with African American groups that had unsuccessfully sought greater support from the Republican-controlled Congress (see Burkhalter 2004). In February 2002, the Christian relief organization Samaritan's Purse hosted a global AIDS conference in Washington that drew leaders from more than 800 Catholic and Protestant churches along with a variety of government leaders. Bush, a born-again Christian with close ties to evangelical groups on a variety of issues (see Fineman 2003), responded in January 2003 with the Emergency Plan for AIDS Relief, which pledged $15 billion in funding over five years.

....

2. The impact of faith-based interest groups is attributable in part to the relatively high level of religiosity in American society. In a survey of forty-three societies conducted in the 1990s, Americans ranked first among all citizens in believing in a "personal God" (Inglehart, Basáñez, and Moreno 1998).

The Tea Party and Occupy Wall Street

Two other social movements—the Tea Party and Occupy Wall Street—emerged in the aftermath of the financial crisis that nearly crippled the U.S. economy in 2008. While both movements rejected "politics as usual" in Washington, their members came from opposite ends of the political spectrum. Whereas members of the Tea Party (named for "taxed enough already" and invoking the Boston Tea Party of 1773) were strongly conservative, the Occupy movement drew much of its support from liberal activists. Both groups focused on domestic issues, primarily the weak U.S. economy, but they also shared strong views regarding U.S. foreign policy.

The Tea Party, formed in 2009, mobilized a large bloc of supporters who viewed themselves as peacefully "reenacting" the American Revolution (Lepore 2010). Drawing also on the populist tradition of President Andrew Jackson, these activists expressed "resentment of the well-bred, the well-connected, and the well-paid" whose close ties to Washington were "both misguided and corrupt" (Mead 2011, 33–34). Members of the group recruited political candidates who shared this view, and they proved adept in attacking candidates, even within the Republican Party, who seemed wedded to "big government."

These viewpoints led members of the Tea Party to espouse distinct foreign policy views. In a 2011 survey of public opinion, 60 percent of Tea Party supporters believed that U.S. military strength rather than "good diplomacy" was the surest path to peace (Pew Research Center for the People and the Press 2011a, 1). Reflecting their nationalist values, most also believed the United States should restrict immigration into the United States and "get tough" with China on trade. The electoral strength of the Tea Party was demonstrated in 2012 when Mitt Romney, the Republican candidate for president, chose Rep. Paul Ryan (R-WI), a Tea Party supporter, as his running mate.

Several other Tea Party members, including Sens. Ted Cruz (R-TX), Marco Rubio (R-FL), and Rand Paul (R-KY), ran in the 2016 presidential election. Paul, the son of a congressman from Texas, gained widespread attention in 2015 when he championed the cause of restricting the U.S. government's ability to engage in domestic surveillance (see Chapters 8 and 12). Striking a tone that appealed to civil libertarians, he warned that this practice "leads us down a slippery slope to where there would be no more freedom left" (quoted in Peters 2015b). Paul, who resorted to a ten-hour filibuster to exhaust his opposition, ultimately swayed enough lawmakers to have the restrictions passed in Congress and signed by President Obama.

The Occupy Wall Street movement was inspired by the mass uprisings in North Africa and the Middle East that were associated with the 2011 Arab Spring (Slaughter 2011). The group's first major demonstration, on September 17 in New York City's Zuccotti Park, resembled the protests in Tahrir Square in Cairo that ultimately toppled Egypt's government. Hundreds of similar demonstrations soon took place across the United States as protesters, often camping out for weeks or even months, denounced the concentration of wealth held by the richest 1 percent of Americans. By mid-October, the Occupy movement had spread to more than 900 cities, including dozens in Europe, where citizens opposed budget cutbacks designed by political leaders to end the Continent's deepening debt crisis. In the United States, prominent activists from the Vietnam War era and other antiwar movements provided moral support for those determined to occupy public spaces until their demands were met (see Chomsky 2012).

■ TYPES OF FOREIGN POLICY NGOs

Social movements in the United States represent coalitions of individual groups that share concerns about foreign and domestic policy. The number of politically active NGOs, which are often loosely connected, cannot be stated with precision. Particularly at the transnational level where much of their foreign policy activism takes place, no formal mechanism exists for licensing or registering the vast majority of these groups. Further complicating matters, NGOs are continuously created and dismantled in response to shifting needs, unforeseen developments, and evolving stages of the policy process. However, the number of NGOs that have gained consultative status with the UN Economic and Social Council (ECOSOC) is known and offers a perspective on the growth of NGOs over the past decade. In 1948, just 40 NGOs held this status; by 2014, the number had grown to 4,045 (see Figure 9.2).

Nonprofit NGOs concerned with U.S. foreign policy assume a variety of institutional forms. Some are small, focus narrowly on single issues, and disappear when their policy preferences are satisfied. Others have large staffs and budgets, promote policies along a broad spectrum of issues, and maintain a permanent presence in Washington, D.C., and foreign capitals. The Worldwide Fund for Nature, for example, boasts a membership of more than 5 million donors and maintained a staff of more than 6,000 in 2015.

Most NGOs are considered to be **particularistic groups**, which serve a limited number of individuals who have a stake in an NGO's mission. The rest are **cosmopolitan groups**, which address transnational problems that affect the general public, such as environmental decay and human rights. Both types of groups have a proven capacity to shape U.S. foreign policy, but they also suffer from four primary weaknesses:

- Limited resources, which forces groups to spend much of their time soliciting private donations to survive
- Lack of formal contacts with governments, which makes gaining access to key decision makers a constant challenge, particularly for smaller groups lacking political or economic muscle

- Inevitable divisions among NGOs with contrary or competing claims on governments, which neutralize the groups' overall impact
- A **democratic deficit** created by a lack of elected representation and openness in decision making, which are hallmarks of democratic states (see Thrandardottir 2015)

The primary strength of these NGOs stems from their direct links to citizens at all levels of government—local, state, national, and transnational. These links often prove stronger than those between states and private citizens because U.S. citizens are more likely to participate politically through NGOs than through government programs or political parties. Furthermore, nonprofit NGOs benefit greatly from a sense of shared values among their members, who are determined to see these values reflected in tangible goals and political action. The high levels of commitment and solidarity within a group are the glue that holds its members together over an extended period of time. Finally, the members of NGOs have expertise in relevant policy areas that lends credibility and leverage when they attempt to influence government officials. Their expertise is also an asset when governments need help implementing or monitoring programs.

Figure 9.2 ■ NGOs and the UN: Members with ECOSOC Consultative Status, 1994–2014

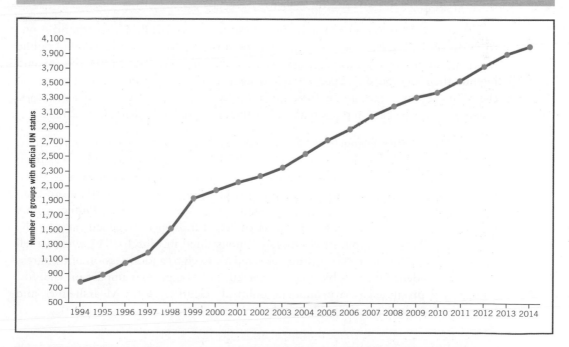

Source: UN Department of Economic and Social Affairs, "Basic Facts about ECOSOC Status," http://csonet.org/?menu=100.

Religious and Ethnic Groups

Religious and ethnic groups play vital roles in the U.S. foreign policy process. Millions of Americans identify themselves as part of a faith community that is represented, in some form, by organizations that advance the group's interests. In the 1990s, religious conservatives "created the largest, best-organized grassroots social movement of the last quarter century" (Putnam 2000, 162). They provided large campaign contributions to political candidates every year along with a steady stream of policy briefs they expected their beneficiaries to follow. Recent surveys suggest that, while Tea Party leaders are driven by a desire for small government, "the rank and file is after a godlier government" (Campbell and Putnam 2012, 38).

As a nation of immigrants, the United States is also sensitive to the needs of ethnic groups, whose members look to Washington for economic and political support. Demographic shifts in the United States elevate the electoral importance of nonwhite Americans, who are projected to increase from 19 to 26 percent of the U.S. population between 2000 and 2050 (Shrestha and Heisler 2011, 20). The proportion of foreign-born residents (12.9 percent in 2010)—equally divided among 40 million naturalized citizens, legal permanent residents, and illegal immigrants—was at the highest level since the early 1900s (Dews 2013). As the ethnic diversity of the United States increases, so will the political clout of minority groups which have distinct interests in domestic and foreign policies.

Religious and ethnic groups form large, cohesive, and politically active organizations to advance the interests of their members. Because support from the general public is crucial in advancing their interests, the groups often espouse causes that extend beyond their membership. Such groups focus their lobbying efforts on Congress, not the White House, because of their greater access to Capitol Hill and legislators' greater responsiveness to parochial, rather than national, concerns (Rytz 2013).

As described earlier, evangelical Christian groups were of particular importance to President George W. Bush, who in 2000 received about 40 percent of his votes from this segment of the population (Bumiller 2003). Jewish Americans have also organized politically to exert strong pressure on U.S. foreign policy. With more than 100,000 members residing in all fifty states, the American Israel Public Affairs Committee (AIPAC) has achieved a level of NGO influence exceeded only by the National Rifle Association. Its clout was demonstrated in March 2015 when Israeli Prime Minister Benjamin Netanyahu delivered a speech to a joint session of Congress without President Obama's blessing (Porter 2015).[3] The group's impact on U.S. foreign policy prompted two prominent political scientists, John Mearsheimer and Stephen M. Walt (2006, 1), to charge that

---

3. After Palestinians petitioned the UN for statehood in 2014, AIPAC gained the assent of 446 of 535 members of Congress to oppose the proposal (Bruck 2014).

the centerpiece of U.S. Middle East policy has been its relationship with Israel. The combination of unwavering U.S. support for Israel and the related effort to spread democracy throughout the region has inflamed Arab and Islamic opinion and jeopardized U.S. security. . . . The overall thrust of U.S. policy in the region is due almost entirely to the activities of the "Israel Lobby." Other special interest groups have managed to skew U.S. foreign policy in directions they favored, but no lobby has managed to divert U.S. foreign policy as far from what the American national interest would otherwise suggest, while simultaneously convincing Americans that U.S. and Israeli interests are essentially identical.[4]

Hispanic Americans, now the largest minority group in the United States, have drawn growing attention by policy makers (Smeltz and Kafura 2015). Certain subgroups have fared especially well. The Cuban American National Foundation (CANF), based in Miami, has long pushed the U.S. government to isolate Cuba's communist regime (Rubenzer 2011). Meanwhile, the organization pushed successfully for the creation of two government-run media outlets, *Radio Martí* (1985) and *TV Martí* (1990), which provide news and entertainment programs directly to the Cuban population. The networks, which supported Washington's hard line against Havana, continued to focus on political repression on the island even as both governments established closer relations in 2015 (Alvarez 2015).

Islamic and Arab American groups have had far more difficulty gaining influence over U.S. foreign policy despite their large numbers in big cities and electorally important swing states such as Michigan. According to political scientist Eric Uslaner (2002), these groups are less cohesive, less affluent, and less politically active than the members of AIPAC. In addition, whereas AIPAC members overwhelmingly support the Democratic Party, Arab Americans are more equally divided between Republicans and Democrats, depriving them of a solid electoral base. Furthermore, the societal stature of these groups suffered, not surprisingly, with the onset of the war on terror, and Arab Americans frequently have been "profiled" and singled out for government scrutiny. Muslim groups such as the Muslim Public Affairs Council responded by framing their appeals for support around the Muslim "suffering at the hands of non-Muslim armed forces or authorities" (Ross 2013, 296).

After the Cold War, ethnic groups linked to the former communist countries in Eastern Europe became actively involved in U.S. foreign policy toward the region. For example, in 1998 Polish American groups mobilized in large numbers to support

---

4. The proven clout of AIPAC—and its hawkish views—led to the creation in 2008 of J Street, a Washington-based NGO dedicated to a two-state solution to the Israeli-Palestinian standoff. In 2014, the Conference of Presidents of Major American Jewish Organizations rejected J Street's application to join the group, citing its policies that were not "pro-Israel" (Paulson 2014).

the eastward expansion of NATO.[5] During the Kosovo conflict of 1999, legislators were careful to address the concerns of Greek Americans about the possible spillover of the conflict into northern Greece. Although it would be an exaggeration to assert that these groups dictated the terms of U.S. foreign policy in these cases, their concerns undoubtedly carried significant weight among elected officials.

Public Interest Groups

As noted earlier, cosmopolitan NGOs confront a wide range of transnational problems ineffectively managed by national governments and intergovernmental organizations. Violations of human rights, threats to the environment, widespread economic disparities, and other problems routinely cross political boundaries and affect entire populations, not parochial interests. Lacking the traditional governing mechanisms to confront these problems, public interest groups appeal to the general public to increase pressure on governments. Shared values play an especially strong role in the mobilization of public interest groups, whose actions cannot be simply reduced to material self-interests. Among other concerns, this activity is prevalent in three areas: human rights, environmental protection, and international development.

Human rights. The protection of human rights is one of the most pervasive concerns of public interest NGOs (Wong 2012). This cause resonates strongly in the United States, where support for global human rights has historically been based on the constitutional foundations of its own government. Attention to human rights intensified during the Cold War. American leaders believed the denial of political and economic freedoms in communist countries amounted to a wholesale violation of human rights. American support for repressive governments around the world, however, prompted charges that the United States did not live up to its own standards of human rights.

In the 1970s and 1980s, lapses of the U.S. government, combined with the widespread abuses of human rights by communist regimes and many developing countries, inspired millions of private citizens worldwide to join NGOs focusing on the issue (Korey 1999). Economic support from foundations, for example, jumped from less than $1 million in the mid-1970s to more than $20 million in the early 1990s (Keck and Sikkink 1998, 99). Rights activists became even more assertive after the Cold War as the East-West conflict gave way to a range of transnational problems that had been neglected, including widespread social inequities and government repression.

Environmental protection. Another primary concern of public interest NGOs is the global environment. Public activism in the environmental arena also increased in the late twentieth century, especially after the Cold War, when security concerns gave

---

5. The U.S. government paid close attention to public opinion in the former Soviet bloc in considering two rounds of NATO expansion after the Cold War (Kostadinova 2000).

way to transnational problems previously neglected by the world powers. Prior to this time, environmental decay in the United States had been considered primarily a domestic problem to be solved by domestic measures such as the Clean Air Act and the Clean Water Act. However, mounting evidence that the effects of pollution could not be contained within political boundaries, along with scientific findings of a "greenhouse effect" and global warming, made it clear that the world needed cooperative solutions (see Chapter 12).

The memberships of environmental NGOs soared in the 1990s, as did financial contributions from members and private foundations. The largest of these groups, including Greenpeace, the Environmental Defense Fund, the Nature Conservancy, and the Natural Resources Defense Council, formed chapters in dozens of countries. The 1992 UN Conference on Environment and Development, more commonly known as the Earth Summit, served as a catalyst for NGO activism. More than 1,400 NGOs and government leaders from more than 170 countries officially took part in the conference, held in Brazil. Thousands of other private groups staged an alternative forum at the Earth Summit, a practice that has since been repeated during annual meetings of the International Monetary Fund (IMF), the World Bank, and the WTO. Ten years later, the World Summit on Sustainable Development, held in Johannesburg, South Africa, also sparked NGO activism and urgent appeals for government action on global warming and other critical issues.

The U.S. government is frequently at odds with environmental groups. As the world's cumulative source of fossil fuel emissions, the United States is among the groups' foremost objects of criticism. Conservation groups, along with many foreign governments, view with disdain the common assertion of U.S. officials that voluntary restrictions on various forms of pollution can make lasting progress in environmental protection. The same critics are well aware that the oil, automotive, and other corporate lobbies have the upper hand in swaying U.S. policy makers. Paradoxically, environmental NGOs owe much of their rapid rise and growing influence to the damaging impact of the United States on the global ecosystem and its refusal to abide by global agreements such as the Kyoto Protocol on climate change.

International development. Hundreds of U.S. and foreign-based NGOs engage daily in the transfer and delivery of humanitarian assistance to people in need. The most prominent of these groups, such as CARE, World Vision International, Oxfam Federation, and Doctors Without Borders, have each controlled more than $500 million of the estimated $8 billion in development aid disbursed annually to poor countries in recent years (Simmons 1998, 92). More than one-half of World Bank loans today involve NGOs in the development process.[6]

----

6. The World Bank, like governments, benefits by outsourcing development projects to private groups rather than managing these projects itself with permanent staff. As the largest source of World Bank funding, the U.S. government has the most to gain from these arrangements.

Groups based in industrialized countries routinely form partnerships with NGOs from developing countries to deliver food aid, conduct health programs, and plan long-term development projects. Government agencies in many developing countries are not equipped to manage the needs of their rapidly growing populations. In these cases, development NGOs fill a void in the public sector, drawing on resources from private sources as well as from wealthy governments that greatly exceed those available to the governments of poor states. The United States has increasingly turned to private contractors to manage the foreign aid programs it sponsors.

A major concern among many development NGOs in recent years has been the foreign debts of developing countries. As noted earlier, a global coalition of private development agencies, church groups, human rights activists, and other groups mobilized around the issue of debt relief through the movement called Jubilee 2000. The movement led the World Bank and the IMF to create the Heavily Indebted Poor Countries Initiative, which coordinated the pledges of debt relief from wealthy countries. By December 2014, their governments had provided $75 billion in debt relief to thirty-six countries. Another $41 billion in relief was provided by multilateral organizations (International Monetary Fund 2014).

Think Tanks and Private Foundations

Public debate on U.S. foreign policy often originates within the many "think tanks" located in Washington and elsewhere across the country. These private groups fill a gap in American politics resulting from a sense, among many citizens, of being excluded from public policies, whether local, national, or global. Staffed by academic specialists, former government and military officials, and outspoken figures from the private sector, think tanks serve as **idea brokers** that aim to influence public opinion and government policy through the dissemination of research findings and the airing of opinions on a variety of national issues (McGann and Sabatini 2011). Think tanks also serve as "governments in waiting," giving those out of power an opportunity to remain active in the policy community while the rival political party controls the White House or Congress (see Figure 9.3).

The "politics of expertise" is particularly important in U.S. foreign policy, which is both highly complex and of limited concern to the general population (Rich 2004). Of the 6,826 think tanks known to exist worldwide in 2013, nearly one-third (1,828) were located in the United States (McGann 2014). These American-made think tanks included eleven of the twenty most prominent in the field of security and international affairs, ten of the top twenty in the field of foreign policy and international affairs, and nine of the top twenty concerned with international development.

Among U.S. foreign policy think tanks, the Council on Foreign Relations (CFR), formed in 1921, is the most influential in informing policy discussions and debates. The council limits its membership, valued as a sign of prestige in the policy

Figure 9.3 ■ Select Foreign Policy Think Tanks: The Ideological Spectrum

Liberal	Centrist	Conservative
Center for Defense Information	Brookings Institution	American Enterprise Institute
Center for Nonproliferation Studies	Carnegie Endowment for International Peace	Cato Institute
Federation of American Scientists	Center for Strategic and International Studies	Ethics and Public Policy Center
Global Policy Forum	Council on Foreign Relations	Family Research Council
Institute for Policy Studies	Economic Policy Institute	Heritage Foundation
Interhemispheric Resource Center	Freedom House	Hoover Institution
Project on Defense Alternatives	Institute for International Economics	Hudson Institute
Union of Concerned Scientists	New America Foundation	Project for the New American Century
World Policy Institute	U.S. Institute of Peace	RAND Corporation

community, to 4,000. Attendance at CFR-sponsored policy forums, which often involve current foreign policy makers and foreign leaders, also serves as an important status symbol. The journal *Foreign Affairs*, edited and published by the council, is a widely read source of elite opinion on U.S. foreign policy. The CFR and other moderate think tanks play a major part in the "revolving door" of policy elites. Richard Haass, for example, left the Brookings Institution in 2001 to become director of policy planning in the State Department and then left the Bush administration to become president of the CFR.

These institutions rely on the public's trust, which was placed sorely in doubt in 2014. Several think tanks were found to be accepting large amounts of money from foreign governments in order to gain influence among U.S. foreign policy makers. "The money is increasingly transforming the once-staid think-tank world into a muscular arm of foreign governments' lobbying in Washington," reported the *New York Times* (Lipton, Williams, and Confessore 2014, A1). At least sixty-four governments contributed $92 million to twenty-eight U.S. think tanks, including the Atlantic Council, the Brookings Institution, and the Center for Strategic and International Studies (see Table 9.2). These payoffs raised questions about the research organizations' allegiances. Also uncertain was whether the groups violated the Foreign Agents Registration Act, which requires foreign officials seeking influence in the U.S. government to register as foreign agents.

Table 9.2 ■ Think Tanks on the Take? Selected Foreign Government Payoffs to the Brookings Institution, 2010–2013

Nation	Year	Payoff
Qatar	2013	$14.8 million
United Arab Emirates	2012	$3 million
Norway	2013	$2.4 million
Australia	2012	$1.2 million
Taipei (Taiwan)	2012	$360,284
Switzerland	2013	$300,000
Denmark	2011	$298,787
Japan	2013	$261,347
South Korea	2010	$170,000
Sweden	2011	$150,000

Source: "Money and Influence in the Think Tank World," *The New York Times*, September 6, 2014, http://www.nytimes.com/interactive/2014/09/07/us/07thinktankdocs1.html.

The Norwegian government was among the most aggressive in funding foreign policy think tanks between 2000 and 2014, spending more than $35 million on grants to various think tanks in Washington, D.C. A report by its Foreign Affairs Ministry (Bjørgaas 2012, p. 33) made its intentions clear: "In Washington, it is difficult for a small country to gain access to powerful politicians, bureaucrats and experts. Funding powerful think tanks is one way to gain such access, and some think tanks in Washington are openly conveying that they can service only those foreign governments that provide funding." The largest single contribution came from Qatar ($14.8 million), a tiny emirate on the Persian Gulf whose government planned to build an affiliate of the Brookings Institution in Doha, its capital.[7]

In many cases, think tanks receiving these funds pursue foreign policy goals that advance those of the U.S. government. Japanese officials, for example, paid the Brookings Institution $1.1 million to support their efforts to gain passage of the Trans-Pacific Partnership, a trade priority of Japan. Members of Congress later met with the think tank and invited one of its analysts to testify in favor of the agreement. Not all lawmakers, however, found this practice acceptable. To Rep. Frank R. Wolf (R-VA),

---

7. Before and after these funds were transferred, Qatar was widely known as a leading supporter of Hamas, a group hostile toward Israel that, since 1997, has been listed by the U.S. State Department as a Foreign Terrorist Organization.

Iran Nuclear Negotiations

Few foreign policy issues in recent years have sparked more debate among think tanks than the negotiations with Iran over its nuclear program. Although the Iranian government claimed to have only peaceful intentions for its program, the technology could be expanded to include the manufacturing of nuclear weapons. If such a step were taken, a nuclear arms race could break out across the Middle East. This is why the P5+1 negotiations, involving Iran and the five permanent members of the UN Security Council along with Germany, have been highly controversial.

Among those in favor of the agreement was Richard Haass, president of the Council on Foreign Relations. "A nuclear agreement of the sort outlined is preferable to Iran possessing nuclear weapons or going to war to prevent that outcome," Haass (2015) argued. "But any agreement must also generate widespread confidence in the United States and the region that it will place a meaningful ceiling on Iran's nuclear program, and that any cheating will be discovered early and dealt with firmly." At the Brookings Institution, analyst Richard Nephew (2015) also believed the negotiations were a safe bet. "If, under the terms of the agreement reached, Iran is not permitted to acquire a nuclear weapon and the U.S. retains the ability to counter that threat into the future, then in my estimation, these negotiations will have been successful by any reasonable standard."

Skeptics of the Iranian negotiations, including Anthony Cordesman of the Center for Strategic and International Studies, voiced several concerns. In his words, "At least in the near term, even the best outcome will have no impact on the massive conventional arms race in the Persian Gulf, Iran's buildup of its missile and asymmetric warfare forces, or Iran's efforts to increase its military and strategic influence in Bahrain, Iraq, Lebanon, Syria, and Yemen." A more critical assessment of the negotiations came from the Heritage Foundation, a conservative think tank. "The deal as it stands now won't arrest Iran's nuclear weapons efforts. It simply slows them down for a while," wrote Edwin J. Feulner (2015). "The administration is more interested in the short-term political benefits of an agreement than in the long-term security goal of making sure the bad guys are safely contained and rendered incapable of hurting a lot of innocent people."

This debate ended in the fall of 2015, when the Obama administration gained enough votes in Congress to ratify the agreement. This critical approval, which followed those of the five other governments engaged in the talks, virtually assured Iran's suspension of its nuclear weapons program. The agreement, which lifted crippling economic sanctions against Teheran, also returned foreign investments to Iran that were of great interest to the negotiating countries.

Sources: Richard N. Haass, "The Future of the Iran Nuclear Deal," *Council on Foreign Relations*, April 3, 2015, http://www.cfr.org/iran/future-iran-nuclear-deal/p36400; Richard Nephew, "The Grand Bargain: What Iran Conceded in the Nuclear Talks," *Brookings Institution*, April 18, 2015, http://www.brookings.edu/blogs/markaz/posts/2015/04/21-nephew-us-iran-nuclear-deal-compromise-diplomacy; Anthony H. Cordesman, "Judging a P5+1 Nuclear Agreement with Iran: The Key Criteria," *Center for Strategic and International Studies*, March 30, 2015, http://csis.org/publication/judging-p51-nuclear-agreement-iran-key-criteria; Edwin J. Feulner, "Fallout from a Bad Deal with Iran," *Heritage Foundation*, May 5, 2015, http://www.heritage.org/research/commentary/2015/5/fallout-from-a-bad-deal-with-iran.

the guidance of foreign policy think tanks is "expected to be in the national interest rather than their special interest" (Lipton 2014, A3).

Alongside think tanks, hundreds of private foundations in the United States provide grants for international research and programs in areas such as public health, global education, environmental protection, and conflict resolution. The Ford Foundation approved more than $413 million in grants in 2011. The Bill and Melinda Gates Foundation, led by the founder and chair of Microsoft Corporation, has provided more than $33 billion in grants since its inception in 1997 in such areas as global health and education (Mathiesen 2015). Recipients urgently needed the funds because of growing income gaps between developed and less-developed countries and cutbacks in government spending in many countries. In 2014, the Gates Foundation announced that its funds helped India become free of polio, a disease that had cost millions of lives. These massive injections of private aid signaled a new era in global governance, with corporations stepping in to fund programs that governments are either unwilling or unable to support. CNN founder Ted Turner, for example, announced in 1997 that he would donate $1 billion to the United Nations over ten years, in part to pay for development programs that faced cutbacks due to lower contributions from the U.S. government. By 2015, 137 billionaires had signed a pledge sponsored by the Giving Pledge NGO to provide more than half of their wealth to global charities (http://givingpledge.org).

■ GROUP STRATEGIES AND TACTICS

As described in this section, the tactics used by NGOs to influence U.S. foreign policy vary widely, depending on the type of NGOs involved, the resources at their disposal, and the foreign policy issues they seek to influence. Generally speaking, NGOs have become far more sophisticated as they have moved from the fringes to the mainstream of the policy process. They are now participating within the process—drafting legislation, serving on international commissions, and implementing government programs in areas previously monopolized by states.[8]

Consciousness Raising

Many NGOs simply want to call attention to their causes. They recognize that before a government will do something about problems such as global warming or the plight of political prisoners, large numbers of private citizens have to make government officials aware of these problems and forcefully call for government action. By **shaming** governments through public information campaigns, NGOs raise moral doubts about the governments in question in the hope that the general public will follow their lead. Such public shaming, combined with other forms of outside pressure, have persuaded many governments to improve their human rights practices (Murdie and Davis 2012).

---

8. Permanent members of the UN Security Council, including the United States, regularly brief NGOs and seek their input on regional problems that may call for UN action.

Arousing public concerns can be difficult, however, as thousands of NGOs compete daily for attention and support in a crowded, often bewildering, media environment. The continued existence of many NGOs depends on their success in taking hold of the media spotlight, if only for a brief time. Amnesty International, for example, contributed to political reforms in Angola after "naming and shaming" its leaders for their unlawful arrests, tortures, and killings of political opponents (Hafner-Burton 2008).

The most effective of these groups exploit advances in communications technology, particularly the Internet, to get their messages across. Their websites serve as crucial sources of information about their organizations, their causes, and the strategies they use to achieve their objectives. These sites commonly provide links to related groups and information sources, encouraging the collaboration of NGOs and collective political action. Groups also use mass e-mail as a low cost means to communicate with their members as well as with influential policy makers. Well-orchestrated media events, such as press conferences and demonstrations, have proved useful in attracting attention as well.

As do government officials, NGOs frame their adopted causes in dramatic and clearly understandable ways to gain media attention and public support. In the NGO campaign to ban land mines, for example, visual images of maimed victims proved more effective than hard numbers on the death toll produced by these weapons (Rutherford 2000). Similarly, members of Amnesty International found that the plight of political prisoners resonated more strongly among the public when individual cases were presented in graphic detail.

Political Pressure and Lobbying

In addition to influencing government agendas, private groups directly intervene in the U.S. foreign policy process. Their tactics include direct-mail campaigns to congressional offices and the White House that ask for support on matters of immediate concern. In the Internet era, interest groups rally their membership to send e-mail en masse in support of their policy goals. Representatives of NGOs also appeal in person to legislators and key executive branch officials. In the process of lobbying, they present these officials with "carrots," or potential rewards, for support of their preferences, as well as "sticks," or potential punishments, for nonsupport.

Carrots and sticks generally come in two forms—electoral and financial. The first relates to the central reality that elected officials need votes to gain and stay in office and that organized groups can deliver more votes than individuals. Politicians listen carefully to private groups, particularly large religious and ethnic NGOs, labor unions, and business groups that can mobilize multitudes of voters. Another way NGOs influence the policy process is by providing, or withholding, contributions to political campaigns through their affiliated **political action committees** (PACs)—the electoral arm of organized groups responsible for fund-raising and distributing money to promote the election of desired candidates. Liberated by court rulings that now permit virtually unlimited campaign contributions from corporations, money speaks volumes in national politics.

Lobbying, a term used to describe activity outside congressional offices and meeting rooms where personal contacts can be made, provides access to the foreign policy process that may not be possible through conventional diplomatic channels. Most foreign embassies, for example, lack the staff and resources necessary to get the attention of top policy makers, let alone members of congressional committees. Lobbying firms, clustered around K Street just a few blocks from the White House and Capitol Hill, can arrange business deals that benefit their foreign clients as well as the politicians who approve the deals. Recent examples of this "privatized" diplomacy abound:

- Americans for Prosperity, a conservative advocacy group, lobbied the White House in 2015 to approve the Keystone XL oil pipeline project that would extend from Canada to the Gulf of Mexico. Billionaires John and David Koch, leaders of the group, held much of the territory in Alberta that would carry the oil (Barron-Lopez 2015).[9]

- In 2014, the Podesta Group signed a contract with South Sudan's leaders that offered to help them gain "relevant U.S. audiences, including Congress, executive branch, media, and policy community" (quoted in Bogardus 2014). The group's clout was assured by its founder, John Podesta, formerly President Bill Clinton's chief of staff.

- Patton Boggs, another prominent lobbying firm, helped the U.S.-India Business Council promote the 2005 agreement between the two countries that called for U.S. shipments of nuclear fuel to India, a deal that alarmed the country's neighbors and nonproliferation advocates (Newhouse 2009).[10]

- The Livingston Group, exploiting its personal links to George W. Bush's foreign policy advisers, worked successfully in 2007 on behalf of its client, the Turkish government, to discourage Congress from condemning Turkey's deadly repression of Armenians in 1915 (Newhouse 2009).

Policy and Program Implementation

A rapidly growing arena of NGO activity is implementation of policies and programs approved by national governments. In these instances, which require shared preferences between the government and groups, NGOs serve as functional extensions of

---

9. President Obama vetoed the project in February 2015 after it was passed by both houses of Congress (see Chapter 12). Obama again rejected the pipeline in November 2015.

10. As part of its effort to secure passage of the deal, which was approved by Congress, the "India lobby" held fund-raisers for key legislators such as Joe Biden (D-DE), chair of the Senate Foreign Relations Committee, and Hillary Clinton (D-NY), co-chair of the Senate India Caucus.

the governments they serve and as instruments of their policy ambitions. Development NGOs, for example, manage the shipment and delivery of U.S. foreign aid to governments in need. Human rights NGOs conduct voter registration drives sponsored by the State Department and monitor elections in countries undergoing transitions to democratic rule.

Government contracting, the "public financing of private provision," is attractive to all parties concerned (Berríos 2000, 23). Through NGOs that have acquired material resources as well as legitimacy in advancing their agendas, the federal government, by far the largest customer of such contracted services in the United States, can pursue its foreign policy goals, such as economic development and political reform, without adding to its permanent workforce. More broadly, the practice of contracting services is consistent with the nation's ideological bias in favor of limited government and free enterprise. **Public choice theory**, which argues that competitive private firms can supply goods and services more efficiently than government agencies, reinforces this bias (see Buchanan 1977).

Recent evidence demonstrates that the U.S. government takes these NGOs seriously in its conduct of foreign policy. After the Kosovo conflict in 1999, the State Department disbursed more than $10 million in grants to NGOs so that they could help refugees return to their homes and rebuild their communities. Shortly before leaving office in January 2001, Secretary of State Madeleine Albright announced nearly $4 million in grants to NGOs so that they could monitor working conditions in overseas sweatshops. Private contractors manage U.S. foreign aid projects so commonly that an "aid lobby" has emerged among competing NGOs in such specialized areas as education, health care, environmental protection, and disaster relief (Lancaster 2007).

As noted earlier, the outsourcing of U.S. foreign policy functions is also routine in the military sector. Of particular interest are **corporate warriors**, private companies that "trade in professional services linked to warfare" (Singer 2003, 8). Dozens of private military firms provide a wide range of military functions once reserved for the government, from food services to maintaining the grounds on U.S. military bases. In Iraq, private contractors built schools and hospitals, installed telephone and satellite systems, and advised Iraqi officials on effective ways in which to pursue political and economic reforms. Other countries have also turned to these companies for assistance, including for combat forces that are in some instances better trained and equipped than their own troops.

The benefits of outsourcing defense come at considerable costs. By their nature, private firms are more secretive and less accountable than public agencies, which must adhere to provisions for legislative oversight and public scrutiny. Controlling corporate warriors can also be difficult, as the U.S. government realized during the 2004 prison abuse scandals in Iraq. Only after the media reported the story did U.S. citizens learn that private contractors serving as prison interrogators had resorted to brutal tactics that violated the Geneva Conventions. Contractors from the United States and other coalition forces became frequent targets of kidnappings in Iraq. Indeed, some of the most publicized U.S. casualties during the Iraq occupation, including the May 2004 beheading of businessman Nicholas Berg, involved private contractors.

Civil Disobedience

When private groups feel their voices are not being heard through conventional channels of political discourse, they may resort to civil disobedience to get attention. According to Howard Zinn (1968, 119), civil disobedience involves "the deliberate, discriminate violation of law for a vital social purpose. It becomes not only justifiable but necessary when a fundamental human right is at stake, and when legal channels are inadequate for securing that right." The tactics of civil disobedience are considered most significant for their symbolic value. Although a protester's arrest may have little immediate consequence for the policy process, protesters expect such arrests to attract public attention and to provoke sympathy, thereby building pressure for reform.

In the United States during the late 1960s and early 1970s, critics of the Vietnam War frequently resorted to civil disobedience to express their displeasure with the government's war effort. For example, the Students for a Democratic Society (SDS), an organization established by campus activists at several major universities, conducted "sit-ins," or the peaceful occupation of public spaces, to express their opposition to the war. Some SDS members burned their draft cards; others staged hunger strikes to raise public consciousness.

Demonstrations against the war, while generally peaceful, sometimes led to violent clashes with police and mass arrests. In the 1980s, organized groups protested the escalation of the arms race and called for a nuclear freeze, much to the dismay of the Reagan administration. As noted earlier, in 2011 members of the Occupy movement deliberately sought to disrupt business as usual in many American cities in order to make their point about corporate greed.

Civil disobedience has long been an important tactic of environmental NGOs. Greenpeace, for example, gained global attention in 1985 by sending boats into restricted areas of the South Pacific where the French government was planning nuclear tests.[11] In response to the massive 2010 oil spill in the Gulf of Mexico, Greenpeace activists scaled the walls of British Petroleum's headquarters and hoisted a flag that renamed the corporation "British Polluters." In 2012, Greenpeace activists penetrated several nuclear power plants in Sweden to demonstrate the facilities' lack

---

11. Membership in Greenpeace soared after the French Secret Services sunk the Greenpeace vessel *Rainbow Warrior* off the coast of New Zealand in 1985.

of security. More recently, in April 2015, six members of Greenpeace chained themselves to an oil rig in the Pacific Ocean in order to demonstrate their opposition to Shell Oil's plans to drill off the coast of Alaska (G. Johnson 2015).

■ BUYING POWER: THE CORPORATE CONNECTION

The largest and most powerful NGOs can be found in the business world. It is not unusual for a company to have its headquarters in one country and its other operations (such as research and development, production, marketing, and sales) in others. Profit-seeking firms with operations, subsidiaries, and markets in more than one country are known as **multinational corporations** (MNCs). In responding to technological advances, primarily in the areas of research and development, telecommunications, and transportation, MNCs are both the by-products and the catalysts of globalization. Indeed, these multinational firms have grown rapidly in number, size, and global reach in the past century, to the point that the annual revenues of today's largest MNCs far exceed the economic output of most countries.

The U.S. government, whose founding principles include a belief in the virtues of free markets and global commerce, has long been an advocate of MNCs. In 2014, six of the world's twenty largest MNCs in terms of total revenues were based in the United States (see Table 9.3). Other leading MNCs have most of their production and support facilities in the United States. Still others, such as electronics firms based in Japan, derive most of their revenues from American consumers. These corporate interests flood the policy process, and political campaigns, with massive financial resources.

More generally, these corporations can serve as agents of U.S. foreign policy by embracing many of the interests, values, and beliefs about political economy held by government leaders. Three areas of convergence can be identified:

- *Shared values.* Corporations and U.S. political leaders share the belief that a free-market economy will foster political freedom. In this view, firms will avoid doing business in countries that cannot guarantee the security of their assets, that tolerate corruption, and that repress political rights to such an extent that mass revolts pose a constant danger.
- *Shared interests.* Corporate leaders and the U.S. government promote a world economy based on private property and open markets. The government's bias toward free trade favors U.S.-based MNCs, which tend to be wealthier and more technologically advanced than their overseas competitors.
- *Economic peace.* Corporate and government officials agree that countries respecting economic and political freedoms most likely will engage in peaceful relations toward one another. This variant of democratic-peace theory (see Chapter 3) is driven by economic necessity, as private investors and firms require a stable, predictable environment, which is impossible in areas prone to violent conflicts and coups.

Table 9.3 ■ The World's Twenty Largest Corporations, 2014

Rank	Company	Nationality	Revenues (billions of U.S. dollars)
1	Wal-Mart Stores	USA	$476
2	Royal Dutch Shell	Netherlands	$460
3	Sinopec	China	$457
4	China National Petroleum	China	$432
5	Exxon Mobile	USA	$408
6	BP	United Kingdom	$396
7	State Grid	China	$333
8	Volkswagen	Germany	$262
9	Toyota Motor	Japan	$256
10	Glencore	Switzerland	$233
11	Total	France	$228
12	Chevron	USA	$220
13	Samsung Electronic	South Korea	$209
14	Berkshire Hathaway	USA	$182
15	Apple	USA	$171
16	AXA	France	$166
17	Gazprom	Russia	$165
18	E.ON	Germany	$163
19	Phillips 66	USA	$161
20	Daimler	Germany	$157

Source: "Global 500: Our Annual Ranking of the World's Largest Corporations," *Fortune*, http://fortune.com/global500/.

Corporate power in the United States increased during the 1980s when many world leaders, including President Reagan and British prime minister Margaret Thatcher, pushed for greater "economic freedom" among investors, merchants, and MNCs. The U.S. government responded by reducing corporate tax rates and by deregulating key financial and commercial sectors of the economy. As a result of these actions, many MNCs recorded record profits while enriching their stockholders and their top executives. The same lack of regulations, however, fueled the reckless lending practices among banks and mortgage brokers that contributed to the financial crisis of 2008 (Rothkopf 2012).

The pervasive role of MNCs in U.S. foreign policy makes them frequent targets of criticism by nonprofit NGOs with more altruistic goals. Animosity is not limited to individuals and groups within the United States; foreign-based groups complain that MNCs are agents of cultural imperialism, force-feeding people consumer products such as Coca-Cola and McDonald's hamburgers through aggressive marketing and advertising campaigns. Exposés of oppressive labor practices in overseas sweatshops by companies such as Nike, Wal-Mart, Walt Disney, and Gap prompted these corporations to establish codes of conduct for their suppliers. Pressure from environmental NGOs such as the Rainforest Network forced major retail stores in the United States, including Home Depot and Lowe's Home Improvement Warehouse, to certify that the lumber they were selling was not furnished by suppliers who were inflicting irreversible damage on the environment.

The Military-Industrial Complex

Among U.S.-based corporations, those involved in the defense industry have the closest ties to the foreign policy process (see Carroll 2006). The U.S. defense industry, by far the largest of its kind in the world, has grown rapidly in recent years, after a decade of post–Cold War cutbacks. Weapons production, a large segment of the U.S. economy, is a leading source of new technologies, many of which find their way into civilian industries.[12] The defense industry currently employs more than 2 million people. As the largest discretionary category of U.S. government spending, the defense budget has a strong impact on the size of the overall federal budget deficit. Sen. Everett Dirksen (R-IL) once observed wryly, "A billion here, a billion there, sooner or later it adds up to real money."

Defense spending is also a major arena of competition for federal dollars. American military contractors, such as Lockheed Martin and Boeing, dominate the global defense industry (see Table 9.4). Although these industry giants produce the largest and most modern weapons systems for the United States and foreign governments, hundreds of smaller MNCs support the defense sector as well, providing ammunition, spare parts, uniforms, food, medical supplies, and other goods to the armed services. Deciding which military contractors receive the massive volumes of money is part of an intense political process within Congress. Its role in the iron triangle (see Chapter 3), which also includes defense contractors and the Pentagon, affects large sectors of the U.S. economy.

------

12. For example, the U.S. Department of Defense sponsored much of the research and development of the Internet during the Cold War.

Table 9.4 ■ Top Ten U.S. Military Contractors, 2014

Rank	Company	Country	Defense Revenue, 2013 (billions of U.S. dollars)	Proportion of Revenue from Defense (%)
1	Lockheed Martin	USA	$41	89
2	Boeing	USA	$32	37
3	BAE Systems	United Kingdom	$28	94
4	Raytheon	USA	$22	93
5	Northrop Grumman	USA	$20	79
6	General Dynamics	USA	$19	60
7	Airbus Group	Netherlands	$17	20
8	United Technologies	USA	$12	19
9	Thales	France	$11	56
10	Finmeccanica	Italy	$11	50

Source: "Defense News Top 100 for 2014," www.defensenews.com.

The latest military buildup, focusing on high-tech weapons systems, accelerated after the terrorist attacks of September 2001. The steady increase in U.S. defense spending, detailed in Chapter 5, benefited hundreds of U.S.-based corporations. In fact, the large size and political clout of these MNCs have been a central feature of U.S. society since World War II. During the Cold War, President Dwight Eisenhower worried that the U.S. **military-industrial complex** posed a danger to the economy by diverting a significant share of output from civilian production (see In Their Own Words box). In his view, the reliance of politically influential corporations on arms manufacturing created a perverse incentive on the government's part to expand the nation's military arsenal. In such an environment, Eisenhower believed, both the arms merchants and their patrons in Congress were tempted to inflate the magnitude of foreign threats.

Eisenhower's warning also highlighted the potential dangers iron triangles pose in the policy process (see Chapter 3). For many former military officers, who retire from active service in their forties and fifties, a logical next step in their careers is a position in the defense industry, with its familiar products and functions. This crossing of career paths creates a strong bond between the Pentagon and defense contractors. Together, they are able to get the attention and support of powerful members of Congress, who receive campaign contributions and other forms of political support from the defense industry and its PACs. The groups in the military-industrial complex, as well as those in countless other areas, have proved to be highly influential in the U.S. foreign policy process.

With such large volumes of money involved, conflicts of interest and potential corruption inevitably emerge, as documented cases of abuse have shown. Some defense contractors have been caught bribing members of Congress in return for lucrative contracts, and former Pentagon officials who have moved into lobbying jobs with military contractors have gained privileged access to legislators.

Defense contractors have a large role in the shaping of U.S. military strategies and tactics. Major corporations such as Lockheed Martin compete for contracts that run into the billions of dollars.

REUTERS/Tami Chappell

Even though measures have been taken to reduce the impact of this "revolving door" on the procurement process—for example, legislators and senior officials must refrain from lobbying their former colleagues for at least one year after leaving government— the incentives of all concerned to maintain these ties persist. At the same time, Pentagon leaders must come to terms with the globalization of defense industries, which are quickly catching up with the United States in such advanced fields as 3D printing, nanotechnology, and robotics (Lynn 2014).

Trade Associations and Labor Unions

Private groups that represent entire sectors of the U.S. economy, or the business community in general, promote business interests in the United States as well. Many of these groups are active in shaping not only U.S. foreign policy but also the policies of governments abroad. Prominent among these groups is the U.S. Chamber of Commerce, which seeks business access to foreign markets by pressuring policy makers in the United States and their counterparts in other countries. In 2002, the Chamber, which represents more than 3 million firms and nearly 1,000 business associations, had a presence in 82 foreign nations. Using many of the same tactics, foreign-based MNCs and trade associations maintain full-time staffs in Washington, D.C., to pursue favorable treatment in U.S. trade policy and other legislation.

Labor unions such as the United Auto Workers, the Teamsters Union, and the Communications Workers of America participate in this process as well, often as adversaries of the MNCs that employ their members. These groups are seeking to keep their workers' jobs in the United States. The clout of this sizable voting bloc, though weakening in recent years as the number and proportion of unionized

Dwight D. Eisenhower *Although Dwight D. Eisenhower's farewell address in 1961 was the first such event to be televised, observers registered surprise not so much at the medium of delivery as at the message sent. The man who had made his name as supreme Allied commander during World War II and then as supreme commander of NATO warned against the defense industry's unchecked influence in the halls of government. Coining the term* military-industrial complex, *Eisenhower offered a cautionary tale about some of the nation's largest and most powerful foreign policy interest groups. While many political and business leaders agreed with Eisenhower, the military-industrial complex is even stronger today.*

A vital element in keeping the peace is our military establishment. Our arms must be mighty, ready for instant action, so that no potential aggressor may be tempted to risk his own destruction. Our military organization today bears little relation to that known by any of my predecessors in peacetime, or indeed by the fighting men of World War II or Korea.

Until the latest of our world conflicts, the United States had no armaments industry. American makers of plowshares could, with time and as required, make swords as well. But now we can no longer risk emergency improvisation of national defense; we have been compelled to create a permanent armaments industry of vast proportions. Added to this, three and a half million men and women are directly engaged in the defense establishment. We annually spend on military security more than the net income of all United States corporations.

This conjunction of an immense military establishment and a large arms industry is new in the American experience. The total influence—economic, political, even spiritual—is felt in every city, every Statehouse, every office of the federal government. We recognize the imperative need for this development. Yet we must not fail to comprehend its grave implications. Our toil, resources, and livelihood are all involved; so is the very structure of our society.

In the councils of government, we must guard against the acquisition of unwarranted influence, whether sought or unsought, by the military-industrial complex. The potential for the disastrous rise of misplaced power exists and will persist.

We must never let the weight of this combination endanger our liberties or democratic processes. . . .

Source: Michael Nelson, ed., "Dwight D. Eisenhower's Farewell Address (1961)," *Historic Documents on the Presidency: 1776–1989* (Washington, DC: Congressional Quarterly, 1989), 350–354.

workers have declined, remains beyond question. Proponents of the steel industry, for example, persuaded President Bush in 2002 to increase tariffs on foreign-made steel to keep domestic producers in business. This was a decision popular in steel-producing regions of the United States, which play a critical role in national elections. However, Bush's decision angered foreign political and business leaders as well as the WTO, which criticized Bush for violating his own standards on free trade and WTO regulations. In the face of this criticism and the threat of imminent WTO and European Union sanctions, Bush lowered the steel tariffs.

The protection of U.S. jobs is a classic intermestic policy, as are other aspects of economic activity, such as environmental regulation and immigration. Policy makers in these cases play a two-level game (Putnam 1988) in which they negotiate simultaneously with representatives of foreign governments and those of U.S. interest groups with a stake in the outcome. Interests at the two levels frequently come into conflict. For instance, after the U.S. government secures access to another country's domestic market, American firms are tempted to move their factories to that country to reduce labor costs, thereby laying off workers in the United States. Decision makers in these cases must walk a political tightrope, trying to find areas of agreement among the interested parties at home and abroad.

The most recent dispute between U.S. labor unions and the federal government involved the Trans-Pacific Partnership (TPP), a proposed regional trading bloc linking twelve countries from the Pacific Rim to North and South America. President Obama declared the trade deal among his highest priorities. As in the case of the North American Free Trade Agreement, signed by President Clinton in December 1993, labor unions charged that the TPP would come at the cost of American jobs. A powerful labor union (AFL-CIO n.d.) made its position clear on its website: "The AFL-CIO provided the Obama administration with ideas to improve U.S. trade positions so that they work for the 99%, not just the 1%. Unfortunately, it is becoming clear the TPP will not create jobs, protect the environment and ensure safe imports." As the final negotiations neared in 2015, Obama also faced pushback from his own Democratic Party, which has long been responsive to the concerns of labor unions. As usual, dozens of interest groups mobilized on both sides of a contentious foreign policy issue.

■ CONCLUSION

This chapter has described the many strategies and tactics pursued by social movements, NGOs, and profit-seeking firms in their attempts to influence U.S. foreign policy. Such activity can be highly effective given the lack of general public interest and engagement in the policy process, a pattern highlighted in Chapters 7 and 8. Whereas broadly based social movements seek policy changes that presumably benefit all citizens, most interest groups seek to advance the interests of a narrower range of stakeholders. The influence of these groups varies widely, and competition among them for resources and access is often fierce. Although their relationship with U.S. foreign policy makers is often contentious, interest groups frequently align with Washington on key issues, producing mutual benefits and a stronger U.S. position in diplomatic bargaining.

Organized group action is entirely consistent with American political values, but there is little doubt that the political and financial pressures imposed by such groups may steer U.S. foreign policy in directions that conflict with and sometimes contradict proclaimed national interests. Privatized diplomacy, which has become commonplace in U.S. foreign policy, reinforces "a uniquely American habit of sustaining the democratic process with money; [foreign governments] see a broad and deepening pattern of corrupt and corruptible members of Congress making self-serving deals with lobbyists working for foreign entities" (Newhouse 2009, 92). The same can be said for the pressure applied by MNCs, military contractors, and other groups with a material stake in security policies, whose proven influence over key decisions fuels the paradox of U.S. world power.

Whereas particularistic groups pose challenges to the democratic conduct of U.S. foreign policy, cosmopolitan groups that promote collective interests must overcome their own "democratic deficits," as described earlier, by permitting outsiders to observe their deliberations or have a voice in selecting their leaders (see McGann and Johnstone 2005). At the same time, the common deficiencies of nonprofit NGOs—their limited political clout compared with that of MNCs, their need for constant fund-raising, and their frequent conflicts with one another—will also persist. These strains will likely continue, even as the spread of democracy to much of the world ensures that members of transnational civil society will become ever more potent political actors (Slaughter 2004).

Broader social movements, including those demanding an end to military interventions or greater U.S. respect for human rights overseas, fail to achieve their goals at least as often as they succeed. Nevertheless, government officials ignore such forces at their peril and must constantly weigh the electoral and material costs and benefits of engagement with large-scale and well-organized advocates for change. The government must contend with the full range of societal actors whose proven capacity to disrupt the status quo and cut political careers short makes them inescapable players in the foreign policy process.

WANT A BETTER GRADE?

Get the tools you need to sharpen your study skills.
Access practice quizzes, eFlashcards, video, and multimedia at
edge.sagepub.com/hook5e.

$SAGE edge™
for CQ Press

KEY TERMS

corporate warriors, p. 317

cosmopolitan groups, p. 304

democratic deficit, p. 305

hyperpluralism, p. 297

idea brokers, p. 310

lobbying, p. 316

INTERNET REFERENCES

The **American Enterprise Institute** (http://www.aei.org), based in Washington, D.C., promotes a variety of causes related to "American freedom and democratic capitalism." Nearly 200 researchers and prominent policy experts publish reports and organize conferences that advocate U.S. foreign policy based on the promotion of national interests rather than global concerns.

The **American Israel Public Affairs Committee** (http://www.aipac.org), one of the most influential lobbying organizations in the United States, promotes U.S. foreign policy in the Middle East that supports Israel. The group's website includes briefings on issues related to regional security and updates on AIPAC efforts to gain U.S. political, economic, and military support for Israel.

The **Brookings Institution** (http://www.brookings.edu) is a think tank that provides scholarly reports and in-depth research on domestic and international sources affecting U.S. foreign policy. Particular attention is paid to defense, the world economy, environmental issues, and global governance.

Foreign Policy in Focus (http://www.fpif.org) is a "think tank without walls" that seeks to educate the public through Internet reports and public conferences on a variety of U.S. foreign policy issues. Sponsored by the Institute for Policy Studies, the group advocates the advancement of human rights and justice as a centerpiece of U.S. foreign policy.

MoveOn (http://www.movcon.org), a coalition of liberal grassroots organizations, gained national stature as a rallying point for critics of the George W. Bush administration's domestic and foreign policies. Through its website, the group sponsors voter registration drives, neighborhood canvassing, and other activities on behalf of liberal candidates.

The **National Council of Churches** (http://www.ncccusa.org) represents an array of U.S.-based Christian denominations in advancing human rights, poverty relief, and other social causes. Recent resolutions have condemned U.S. mistreatment of prisoners and increased domestic surveillance in the war on terror.

ONE (http://www.one.org), an Internet-based advocate for humanitarian relief, derives its influence from the more than 2 million signatories of its declaration to end extreme poverty. The group's petitions reveal mass-based support for debt forgiveness, increased treatment of HIV/AIDS, and the protection of human rights in the developing world.

NATIONAL SECURITY AND DEFENSE POLICY

Vasily Fedosenko/Reuters/Corbis

Ukrainian citizens seeking closer ties to the European Union confront fierce resistance from police and armed forces. Civil unrest soon spread to eastern Ukraine, where violent protesters fought for annexation into neighboring Russia.

10.1   Discuss strategy as it concerns U.S. foreign policy and policy making.

10.2   Explain different rationales that justify the use of force.

10.3   Describe the role of nuclear weapons in U.S. foreign policy strategy.

10.4   Summarize the ideologies and institutions involved in combatting terrorism.

The final three chapters of this book examine the primary domains of U.S. foreign policy—that is, the substantive issue areas that affect the nation's relations with governments and citizens overseas. The three domains—national security, global economic relations, and transnational issues—capture the diversity of foreign policy problems facing the United States today. They do not, however, exhaust the full range of issues that confront policy makers, who must respond to unanticipated events while managing routine functions and pursuing their long-term objectives on a daily basis.

This chapter considers the foreign policy problems related to **national security**, the freedom a nation-state enjoys from threats to its sovereignty, territory, and political autonomy. This term is inherently controversial because of the tendency of political leaders to justify their actions on security grounds. Dwight Eisenhower, for example, created the interstate highway system on the basis of national security, and Richard Nixon used the same rationale to defend his secret bombings of Cambodia during the Vietnam War. Yet, despite its ambiguities, the term *national security* "has come into such broad usage since World War II that, like a boomerang, we cannot throw it away" (Jordan, Taylor, and Mazarr 1999, 3).

The security that states and their citizens experience derives from a variety of sources. Canadian scholar Barry Buzan (1991, 19–20) found that five elements combine to create a sense of national security:

- *Military security*—the strength and effectiveness of the armed forces
- *Economic security*—the productive use of natural and human resources, financial assets, technological advancements, and foreign markets
- *Political security*—the stability and legitimacy of government institutions

- *Societal security*—the vitality of civil society, including interest groups, mass culture, and the news media

- *Environmental security*—the degree to which natural resources are protected and human activity takes place on an ecologically sustainable basis

The Pentagon, with its massive budget and worldwide troop presence, has assumed greater responsibility for all aspects of U.S. national security in recent years. The nation's ongoing struggle against terrorists fuels this militarization of U.S. foreign policy. Even the provision of development aid is increasingly a Pentagon function. Indeed, U.S. foreign policy today is unique to the extent that it "is being crafted and implemented by the military" (M. A. Cohen 2009, 69). "Whether it's waging the war on terror or the war on drugs; nation-building in post-conflict environments; development, democracy promotion, or diplomacy; fighting cyber-criminals or training foreign armies, the global face of the United States is generally that of a soldier."

The balance of military power among the world's nations offers a useful starting point in any analysis of U.S. defense policy (see Table 10.1). While China has the most soldiers in uniform and Russia has the most nuclear warheads, the United States on the whole maintains a wide lead over other great powers in hard and soft power. As noted in Chapter 1, U.S. defense spending of more than $600 billion in recent years nearly exceeds the spending of all other countries combined. Only the United States maintains a worldwide military presence that carves the globe into separate regional commands (see Map 6.1 in Chapter 6, Department of Defense Regional Commands). Through this pervasive reach, the United States dominates the "commons" of air, sea, and space (Posen 2003). Advances in U.S. military technology, even in the midst of globalized competition, significantly widen this advantage in U.S. world power.

These indicators highlight the importance of military strength in the global balance of power. To Hans Morgenthau (1967, 26), who equated *world* politics with *power*

GET THE EDGE ON YOUR STUDIES

edge.sagepub.com/hook5e

- Take a quiz to find out what you've learned.
- Review key terms with eFlashcards.
- Watch videos that enhance chapter content.

Table 10.1 ■ Global Military Balance of Power, 2014

Country	Military Spending (billions of U.S. dollars)*	Armed Forces (total thousands of active personnel)	Military Aircraft	Navy Ships	Land-Based Weapons	Nuclear Warheads
United States	609.9	1,400	13,892	473	54,474	7,200
China	216.3	2,300	2,860	673	23,664	250
Russia	84.4	766	3,429	352	61,086	7,500
Saudi Arabia	80.7	234	675	55	7,960	0
France	62.3	203	1,264	113	7,888	300
United Kingdom	60.5	147	936	66	6,624	215
India	49.9	1,325	1,905	202	21,164	90–110
Germany	46.5	179	663	81	6,481	0
Japan	45.8	247	1,613	131	4,329	0
South Korea	36.7	625	1,412	166	12,619	0
Brazil	31.8	327	749	113	3,048	0
Italy	30.9	320	760	174	7,835	0
Australia	25.4	58	408	52	2,174	0

* Military spending is as of 2014.

Sources: Stockholm International Peace Research Institute, SIPRI Military Expenditures Database; Global Firepower .com, "Aircraft Strength by Country," "Total Naval Ship Power by Country," "Available Military Manpower by Country"; Federation of Atomic Scientists, "Status of World Nuclear Forces."

politics, "armed strength as a threat or a potentiality is the most important material factor making for the political power of a nation." In this regard, power represents more than a tangible resource, the identifiable and measurable sum of a country's military assets. It also represents an intangible capability to "effect the outcomes you want, and if necessary, to change the behavior of others to make this happen" (Nye 2002, 4).

Throughout its history, the United States has frequently employed its military forces to achieve a variety of foreign policy goals. These forces engaged in 374 instances of overt military force between 1798 and January 2015, an average of more than 1.7 military actions per year. In recent years, U.S. troops have been deployed, sometimes on a regular basis, to Iraq, Afghanistan, Kosovo, Jordan, and several countries in sub-Saharan Africa. In many cases, including Haiti (2004) and Yemen (2012), additional U.S. forces were required to protect U.S. citizens and diplomats in the midst of civil unrest. In the midst of the U.S. war on terror, the reported military engagements became more ambiguous. President Bush reported to Congress in 2004 that "combat-equipped and combat-support forces" were deployed "to a number of locations in the Central, Pacific, European, and Southern Command areas of operation." Five years later, President Obama reported that naval forces were engaged in "maritime interception operations on the high seas" (Salazar 2015, 26).

The terrorist attacks of September 2001 forced military planners to reshape U.S. strategy around the concept of asymmetric warfare—that is, wars fought between adversaries of highly uneven material strength (see Chapter 1). The *National Defense Strategy* (U.S. Department of Defense 2008, 2) found the global security environment to be "defined by a global struggle against a violent extremist ideology that seeks to overturn the international state system." The advantages of even the most muscle-bound states, including the United States, may be undercut by weaker but highly determined terrorist groups that prey on civilian targets and mass psychology, staging attacks at times and places of their choosing.

Real and potential military challenges confront U.S. leaders along a spectrum of armed conflict in which the chance of each type of conflict occurring is inversely proportionate to its destructiveness (see Figure 10.1). Nuclear war is the most lethal, yet least likely, form of warfare. Conversely, "military operations other than war" are less destructive but more common, as in the 2010 relief effort in Haiti or in the 2011 U.S. peacekeeping effort in Liberia following elections in that African country. Conventional wars, such as those fought in Korea and Vietnam during the Cold War, fall in the middle of this spectrum. Military planners and their political masters must carefully gauge these ratios in considering the use of force.

The Pentagon today must respond to a more complex variety of challenges to the United States than ever before. Major concerns now include the continued presence of U.S. troops in Afghanistan who were unable, over more than a decade, to achieve their goals of transforming their government into a stable democracy. Other key challenges include those posed by Russia, which in 2014 launched an attempt to expand its territory into Ukraine, and by the Islamic State of Iraq and Syria (ISIS), whose vows to create an Islamist caliphate across the Middle East were backed by acts of unspeakable brutality. As the United States directs more attention to the Asia-Pacific region, its foremost concern is the rapid rise of China, described by a former U.S. national security adviser as "the most dramatic change in the world's geopolitical and economic pecking order" (Brzezinski 2012, 18).

Figure 10.1 ■ Spectrum of Armed Conflict

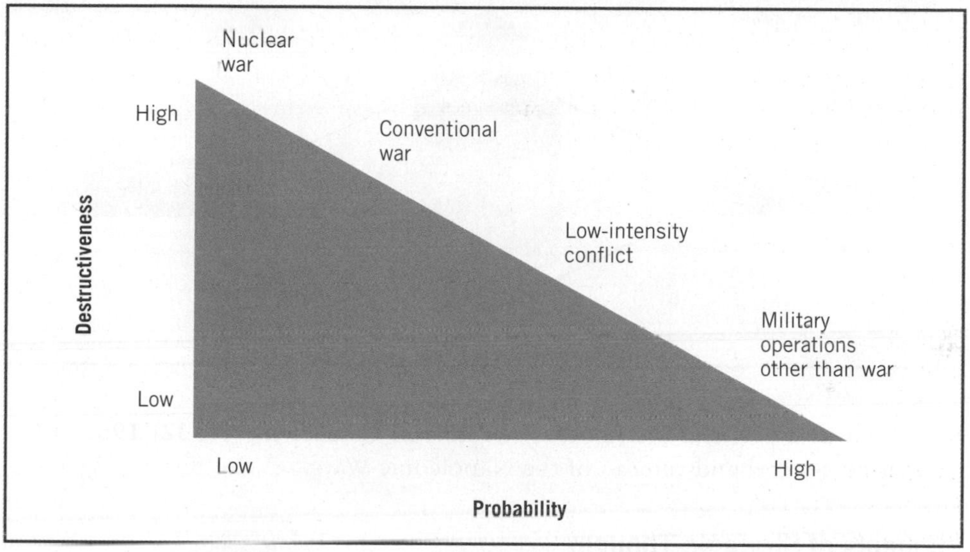

Source: Peter L. Hays, Brenda J. Vallance, and Alan R. Van Tassel, eds., with a foreword by Brent Scowcroft. *American Defense Policy,* 7th ed. (Baltimore: Johns Hopkins University Press), 8 (figure 1). © 2005 The Johns Hopkins University Press. Reprinted by permission.

■ THE FOUNDATION OF STRATEGY

Conflicts of interest, real and potential, are central realities of world politics and must be confronted and overcome on a regular basis. In facing such conflicts, political leaders devise a **grand strategy**—that is, a statement of the nation's essential objectives in world politics and the means of achieving those objectives. A clear statement of grand strategy includes "an integrated conception of interests, threats, resources, and policies" (Brands 2012, 4). The chosen strategy is based upon a government's global objectives as seen through the lens of its perceived threats and available resources (see Figure 10.2).

In the absence of a grand strategy, states approach international conflicts without a sense of purpose, and their military tactics, or means, bear little relation to the ends pursued in a given conflict (Liddell Hart 1967). Carl von Clausewitz, who nearly two centuries after his death remains the most influential military strategist in history, believed that nations sever the link between politics and war at their peril. "Under all circumstances War is to be regarded not as an independent

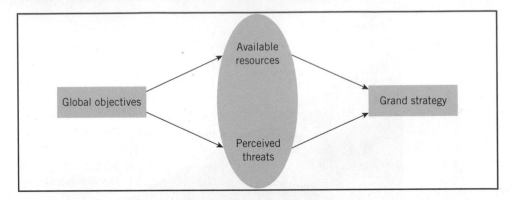

Figure 10.2 ■ The Strategic Matrix

Global objectives

Available resources

Perceived threats

Grand strategy

thing, but as a political instrument," wrote von Clausewitz ([1832] 1982, 121), a Prussian general and veteran of the Napoleonic Wars.

Elements of Strategic Thought

A state derives the elements of its grand strategy from a variety of external and internal sources. Among external sources, the **strategic environment** provides the context in which strategy must be applied. This term incorporates trends in global and regional balances of power and the degree to which a state considers other powerful nations and politically mobilized private groups to be friends or foes. Important developments in world politics, particularly those that challenge the state's vital security assets, are also elements of the strategic environment and, as such, require immediate as well as long-term accommodation. The terrorist attacks of September 2001, for example, altered the strategic environment for the United States and called for a recasting of its foreign policy priorities and diplomatic relations. Of novel significance was the elevation of nonstate actors, in the form of Islamic terrorist groups, as proven threats to U.S. security, and the tactical challenges posed by terrorism as a form of warfare.

Still, U.S. global primacy remains the defining feature of the strategic environment. Even under the strains of multiple military commitments and a stagnant economy, the unipolar balance of world power dominated by the United States has endured. Rather than expand their military forces (**internal balancing**) or form rival alliances (**external balancing**), other major powers have generally remained on the U.S. bandwagon—even as their leaders have openly disputed and opposed U.S. foreign policies (Lieber and Alexander 2005). Even the most brazen actions by the White House have not threatened most foreign governments, many of which enjoy considerable material benefits and security protections from their bilateral relations with Washington. In addition to these external sources of grand strategy, several internal factors must be taken into account for a fuller understanding of strategic thought. These include geopolitical assets, strategic culture, state-society relations, and structural arrangements.

Geopolitical assets. Grand strategy also involves geopolitics, which reflects the spatial and territorial factors that separate states physically. The most basic of these geopolitical assets—the size, location, and natural resources of the state—establish its possibilities, limitations, and strategic options. The United States' early grand strategy of strategic detachment was possible only because the young nation lay a considerable distance from the great powers of Europe and Asia. Other, more changeable factors include the size, structure, and growth of the country's economy; the perceived legitimacy of the government; the health and morale of the population; and some elements of "soft power" such as national education and cultural influence (Nye 2004). Technological advances, particularly those in the information and military sectors, are increasingly vital to U.S. security. Finally, military alliances combined with the worldwide deployment of U.S. troops (see Table 10.2) are an additional geopolitical asset of the United States.

Table 10.2 ■ Geographical Distribution of Active-Duty U.S. Military Personnel, March 2015

Geographic Location	Number of Active-Duty U.S. Military Personnel
United States and territories	1,148,530
Japan	49,430
Germany	38,015
South Korea	29,041
Afghanistan	14,452
Italy	11,425
Kuwait	11,313
United Kingdom	9,078
Iraq	2,677
Other foreign countries	19,773

Source: "Active Duty Military Personnel by Regional Area and by Country, March 30, 2015." Washington DC: U.S. Department of Defense, Defense Manpower Data Center.

Strategic culture. This element of strategic thought refers to widely shared normative beliefs, attitudes, and policy preferences as they pertain to a country's foreign relations and decisions regarding war and peace (see Snow 2004, ch. 3). As noted in Chapter 1, the United States has exhibited several distinct cultural traits throughout its history. These include a sense of exceptionalism, or standing apart from "ordinary" nation-states; a related sense of moralism, or a conception of world politics as a struggle between good and evil; and ambivalence toward the nature and extent of U.S. global engagement (see Hook and Spanier 2016). These cultural traits together help to explain the nation's erratic approach to foreign affairs: at times ignorant of and indifferent toward events abroad and at other times committed passionately to reforming foreign governments and international order, whatever the costs.[1]

State-society relations. A grand strategy stems, too, from **state-society relations**, or the interaction of government and private actors in matters of foreign policy. As described earlier, the United States maintains a vibrant civil society, including private interest groups and a pervasive mass media, which exerts great influence over the foreign policy process. This culture, however, stands in contrast to the strict discipline and unquestionable allegiance to national objectives that are required by the armed forces. According to Samuel Huntington, an early expert on state-society relations, "the tension between the demands of military security and the values of American liberalism can, in the long run, be relieved only by the weakening of the security threat or the weakening of liberalism" (Huntington 1957).

Structural arrangements. The governing bodies and legal systems of every nation shape grand strategy as well. In democracies, constitutional provisions constrain the options available to military strategists. Powers shared by the executive and legislative branches in the United States extend beyond legal authority to include the appropriation of resources by Congress that presidents require to fulfill their strategic objectives. Of consequence, too, are the authorities granted to the diplomatic corps, defense forces, and intelligence services, all of which must be in sync with the government's foreign policy objectives. The decentralized nature of U.S. foreign policy decision making, and the closely followed interagency rivalries that permeate the bureaucracy, have high costs for the orderly implementation of grand strategy.

The Evolution of U.S. Grand Strategy

Debates over U.S. grand strategy occur along two dimensions. The first dimension relates to the *degree* of U.S. involvement in foreign affairs. Should the United States impose its will on other states through an activist foreign policy? Or is the nation sufficiently secure to permit a more restrained posture, allowing most troubles

---

1. Meanwhile, American foreign policy makers must come to grips with the strategic cultures of their adversaries, which often reflect very different values, priorities, and long-term objectives (see Donnelly 2006).

U.S. Department of Defense *The U.S. Congress requires that the Department of Defense prepare a summary of U.S. national security priorities and military objectives every four years. The Quadrennial Defense Review provides lawmakers, along with interested citizens, a detailed description of the security environment facing the United States and how the Pentagon will respond to existing and potential threats to the nation. In this introductory statement, the Defense Department describes U.S. responses to ongoing and emerging challenges.*

The United States faces a rapidly changing security environment. We are repositioning to focus on the strategic challenges and opportunities that will define our future: new technologies, new centers of power, and a world that is growing more volatile, more unpredictable, and in some instances more threatening to the United States.

Reflecting this diverse range of challenges, the U.S. military will shift focus in terms of what kinds of conflicts it prepares for in the future, moving toward greater emphasis on the full spectrum of possible operations. Although our forces will no longer be sized to conduct large-scale prolonged stability operations, we will preserve the expertise gained during the past ten years of counterinsurgency and stability operations in Iraq and Afghanistan. We will also protect the ability to regenerate capabilities that might be needed to meet future demands.

The Joint Force must also be prepared to battle increasingly sophisticated adversaries who could employ advanced warfighting capabilities while simultaneously attempting to deny U.S. forces the advantages they currently enjoy in space and cyberspace. We will sustain priority investments in science, technology, research, and development both within the defense sector and beyond. . . . We will actively seek innovative approaches to how we fight, how we posture our force, and how we leverage our asymmetric strengths and technological advantages. Innovation is paramount given the increasingly complex warfighting environment we expect to encounter.

Source: U.S. Department of Defense, 2014, *Quadrennial Defense Review*, pp. iii, vii, http://archive.defense.gov/pubs/2014_Quadrennial_Defense_Review.pdf.

abroad to work themselves out? The second dimension relates to the *nature* of U.S. involvement. Should the United States be concerned primarily with attaining its own national interests? Or does it have a greater responsibility to pursue transnational interests, some with little or no direct effect on the security or prosperity of American citizens?

As noted in Chapter 2, the geopolitical good fortune of the newly founded United States was the basis for its initial grand strategy of **strategic detachment**. Facing no large-scale military threat at home and protected at sea through a tacit naval alliance with Great Britain, the U.S. government did not have to build a large, permanent military force or even establish and deploy a large diplomatic corps. American strategic thought in the late nineteenth century was influenced profoundly by the capture of the continental frontier and the end of direct U.S. territorial expansion in the Western Hemisphere. Westward expansion did continue, however, by sea, into the Eastern Hemisphere. The principal figure behind this maritime strategy was Capt. Alfred Thayer Mahan (1897), who called for a rapid increase of U.S. naval forces and the creation of a network of U.S. bases across the Pacific Ocean.

Foreign events drove the nation's grand strategy during the world wars (see Layne 2006). When the European powers descended into mass violence, the United States altered its grand strategy, basing the new approach on the geopolitical premise that Americans would be secure only if no single power dominated Europe. After Germany's launch of its continental conquests in 1914 made the possibility of such domination all too real, the United States entered the war in 1917 and helped to end the threat. Between the world wars, the United States relapsed into strategic detachment, which lasted until Germany overran Europe once again and U.S. forces became the targets of submarine attacks in the Atlantic Ocean. The direct impetus for U.S. entry into World War II—the Japanese attack on Pearl Harbor—extended this strategic logic to East Asia, which, like Europe, the United States considered hospitable to its foreign policy only so long as a balance of power existed among the region's strongest countries.

The arrival of the United States as the world's predominant power after World War II demanded a new U.S. grand strategy. Though not explicitly, the government adopted a strategy of **sustained primacy**, which called for preserving the nation's military and economic predominance in the interstate system. This strategy, enabled by the emerging balance of power, had a strong historical foundation in the nation's exceptional self-image (see Chapter 2). Its sense of "manifest destiny," which many believed was affirmed with every advance in living conditions and territorial expansion, made U.S. leadership of the postwar order seem preordained (P. D. Miller 2012).

During the Cold War, American officials devised two overriding tactics—global engagement and communist containment—to serve this strategy.

First, the U.S. government would solidify its primacy by maintaining military activism, pursuing market-led economic expansion, and fostering the creation of multilateral organizations in which the United States would play a lead role. By doing so, the nation would preserve its advantages in relative power while reassuring its allies through promises of economic aid, military protection, and the pursuit of shared social and political goals (see Ikenberry 2001).

Second, the United States would adopt George Kennan's containment doctrine as the tactical blueprint for waging the Cold War. This doctrine would help the nation avoid the pitfalls of renewed strategic detachment on the one hand and a potentially cataclysmic "hot war" on the other. Kennan's predication that the Soviet Union would self-destruct due to the flaws of its communist system came true half a century later.

After the Soviet Union's collapse in 1991 ended the communist challenge, the U.S. government was determined to exploit the unipolar world that defined the new era. Under President George H. W. Bush, the United States adopted a defense strategy whose primary goal was "convincing potential competitors that they need not aspire to a greater role" (*New York Times* 1992, A14). The terrorist attacks of September 2001 altered the strategic environment while leaving intact the U.S. grand strategy of sustained primacy. According to the National Security Council (NSC), "Our forces will be strong enough to dissuade potential adversaries from pursuing a military build-up in hopes of surpassing, or equaling, the power of the United States" (White House 2002, 21).

Although President Obama did not reject sustained primacy, he called for a security policy that recognized the limits of U.S. world power. Even as he announced the surge of U.S. troops to Afghanistan in December 2009, the president told cadets at West Point that "we must rebuild our strength here at home. Our prosperity provides a foundation for our power. It pays for our military. It underwrites our diplomacy. . . . That's why our troop commitment in Afghanistan cannot be open-ended—because the nation that I'm most interested in building is our own" (Obama 2009a).

From Strategy to Tactics

The fate of nations is often decided on the battlefield. A grand strategy, therefore, is effective only if it provides direction for military action. The organization of the armed services, in terms of size as well as tactical capabilities, must be compatible with the nation's strategic goals. This force structure, in turn, must deter external challenges to these goals or, if deterrence fails, overcome those challenges with superior military force. "To neglect strategy in defense planning or the conduct of war would be like trying to play chess without kings on the board; there would be no point" (C. Gray 1999, 44). Similarly, a military strategy must lead deductively to effective tactics—the translation of political ends into military means. In short, strategists *plan* and tacticians *do*. A functional relationship therefore exists among all these elements of security policy. Only when grand strategy, force structure, and military tactics are aligned can the United States or any other country pursue a sound defense policy.

How do these functional relationships apply to the ways in which the United States wages war? Modern warfare is fought on the ground, at sea, and in the air. The relative significance of each method varies over time, largely in response to technological developments. The U.S. military strategy during its first century was based on discouraging threats to the nation's territory while consolidating new acquisitions. Naval power, traditionally associated with the projection of power, became vital to the United States as it sought economic markets around the world.

The U.S. Army has traditionally represented the core of the U.S. military. Soldiers on the ground are first and foremost prepared to defend the mainland and U.S. allies overseas. In wartime, they provide the Pentagon with the largest contingent of battle-ready fighters. Mandatory cutbacks in the Pentagon's budget, however, have reduced the size and operational scope of the U.S. Army, whose number of active-duty forces fell below 500,000 for the first time in a decade (Tice 2015). The Pentagon argued that this drawdown would not damage U.S. national security as innovations in military technology would make up for the loss of Army personnel.

The United States maintains the world's most lethal navy, although its size has steadily decreased since its peak in World War II (see Figure 10.3). Today's warships are far more powerful than those in the past, and modern submarines maintained by the U.S. Navy are the least vulnerable elements of the nation's nuclear arsenal. Most other countries with large navies, including those managed by NATO members and U.S. allies in East Asia, effectively bolster rather than threaten U.S. security on the high seas. Among potential rivals, Russia's navy is far less potent than its Soviet predecessor, and China has only recently begun creating a naval force that can serve more than a defensive role. Meanwhile, the U.S. Marines operate as an adjunct to the Navy, taking the lead on assaults against enemy armed forces and installations.

Finally, air power emerged as a critical instrument of power projection during the world wars, and during the Cold War the U.S. Air Force adopted the critical role of managing the nation's growing nuclear arsenal. The Pentagon's reliance on air power has steadily grown given its ability to move swiftly and deliver catastrophic losses to enemies on the ground. Still, air power has only been as effective as its underlying strategic logic. No amount of bombing could bring down the Vietnamese forces. The 1991 Persian Gulf War featured a fierce show of U.S. air power. Its firepower, though, did not establish a stable political order because Saddam Hussein remained Iraq's leader. The "shock and awe" blitzkrieg of Operation Iraqi Freedom in 2003 achieved its immediate objective of ousting Saddam's government, but the low-tech mission of occupying a demoralized and antagonistic population overshadowed the initial success. In the Libya uprising of 2011, coalition bombings of government offices, media centers, and military bases cleared the way for antigovernment rebels to overthrow Muammar Qaddafi. With no plans in place to create a new government in Qaddafi's absence, Libya became a lawless failed state.

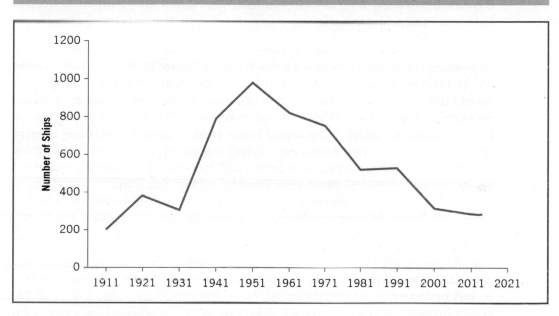

Figure 10.3 ■ Smaller but Stronger: The Shrinking American Navy

Source: Naval History and Heritage Command, "U.S. Navy Active Ship Force Levels, 1886–Present," http://www.history.navy.mil/ research/histories/ship-histories/us-ship-force-levels.html.

High-Tech Tactics: Drones and Cyberwarfare

For all of recorded history, advances in technology have changed the face of warfare. In the past century alone, armored tanks neutralized the collective force of large armies in World War I, nuclear weapons brought imperial Japan to its knees in World War II, and submarine-launched ballistic missiles assured nuclear deterrence during the Cold War. More recently, advances in satellite telecommunications expanded from enemy surveillance during the Balkan wars of the 1990s to include high robotics, and other high-tech research sectors that have made major powers "wired for war" (see Singer 2009).

As noted earlier, President George W. Bush's response to the September 2001 terrorist attacks included a growing role for aerial drones, whose missions have increasingly involved bombing raids, against enemies and their facilities in the war on terror. President Bush approved 46 targeted killings on his watch, most of which were focused on the Afghan-Pakistani border. By the end of 2014, the Obama administration had ordered 456 drone attacks (Serle 2015). The death toll from these attacks through 2012 was estimated at 3,430 enemies, with an additional 401 civilians killed in the crossfire (Zenko 2013, 13).[2] The bombing attacks, which initially focused on Iraq and Afghanistan, also struck hundreds of targets in Pakistan, Yemen, and Somalia.

This latest military innovation represented a "radically new and geographically unbounded use of state-sanctioned lethal force" (J. Mayer 2009; see also Klaidman 2012). On their missions, Predator and Reaper drones are equipped with satellite-based tracking and communication systems, surveillance cameras, and laser-guided air-to-ground missiles. The drones take off from distant U.S. air bases and are guided to their targets by "pilots" in the United States. Unlike fighter jets and other military aircraft, the slow-moving drones can "loiter" directly over the target zone, which may be a paramilitary compound, a commercial building, or a home in a residential neighborhood. Under the system established to conduct drone attacks, the National Counterterrorism Center prepares lists of specific targets, which are then reviewed by the NSC and the CIA directors. The president then decides whether or not to launch attacks on recommended targets.

For all their proclaimed advantages as an instrument of war, the use of drones has sparked a fierce debate among politicians, UN officials, NGOs, and scholars (see Point/Counterpoint). The highly secretive use of the weapons makes it difficult for citizens to make clear judgments of U.S. actions, especially when it comes to civilian casualties. According to a report by the *New York Times*, "Every independent investigation of the strikes has found far more civilian casualties than administration officials admit" (Shane 2015, A1). A January 2015 drone strike in Pakistan, which accidentally killed two hostages, including the American Warren Weinstein, fueled further concerns.

A final question concerns the unpredictable future of robotic warfare generally. Drone technology is being developed by more than most industrialized countries. The use of drone warfare is being prepared in several military arsenals, including those of China, France, Great Britain, Italy, Iran, Israel, Russia, South Korea, and Turkey (Singer 2013). This "global swarm" also includes robotic ground vehicles that penetrate minefields and other hazardous war zones without placing troops at risk. As this technology advances, American citizens are likely to see drones operating in or near their communities. Drones have been used to monitor the U.S. border with Mexico, deliver water and pesticides to crops, track wildlife, conduct searches and rescues, and showcase real estate in remote areas. The prospect of police agencies using drones for domestic surveillance has prompted privacy-rights activists to seek state and federal restrictions on using drones for this purpose.

---

2. As of 2013, the United States managed a fleet of more than 8,000 unmanned aircraft along with about 12,000 unmanned ground vehicles. Whereas 95 percent of U.S. assault aircraft were manned in 2005, more than 40 percent had no pilots by 2012 (Gertler 2012, 9).

Afghan citizens survey the damage caused by the crash of a U.S. aerial drone east of Kabul in August 2011. The U.S. military's use of unmanned bombers (see inset), which has become common in recent years, is highly controversial overseas. While the Pentagon blamed the crash on equipment failure, the Taliban in Afghanistan claimed they shot down the drone.

A second high-tech U.S. military tactic involves **cyberwarfare**, or the contested ownership, possession, storage, and use of digital information. As with other war tactics, cyberwarfare takes on offensive and defensive missions as governments seek to gain vital classified information from other states or non-state actors within their territory. The addition of cyberwarfare to the U.S. arsenal expands the scope of military actions far beyond the battlefield, where mathematicians may determine foreign policy outcomes alongside politicians, cabinet secretaries, and generals. As in the case of nuclear weapons during the Cold War and drone bombers today, the threat of U.S. digital dominance provokes other governments to advance their own cyberwar capabilities. This high-tech competition prompted Defense Secretary Leon Panetta (2012) that an attack on the United States could produce a "cyber Pearl Harbor—an attack that would cause physical destruction and loss of life, paralyze and shock the nation, and create a profound sense of vulnerability." The creation of the U.S. Cyber Command in 2010 gave such concerns institutional form.[3]

3. The Cyber Command, located near the National Security Agency in Fort Meade, Maryland, is joined with the other specialized units of the U.S. Strategic Command, which manage the use of nuclear forces, missile-defense programs, military operations in space, and other security functions (see www.stratcom.mil).

Chapter 10: National Security and Defense Policy ■ 343

Russia's Power Play in Ukraine

Conflicts in the Middle East offered an opening for Vladimir Putin, Russia's president, to stage a show of force on his western border. In February 2014, Putin sparked an uprising among ethnic Russians in eastern Ukraine, which during the Cold War was part of the Soviet Union. Putin, who weeks earlier hosted the Winter Olympics, ordered his troops to seize the strategically vital Crimean Peninsula, home to a major naval base that quickly became property of the Kremlin. After this power play, Putin supported widespread political violence among ethnic Russians who sought annexation into Russia. This action, which President Obama declared a threat to U.S. national security, raised further questions about the source of the crisis.

To John Mearsheimer, a professor at the University of Chicago, "The United States and European allies share most of the responsibility for the crisis." In his view, these governments provoked the Kremlin by expanding the North Atlantic Treaty Organization (NATO) eastward to Russia's border. The same governments, Mearsheimer argued, encouraged Ukraine's government to approve a trade deal with the European Union and to depose their leader, Viktor Yanukovych, an ethnic Russian who declared that his country would rely on Russia as its economic partner. "For Putin, the illegal overthrow of Ukraine's democratically elected and pro-Russian president—which he rightly labeled a 'coup'—was the final straw. He responded by taking Crimea, a peninsula he feared would host a NATO naval base, and worked to destabilize Ukraine until it abandoned its efforts to join the West."

This position was widely rejected by other strategic analysts. Michael McFaul, the U.S. ambassador to Russia from 2012 to 2014, countered that NATO expansion had little to do with Putin's aggression. He recalled that Russian officials, despite their occasional protests of NATO expansion, offered little resistance. "Russian foreign policy did not grow more aggressive in response to U.S. policies; it changed as a result of Russian internal political dynamics," McFaul asserted. Putin was struggling politically after elections in December 2011 proved fraudulent, inciting public protests. "To sustain his legitimacy at home, Putin continued to need the United States as an adversary. He also genuinely believed that the United States represented a sinister force in world affairs." Putin's self-inflicted political problems prompted him to act out militarily, according to Stephen Sestanovich. "Putin's seizure of Crimea was first and foremost an attempt to recover from his own egregious mistakes."

Sources: John Mearsheimer, "Why the Ukraine Crisis Is the West's Fault," *Foreign Affairs* (September/October 2014); Michael McFaul, "Moscow's Choice," *Foreign Affairs* (November/December 2014); Stephen Sestanovich, "How the West Was Won," *Foreign Affairs* (November/December 2014).

The pace of technological change creates a cat-and-mouse game with government officials trying to stay a step ahead of hackers. The U.S. government turned to cyberwarriors when in 2010 it targeted Iran's nuclear enrichment facilities by planting a "worm" in the system and disabling several of the facilities' functions. The National Security Agency hoped to delay Iran's feared conversion of its nuclear energy program into a bomb factory. The covert U.S. operation in Iran, code-named *Stuxnet*, was aided by the Israeli government. While taking the offensive against Iran, American leaders were forced to contend with a large-scale hacking campaign by agents within the People's Republic of China (PRC) that penetrated U.S. government as well as corporate networks. These attacks, based within the People's Republican Army, extended to computer sites within financial institutions and public offices engaged in various functional areas, including transportation, energy, and aerospace. These findings followed an earlier Chinese cyberattack on the offices of the *New York Times*.

Obama spoke out on the problem in his 2013 State of the Union address: "We know foreign countries and companies swipe our corporate secrets. Now our enemies are also seeking the ability to sabotage our power grid, our financial institutions, and our air traffic control systems." Despite these threats, government officials claimed that they had fended off hundreds of attempts to disrupt the federal mainframe. While most efforts are thwarted, others create serious problems for the government. This was the case early in 2015, when Russian hackers gained access to the president's e-mails (Schmidt and Sanger 2015). Given the widespread efforts by governments to penetrate enemy networks, and lacking formal treaties designed to render these attacks illegal, the Internet remained a digital free-fire zone.

■ JUSTIFYING THE USE OF FORCE

The most crucial decision facing the leader of any country is whether to send military forces into combat. The outcome of armed conflicts is never certain, and unintended consequences—sneak attacks by the enemy, third-party interventions, domestic uprisings—shroud military calculations in the "fog of war" (see Betts 2002). In contrast to this ambiguity, leaders on the brink of war face the near certainty of casualties, widespread physical destruction, and economic liabilities. The choices they make at critical junctures "between peace and war" determine the fate of nations for decades (Lebow 1981), and misperceptions of foreign threats can lead to unfounded wars (Duelfer and Dyson 2011). The acceptable moral rationales for using force have changed over time and differ across cultures, making these vital decisions even more complicated (see Finnemore 2003; Gray 2004).

Similarly, the context and motivations of U.S. military interventions vary widely. At times, such as in World War II, the United States fights **wars of necessity**, or conflicts arising from direct and unambiguous challenges to the nation's security. More commonly, such as in Panama in 1989, Kosovo in 1999, and Libya in 2011, U.S. forces fight **wars of choice**, or conflicts over nonvital interests.[4] Most frequently, U.S. power and influence are employed without the use of violence. Yet the nation's military clout never lies far from the surface in negotiations with its adversaries.

Long ago, theologians St. Augustine (354–430) and St. Thomas Aquinas (1225–1274) crafted the **just-war doctrine**, which established appropriate rationales to engage in wars and how they should be fought morally. Historically, most nations have adhered to these rationales despite their hatred toward their enemies. It is worth considering this doctrine in the context of the U.S. struggle against terrorism and its policies regarding nuclear weapons, respectively.

In the first category, wars should only be fought as a last resort, the cause should be just and well intentioned, and war must be declared by proper authorities (of governments). From Washington's standpoint, terrorist groups have not sought peaceful means of resolving their differences, their causes are not just, and they are rarely directed by sovereign states. The second category of just war sets standards for fighting wars once started. Two standards were established: military actions should be *proportionate* to the damage inflicted by the initial attack. The second standard, *discrimination*, calls for military attacks to spare the lives of noncombatants to the fullest extent possible. In practice, the first use of nuclear weapons would, by its very nature, be disproportionate to any attack using conventional weapons, and nuclear weapons target civilians and military personnel alike. Taken together, these standards call into question the morality of the U.S. government's nuclear attacks on Japan in 1945 (Schell 1983).

Decisions on War and Peace

The reshaped institutions of U.S. power after World War II—including the newly created Department of Defense, National Security Council, and CIA—ensured the presence of U.S. global military might for decades to come. Less clear, however, was under what circumstances that power should be used to protect the nation's worldwide interests. The containment doctrine set forth a singular rationale for U.S. intervention—attempted expansion of the communist sphere of influence—that most Americans found acceptable, although some considered it too passive (see Lippmann 1947). The Soviet Union's achievement of nuclear parity in the 1960s, combined with the frustrations associated with the Vietnam War, ruptured any prospects for national consensus in the late 1960s and 1970s. Successive U.S. presidents tried, but failed, to

---

4. The Obama administration depicted its mission in Libya as something less than a war. According to Ben Rhodes, a senior military adviser, in protecting the Libyan people, averting a humanitarian crisis, and setting up a no-fly zone, U.S. troops and their allies were engaged in "kinetic military action" (Allen 2011).

outline a coherent rationale for the U.S. intervention in Vietnam, and the military tactics they devised ultimately made for a slow and debilitating defeat. Public protests, some of which turned violent, further ensured a lengthy period of introspection on the future course of U.S. defense policy.

Recognizing the persistent uncertainty about the use of force, Caspar Weinberger, Ronald Reagan's secretary of defense, demanded that military interventions be planned thoroughly and have domestic support before any offensive action is initiated. His successor, Gen. Colin Powell (1992–1993), took these guidelines a step further. As chair of the Joint Chiefs of Staff in the George H. W. Bush and Clinton administrations, he insisted that U.S. armed forces, once committed to using force, must prevail decisively. The **Powell Doctrine**, as it became known, was executed in the 1991 Persian Gulf War, when he called for at least 500,000 troops to ensure quick victory. He proved correct in his war plan when Iraqi forces quickly surrendered when they encountered the U.S. onslaught. A Vietnam veteran, Powell also demanded that an exit strategy be prepared so that U.S. troops would not be mired in another regional conflict. His greatest fear was **mission creep**, the tendency of limited deployments to expand incrementally and take on new and ill-conceived commitments.

President George W. Bush came to power in 2001 favoring these more restrictive conditions for using military force. Two years later, his invasion of Iraq violated three elements of the Powell Doctrine. First, the political objective of the invasion, removing Iran's weapons of mass destruction, proved unfounded after no such weapons were found. Second, the U.S. ground forces, less than half the size of those used to eject Saddam from Kuwait, were insufficient to ensure a swift and resounding victory. Finally, as the prospects of a stable political settlement eroded, no appealing exit strategy could be found. Barack Obama returned to Powell's military strategy upon his election in 2008, overseeing the withdrawal of U.S. forces after more than a decade of futile state building. Obama's resistance to military intervention against ISIS, a mission that had little support at home, also followed Powell's approach to national security.

Threats and Coercive Diplomacy

Short of resorting to military force, U.S. officials often pursue their foreign policy goals through **coercive diplomacy**—the threat to use force to reverse an adversary's offensive action. "The attractiveness of coercive diplomacy as a tool of foreign policy is quite clear," political scientist Alexander L. George (2000, 80) observed. "It offers the possibility of achieving one's objective economically, with little bloodshed, fewer political and psychological costs, and often with much less risk of escalation than does resort to military action to reverse an adversary's encroachment." The Cuban missile crisis, which ended peacefully in 1962 largely on U.S. terms, is viewed widely as a textbook example of effective coercive diplomacy. The Kennedy administration skillfully combined five elements of this tactic to prevent the crisis from leading to a nuclear holocaust (George 2000, 84–85):

- *Clear demands.* The U.S. government issued clear demands with specific deadlines and penalties if the Soviet Union refused to remove its newly installed nuclear missiles from Cuba.

- *Severe penalty.* The penalty identified by President Kennedy—that the missiles would be removed forcefully and the Cuban government overthrown by U.S. forces— would obviously have "hurt" the Soviet Union and its leader, Nikita Khrushchev.

- *Credible demands.* The U.S. demands were credible. The presence of the nuclear warheads in Cuba clearly threatened U.S. security, and Kennedy had the political support and military capability to make good on his threat.

- *Coherent plan.* The United States had a well-laid plan of action to remove the missiles if Kennedy's threats were ignored, a fact made known to the Soviet leader.

- *Flexible application.* Kennedy offered Khrushchev a "carrot" as well as the "stick" of military retaliation. By offering to remove U.S. nuclear missiles from Turkey, an action already decided privately by the U.S. government, Kennedy provided the Soviet leader with a face-saving exit from the crisis.

Not all adversaries respond so well to coercive diplomacy. The United States has failed to resolve conflicts through coercive diplomacy more often than it has succeeded. Foreign leaders, even those of very weak states, commonly resist such threats, vowing instead to withstand U.S. pressure and hoping to call the bluff of their American counterparts. In doing so, adversaries present a threat of their own—a blow to the credibility of the United States should its threats be defied successfully. In 1989, for example, Manuel Noriega of Panama ignored U.S. demands to step down as president; ousting him required a large-scale invasion of the country (see Buckley 1991). Four years later, U.S. threats against Somali warlords merely sparked more violent attacks on U.S. forces. The deaths of eighteen U.S. soldiers in Mogadishu, which sharpened U.S. domestic opposition to the mission, prompted President Clinton to withdraw from Somalia, thereby suffering a humiliating defeat.[5]

This pattern of U.S. threats, foreign resistance, and subsequent U.S. military interventions continued in Haiti (1994) and in the former Yugoslavia (1993–1995, 1999). In Haiti, rebels exploited the "Somalia syndrome," calculating—wrongly—that Clinton would not risk a second military humiliation. In the Yugoslav conflicts, President Milosevic gambled that domestic opposition in the United States and Europe would undermine Clinton's effort to stop the ethnic cleansing of Muslims. In the end,

---

5. "We have studied Vietnam and Lebanon and know how to get rid of Americans, by killing them so that public opinion will put an end to things," remarked Somali warlord Mohamed Farah Aideed, the primary target of Operation Restore Hope (quoted in Blechman and Wittes 1999, 6).

Milosevic was defeated, but NATO intervened only after his country suffered large-scale bloodletting, physical devastation, and the displacement of millions of civilians.

Coercive diplomacy also failed to prevent the two U.S.-led wars against Saddam Hussein's Iraq in 1991 and 2003. In both conflicts, Saddam refused to meet the full range of U.S. demands and then suffered overwhelming military defeat and, ultimately, his overthrow from power. Speculation persists about his rationales for inviting such calamities. In one account, Saddam was always more worried about threats from Shiite Muslims in Iran than an attack by the United States. Among his tactics in this war of wills was acting as though Iraq had something to hide, including weapons of mass destruction, but this was a ruse he intended to scare off Iran, not the United States. By exaggerating Iraq's threat to Iran, Saddam led U.S. leaders to overestimate his threat to Washington (Duelfer and Dyson 2011).

Preemptive and Preventive War: The Iraq Precedent

Countries engage in interstate wars for many reasons. In offensive wars, they disrupt the status quo to gain resources, tangible or intangible, unavailable through peaceful or legal means. In defensive wars, states act in the face of external aggression. In outright attacks, they face the grim choice of responding with armed resistance to the attack or submitting to the demands of the attackers.

Not all defensive wars, however, are responses to outright, clear-cut attacks (see Walzer 1977, 74–85). Foreign intelligence may signal that an external attack is imminent, perhaps only days away, tempting leaders to strike first against the would-be invader. This recourse to **preemptive war**, rare in modern history, is justified only when a clear and present danger is literally on the horizon. More commonly, a more powerful rival may perceive an emerging challenger as presenting a long-term threat to the security of the dominant nation or the security of its allies, tempting the stronger state to launch a **preventive war** to eliminate the threat before it materializes (see Levy 1987). This approach is widely denounced because the longer time horizons afford opportunities for diplomatic solutions. "We do not believe in aggressive or preventive war," President Harry Truman proclaimed. "Such war is the weapon of dictators, not of free democratic societies" (quoted in Jordan, Taylor, and Mazarr 1999, 57).

George W. Bush rejected this perspective, claiming that the United States must take the offensive in his war on terror. His support for preemptive and preventive war formed a key element of his National Security Strategy released in September 2002.[6] Although not using the term explicitly, the Bush administration launched a preemptive war against Iraq designed to stem the nation's development of weapons of mass destruction. In justifying the war, Bush characterized Saddam Hussein's regime as an

---

6. According to political scientist Dan Reiter (1995), only three armed conflicts globally prior to 1995 qualify as preemptive wars: the start of World War I, China's 1950 intervention in the Korean War, and Israel's attack on Egypt in 1967.

immediate threat to Iraq's neighbors and the United States. Saddam's secret arsenal of biochemical weapons, Bush warned, could be unleashed at any time. The president's decision to invade Iraq preemptively, without sanction from the UN Security Council, angered most foreign governments. Even close U.S. allies distanced themselves from Washington, especially after Bush's warnings proved unfounded. The Iraq precedent revealed the problems that arise when governments strike first in the absence of concrete evidence that vital interests are at stake.

■ THE NUCLEAR SHADOW

A central task of U.S. security policy is to manage the nation's nuclear arsenal, by far the largest in the world. Nuclear weapons, which are strategic forces, play a vital role in military strategy that fundamentally departs from the role played by nonnuclear, or conventional, forces. Since their first and only wartime use by the United States against Japan in August 1945, nuclear weapons have remained unused but "absolute weapons," capable of obliterating foreign enemies—and possibly millions of citizens—in one swift blow (Brodie 1946). The Soviet Union's successful test of a nuclear bomb in 1949 transformed the Cold War balance of power into a "delicate balance of terror" (Wohlstetter 1959). Great Britain joined the "nuclear club" in 1952, followed by France (1960) and China (1962). Coincidentally, these first five nuclear powers were also the lone permanent members of the UN Security Council.

Despite the peaceful ending of the U.S.-Soviet arms race, the perils posed by nuclear weapons are more acute than ever. As of 2015, nine governments had the materials and means to deliver nuclear weapons (see Map 10.1, Nuclear Threats and U.S. Defense Installations). These countries include India (1974) and Pakistan (1998), bitter rivals in South Asia, and North Korea (2006), an impoverished dictatorship with an affinity for ballistic missile exports and nuclear blackmail. Israel (unknown date) also maintains a nuclear arsenal, although its government refuses to confirm this worst-kept secret in world politics. Meanwhile, Iran's government has long since proclaimed its "nuclear rights," although it agreed in 2015 to suspend its weapons program in return for the phasing out of crippling economic sanctions.

Deterrence in Theory and Practice

The enduring menace posed by nuclear weapons, a defining feature of twenty-first-century world politics, was not inevitable. Just after World War II, the United States proposed placing all the world's nuclear materials, including its own, under the control of a UN-sponsored international authority. However, the Soviet Union opposed this Baruch Plan, named after U.S. financier and presidential adviser Bernard Baruch, because it allowed the U.S. government to maintain its monopoly of nuclear weapons technology. Soviet leaders, who were three years away from testing their own nuclear weapon, also distrusted the United Nations and U.S. allies in the Security Council.

Map 10.1 ■ Nuclear Threats and U.S. Defense Installations

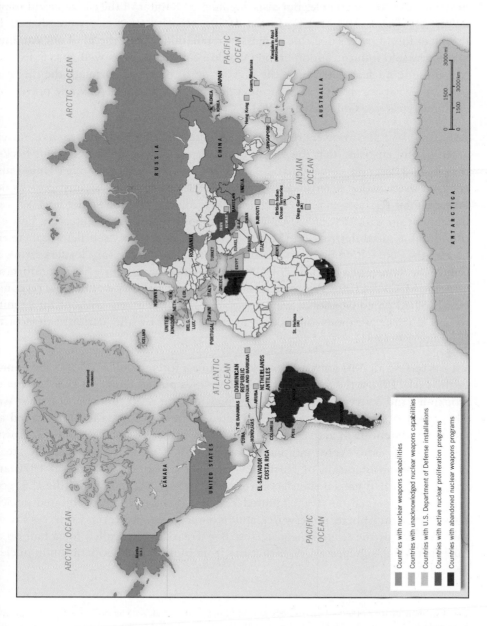

Source: "Department of Defense Base Structure Report: Fiscal Year 2009 Baseline (A Summary of DoD's Real Property Inventory)" (Washington, DC: Office of the Deputy Under Secretary of Defense, Installations and Environment), http://www.defense.gov/Portals/1/Documents/pubs/BSR2009Baseline.pdf.

Since the 1945 bombings of Hiroshima and Nagasaki, nuclear weapons have had a unique functional distinction among military weapons—they are not meant to be used. Such use would not only invite nuclear retaliation from the target government or its nuclear-equipped allies but also threaten the habitat of the entire world population (see Sagan 1983/1984). In the 1950s, security strategies were shaped by President Eisenhower's doctrine of **massive retaliation**, whose threat of nuclear annihilation would induce caution among would-be adversaries as well as U.S. leaders. Maintaining **nuclear deterrence**, the prevention of hostilities through the threat of using the weapons, is vital to securing a nuclear power's interests while preventing an apocalypse (see G. H. Snyder 1961).

Both Cold War superpowers refined nuclear deterrence by building massive nuclear arsenals and ensuring that the victim of a first strike would survive to hit back—that is, had "second-strike capabilities." The United States and Soviet Union also engaged in *extended* deterrence by vowing nuclear retaliation against attacks not only on their territory but also on that of their allies. Once the Soviet nuclear arsenal caught up with that of the United States, both superpowers entered a new era of **mutual assured destruction (MAD)**: both sides had to be "self-deterred." In the face of the compelling prospect of nuclear Armageddon, military leaders strove to reduce the danger of a head-on collision between the two countries.[7] Uncomfortable with the MAD doctrine, President Kennedy adopted a strategy of **flexible response**, which relied on conventional war tactics in regional conflicts without threatening to use nuclear weapons or risking nuclear attack by the nation's adversaries (Daalder 1991).

Efforts to restrain this arms race quickly became a foreign policy priority. Beginning in the early 1970s, the SALT and START treaties placed limits on U.S. and Soviet stockpiles and delivery systems and then provided for deep cuts after the Cold War. The Treaty of Moscow, signed by the United States and Russia in 2002, called for ten-year reductions in active nuclear stockpiles to between 1,700 and 2,200 warheads on each side.[8] As for multilateral accords, the United States signed the Treaty on the Non-proliferation of Nuclear Weapons that came into force in 1970 and that by 2010 had gained the signatures of 189 governments. Earlier the U.S. government had signed the 1963 Limited Test Ban Treaty, which prohibited nuclear tests in the atmosphere, underwater, and in outer space. However, Congress's rejection in 1998 of the Comprehensive Test Ban Treaty, which called for a ban on all nuclear testing, signaled a U.S. turn away from multilateral cooperation in nuclear arms control.

---

7. For prominent studies of nuclear strategy during this critical period, see Henry Kissinger (1957), Robert Osgood (1957), Thomas Schelling (1960), and Morton Halperin (1963). Lawrence Freedman (2003) provides a useful review of Cold War nuclear strategies.

8. The treaty allowed both sides to store thousands of inactive warheads, which could be reactivated quickly in a crisis.

This trend continued under George W. Bush, who also widened the possible uses of nuclear weapons by abolishing the long-held "firewall" between these and conventional weapons. Under the revised plan, "low-yield" nuclear warheads would be used to destroy underground military facilities in such countries as Iran, which was busily constructing such sites during the Bush years. Meanwhile, calls for nuclear abolition grew louder and came from unlikely sources. Henry Kissinger, an architect of U.S. nuclear strategy long before his appointment as Richard Nixon's national security adviser in 1969, joined other former leaders in advocating disarmament.[9]

Upon taking office in 2009, President Obama vowed to reverse this trend and called for the destruction of all nuclear stockpiles—including those of the United States. Obama reached an agreement with Russia in March 2010 to reduce the number of deployed nuclear warheads on both sides to 1,550. The revised START treaty, ratified by the Senate in December, would take several years to take effect. Meanwhile, the United States in 2015 maintained an arsenal of nearly 5,000 nuclear warheads, either actively deployed or in reserve (see Table 10.3).

Nuclear weapons today remain vital elements of national security, if only in their awesome potential to wreak havoc on a global scale. Russia's aggression in neighboring Ukraine revived tensions between the former Cold War superpowers. When NATO

Table 10.3 ■ America's Nuclear Arsenal, 2015

Type	Number of Nuclear Weapons
Intercontinental ballistic missiles (ICMBs, land based)	450
Submarine-launched ballistic missiles (SLBMs, sea based)	288
Strategic bombers (air based)	113
Nonstrategic forces	180
Total deployed	2,080
Total in reserve	2,680
Retired warheads	2,340
Total inventory	7,100

Source: Hans B. Kristensen and Robert S. Norris, 2015, "U.S. Nuclear Forces, 2015. *Bulletin of the Atomic Scientists* 71 (2), 107–119.

9. See George P. Shultz, William J. Perry, Henry A. Kissinger, and Sam Nunn, "Toward a Nuclear-Free World," *Wall Street Journal*, January 15, 2008, A15. Their embrace of the "zero option" was later endorsed by most former secretaries of defense, secretaries of state, and national security advisers.

allies on Ukraine's border "pre-positioned" armed forces in 2015, Vladimir Putin announced that he would expand his nuclear arsenal. This threat was largely symbolic, however, given its nation's existing, and clearly adequate, stockpile of warheads. With the exception of Iran, no other countries in recent years have sought to develop their own nuclear weapons program. Rational leaders know that such a move is costly, provocative, and likely to be offset by punitive countermeasures.

Despite the slim chance of a nuclear breakout, the U.S. Defense Department remains determined to "pursue programs that will allow it to modernize and adjust its strategic forces so that they remain capable in coming years" (Woolf 2013, 1). According to Thomas M. Nichols (2014, 182), a national security expert at the U.S. Naval War College, nuclear brinkmanship has become habit-forming in the Pentagon. "We have continued to accept the presence of huge numbers of nuclear weapons in our midst *because we have just gotten used to them* (emphasis in original). The people who lived through the Cold War felt they have no choice but to endure the dangers of nuclear deterrence. Maybe they were right, in their time. Today, we have a choice."

The Missile Defense Controversy

Technological advances in strategic missile defense make the balance of terror more uncertain. Among other paradoxes of nuclear strategy, for deterrence to succeed, states must be defenseless against nuclear attacks. "Shielded" nations would be free to inflict overwhelming harm on their enemies without fear of retaliation. Recognizing this paradox, the United States and Soviet Union signed the Anti-Ballistic Missile (ABM) Treaty in 1972, which kept both superpowers vulnerable to nuclear attack beyond the end of the Cold War. In the United States, critics of the ABM Treaty longed for the day they would no longer be held hostage to threats of nuclear annihilation. Among these critics was President Ronald Reagan, whose 1983 Strategic Defense Initiative (SDI), better known as "Star Wars," called for space-based interceptors that would destroy long-range nuclear missiles in midflight. Congress approved $26 billion for the development of SDI, which Reagan promised to share with other nuclear powers once the system became operational.

Reagan's Star Wars program marked the beginning of the end of the ABM Treaty. Research on missile defense continued under President Clinton, then accelerated under George W. Bush. The United States officially withdrew from the ABM Treaty in 2002, the first U.S. renunciation of an arms control treaty in the nuclear era. With the consent of Congress and appropriations that reached $10 billion in fiscal year 2005, the White House created the Missile Defense Agency within the Department of Defense to develop and deploy a ballistic missile defense system that would be "layered" to intercept missiles in all phases of their flight, from liftoff through reentry into the lower atmosphere (Hildreth 2005).

Opponents of missile defense, including an issue network of legislators, strategic analysts, and peace groups, challenged the president's arguments for missile defense with three arguments. The first challenged the presumed reliability of missile defense, a presumption that leaves no margin for error. Critics point out that experimental tests have thus far produced, at best, mixed results. Tests of missile interceptors failed to destroy their targets; in two such tests, the interceptors never got off the ground (Coyle 2006). Second, critics warn that even a perfect ABM system would leave the United States vulnerable to nuclear attacks not delivered by missile. "Suitcase bombs" made in the United States or smuggled into its territory could prove just as deadly. Finally, it is not clear how other governments would react if the United States came close to having both a massive nuclear arsenal and the certainty of nuclear defense.

Despite these concerns, the United States under President Obama moved forward with research into and deployment of missile defenses. Where they would be stationed, however, became the focus of concern (Sanger and Broad 2009). Obama delayed the deployment of missile interceptors in Poland, which were widely perceived to be targeted against a hypothetical Russian nuclear attack on Europe or even the United States. Instead, Obama signed an agreement with the Romanian government to install twenty-four interceptors whose targets would include potential attacks by Iran. The United States also gained Turkey's approval to place a sophisticated radar system on its soil, and a similar deal was reached with Japan's government. In the spring of 2013, threats of aggression by North Korea's government prompted the White House to place U.S. defense systems in the northern Pacific region on full alert.

These efforts aside, it is highly unlikely that nuclear defenses can credibly protect the American homeland. "A reliable and affordable defense that could protect America against a Russian force that could launch some 1,500 ballistic missile warheads simply does not exist," argued Steven Pifer (2015), a strategic analyst. "For the foreseeable future, offense wins the offense-defense relationship. Offensive ballistic missile technology is far more mature than that of missile defense, and cost considerations favor the offense." The evidence, however, has not prevented the Pentagon from developing refining nuclear defenses. From the standpoint of strategic planners, a breakthrough in such technologies, however unlikely, would extend American primacy for decades to come (see M. Mayer 2015).

■ WAGING WAR ON TERROR

Since September 2001, U.S. foreign policy makers have elevated terrorism to the top of the U.S. security agenda. President Bush immediately declared the attacks to be acts of war, not incidents to be turned over to criminal investigators and courts. Rather than taking on a sovereign state, the global war would involve loosely connected private groups whose members shared an intense hatred of the United States and its Western allies. The groups, most prominently al Qaeda after 9/11, also shared a determination to resist the political, economic, and cultural influence of these states by any means, including mass violence against civilians. Since most

Islamic State militants released a graphic video allegedly depicting the beheading of American photojournalist James Wright Foley, who has been missing since 2012 after being kidnapped in Syria.

terrorists are not affiliated with any governments, they are especially difficult to identify, locate, and defeat.[10]

Between 2001 and 2014, approximately 70,000 terrorist incidents—large and small—occurred worldwide (Global Terrorism Database 2015). These numbers remained consistent during the first decade of the millennium and then grew rapidly between 2010 and 2014 (see Figure 10.4). The steep escalation had two sources, both originating in the Middle East: the regional chaos that followed the 2011 Arab Spring; and the rise of the Islamic State, whose reign of terror began in 2014. The attacks most often took the form of short-range bombings that targeted government offices, military posts, and commercial outlets. In the United States, fewer than 300 terrorist attacks occurred during this period. In contrast to the 9/11 attacks, which killed nearly 3,000 people, most of these domestic attacks did not have foreign policy concerns and did not produce casualties.[11]

Until 2001, foreign terrorists had spared the U.S. homeland from large-scale attacks. When they did strike, the terrorists generally chose targets overseas, such as in the 1995 and 1996 attacks on U.S. troops in Saudi Arabia, the 1998 bombings of U.S.

---

10. Simply defining terrorism has proven difficult because one person's "terrorist" may be another's "freedom fighter." According to the U.S. government, terrorism is "the unlawful use of force and violence against persons or property to intimidate or coerce a government, the civilian population, or any segment thereof, in furtherance of political or social objectives (U.S. Code of Federal Regulations, 28 C.F.R. Section 0.85).

11. The most frequent domestic attacks during this period were committed by two groups of self-proclaimed "eco-terrorists": the Earth Liberation Front and the Animal Liberation Front, which launched 84 nonlethal attacks in the United States.

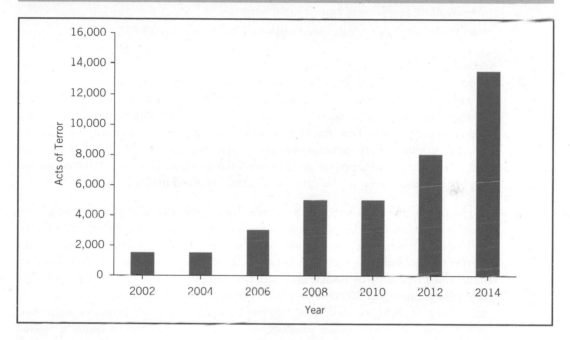

Figure 10.4 ■ Acts of Terror Worldwide, 2001–2014 (approximations in thousands)

Source: Global Terrorism Database, University of Maryland; accessed June 2015.

embassies in Kenya and Tanzania, and the 2000 attack on the USS *Cole* off the coast of Yemen. The most prominent exception to this rule, a failed initial attempt by Islamic militants to topple the World Trade Center with an underground detonation in February 1993, left six people dead and more than 1,000 injured.

As the war on terror deepened in 2002 and 2003, nearly half of the attacks and related deaths occurred in Iraq and Afghanistan. Beyond these two frontline states, the number of large-scale terrorist attacks remained relatively stable in the years following the attacks of September 11. Prominent exceptions included grisly attacks in Istanbul (2003), Madrid (March 2004), and London (July 2005) and a series of coordinated attacks in Mumbai, India's largest city, which left nearly 500 people killed or wounded in November 2008. Two subsequent terrorist attacks targeted the United States: the attack on the U.S. consulate in Benghazi, Libya (2012), that killed U.S. ambassador Christopher Stevens and three other U.S. nationals; and the bombing of the Boston Marathon (2013), which was committed by two domestic terrorists who left three dead and 264 injured while reviving many Americans' fears about their own domestic security.

As noted above, the pace of terrorist attacks has accelerated in recent years. Among the statistics from 2014 compared with 2013 (Global Terrorism Database 2015) are

- 13,463 terrorist attacks occurred (up 35%);
- 32,727 people were killed (up 81%);
- 34,4791 people were injured (up 6%); and
- 9,428 people were kidnapped and/or taken hostage (up 300%).

According to the U.S. Department of State (2015b), "weak or failed governance continued to provide an enabling environment for the emergence of extremist radicalism and violence." While nearly 100 countries suffered terrorist attacks in 2014, nearly two-thirds of the carnage occurred in just five countries (Afghanistan, India, Iraq, Nigeria, and Pakistan). The attacks were also unusually lethal, as twenty killed more than 100 people, a sharp increase over 2013, when just two attacks had left so many dead. The spike in kidnappings and hostage taking was largely concentrated within Iraq, Nigeria, and Syria, where many such cases involved multiple captives.

The rise of ISIS created a terrorist threat which dwarfed that of al Qaeda. The group, which emerged late in 2013, moved swiftly in its effort to create a *caliphate*, or a theocracy based on Islamic law. Its offensive, launched early in 2014, filled a power vacuum in Syria and Iraq, both of which were consumed by civil wars (see Map 10.2). The Syrian regime, ruled ruthlessly by Bashar al-Assad, clung to power after the 2011 Arab Spring while killing more than 300,000 people and opening the door for ISIS to take over its northern tier. By 2015, more than 16,000 foreign fighters from 90 countries had joined swelling bands of home-grown **jihadists**, or militants determined to create a "pure" Islamic society by force (see U.S. Department of State 2015b). Iraq's government effectively collapsed after U.S. troops withdrew in December 2011, leaving a new government dominated by a Shiite regime that repressed minority Sunnis and ethnic Kurds for three years. As Iraq became a failed state, unable to provide basic services to its people, thousands of Sunni fighters gave up on their army and joined ISIS. Their tactics, including beheadings, crucifixions, massacres, and multiple forms of torture, were designed to enrage citizens worldwide—and to recruit even more jihadists drawn to the bloodshed.

The U.S. government was caught off guard as ISIS expanded its blitzkrieg that would, by mid-2015, claim a landmass nearly the size of Great Britain. In January 2014, President Obama referred to the group as a "JV team" and considered it little more than an obscure new player in the sectarian struggles that plagued the Middle East for centuries. He looked to Iraq's leader, Nuri al-Maliki, to suppress the group with his army despite its poor training and low morale (Baker and Schmitt 2014). As for Syria, Obama knew that Assad was beset by countless adversaries and assumed their focus was directed toward toppling the dictator, not redrawing the regional map.

By late 2015, the president had devised several strategies to "degrade and ultimately destroy" ISIS: conducting aerial attacks, training Iraqi Security Forces, assisting Kurds in the north, preventing American citizens from joining ISIS, and disrupting financial flows (Blanchard et al. 2015). Obama's plan also called for strikes by

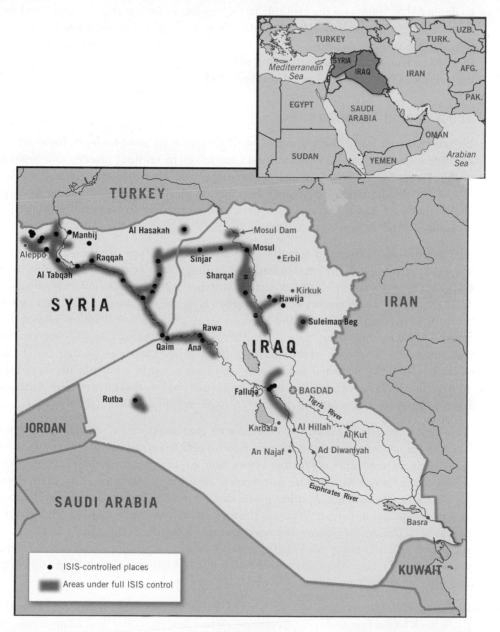

Source: Steven W. Hook and John Spanier, *American Foreign Policy Since World War II,* Twentieth Edition, 319, CQ Press (2016).

Special Forces, highly trained military units that undertake covert operations. Finally, he enlisted a coalition of other governments, including NATO allies and others in the Mideast, to create a united front against the Islamic State.[12] Obama, however, refused to deploy U.S. "boots on the ground" in the region, an option that was opposed by a war-weary population. By late 2015, however, the regional governments had yet to take on ISIS directly. Meanwhile, ISIS launched a series of attacks against targets that included a Russian commercial jet and multiple locations in Paris that left more than more than 100 people dead in November 2105.

The Nature of Terrorism

By nature, terrorist groups are highly motivated and unswervingly loyal to one another and their cause. They conceal themselves in remote, inaccessible areas or within the political and social chaos of failed states. They also effectively limit their internal communications to prevent detection. With their widely disbursed memberships and "flat" organizational structures, terrorist groups are especially elusive (see Arquilla, Ronfeldt, and Zanini 1999).

The psychological effects of terrorism are crucial to this type of warfare. The perpetrators of random acts of violence find that raising public anxieties and doubts about the government's ability to protect its citizens is a victory in and of itself (Wardlaw 1989). Another distinctive aspect of terrorism is its use of a single violent act to send a symbolic message. In Greece and Peru, for example, antiglobalization groups have bombed McDonald's, Pizza Hut, and other restaurant chains that they see as being the embodiment of U.S. economic and cultural imperialism. Osama bin Laden acknowledged the symbolic function of terrorism when he said that the September 11 attacks "were not targeted at women and children. The real targets were America's icons of military and economic power" (quoted in Esposito 2002, 22).

Although terrorism is usually associated with non-state actors, **state terrorism,** too, has been practiced throughout history. Roman and Byzantine emperors publicly tortured their rivals to scare off further opposition. And during the "reign of terror" that followed the French Revolution, Robespierre found the guillotine a convenient device for pacifying his enemies. Another useful distinction can be made between domestic and international terrorism. Whereas the terrorist attacks of September 11, 2001, the deadliest in U.S. history, came from overseas, the second deadliest came from within. Six years earlier, Timothy McVeigh revealed the dangers posed by **domestic terrorism** when he bombed the Murrah Federal Building in Oklahoma City, killing 168 people and injuring hundreds more.

Religious beliefs have long driven attacks by terrorists. This perverse relationship dates back to the first and second centuries, when Jewish zealots and Islamic assassins

----

12. Saudi Arabia, for example, conducted multiple bombing raids in Yemen, a terrorist hotbed, and the Turkish government bombed suspected terrorists within its borders.

used terror tactics to advance their spiritual ideals. In the sixteenth and seventeenth centuries, followers of Catholicism and Protestantism waged the "Wars of Religion", that saw much of Europe's population injured or killed. Terrorism in the nineteenth and early twentieth centuries focused more on secular causes, as anarchists and Marxist revolutionaries attempted to overthrow governments through assassinations and other acts of terrorism. Throughout this period, violent conflicts within the Islamic faith reflected "a deep disagreement among Muslims over the degree to which Islam ought to shape the laws and institutions of society" (Owen 2015, 77). The revival of "sacred terror" came late in the twentieth century, as ideological conflicts associated with the Cold War gave way to renewed tensions between the proponents among and within world religions (Benjamin and Simon 2002; see also Hoffman 1998 and Laqueur 1999).

Religious justification for deadly attacks renders suicide terrorism—the detonation of bombs that take the lives of perpetrators as well as targets—an act of ultimate sacrifice. These attacks, often committed by young people recruited by terrorist organizations with the blessing of their parents and local clerics, commonly seek the liberation of territories that are seen as unjustly occupied by foreign powers (Pape 2005). Suicide terrorists, who attach the explosives to their bodies before igniting them in population centers such as markets and cafés or who detonate vehicles laden with explosives in crowded areas while driving them, may also be driven by ideological passion, a desire for vengeance, and a belief that their sacrifice will be rewarded by a utopian afterlife (Moghadam 2008/2009).[13] While such a practice is viewed as abhorrent in the United States and most other countries, terrorist groups relish the attention they gain from suicide attacks and the fear they incite among those who may consider siding with the enemy.

Elements of U.S. Counterterrorism

Upon taking office in 2001, Defense Secretary Donald Rumsfeld made it clear that the gradual downsizing of U.S. military facilities served his overriding goal of competing more effectively on the battlefields of the future (see MacGregor 2003). Like his predecessors, Rumsfeld believed the DoD should exploit the **revolution in military affairs** that would change the nature of conventional warfare (Galdi 1995; O'Hanlon et al. 2002). Rapid changes in military technology would fuel this revolution by allowing modern militaries to increase the potency of their armed forces while greatly reducing the number of soldiers deployed to battle zones. In contrast to Operation Desert Storm in 1991, when 500,000 U.S. troops were deployed to liberate Kuwait from Iraqi control, fewer than 150,000 U.S. troops, along with 45,000 British troops, mounted the 2003 invasion of Iraq. Although the "shock-and-awe"

---

13. Contrary to widespread beliefs that the most notorious terrorists tend to be affluent—as in the case of Osama bin Laden—most come from modest means and thus have "less to lose" by committing acts of terrorism (Lee 2011).

IN THEIR OWN WORDS

Donald Rumsfeld *The 9/11 terrorist attacks on the United States forced military planners in the Pentagon to rethink their approach to fighting wars. Defense Secretary Donald Rumsfeld made this clear in a September 27, 2001, commentary in the* New York Times. *In the excerpt below, Rumsfeld detailed the many differences in military tactics that would define President George W. Bush's "global war on terror."*

This war will not be waged by a grand alliance united for the single purpose of defeating an axis of hostile powers. Instead, it will involve floating coalitions of countries, which may change and evolve. Countries will have different roles and contribute in different ways. Some will provide diplomatic support, others financial, still others logistical or military. Some will help us publicly, while others, because of their circumstances, may help us privately and secretly. . . . This war will not necessarily be one in which we pore over military targets and mass forces to seize those targets. Instead, military force will likely be one of many tools we use to stop individuals, groups and countries that engage in terrorism.

Our response may include firing cruise missiles into military targets somewhere in the world; we are just as likely to engage in electronic combat to track and stop investments moving through offshore banking centers. The uniforms of this conflict will be bankers' pinstripes and programmers' grunge just as assuredly as desert camouflage. . . .

Even the vocabulary of this war will be different. When we "invade the enemy's territory," we may well be invading his cyberspace. There may not be as many beachheads stormed as opportunities denied. Forget about "exit strategies"; we're looking at a sustained engagement that carries no deadlines. We have no fixed rules about how to deploy our troops; we'll instead establish guidelines to determine whether military force is the best way to achieve a given objective.

Source: Donald Rumsfeld, "A New Kind of War," *The New York Times*, September 27, 2001, A21.

campaign quickly succeeded in ousting the regime of Saddam Hussein, U.S. military forces were unable to contain the insurgency and sectarian conflicts that prevented the swift transition to democratic rule anticipated by the White House.

The Bush administration then sought victory in Iraq and Afghanistan by turning to **counterinsurgency,** a tactic designed to win the "hearts and minds" of civilians caught in the crossfire of sectarian militants and Islamist terrorists. Gen. David Petraeus, leader of the coalition forces, used this tactic in the 2007 surge in Iraq, which proved successful in reversing a series of previous setbacks. While the new tactic was far less expensive and perilous for U.S. troops, it failed to create security in Afghanistan, whose fledgling armed forces were left to their own devices in resisting Taliban insurgents across the country. The counterinsurgency also failed to prevent regional warlords from controlling most of the country by 2012 (Mann 2012, ch. 9).

Faced with these disappointing outcomes, Obama adopted a new strategy based on **counterterrorism**, which combined heightened intelligence gathering, clearly targeted aerial bombings, and sneak attacks by Special Forces such as the Navy Seals and Delta Forces. This capital- rather than labor-intensive approach to warfare, a high-tech extension of Rumsfeld's revolution in military affairs, "marked a reversal of the American calculus in the region" and became the basis of Obama's overall military strategy (Sanger 2012a, 129). The president's shift to a smaller military "footprint" in conflict zones was also driven by budget concerns, as the new approach was far less costly to American taxpayers. As Defense Secretary Robert Gates (quoted in Shanker 2011, A7) told West Point cadets in February 2011, "Any future defense secretary who advises the president to again send a big American land army into Asia or into the Middle East or Africa should have his head examined." Obama heeded this wisdom and maintained his counterterrorism policies into his second term.

Because of the increasing destructiveness and sophistication of international terrorism, as well as its religious character, it is difficult to contain and virtually impossible to eliminate (see Lesser et al. 1999). In cutting across political jurisdictions and state-societal boundaries, terrorists hinder their enemies' efforts to identify, pursue,

Senior members of the Obama administration's security team watch anxiously as the U.S. raid on the suspected hideout of Osama bin Laden unfolds in May 2011. The successful raid by U.S. Special Forces, which occurred in Pakistan without the prior knowledge or permission of its government, ended more than a decade of fruitless pursuit and marked a major foreign policy success for President Obama.

AP Photo/The White House, Pete Souza

apprehend, and prosecute suspects. In this respect, the United States faces greater difficulties in crushing terrorists than in defeating states in conventional wars. Historically, war planners are prone to fighting "the last war" rather than the one currently being fought. Their approach to counterterrorism, however, established a foundation for fighting back at terrorist groups. The White House would support this effort through many other measures, each of which had its strengths and weaknesses. These measures included the following:

Military combat. In declaring "war" on terrorism after September 11, the White House granted the nation's military forces a lead role in the counteroffensive. The invasions of Afghanistan and Iraq required large-scale deployments of U.S. and allied troops, complex tactical alliances with supportive indigenous forces, and long-term military occupations in hostile environments. The initial military offensives effectively routed the state sponsors of terrorism (Afghanistan) and the state terrorists themselves (the ruling Baath Party in Iraq). By engaging in asymmetric warfare, however, the terrorists prevented occupying forces from gaining full control of both countries. In sum, the U.S. attempt to treat the war on terror using conventional means proved inadequate and highly costly on several levels.

Law enforcement. The United States employed its domestic law enforcement agencies at all levels—federal, state, and local—to support the counterterrorism effort. Most prominently, the FBI assumed substantial authority to investigate terrorist attacks in the United States and abroad. The government encouraged cooperation between the FBI and local law enforcement agencies, which previously was limited, to create a more united front against domestic terrorist cells. On another front, Attorney General John Ashcroft expanded domestic surveillance, the "profiling" of potential terrorists, and other measures authorized by the USA PATRIOT Act, which was approved by Congress shortly after the September 11 terrorist attacks.

Diplomacy. Conventional diplomacy has little value in resolving differences directly with terrorist groups, which, as noted earlier, typically operate outside the standard channels of statecraft. National governments may benefit, however, by cooperating with each other in counterterrorist efforts and engaging in public diplomacy (see Chapter 6) that isolates terrorists politically. Obama revived the U.S. diplomacy effort, although turmoil associated with the 2011 Arab Spring produced new governments in North Africa and the Middle East that were skeptical of, if not antagonistic toward, the United States. Still, many regional governments, such as Jordan, Saudi Arabia, and the small Persian Gulf states, maintained close contact with the United States, although they also pursued their own self-interests.

Intelligence. A central goal of counterterrorism, as of conventional wars, is to "know thine enemy." But it is especially difficult to "know" terrorists, because they rely on stealth and deception to protect themselves. High-tech electronic intelligence may prevent al Qaeda operatives from communicating by phone or computer, but only human intelligence can penetrate terrorist cells and expose them to retaliation by the U.S. government. As described in Chapter 6, the tangle of U.S. intelligence agencies, with their many overlapping portfolios, and their traditional reluctance to compare notes with one another, greatly hinder the potential role of intelligence in fighting terrorism. The selective use of intelligence for political purposes creates another problem, as members of Congress learned in their multiple investigations of prewar intelligence on Iraq (J. Burke 2011).

Finance. The U.S. and other governments attempt to weaken terrorist groups by seizing control of their financial assets. This form of **financial statecraft**, or the manipulation of capital flows to achieve foreign policy goals, commonly involves seizing any assets of terrorists that are "laundered" in bank accounts, often in the United States (Steil and Litan 2006, ch. 3). Federal agents have long relied on this tactic in battling organized crime and drug traffickers, whose leaders similarly funnel huge volumes of cash through U.S. financial institutions. As noted earlier, this tactic was adopted in the U.S. struggle against ISIS. Another common target of U.S. agents is the network of charitable organizations that frequently serve as fronts for terrorist groups, including Hamas and Hezbollah in the Middle East.

Foreign aid and arms sales. The U.S. and other governments have increased their economic and security assistance to "frontline" states in the war on terror. Bolstering the governments of Pakistan, Egypt, and other countries, officials believe, allows these governments to support U.S. efforts and prepare better for terrorist attacks on their own soil. As noted previously, the United States has virtually cornered the $60 billion market for commercial weapons sales, many of which are directed toward developing countries that lack sufficient defenses against terrorist movements and attacks (Grimmett and Kerr 2012). The citizens of poor countries, moreover, tend to be helpless in the face of intimidation by radical militants who demand their moral and practical support. It is not unusual for villagers to be bullied into providing militants with food, shelter, and other sources of material support. A constant danger, however, is that the weapons will later fall into enemy hands, creating a high risk of "blowback" against the United States (Johnson 2000).

Homeland security. The September 2001 attacks proved especially traumatic for Americans because they demonstrated, once and for all, that the geographical separation of the United States from other world power centers no longer guaranteed the nation's security. The heightened sense of vulnerability required "new vigilance in the most fragile corners of the transportation, energy, power, and communications systems and closer attention to the security of government buildings" (Posen 2001/2002, 45). Despite chronic morale problems at the newly created Department of Homeland Security, the new agency created a more coherent structure for managing the new threats facing Americans at home.

Taken together, these responses to terrorism have transformed the landscape of U.S. foreign policy. Although the absence of a "second 9/11" is a source of relief, recent attacks by al Qaeda and other terrorist groups in India (2008), Indonesia (2009), Russia (2010), and Nigeria (2014) revealed the staying power of terrorist threats around the world. Late in 2012, the deadly al Qaeda attack on the U.S. consulate in Benghazi, Libya, sent this clear message to American citizens. The attack made it clear that the U.S. "targeted killings" of al Qaeda operatives "will not end the war of the terrorists. Bin Laden's ideas have circulated widely and will continue to attract adherents for years to come" (Bergen 2011, 349). The April 2013 terrorist attacks on the Boston Marathon provided grisly new evidence that Americans' domestic security was at risk.

The United States faces unique obstacles in combating terrorism, including the very global primacy that represents the foundation of American world power. Washington's claims to dominance naturally fuel resentment within foreign countries, particularly among frustrated societal groups in the developing world that link their impoverished living standards to U.S. wealth and power. Such groups may mobilize against all forms of U.S. primacy—military, economic, and cultural—and resort to terrorism whenever they feel other avenues of protest are closed to them. The thousands of Americans stationed in overseas military bases and diplomatic posts, along with thousands more conducting business overseas, are attractive targets for anti-American terrorists.

With its open, liberal government and civil society, the United States finds it difficult to gain the upper hand against terrorists. The fragmented U.S. political system—its checks and balances, federalism, and loosely connected bureaucracies—hampers effective planning and coordination. Private groups, including those bent on harming the government and its citizens, have considerable freedom to organize, gather information about the United States, express their views, and recruit new members. Even after new restrictions were imposed, these groups retained ample access to government facilities. Further obstacles are posed by the general public, which has grown weary of the seemingly endless U.S. military interventions overseas and would like political leaders in Washington to focus on the nation's economic problems at home.

■ CONCLUSION

Like other countries, the U.S. government considers the protection of national security to be its essential function, one that makes other policy goals at home and abroad attainable. This chapter has focused on the ends and means of security and defense policy and its relationship to the nation's evolving grand strategy. As the chapter has described, for more than half a century, this strategy has focused on sustaining U.S. primacy in the interstate system. A combination of hard-power assets—including vast natural resources, a productive population, and cutting-edge military power—made this primacy possible after World War II. These resources and the nation's soft-power assets—the legitimacy of its governmental institutions, economic freedoms, and a dynamic civil society—extended the unipolar balance of power past the Cold War and well into the new millennium.

Many warning signs, however, suggest that sustained U.S. primacy cannot be taken for granted. The readiness of U.S. military forces eroded during the Iraqi and Afghan conflicts, and active forces were strained by accelerated rotations and multiple combat tours. The costs of these wars, combined with the lasting effects of the 2008 financial crisis, eroded the economic foundations of U.S. military power. More recently, the escalation of terrorist attacks, combined with shows of force by Russia and China, are widely viewed as evidence of American decline. Revelations of U.S. surveillance of private citizens, along with such close allies as Germany and France, have raised doubts about the nation's moral leadership. Although claims of impending U.S. decline have been commonplace since the arrival of "Pax Americana" after World War II, the hazards in the current strategic environment are unprecedented in their scope and complexity.

All this suggests that preserving U.S. national security will depend on learning the lessons of the past that provided foreign policy makers with both the blessings and burdens of world power. Of these lessons, perhaps the most important is that "capabilities do not easily translate into influence" (Pressman 2009, 151). American primacy is not reducible to tanks and nuclear warheads. These instruments of destruction may subdue enemies, but they do not create the conditions that will ultimately make the United States secure.

In fighting terrorism on multiple fronts, the United States has entered into a "perpetual war which has made it clear that presidents should resist the urge to unleash U.S. combat power" (Betts 2014, 16). These and other lessons—the importance of U.S. moral leadership, for example, and the dangers of searching "for monsters to destroy"—may yet right the course of a nation that has consistently overcome threats to its national security.

10

INTERNET REFERENCES

The **Center for Strategic and International Studies** (http://www.csis.org) is a bipartisan, non-profit organization whose website includes numerous reports on defense and security issues and related policy problems regarding demographics and population, energy security, and the international financial and economic system. The center publishes the *Washington Quarterly* (http://www.twq.com), which analyzes global changes and foreign policies with an emphasis on the U.S. role in the world, defense procurement, terrorism, nuclear proliferation, and regional issues.

The **Federation of American Scientists** (FAS; http://www.fas.org) is a nonprofit organization committed to researching the causes and tactics of war. Areas of research featured on the group's website include nuclear arms, terrorism, intelligence gathering and reporting, government secrecy, small arms trade, and the connection between technology and weaponry. In addition to providing facts and figures on these areas, FAS also publishes a newsletter, *Arms Sales Monitor* (http://www.fas.org/asmp/), and a journal, *Public Interest Report* (http://www.fas.org/faspir/), along with short books on each research topic.

The **International Institute for Strategic Studies** (IISS; http://www.iiss.org), a London-based company and registered charity, conducts research on political and military conflict. The IISS, which publishes the journal *Survival*, focuses its research on grand strategy, armed forces, technological and military equipment, and regional relations. The group's website, featuring updates on the global balance of power and recent reports on other security issues, is available only to members, however.

The **North Atlantic Treaty Organization** (NATO) is the world's largest international defense organization. Its website (http://www.nato.int) hosts an online electronic library (http://www.nato.int/cps/en/natolive/publications.htm) with links to numerous reports detailing NATO activities around the globe. Also available for additional research are platforms and data on, among other things, NATO's history, missions, partnerships, organizational capabilities, command structure, and defense expenditures.

The **RAND Corporation** (http://www.rand.org) is a private, nonprofit think tank established by the U.S. Air Force in the 1940s. It specializes in international affairs, terrorism, and U.S. national security issues. The group's website also maintains a database on international terrorism that is a vital resource for researchers. RAND, an acronym for *research and development*, also publishes the *RAND Review* (www.rand.org/publications/randreview/), a magazine that covers current security and defense issues.

The **World Policy Institute** (http://www.worldpolicy.org) is a research organization that focuses on the connection between the domestic and international factors that drive foreign policy. WPI's research topics, which are also covered in its *World Policy Journal* (www.worldpolicy.org/journal/), include counterterrorism, arms trade, U.S. grand strategy, cultural relations, and relationships between military superpowers. The group's website highlights its most recent activities and includes links to other sources of information on international security.

CHAPTER 11

ECONOMIC STATECRAFT

AP Photo/Lee Jin-man

South Korean citizens wave flags of the United States and South Korea as they celebrate the free trade agreement (FTA) signed by the two governments in March 2012. Such FTAs have become popular instruments of U.S. foreign economic policy as they provide for open markets in bilateral trade while allowing both members to keep their trade restrictions in place against other countries.

11.1 Describe three different types of political economy adopted in modern times.

11.2 Summarize the dominant role of the United States in the balance of economic power.

11.3 Discuss global and domestic trade politics as aspects of U.S. foreign economic policy.

11.4 Explain the motivations behind foreign aid in U.S. foreign economic policy.

11.5 Identify the forms and functions of economic sanctions as a policy tool.

American leaders, like their counterparts overseas, consider national prosperity essential to achieving their foreign policy goals. The military preponderance currently enjoyed by the United States would not be possible in the absence of a productive population, vast natural resources, advanced technology, and commercial links to other markets. "Trade is what most international relations are about," economist Thomas Schelling (quoted in Froman 2014, 111) observed. "For that reason trade policy is national security policy."

Economic strength is a source of the nation's soft power, much of which is wielded by consumers and reflected in their material well-being. Close trade ties are also known to encourage a "capitalist peace" among governments that "anticipate a lessening of militarized disputes or wars" (Gartzke 2007, 166). This point was made in 1947 by President Truman, who noted that free trade creates "an atmosphere congenial to the preservation of peace." At home, commercial activity harnesses the energies of private citizens, whose pursuit of material self-interest contributes to the realization of national goals. In this respect, the domain of foreign economic policy may be considered more democratic than security policy, usually often takes place beyond the view or reach of civil society. The notion that "the business of America is business" is deeply engrained in the nation's cultural identity. Alexis de Tocqueville, who toured the United States in 1831 and 1832, captured this materialistic spirit in his classic cultural study *Democracy in America*:

> The desire to acquire the good things of this world is the dominant passion among Americans. . . . It is odd to watch with what feverish ardor the Americans pursue prosperity and how they are ever tormented by the shadowy suspicion that they may not have chosen the shortest route to get it. Americans cleave to the things of this world as if assured that they will never

die, and yet are in such a rush to snatch anything that comes within their reach, as if expecting to stop living before they have relished them. They clutch everything but hold nothing fast, and so lose grip as they hurry after some new delight (Tocqueville [1835] 1988, 534, 536).

As we will find, regulating commerce is a highly political enterprise because of the routine interaction of public and private actors in the U.S. economic complex (see Chapter 6). The makeup of Congress is determined in large part by the economic interests of constituents (Fordham and McKeown 2003), and presidential candidates know that "pocketbook" issues typically concern voters more than any others. Political intervention in private markets is inevitable because the economic affairs of Americans, diffused across business sectors, routinely come into conflict and cannot be fully reconciled. Amid the cross-pressures imposed by competing, self-interested investors, firms, and workers, the U.S. government must act as the final arbiter of these conflicts of interest (see Ikenberry, Lake, and Mastanduno 1988).

Still, the U.S. government has only limited control over the market-driven world economy that it played a central role in creating. Economic globalization, which melds national and regional markets into a single world market, expands the field of competition and favors emerging economies that adopt new technologies created elsewhere and produce manufactured goods with lower labor costs.[1] The flow of private capital across national borders, a crucial part of globalization, also hinders the U.S. government's economic ability to control its fortunes in the global marketplace. As U.S.-based multinational corporations (MNCs) expand into new markets and join forces with foreign firms, they are less likely to align themselves automatically with U.S. foreign policy goals. All these trends suggest that, as in other areas of foreign policy, the United States may be the victim of its own success.

1. See Steger (2010) for a volume of classic essays on economic globalization.

Like his predecessors, President Obama viewed economic growth a major priority eclipsed only by national security. He also followed past practice by demanding that U.S. trade partners follow "the rules of the road," especially their openness to U.S. exports and foreign investments. The president also pushed for free-trade agreements with like-minded governments and for the creation of multilateral trade pacts. Aside from these ongoing objectives, Obama was forced to spend the first year of his presidency containing a financial crisis that quickly reached global proportions (see below).

This chapter begins by identifying the key models of political economy and then reviews the current status of the United States in the world economy. It then considers the two dimensions—global and domestic—of U.S. trade policy. Finally, the chapter examines two other aspects of U.S. foreign economic policy, foreign aid and economic sanctions, both of which are designed to advance the nation's global interests. As we will find, all these elements of **economic statecraft** (Baldwin 1985) are crucial to the overall success or failure of U.S. foreign policy.

■ MODELS OF POLITICAL ECONOMY

Understanding U.S. foreign economic policy requires a firm grasp of **political economy**, an arena of public life located at the crossroads of governments and markets. As noted earlier, regulating commerce is inherently a political process because of the state's role in deciding which economic system will be in place at any particular time, what the rules of the system will be, and how its costs and benefits will be distributed across society. These questions become matters of foreign economic policy when they involve the government's commercial, financial, and regulatory ties with other countries. The **international political economy** is the arena in which states engage with an array of private actors—small firms, corporations, workers, investors, and interest groups—as well as foreign governments and intergovernmental organizations such as the World Bank and the World Trade Organization (WTO). This engagement is partly competitive, as each nation seeks benefits for itself at the expense of others, but cooperation is also needed if the global economy is to function efficiently.

An essential function of all governments is to organize economic activity within their societies and establish the relationships among economic actors in the public and private sectors. In doing so, political leaders adopt different models of political economy that feature distinctive trade-offs between labor and capital, political liberty and economic equality, and the power of states versus civil society. The model of political economy chosen by each nation determines the role it will play in the global economy and the broader relations it will maintain with other governments. Three models of political economy have been adopted in modern times: **economic liberalism (or capitalism)**, socialism, and economic nationalism (or mercantilism).[2] In managing economic affairs, governments commonly draw on the elements of more than one model.

The United States is widely considered the primary proponent of **capitalism**, a system of free enterprise that protects private property and commercial activity from government intervention (see Lal 2006). Adam Smith ([1776] 2000), a leading proponent of this model during the Enlightenment era, believed that free markets offer an ideal environment in which entrepreneurs can take risks, introduce technological innovations, and expand production, thereby improving societal living standards beyond what governments can provide. In this view, a natural "harmony of interests" exists between states and markets, and among the producers and consumers of goods and services. For many years, American leaders demanded that recipients of U.S. foreign aid adhere to the "**Washington consensus**," which emphasized minimal state intervention, balanced budgets, and open trade markets.

The second model of political economy, **socialism**, rejects the liberal notion of a harmony of interests and argues instead that free markets inevitably produce disparities in wealth and the exploitation of workers by business owners and managers. This critique, identified with Karl Marx and known today as Marxism, considers the political leaders of liberal states to be co-conspirators with banks and business firms in the exploitation of workers. A socialist system seeks to ensure economic equality through social welfare programs and government ownership of vital enterprises, while also allowing citizens to own private property and operate firms. The Soviet Union pursued a stronger version of this model, **communism**, by seeking complete economic and political control of the nation. Communism, along with the most rigid forms of socialism, has failed to improve living standards while keeping governments solvent. Still, in light of growing gaps between rich and poor in much of the world—including the United States—the Marxist critique of liberal economics persists.

Finally, **mercantilism** considers commercial activity fruitful only if it serves the interests of the state, whose power depends on the accumulation of wealth. Political actors adopting this model view the world economy as a "zero-sum game" in which the losses suffered by one country offset the gains enjoyed by another. During the Renaissance era, the maritime empires of Europe adopted this model by accumulating vast amounts of specie, or mineral wealth, which they used to enhance their military defenses and domestic political power. The revival of **economic nationalism** in the 1920s led to the closing of world trade markets, a severe global depression, and the onset of World War II. Since the 1980s, Japan and other East Asian countries have been accused of "neo-mercantilism" by flooding global markets with their goods while protecting domestic producers from foreign competition.

---

2. See Gilpin and Gilpin (1987) for a similar breakdown of political economic models.

The Chinese government, meanwhile, has established a hybrid model of political economy. Under **state capitalism**, the ruling Chinese Communist Party (CCP) satisfies the material interests of a growing number of citizens while continuing to deny them basic political freedoms and civil rights (see Halper 2010). To Chinese leaders, such freedoms only invite political turmoil and threats to established governmental practices. With a tight grip on civil society, the CCP ensures domestic tranquility along with the economic growth that has boosted living standards among China's massive population. This model has appealed to many developing countries that embrace the "Beijing consensus" as a path to prosperity.

The United States first adopted the mercantile approach when it created a strong manufacturing base that, while restricting imports, produced sufficient profits to finance national expansion and security. This behavior changed as the nation emerged from World War I as the world's economic powerhouse. Woodrow Wilson, who included free trade as one of his fourteen points for restoring global stability, pledged to dismantle U.S. trade barriers and respect other tenets of capitalism. The calamity of the Great Depression and World War II prompted Franklin Roosevelt's secretary of state, Cordell Hull, to observe that "If we could get a freer flow of trade—freer in the sense of few discriminations and obstructions . . . we might have a reasonable chance of lasting peace" (quoted in Gardner 1980, 9). During this time, Washington also adopted programs of social security, health care for the elderly, minimum wages, and unemployment compensation that resembled the practices of socialist states.

Institutional arrangements play a central role in shaping the foreign economic policies of all countries. In the United States, for example, financial regulations are often overlooked and corporations enjoy a privileged place in the policy process. Workers in Great Britain and Germany, meanwhile, have greater political influence over trade and foreign investment than their American counterparts. Meanwhile, the central governments of Japan and France are better equipped to overcome pressure from either of these societal groups (J. A. Hart 1992). Among developing states, India has spurred economic growth by protecting political rights in a multiparty system while becoming a global hub of services related to information technology (Dahlman 2012). These comparisons demonstrate the extent to which foreign economic policies reflect the bargains struck daily among contending actors in domestic society.

■ THE BALANCE OF ECONOMIC POWER

The United States has managed the world's largest economy for the past century. Its output first exceeded that of Great Britain and other economic rivals early in the twentieth century, and the lead widened with the damage suffered by other industrial

POINT/COUNTERPOINT

The United States and China: Partners or Rivals?

A vital question in world politics today concerns future relations between the United States and the People's Republic of China (PRC). From 1979 through 2010, the Chinese economy grew by about 10 percent annually, making the nation a first-tier economic power. This soaring wealth, in turn, allowed Chinese leaders to boost defense spending from $30 billion in 2000 to $145 billion in 2015. An open question is whether China and the United States, which share lucrative financial and trade ties, will be geopolitical partners or rivals in the years to come.

For China optimists, their leaders have strong incentives to be part of the international community rather than challenge the existing order. Further, the PRC's central role in the globalized world economy makes it dependent on stable relations with the United States and other industrialized countries. To Loren Thompson, China is constrained by its lack of regional allies and by its repressive government. In a 2015 study by the RAND Corporation, Lloyd Thrall concluded that China's growing engagement in Africa "is not a strategic threat to U.S. security interests. In fact, both countries have a primary interest in a stable and secure Africa." Summing up this case, Joseph S. Nye Jr. argued that the United States "remains decades ahead of China in overall military, economic, and soft power resources at the global level."

China pessimists, meanwhile, view China as an imminent rival of the United States, and its recent provocations in the East and South China should be of great concern to U.S. foreign policy makers. According to strategic analyst Aaron Friedberg, both countries have "strategic objectives that threaten the fundamental interests of the other side." Adam Liff and G. John Ikenberry find Sino-American relations being driven by a "security dilemma" that compels them to strengthen their military forces to protect them in case the other side takes aggressive action. Finally, Evan Braden Montgomery assessed China's military power and concluded that "the PRC has been developing, acquiring, and fielding a variety of capabilities that could enable it to pose a genuine challenge to U.S. military power across its home region and in the global commons."

Sources: Loren Thompson, "Five Reasons China Won't Be a Big Threat to America's Global Power," *Forbes*, June 6, 2014; Lloyd Thrall, "China Not a Threat to U.S. National Security Interests in Africa," RAND Corporation, April 22, 2015; Joseph S. Nye Jr., *Is the American Century Over?* Cambridge, MA: Polity Press, 2015: 69; Aaron Friedberg, *A Contest for Supremacy: China, America and the Struggle for Mastery in Asia* (New York: Norton, 2012); Adam P. Liff and G. John Ikenberry, "Racing toward Tragedy," *International Security* 39 (Fall 2014); Evan Braden Montgomery, "Contested Primacy in the Western Pacific: China's Rise and the Future of U.S. Power Projection," *International Security* 38 (Spring 2014): 130.

powers in the two world wars. By 1946, U.S. firms were producing as much economic output as the rest of the world combined. Although this edge predictably receded while the other states recovered, U.S. economic clout, which is propelled by robust research universities and a strong workforce, remains unsurpassed today.

Strengths and Weaknesses of the U.S. Economy

As noted in Chapter 1, the **gross domestic product (GDP)** of the United States amounted to more than $17 trillion in 2014, or 22 percent of the global total of $77 trillion (International Monetary Fund 2015).[3] This proportion is especially striking because the U.S. population of 321 million in 2015 represented less than 5 percent of the global population of 7.2 billion. The People's Republic of China, which managed the world's second-largest national economy in 2014, produced just 60 percent of U.S. output.[4] The volume of U.S. output exceeded the combined totals of more than 140 lower-income countries. As for Russia, the geopolitical rival of the United States in the Cold War, a half century of economic and political stagnation has cut Moscow's GDP to 11 percent of U.S. levels.

Other statistics illustrate the magnitude of U.S. economic abundance. The per capita income of the United States, the nation's economic output divided by its population, amounted to $55,200 in 2011 (World Bank 2015). Only fourteen other countries exceeded this level of affluence. The average life expectancy of Americans reached 80 years in 2014, significantly higher than the world average of 68 years. The combined total of U.S. goods and services produced, along with the nation's robust import activity, exceeded that of China, the second-largest trading power (World Trade Organization 2015). Finally, U.S.-based transnational corporations, with offices worldwide, have a commanding technological lead in such vital sectors as defense, banking, computers, electronics, and health care (Starrs 2013).

Despite its strengths in the world economy, the United States confronts profound changes in the world economy that pose direct challenges to its sustained primacy. For more than twenty-five years, the United States maintained a favorable **balance of trade**, or an equilibrium between imports and exports. But in the 1970s, the nation began buying more goods from foreign countries than it was selling to them (see Figure 11.1). These trade deficits have widened ever since. Other cracks in the post-war U.S. economy appeared in the same period, when a spike in oil prices created double-digit inflation, high unemployment, and stagnant levels of output. American manufacturing firms, meanwhile, faced growing competition from lower-wage economies overseas. By 2013, Chinese exports exceeded those of the United States by more than $600 billion (see Table 11.1).

The U.S. relationship with the PRC is close but contradictory. China, for example, is both a chief *competitor* of the United States and a *partner* in maintaining a stable global economy. The Chinese economy, which grew by an astonishing 10 percent

---

3. A country's GDP is based on its total income earned in a given year. A closely related measure, Gross National Product, also includes income from overseas ventures.

4. The ratio of Chinese to U.S. GDP may be deceiving, as Beijing sets its currency value at an artificially low rate, which makes its exports cheaper. If yet another measure, purchasing power parity, is used, China's output in 2014 was slightly above that of the United States (World Bank 2015).

Table 11.1 ■ Top Ten World Merchandise Traders, 2013 (all figures in billions of U.S. dollars)

Exporter	Value of Exports	Importer	Value of Imports
China	2,209	United States	2,329
United States	1,580	China	1,950
Germany	1,453	Germany	1,189
Japan	715	Japan	833
Netherlands	672	France	681
France	580	United Kingdom	655
South Korea	560	Netherlands	590
United Kingdom	542	South Korea	516
Russia	523	Italy	477
Italy	518	Canada	474

Source: World Trade Organization, *World Trade Developments* (2014).

annually between 1979 and 2008 (Morrison 2009), benefited greatly from the export of manufactured goods. China has also emerged as a leading destination of development assistance and foreign direct investment, particularly in Africa, where the PRC has lavished many poor countries with soccer stadiums, highways, and other infrastructure projects, often in return for access to oil, mineral resources, or other raw materials. The bilateral link between the two countries is often strained, as the U.S. government frequently complained about China's trade policies. By 2014, however, the PRC's economic growth had slowed dramatically, a result of excessive supply of production and slumping demand from consumers. As in the case of the U.S.-based financial crisis of the previous decade, the unforeseen economic slowdown in China produced a sharp fall in the nation's economic vitality.

Alongside these complexities in the Sino-American relationship, three sets of problems face the U.S. economy today:

- **Globalization:** As described in Chapter 1, the U.S. economic model lends itself to the free flow of capital, labor, and overseas trade. This model of open markets, however, encourages U.S.-based MNCs to move their operations overseas where they can find the lowest production costs of their merchandise. Further, rising economic powers such as China, India, and Brazil have benefited by adopting technologies pioneered by U.S. firms. The United States also has become a prime victim of foreign governments that violate U.S. intellectual property rights.

- **Debts and deficits:** As of July 2015, the U.S. government held a national debt of $18 trillion, an amount greater than the nation's output in 2014. Payments on the interest of this debt have become one of the fastest-growing federal expenditures. The United States also suffers from a chronic trade deficit (see Figure 11.1). This deficit, which stood at $504 billion at the end of 2014, effectively resulted in the export of American wealth (R. E. Scott 2012). Consumer spending fuels an

Figure 11.1 ■ U.S. Balance of Trade, 1970–2014 (figures in millions of U.S. dollars)

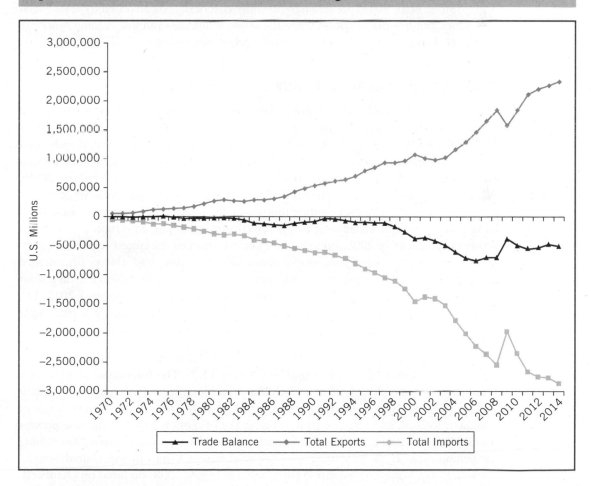

Source: Bureau of Economic Analysis, "Trade in Goods and Services," www.bea.gov/international/.

ongoing import binge as Americans rush to buy the lowest-cost goods they can find, regardless of national origin. By July 2015, U.S. consumers accumulated nearly $12 trillion in debt, including $1.2 trillion in student loans and $900 million in credit cards (Chen 2015).

- **Income Inequality.** Once known as a nation founded on its middle class, the United States has become the most unequal industrialized state in the world. This shift "undermines a critical component of U.S. soft power and is a model for societal engineering that few would choose to emulate" (J. Campbell 2014). The Gini Index, used to measure levels of national inequality, found the United States in 2014 ranking forty-first of 141 countries in inequality. Of the forty nations with higher levels of inequality, all were developing rather than industrial economies. In 2013, 3 percent of the American public held 54 percent of the nation's wealth (Stone et al. 2015). Increasingly, wealthy corporate executives enjoy lavish salaries and five-digit bonuses while the wages of middle- and low-income American workers enjoyed watched their buying power decreasing.

The Financial Crisis and Recovery

These worrisome trends paled in comparison to the disruption of the U.S. and world economies that followed the financial crisis of 2008. The economic recession began a year earlier when a "bubble" burst in the real estate market that experienced such rapid growth in property values that mortgage brokers offered home loans at sub-prime interest rates with little regard for the creditworthiness of borrowers (see Schwartz 2009). When millions of these homeowners, faced with unexpected job losses or other economic problems, suddenly defaulted on their mortgages, the foreclosures triggered a cascade of bank failures and the collapse of major investment firms. The bankruptcy of Lehman Brothers in September 2008, valued at $639 billion, marked the largest such bankruptcy in U.S. history. President Bush, whose economic philosophy had always discouraged government intervention, pleaded with Congress to approve a $700 billion federal bailout to prevent the collapse of the U.S. financial system. To one analyst (Bremmer 2012, 11), the U.S. debt crisis "is a slow-motion emergency that has been developing in plain sight for decades under presidents and congressional majorities of both parties."

The crisis quickly assumed global proportions, as global stock markets tumbled alongside steep declines in national output (see Figure 11.2). The International Monetary Fund (IMF), which along with the World Bank had long served as an agent of globalization (Woods 2006), provided emergency loans to prevent the governments of Hungary, Iceland, and Ukraine from running out of money. Major economic powers such as Australia, India, and Russia also endured months of financial chaos. "Everything happening now in the economic and financial sphere began in the United States," Russian Prime Minister Vladimir Putin (quoted in Jagger 2008) declared on October 2. "This is not the irresponsibility of specific individuals but the irresponsibility of the system that claims leadership."

Christopher Dodd *The U.S. financial crisis of 2008 shocked the global economy, creating a deep recession that left millions of citizens in the United States and overseas with lost savings and jobs. Sen. Christopher Dodd (D-Conn.), chairman of the Senate's banking committee, played a key role in the U.S. response to the crisis. He was clearly shocked when, on September 18, 2008, Secretary of the Treasury Henry Paulson and Federal Reserve chair Ben Bernanke informed Dodd and other leading members of Congress that drastic measures—including a $700 billion government bailout—were needed to avoid a catastrophe. Dodd described his feelings in a 2009 documentary entitled "Inside the Meltdown."*

It's the economic equivalent of 9/11 in my view, having been here for both events . . . Sitting in that room with Hank Paulson saying to us, in very measured tones, no hyperbole, no excessive adjectives, that unless you act, the financial system of this country and the world will melt down in a matter of days. There was literally a pause in that room where the oxygen left. . . . Literally, I know I'm drawing too close of an analogy here given the lives lost on 9/11, but it's that kind of moment. This is not some analyst. This is not some functionary at the Treasury. This is the chairman of the Federal Reserve Bank, the most important central bank in the world, announcing to the leadership, Republicans and Democrats of Congress, "Unless we act within days, the financial system will melt down."

Source: Public Broadcasting Service, *Frontline: Inside the Meltdown*, February 17, 2009.

The U.S. budget deficit grew rapidly under President Bush due to sweeping tax cuts in 2001 and the costs of fighting the war on terror after September 11. The financial crisis in Bush's last year sent this deficit soaring further—from $459 billion in 2008 to nearly $1.6 trillion in 2009. This total represented 11.2 percent of national output, the highest such level since World War II (Congressional Budget Office 2009a). Trade levels between the United States and other countries plummeted from $4.3 trillion in 2008 to $3.5 trillion in 2009, a clear sign that the financial crisis had "gone global." Taken together, the U.S. and other governments spent a combined total of $12 trillion in recovery costs, a price tag that amounted to almost $2,000 for every woman, man, and child on the planet (Jess 2009).

President Obama avoided a greater calamity with the help of a second stimulus package from Congress, this one directed toward construction and other projects that would stem rising unemployment across the United States. Above and beyond these staggering costs, the financial crisis raised worldwide doubts about the liberal model of political economy and its most boisterous advocate, the United States. The deregulation of financial practices, which began in the Reagan years and continued under George W. Bush, "unleashed" private enterprise to such an extent that

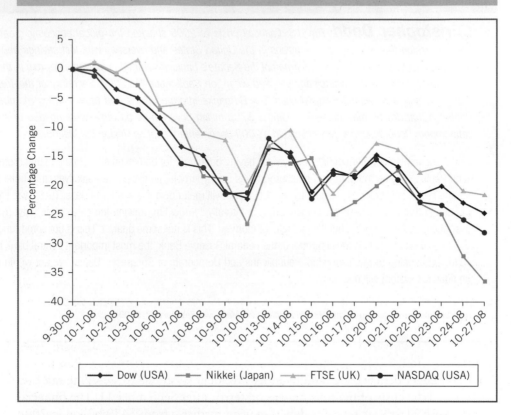

Figure 11.2 ■ Falling Fortunes: Index of Four Global Stock Markets, September 30–October 27, 2008

Source: Data from MSN.com "Money" webpage, http://moneycentral.msn.com/detail/stock_quote.

market discipline broke down. A 646-page report by the U.S. Senate Permanent Subcommittee on Investigations (2011) laid the blame on irresponsible mortgage lenders and investment banks, negligent federal regulators, and credit rating agencies that failed to anticipate the crisis. The U.S. Office of Thrift Supervision, for example, identified more than 500 serious problems with the Washington Mutual holding company but failed to take action against the aggressive lender (Morgenson and Story 2011).

This Great Recession ultimately eased, although millions of Americans remained crippled by joblessness and shattered finances. Contrary to expectations of prolonged economic misery, the U.S. economy grew by 2.4 percent in 2014, the largest one-year increase since the financial crisis began. At the global level, the world economy grew by 9 percent between 2010 and 2012, and worldwide industrial output in 2012 was 10 percent higher than its 2007 level (Drezner 2014, 131). Central banks around the world provided ample funding to keep governments solvent, and the Group of 20 nations tripled their contributions to the International Monetary Fund.[5] The U.S. rebound came with a more rigid set of financial regulations, including those spelled out in the Dodd-Frank Wall Street Reform Act of July 2010 that restored faith in the shaken U.S. financial system. Still, the hard lesson was learned that "even the U.S. was not immune to the dangers of unbridled finance. . . . Given the damage wrought, the crisis ended the widespread assumption that the American model was the only way, or even that it was the right way" (J. Kirshner 2015).

■ TRADE POLICY AS A "TWO-LEVEL GAME"

The conduct of trade policy is a prime example of a "two-level game" (Putnam 1988). In this game, officials in the executive branch negotiate simultaneously with foreign leaders and domestic stakeholders, including business firms, labor unions, and members of Congress. Because the terms of prospective trade agreements must be acceptable to parties at both levels if those agreements are to be approved and ratified, negotiators must be sure to resolve everyone's concerns to the greatest extent possible. At the same time, the foreign governments and domestic actors involved recognize the benefits of expanded trade and know compromises and trade-offs have to be made (see Chapter 3).

By far the most important aspect of U.S. foreign economic policy is trade with other countries. As noted earlier, Americans have robust appetites for foreign goods, even those that come at the cost of shuttered factories in U.S. cities. Although the United States is no longer the world's dominant exporter, the nation enjoys a commanding lead in many sectors of foreign trade, particularly services, military equipment, and the high-technology goods associated with the computer industry. Whereas trade accounted for about 10 percent of U.S. economic output in 1960, about one-fourth of the goods and services produced today are destined for foreign customers.

An examination of U.S. bilateral trade flows reveals the far reaches of the nation's trade deficit (see Table 11.2 and Map 11.1, U.S. Foreign Economic Relations). Of the top ten U.S. trading partners in 2014, all but Brazil maintained a trade surplus with the United States. The trade gap was most severe in the case of the PRC, whose imports to the United States amounted to nearly four times the value of U.S. exports

---

5. The G-20 is an expanded alternative to the Group of 8 (G-8), whose member states (Canada, France, Germany, Italy, Japan, Russia, the United Kingdom, and the United States) had dominated global economic discussions. Through the G-20, such talks have included a more diverse group of countries, including Argentina, Australia, Brazil, China, India, Indonesia, Mexico, Saudi Arabia, South Africa, South Korea, and Turkey along with the European Union. Russia, however, was expelled from G-20 after its government in 2014 forcefully captured the Crimean Peninsula, which was part of Ukraine.

to China. Canada and Mexico, wedded to the U.S. markets by proximity and the North American Free Trade Agreement (NAFTA), remained the leading destinations of U.S. exports while adding a combined $88 billion to the U.S. trade deficit. The United States, meanwhile, continued to manage close trade relations—and a chronic trade deficit—with Japan, despite long-standing efforts by Washington to ensure "fair trade."

Global Trade Politics

For U.S. foreign policy, the effective management of global trade politics is a national priority. These pressures began with the nation's founding and continued as the United States established itself as a formidable agricultural and industrial power early in the twentieth century. The nation's population had recently surpassed 100 million, in large part because of a wave of European immigration at the turn of the century, which brought a much-needed influx of workers to support the country's rapid industrial expansion. By the early 1920s, the United States was producing more steel, oil, and automobiles than the rest of the world combined. After World War II, the United States and other industrial powers adopted trade rules through the General

Table 11.2 ■ Top Ten U.S. Trading Partners, 2014 (figures in billions of U.S. dollars)

Country	Total Trade	Import Volume	Export Volume	Bilateral Trade Balance
Canada	658.1	346.1	312.0	–34.1
China	590.7	466.7	124.0	–342.7
Mexico	534.5	294.2	240.3	–53.9
Japan	200.9	133.9	67.0	–66.9
Germany	172.6	123.2	49.4	–73.8
South Korea	114.1	69.6	44.5	–25.1
United Kingdom	107.9	54.0	53.9	–.1
France	78.2	47.0	31.2	–15.8
Brazil	72.8	30.3	42.4	12.1
Taiwan	67.4	40.6	26.8	–13.8

Source: U.S. Census Bureau, "Top Trading Partners—December 2014," Year-to-Date Total Trade, Exports, Imports, http://www.census.gov/foreign-trade/statistics/highlights/top/top1412yr.html.

Agreement on Tariffs and Trade (GATT), which later served as the primary vehicle of market reforms and the forerunner of the World Trade Organization. The GATT negotiations, or "rounds," were based on the principle of **most-favored-nation trading status**—that is, the provision of equal market access and terms of trade to all states participating in the GATT system.

The United States laid the foundation of the post–World War II trading system and assumed primary responsibility for managing global monetary policies through the World Bank and International Monetary Fund (IMF). The United States supported foreign currencies by basing their values on the U.S. dollar, which the nation backed up with its gold reserves. In 1971, however, rising inflation along with the high costs of the Vietnam War prompted President Richard Nixon to abandon this **gold standard**. In its absence, a system of **floating exchange rates** came into being that determined the value of one country's currency on the basis of the value of other currencies on foreign exchange markets.

Meanwhile, the U.S. government still provided the largest share of IMF and World Bank funds and maintained the greatest influence over their policies. In 1973, the Nixon administration confronted an economic challenge posed by the Organization of the Petroleum Exporting Countries (OPEC), a cartel whose embargo on oil exports sparked high inflation and a protracted economic recession across the industrialized world for the next decade. Subsequent strains in the 1980s chipped away at the nation's commitment to free trade. The United States became a victim of its own success during this period as newly industrialized countries took advantage of open U.S. markets to hasten their own economic growth. Japan and other East Asian states kept their markets largely closed to foreign competition while flooding export markets with low-cost, highly subsidized goods. The result was a rapidly growing trade deficit in the United States, whose industries stagnated in several key sectors such as steel, textiles, and consumer electronics.

The end of the Cold War in 1991 prompted President Clinton to base U.S. foreign policy on geoeconomics. Bolstered by his 1993 success in launching the NAFTA trade bloc, in 1995, Clinton gained congressional support for U.S. membership in the World Trade Organization, which replaced the GATT as the key forum for resolving trade disputes (see Lanoszka 2009). His push for free trade, however, produced its own counterreaction in the form of the antiglobalization movement. Protesters, supported by mass publics in many developing countries, argued that the WTO-sponsored trade agreements neglected environmental concerns and the rights of workers. Furthermore, these critics charged, open markets were fine for the United States, with its huge corporations, technological superiority, and economies of scale, but perilous for their own countries. *Globalization*, in this view, was a code word for *Americanization* (see Hayden and el-Ojeili 2005). The resulting tensions boiled over in September 2003, when the representatives of dozens of developing countries walked out of the WTO talks in Cancun, Mexico. The formal suspension of trade

Map 11.1 ■ U.S. Foreign Economic Relations

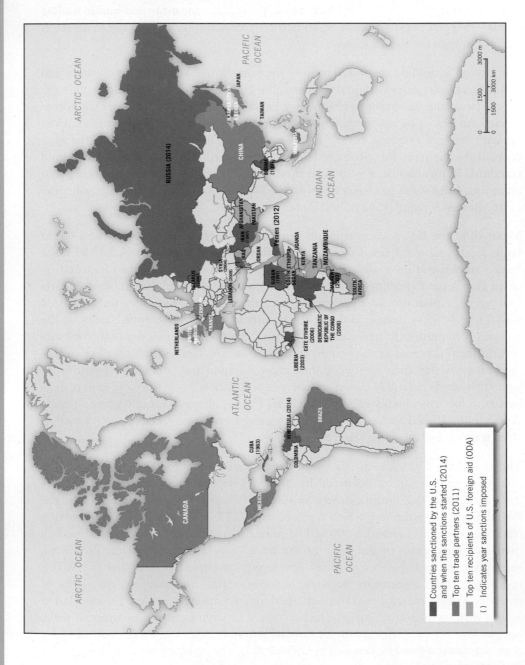

Source: U.S. Department of the Treasury, Office of Foreign Assets Control, www.ustreas.gov/offices/enforcement/ofac/programs; U.S. Department of Commerce, Census Bureau, *Foreign Trade Statistics,* www.census.gov/foreign-trade/statistics/index.html; Organisation for Economic Co-operation and Development, *Statistical Annex of the 2010 Development Co-operation Report* (Paris: OECD, 2010), http://www.oecd-ilibrary.org/development/development-co-operation-report-2010/statistical-annex_dcr-2010-40-en.

talks in 2006 halted a half-century of progress toward open trade markets, a primary catalyst of economic globalization.

With 161 member states in 2015, the WTO wields enormous supranational, or legal, authority over its member states. Just as Congress effectively waived its constitutional power to regulate trade, the White House routinely defers to the organization's demands for changes in U.S. trade policies, even when they

Heng/International New York Times

have harmed important domestic groups. In its first decade, the WTO ruled against the United States in sixty-eight of seventy-one cases brought before the trade body. The fact that the U.S. government made the required changes in fifty-nine of those cases, opening its markets more fully to foreign competition, represented a "triumph of globalism" over domestic politics in U.S. trade policy (Kirshner 2005, 498).

China's rapid economic growth and global trade and investment ties encouraged the PRC to create its own multilateral institution, the Asia Infrastructure Investment Bank, which was created in 2015 to provide capital to developing countries. This bank, considered by Washington a potential rival to its World Bank and Asian Development Bank, soon attracted forty-six member states, including many European allies, by June 2015. To one regional expert, this unexpected outpouring recognized "economic reality. China has deep pockets, and the institutions backed by the United States have not met the growing demands for roads, railroads and pipelines in Asia" (Perlez 2015, A5). With the United States looking from the outside in, the new bank also raised fears among foreign policy makers that China would attempt to create its own version of the IMF.

Domestic Trade Politics

Early in the history of the United States, two opposing views of trade policy vied for government support. Economic nationalists believed the nation should protect its domestic market from foreign competition and seek to become economically self-sufficient. Alexander Hamilton, the first U.S. Treasury secretary and a strong proponent of this view, felt the United States required a strong industrial base that could be used for military purposes in case of a challenge from abroad. By contrast, economic liberals favored a free trade policy more in keeping with the nation's distrust of an activist federal government, especially in economic affairs. Thomas Jefferson, for example, believed that living standards everywhere would be enhanced by the creation of a global division of labor in which each country's producers would contribute in areas drawing on their unique strengths. David Ricardo and other early advocates of economic globalization later refined this notion of **comparative advantage** (see Heilbroner 1999).

Congress, despite its constitutional power to "regulate commerce," has largely deferred to the executive branch. This deference stemmed from a painful chapter in the 1920s, when trade wars broke out among the major industrial powers. Members of Congress jumped into the fray in 1930 by passing the **Smoot-Hawley Tariff Act**, which dramatically increased tariffs on goods coming into the country.[6] The act, designed to strengthen domestic firms and bolster the nation's economic strength, instead reduced the volume of U.S. trade by nearly 70 percent and helped to plunge the U.S. and world economies into the Great Depression.

Two lessons emerged from the Smoot-Hawley debacle. First, members of Congress learned that the United States bore the primary responsibility for promoting and sustaining global economic growth. As the locomotive of the world economy, the United States could not engage in the trade wars so common among the smaller economic powers. Second, legislators recognized that constituent pressure for trade protections prevented them from living up to this global responsibility. Congress responded by passing the Reciprocal Trade Agreement of 1934, which shifted responsibility for trade agreements to the executive branch. The legislation presumed that presidents, in representing the national interest, could better withstand the parochial pressures than legislators with their closer contact to constituents.

Heightened trade competition in the 1970s prompted Congress to provide presidents with "fast-track authority," later renamed **trade promotion authority,** for use in negotiating trade agreements with foreign governments. As plants closed across the United States, eliminating the jobs of millions of U.S. workers, the free trade consensus quickly gave way to "a recurring suspicion that free trade is not necessarily desirable at all costs" (Gibson 2000, 114). The Omnibus Trade and Competitiveness Act of 1988 required presidents to identify the most serious violations of free trade either through tariffs or **nontariff barriers;** the latter include the "dumping" of goods overseas or selling them at lower costs than domestic consumers pay. The bitter domestic politics of the Clinton years extended to the trade realm, as Republicans joined with labor-backed Democrats in denying Clinton the trade promotion authority granted to his predecessors.

After George W. Bush came to power in 2001, the Republican-led Congress promptly granted him trade promotion authority. While pledging allegiance to free trade, Bush

---

6. This measure raised the average tax on imports from 39 percent to 53 percent of their value. Other countries retaliated with higher tariffs of their own, prompting the volume of global exports to plummet from $5.2 billion in 1929 to $1.6 billion in 1932. Unemployment in the United States soared, peaking at 32 percent in 1932 and idling nearly one in every three workers (Rothgeb 2001, 38–39).

maintained the agricultural subsidies and tariffs that angered developing countries and led to the collapse of WTO talks. President Obama supported this position when he took office, although his energies were focused initially on stabilizing U.S. financial institutions. The U.S. government, for example, assumed primary ownership of the ailing automakers General Motors and Chrysler, whose imminent bankruptcies would have greatly increased unemployment while sharply accelerating the erosion of America's manufacturing sector.[7] The United States, meanwhile, continued to pursue **free trade agreements (FTAs)** and established FTAs with twenty countries by 2013. In such agreements, both partners eliminate their mutual trade barriers while maintaining restrictions elsewhere (see W. H. Cooper 2012). The White House also pursued multilateral trade pacts based on the NAFTA model. In 2014, the United States joined eleven other nations in creating the Trans-Pacific Partnership (TPP) that would link the trade markets of East Asia and the Western Hemisphere. A similar arrangement was in the works for Europe and the Western Hemisphere, which would solidify the already close trade relations on both sides of the Atlantic Ocean. Finally, Obama supported the African Growth and Opportunity Act that blended U.S. development aid with stepped-up U.S. imports from sub-Saharan Africa, where many countries have recently spurred rapid economic growth (see B. R. Williams 2015). In all of these ways, U.S. leaders became further immersed in the global economy.

■ NATIONAL INTERESTS AND FOREIGN AID

Another instrument of U.S. foreign economic policy is **foreign aid**, or economic resources made available to poor countries on terms unavailable to them in commercial markets.[8] Virtually every nation-state, rich or poor, either provides or receives this aid. Despite recent growth rates, 30 percent of the world's population still lives on less than $2 a day across the **Global South**—a region that roughly includes Africa, Latin America, and southern Asia. More than 80 percent of the world's population lives in developing rather than industrial countries, yet they own less than a quarter of global wealth. Their starvation, disease, and despair necessitate this global aid network. The higher aid volumes of recent years, provided by individual states as well as the United Nations and many development NGOs, are directed toward six general objectives:

- Providing immediate relief to those living in extreme poverty (less than $1.25 of income per day);
- Stimulating market-based economic growth;

---

7. Both companies repaid their government loans and regained profitability by 2012, boosting U.S. employment along with Obama's prospects for reelection.

8. In this discussion, foreign (or development) aid is separate from military aid, which the United States and other major powers provide to allies in order to bolster their national security.

- Combating the spread of HIV/AIDS and other infectious diseases;
- Easing the burden of international debt;
- Supporting emergency response and reconstruction after natural disasters; and
- Countering the threat of international terrorism.

This activity took place in the context of the **Millennium Development Goals** established at a September 2000 UN summit, the largest gathering of world leaders in history. The eight goals included deep reductions in poverty, child mortality, and HIV/AIDS; improved education and maternal health, gender equity, and environmental sustainability; and the drafting of a long-term strategy to eradicate extreme poverty (see http://www.unmillenniumproject.org/). The worldwide effort, combined with robust growth in many developing states, paid off. By 2015, the number of people living in extreme poverty had declined by more than half, from 1.9 billion in 1990 to 836 million in 2015. Child and maternal mortality rates also fell by one-half, and an estimated forty-three million people were saved from diseases (United Nations 2015). This progress, however, still left much of the world without work or even the basic needs to survive.

The United States, which has provided the largest volume of foreign aid since World War II, continues to maintain that status today. Its $33 billion contribution of development aid in 2014 was more than $13 billion above the level provided by the United Kingdom, the second largest aid provider (see Figure 11.3). Still, the United States ranked near the bottom of aid donors in terms of the proportion of national output devoted to foreign aid (1.9 percent). As a result, the world's most prolific aid donor was also widely considered its biggest miser.[9]

Although foreign aid represents less than 1 percent of the U.S. federal budget, this highly controversial program generates strong opposition from many political leaders and private citizens. As John D. Montgomery (1962, 197) observed more than a century ago, "In few areas of American public life is there so little national consensus on purposes as in foreign aid." Today's critics of foreign aid make four central arguments: (1) domestic needs should be taken care of first; (2) aid funds only reward incompetence and corruption abroad; and (3) past programs have not prevented the developing world from slipping further into poverty and social distress (Easterly 2006). The fourth related argument is that the private agencies delivering the most aid-funded programs place their institutional interests above the interests of the starving and war-torn societies they serve.

As a leading contributor of foreign aid on an absolute level, the United States closely ties its aid contributions to the pursuit of its own prosperity and military security.

---

9. Among other standards, members of the OECD's Development Assistance Committee are urged to devote at least 0.7 percent of national output to development aid. Only a few countries, mostly located in Scandinavia, have surpassed this level on a regular basis.

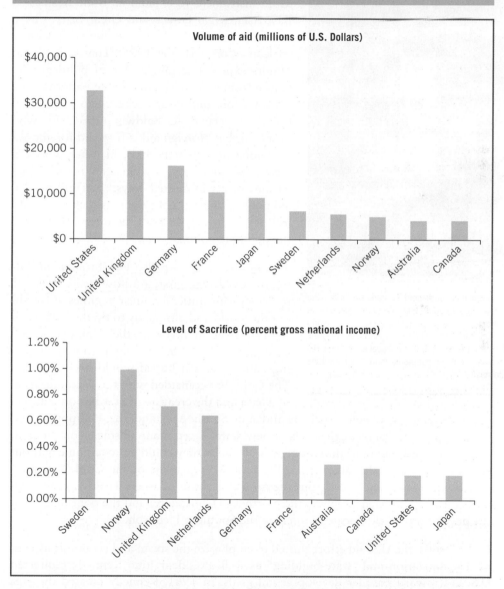

Figure 11.3 ■ Quantity vs. Quality: Development Aid Volume and Levels of Sacrifice among Top Ten Donors, 2014

Volume of aid (millions of U.S. Dollars)

(Bar chart, from left to right: United States, United Kingdom, Germany, France, Japan, Sweden, Netherlands, Norway, Australia, Canada. Y-axis from $0 to $40,000.)

Level of Sacrifice (percent gross national income)

(Bar chart, from left to right: Sweden, Norway, United Kingdom, Netherlands, Germany, France, Australia, Canada, United States, Japan. Y-axis from 0.00% to 1.20%.)

Source: Organisation for Economic Co-operation and Development, Aid Statistics, "Development Aid Stable in 2014 but Flows to Poorest Countries Still Falling," April 8, 2015. http://www.oecd.org/dac/stats/development-aid-stable-in-2014-but-flows-to-poorest-countries-still-falling.htm.

Mahmoud Ahmadinejad, president of Iran, addresses the 67th session of the United Nations General Assembly on September 26, 2012. As in past addresses to the world body, Ahmadinejad lashed out at the United States, its allies, and the UN itself for blocking Iran's political aspirations. His successor, Hassan Rouhani, adopted a more moderate tone in his UN addresses.

This linkage between self-interest and the needs of aid recipients is not unique to the United States. Japan, for example, has routinely used foreign aid as an instrument to expand its trade ties across East Asia, while France and Great Britain have used aid to retain influence within their former African colonies (Hook 1995). That said, all aid donors expect a certain degree of political allegiance from their recipients. These patterns were evident more than four decades ago to political economist David A. Baldwin (1966, 3), who observed that "foreign aid is first and foremost a technique of statecraft. It is, in other words, a means by which one nation tries to get other nations to act in desired ways. . . . Thus, foreign aid policy is foreign policy, and as such it is a subject of controversy in both the international and the domestic political arenas."

Two motivations propelled U.S. foreign aid during the Cold War. First, aid flows were designed to strengthen anticommunist regimes throughout the world and ultimately to tip the balance of world power in favor of the capitalist states. Second, the United States sought to help emerging nation-states it hoped would become allies. The Cold War coincided with the decolonization of Africa and the creation of new nation-states in other developing regions, such as India in South Asia and the Philippines and Indonesia in the Pacific region. These new states faced many obstacles on the path to political and economic development—obstacles they could not overcome without external assistance. In this respect, the East-West struggle of the Cold War intersected with emerging North-South tensions, or those between wealthy, industrialized countries (located largely in the Northern Hemisphere) and the poor nations of the developing world (located largely in the Southern Hemisphere).

In the 1960s, the U.S. aid effort shifted to emphasize the social and economic aspects of decolonization and "state-building" as well. President John Kennedy redirected U.S. aid toward broader developmental goals. In 1961, Kennedy created the U.S. Agency for International Development (USAID), which served the State Department's commitment to foreign aid. The Foreign Assistance Act of 1961 also created the Alliance for Progress, the Peace Corps, and other initiatives aimed at promoting improved living standards in poor countries. However, the United States became mired in the Vietnam War, which claimed nearly half of all U.S. aid flows until the mid-1970s. The second motivation of the U.S. during the Cold War involved Middle East politics. President Jimmy Carter hoped to revive the humanitarian elements of U.S. foreign aid, but strategic concerns overtook his plans. The 1978 Camp David Accords between Israel and Egypt, although a major foreign policy achievement, came at a huge price tag: about $5 billion annually in foreign aid to the two countries.

The Cold War's demise in 1991 deprived many bilateral aid programs—and U.S. foreign policy in general—of their previously stated rationales. Lacking the containment of communism as a primary U.S. concern, President George H. W. Bush offered assistance to former clients of the Soviet Union in Eastern Europe, and then to the newly created countries in the former Soviet Union. The 2001 terrorist attacks and subsequent global war on terror forced radical changes in U.S. development aid. Nations embroiled in the war on terror became the primary destinations of U.S. assistance. By 2013, U.S. aid flows were distributed more broadly, with six of the ten leading aid recipients located in sub-Saharan Africa (see Table 11.3). Still, the United States provided billions in development and military assistance to its strategic allies in the Middle East.

Table 11.3 ■ Top Ten Recipients of U.S. Foreign Aid, 1993–2013

1993	2003	2013
Israel	Egypt	Afghanistan
Egypt	Iraq	Kenya
El Salvador	Democratic Rep. of Congo	South Sudan
Somalia	Pakistan	Ethiopia
Philippines	Jordan	Pakistan
Colombia	Colombia	Iraq
India	Afghanistan	Tanzania
Jamaica	Ethiopia	Jordan
Pakistan	Serbia and Montenegro	South Africa
Panama	Indonesia	Mozambique

Sources: Organisation for Economic Co-operation and Development, *2014 Development Co-operation Report*, Major Recipients of Individual DAC Members' Aid, Figure 52.7, 379 (Paris, OECD, 2014); Organisation for Economic Co-operation and Development, *Statistical Annex of the 2010 Development Co-operation Report*, Table 32: Major Recipients of Individual DAC Members' Aid, 256 (Paris, OECD, 2010); Organisation for Economic Co-operation and Development, *Statistical Annex for the 2004 Development Co-operation Report*, Table 34: Major Recipients of Individual DAC Members' Aid, 218 (Paris, OECD, 2004).

In keeping with the UN aid initiative, President Bush in 2002 created a Millennium Challenge Corporation (MCC) to provide development aid only to countries with a proven track record of economic reform (see www.mcc.gov). Unlike USAID, with its large staff of development experts and its global network of private consultants, the MCC would resemble a philanthropic foundation whose "lean" staff would be limited to considering and approving grant applications, known as development "compacts." Also unlike USAID, the MCC would be free of the political concerns or foreign policy interests closely associated with other aid programs. For their part, recipients of its aid would be left alone in proposing and carrying out approved projects such as modernizing farms, improving transportation networks, or expanding media coverage. By the end of 2014, the MCC had approved $10 billion in five-year "compacts" with twenty-nine developing nations.

Foreign policy makers in recent years have regarded global development as one of three "pillars" of U.S. foreign policy, alongside defense and diplomacy. They recognized that extreme poverty is not only a humanitarian problem, but also a potential security threat when terrorists prey on the desperation of starving populations, or when failed states such as Somalia and Libya lose control of their populations. Increasingly, the Pentagon has worked with USAID in providing relief to victims of natural disasters while USAID has delivered food and medicine to citizens caught in U.S. military interventions. Secretary of State Clinton (quoted in Epstein 2011, 4), an advocate for the "whole-of-government" approach, said, "What we will do is leverage the expertise of our diplomats and military on behalf of development, and vice versa. The three Ds (defense, diplomacy, development) must be mutually reinforcing."

■ ECONOMIC SANCTIONS AS A POLICY TOOL

Increasingly, the U.S. government attempts to resolves foreign policy conflicts by using **economic sanctions,** or material penalties imposed on target countries in the areas of trade, aid, investments, and financial holdings (see Zarate 2013). Presidents may impose sanctions by executive order, or sanctions may originate in congressional legislation. The United States, whose vast wealth and domestic markets make its sanctions especially costly, uses its economic leverage in these cases to force policy changes in foreign governments engaged in threatening or illegal actions. As of July 2015, the U.S. officials maintained twenty-six sanctions against such countries as Iran, Russia, Syria, and other nations (Masters 2015). The Treasury Department's Office of Foreign Assets Control (OFAC) also approves and enforces "targeted" sanctions against individuals rather than entire governments (see Rathbone, Jeydel, and Lentz 2014, 1058).[10]

To Treasury Secretary Jacob J. Lew (2014), financial sanctions have "opened up a new battlefield for the United States, one that enables us to go after those who wish

10. In June 2014, the U.S. government maintained an estimated 6,000 sanctions against individuals and political institutions (Lowrey 2014).

us harm without putting our troops in harm's way or using lethal force." In this sense, sanctions send a signal to their targets that the U.S. government is serious about the dispute in question (Peterson 2013). Sanctions play a strategic role when they are backed up by promises of military action in the event the sanctions do not produce the desired changes in behavior. Sanctions also serve a symbolic function by identifying the target state and establishing the moral supremacy of the "sanctioning community" (Addis 2003). Finally, sanctions may provide political benefits for those who impose them by serving as a "low cost way of displaying strong leadership during international conflicts" (Whang 2011, 787).

Forms and Functions of Sanctions

Economic sanctions, which may assume several forms, are often used by governments in various combinations (see Table 11.4). The most common types of sanctions are trade embargoes and boycotts, increases in export quotas, revocation of most-favored-nation status, and other measures that restrict bilateral trade. These measures are *negative* in nature, involving the "stick" of economic penalties. The United States also may employ the "carrot" of *positive* sanctions, such as increases in foreign aid or trade, to modify the behavior of other governments (Baldwin 1985, 40–44).

Economic sanctions vary in other ways as well. In some instances, the United States joins with other countries, intergovernmental organizations, or both to impose *multilateral* sanctions. This has been the case most recently with Iran, Russia, and Syria, among other targeted governments. Otherwise, the United States acts alone in imposing *unilateral* sanctions. Although other countries may act independently to impose their own sanctions against the offending state, there is no concerted effort to do so in these cases. Finally, sanctions may be imposed with very specific demands—that a country withdraw from a country it invaded recently, for example. Or the sanctions may be accompanied by broader demands, such as when the imposing state insists on a change in the policies, or even the leadership, of the offending state.

Prominent Cases of U.S. Sanctions

Given the growing interdependence of global finance, U.S. officials have relied more heavily on economic sanctions in recent years. Since the Cold War, the use of sanctions has preceded U.S. military actions against nations such as Iraq (2003) and Libya (2011).[11] In many other instances, such as in Pakistan, threats of sanctions have become a routine part of bilateral diplomacy. Among the prominent examples are the following:

Iran. Since the Iranian Revolution of 1979, the United States has imposed a wide variety of sanctions against the government and its people. Early sanctions focused

---

11. Other targets include, among others, Burma, Cuba, Iran, Libya, North Korea, Syria, Venezuela, Yemen, and Zimbabwe (U.S. Department of the Treasury 2015).

Table 11.4 ■ Types and Examples of U.S. Economic Sanctions

Type	Description	Historical Example
Boycott	Restriction on the import of another country's goods or services	Ban on diamond imports from Sierra Leone, used to finance domestic insurrection (2001)
Divestment	Withdrawal of assets from a foreign country; ban on future investments	Ban on investments from South Africa to penalize its apartheid policy of minority rule (1986)
Embargo	Refusal to provide one's own goods and services to a potential customer abroad	Grain embargo against the Soviet Union following its invasion of Afghanistan (1979)
Freezing assets	Impoundment of domestically held financial assets owned by the government or citizens of target country	Freezing of all Syrian assets held in U.S. banks (2012); targeted seizures of wealth among Russian elites after Crimea takeover (2014)
Suspending foreign aid	Refusal to honor previous commitments to provide economic or military assistance	Cutoffs of $70 million in foreign aid to the poor African nation of Mali after the violent overthrow of its president (2012)

on Iran's connection to terrorist groups such as *Hezbollah* in Lebanon. More recently, the sanctions resulted from Teheran's development of nuclear power and the related threat that this capability would lead to a nuclear weapon. Since 2002, the United States has joined most European governments, Japan, South Korea, and many other states in effectively paralyzing the Iranian economy, which is almost entirely dependent on its oil industry. A group of major powers—including the five permanent members of the UN Security Council along with Germany—began meeting in 2006 with Iranian leaders in order to resolve this escalating standoff. The "P5+1" negotiators finally came to an agreement that called for a suspension of Iran's nuclear weapons program in return for an easing of the multilateral sanctions (see Gordon and Sanger 2015). To President Obama, the agreement would encourage Iran to assume an active—and constructive—role in the international community. In September 2015, Obama received the necessary votes from Congress to approve the nuclear deal.

Russia. The international community was shocked early in 2014 when Russia's military overran the Crimean Peninsula and laid claim to the strategically vital province, which had been part of Ukraine. Other provocative actions by President Vladimir Putin led Western governments, including the United States and those in the European Union, to impose sanctions on Russia rather than attempt to resolve the dispute through military means. These sanctions were unique in their targeting of wealthy individuals close to the president rather than entire sectors of Russia's economy. To Obama and his partners, putting personal pressure on the Russian leader would force him to stop his aggression. Putin, meanwhile, retaliated by imposing his own sanctions on his adversaries, primarily by restricting shipments of heating oil to European states. He refused to budge even as Russia's economy suffered from falling economic output and stock values. Putin was also hampered by a worldwide plunge in oil prices, the primary source of Russia's exports.

Pakistan. The case of Pakistan reveals how far the U.S. will go to avoid alienating strategically vital governments (see Kux 1998). The United States supported Pakistan during and after the Cold War, showering its government with economic and military aid. Pakistan's detonation of a nuclear device in 1998, however, prompted the United States and other UN members to impose sanctions against both Pakistan and India, whose own nuclear weapons test had provoked the Pakistani response. The terrorist attacks of September 11, 2001, elevated Pakistan once again to the status of a U.S. "strategic partner"; the Bush administration lifted the sanctions shortly after the attacks. President Obama continued this practice despite his frustration with Pakistan over alleged harboring of terrorists and the 2011 discovery of Osama bin Laden in hiding close to Islamabad, the capital. Still, Pakistan has avoided U.S. economic sanctions and has instead received an average of $3.5 billion in U.S. economic and security assistance (Epstein and Kronstadt 2012, 20–21).

Cuba. Fidel Castro's rise to power in 1959 and his creation of a communist government in Cuba prompted sweeping economic sanctions by the United States. The Trading with the Enemy Act of 1963 prohibited nearly all trade with the Castro regime. The penalties for breaking these laws were substantial: up to ten years in prison, $1 million in corporate fines, and $250,000 in individual fines. The Helms-Burton Act, passed by Congress in March 1996, imposed even stronger penalties. The act targeted foreign countries benefiting economically from confiscated U.S. property in Cuba. The fifty-five years of stalemate suddenly ceased in 2014 when President Obama and Raul Castro, Cuba's leader, announced that they had restored full diplomatic relations. This political breakthrough, however, did not fully boost Cuba's struggling economy, which remained subject to most U.S. economic sanctions. The White House and Congress continued to demand that the island nation respect human rights before full economic relief would arrive.

Taken together, the track record of economic sanctions provides four important lessons about the utility of these measures:

- Sanctions rarely have the immediate impact their advocates desire. Examples include collapse of Cuba's communist government, for example, and Saddam Hussein's withdrawal from Kuwait in 1990. Sanctions, however, may weaken leaders in target countries, and the mere threat of sanctions often compels them to change their behavior (Drezner 2003). A key factor is whether the sanctioning country has the willpower to enforce sanctions that affect its own citizens negatively (Blanchard and Ripsman 2008).

- The leaders of targeted states rarely suffer directly from sanctions, which instead tend to victimize citizens with little political power (Peksen 2011). American sanctions against Myanmar in 2003, for example, produced sharply higher poverty rates (Rarick 2006). Even **smart sanctions**, designed to punish elites rather than their most vulnerable citizens, frequently have limited effects, as in the case of Russia's Putin's (Shishkin and Schectman 2014).

- Multilateral sanctions have a greater probability of succeeding than unilateral measures. When the United States acts alone, its targets can readily turn to other trading partners to fill the gap. Sanctions imposed by the United States against Iran, for instance, had little effect without similar sanctions from other countries. More success came after the European Union in July 2012 imposed its own boycott of Iranian oil, which reduced its daily exports from 2.5 million to about one million barrels (Katzman 2012).[12]

- A combination of "carrots" and "sticks" can encourage targeted governments to discontinue their bad behavior (Masters 2015). The United States, for example, successfully offered development aid to the government of Libya in 2000 if its leader, Muammar Qaddafi, would stop supporting terrorism. Early in 2014, the United States and European Union offered modest financial relief to Iran's government in return for its continuing negotiations with the P5+1 countries regarding its potential nuclear weapons breakout (Stanglin 2014).

■ CONCLUSION

As this chapter has shown, the U.S. government pursues commerce abroad with the same vigor it promotes economic development within its borders. American leaders have always looked forward to a world in which people and governments will be intimately connected to one another by the bonds of trade and foreign investments. They have envisioned the United States as a catalyst of global commerce by producing an abundance of goods for export while craving goods from abroad and stimulating foreign economies. This vision appeared to be realized with the victory of the United States in the Cold War and the triumph of capitalism over communism as the superior form of political economy.

---

12. While the widening sanctions left Iran virtually isolated, several holdouts—including China and Russia—helped sustain the nation's economy along with the defiance of its leaders for whom sanctions had long been "integrated within the regime's ideological narrative" (Takeyh and Maloney 2011, 1306).

Recent developments, however, place this economic superiority in doubt. The United States itself has suffered the downside of globalization as millions of manufacturing jobs have moved to foreign countries with lower wage rates. The nation's chronic trade deficits still being experienced today provide further evidence that globalization is a mixed blessing for the United States. Another cause for concern is the nation's budget deficit—a result, in part, of the security costs borne by the United States to keep the peace globally and to keep oil flowing to other industrialized countries. These problems were compounded by the financial crisis of 2008 that battered the U.S. and other major economies.

Meanwhile, growing challenges from overseas, however consistent with the transnational logic of capitalism, may ignite pressures at home to resurrect trade barriers in order to prevent further hemorrhaging of American jobs. Political leaders know their careers depend on economic growth that benefits a broad cross section of the U.S. population, not simply corporate leaders and stockholders. Despite the decline in union membership in the United States, from its high of 20 percent of the U.S. workforce in 1983 to 11.1 percent in 2014, "big labor" still provides a strong voice for economic nationalism (U.S. Department of Labor 2015). Avoiding a return to protectionism and trade wars requires effective restructuring of the U.S. economy and continued cooperation with trading states either alone or through multilateral pacts.

As globalization inevitably spreads, the U.S. government stands to lose the considerable leverage it enjoyed during its peak years of economic hegemony just after World War II. The nation must now contend with other states, as well as foreign-based corporations and rival financial systems, on a more equal footing. In short, the United States must come to grips with a globalized world economy of its own making. As in the past, the outcome of the ongoing struggle over U.S. foreign economic policy will be decided in the political arena.

11

KEY TERMS

balance of trade, p. 377

capitalism, p. 374

communism, p. 374

comparative advantage, p. 388

economic liberalism, p. 373

economic nationalism, p. 374

economic sanctions, p. 394

economic statecraft, p. 373

floating exchange rates, p. 385

foreign aid, p. 389

free trade agreements (FTAs), p. 389

Global South, p. 389

gold standard, p. 385

gross domestic product (GDP), p. 377

international political economy, p. 373

mercantilism, p. 374

Millennium Development Goals, p. 390

most-favored-nation trading status, p. 385

nontariff barriers, p. 388

political economy, p. 373

smart sanctions, p. 398

Smoot-Hawley Tariff Act, p. 388

socialism, p. 374

state capitalism, p. 375

trade promotion authority, p. 388

Washington consensus, p. 374

INTERNET REFERENCES

The **Economic Policy Institute** (EPI; www.epi.org) conducts research on global trade, globalization, NAFTA, and U.S.-China relations, as well as on other economic and budgetary policies. EPI's website presents statistics and policy reports on various research topics, including free trade, U.S. agricultural/commercial relations, and fast-track powers.

The **Peterson Institute for International Economics** (IIE; www.iie.com) is a nonprofit, nonpartisan research center that focuses on international economic policy. In addition to offering statistics and information on globalization, U.S. economic policy, debt, international trade, and international investment, IIE's website includes policy briefs, speeches, working papers, and links to relevant topics.

The **International Monetary Fund** (www.imf.org) is a 186-member international organization that seeks to ensure international monetary cooperation, financial stability, and temporary financial assistance to needy countries. IMF's website provides fact sheets on lending, country statistics, glossaries of financial terms, and links to other banks and international organizations.

The **International Trade Administration** (ITA; www.trade.gov) is a government agency committed to providing U.S. export and import data. ITA's website includes data on export growth and market expansion as well as on national and state trade levels, balances, sectors, and regions.

The home page of the **Office of the United States Trade Representative** (www.ustr.gov) offers links and access to bilateral and multilateral trade data and events. The information on NAFTA, the

WTO, and free trade negotiations in addition to speeches, testimony, trade legislation, and daily updates on international trade is particularly helpful for further research.

The **Organisation for Economic Co-operation and Development** (www.oecd.org) is an international organization of thirty-one member countries that share a commitment to democracy and free economic markets. Included on this website are data links on national wealth, foreign aid and investment, and development regimes.

The **U.S. Agency for International Development** (www.usaid.gov) provides information and statistics on U.S. foreign and military aid to other countries. USAID's website includes detailed information on humanitarian efforts and specific mission programs to other countries. Additional research topics covered are agriculture, democratization, global health, and humanitarian mission projects. A full database of U.S. foreign aid is available for all years of aid allocation.

The mission of the **World Bank** (www.worldbank.org) is to reduce poverty and economic disparities by providing loans and financial assistance to countries around the globe. The World Bank's website describes the bank's specific projects and missions and provides statistics on trade, aid, poverty, and other demographic issues.

The **World Health Organization** (WHO; www.who.int), based in Geneva, Switzerland, is a significant UN agency that seeks the "attainment by all peoples of the highest possible level of health." WHO's website offers links describing health issues in each member country as well as detailed summaries of health care topics and problems concerning all countries.

The **World Trade Organization** (www.wto.org) is an international organization that promotes open trade relations among countries. The WTO's website includes information on trade regulations, industry and business sector descriptions, currency and trade statistics, and annual growth reports.

CHAPTER 12

TRANSNATIONAL POLICY PROBLEMS

Paul Goldstein/Exodus/REX Shutterstock

A polar bear has difficulty navigating an ice floe in Spitsbergen, Norway, a region that has witnessed glaciers retreating at a rapid pace. This tragedy in the making is one of many ecological problems that will affect the global commons and U.S. foreign policy.

The United States manages foreign policies that extend beyond national defense and the pursuit of gains in the global economy. Transnational policy problems, which do not respect political boundaries and cannot be solved in isolation from other states, also confront U.S. leaders.[1] This chapter examines the U.S. government's response to four sets of transnational problems: (1) threats to the global commons, (2) illegal immigration, (3) weapons proliferation, and (4) restrictions on human rights and democratic freedoms. Although a matter of domestic governance, the fourth problem is also transnational because of the presumed link between the treatment of citizens at home and the promotion of national values abroad. The spread of democracy has always been a stated goal of U.S. leaders, who pursue political reforms overseas by a variety of means, including military force.

The United States has a mixed record in managing transnational problems. Although government officials rhetorically support cooperative problem solving in the four areas listed, domestic self-interests often stand in the way. This is particularly true when solutions require sacrifices by influential domestic groups or reelection-minded politicians. Throughout his presidency, George W. Bush viewed transnational civil society, including the UN and public interest groups such as Amnesty International, as a threat to U.S. sovereignty—an paradoxical twist given that the United States had played a catalytic role in the rise of these actors.

This detachment prevented Washington from using its vast resources to solve global problems, while giving smaller powers a ready excuse to neglect such problems themselves. Despite President Obama's efforts, domestic politics prevented him from making good on many of his pledges to the international community during his first term.

----

1. Globalization has expanded the scope of transnational law, connecting legal systems at a rapid pace. Justice Stephen Breyer discusses these issues in relation to the Supreme Court in *The Court in the World: American Law and the New Global Realities* (New York: Alfred A. Knopf, 2015).

Economic recovery at home preoccupied the president, along with national security problems associated with terrorism and the withdrawal of U.S. military forces from Iraq and Afghanistan. Although Obama embraced global governance and multilateral cooperation, his initiatives were stymied by nationalists in Congress and powerful interest groups. The president had greater success on environmental issues in his second term. Still, he could not overcome resistance from Congress on many other transnational issues.

■ MANAGING THE GLOBAL COMMONS

The **global commons** is the fragile ecosystem that sustains the earth's plant and animal life. That system is being threatened by the world's soaring population, the depletion of finite natural resources, rampant deforestation, and fouling of the air and water—all of which have forced countries to confront environmental decay as a major foreign policy issue. These problems are inherently transnational in scope in that pollution, as well as the loss of habitat and nonrenewable resources, ultimately affects the entire human population, not just a single nation.

As with other U.S. foreign policy issues, judgments about environmental protection can be viewed through the theoretical lenses of realism, liberalism, and constructivism. To realists, the lack of a world government compels political leaders to maximize their self-interests by refusing to make sacrifices on environmental policies. Those who embrace liberalism, meanwhile, argue that such sacrifices are morally justified on the basis of global rather than national self-interests. Finally, constructivists maintain that states' environmental policies are informed not only by hard science but also by the ideological and cultural perspectives of powerful lawmakers. Their decisions are "also shaped by context, as the science and politics of each environmental issue are different" (Bryner 2011, 43–44).

The rapid destruction of the Amazon rain forest provides both warnings and hope for the global commons. At one level, the Amazon case represents a classic **tragedy of the commons**, a situation in which a population stands to lose an essential common resource due to overuse unless limiting measures are taken by a governing authority. Covering more than 2 million square miles, the forest's rich vegetation plays a crucial role in absorbing the toxic gases that contribute to global warming. However, the immediate needs of Brazil and other impoverished South American countries have taken priority over the long-term needs of the global population. As a result, nearly a quarter of the rain forest has been cleared for development in the past several decades—mostly for farms but also for homes and commercial enterprises. Recognizing this "tragedy," since 2004, political and business leaders in the region have worked with UN agencies and hundreds of environmental groups to slow the rate of Amazon deforestation by 75 percent (Vaughan 2012).

The U.S. environmental protection movement was launched at the grassroots level in the 1960s and 1970s. Citizens demanded that the government give priority to regulating and enforcing environmental quality. Rapid industrial growth earlier in the century had left urban areas shrouded in smog and many waterways so contaminated that they could not sustain marine life. Congress responded by passing landmark legislation in the early 1970s, including the Clean Air Act and the Clean Water Act, that improved the quality of both public goods. The Environmental Protection Agency (EPA) also came into being during this period, as did similar state and local agencies.

Washington, however, has resisted global remedies to the tragedy of the global commons (see Leggett 2011). Many political leaders, particularly conservatives and foreign policy "realists," view multilateral pacts as threats to U.S. sovereignty and economic well-being. At the 1992 **Earth Summit** in Brazil, the largest gathering of heads of state in history, delegates singled out the United States as the primary obstacle to a healthier global environment. Subsequent U.S. actions merely fueled these charges. For example, the United States has opposed the Convention on Biological Diversity, whose chief mission is to promote "sustainable development" in poor countries. By 2015, nearly all the nations of the world had signed the conventions (Convention on Biological Diversity 2015). The United States, however, failed to ratify the convention due to domestic opposition from property rights activists and the American Sheep Industry Association.

Obama promised to reverse the U.S. government's antagonistic approach to environmental policy. His first months in office witnessed several achievements, including greater fuel efficiency requirements for cars and trucks, an explicit EPA recognition of the harmful effects of greenhouse gas emissions, and a prohibition of expanded oil drilling on public lands.[2] The House of Representatives, meanwhile, approved a

---

2. The U.S. Environmental Protection Agency (2009) found that "the current and projected concentrations of the six key well-mixed greenhouse gases . . . in the atmosphere threaten the public health and welfare of current and future generations."

"cap-and-trade" program for emission control similar to that established by the European Union.[3] This early momentum halted, however, as Obama struggled with the financial crisis and launched a reform of the U.S. health care system. Amid the ensuing surge of partisan strife—not a single Republican voted for the health reform legislation—Obama later turned to reforms in regulations and executive order to fulfill his environmental goals.

Population Growth and Family Planning

One of the most critical problems facing the global commons today is the world's burgeoning population, which during the past century more than tripled, reaching 7.3 billion in mid-2015. The population level is expected to increase to nearly 10 billion by 2050 before leveling off by the century's end. The population explosion raises questions about the world's **carrying capacity**—that is, the limits to which existing natural resources can meet the demands and withstand the strains imposed on them by human development (see J. E. Cohen 2003).

The most rapid rates of population growth are concentrated in the world's poorest regions (see Figure 12.1). These trends illustrate the effects of the **demographic transition** that societies experience as their birthrates fall and life expectancies rise during the process of industrialization. The reason for this transition is clear. Families in traditional (agricultural) nations rely on large families for their sustenance while adults in industrialized states tend to favor smaller families for professional reasons. The growing number of females in commercial and other workforces further reduces family sizes. In 2014, for example, population growth rates in the poorest countries stood at 2.4 percent in 2014 while those in the most affluent states had a growth rate of just 0.1 percent (Population Reference Bureau 2014). Fertility rates, or the average number of births per woman, were nearly three times as high in low-income countries (4.3) as in the most affluent countries (1.6).

The United Nations and other international organizations also recognize the links that connect population growth, living conditions, and long-term economic development. The first UN-sponsored global conference on family planning was held in 1974, and subsequent meetings in 1984 and 1994 placed the issue squarely in the context of development. Family planning and medical care for reproductive health are vital given that nearly 300,000 women die annually due to complications in pregnancies and childbirths (Henry J. Kaiser Family Foundation 2015). Hundreds of nonprofit nongovernmental organizations (NGOs) offer family-planning services in the developing world, focusing their efforts on the distribution of contraceptives and the education of women about their reproductive rights and options.

---

3. Under this program, nations establish a "cap" on carbon emissions, assign credits to major industrial sources of these emissions, and then allow heavy polluters to "trade" these credits with cleaner firms in order to stay within the national limits.

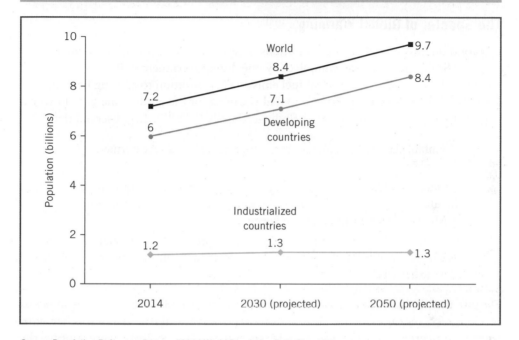

Figure 12.1 ■ Trends in Global Population Growth

Population (billions)

World
7.2
8.4
9.7

Developing
countries
6
7.1
8.4

Industrialized
countries
1.2
1.3
1.3

2014   2030 (projected)   2050 (projected)

Source: Population Reference Bureau, "2014 World Population Data Sheet," 7.

Americans generally agree about the merits of family planning, but the funding of programs that include abortion counseling and services continues to be highly controversial. Opposition to abortion in many segments of U.S. society has not subsided since the Supreme Court's *Roe v. Wade* decision in 1973, which ruled that abortion is constitutional in most cases. Since *Roe*, the opposition to abortion has been well represented in Congress and the White House, and it has emerged as a foreign policy issue as well.

The Reagan administration first took the offensive against abortion funding overseas at the 1984 UN International Conference on Population, held in Mexico City. Reagan's adoption of the **Mexico City policy** was significant because of the lead role played by the United States in providing family-planning funds in the Global South. The policy became a fixture of interest-group politics in the United States, with Republicans siding with religious and pro-life groups and Democrats drawing support from women's groups and civil libertarians. Since the Reagan years, Democratic presidents have rejected the policy by executive order—usually on the first day in office—while Republican presidents have adopted it.[4] President Obama

---

4. Obama also gained legislative approval for family-planning programs in many developing countries.

continued this pattern while also restoring funds for the UN Population Fund and supporting worldwide calls for universal access to reproductive health.[5]

The Specter of Global Warming

A second threat facing the global commons is the effects of air pollution on the world's climate. Scientific evidence compiled by the Intergovernmental Panel on Climate Change (IPCC) suggests that fossil fuel emissions, in addition to causing health problems and habitat loss, contribute to **global warming**, or the gradual increase in world surface temperatures. Among other findings, the IPCC (2007, 12) observed that

- Mountain glaciers and snow cover are "retreating" across the northern and southern hemispheres
- Sea levels are likely to increase by between seven and twenty-three inches by 2100, threatening crowded urban areas along shorelines, including American cities such as Miami, New Orleans, and San Diego
- Many parts of the world have experienced "more intense and longer droughts" in recent years, while others have suffered flood-producing rains and "intense cyclone activity"

Despite the doubts raised by global-warming skeptics, including many Republicans in Congress, recent evidence clearly supports a call for alarm. Among other worrisome indicators, from 1997 to 2014 every year except 2005 were among the hottest years on record, with 2014 being the hottest (see Table 12.1). If this unprecedented heat wave continues, global surface temperatures will increase by four to eight degrees over the next century and continue rising in the absence of reductions in heat-trapping greenhouse emissions. A study in the respected journal *Science* concluded that projections of steadily rising surface temperatures appear more accurate than those that project little or no change (Fasullo and Trenberth 2012).

Earlier signs of global warming prompted delegates at the 1992 Earth Summit to ratify the UN Framework Convention on Climate Change. The agreement, supported by the U.S. government, called on industrialized countries to voluntarily reduce their emissions of greenhouse gases.[6] These governments met again in Kyoto, Japan, in 1997 to strengthen the earlier agreement with legally binding standards and timetables for emission cutbacks. The **Kyoto Protocol**, signed by eighty-four

---

5. "Providing universal access to reproductive health care—including voluntary family planning—is one of the great human rights of the 21st century," wrote policy analyst Kathy Calvin (2014) of the Bill and Melinda Gates Foundation. "It is also one of the smartest investments we can make to create a more equitable and prosperous world."

6. These greenhouse gases include carbon dioxide, methane, nitrous oxide, hydrofluorocarbons, perfluorocarbons, and sulfur hexafluoride. The primary sources of these gases are gasoline-powered vehicles, coal-burning electric utilities, and large factories. The gases raise the earth's surface temperature by trapping the sun's heat and preventing it from returning to space, similar to the process that occurs in a greenhouse.

Table 12.1 ■ Hard Evidence of Global Warming? Fifteen Hottest Years on Record, 1880–2014

Rank	Year	Deviation from Norm (degrees Celsius)
1	2014	0.67
2	2010	0.66
3	2007	0.62
4–5	1998	0.61
	2002	0.61
6–7	2003	0.60
	2013	0.60
8–9	2006	0.59
	2009	0.59
10	2012	0.57
11	2011	0.55
12	2001	0.53
13	2004	0.51
14	2008	0.49
15	1997	0.45

Source: National Aeronautics and Space Administration, "Combined Land-Surface Air and Sea-Surface Water Temperature Anomalies," 2015.

governments in 1998 and 1999, required industrialized nations to reduce these emissions to 5 percent below their 1990 levels by 2012.

The United States signed the Kyoto Protocol in December 1998. Its support was crucial because, at the time, the United States was the leading source of greenhouse gases—a status now held by China (see Figure 12.2). The hopes of all countries for coming to grips with global warming thus hinged on U.S. actions. The treaty, however, faced strong opposition in Congress. Earlier, the Senate had passed, 95–0, a nonbinding resolution rejecting the Kyoto Protocol if it would harm the U.S. economy. Lawmakers also refused to ratify the agreement if it exempted major developing countries, including China and India, from the required cutbacks.[7] With these

7. These nations were allowed to waive the Kyoto restrictions for a limited time on the grounds that other economic powers, including the United States, had not faced such barriers during their periods of "dirty" industrialization.

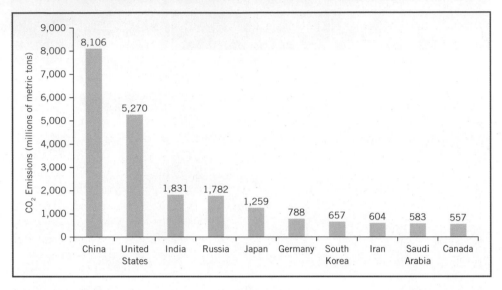

Figure 12.2 ■ Top Ten Sources of Carbon Dioxide Emissions, 2015

Source: U.S. Energy Information Administration, "International Energy Statistics: Total Carbon Dioxide Emissions from the Consumption of Energy (Million Metric Tons)," July 2015. http://www.eia.gov/cfapps/ipdbproject/IEDIndex3.cfm?tid=90&pid=44&aid=8.

exemptions written into the protocol, Clinton knew the treaty would be dead on arrival and did not submit it to the Senate.

As a presidential candidate, George W. Bush expressed concern about global warming and pledged to seek reductions in carbon dioxide (CO_2) emissions, which most scientific studies linked directly to global warming. However, Bush reversed his position in March 2001 when he announced that the U.S. government would not seek to reduce CO_2 emissions. The White House later declared the Kyoto Protocol to be so "fatally flawed" that the United States would no longer participate in climate change negotiations. The president restated the objections widely held in Congress, questioning the scientific evidence that included CO_2 among greenhouse gases and disputing the dire forecasts of climatologists.

Despite the U.S. government's withdrawal, the Kyoto Protocol gained new signatories and came into force in February 2005. Hopes that the United States would reverse its stance under Obama were already dashed by the time world leaders met at the Copenhagen climate summit in December 2009. Instead of strengthening the treaty, the leaders pledged to honor their existing commitments to the Kyoto Protocol and to further reduce their emissions of greenhouse gases voluntarily. The 2011 climate summit in Durban, South Africa, also produced little beyond complaints about the lack of U.S. leadership. By the end of 2015, the United States stood apart from the 192 other countries (plus the European Union) that had approved the protocol.

Obama's attempts to gain support for measures to curb global warming continued to fall on deaf ears. A strong U.S. role on global action required approval from Congress, which proved impossible while political gridlock stymied the federal government (Broder 2011). Sen. Jim Inhofe (R-OK), a prominent skeptic on the Senate Environment and Public Works Committee, triumphantly proclaimed in August 2012 that the "global warming movement has completely collapsed" (quoted in Hewitt 2012).

Although global warming is generally considered a long-term problem, it has already been linked to "changes in the frequency, intensity, spatial extent, duration, and timing of extreme weather and climate events" (IPCC 2012). This finding calls attention to climate change as a tangible by-product of global warming. Those looking for evidence of climate change in the United States have many examples to choose from, including Hurricane Katrina in 2005 and a 2011 drought in several Western states that sparked massive wildfires. The diminishing pool of climate-change skeptics was hard-pressed to dismiss the onslaught of "Superstorm Sandy" in October 2012. The hurricane, whose

Petty Officer Sukarno H. Reyes loads relief supplies onto helicopters in Aceh, Indonesia, where an earthquake battered more than 4,000 homes. This and other natural disasters have become commonplace in recent years, leaving millions of victims in their wake.

diameter spanned 1,800 miles, crippled dozens of heavily populated communities along the East Coast and, on its path inland, delivered a snowstorm that left much of West Virginia without power and produced gale-force winds as far west as Lake Michigan.

In place of legislation, Obama turned to regulation to slow the pace of global warming. In August 2012, he ordered the U.S. auto industry to raise average fuel efficiency to 54.5 miles per gallon by 2025. He also affirmed new EPA limits on CO_2 emissions from power plants—a move that led in 2015 to even more strict restrictions on coal-fired plants. In November 2014, Obama signed a bilateral agreement with China that required both governments to reduce their carbon emissions significantly by 2025 and 2030, respectively. Along with Chinese President Xi Jinping, Obama hoped that the agreement would prompt all governments to make the same commitment, a successor to the Kyoto Protocol, at a UN-sponsored global environmental summit held in 2015 (Davenport 2015).

Energy and the Environment

Concerns over global warming and climate change are linked closely to U.S. energy policy. Historically, Americans have enjoyed a steady and relatively inexpensive energy supply. While vast coal fields have powered electrical grids across the country, seemingly limitless petroleum deposits have satisfied the appetites of motorists (see Yergin 1991, 2011). Periodic oil shocks, however, along with every new sign of global warming and climate change, reveal gaps in U.S. "energy security" (Lovins 2012). Changing course on fossil fuels would be difficult for the U.S. government given the clout of oil companies, the auto industry, and other interest groups in Washington that benefit from the status quo.

Statistics reveal the towering presence of oil consumption in U.S. energy policy. Americans consumed nearly 19 million barrels of oil a day in 2014, about 21 percent of the global total (British Petroleum 2015, 9). The nation's seemingly insatiable appetite for oil has spread to newly industrialized countries with much larger populations, namely China and India. Although a growing share of U.S. oil comes from domestic sources, the reliance of U.S. allies on Middle East oil is well known and highly relevant to the global power balance (see Figure 12.3). The United States, which has attained energy self-sufficiency for reasons described below, has benefited from lower oil costs in recent years that have pleased consumers while harming the economies of nations hostile toward Washington, including Russia and Venezuela (Higgins 2014).

For more than a century, U.S. oil companies, in cooperation with government officials, have aggressively pursued access to these fields (Randall 2005). As noted in the previous chapter hazards of such dependence were first revealed in 1973, when the members of the Organization of the Petroleum Exporting Countries (OPEC) embargoed oil exports to the United States and other allies of Israel and then greatly increased the wholesale price of crude oil. The OPEC embargo, combined with fiscal problems

Figure 12.3 ■ Global Oil Reserves by Region, 2015 (percentage of total known global reserves)

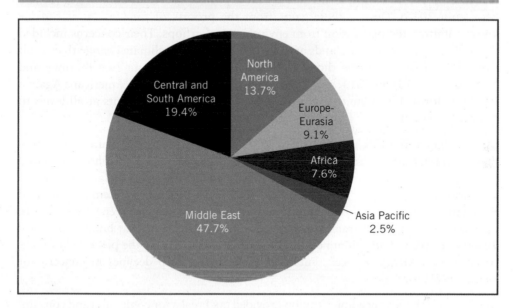

North
America
13.7%

Europe-
Eurasia
9.1%

Africa
7.6%

Asia Pacific
2.5%

Middle East
47.7%

Central and
South America
19.4%

Source: BP Statistical Review of World Energy, June 2015, "Oil Proved Reserves," 6.

in the United States linked to the war in Vietnam, plunged the U.S. and European economies into a prolonged economic recession. A second oil shock occurred in 1979–1980, when the revolution in Iran led to another disruption in OPEC supplies.

Although these oil shocks spurred efforts to improve energy conservation, the U.S. government and consumers later relaxed their conservation measures when oil prices began to fall. A decline in fuel prices during the 1980s prompted the Reagan administration to cut federal funding for conservation by 70 percent; federal support for the research on and development of new energy sources was cut by nearly two-thirds (Prestowitz 2003). The fuel efficiency of U.S. automobiles peaked at 26 miles per gallon (mpg) in 1987 but then fell to 24 mpg by 2002 (Joskow 2002). In 2009, Obama's executive order to raise fuel efficiency standards to 36 mpg made a reversal of this trend mandatory. The Environmental Protection Agency, meanwhile, raised emission standards for light trucks and family vans while monitoring steps by automakers to reach the mandatory 55 mpg average for cars by 2025 (Eilperin 2012).

The global energy picture changed dramatically during this period due to large-scale extraction in the United States of shale oil and natural gas from remote underground fields. Using new technologies, energy firms fractured underground rock beds in order to allow oil and gas deposits to flow to the surface. By 2015, the United States had surpassed Saudi Arabia as the world's largest source of oil. American energy firms also replaced Russia as the world's most prolific source of natural gas (British Petroleum 2015). Despite these gains from the process of *fracking*, as it became known, it attracted opposition from environmental groups. Their concerns included the fouling of pristine woodlands and the contributions to climate change that result from the release of carbon dioxide methane gasses into the air (see Brantley and Meyendorff 2013). In 2014, a coalition of environmental groups, Americans Against Fracking, formed in more than thirty states to pressure governments at all levels to outlaw the practice.

Under Obama, the U.S. government sought to harness renewable sources of energy that drew their power from rivers, the wind, and the sun. His effort, however, faced two obstacles. First, Obama's attempt to foster "green" technologies faced enormous institutional resistance as "everything about the modern electrical system is predicated on the use of fossil fuels: the coal mines and gas fields that produce them; the railroads, pipelines, and ships that transport them; and the power plants that burn them" (Ball 2012, 124). Second, the plummeting cost of gas and oil reduced the perceived urgency of renewable energy research. Public polls registered deep declines in concern for energy security.

Meanwhile, the Obama administration provided tax breaks for companies and consumers to exploit solar and wind power. This transition would not only reduce U.S. reliance on oil, but would also reduce the nation's cost of electricity.[8] This effort paid off in the case of solar power, whose use increased by 30 percent between 2013 and 2014 (Cusick 2015). Wind power also increased from 3.5 to 4.1 percent of the U.S. share of U.S. electricity generation (U.S. Energy Information Administration 2014). Finally, U.S. utilities continued to produce hydroelectric power, though at a level that remained static. Still, the United States today remains wedded to oil, gas, and coal for most of its power.

Another alternative source, nuclear power, provides about 20 percent of U.S. energy and represents the nation's largest source of electricity not drawn from fossil fuels (Moniz 2011). The construction of U.S. nuclear power plants halted, however, after two serious accidents at facilities in the United States (1979) and the former Soviet Union (1986). Heightened concerns over global warming sparked new interest in nuclear power until March 2011, when a massive tsunami and earthquake in Japan damaged the Fukushima nuclear plant. The partial meltdown of three reactors and subsequent releases of deadly radiation prompted some governments, including Germany's, to abandon nuclear energy altogether. The U.S. government sought only to bolster the security of its sixty-five nuclear plants still functioning.

---

8. Globally, the use of renewable energy sources soared from 76 million tons of oil equivalence to 283 million in 2014 (British Petroleum 2015, 38).

■ THE IMMIGRATION DEBATE

Americans have long relished the nation's rich history as a melting pot for immigrants seeking economic opportunities and greater political freedom. The rapid industrial expansion of the United States a century ago would have been impossible without millions of European immigrants. After World War II, Latin Americans became the largest group of immigrants, representing about one-half of the 40 million foreign-born U.S. citizens in 2010. Eleven million Asians also were part of this group, with smaller numbers coming from Europe, Africa, and other parts of the world.

For U.S. foreign policy, immigration is a classic **intermestic policy** that fuses international and domestic elements. Between 1970 and 2010, the number of immigrants in the United States soared from 10 million to more than 40 million. Whereas 5 percent of U.S. citizens came from other countries in 1970, that percentage grew to 13 percent by 2010 (Migration Policy Institute 2014). This rate of immigration is expected to grow to 78 million by 2060, raising the percentage of foreign-born citizens to nearly 20 percent (Colby and Ortman 2015, 2).

The United States, home to the largest share of the world's immigrants, faces a double-edged sword in its approach to immigration. To many observers, the system is "broken" because the U.S. government cannot exercise much control over the influx of workers. An estimated 11.3 million people, more than a quarter of the foreign-born citizens living in the United States in 2013, entered the country illegally (Krogstad and Passel 2015). Most of these undocumented aliens are migrant workers who toil for low wages on American farms or in factory and service jobs and then send, or "repatriate," their earnings home to their families. The size of their paychecks is paltry by American standards. Still, the funds sent to their families greatly exceed what the workers would have earned in their own communities.

Syrian refugees resort to desperate measures in order to protect themselves from the nation's long and brutal civil war. Their effort to find safety in Turkey was shared by more than 4 million other Syrians who fled their homes since 2011. In September 2015, this exodus led U.S. leaders to accept thousands of refugees from Syria.

AP Photo/Lefteris Pitarakis

POINT / COUNTERPOINT

Strains in the Melting Pot?

The soaring rates of U.S. immigration have become a major source of controversy among U.S. citizens, interest groups, and policy makers. The national debate over immigration is not likely to be resolved any time soon, especially as no consensus on this issue has emerged among legislators and White House policy makers.

Among concerns raised by critics of rapid immigration, the practice opens U.S. citizens to unknown dangers and social changes. "Open borders are particularly unwise because of the threat of global terrorism," observed Derrick Morgan and David Inserra of the Heritage Foundation. "Unlimited immigration is also a concern in a constitutional republic like the United States that is ultimately governed by the people." Regarding the terrorism issue, Texas governor Rick Perry claimed that "the government has a biblical responsibility to protect our people against those who come to America not to be a part of it, but to tear it apart." Finally, the conservative group American Principles in Action made it clear that illegal immigrants have broken the law. They should, therefore, not be rewarded with a special path to citizenship."

Advocates of open doors make several points. As author Darrell West wrote, "Many of America's greatest artists, scientists, inventors, educators, and entrepreneurs have come from abroad. Rather than suffering from the 'brain drain' of talented and educated individuals emigrating, the United States has benefited greatly over the years from the 'brain gain' of immigration. To stay competitive, the United States must institute more of an open-door policy to attract unique talents from other nations." According to Alex Nowrasteh of the CATO Institute, "the benefits of increased immigration are fiscally positive for the United States." Walter Ewing of the American Immigration Council argued that "the broken machinery of the U.S. immigration system continues to destroy lives and families while draining the federal budget and undermining the economy. But this cannot go on forever. The cost of doing nothing is too great."

Sources: Derrick Morgan and David Inserra of Heritage Foundation, "Administrative Amnesty: Unjust, Costly, and an Incentive for More Illegal Immigration," August 14, 2014; "Family Research Council Links 'Lawless' Immigration and Marriage Equality to ISIS," Frontiers Media, March 6, 2015; American Principles in Action, "5 Point Conservative Immigration Plan," May 19, 2015; CATO Policy Report, "Is Immigration Good for America?" September-October 2013; Darrell West, *Brain Gain: Rethinking U.S. Immigration Policy*, Brookings Institution Press, 2011; Walter Ewing, "The Cost of Doing Nothing," American Immigration Council, September 23, 2013.

Immigrants engage in a broader process of migration that has endured since the dawn of civilizations. In some cases, these migrations have occurred unexpectedly and tragically. According to the UN Refugee Agency (2015), nearly 60 million people were forced out of their homes and communities in 2014, a record unsurpassed in world history. Put another way, this total was "roughly the equivalent the entire

Table 12.2 ■ Top Ten Populations Granted U.S. Permanent Residence Status, 2013

Country of Origin	Number of Immigrants (to nearest thousand)
Mexico	135
China	72
India	68
Philippines	54
Dominican Republic	41
Cuba	32
Vietnam	27
South Korea	23
Colombia	21
Haiti	20

Source. Randall Monger and James Yankey, "U.S. Lawful Permanent Residents, 2013," U.S. Department of Homeland Security, Office of Immigration Statistics, 2014. http://www.dhs.gov/sites/default/files/publications/ois_lpr_fr_2013.pdf.

population of Italy being pushed out of their homes" (Graham 2015). In Syria alone, nearly 12 million people were displaced within or outside the country. These disruptions not only traumatized entire communities; they also created massive refugees camps in nations such as Turkey and Jordan that required funding from around the world. In September 2015, President Obama pledged to accept as least 10,000 Syrian refugees into the United States.

The focal point of the U.S. immigration controversy is Mexico, the birthplace of the largest number of foreign-born citizens in recent years (see Table 12.2). According to the Pew Hispanic Center (2012), more than 6 million Mexicans worked illegally in the United States in 2011, a total that represented nearly 60 percent of all undocumented aliens. These illegal Mexican workers greatly outnumbered those with "green cards," or work permits. Further aggravating U.S.-Mexico ties, it is widely understood that border cities such as Tijuana serve as major transit points for smuggling narcotics into the United States from Latin America. From the Mexican perspective, access to the U.S. labor market is an economic necessity, as migrant and seasonal workers send billions of dollars to their families in Mexico annually, an infusion of foreign capital surpassed only by that produced by the nation's oil industry.

In Congress, labor "nationalists" effectively gained control of U.S. immigration policy in the 1990s. The 1996 Illegal Immigration Reform and Immigrant Responsibility

Act gave the attorney general greater authority to fortify the U.S. border with Mexico. With the September 2001 terrorist attacks adding further urgency to the need for greater border control, Congress passed in 2005 the REAL ID Act, which authorized the attorney general to waive all legal impediments to securing the U.S. border from terrorists. President Bush deployed thousands of U.S. National Guard troops to support this effort, and thousands of armed private citizens, known as *Minutemen*, organized their own border patrols. Under the Secure Fence Act of 2006, the U.S. government would erect 700 miles of fencing along Mexico's border with California, Arizona, New Mexico, and Texas. The project, to cost an estimated $1.2 billion, included remote cameras and aerial drones to patrol the border. To Mexican president Felipe Calderón (quoted in Stout 2006), "Humanity made a huge mistake by building the Berlin Wall, and I believe the United States is committing a grave error in building the wall on our border."

For Obama, a "pluralist" on immigration policy, the nation would be better served by providing young undocumented residents an opportunity to gain legal status and possibly U.S. citizenship. The president supported the DREAM Act (an acronym for Development, Relief, and Education for Alien Minors), which was first introduced by Congress in 2001. The 2010 version of the bill, which had stalled in the legislature, would make citizenship possible for aliens who had come to the United States as children and had since demonstrated "good moral character," graduated from a U.S. high school, and spent at least two years in college or the military, among other requirements. Despite support from many Republicans, the DREAM Act still failed to gain approval in the U.S. Senate.

Obama responded in June 2012 with an executive order that stopped the deportation of young illegal immigrants who had established productive lives in the United States. The president (quoted in Cohen 2012) noted that since the children of illegal immigrants "study in our schools, play in our neighborhoods, befriend our kids, pledge allegiance to our flag, it makes no sense to expel talented young people who are, for all intents and purposes, Americans." In 2014, border agents confronted a sudden influx of more than 52,000 children from Central America who sought protection in the United States from violence in their homelands. This surge magnified the U.S. government's challenge in managing its southern border.

■ THE DANGERS OF WEAPONS PROLIFERATION

Another transnational problem facing all governments today is the proliferation of weapons, from small arms to weapons of mass destruction. The spread of these weapons, whose accuracy and destructive power increase each year, aggravates internal and regional power balances, while diverting scarce economic resources from productive uses. A more militarized world poses clear risks to the United States, a primary target of resentment among many foreign governments and terrorist groups.

Yet, the United States has sent mixed messages on this front, serving as both a vocal opponent and an enabler of global weapons proliferation.

The prospect of nuclear proliferation is a paramount global concern, and preventing rogue states and terrorist groups from gaining access to such weapons is a central goal of U.S. foreign policy. As described in Chapter 10, for most of the late twentieth century, the number of acknowledged nuclear powers stood at five: the United States, Great Britain, France, China, and the Soviet Union/Russia. As noted in Chapter 10, Israel's nuclear arsenal raised the membership of the nuclear club to six.[9] The group reached eight in 1998 when India and Pakistan conducted underground tests, and North Korea joined the club with similar tests in 2006 (see Sutcliffe 2006).

The United States supports multilateral efforts to prevent the spread of these weapons through the Nuclear Non-Proliferation Treaty (NPT), which by 2015 had been signed by the leaders of 191 countries.[10] Since the NPT was first signed in 1968, many would-be nuclear powers have later shunned these weapons (see Joyner 2011; S. Sagan 2011). These states include the major regional powers in South America and Africa, which feel more secure in nuclear-free zones. Yet U.S. leaders worry that Russia may sell nuclear material to the highest bidder on the black market or that China may export ballistic missile technology to state sponsors of terrorism. As detailed earlier, the fear of an Iranian bomb compelled major world powers in 2015 to reach an agreement to ease economic sanctions on Iran in return for its suspension of activities that could lead to a nuclear weapon.

As with environmental issues, arms control featured prominently in Obama's presidential campaign and early public statements from the White House. "The existence of nuclear weapons is the most dangerous legacy of the Cold War," he told a public audience in Prague in April 2009. "I state clearly and with conviction America's commitment to seek the peace and security of a world without nuclear weapons" (2009a). The president's *Nuclear Posture Review*, released in April 2010, proclaimed that "the United States will not use or threaten to use nuclear weapons against non-nuclear weapons states that are party to the Nuclear Non-Proliferation Treaty (NPT) and in compliance with their nuclear non-proliferation obligations" (U.S. Department of Defense 2010, 15). The "fundamental role" of nuclear weapons would be "to deter nuclear attack on the United States, our allies, and partners," a statement that seemed to rule out the use of nuclear weapons for tactical use, in small-scale conflicts, or against countries that used chemical or biological weapons but did not pose a direct threat to the United States.

---

9. Although U.S. officials have declared nuclear proliferation in North Korea and Iran to be unacceptable, they have tolerated Israel's nuclear arsenal. This double standard in U.S. nuclear policy angers Arab nations, which would be the likely targets of an Israeli nuclear attack.

10. The few holdouts included India, Israel, and Pakistan, along with North Korea, which withdrew from the treaty in 2003.

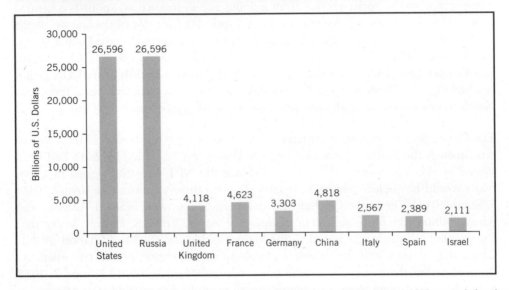

Figure 12.4 ■ Top Ten Global Arms Merchants, 2014 (value of worldwide arms agreements in billions of U.S. dollars)

Source: Stockholm International Peace Research Institute, "SIPRI Arms Transfers Database," 2015, www.sipri.org/databases/armstransfers.

While he expressed doubts that global nuclear disarmament would be achieved in his lifetime, Obama and his Russian counterparts agreed in March 2010 to further cuts in their strategic warheads. More frustrating for the president was his effort to gain the Senate's support of the Comprehensive Test Ban Treaty, whose defeat on Capitol Hill in 1999 had crippled Bill Clinton's nonproliferation efforts. A decade later, with Republicans voting in lockstep against most of Obama's policies, getting the sixty-seven votes needed to ratify the treaty was an impossible dream for the White House.

The U.S. government has also turned to global agreements to discourage the proliferation of chemical and biological weapons. The Chemical Weapons Convention, ratified by the Senate in 1997, prohibits the "development, production, acquisition, stockpiling, transfer, and use" of such weapons. By July 2015, 190 governments had made this pledge. The United States, along with more than 171 other governments, is also a signatory of the Biological Weapons Convention, which was ratified by Congress in 1975. The U.S. government's support for both measures has been controversial, however. Its own use of chemical and biological agents in Vietnam is often cited by critics, as are U.S. shipments in the 1980s of such agents to Saddam Hussein, who later used them against Iranian troops and his own Kurdish population (see Arms Control Association 2006).

The credibility of the United States has also been questioned in three other areas of weapons proliferation:

- *Arms sales.* As in other areas of military capacity, the United States maintains a dominant position in the global arms industry. In 2014, arms merchants posted sales of $85 billion worth of major weapons. Of that total, the United States ($27 billion) and China ($23 billion) accounted for nearly 60 percent of these exports (see Figure 12.4). All post–Cold War presidents have defended exports as a means of strengthening U.S. allies overseas and closing the U.S. trade deficit. Critics of arms sales argue that these transactions contribute to militarized violence within and between governments while opening black markets for terrorist groups such as the Islamic State that acquire weapons illegally.

- *Trafficking in small arms.* These are the weapons of choice in most military conflicts due to their relatively low costs and versatility. Global sales of these weapons have soared in recent years, exceeding $5 billion due largely to the widespread political violence in the Middle East (Small Arms Survey 2015). The United States has consistently exported the largest volumes of these weapons, which are often sold on the black market once they reach their destinations. American leaders, under pressure from domestic suppliers and the National Rifle Association, have resisted pressures to restrict the commercial sale of these convenient weapons.

- *Weapons in space.* In 1967, most governments signed the Outer Space Treaty urging them to use this new frontier for "peaceful purposes" (see Hu 2014). In 2006, however, the U.S. adopted a National Space Policy declaring that "Freedom of action in space is as important to the United States as air power and sea power. . . . The United States will oppose the development of new legal regimes or other restrictions that seek to prohibit or limit U.S. access to or use of space" (U.S. Office of Science and Technology Policy 2006, 1–2). Obama announced a new space policy in 2010 that called for a new global treaty banning weapons in space. Little has come of this initiative, however.

■ PROMOTING HUMAN RIGHTS AND DEMOCRACY

As detailed in Chapter 2, American leaders historically believed that the nation could not be secure as a democratic island in a sea of despotic regimes. The twin victories of the United States during the twentieth century, first against the fascist powers of World War II and then against Soviet communism in the Cold War, reinforced the consensus among U.S. foreign policy makers that repression at home leads to adventurism abroad. Since then, the "most consistent tradition in American foreign policy . . . has been the belief that the nation's security is best protected by the expansion of democracy worldwide" (T. Smith 1994, 9).

Map 12.1 ■ Freedom in the World, 2014

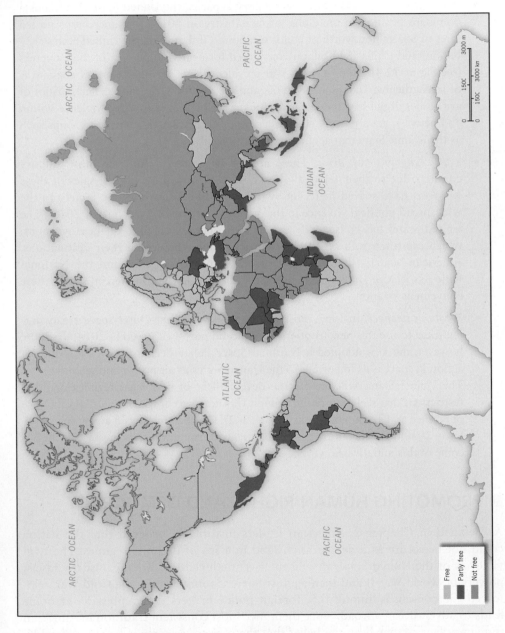

Free

Partly free

Not free

Source: "Freedom in the World, 2014: The Annual Survey of Political Rights and Civil Liberties," Freedom House (Washington, DC: Freedom House, 2014).

This formula for **democratization** received new validation with the terrorist attacks of September 2001—but with a significant twist. The attackers on that day were not agents of a foreign government but rather Islamic terrorists who harbored intense hostility toward the United States and Western society in general. Most of the al Qaeda terrorists were from Saudi Arabia, whose ruling monarchy had long excluded rival groups from power while maintaining cordial relations with the United States, the primary destination of its petroleum exports and the primary source of the royal family's extravagant wealth and corresponding military power (Yergin 1991). Thus the attacks on the United States were linked, however indirectly, to a dictatorial regime overseas.

Until recently, the number of democracies grew steadily in number and global influence. This progress, however, halted abruptly in 2005 and has fallen steadily since. According to Freedom House, whose index of political freedoms is watched closely by governments and human rights NGOs, the erosion of political freedoms from 2006 through 2014 was the steepest of its kind in nearly five decades. In 2014, just 40 percent of the world's population lived in "free" countries. Nearly three billion people lived in countries that were denied basic political and human rights. "In a year marked by an explosion of terrorist violence, autocrats' brutal tactics, and Russia's invasion and annexation of a neighboring country's territory, the state of freedom in 2014 worsened in nearly every part of the world," wrote analyst Arch Paddington (Freedom House 2015, 1). "Indeed, acceptance of democracy as the world's dominant form of government—and of an international system built on democratic ideals—is under greater threat than at any point in the last 25 years."

In response to threats posed by autocratic regimes and failed states in the developing world, U.S. foreign policy makers regularly support the promotion of democracy. But this is largely an act of enlightened self-interest, not of altruism. According to democratic peace theory, a more democratic world would be a more peaceful one (see M. W. Doyle 1986; Rasler and Thompson 2005). Governments that uphold political freedoms will escape the ravages of war with like-minded states and are likely to complement profitable trade relations.

Heightened concerns about human rights have spawned new efforts to punish governments for the most egregious crimes they commit against their citizens and those of other countries. Legal precedents for the International Criminal Court (ICC), which came into being in 2002, date back to the Nuremberg and Tokyo tribunals after World War II (see D. V. Jones 2002). In the mid-1990s, international support for such a court was revived when ad hoc tribunals were established for the former Yugoslavia and Rwanda, scenes of large-scale ethnic warfare that together left more than 1 million people dead, almost all civilians. Under a multilateral agreement approved in 1998, known as the **Rome Statute**, the ICC would consider only those cases that governments were unable or unwilling to handle on their own. The statute identified four categories of crimes that would be considered by the proposed ICC (see Schmitt and Richards 2000):

- *Genocide*, which includes mass attacks "with intent to destroy, in whole or part, a national ethnic, racial, or religious group";
- *Crimes against humanity*, a category that covers systematic violence against citizens, including murder, enslavement, torture, rape, and other inhumane acts;
- *War crimes*, or the use of indiscriminate violence against civilians in pursuit of military goals;
- *Unlawful acts of foreign aggression*, coercive actions that challenge the sovereign rights of other governments,

As of January 2015, 123 countries had ratified the Rome Statute and become active members of the court (International Criminal Court 2015a). As in the cases of other global agreements, the United States has been conspicuously absent from the ICC. American leaders, who once championed such a court, claimed it would violate U.S. sovereignty. Their opposition was rooted in fears that the nation's primacy inevitably creates resentments elsewhere (see Brooks and Wohlforth 2008, ch. 6). Specifically, the deployment of U.S. troops in military interventions, most with UN support, gives adversaries opportunities to target the United States with charges of war crimes and foreign aggression. Absent direct U.S. engagement, as of late 2015, the ICC was investigating twenty-two cases involving eight countries, all located in Africa.[11] In other war zones, such as Syria and Iraq with backers in Russia and the United States, respectively, the ICC had virtually no clout.

A Distinctive View of Human Rights

American political culture historically maintains a conception of human rights that differs from that adopted by most other countries. From the U.S. view, human rights apply primarily to the protection of *political* and *civil* rights, which focus on constraints on government power so citizens can enjoy their "inalienable rights to life, liberty, and the pursuit of happiness." The more widely accepted view of human rights is broader, encompassing *social* and *economic* rights as well as political freedoms. To advocates of this model, citizens cannot be truly free if many of them suffer from poverty and a lack of basic government services such as health care and education. This more inclusive perspective was written into the Universal Declaration of Human Rights, adopted by UN members in 1948. Its thirty articles include the political rights familiar to Americans, such as freedom of thought and assembly and the ownership of private property. The declaration also includes social and economic rights, including the right to equal pay for equal work, an "adequate" standard of living, assistance for child care, and sufficient opportunities for "rest and leisure."

---

11. These countries included the Central African Republic, Côte d'Ivoire, Democratic Republic of the Congo, Kenya, Libya, Mali, Sudan, and Uganda (International Criminal Court 2015b).

In the late 1970s, Congress began to raise the profile of human rights as a foreign policy priority. Among other things, it suspended foreign aid to countries that engaged in "gross violations" of human rights, it created an Office of Humanitarian Affairs, and it required the secretary of state to submit annual reports on the human rights behavior of all foreign governments. President Carter, with the Vietnam War fresh in his memory, identified human rights as a top foreign policy priority. "Because we are free we can never be indifferent to the fate of nations elsewhere," Carter declared in his 1977 inaugural address. "Our commitment to human rights must be absolute" (quoted in Schlesinger 1978, 514). But even Carter could not avoid double standards. His support for the despotic shah of Iran not only contradicted the president's moral standards but also led to the shah's overthrow in 1979 and replacement by an Islamic theocracy that remains hostile to the United States.

More recently, the U.S. government has been widely criticized for its treatment of war prisoners in Afghanistan and Iraq during President Bush's first term. To critics, these interrogations, many of which were conducted in "black sites" abroad, constituted war crimes. In April 2014, the United Nations Refugee Agency (2014) criticized the U.S. government on these grounds along with several other practices considered to be violations of human rights. Aside from domestic concerns such as the death penalty and gun violence, the UN's grievances regarding U.S. foreign policy included

- Targeted killings using aerial drones
- Racial profiling and surveillance of Muslims
- Continued detentions at Guantánamo Bay
- Mistreatment of immigrants in the United States
- Secret domestic surveillance by the NSA

Political theorist Andrew Moravcsik (2005) believes these gaps between U.S. principles and practices represent a "paradox of American exceptionalism" in which the U.S. government serves as the world's most outspoken champion of human rights while actively resisting legal restraints on its own power to uphold them. Stated more simply, the United States is "simultaneously a leader and an outlier" in the area of human rights (Ignatieff 2005, 2). This paradox has two primary sources. First, U.S. primacy encourages its leaders to take or leave global commitments to human rights and other issues—a luxury not available to weaker states that benefit more from multilateral ties. A second source of the paradox is the messianic nature of U.S. political culture, which traditionally views the United States as an exemplar of political and economic freedom whose model can be readily adopted in other nations.

The United States today remains caught between "two worlds" that cannot be reconciled (Forsythe 1995). The first world relates to the liberal tradition of U.S. moral exceptionalism and to the nation's self-image as an inspiring "city upon a hill." The second world corresponds to the bleak vision of realism that foresees endless conflicts among states and the primacy of national defense above other foreign policy goals, including the promotion of human rights. Moral appeals to human rights, which have contributed to democratic reforms in many countries, are as central to American political culture as its resort to the "law of the jungle." This dilemma cannot be overcome easily. The United States, a vocal advocate of global human rights, is widely seen overseas as a serial violator of its own values, producing an ongoing tension that contributes to the paradox of U.S. world power.

Prospects for "Exporting" Democracy

American leaders often feel compelled to impose "democracy by force" (von Hippel 2000). The 2003 U.S.-led invasion of Iraq was only the latest in a long U.S. project of **state building**, or the creation of the political institutions that facilitate the orderly and democratic conduct of governance (see Fukuyama 2004). A similar project, **nation building**, refers to the development of a harmonious civil society in which freedom flourishes. In both cases, most industrialized countries have pursued democratization as an important venture, particularly in aiding small and poor countries that do not have the resources needed to manage the task themselves.

The U.S. government does not merely proclaim the benefits of human rights, American style; it actively supports political reforms in other countries. This proactive effort, which has been a central element of U.S. foreign policy in recent decades, stands in contrast to the more passive approach favored earlier in the country's history, when the United States sought to inspire democratic revolutions by example. As Secretary of State John Quincy Adams declared about the United States in 1821: "Where the standard of freedom and independence has been unfurled, there will her heart, her benedictions and her prayers be. But she goes not abroad, in search of monsters to destroy. She is the well-wisher to the freedom and independence of all. She is the champion and vindicator only of her own" (quoted in Merrill and Paterson 2000, 167). More than a century later, President Franklin Roosevelt framed the growing U.S. involvement in World War II in the context of a global conflict between tyranny and democracy (see In Their Own Words box).

The U.S. occupations of the western portion of Germany and of Japan after World War II are still regarded as the most successful state-building enterprises to date. The United States built new governments virtually from scratch in these countries. Constitutions were written that separated powers; produced independent judiciaries; and protected the freedoms of speech, press, and religion. Foreign aid funds were then used to construct government buildings and to train civil servants, military and police officers, journalists, and trade unionists. The German and Japanese efforts became role models for subsequent state-building missions, although none would compare in the scope or significance of their outcomes.

The postwar hegemony of the United States later encouraged its leaders to pursue dozens of state-building missions. This effort took on a new urgency in the early

Franklin D. Roosevelt *American presidents have historically cast U.S. military interventions in the context of the nation's moral ideals. Franklin Roosevelt, while avoiding the sweeping rhetoric of Woodrow Wilson, told Congress in January 1941 that the United States would strive to ensure that "four freedoms" were protected by all governments after World War II. In seeking this support, the president made it clear that the United States would pursue outcomes in the war that extended beyond national self-interests.*

In the future days which we seek to make secure, we look forward to a world founded upon four essential human freedoms.

The first is freedom of speech and expression everywhere in the world.

The second is freedom of every person to worship God in his own way—everywhere in the world.

The third is freedom from want, which, translated into world terms, means economic understanding which will secure to every nation a healthy peacetime life for its inhabitants—everywhere in the world.

The fourth is freedom from fear, which, translated into world terms means a world-wide reduction of armaments to such a point and in such a thorough fashion that no nation will be in a position to commit an act of physical aggression against any neighbor—anywhere in the world. . . . Since the beginning of our American history we have been engaged in change, in a perpetual, peaceful revolution, a revolution which goes on steadily, quietly, adjusting itself to changing conditions without the concentration camp or the quicklime in the ditch. The world order which we seek is the cooperation of free countries, working together in a friendly, civilized society.

Source: Michael Nelson, ed., *Historic Documents on the Presidency, 1776–1989* (Washington, DC: Congressional Quarterly, 1989), 283–284.

1960s with the decolonization of Africa and growing concerns about poverty and potential communization in Latin America. President John Kennedy's Peace Corps, Alliance for Progress, and foreign aid programs supported U.S.-style political reforms alongside public health programs and economic development. The focus of U.S. foreign policy, however, soon shifted to Cold War concerns in Vietnam, which consumed most of the foreign aid budget. In the late 1970s, Jimmy Carter revived the State Department's democracy programs, and later the Reagan administration created the National Endowment for Democracy, a federally funded NGO designed to fund political reforms abroad, primarily in the developing world. After the Cold War, Bill Clinton sought to "enlarge the circle of nations that live under free institutions" as a central element of his grand strategy (Clinton quoted in Brinkley 1997, 119).

After the September 2001 terrorist attacks, President Bush launched his "freedom agenda" to further the spread of democratic rule. The U.S. takeover of Afghanistan, home to the al Qaeda terrorists who attacked the United States, had two objectives: capturing the terrorists and creating a new government based on democratic principles. As described earlier, the 2003 U.S. invasion of Iraq, first justified on security grounds, morphed into a quest to remake Iraq as a democratic state that would spark freedom throughout the Middle East. Subsequent failures in both countries raised serious questions in Washington about the future of exporting democracy.

For his part, President Obama promoted global democracy by declaring a "renewal" of U.S. moral leadership and by turning to diplomacy and "soft power" rather than military force to advance this effort. As did his predecessors, however, Obama made vital exceptions to his calls for political reform. The United States, for example, continued to embrace the government of Saudi Arabia, considered by Freedom House to be one of the world's most repressive states. Obama was also selective during the Arab Spring, assisting democratic transitions in Tunisia and Egypt while continuing to embrace autocratic rulers in Bahrain and Qatar that hosted U.S. military bases. Four lessons can be drawn from these U.S. attempts to export democracy:

- State-building efforts are unlikely to succeed without public support. President Clinton's efforts to "enlarge" global democracy occurred at a time when the public had little interest in foreign policy activism.

- Free and fair elections do not ensure that democratic leaders will come to power. Elections may instead produce an **illiberal democracy** in which elected leaders such as Russia's Vladimir Putin imprison political enemies, crush press freedoms, and generally ignore the rule of law.[12]

- Security concerns almost always override concerns about democratic governance in the allocation of foreign aid. The top recipients of U.S. foreign aid in recent years—Afghanistan, Iraq, and Pakistan—did not rule justly or protect basic political and human rights.

- External support is most helpful to governments that have already initiated their democratic transitions. In countries in which attempted transitions "are stagnating or slipping backward, democracy aid has few chances of reversing this trend" (Carothers 1999, 306).

This final lesson offers a crucial reminder that democracy must begin at home. Political leaders and their citizens must have a strong commitment to undertake these difficult transitions. Although aid for infrastructure and training in modern public administration can increase the chances that democratic reforms will succeed, no amount of outside support can transform a repressive state into a viable democracy.

---

12. This point was demonstrated further in 2006, when Palestinian voters in Gaza elected candidates from Hamas, a militant organization linked to terrorist attacks on Israel, to lead their legislature.

Central to this effort, the empowerment and tolerance of civil society must be in place. Attaining this degree of national unity and social engagement can take years, and sometimes decades, to achieve.

Threats to Democracy at Home

The September 2001 terrorist attacks caused a seismic shift in how Americans perceived threats to the nation. Among these changes was a greater willingness to grant the federal government more powers to combat terrorism within the nation's borders. In surveys, a majority of Americans consistently felt that government officials at all levels should have stronger powers to prevent a recurrence of terrorist attacks, even if the new measures encroached upon individual freedoms and civil rights. Reflecting this shift in the national mood, Congress quickly and overwhelmingly passed the USA PATRIOT Act in October 2001, which expanded federal powers of surveillance, detention, and search and seizure.[13]

Among the PATRIOT Act's most contested provisions was Section 215, which expanded the kinds of records the federal government can search when investigating suspected terrorists. Before the act, the FBI had to demonstrate probable cause when requesting search warrants against such suspects, and the domains of FBI searches were largely limited to hotels, airlines, storage lockers, and car rentals. The PATRIOT Act, however, expanded the list of searchable items to include "any tangible thing," such as financial statements, library records, travel receipts, telephone logs, medical information, and memberships in religious institutions. Under the act, rather than having to make the case for probable cause, FBI agents had to merely assert that the requested search would protect the United States against terrorism.

Despite being passed by huge margins in Congress, the act drew fire from civil libertarians. The American Civil Liberties Union (ACLU) sued the federal government, charging that many stipulations of the PATRIOT Act violated constitutional guarantees to privacy and equal protection under the law. "Congress and the Administration acted without any careful or systematic effort to determine whether weaknesses in our surveillance laws had contributed to the attacks," the ACLU (2010) argued. In May 2011, these and other criticisms did not stop Congress and President Obama from extending the act through 2015.

Such actions are not new to the U.S. security establishment. The Alien and Sedition Acts of 1798, passed by Congress in anticipation of a war with France, made it illegal

---

13. Considering its vast scope, the rapid passage of the PATRIOT Act was unprecedented. The act was introduced in the House of Representatives on October 23, 2001, and passed the next day by a 357–66 vote. On October 26, the Senate approved the bill without amendment by a 98–1 vote.

to "print, utter, or publish" criticism of government policies. During World War II, the U.S. government placed Japanese Americans in detention camps solely on the grounds of their heritage. Some two decades later, Richard Nixon's efforts to suppress criticism during the Vietnam War provoked Supreme Court intervention on behalf of press freedoms in the *Pentagon Papers* case (see Chapter 4).

Other U.S. responses to the September 11 attacks raised concerns about the government's adherence to the democratic values that distinguished the United States from despotic regimes and terrorist groups. As described in Chapter 8, the Bush and Obama administrations secretly permitted the National Security Agency (NSA) to eavesdrop on U.S. citizens' private information, including travels, telephone calls, e-mail and text messages, purchases, bank records, and the use of social media outlets such as Facebook and YouTube. The White House first justified this practice as being limited in scope: only suspected terrorists were being monitored. It later became known, however, that the NSA had amassed "metadata" on nearly all ordinary Americans.

The growing web of secrecy was reflected in the fact that nearly 5 million Americans, including public servants and private contractors, were given security clearances in 2011 (U.S. Office of the Director of National Intelligence 2012). More than 1 million held "top secret" security clearances. This select group included Edward Snowden, the NSA contractor whose press leaks of details regarding rampant domestic surveillance forced him to flee the United States and seek refuge in Russia (see Harding 2014). "Threats and alarms about terrorism gave the NSA room to expand domestic surveillance in the aftermath of 9/11," journalist James Risen (2014, 265) argued. "Now threats posed by cyberattacks have given the NSA maneuvering room once again."[14]

■ CONCLUSION

The United States has long been a catalyst for the two most vital forces in modern world politics: democratization and economic globalization. The first of these forces empowers citizens and civil societies, inviting them to serve as counterweights to the power of the state. The second of these forces provides the technological means for these private actors to connect with each other, both within their polities and increasingly across national borders. While enabling mass movements to gather momentum, globalization also encourages the dissemination of weaponry and techniques of political violence. Paradoxically, the greatest threat to continued U.S. primacy comes from the very political, social, and economic forces the United States inspired and actively supports.

---

14. Terrorist attacks against France in September 2015, committed by ISIS extremists, raised new demands for unlimited surveillance of American citizens.

Amid these changes in world politics, the United States maintains a system of governing institutions largely unchanged from the days of its founding. Here as well, the objective is to fragment and fracture state power in order to prevent tyranny. The diffusion of policy-making authority across a widening array of federal agencies, however, inhibits the government from advancing a coherent set of principles and priorities. This pattern is especially visible in the formulation and conduct of U.S. foreign policy, a domain that features multiple centers of decision making within the diplomatic, security, intelligence, and economic bureaucracies.

Meanwhile, little guidance on foreign policy can be expected from public opinion because many Americans not only pay little attention to world politics but also are the products of an educational system that has long neglected world history and geography. As described in Chapter 8, the most recent revolution in mass communications—including the tidal wave of Internet and social media outlets—has been accompanied by reduced coverage of, and interest in, world news. These trends reinforce the nation's political culture, which still exhibits a chronic ambivalence about the global roles and responsibilities of the United States. As in the nation's early years, Americans and their leaders alternately seek to free the nation from "foreign entanglements" and to transform that world in the nation's own image (Hook and Spanier 2016). A middle ground between the two, cooperating with other states on the basis of sovereign equality, seems to be ruled out by an ingrained sense of American exceptionalism, which leaves U.S. foreign policy caught "between virtue and power" (Kane 2008).

For now, no single foreign government or rival coalition appears capable of upending the current balance of world power and its defining feature, U.S. primacy. Aside from his bids for off-shore islands, China's Xi Jinping must come to grips with the downside of the nation's economic boom: overproduction, widespread pollution, rampant corruption, and, most of all, the rising democratic expectations of its increasingly "wired" population. Russia's government, largely isolated from other world powers, has become a "kleptocracy" led by Putin and oligarchs whose primary objective is amassing massive wealth at the expense of citizens. India and Japan also remain preoccupied with domestic concerns, and the European Union has been beset by economic failures in several member states, particularly Greece. In this environment, most middle powers continue to "bandwagon" rather than challenge the United States, reaping the material benefits of their alignments with Washington.

Managing U.S. world power in the future will be more difficult despite these many strengths. As noted in Chapter 1, U.S. intelligence agencies openly concede the shift in relative power that will make China the most productive nation the 2040s, with India not far behind. Even with its preponderance of power, Washington will need to prepare for, and accommodate, a more congested and turbulent world that is gradually more diffused in the exercise of global authority by state and non-state actors. Such a power shift, though likely to concern students and practitioners of U.S. foreign policy, may bolster rather than weaken America's world power.

It is often said that the United States cannot and should not "go it alone" in foreign affairs. The years ahead afford the American leaders the opportunity to follow this advice and encourage other governments to take a more active role in sharing the burdens of global governance. By following this course, policy makers would be honoring the public's clear preference for domestic prosperity and democratic freedoms as the clearest path toward sustained U.S. primacy.

America's success will ultimately depend on its management of a world order that is largely of its own making. The current interstate system is at once more closely interconnected and more disjointed than ever before. Such contradictions, integral elements of America's own political system and society, are intimately familiar to foreign policy makers. The ability of past leaders to embrace and reconcile these contradictory forces at home offers a hopeful lesson for the future navigation of U.S. foreign policy.

WANT A BETTER GRADE?

Get the tools you need to sharpen your study skills.
Access practice quizzes, eFlashcards, video, and multimedia at
edge.sagepub.com/hook5e.

 **SAGE edge**™ for CQ Press

KEY TERMS

carrying capacity, p. 406

climate change, p. 404

democratization, p. 421

demographic transition, p. 406

Earth Summit, p. 405

global commons, p. 404

global warming, p. 408

illiberal democracy, p. 428

intermestic policy, p. 415

Kyoto Protocol, p. 408

Mexico City policy, p. 407

nation building, p. 426

Rome Statute, p. 423

state building, p. 426

tragedy of
the commons, p. 405

INTERNET REFERENCES

The **Carnegie Council for Ethics in International Affairs** (http://www.carnegiecouncil.org) is an independent, nonpartisan organization that focuses on ethics, war and peace, global social justice, and religion in politics. The Carnegie Council produces, among its other publications, the journal *Ethics and International Affairs*, with many articles available online through the link to "publications" on its home page.

The **Carnegie Endowment for International Peace** (http://www.carnegieendowment.org) is a private, nonprofit, and nonpartisan organization with offices in Moscow, Beijing, Beirut, Brussels, and Washington, D.C. The endowment promotes international cooperation among nations and greater U.S. involvement in international affairs. The organization also addresses global change by examining international organizations, bilateral relations, and the various political-economic forces affecting change.

Europa (http://europa.eu), the portal to the main website for the European Union, offers information on the integration of European countries. It provides links to maps, to an online library of EU documents, and to institutions such as the European Parliament and the EU's central bank.

The **Foreign and International Law Library** (http://www.washlaw.edu/forint/), maintained by Washburn University School of Law Library, provides access to international and foreign law topics and journals as well as links to sites to facilitate further research.

Foreign Policy in Focus (FPIF; http://www.fpif.org) is a think tank allied with "progressive" interests that emphasizes citizen based foreign policy issues. FPIF researchers compose short policy briefs on U.S. foreign policy issues and global involvement such as trade, energy, environment, security, human rights, and labor. Much of their work is directed toward understanding the connection between private actors and the government.

Freedom House (https://www.freedomhouse.org) is an independent, nongovernmental research organization committed to promoting and understanding civil and political freedoms around the world. The organization conducts research at the national, regional, and global levels of analysis. Many of its publications, including *Freedom in the World*, which uses an ordinal scale to measure civil and political freedoms, are available on the Freedom House website.

The **Global Policy Forum** (https://www.globalpolicy.org) integrates information and research on globalization, security issues, and the United Nations. Resources on the website focus on UN and state accountability, issues of sovereignty, questions of empire, and the crisis in Iraq.

The **Globalization Website** (http://sociology.emory.edu/faculty/globalization/), maintained by Emory University, provides links to international organizations, NGOs, and other resources related to globalization such as data links, newsletters, quick reference guides, glossaries, and debates on international governance and globalization.

The **Institute for Global Communications** (http://www.igc.org) is a network for NGOs wishing to discuss, promote, and influence transnational policies. Subject areas on the website include human rights, peace promotion, environmental protection, women's rights, and workers' rights. These are found through the portals of four central networks: PeaceNet, AntiRacismNet, WomensNet, and EcoNet.

The list of **International Affairs Resources** (http://www.etown.edu/vl/research.html) from the World Wide Web Virtual Library provides links to think tanks, international organizations, and NGOs to facilitate research into matters pertaining to international law, global governance, human rights, peacekeeping operations, and international economic affairs. The site is organized by data, journal, and electronic resources, with full descriptions of each link.

The **United Nations** (http://www.un.org) is the largest intergovernmental organization in the world. The UN's website provides links to further information on its councils, bureaus, and governing resources. Data resources on member countries and missions are also included.

U.S. Public Interest Research Group (U.S. PIRG; http://www.uspirg.org), the federation of state Public Interest Research Groups, seeks to represent the interests of the American public on large-scale policy issues. U.S. PIRG focuses on the environment, energy, democratic governance, and health care among other issues. Research reviews and policy reports, as well as congressional and presidential "scorecards" on multiple issues, are available on the website.

U.S. ADMINISTRATIONS SINCE WORLD WAR II

President	Secretary of State	Secretary of Defense	National Security Adviser
Harry Truman 1945–1953	Edward Stettinius James Byrnes George Marshall Dean Acheson	James Forrestal Louis Johnson George Marshall Robert Lovett	
Dwight Eisenhower 1953–1961	John Dulles Christian Herter	Charles Wilson Neil McElroy Thomas Gates	Robert Cutler Dillon Anderson Robert Cutler Gordon Gray
John F. Kennedy 1961–1963	Dean Rusk	Robert McNamara	McGeorge Bundy
Lyndon Johnson 1963–1969	Dean Rusk	Robert McNamara Clark Clifford	McGeorge Bundy Walt Rostow
Richard Nixon 1969–1974	William Rogers Henry Kissinger	Melvin Laird Elliot Richardson James Schlesinger	Henry Kissinger
Gerald Ford 1974–1977	Henry Kissinger	James Schlesinger Donald Rumsfeld	Henry Kissinger Brent Scowcroft
Jimmy Carter 1977–1981	Cyrus Vance Edmund Muskie	Harold Brown	Zbigniew Brzezinski

(Continued)

(Continued)

President	Secretary of State	Secretary of Defense	National Security Adviser
Ronald Reagan 1981–1989	Alexander Haig George Shultz	Caspar Weinberger Frank Carlucci	Richard Allen William Clark Robert McFarlane John Poindexter Frank Carlucci Colin Powell
George H. W. Bush 1989–1993	James Baker Lawrence Eagleburger	Dick Cheney	Brent Scowcroft
Bill Clinton 1993–2001	Warren Christopher Madeleine Albright	Les Aspin William Perry William Cohen	Anthony Lake Samuel Berger
George W. Bush 2001–2009	Colin Powell Condoleezza Rice	Donald Rumsfeld Robert Gates	Condoleezza Rice Stephen Hadley
Barack Obama 2009–	Hillary Clinton John Kerry	Robert Gates Leon Panetta Chuck Hagel	James Jones Tom Donilon

THE WAR POWERS RESOLUTION OF 1973

■ JOINT RESOLUTION CONCERNING THE WAR POWERS OF CONGRESS AND THE PRESIDENT

Resolved by the Senate and House of Representatives of the United States of America in Congress assembled,

Short Title

SECTION 1. This joint resolution may be cited as the "War Powers Resolution."

Purpose and Policy

SEC. 2. (a) It is the purpose of this joint resolution to fulfill the intent of the framers of the Constitution of the United States and insure that the collective judgment of both the Congress and the President will apply to the introduction of the United States Armed Forces into hostilities, or into situations where imminent involvement in hostilities is clearly indicated by the circumstances, and to the continued use of such forces in hostilities or in such situations.

(b) Under article I, section 8, of the Constitution, it is specifically provided that the Congress shall have the power to make all laws necessary and proper for carrying into execution, not only its own powers but also all other powers vested by the Constitution in the Government of the United States, or in any department or officer thereof.

(c) The constitutional powers of the President as Commander-in-Chief to introduce United States Armed Forces into hostilities, or into situations where imminent involvement in hostilities is clearly indicated by the circumstances, are exercised only pursuant to (1) a declaration of war, (2) specific statutory authorization, or (3) a national emergency created by attack upon the United States, its territories or possessions, or its armed forces.

Consultation

SEC. 3. The President in every possible instance shall consult with Congress before introducing United States Armed Forces into hostilities or into situations where imminent involvement in hostilities is clearly indicated by the circumstances, and after every such introduction shall consult regularly with the Congress until United States Armed Forces are no longer engaged in hostilities or have been removed from such situations.

Reporting

SEC. 4. (a) In the absence of a declaration of war, in any case in which United States Armed Forces are introduced—

(1) into hostilities or into situations where imminent involvement in hostilities is clearly indicated by circumstances;

(2) into the territory, airspace or waters of a foreign nation, while equipped for combat, except for deployment which relate solely to supply, replacement, repair, or training of such forces; or

(3) in numbers which substantially enlarge United States Armed Forces equipped for combat already located in a foreign nation; the President shall submit within 48 hours to the Speaker of the House of Representatives and to the President pro tempore of the Senate a report, in writing, setting forth—

   (A) the circumstances necessitating the introduction of United States Armed Forces;

   (B) the constitutional and legislative authority under which such introduction took place; and

   (C) the estimated scope and duration of the hostilities or involvement.

(b) The President shall provide such other information as the Congress may request in the fulfillment of its constitutional responsibilities with respect to committing the Nation to war and to the use of United States Armed Forces abroad.

(c) Whenever United States Armed Forces are introduced into hostilities or into any situation described in subsection (a) of this section, the President shall, so long as such armed forces continue to be engaged in such hostilities or situation, report to the Congress periodically on the status of such hostilities or situation as well as on the scope and duration of such hostilities or situation, but in no event shall he report to the Congress less often than once every six months.

Congressional Action

SEC. 5. (a) Each report submitted pursuant to section 4 (a) (1) shall be transmitted to the Speaker of the House of Representatives and to the President pro tempore of the

Senate on the same calendar day. Each report so transmitted shall be referred to the Committee on Foreign Affairs of the House of Representatives and to the Committee on Foreign Relations of the Senate for appropriate action. If, when the report is transmitted, the Congress has adjourned sine die or has adjourned for any period in excess of three calendar days, the Speaker of the House of Representatives and the President pro tempore of the Senate, if they deem it advisable (or if petitioned by at least 30 percent of the membership of their respective Houses) shall jointly request the President to convene Congress in order that it may consider the report and take appropriate action pursuant to this section.

(b) Within sixty calendar days after a report is submitted or is required to be submitted pursuant to section 4 (a) (1), whichever is earlier, the President shall terminate any use of United States Armed Forces with respect to which such report was submitted (or required to be submitted), unless the Congress (1) has declared war or has enacted a specific authorization for such use of United States Armed Forces, (2) has extended by law such sixty-day period, or (3) is physically unable to meet as a result of an armed attack upon the United States. Such sixty-day period shall be extended for not more than an additional thirty days if the President determines and certifies to the Congress in writing that unavoidable military necessity respecting the safety of United States Armed Forces requires the continued use of such armed forces in the course of bringing about a prompt removal of such forces.

(c) Notwithstanding subsection (b), at any time that United States Armed Forces are engaged in hostilities outside the territory of the United States, its possessions and territories without a declaration of war or specific statutory authorization, such forces shall be removed by the president if the Congress so directs by concurrent resolution.

Congressional Priority Procedures for Joint Resolution or Bill

SEC. 6. (a) Any joint resolution or bill introduced pursuant to section 5(b) at least thirty calendar days before the expiration of the sixty-day period specified in such section shall be referred to the Committee on Foreign Affairs of the House of Representatives or the Committee on Foreign Relations of the Senate, as the case may be, and such committee shall report one such joint resolution or bill, together with its recommendations, not later than twenty-four calendar days before the expiration of the sixty-day period specified in such section, unless such House shall otherwise determine by the yeas and nays.

(b) Any joint resolution or bill so reported shall become the pending business of the House in question (in the case of the Senate the time for debate shall be equally divided between the proponents and the opponents), and shall be voted on within three calendar days thereafter, unless such House shall otherwise determine by yeas and nays.

(c) Such a joint resolution or bill passed by one House shall be referred to the committee of the other House named in subsection (a) and shall be reported out not later than fourteen calendar days before the expiration of the sixty-day period specified in section 5 (b). The joint resolution or bill so reported shall become the pending business of the House in question and shall be voted on within three calendar days after it has been reported, unless such House shall otherwise determine by yeas and nays.

(d) In the case of any disagreement between the two Houses of Congress with respect to a joint resolution or bill passed by both Houses, conferees shall be promptly appointed and the committee of conference shall make and file a report with respect to such resolution or bill not later than four calendar days before the expiration of the sixty-day period specified in section 5 (b). In the event the conferees are unable to agree within 48 hours, they shall report back to their respective Houses in disagreement. Notwithstanding any rule in either House concerning the printing of conference reports in the Record or concerning any delay in the consideration of such reports, such report shall be acted on by both Houses not later than the expiration of such sixty-day period.

Congressional Priority Procedures for Concurrent Resolution

SEC. 7 (a) Any concurrent resolution introduced pursuant to section 5 (c) shall be referred to the Committee on Foreign Affairs of the House of Representatives or the Committee on Foreign Relations of the Senate, as the case may be, and one such concurrent resolution shall be reported out by such committee together with its recommendations within fifteen calendar days, unless such House shall otherwise determine by the yeas and nays.

(b) Any concurrent resolution so reported shall become the pending business of the House in question (in the case of the Senate the time for debate shall be equally divided between the proponents and the opponents) and shall be voted on within three calendar days thereafter, unless such House shall otherwise determine by yeas and nays.

(c) Such a concurrent resolution passed by one House shall be referred to the committee of the other House named in subsection (a) and shall be reported out by such committee together with its recommendations within fifteen calendar days and shall thereupon become the pending business of such House and shall be voted upon within three calendar days, unless such House shall otherwise determine by yeas and nays.

(d) In the case of any disagreement between the two Houses of Congress with respect to a concurrent resolution passed by both Houses, conferees shall be promptly appointed and the committee of conference shall make and file a report with respect to such concurrent resolution within six calendar days after the legislation is referred to the committee of conference. Notwithstanding any rule in either House concerning the printing of conference reports in the Record or concerning any delay in the consideration of such reports, such report shall be acted on by both Houses not later than six calendar days after the conference report is filed. In the event the conferees are unable to agree within 48 hours, they shall report back to their respective Houses in disagreement.

Interpretation of Joint Resolution

SEC. 8. (a) Authority to introduce United States Armed Forces into hostilities or into situations of wherein involvement in hostilities is clearly indicated by the circumstances shall not be inferred—

(1) from any provision of law (whether or not in effect before the date of the enactment of this joint resolution), including any provision contained in any appropriation Act, unless such provision specifically authorizes the introduction of United States Armed Forces into hostilities or into such situations and states that it is intended to constitute specific statutory authorization within the meaning of this joint resolution; or

(2) from any treaty heretofore or hereafter ratified unless such treaty is implemented by legislation specifically authorizing the introduction of United States Armed Forces into hostilities or into such situations and stating that it is intended to constitute specific statutory authorization within the meaning of this joint resolution.

(b) Nothing in this joint resolution shall be construed to require any further specific statutory authorization to permit members of United States Armed Forces to participate jointly with members of the armed forces of one or more foreign countries in the headquarters operations of high-level military commands which were established prior to the date of enactment of this joint resolution and pursuant to the United Nations Charter or any treaty ratified by the United States prior to such date.

(c) For purposes of this joint resolution, the term introduction of United States Armed Forces includes the assignment of members of such armed forces to command, coordinate, participate in the movement of, or accompany the regular or irregular military forces of any foreign country or government when such military forces are engaged, or there exists an imminent threat that such forces will become engaged, in hostilities.

(d) Nothing in this joint resolution—

(1) is intended to alter the constitutional authority of the Congress or the President, or the provisions of existing treaties; or

(2) shall be construed as granting any authority to the President with respect to the introduction of United States Armed Forces into hostilities or into situations wherein involvement in hostilities is clearly indicated by the circumstances which authority he would not have had in the absence of this joint resolution.

Separability Clause

SEC. 9. If any provision of this joint resolution or the application thereof to any person or circumstance is held invalid, the remainder of the joint resolution and the application of such provision to any other person or circumstance shall not be affected thereby.

Effective Date

SEC. 10. This joint resolution shall take effect on the date of its enactment.

Source: Statutes at Large, 93rd Cong., 1st session, Nov. 7, 1973, 555–560.

advisory system: A closely knit network of trusted aides and confidants who have the most immediate impact on the president's foreign policy decisions.

aerial drone: A remote-controlled aircraft devised by the U.S. government to conduct surveillance and later to conduct airstrikes on enemy positions.

Almond-Lippmann consensus: A widespread negative view jointly articulated by Gabriel Almond and Walter Lippmann that U.S. public opinion is volatile, incoherent, and irrelevant to the policy-making process.

anarchy: The lack of a world government to regulate and restrain the behavior of countries, a condition emphasized by structural realists as the defining feature of world politics.

Arab Spring: Otherwise known as the "Arab Awakening," a period in 2011 when the citizens of several countries in North Africa and the Middle East mobilized in mass numbers to denounce, and in some cases remove, their repressive political leaders from power.

asymmetric warfare: A type of armed conflict between two sides of unequal strength characterized by the weaker side's exploiting the vulnerabilities of the stronger.

attentive public: The small segment of the U.S. general public that pays close attention to foreign policy issues but has little influence on the government's policy making.

balance of power: The distribution of resources and capabilities among nation-states. Also, in realist theory, a belief that global stability can be maintained when the strongest nation-states have roughly equal levels of power.

balance of trade: The relationship between the value of a state's imports and exports. A surplus indicates a higher level of exports, whereas a deficit indicates a higher level of imports.

bandwagon: A strategy by which less powerful states align diplomatically with a global or regional hegemon in exchange for security and economic benefits provided by the hegemon.

belief systems: Individual worldviews, formed early in life, that directly influence decision makers' foreign policy goals and strategies as well as their responses to specific problems.

bipolar: A power balance dominated by two states, most recently the United States and the Soviet Union.

blowback: Hostile actions against a powerful state that are motivated largely by perceived wrongdoings and mistreatment by the targeted state.

bounded rationality: A decision-making environment characterized by an influx of more information than can be managed effectively, leading to policy decisions that do not fully conform to standards of rationality.

Bretton Woods agreements: A series of agreements approved by the United States and other market economies in 1944 that led to the creation of the World Bank and the International Monetary Fund.

bully pulpit: A term coined by Theodore Roosevelt to describe a president's unique ability to shape public opinion by speaking out forcefully on important issues.

bureaucratic politics: A model of policy making that emphasizes inherent conflicts of interest among government agencies. The state is perceived as an arena of bureaucratic struggle rather than a "unitary actor."

Bush Doctrine: A set of foreign policy principles and strategies, including the possible launching of preventive wars, devised by President George W. Bush in the aftermath of the September 2001 terrorist attacks.

capitalism: A system of free enterprise that protects private property and commercial activity from government intervention.

carrying capacity: The physical limit of the earth's ecosystem to sustain human life, which is threatened by population growth, resource depletion, and environmental degradation.

Case-Zablocki Act: Congressional bill passed in 1972 requiring presidents to report all international agreements to Congress within sixty days of their entering into force.

causal beliefs: The perceptions that an individual decision maker holds regarding the most likely functional links among policy problems, their sources, and alternative solutions to solve them.

celebrity diplomacy: The involvement of famous actors, musicians, and other celebrities in foreign policy issues such as HIV/AIDS and the genocide in Darfur that raises public awareness of the issues and often spurs government action.

Church Committee: A select committee of the U.S. Senate created by Sen. Frank Church, D-ID, in 1975 to investigate a wide range of recent operations conducted by the CIA and other intelligence agencies, many of which were determined by the committee to be abuses of power. A series of intelligence reforms were enacted in response to these findings.

clientitis: State Department employees' overly close relationships with foreign governments and citizens that may cloud their judgment about U.S. global priorities.

climate change: "Changes in the frequency, intensity, spatial extent, duration, and timing of extreme weather and climate events" (IPCC 2012).

CNN effect: A pattern in which globalized news coverage of a crisis abroad prompts the U.S. government to take foreign policy action.

codetermination: A principle expressed in the U.S. Constitution calling for the sharing of foreign policy powers between the executive and legislative branches of government.

coercive diplomacy: The threat to use force to reverse an adversary's offensive action. Often used by stronger powers to achieve foreign policy goals without violence.

Cold War: The protracted conflict between the United States and the Soviet Union, and their respective allies, from World War II until 1991 that was labeled "Cold" because it never led to direct military combat between the nuclear superpowers.

collective security: A system of preventing interstate conflict in which world leaders renounce war as an instrument of statecraft and then pledge to defend each other in the case of aggression. A hallmark of the League of Nations.

collegial model: A management style that encourages open dialogue among presidential advisers in order to gain consensus.

communism: An economic system in which the state owns the primary means of production in order to ensure the equitable division of wealth among a nation's population, as in the case of the former Soviet Union.

comparative advantage: A global division of labor in which each country's producers contribute to the world economy in areas that draw on their unique strengths. According to Ricardian economics, such a division would lead to a prosperous global market economy.

competitive model: A management style that encourages open debate among advisers, often without regard to rank, allowing the president to

select the policy that is defended most persuasively.

congressional diplomacy: Efforts by the president to consult members of Congress at various stages of the foreign policy process. Seen as crucial to achieving White House goals in foreign policy.

constituent service: Legislators' attention to the needs of citizens in their states and districts as opposed to more general national concerns.

constructivism: A critical body of social and political thought that argues that public problems, including those related to foreign policy, do not have fixed or "objective" properties but rather are socially constructed, primarily through public discourse.

containment: The U.S. strategy devised by U.S. diplomat George Kennan at the start of the Cold War to prevent Soviet expansion. A midrange alternative to the extremes of U.S. withdrawal from global activism and direct military conflict with the Soviet Union.

cooperative internationalism: A form of active engagement in foreign policy that emphasizes diplomacy and multilateral collaboration rather than military confrontation.

corporate warriors: Private contractors engaged in the provision of military services, from cooking meals to interrogating prisoners, in theaters of armed conflict. Used increasingly by the United States and some other governments.

cosmopolitan groups: Nongovernmental organizations that seek to influence transnational problems in world politics, such as environmental decay and weapons proliferation, which affect people globally.

counterinsurgency: The ongoing effort by the United States and other governments to anticipate, resist, and destroy insurgent groups, as in the ongoing U.S. military efforts in Afghanistan and Pakistan.

counterintelligence: Efforts by intelligence agents to obstruct attempts by foreign agents to infiltrate

a country's political process or compromise its national interests.

counterterrorism: Efforts to fight terrorism through the use of timely intelligence, small commando units, and stepped-up measures of homeland security.

covert operations: Secret efforts by U.S. intelligence agencies to effect changes that are favorable to the United States within foreign governments.

Cuban missile crisis: A dangerous standoff between the United States and the Soviet Union in October 1962 sparked by Soviet shipments of nuclear missiles to Cuba. The crisis, which brought the superpowers as close as they ever came to nuclear war, was settled peacefully after two weeks of tense negotiations.

cyberwarfare: The contested ownership, possession, storage, and use of digital information.

delegate model: One of two models of political representation (the other is the trustee model). Holds that elected officials should act according to the general public's preferences on a given policy issue.

democratic deficit: The lack of legal requirements for openness and elected representation in many nongovernmental organizations.

democratic peace: A liberal theory holding that representative governments maintain peace with each other through joint efforts.

democratization: The process by which states adopt and implement democratic reforms. Also, a foreign government's promotion of democratic reforms in other states, often through the use of foreign aid or moral suasion.

demographic transition: The process by which societies experience falling rates of population growth and rising life expectancies as they undergo the transition from agricultural to industrial economies.

demographics: The characteristics (for example, ethnicity, religion, age, and wealth) of a given population that are known to affect opinions on foreign policy and other matters.

détente: A policy devised by Henry Kissinger, national security adviser and secretary of state under Presidents Richard Nixon and Gerald Ford, to ease tensions between the United States and the Soviet Union.

digital diplomacy: Increased contact among governments made possible by advances in telecommunications technology.

diplomacy: Negotiations among representatives of two or more sovereign states involving official matters of mutual or collective concern.

diversionary theory of war: A possible cause of war in which political leaders provoke armed conflicts to divert public attention from domestic problems or to boost their public approval ratings.

divine divide: The consistently reported differences in public opinion between religiously devout Americans and others. This gap was reflected during the Iraq War, whose greatest source of public support came from evangelical Christians.

domestic terrorism: Acts of terrorism in which the perpetrators and their targets are located within the same nation-state.

Earth Summit: A major UN-sponsored environmental conference held in 1992 in Brazil that identified "sustainable development" as a central objective in the post–Cold War era.

economic liberalism: A political-economic system that protects private property and commercial activity from government intervention. Identified with Adam Smith, an Enlightenment theorist.

economic sanctions: Material penalties involving trade, aid, foreign investments, or other aspects of economic relations that states or intergovernmental organizations impose on foreign countries to force adherence to political demands.

economic statecraft: The use by national governments of a variety of economic tools, including trade, foreign aid, and sanctions, to advance their foreign policy goals.

elitism: A challenge to pluralist theory that argues that political power even in democratic systems is highly concentrated among a few government leaders and the wealthiest citizens.

embeds: Reporters "embedded" with U.S. military troops during the 2003 invasion of Iraq to provide firsthand accounts in a practice accurately anticipated by government leaders to produce more favorable media coverage.

empire: A form of domination by a world power that includes direct control over the domestic and foreign policies of other political entities.

exceptionalism: A widely held sense of national distinctiveness or superiority, exemplified by Americans' traditional view of their nation as a "city upon a hill."

executive agreements: Formal agreements negotiated by the executive branch with foreign governments that do not require Senate ratification. Often serve as an alternative to treaties.

external balancing: The formation of military alliances and other tactics that allow relatively weak states to counter the ambitions and influence of a dominant power.

failed states: National governments that are incapable of maintaining order or providing even minimal services to their citizens.

flexible response: A security strategy adopted by the U.S. government during the Cold War that allowed for a range of military actions—nuclear and conventional—in response to offensive threats posed to the United States and its allies.

floating exchange rates: A system in which the value of a country's currency is determined by market forces and based largely on the relative value of other currencies rather than by government intervention.

foreign aid: Economic resources provided by affluent governments to developing countries on terms unavailable to the recipients through commercial markets. May take the form of development or security assistance.

foreign policy elite: The small segment (less than 5 percent) of the U.S. population that has both the interest and the means to influence U.S. foreign policy.

foreign policy entrepreneurs: Members of Congress who adopt U.S. foreign policy as a major concern and take individual actions to advance their policy agendas.

foreign service officers: Permanent State Department officials who work in overseas embassies and consulates on routine matters such as handling visas, hosting delegations, and advancing U.S. foreign policy priorities in their "host" countries.

formalistic model: A presidential management style characterized as orderly and hierarchical, featuring the structured discussion of issues following well-defined procedures, roles, and communication channels.

framing: Government attempts to simplify and represent foreign policy problems so that they are understood by citizens in ways that favor the government's position. Generally supported and perpetuated by news organizations.

free trade agreements (FTAs): Bilateral trade pacts between the United States and foreign governments that provide for preferential terms of trade on a mutual basis while not restricting trade practices toward other governments.

gender gap: The consistently reported differences between men and women in public opinion regarding U.S. foreign policy, with women found to be more supportive of diplomacy and other nonmilitary approaches to conflict resolution.

geoeconomics: The interaction of national economies in the world economy. Also, the global production and distribution of economic output as a national priority.

geopolitics: The impact of geographical factors on the distribution of global power and the foreign policies of states.

global commons: The earth's fragile ecosystem that sustains animal and plant life. Generally includes physical resources shared by all inhabitants.

global governance: Combines traditional state-to-state diplomacy with policy collaboration among private groups and intergovernmental organizations.

Global South: An informal designation for developing countries in the Southern Hemisphere and South Asia that house most of the world's population while also suffering the most from extreme poverty.

global warming: The rising average temperatures on the earth's surface produced by population growth, industrialization, and the resulting fossil fuel emissions.

globalization: The melding of national and regional markets into a single world market with limited political barriers to commerce.

gold standard: A system of "fixed" exchange rates in which the values of national currencies are based on the value of gold. An alternative to the "floating" exchange rates that currently set currency values.

Goldwater-Nichols Act: Legislative measure approved in 1986 that altered the balance of power within the Pentagon by strengthening the power of the chair of the Joint Chiefs of Staff and increasing the power of regional commanders in chief who manage forces across the armed services.

grand strategy: A statement of a nation's essential objectives in world politics and the means to achieve those objectives.

gross domestic product (GDP): A key measure of a nation's wealth, the sum total of goods and services produced in that nation during a given year.

group identity: The tendency of individual citizens to adopt opinions regarding U.S. foreign policy and other issues that reflect their affiliation with larger groups such as churches, professional associations, and public interest groups.

groupthink: Dysfunctional collective decision making characterized by a strong sense of a group's moral righteousness, closed-mindedness, and pressures toward conformity.

Gulf of Tonkin Resolution: Resolution approved by Congress in 1964 authorizing President Lyndon Johnson to "take all necessary measures" to protect U.S. forces supporting the government of South Vietnam.

gunboat diplomacy: The use of deployed military forces as a means of political intimidation in order to achieve a nation's foreign policy preferences without resorting to violence.

guns-or-butter debates: Ongoing policy disputes about federal spending for defense versus social programs and domestic needs.

habeas corpus: A centuries-old legal principle that prisoners must be able to challenge the lawfulness of their arrests before an independent court.

hegemon: One nation-state that exerts a controlling influence over other countries and societies that falls short of formal political authority.

human intelligence (HUMINT): Information gained by intelligence agencies from foreign informants working undercover.

hyperpluralism: A potential problem for democratic governance in which organized interest groups become sufficiently influential to weaken the power of the state to adopt policies that serve the common good.

idea brokers: Nongovernmental actors in policy debates who attempt to influence public opinion and government action through disseminating research findings and airing opinions on a variety of issues.

ideological factors: Aspects of policy makers' worldviews that influence their foreign policy decisions.

illiberal democracy: A form of government in which an elected governmental regime adopts policies that repress political freedoms and human rights.

image intelligence (IMINT): Information gathered by the CIA and other U.S. intelligence agencies that provides imagery of buildings, troop deployments, potential military targets, and other items that are of interest to the United States.

imperial overstretch: A pattern noted by historian Paul Kennedy in which great powers have consistently expanded their foreign commitments beyond their ability to remain economically solvent and militarily secure.

imperial presidency: A critique of the U.S. political system advanced in the 1970s by historian Arthur M. Schlesinger Jr., who described the president as governing virtually "by decree."

influence operations: Efforts by U.S. military, diplomatic, and intelligence agencies to shape public opinion in foreign countries in a way that enhances their governments' and citizens' support for the United States.

infotainment: The common result of "soft news" that blends information regarding public affairs, including U.S. foreign policy, and media content designed to entertain an audience, as in *The Daily Show* with Jon Stewart.

intelligence cycle: The five-stage intelligence process, moving from planning and direction to collection, processing, analysis, and, finally, dissemination to policy makers.

intelligence gap: The stark contrast between the openness of democracies such as the United States and repressive societies such as North Korea, a gap that makes democracies more vulnerable to penetration by foreign intelligence services.

Intelligence Oversight Act of 1980: Legislative measure empowering House and Senate committees to oversee U.S. intelligence activities and requiring presidents to notify Congress about covert operations in foreign countries.

interdependence: In contrast to anarchy, a model of world politics devised by liberal theorists based on mutual reliance among states and their need to cooperate in solving shared problems.

intermestic policy: A policy that merges international and domestic concerns, such as trade and environment policies.

internal balancing: The strengthening of military forces and other domestic measures used by relatively weak states to counter the ambitions and influence of a dominant power.

international political economy: The domain of political economy in which governments seek to manage economic activity beyond their borders in ways that advance their policy goals and principles.

international trust: A perception among some political leaders that other governments customarily behave in accordance with commonly accepted rules, norms, and laws of world politics.

iron curtain: A term coined by British prime minister Winston Churchill in 1946 to describe the metaphorical line separating communist countries under Soviet control from the capitalist countries of Western Europe supported by the United States. Remained intact throughout the Cold War.

iron triangle: The alliance of influential interest groups, congressional committees, and corresponding executive branch agencies to carry out policies of mutual concern to the exclusion of other policy actors or outside interests.

issue networks: A model of decision making that involves more actors and is more open to competing viewpoints than the iron triangle model. Brings together interested governmental and private actors with shared expertise in a given area of public policy.

Jackson-Vanik Amendment: A legislative measure approved in 1974 that prevented presidents from granting most-favored-nation trade status to foreign countries that restricted the emigration of their citizens.

jihadists: Militants determined to create a "pure" Islamic society by force.

judicial noninterference: The judicial branch's reluctance to intervene in conflicts between the executive and legislative branches due to its traditional view of these interbranch conflicts as "political" in nature.

just-war doctrine: A code of conduct originating in the Middle Ages that establishes moral and ethical standards for the use of military force.

Kellogg-Briand Pact: A 1928 agreement among fifteen countries, including the United States, that condemned "recourse to war for the solution of international controversies [and] as an instrument of national policy."

Kyoto Protocol: An intergovernmental agreement approved in 1997 that called on signatories to reduce the greenhouse gas emissions linked to global warming. Not approved by the United States.

lend-lease program: A program devised by the United States during World War II to provide military assets to Great Britain in exchange for U.S. access to British military bases.

levels of analysis: The systemic, societal, governmental, and individual factors that shape foreign policy decisions and outcomes.

liberal internationalism: A key aspect of President Jimmy Carter's foreign policy that called for U.S. global involvement consistent with the country's moral principles and political ideals.

living-room war: A term that originated during the Vietnam War to describe a U.S. military conflict brought to American homes graphically and daily through extensive television coverage.

lobbying: A tactic, commonly employed by interest groups, of appealing directly to government officials for support of policy preferences.

logrolling: The practice of "trading" legislative votes in which a member of Congress supports one measure with the expectation of garnering support from other legislators for a separate measure.

long cycle theory: A view of world history that highlights recurring periods of dominance of imperial or hegemonic powers.

management style: The working relationship a president establishes with and among his subordinates that reflects the president's worldview and personality.

manifest destiny: A belief popular in the early history of the United States that the nation had God's blessing to expand and assume political control of a wider population.

Marshall Plan: Named after President Harry Truman's secretary of state, George Marshall, a U.S. foreign policy initiative approved in 1947 that provided U.S. allies with economic aid to hasten their recovery after World War II.

mass public: The large segment of the U.S. population that is neither well informed nor strongly interested in most foreign policy issues and thus has little direct impact on the policy process.

massive retaliation: A security strategy based on the promise of the nuclear annihilation of the sponsor of an attack on the vital interests of the state that adopts the strategy.

mercantilism: An economic model whose primary aim is to enhance the wealth of national firms and the government, often at the expense of foreign competitors, rival states, and a market-driven global economy.

Mexico City policy: A policy first approved by the Reagan administration prohibiting U.S. economic assistance to foreign family-planning agencies that offer abortion counseling or services.

militant internationalism: A form of activism in foreign policy that emphasizes coercive measures, including the use of force, over diplomacy and other peaceful means of statecraft.

military-industrial complex: An alignment of U.S. defense and private economic interests identified by President Dwight Eisenhower in 1961 as a potential threat to the nation's democracy and security.

Millennium Development Goals: A set of objectives adopted in 2000 by all 191 UN member states to reduce global poverty and improve living conditions in the poorest states.

mission creep: The tendency of armed forces in limited military deployments to take on new tasks and open-ended commitments.

Monroe Doctrine: Proclamation by President James Monroe in 1823 that politically separated the United States from Europe and declared future colonization in the Western Hemisphere a threat to U.S. national security.

most-favored-nation trading status: The provision of equal market access and terms of trade to all states participating in the General Agreement on Tariffs and Trade (GATT) system.

multinational corporations (MNCs): Profit-seeking firms with operations, subsidiaries, and markets in more than one country. The largest and arguably most politically powerful type of nongovernmental organization.

multiple advocacy: A formal decision-making structure in which participants with differing viewpoints articulate and defend their positions openly as a means to ensure that the merits and weaknesses of all policy options are considered.

multipolar: A world order dominated by several states.

mutual assured destruction (MAD): A nuclear stalemate that occurs when two nuclear-equipped adversaries credibly promise massive retaliation against each other in the event of an attack.

nation building: The process by which an external government, intergovernmental organization, or nongovernmental organization attempts to create the conditions necessary for a nation to gain internal cohesion and solidarity.

national interest: A self-justifying rationale for foreign policy actions that presumes an inherent "interest" maintained by the state that overrides the parochial interests of government bureaucracies or societal groups.

national security: The freedom a nation-state enjoys from threats to its sovereignty, territory, and political autonomy.

national security adviser: Technically known as the special assistant for national security affairs. A top aide who advises the president on a regular basis and coordinates the input of other foreign policy advisers.

national style: The expression of cultural influences that have historically shaped a country's identity and approach to international relations.

Nelson-Bingham Amendment: A legislative measure approved in 1974 authorizing Congress to review foreign arms sales of more than $25 million and to reject such sales through a concurrent resolution of both chambers.

neorealism: A variant of realist theory focusing on the anarchic nature of the international system as the ultimate and inevitable cause of interstate conflicts.

New Look: President Dwight Eisenhower's shift in security strategy that enlarged the role of nuclear weapons and created new military alliances to contain the Soviet Union and China.

new world order: President George H. W. Bush's characterization of the emerging post–Cold War international system, emphasizing democratization, economic globalization, and multilateral cooperation.

nontariff barriers: An array of trade measures, including industrial subsidies and favorable regulations, which heighten a country's competitive advantages in world markets while ostensibly respecting the rules of "free trade."

nuclear deterrence: The prevention of hostilities through the threat of using nuclear weapons.

Obama Doctrine: A security strategy adopted by the president combining military restraint in undertaking military interventions, greater support from allies, heightened intelligence, covert operations by Special Forces, and air strikes against enemies.

Open Door policy: A policy adopted by the U.S. government in 1899 that called for free trade access to China and discouraged other trading states from dividing China into spheres of influence.

Operation Desert Storm: The name of the 1991 U.S.-led counteroffensive against Iraq to eject its forces from Kuwait.

operational code: An individual's integrated set of conceptions about political life that informs his or her calculations of appropriate and effective policy.

organizational culture: The set of shared values, goals, and functional priorities of the members of a government agency.

organizational process: A model of decision making characterized by standard operating procedures and fragmented centers of authority that hinders unified, consistent, and effective government policies.

oversight: Congress's ability, enhanced in the 1970s and 1980s, to monitor the president's conduct of foreign policy.

parachute journalism: A pattern of news coverage in which reporters descend on a trouble spot and then move on, never gaining a deep understanding of the problems in the area that would give their reporting greater substance.

particularistic groups: Nongovern-mental organizations seeking to influence U.S. foreign policy that serve a limited number of individuals with stakes in the groups' missions. An alternative to cosmopolitan groups.

passing the buck: A tendency of Congress to defer to the president in foreign policy given that the White House, not Congress, will likely receive credit for major breakthroughs as well as blame for failures.

path dependency: A pattern by which past structural choices, with their underlying values and goals, push future policies in particular directions.

political action committees (PACs): The electoral arms of organized groups that are responsible for fund-raising and distributing money to promote the election of desired candidates.

political economy: An arena of public life, located at the crossroads of states and markets, in which governments seek to organize domestic economic activity in ways that advance their policy goals and principles.

Powell Doctrine: Policy articulated in the early 1990s by Gen. Colin Powell when he was chair of the Joint Chiefs of Staff that calls for the United States to prevail decisively in military conflicts and to have a clear exit strategy.

power politics: An aggressive form of statecraft that relies on threats of aggression and shows of force based on the military strength of rivals.

preemptive war: A military attack initiated by one country whose leaders believe an attack from another country is imminent.

prerogative powers: A president's freedom to make independent and binding judgments, extending beyond national emergencies to include day-to-day decisions, which do not require the approval of Congress or the courts.

press leaks: The widespread and private transfer of sensitive information regarding government policy from official sources to the news media, often in the hope that the released information will change policies.

preventive war: A military attack initiated by a country whose leaders believe an emerging challenger presents a long-term threat to eliminate the threat before it materializes.

primacy: A country's predominant stature in the hierarchy of global power.

principled beliefs: In contrast to causal beliefs, structured perceptions toward political problems that are informed primarily by such normative principles as liberty, justice, and equality.

propaganda: False or misleading public information designed to enhance the stature of the originating government or its policies.

public choice theory: A model of public policy arguing that competitive private firms supply goods and services more efficiently than government agencies.

public diplomacy: Efforts by the U.S. government, often through the mobilization of private citizens and groups, to appeal directly to foreign citizens and strengthen international support for the United States.

public relations presidency: A governing style in which the U.S. president is guided primarily by public opinion in making policy decisions.

rally around the flag effect: The sharp increase in a president's public approval rating that occurs when the nation faces a military crisis. Generally attributed to a patriotic sense among citizens that national unity must be maintained in times of crisis.

rational choice: A behavioral approach to public policy that reduces decision making to objective calculations of costs and benefits.

raw intelligence: Unprocessed information about foreign governments and developments abroad collected by intelligence agents from various sources and shared with policy makers after it has been processed.

recess appointment: The ability of a president to make political appointments without the advice and consent of Congress when the legislative body is not in session, as in George W. Bush's controversial August 2005 appointment of John Bolton as U.S. ambassador to the United Nations.

regimes: Areas of interstate cooperation in foreign policy, such as arms control, in which decision makers enjoy positive-sum gains by adopting common norms, objectives, and institutionalized means of problem solving.

regional integration: The process by which close economic and political cooperation among states in a particular region offers a remedy for chronic military conflicts. Most often applied to the evolution of the European Union.

revolution in military affairs: A fundamental shift in the U.S. military's structure and strategic doctrine as the result of advances in technology in the United States and overseas.

Rome Statute: An intergovernmental agreement approved in 1998 in which signatories identified a variety of crimes—genocide, crimes against humanity, war crimes, and foreign aggression—that would fall under the jurisdiction of the proposed International Criminal Court.

rooftop journalism: Style of war reporting in which journalists provide accounts of military conflicts from nearby vantage points, often the tops of buildings. Became a staple of televised war coverage during the 1991 Persian Gulf War.

Roosevelt Corollary: President Theodore Roosevelt's 1904 expansion of the Monroe Doctrine proclaiming that the United States had authority to act as an "international police power" outside its borders in order to maintain stability in the Western Hemisphere.

saber rattling: A tactic used by foreign policy makers to gain concessions from rival states by escalating tensions through threats of imminent military attack.

security community: A region of the world in which governments form close political, economic, and military ties to such an extent that war among them becomes unthinkable. Often associated with the European Union.

security dilemma: The destabilizing effect of military expansion by one state, even for defensive purposes, as other states respond by expanding their armed forces.

selective exposure: The tendency of news consumers to rely on sources of information that conform to their preexisting values and opinions, a practice that tends to reinforce rather than inform public opinion.

shaming: A tactic by which critics of governments, corporations, and other political actors raise moral or ethical doubts about the actions of these entities in hopes of heightening public pressure for policy reform.

signal intelligence (SIGINT): Information gathered by U.S. and other intelligence agencies through the interception of foreign radio broadcasts, telephone conversations, e-mail messages, and other electronic transmissions.

situational factors: The objective details of a given problem facing Congress and the calculated costs and benefits of proposed legislative solutions.

smart sanctions: Economic penalties designed to punish government elites rather than the most vulnerable citizens in the target state.

Smoot-Hawley Tariff Act: Congressional measure passed in 1930 and signed by President Herbert Hoover that dramatically increased tariffs on goods coming into the United States. A central factor in the onset of the Great Depression.

social movement: The mobilization of broad-based private groups, usually around shared concerns or grievances related to public policy on a specific issue and a desire to alter the policy through mass pressure.

socialism: A political economy model that seeks to ensure economic equality through social welfare programs and government ownership of vital enterprises while also allowing citizens to own private property and operate firms.

soft balancing: A strategy by second-tier powers to accept the preponderant influence of hegemons while taking modest steps, such as antagonistic speeches before the UN General Assembly and appeals to global public opinion, that signal their dissatisfaction with the status quo.

soft news: The presentation of public issues, such as political scandals, foreign policy crises, and social problems, in media venues designed to entertain rather than inform, often with considerable impact on public opinion.

soft power: The attractiveness of a nation's political and cultural values to other states and societies that enhances the nation's ability to gain support from other governments for its policy goals.

sovereignty: The highest level of political authority maintained by secular nation-states. Affirmed in the 1648 Treaty of Westphalia, which rejected political control by religious authorities and the divine right of kings.

sovereignty gap: A consequence of the anarchic state system, whose lack of centralized, authoritative body inhibits solutions to collective problems such as nuclear proliferation and climate change.

Special Forces: Small but highly trained military units that undertake covert special operations, which may include assassinations, attacks on physical assets, the rescue of prisoners, or other actions.

spin control: Action by government officials to shape news coverage so that it shows them in the best possible light.

standard operating procedures (SOPs): Consistent, routine measures for addressing commonly encountered problems in public policy. Stress continuity over change and a high level of internal order.

state building: The process by which an external government, intergovernmental organization, or nongovernmental organization attempts to create the conditions necessary for a state to establish a stable and democratic government.

state capitalism: A model of political economy that combines market-driven economic policies and illiberal political rule. Often applied in recent years to China and Russia, among other states.

stewardship theory: A view of the U.S. presidency advanced by Theodore Roosevelt that provided the head of state, as the "steward" of the nation, broad discretion to act in foreign policy without regard for domestic opposition.

strategic communications: Officially sanctioned messages originating from the U.S. government and disseminated through various channels to foreign governments, news outlets, and carefully selected interest groups in order to advance U.S. foreign policy goals.

strategic detachment: An early grand strategy adopted by the United States that featured national self-reliance and avoidance of binding commitments to other countries.

strategic environment: The context in which security policy is devised. Reflects trends in global and regional balances of power and the degree to which a state considers other powerful nations and mobilized private groups to be friends or foes.

structural arrangements: The governing bodies and legal system within which policy making takes place and that shape a grand strategy.

structural realism: Also known as neorealism, a theory of international relations that emphasizes global anarchy, persistent fears and distrust, and a balance of power among states as the most reliable guarantor of world peace.

sustained primacy: A grand strategy adopted by the United States after World War II based on preservation of the nation's predominance in the interstate system. Adopted explicitly by the George W. Bush administration in 2002.

targeted killing: A military tactic adopted by the Obama administration that uses and justifies aerial attacks to kill "high-value" enemies of the United States and its allies.

terrorism: A tactic of unconventional warfare that uses threats and acts of violence to raise mass fear as a means of achieving political objectives.

Track II diplomacy: An informal approach to international relations that engages private citizens and nongovernmental organizations on a variety of transnational issues.

trade promotion authority: Formerly known as "fast-track" authority, a measure that strengthens the executive branch's ability to conclude trade agreements with other governments by restricting the time allotted for the consideration of such agreements in Congress.

tragedy of the commons: A situation in which a group of people stands to lose a common resource because of overuse unless some limiting measures are taken. A "tragedy" because of the many constraints on undertaking collective action and the stark consequences of inaction.

transnational advocacy networks: Large, well-organized coalitions of groups from two or more countries that apply political pressure on several governments at once to achieve their policy preferences.

transnational civil society: Societal forces that extend beyond the political boundaries of a nation-state, including interest groups, public opinion, the news media, and intergovernmental organizations.

Treaty of Westphalia: An agreement signed in 1648 ending the Thirty Years' War that helped establish and codify the nation-state system that exists today.

Truman Doctrine: President Harry Truman's pledge to provide military aid to Greece and Turkey to help overcome internal communist revolts and, more broadly, to support "free peoples who are resisting attempted subjugation by armed minorities or by outside pressures."

trustee model: One of two general models of political representation, it is based on a political leader's presumed superior judgment. Provides for greater freedom of thought and autonomous decision making by elected officials than the delegate model.

two-level game: A situation in which foreign policy makers simultaneously negotiate with their foreign counterparts and domestic actors (public and private) who have a stake in the policy process.

two presidencies: A model of U.S. government developed by political scientist Aaron Wildavsky that describes the president as constrained on domestic issues while reigning supreme in foreign affairs.

unilateralism: The pursuit of foreign policy objectives without the collaboration or assistance of other governments.

unipolar: A global power structure in which one nation-state maintains a predominant share of the economic, military, and other resources needed to advance its interests in the interstate system.

unitary actors: A model of national decision making that assumes that foreign policy makers act in a united fashion to make decisions in the name of the "national interest." A central tenet of realist theory.

USA PATRIOT Act: Sweeping legislation passed after the September 11, 2001, attacks that increased the federal government's ability to investigate suspected terrorists in the United States. An acronym for "Uniting and Strengthening America by Providing Appropriate Tools Required to Intercept and Obstruct Terrorism."

Vietnam syndrome: National self-doubt in the United States in the late 1960s and 1970s as the nation's involvement and defeat in the Vietnam War led to a weakened sense of U.S. primacy and moral superiority.

war on terror: A term formally adopted by President George W. Bush to describe the U.S. government's response to the September 2011 terrorist attacks.

War Powers Resolution: A legislative measure approved by Congress in 1973 requiring presidents to inform Congress about imminent U.S. military deployments and authorizing Congress to order the troops home after sixty days if a majority of legislators oppose the deployments. Rarely invoked and routinely dismissed by presidents as unconstitutional.

wars of choice: Military conflicts concerning nonvital national interests.

wars of necessity: Military conflicts resulting from direct challenges to a nation's vital interests.

WikiLeaks: Internet site founded in 2006 by Julian Assange that publishes secret information leaked from anonymous sources.

zone of twilight: A conception of U.S. foreign policy often adopted by the courts that emphasizes the lack of explicit powers granted to the executive and legislative branches and that sees interbranch conflict as largely "political."

Abramowitz, Alan I. 2010. *The Disappearing Center: Engaged Citizens, Polarization, and American Democracy.* New Haven, CT: Yale University Press.

Abramson, Mark A., and Paul R. Lawrence, eds. 2001. *Transforming Organizations.* Lanham, MD: Rowman & Littlefield.

Addis, Adeno. 2003. "Economic Sanctions and the Problem of Evil." *Human Rights Quarterly* 25 (3): 573–623.

Adler, David Gray. 1996a. "Constitutional Principles and Democratic Norms: Court, Constitution, and Foreign Affairs." In *The Constitution and the Conduct of American Foreign Policy,* edited by David Gray Adler and Larry Nelson George, 19–56. Lawrence: University Press of Kansas.

———. 1996b. "President's Recognition Power." In *The Constitution and the Conduct of American Foreign Policy,* edited by David Gray Adler and Larry Nelson George, 133–157. Lawrence: University Press of Kansas.

———. 2006. "The Law: George Bush as Commander in Chief: Toward the Nether World of American Constitutionalism." *Presidential Studies Quarterly* 36 (3): 525–540.

AFL-CIO. n.d. "Trans-Pacific Partnership Free Trade Agreement (TPP)." http://www .aflcio.org/Issues/Trade/Trans-Pacific-Partnership-Free-Trade-Agreement-TPP.

Allan, Stuart. 2006. *Online News: Journalism and the Internet.* New York: Open University Press.

Allen, Jonathan. 2011. *'Kinetic Military Action' or 'War'?* March 24. http://www.politico.com/news/stories/0311/51893.html.

Allison, Graham T. 1971. *Essence of Decision: Explaining the Cuban Missile Crisis.* Boston: Little, Brown.

Allison, Graham T., and Philip Zelikow. 1999. *Essence of Decision: Explaining the Cuban Missile Crisis,* 2nd ed. New York: Longman.

Almond, Gabriel. A. 1950. *The American People and Foreign Policy.* New York: Harcourt, Brace.

Alston, Philip. 2010. *Report of the Special Rapporteur on Extrajudicial, Summary or Arbitrary Executions: Report to the United Nations.* http://www2.ohchr.org/english/bodies/hrcouncil/docs/14session/A.HRC.14.24.Add6.pdf.

Althaus, Scott L., and Kevin Coe. 2011. "Priming Patriots: Social Identity Processes and the Dynamics of Public Support for War." *Public Opinion Quarterly* 75 (1): 65–88.

Alvarez, Lizette. 2015. "Radio and TV Martí, U.S. Broadcasters to Cuba, Emerge from Cold War Past Facing Uneasy Future." *New York Times,* March 24, A1.

American Civil Liberties Union. 2010. "Surveillance under the USA PATRIOT Act." December 10. http://www.aclu .org/national-security/surveillance-under-usa-patriot-act/.

American Presidency Project. n.d. "Executive Orders." http://www.presidency.ucsb .edu/data/orders.php.

American Press Institute. 2014. "The Personal News Cycle: How Americans Choose to Get Their News." March 17. http://www.americanpressinstitute .org/publications/reports/survey-research/personal-news-cycle/.

Anderson, Fred, and Andrew Cayton. 2005. *The Dominion of War: Empire and Liberty in North America, 1500–2000.* New York: Viking.

Anderson, Monica, and Andrea Caumont. 2014. "How Social Media Is Reshaping News." Washington, DC: Pew Research Center, September 24. http://www .pewresearch.org/fact-tank/2014/09/24/how-social-media-is-reshaping-news/.

Annenberg Public Policy Center. 2014. "Americans Know Surprisingly Little about Their Government, Survey Finds." September 17.

Arms Control Association. 2006. "The 2006 Biological Weapons Convention Review Conference: Articles and Interviews on Tackling the Threats Posed by Biological Weapons." Washington, DC: Arms Control Association.

Arquilla, John, David Ronfeldt, and Michele Zanini. 1999. "Networks, Netwar, and Information-Age Terrorism." In *Countering the New Terrorism,* edited by Ian O. Lesser, Bruce Hoffman, John Arquilla, David Ronfeldt, and Michele Zanini, 39–84. Santa Monica, CA: RAND.

Art, Robert J. 1973. "Bureaucratic Politics and American Foreign Policy: A Critique." *Policy Sciences* 4 (4): 467–490.

———. 2003. *A Grand Strategy for America.* Ithaca, NY: Cornell University Press.

Ash, Timothy Garton. 2002. "The Peril of Too Much Power." *New York Times,* April 9, A25.

Ashkenas, Jeremy, Hannah Fairfield, Josh Keller, and Paul Volpe. 2014. "7 Key Points from the CIA Torture Report." *New York Times,* December 9.

Asmus, Ronald D. 2002. *Opening NATO's Door: How the Alliance Remade Itself for a New Era.* New York: Columbia University Press.

Auerswald, David P., and Stephen M. Saideman. 2014. *NATO in Afghanistan: Fighting Together, Fighting Alone.* Princeton, NJ: Princeton University Press.

Auster, Bruce B., and David E. Kaplan. 1998. "What's Really Gone Wrong with the CIA?" *U.S. News & World Report,* June 1, 27.

Bacevich, Andrew J. 2010. *Washington Rules: America's Path to Permanent War.* New York: Metropolitan Books.

Badie, Dina. 2010. "Groupthink, Iraq, and the War on Terror: Explaining U.S. Policy Shift toward Iraq." *Foreign Policy Analysis* 6 (4): 277–296.

Bailey, Thomas A. 1948. *The Man in the Street: The Impact of American Public Opinion on Foreign Policy.* New York: Macmillan.

Baker, James A., III. 1995. *The Politics of Diplomacy: Revolution, War, and Peace, 1989–1992*. With Thomas M. DeFrank. New York: Putnam.

Baker, Peter, and Eric Schmitt. 2014. "Many Missteps in Assessment of ISIS Threat." *New York Times*, September 29.

Baker, William D., and John R. Oneal. 2001. "Patriotism or Opinion Leadership? The Nature and Origins of the 'Rally' Round the Flag' Effect." *Journal of Conflict Resolution* 45 (5): 661–687.

Baldwin, David A. 1966. *Foreign Aid and American Foreign Policy: A Documentary Analysis*. New York: Praeger.

———. 1985. *Economic Statecraft*. Princeton, NJ: Princeton University Press.

Ball, Jeffrey. 2012. "Tough Love for Renewable Energy: Making Wind and Solar Power Affordable." *Foreign Affairs* 91 (May-June): 122–133.

Ballasy, Nicholas. 2014. "Brzezinski, Scowcroft: Obama Should Shrink 300-Plus National Security Staff." *PJ Media*, November 14.

Barber, James D. 1992. *The Presidential Character: Predicting Performance in the White House*, 4th ed. Englewood Cliffs, NJ: Prentice Hall.

Bardes, Barbara. 1997. "Public Opinion and Foreign Policy: How Does the Public Think about America's Role in the World?" In *Understanding Public Opinion*, edited by Barbara Norrander and Clyde Wilcox, 150–169. Washington, DC: CQ Press.

Barnett, Roger W. 2003. *Asymmetrical Warfare: Today's Challenge to U.S. Military Power*. Washington, DC: Brassey's.

Barone, Michael, and Grant Ujifusa. 1999. *The Almanac of American Politics 2000*. Washington, DC: National Journal Group.

Barron-Lopez, Laura. 2015. "Americans for Prosperity Launch Push for White House to Sign Keystone Bill." *The Hill*, February 13.

Bauerlein, Mark. 2008. *The Dumbest Generation: How the Digital Age Stupefies Young Americans and Jeopardizes Our Future (Or, Don't Trust Anyone under 30)*. New York: Penguin.

Baum, Matthew A. 2002. "The Constituent Foundations of the Rally-Round-the-Flag Phenomenon." *International Studies Quarterly* 46 (2): 263–298.

Baum, Matthew A., and Tim J. Groeling. 2010. *War Stories: The Causes and Consequences of Public Views of War*. Princeton, NJ: Princeton University Press.

Baum, Matthew A., and Angela Jamison. 2011. "Chapter 8: Soft News and the Four Oprah Effects." In *The Oxford Handbook of American Public Opinion and the Media*, edited by Robert Y. Shapiro and Lawrence R. Jacobs. Oxford: Oxford University Press.

Baumgartner, Jody C., Peter L. Francia, and Jonathan S. Morris. 2008. "A Clash of Civilizations? The Influence of Religion on Public Opinion of U.S. Foreign Policy in the Middle East." *Political Research Quarterly* 61 (2): 171–179.

Baumgartner, Jody C., and Jonathan S. Morris. 2006. "*The Daily Show* Effect: Candidate Evaluations, Efficacy, and American Youth." *American Politics Research* 34 (3): 341–367.

Bax, Frank R. 1977. "The Legislative-Executive Relationship in Foreign Policy: New Partnership or New Competition?" *Orbis* 20 (winter): 881–904.

Becker, Jo, and Scott Shane. 2012. "Secret 'Kill List' Proves a Test of Obama's Principles and Will." *New York Times*, May 29.

Beevor, Antony. 2012. *The Second World War*. Boston: Little, Brown.

Belasco, Amy. 2011. *The Cost of Iraq, Afghanistan, and Other Global War on Terror Operations Since 9/11*. Washington, DC: Congressional Research Service, March 29.

———. 2014. *The Cost of Iraq, Afghanistan, and Other Global War on Terror Operations Since 9/11*. Washington, DC: Congressional Research Service, December 8.

Below, Amy. 2008. "U.S. Presidential Decisions on Ozone Depletion and Climate Change: A Foreign Policy Analysis." *Foreign Policy Analysis* 4 (1): 1–20.

Bendor, Jonathan, and Thomas H. Hammond. 1992. "Rethinking Allison's Models." *American Political Science Review* 86 (2): 301–322.

Benjamin, Daniel, and Steven Simon. 2002. *The Age of Sacred Terror*. New York: Random House.

Bennett, John C. 1966. *Foreign Policy in Christian Perspective*. New York: Scribner.

Bennett, W. Lance, and David L. Paletz, eds. 1994. *Taken by Storm: The Media, Public Opinion, and U.S. Foreign Policy in the Gulf War*. Chicago: University of Chicago Press.

Bergen, Peter L. 2011. *The Longest War: The Enduring Conflict Between America and Al Qaeda*. New York: Free Press.

Bergen, Peter L., and Daniel Rothenberg, eds. 2014. *Drone Wars: Transforming Conflict, Law, and Policy*. New York: Cambridge University Press.

Bergen, Peter L., and Katherine Tiedemann. 2011. "Washington's Phantom War: The Effects of the U.S. Drone Program In Pakistan." *Foreign Affairs* 90 (4): 12–18.

Berríos, Rubén. 2000. *Contracting for Development: The Role of For-Profit Contractors in U.S. Foreign Development Assistance*. Westport, CT: Praeger.

Best, James J. 1992. "Who Talked with President Kennedy? An Interaction Analysis." *Presidential Studies Quarterly* 22 (2): 351–369.

Best, Richard A., Jr. 2011. *Intelligence Issues for Congress*. Washington, DC: Congressional Research Service, December 28. http://www.fas.org/sgp/crs/intel/RL33539.pdf.

Best, Richard A., Jr., and Elizabeth B. Bazan. 2006. *Intelligence Spending: Public Disclosure Issues*. Washington, DC: Congressional Research Service, September 25.

Best, Samuel J., Brian Chmielewski, and Brian S. Krueger. 2005. "Selective Exposure to Online Foreign News during the Conflict with Iraq." *International Journal of Press/Politics* 10 (4): 52–70.

Betts, Richard K. 2002. *Conflict after the Cold War: Arguments on Causes of War and Peace*, 2nd ed. New York: Longman.

———. 2014. "Ending America's Era of Permanent War." *Foreign Affairs* 93 (November-December): 15–24.

Binder, Sarah A. 1996. "The Disappearing Political Center: Congress and the Incredible Shrinking Middle." *Brookings Review* 14 (4): 36–39.

Birnbaum, Michael, and Karen DeYoung. 2012. "Anti-U.S. Protests Spread through Muslim World." *Washington Post,* September 14. http://articles .washingtonpost.com/2012-09-14/ world/35495624_1_protests-spread-embassy-walls-tunisian-security/.

Bjørgaas, Tove. 2012. *From Contributor to Partner? Norway's Role in Foreign Policy Research and Implementation in the United States.* Oslo: Norwegian Peacebuilding Research Center.

Blanchard, Christopher M., Carla E. Humud, Kenneth Katzman, and Matthew C. Weed. 2015. "The 'Islamic State' Crisis and U.S. Policy." Congressional Research Service, June 11.

Blanchard, Jean-Marc F., and Norrin M. Ripsman. 2008. "A Political Theory of Economic Statecraft." *Foreign Policy Analysis* 4 (4): 371–398.

Blechman, Barry M., and Tamara C. Wittes. 1999. "Defining Moment: The Threat and Use of Force in American Foreign Policy." *Political Science Quarterly* 114 (1): 1–30.

Bloodgood, Elizabeth A. 2011. "The Interest Group Analogy: International Non-governmental Advocacy Organizations in International Politics." *Review of International Studies* 37 (1): 93–120.

Bogardus, Kevin. 2014. "Podesta Group Lands $480K Contract." *The Hill,* March 17.

Bowen, Stuart W., Jr. 2013. *Learning from Iraq: A Final Report from the Inspector General for Iraq Reconstruction.* Washington, DC: U.S. Department of Defense, Office of the Special Inspector General for Iraq Reconstruction. http://www.sigir.mil/ learningfromiraq/.

Bowser, Benjamin P. 2003. "A Meaning of 9/11: Failure in Race Relations at Home Has Led to a Failed U.S. Foreign Policy Overseas." *SAGE Race Relations Abstracts* 28 (3/4): 19–24.

Brace, Paul, and Barbara Hinckley. 1993. *Follow the Leader: Opinion Polls and the Modern Presidents.* New York: Basic Books.

Bracken, Paul. 2012. *The Second Nuclear Age: Strategy, Danger, and the New Power Politics.* New York: Times Books.

Brands, H. W. 1998. *What America Owes the World: The Struggle for the Soul of Foreign Policy.* New York: Cambridge University Press.

Brands, Hal. 2012. *The Promise and Pitfalls of Grand Strategy.* Carlisle, PA: Strategic Studies Institute, U.S. Army War College.

Brantley, Susan L., and Anna Meyendorff. 2013. "The Facts on Fracking." *New York Times,* March 13.

Braumoeller, Bear F. 2010. "The Myth of American Isolationism." *Foreign Policy Analysis* 6 (4): 349–371.

Bremmer, Ian. 2012. *Every Nation for Itself: Winners and Losers in a G-Zero World.* New York: Penguin.

Brenner, Carl N. 1999. "Modeling the President's Security Agenda." *Congress and the Presidency* 26 (2): 171–191.

Brewer, Paul R., Kimberly Gross, Sean Aday, and Lars Willnat. 2004. "International Trust and Public Opinion about World Affairs." *American Journal of Political Science* 48 (1): 93–109.

Brinkley, Douglas G. 1997. "Democratic Enlargement: The Clinton Doctrine." *Foreign Policy* (spring): 111–127.

British Petroleum. 2015. "Statistical Review of World Energy." June. http://www .bp.com/statisticalreview/.

Broder, John M. 2011. "Obama Administration Abandons Stricter Air-Quality Rules." *New York Times,* September 3, A1.

Brodie, Bernard, ed. 1946. *The Absolute Weapon: Atomic Power and World Order.* New York: Harcourt, Brace.

Brooks, Deborah Jordan, and Benjamin A. Valentino. 2011. "A War of One's Own: Understanding the Gender Gap in Support for War." *Public Opinion Quarterly* 75 (2): 270–286.

Brooks, Stephen G., G. John Ikenberry, and William C. Wohlforth. 2012–2013. "Don't Come Home America: The Case Against Retrenchment." *International Security* 37 (3): 7–51.

Brooks, Stephen G., and William C. Wohlforth. 2008. *World Out of Balance: International Relations and the Challenge of American Primacy.* Princeton, NJ: Princeton University Press.

Bruck, Connie. 2014. "Friends of Israel." *New Yorker,* September 1.

Brunk, Darren C. 2008. "Curing the Somalia Syndrome: Analogy, Foreign Policy Decision Making, and the Rwandan Genocide." *Foreign Policy Analysis* 4 (3): 301–320.

Bryner, Gary C. 2011. *Protecting the Global Environment.* Boulder, CO: Paradigm.

Brzezinski, Zbigniew. 1997. *The Grand Chessboard: American Primacy and Its Geostrategic Imperatives.* New York: Basic Books.

———. 2012. *Strategic Vision: America and the Crisis of Global Power.* New York: Basic Books.

Buchanan, James M. 1977. "Why Does Government Grow?" In *Budgets and Bureaucrats: The Sources of Government Growth,* edited by Thomas E. Borcherding. Durham, NC: Duke University Press.

Buckley, Kevin. 1991. *Panama: The Whole Story.* New York: Simon & Schuster.

Bueno de Mesquita, Bruce. 2009. *Principles of International Politics,* 4th ed. Washington, DC: CQ Press.

Bumiller, Elizabeth. 2003. "Evangelicals Sway White House on Human Rights Issues Abroad." *New York Times,* October 26, A1.

Burgin, Eileen. 1993. "The Influence of Constituents: Congressional Decision-Making on Issues of Foreign and Domestic Policy." In *Congress Resurgent: Foreign and Defense Policy on Capitol Hill,* edited by Randall B. Ripley and James M. Lindsay, 67–88. Ann Arbor: University of Michigan Press.

Burke, Jason. 2011. *The 9/11 Wars.* London: Allen Lane.

Burke, John P. 2009. *Honest Broker? The National Security Adviser and Presidential Decision Making.* College Station: Texas A&M Press.

Burkhalter, Holly. 2004. "The Politics of AIDS: Engaging Conservative Activists." *Foreign Affairs* 83 (January-February): 8–14.

BurrellesLuce. 2015. "Top U.S. Consumer Magazines." New York: BurrellesLuce.

Burton, Daniel F., Jr. 1997. "The Brave New Wired World." *Foreign Policy* 106 (spring): 22–37.

Bush, George H. W. 1991. "Address before a Joint Session of Congress on the End of the Gulf War," March 6, Washington, DC: http://millercenter.org/president/ speeches/detail/3430/.

Bush, George W. 2001. Address to a Joint Session of Congress and the American People, September 20, Washington, D.C. http://georgewbush-whitehouse.archives.gov/news/releases/2001/09/20010920-8.html.

———. 2002. State of the Union Address, January 29, Washington, D.C. http://georgewbush-whitehouse.archives.gov/news/releases/2002/01/20020129-11.html.

———. 2004. Interview by Tim Russert. Meet the Press, NBC, February 7. http://www.msnbc.msn.com/id/4179618/ns/meet_the_press/t/transcript-feb-th/.

Bushnell, Prudence. 2012. "Our Diplomats Deserve Better." New York Times, September 14, A29.

Buzan, Barry. 1991. "New Patterns of Global Security in the Twenty-First Century." International Affairs 67 (3): 431–451.

Calabresi, Massimo. 2011. "Head of State." Time, November 7, 28–33.

Calvin, Kathy. 2014. "Universal Access to Reproductive Health Care: A Global Obligation and Opportunity." Bill and Melinda Gates Foundation, September 23.

Campbell, Angus, Philip E. Converse, Warren E. Miller, and Donald E. Stokes. 1960. The American Voter. New York: Wiley.

Campbell, David E., and Robert D. Putnam. 2012. "God and Caesar in America: Why Mixing Religion and Politics Is Bad for Both." Foreign Affairs 91 (March-April): 34–43.

Campbell, John. 2014. U.S. Policy to Counter Nigeria's Boko Haram. New York: Council on Foreign Affairs. http://www.cfr.org/nigeria/us-policy-counter-nigerias-boko-haram/p33806.

Cantir, Cristian, and Juliet Kaarbo. 2012. "Contested Roles and Domestic Politics: Reflections on Role Theory in Foreign Policy Analysis and IR Theory." Foreign Policy Analysis 8 (1): 5–24.

Caprioli, Mary. 2000. "Gendered Conflict." Journal of Peace Research 37 (1): 51–68.

Carothers, Thomas. 1999. Aiding Democracy Abroad: The Learning Curve. Washington, DC: Carnegie Endowment for International Peace.

Carroll, James. 2006. House of War: The Pentagon and the Disastrous Rise of American Power. Boston: Houghton Mifflin.

Carroll, Toby. 2010. Delusions of Development: The World Bank and the Post-Washington Consensus in Southeast Asia. New York: Palgrave Macmillan.

Carter, Ralph G. 1989. "Senate Defense Budgeting, 1981–1988: The Impacts of Ideology, Party, and Constituency Benefit on the Decision to Support the President." American Politics Quarterly 17 (3): 332–347.

Carter, Ralph G., and James M. Scott. 2009. Choosing to Lead: Understanding Congressional Foreign Policy Entrepreneurs. Durham, NC: Duke University Press.

Caruson, Kiki, and Victoria A. Farrar-Myers. 2007. "Promoting the President's Foreign Policy Agenda: Presidential Use of Executive Agreements as Policy Vehicles." Political Research Quarterly 60 (4): 631–644.

Cashman, Greg, and Leonard C. Robinson. 2007. An Introduction to the Causes of War: Patterns of Interstate Conflict from World War I to Iraq. Lanham, MD: Rowman & Littlefield.

Castle, Stephen. 2010. "As the E.U. Does More, Fewer Tell about It." New York Times, March 22.

Cauley, Leslie. 2006. "NSA Has Massive Database of Americans' Phone Calls." USA Today, May 11. http://usatoday30.usatoday.com/news/washington/2006-05-10-nsa_x.htm.

Central Intelligence Agency. 2004. "Special Review: Counterterrorism, Detention, and Interrogation Activities (September 2001–October 2003)." Office of Inspector General, May 7. http://www.aclu.org/torturefoia/released/052708/052708_Special_Review.pdf.

———. 2013. CIA World Factbook. "United States." Updated March 26, 2013. https://www.cia.gov/library/publications/the-world-factbook/geos/us.html.

Chait, Jonathan. 2002. "Defense Secretary: The Peculiar Duplicity of Ari Fleischer." New Republic, June 10, 20–23.

Checkel, Jeffrey T. 2008. "Constructivism and Foreign Policy." In Foreign Policy: Theories, Actors, Cases, edited by Steve Smith, Amelia Hadfield, and Timothy Dunne, 71–82. New York: Oxford University Press.

Chen, Tim. 2015. "American Household Credit Card Statistics." San Francisco: NerdWallet. http://www.nerdwallet.com/blog/credit-card-data/average-credit-card-debt-household/.

Cheney, Dick. 2001. Interview by Tim Russert. Meet the Press, NBC, September 16. http://georgewbush-whitehouse.archives.gov/vicepresident/news-speeches/speeches/vp20010916.html.

Chicago Council on Global Affairs. 2008. "Anxious Americans Seek a New Direction in Foreign Policy: Results of a 2008 Survey of Public Opinion."

———. 2012. "Foreign Policy in the New Millennium: Results of the 2012 Chicago Council Survey of American Public Opinion and U.S. Foreign Policy." http://www.thechicagocouncil.org/sites/default/files/2012_CCS_Report.pdf.

———. 2014. "Foreign Policy in the Age of Retrenchment: Results of the 2014 Chicago Council Survey of American Public Opinion and U.S. Foreign Policy." http://www.thechicagocouncil.org/sites/default/files/2014_CCS_Report_1.pdf.

Chomsky, Noam. 2012. Occupy. New York: Zuccotti Park Press.

Chong, Dennis, and James N. Druckman. 2007. "Framing Theory." Annual Review of Political Science 10: 103–126.

Chothia, Farouk. 2015. "Who Are Nigeria's Boko Haram Islamists?" May 4. http://www.bbc.com/news/world-africa-13809501.

Churchill, Winston. 1946. Commencement address at Westminster College (Iron Curtain Speech), Fulton, Mo., March 5. http://www.nationalcenter.org/ChurchillIronCurtain.html.

Clark, Wesley K. 2001. Waging Modern War: Bosnia, Kosovo, and the Future of Combat. New York: Public Affairs.

Clawson, Rosalee A., and Zoe M. Oxley. 2013. Public Opinion: Democratic Ideals, Democratic Practice, 2nd ed. Washington, DC: CQ Press.

"Cleveland City Council Resolution against War on Iraq." WKYC-TV. February 11, 2003. http://www.wkyc.com/news/story.aspx?storyid=2691.

Clinton, Hillary. 2010. "Remarks on United States Foreign Policy." Address to the Council on Foreign Relations, September 8. http://www.state.gov/secretary/rm/2010/09/146917.htm.

———. 2011. "Internet Rights and Wrongs: Choices and Challenges in a Networked World." Remarks at George Washington University, February 15. http://www.state.gov/secretary/rm/2011/02/156619.htm.

Clinton, William J. 1997. "Second Inaugural Address." January 20.

Cohen, Joel E. 2003. "The Future of Population." In *What the Future Holds: Insights from Social Science,* edited by Richard N. Cooper and Richard Layard, 29–75. Cambridge: MIT Press. Article originally published in 2001.

Cohen, Michael A. 2009. "Arms for the World: How the U.S. Military Shapes American Foreign Policy." *Dissent* 56 (fall): 69–74.

Cohen, Roger. 2013. "Diplomacy Is Dead." *New York Times*, January 21.

Cohen, Tom. 2012. "Obama Administration to Stop Deporting Some Young Illegal Immigrants." *CNN Politics*, June 16. http://www.cnn.com/2012/06/15/politics/immigration/index.html.

Coker, Christopher. 2015. *The Improbable War: China, the United States, and the Logic of Great Power Conflict.* New York: Oxford University Press.

Colby, Elbridge, and Paul Lettow. 2014. "Have We Hit Peak America? The Sources of U.S. Power and the Path to National Renaissance." http://foreignpolicy.com/2014/07/03/have-we-hit-peak-america/.

Colby, Sandra L., and Jennifer M. Ortman. 2015. *Projections of the Size and Composition of the U.S. Population: 2014–2060.* Washington, DC: U.S. Census Bureau.

Cole, Patrick. 2010. "Rockefeller, Perelman Join Buffett's Charity Pledge." *Bloomberg,* August 4. http://www.bloomberg.com/news/2010-08-04/rockefeller-ellison-weill-turner-allen-join-buffett-s-charity-pledge.html.

Coll, Steve. 1992. "Anatomy of a Victory: CIA's Covert Afghan War." *Washington Post*, July 19.

———. 2004. *Ghost Wars: The Secret History of the CIA, Afghanistan, and bin Laden, from the Soviet Invasion to September 10, 2001.* New York: Penguin Books.

———. 2014. "The Unblinking Stare: The Drone War in Pakistan." *New Yorker*, November 24.

Collins, Stephen D. 2009. "Can America Finance Freedom? Assessing U.S. Democracy Promotion via Economic Statecraft." *Foreign Policy Analysis* 5 (4): 367–389.

Combs, Cindy C. 2003. *Terrorism in the 21st Century,* 3rd ed. Upper Saddle River, NJ: Prentice Hall.

Compaine, Benjamin M., and Douglas Gomery. 2000. *Who Owns the Media? Competition and Concentration in the Mass Media Industry,* 3rd ed. Mahwah, NJ: Lawrence Erlbaum.

Congressional Budget Office. 2009a. *The Budget and Economic Outlook: An Update.* Washington, DC: CBO, August 25.

Convention on Biological Diversity. 2013. "Convention on Biological Diversity." http://www.eoearth.org/view/article/151444.

Converse, Philip. 1964. "The Nature of Belief Systems in Mass Publics." In *Ideology and Discontent,* edited by David E. Apter, 206–261. New York: Free Press.

Cooper, Andrew F. 2008. *Celebrity Diplomacy.* Boulder, CO: Paradigm.

Cooper, Phillip J. 2014. "Playing Presidential Ping-Pong with Executive Orders." The *Washington Post*, January 31.

Cooper, William H. 2012. *Free Trade Agreements: Impact on U.S. Trade and Implications for U.S. Trade Policy.* Washington, DC: Congressional Research Service, June 18.

Cordesman, Anthony H. 2015. "Judging a P5+1 Nuclear Agreement with Iran: The Key Criteria." *Center for Strategic and International Studies*, March 30. http://csis.org/publication/judging-p51-nuclear-agreement-iran-key-criteria.

Corwin, Edward S. 1957. *The President, Office and Powers, 1787–1957: History and Analysis of Practice and Opinion,* 4th ed. New York: New York University Press.

Council on American-Islamic Relations Research Center. 2006. "American Public Opinion about Islam and Muslims: 2006." http://www.cair.com/cairsurveyanalysis.pdf.

Cowan, Geoffrey, and Nicholas J. Cull. 2008. "Public Diplomacy in a Changing World." *Annals of the American Academy of Political and Social Science* 616 (1): 6–8.

Cox, Dan G., and Cooper A. Drury. 2006. "Democratic Sanctions: Connecting the Democratic Peace and Economic Sanctions." *Journal of Peace Research* 43 (November): 709–722.

Coyle, Philip E. 2006. "Missile Defense: An Expensive Bluff?" *Defense Monitor* 35 (4): 1–2.

Crabb, Cecil V., Jr., and Kevin V. Mulcahy. 1995. "George Bush's Management Style and Operation Desert Storm." *Presidential Studies Quarterly* 25 (2): 251–265.

Craig, Campbell. 2009. "American Power Preponderance and the Nuclear Revolution." *Review of International Studies* 35 (1): 27–44.

Crockett v. Reagan, 558 F. Supp. 893 (D.D.C. 1982).

Cronin, Patrick, and Benjamin O. Fordham. 1999. "Timeless Principles or Today's Fashion? Testing the Stability of the Linkage between Ideology and Foreign Policy in the Senate." *Journal of Politics* 61 (4): 967–998.

Crowley, Michael. 2004. "Playing Defense: Bush's Disastrous Homeland Security Department." *New Republic,* March 16, 17–21.

Cumming, Alfred. 2006. *Covert Action: Legislative Background and Possible Policy Questions.* Washington, DC: Congressional Research Service, November 2.

Cusick, Daniel. 2015. "Solar Power Sees Unprecedented Boom in U.S." *Scientific American*, March 10.

Daalder, Ivo H. 1991. *The Nature and Practice of Flexible Response: NATO Strategy and Theater Nuclear Forces since 1967.* New York: Columbia University Press.

Daalder, Ivo H., and I. M. Destler. 2000. *A New NSC for a New Administration.* Brookings Policy Briefs No. 68. Washington, DC: Brookings Institution Press.

———. 2011. *In the Shadow of the Oval Office: Profiles of the National Security*

Advisers and the Presidents They Served—From JFK to George W. Bush. New York: Simon and Schuster.

Daalder, Ivo H., and James M. Lindsay, eds. 2003. *America Unbound: The Bush Revolution in Foreign Policy.* Washington, DC: Brookings Institution Press.

Daalder, Ivo H., and Michael E. O'Hanlon. 2000. *Winning Ugly: NATO's War to Save Kosovo.* Washington, DC: Brookings Institution Press.

Dafoe, Allan O., John R. Oneal, and Bruce Russett. 2013. "The Democratic Peace: Weighing the Evidence and Cautious Inference." *International Studies Quarterly* 57 (1): 201–224.

Daggett, Stephen, and Pat Towell. 2012. *FY2013 Defense Budget Request: Overview and Context.* Washington, DC: Congressional Research Service, April 20.

Dahlman, Carl J. 2012. *The World under Pressure: How China & India Are Influencing the Global Economy and Environment.* Stanford, CA: Stanford University Press.

Dale, Catherine, Nina Serafino, and Pat Towell. 2008. *Organizing the U.S. Government for National Security: Overview of the Interagency Reform Debates.* Washington, DC: Congressional Research Service, April 18.

Dalgeish, Sarah. 2014. "The Biggest U.S. Foreign Aid Recipients." Washington, DC: U.S. Agency for International Development, August 26.

Dallek, Robert. 1989. *The American Style of Foreign Policy: Cultural Politics and Foreign Affairs.* New York: Oxford University Press.

Davenport, Coral. 2015. "U.S. and Chinese Climate Change Negotiators to Meet in Los Angeles." *New York Times,* September 15.

Davidson, Roger H., and Walter J. Oleszek, eds. 2004. *Congress and Its Members,* 9th ed. Washington, DC: CQ Press.

———. 2006. *Congress and Its Members,* 10th ed. Washington, DC: CQ Press.

Davies, Graeme A. M. 2012. "Coercive Diplomacy Meets Diversionary Incentives: The Impact of U.S. and Iranian Domestic Politics during the Bush and Obama Presidencies." *Foreign Policy Analysis* 8 (3): 313–331.

de Wijk, Rob. 2002. "The Limits of Military Power." *Washington Quarterly* 25 (1): 75–92.

Deace, Steve. 2014. "Just War Theory and ISIS." *Townhall.com,* September 13. http://townhall.com/columnists/stevedeace/2014/09/13/just-war-theory-and-isis-n1889814.

Deering, Christopher J. 1993. "Decision Making in the Armed Services Committees." In *Congress Resurgent: Foreign and Defense Policy on Capitol Hill,* edited by Randall B. Ripley and James M. Lindsay, 155–182. Ann Arbor: University of Michigan Press.

———. 1996. "Congress, the President, and Automatic Government: The Case of Military Base Closures." In *Rivals for Power: Presidential-Congressional Relations,* edited by James A. Thurber, 153–169. Washington, DC: CQ Press.

Deering, Christopher J., and Steven S. Smith. 1997. *Committees in Congress,* 3rd ed. Washington, DC: CQ Press.

Defense Science Board. 2004. *Report of the Defense Science Board Task Force on Strategic Communication.* Washington, DC: Office of the Secretary of Defense. http://www.fas.org/irp/agency/dod/dsb/commun.pdf.

Delany, Colin. 2011. "How Social Media Accelerated Tunisia's Revolution: An Inside View." *Huffington Post,* February 13.

Destler, I. M. 1995. *American Trade Politics: System under Stress,* 3rd ed. Washington, DC: Institute for International Economics.

———. 2001a. "Congress and Foreign Policy at Century's End: Requiem or Cooperation?" In *Congress Reconsidered,* 7th ed., edited by Lawrence C. Dodd and Bruce I. Oppenheimer, 315–333. Washington, DC: CQ Press.

———. 2001b. "The Reasonable Public and the Polarized Policy Process." In *The Real and the Ideal: Essays on International Relations in Honor of Richard H. Ullman,* edited by Anthony Lake and David Ochmanek, 75–90. Lanham, MD: Rowman & Littlefield.

Destler, I. M., Leslie H. Gelb, and Anthony Lake. 1984. *Our Own Worst Enemy: The Unmaking of American Foreign Policy.* New York: Simon and Schuster.

Deutsch, Karl W., S. A. Burrell, R. A. Kann, M. Lee Jr., M. Lichterman, R. E. Lindgern, F. L. Loewenheim, and R. W. Van Wagenen. 1957. *Political Community and the North Atlantic Area: International Organization in the Light of Historical Experience.* Princeton, NJ: Princeton University Press.

Dews, Fred. 2013. "What Percentage of U.S. Population Is Foreign Born?" *Brookings Institution,* October 3. http://www.brookings.edu/blogs/brookings-now/posts/2013/09/what-percentage-us-population-foreign-born/

DeYoung, Karen. 2015. "How the Obama White House Runs Foreign Policy." *Washington Post,* August 4.

Diamond, John. 2008. *The CIA and the Culture of Failure: U.S. Intelligence from the End of the Cold War to the Invasion of Iraq.* Stanford, CA: Stanford University Press.

Diani, Mario. 2012. "Interest Organizations in Social Movements: An Empirical Exploration." *Interest Groups and Advocacy* 1: 26–47.

Dimaggio, Anthony. 2009. *When Media Goes to War: Hegemonic Discourse, Public Opinion, and the Limits of Dissent.* New York: Monthly Review Press.

Diven, Polly. 2006. "A Coincidence of Interests: The Hyperpluralism of U.S. Food Aid Policy." *Foreign Policy Analysis* 2 (4): 361–384.

Dizard, Wilson P. 2001. *Digital Diplomacy: U.S. Foreign Policy in the Information Age.* Westport, CT: Greenwood.

Domscheit-Berg, Daniel. 2011. *Inside WikiLeaks: My Time with Julian Assange at the World's Most Dangerous Website.* With the assistance of Tina Klopp. Translated by Jefferson Chase. New York: Crown.

Donnelly, Thomas. 2006. "Countering Aggressive Rising Powers: A Clash of Strategic Cultures." *Orbis* 50 (summer): 413–428.

Donno, Daniela. 2010. "Who Is Punished? Regional Intergovernmental Organizations and the Enforcement of Democratic Norms." *International Organization* 64 (4): 593–625.

Dorman, Shawn, ed. 2003. *Inside a U.S. Embassy: How the Foreign Service Works for America.* Washington, DC: American Foreign Service Association.

Douthat, Ross. 2012. "The Mystery of Benghazi." *New York Times*, October 14.

Dower, John. 1986. *War without Mercy: Race and Power in the Pacific War*. New York: Pantheon.

Doyle, Charles. 2006. *Federal Habeas Corpus: An Abridged Sketch*. Washington, DC: Congressional Research Service, April 28.

Doyle, Michael W. 1986. "Liberalism and World Politics." *American Political Science Review* 80 (4): 1151–1169.

———. 2008. "Liberalism and Foreign Policy." In *Foreign Policy: Theories, Actors, Cases,* edited by Steve Smith, Amelia Hadfield, and Tim Dunne, 49–70. New York: Oxford University Press.

Dreazen, Yochi, and Sean D. Naylor. 2015. "Mission Unstoppable." *Foreign Policy* 212 (May-June): 36–43.

Drezner, Daniel W. 2000. "Ideas, Bureaucratic Politics, and the Crafting of Foreign Policy." *American Journal of Political Science* 44 (4): 733–749.

———. 2003. "The Hidden Hand of Economic Coercion." *International Organization* 57 (3): 643–659.

———. 2006. *U.S. Trade Strategy: Free versus Fair*. New York: Council on Foreign Relations.

———. 2014. "The System Worked: Global Economic Governance during the Great Recession." *World Politics* 66 (January): 123–164.

Dryden, Steve. 1995. *Trade Warriors: USTR and the American Crusade for Free Trade*. New York: Oxford University Press.

Dueck, Colin. 2010. *Hard Line: The Republican Party and U.S. Foreign Policy since World War II*. Princeton, NJ: Princeton University Press.

Duelfer, Charles A., and Stephen Benedict Dyson. 2011. "Chronic Misperception and International Conflict: The U.S.-Iraq Experience." *International Security* 36 (1): 73–100.

Dumbrell, John. 2002. "Was There a Clinton Doctrine? President Clinton's Foreign Policy Reconsidered." *Diplomacy and Statecraft* 13 (2): 43–56.

Dyson, Stephen B. 2009. "'Stuff Happens': Donald Rumsfeld and the Iraq War." *Foreign Policy Analysis* 5 (4): 327–347.

Easterly, William. 2006. *The White Man's Burden: Why the West's Efforts to Aid the Rest Have Done So Much Ill and So Little Good*. New York: Penguin Books.

Eland, Ivan. 2014. "Despite Criticism, Obama's Foreign Policy Is Better than That of Recent Presidents." *Huffington Post*, May 5.

Elliott, Justin. 2010. "The Ten Most Important WikiLeaks Revelations. *Salon*, November 29. http://www.salon.com/2010/11/29/wikileaks_roundup/.

Eilperin, Juliet. 2012. "Autos Must Average 54.5 mpg by 2025, New EPA Standards Say." *Washington Post*, August 28.

Engelbrecht, Helmuth Carol, and Frank Cleary Hanighen. 1934. *Merchants of Death: A Study of the International Armament Industry*. New York: Dodd, Mead.

Entman, Robert M. 2004. *Projections of Power: Framing News, Public Opinion, and U.S. Foreign Policy*. Chicago: University of Chicago Press.

Epstein, Susan B. 2011. *Foreign Aid Reform, National Strategy, and the Quadrennial Review*. Washington, DC: Congressional Research Service, February 15.

Epstein, Susan B., and K. Alan Kronstadt. 2012. *Pakistan: U.S. Foreign Assistance*. Washington, DC: Congressional Research Service. http://www.fas.org/sgp/crs/row/R41856.pdf.

Eshbaugh-Soha, Matthew, and Christopher Linebarger. 2014. "Presidential and Media Leadership of Public Opinion on Iraq." *Foreign Policy Analysis* 10 (4): 351–369.

Esposito, John L. 2002. *Unholy War: Terror in the Name of Islam*. New York: Oxford University Press.

Etheridge, Lloyd. 1978. "Personality Effects on American Foreign Policy, 1898–1968: A Test of Interpersonal Generalization Theory." *American Political Science Review* 72 (2): 434–451.

Farnham, Barbara. 2004. "Impact of the Political Context on Foreign Policy Decision-Making." *Political Psychology* 25 (3): 441–463.

Fasullo, John T., and Kevin E. Trenberth. 2012. "A Less Cloudy Future: The Role of Subtropical Subsidence in Climate Sensitivity." *Science* 338 (6108): 792–794.

Federation of American Scientists, Intelligence Resource Program. 2015. Intelligence Budget Data. Washington, DC: Federation of American Scientists. http://fas.org/irp/budget/.

Feaver, Peter D., and Christopher Gelpi. 2004. *Choosing Your Battles: American Civil-Military Relations and the Use of Force*. Princeton, NJ: Princeton University Press.

Feulner, Edwin J. 2015. "Fallout from a Bad Deal with Iran." *Heritage Foundation*, May 5. http://www.heritage.org/research/commentary/2015/5/fallout-from-a-bad-deal-with-iran.

Fineman, Howard. 2003. "Bush and God: A Higher Calling." *Newsweek,* March 10, 22–30.

Finnemore, Martha. 2003. *The Purpose of Intervention: Changing Beliefs about the Use of Force*. Ithaca, NY: Cornell University Press.

———. 2009. "Legitimacy, Hypocrisy, and the Social Structure of Unipolarity: Why Being a Unipole Isn't All It's Cracked Up to Be." *World Politics* 61 (1): 58–85.

Fischer, Eric A., Edward C. Liu, John Rollins, and Catherine A. Theohary. 2013. *The 2013 Cybersecurity Executive Order: Overview and Consideration for Congress*. Washington, DC: Congressional Research Service.

Fisher, Louis. 2004. "The Way We Go to War: The Iraq Resolution." In *Considering the Bush Presidency,* edited by Gary L. Gregg II and Mark J. Rozell, 107–124. New York: Oxford University Press.

———. 2007. "The Scope of Inherent Powers." In *The Polarized Presidency of George W. Bush*, edited by George C. Edwards III and Desmond S. King, 31–64. New York: Oxford University Press.

Fisher, Max. 2013. "Who Loves and Hates America: A Revealing Map of Global Opinion toward the United States." *Washington Post*, January 11.

Flanik, William. 2011. "'Bringing FPA Back Home': Cognition, Constructivism, and Conceptual Metaphor." *Foreign Policy Analysis* 7 (4): 423–446.

Fleisher, Richard, Jon R. Bond, and B. Dan Wood. 2008. "Which Presidents Are Uncommonly Successful in Congress?" In *Presidential Leadership: The Vortex of Power*, edited by Bert A. Rockman and Richard W. Waterman, 191–214. New York: Oxford University Press.

Ford, Jess T. 2009. "Department of State: Persistent Staffing and Foreign Language Gaps Compromise Diplomatic Readiness." Washington, DC: U.S. Government Accountability Office, September 24. http://www.gao.gov/assets/130/123400.html.

Fordham, Benjamin O., and Timothy McKeown. 2003. "Selection and Influence: Interest Groups and Congressional Voting on Trade Policy." *International Organization* 57 (3): 519–549.

Forsythe, David P. 1995. "Human Rights and U.S. Foreign Policy: Two Levels, Two Worlds." *Political Studies* 43 (S1): S111–S130.

Foster, Dennis M., and Jonathan W. Keller. 2014. "Leaders' Cognitive Complexity, Distrust, and the Diversionary Use of Force." *Foreign Policy Analysis* 10 (3): 205–223.

Franck, Thomas M., and Edward Weisband. 1979. *Foreign Policy by Congress.* New York: Oxford University Press.

Freedman, Lawrence. 2003. *The Evolution of Nuclear Strategy* (3rd ed.). New York: Palgrave Macmillan.

Freedom House. 2011. *A Contest for Supremacy: China, America, and the Struggle for Mastery in Asia.* New York: W. W. Norton.

———. 2012. *Freedom in the World 2012: The Arab Uprisings and their Global Repercussions.* http://www.freedomhouse.org/article/freedom-world-2012-arab-uprisings-and-their-global-repercussions/.

———. 2015. *Freedom in the World 2015.* Washington, DC: Freedom House. https://freedomhouse.org/sites/default/files/01152015_FIW_2015_final.pdf.

Friedberg, Aaron L. 2011. *A Contest for Supremacy: China, America and the Struggle for Mastery in Asia.* New York: Norton.

Froman, Michael. 2014. "The Strategic Logic of Trade: New Rules of the Road for the Global Market." *Foreign Affairs* 93 (November-December): 111–118.

Fry, Earl H. 1998. *The Expanding Role of State and Local Governments in U.S. Foreign Affairs.* New York: Council on Foreign Relations.

Fukuyama, Francis. 1989. "The End of History?" *National Interest* 16 (summer): 3–18.

———. 2004. *State-Building: Governance and World Order in the 21st Century.* Ithaca, NY: Cornell University Press.

Gadarian, Shana K. 2010. "Foreign Policy at the Ballot Box: How Citizens Use Foreign Policy to Judge and Choose Candidates." *Journal of Politics* 72 (4): 1046–1062.

Gaddis, John L. 2005. *Surprise, Security, and the American Experience.* Cambridge, MA: Harvard University Press.

Gagliano, Joseph A. 2015. *Congressional Policymaking in Sino-U.S. Relations during the Post–Cold War Era.* New York: Routledge.

Galdi, Theodor W. 1995. *Revolution In Military Affairs? Competing Concepts, Organizational Responses, Outstanding Issues.* Washington, DC: Congressional Research Service, December 11.

Gallagher, Maryann E., and Susan H. Allen. 2014. "Presidential Personality: Not Just a Nuisance." *Foreign Policy Analysis* 10 (1): 1–21.

Gao, George. 2015. "Scientists More Worried than Public about World's Growing Population." Washington, DC: Pew Research Center, June 8.

Gardner, Richard N. 1980. *Sterling-Dollar Diplomacy in Current Perspectives: The Origins and Prospects of Our International Economic Order*, Exp. ed. New York: Columbia University Press.

Garrison, Jean. 1999. *Games Advisors Play: Foreign Policy in the Nixon and Carter Administrations.* College Station: Texas A&M University Press.

Gartner, Scott S. 2011. "On Behalf of a Grateful Nation: Conventionalized Images of Loss and Individual Opinion Change in War." *International Studies Quarterly* 55 (2): 545–561.

Gartzke, Erik. 2007. "The Capitalist Peace." *American Journal of Political Science* 51 (1): 166–191.

Gates, Robert M. 1996. *From the Shadows: The Ultimate Insider's Story of Five Presidents and How They Won the Cold War.* New York: Simon & Schuster.

———. 2014. *Duty: Memoirs of a Secretary at War.* New York: Knopf.

Gelman, Barton. 2013. "Code Name 'Verax': Snowden, in Exchanges with Post Reporter, Made Clear He Knew Risks." *Washington Post*, June 9.

Genovese, Michael A. 2011. *Presidential Prerogative: Imperial Power in an Age of Terrorism.* Stanford, CA: Stanford University Press.

George, Alexander L. 1972. "The Case for Multiple Advocacy in Making Foreign Policy." *American Political Science Review* 66 (3): 751–785.

———. 1980. *Presidential Decisionmaking in Foreign Policy: The Effective Use of Information and Advice.* Boulder, CO: Westview Press.

———. 1989. "The 'Operational Code': A Neglected Approach to the Study of Political Leaders and Decision Making." In *American Foreign Policy: Theoretical Essays,* edited by G. John Ikenberry, 483–506. New York: HarperCollins.

———. 2000. "The Role of Force in Diplomacy: A Continuing Dilemma for U.S. Foreign Policy." In *The Use of Force after the Cold War,* edited by H. W. Brands, 59–92. College Station: Texas A&M University Press.

George, Alexander L., and Juliette L. George. 1956. *Woodrow Wilson and Colonel House: A Personality Study.* New York: J. Day.

Gertler, Jeremiah. 2012. *U.S. Unmanned Aerial Systems.* Washington, DC: Congressional Research Service, January 3.

Gibson, Martha L. 2000. *Conflict amid Consensus in American Trade Policy.* Washington, DC: Georgetown University Press.

Gilpin, Robert. 1981. *War and Change in World Politics.* New York: Cambridge University Press.

Gilpin, Robert, and Jean Millis Gilpin. 1987. *The Political Science of International Relations.* Princeton, NJ: Princeton University Press.

Ginsberg, Benjamin. 1986. *The Captive Public: How Mass Opinion Promotes State Power.* New York: Basic Books.

Glad, Betty. 1983. "Black-and-White Thinking: Ronald Reagan's Approach to Foreign Policy." *Political Psychology* 4 (1): 33–76.

Glain, Stephen. 2011. *State vs. Defense: The Battle to Define America's Empire.* New York: Crown.

Glassman, James K. 2012. "Send Public Diplomacy into Battle." *The Hill*, August 1. http://thehill.com/opinion/op-ed/241739-send-public-diplomacy-into-battle/.

Global Terrorism Database. 2015. National Consortium for the Study of Terrorism and Responses to Terrorism, June. College Park: University of Maryland.

Golan, Guy G. 2010. "Determinants of International News Coverage." In *International Media Communications in a Global Age,* edited by Guy Golan, Thomas J. Johnson, and Wayne Wanta, 125–144. New York: Routledge.

Goldberg, Jeffrey. 2014. "Hillary Clinton: 'Failure' to Help Syrian Rebels Led to the Rise of ISIS." *The Atlantic,* August 10.

Goldman, David. 2012. "Facebook Tops 900 Million Users." *CNN Money,* April 23. http://money.cnn.com/2012/04/23/technology/facebook-q1/index.htm.

Goldsmith, Benjamin E., and Yusaku Horiuchi. 2012. "In Search of Soft Power: Does Foreign Public Opinion Matter for U.S. Foreign Policy?" *World Politics* 64 (3): 555–585.

Goldsmith, Jack. 2012. *Power and Constraint: The Accountable Presidency after 9/11*. New York: Norton.

Goldsmith, Jack, and Matthew Waxman. 2014. "Obama, Not Bush, Is the Master of Unilateral War." *The New Republic*, October 14.

Goldstein, Judith, and Robert O. Keohane. 1993. *Ideas and Foreign Policy: Beliefs, Institutions, and Political Change*. Ithaca, NY: Cornell University Press.

Goldwater et al. v. Carter, 444 U.S. 996 (1979).

Goodman, Melvin A. 2008. *Failure of Intelligence: The Decline and Fall of the CIA*. Lanham, MD: Rowman & Littlefield.

Goodwin, Jacob. 1985. *Brotherhood of Arms: General Dynamics and the Business of Defending America*. New York: Times Books.

Gordon, Michael R. 2013. "Report Details Mistakes Made by U.S. in Improvement Projects for Iraq." *New York Times*, March 6.

———. 2015. "Armed with Google and YouTube, Analysts Gauge Russia's Presence in Ukraine." *New York Times*, A6.

Gordon, Michael R., and David E. Sanger. 2015. "Deal Reached on Nuclear Program: Limits on Fuel Would Lesson with Time." *New York Times,* July 14.

Gordon, Michael R., and Bernard E. Trainor. 2006. *Cobra II: The Inside Story of the Invasion and Occupation of Iraq*. New York: Pantheon Books.

Graber, Doris A., and Johanna Dunaway. 2015. *Mass Media and American Politics*, 9th ed. Washington, DC: CQ Press.

Graebner, Norman A., ed. 1964. *Ideas and Diplomacy: Readings in the Intellectual Tradition of American Foreign Policy*. New York: Oxford University Press.

Graham, David A. 2014. "Defense Secretary Chuck Hagel: Get Used to Endless War." *The Atlantic*, October 29.

———. 2015. "Violence Has Forced 60 Million People from Their Homes." *The Atlantic*, June 17.

Gray, Christine D. 2004. *International Law and the Use of Force,* 2nd ed. New York: Oxford University Press.

Gray, Colin S. 1999. *Modern Strategy*. New York: Oxford University Press.

Greenberger, Robert S. 1995/1996. "Dateline Capitol Hill: The New Majority's Foreign Policy." *Foreign Policy* 101 (winter): 159–169.

Greenwald, Glenn. 2013. "NSA Collecting Phone Records of Millions of Verizon Customers Daily." *The Guardian*, June 5.

Greenwald, Glenn, and Ewen MacAskill. 2013. "NSA Prism Program Taps in to User Data of Apple, Google, and Others." *The Guardian*, June 6.

Greenwald, Glenn, Ewen MacAskill, and Laura Poitras. 2013. "Edward Snowden: The Whistleblower behind the NSA Surveillance Revelations." *The Guardian*, June 9.

Gregg, Gary L., II. 2004. "Dignified Authenticity: George W. Bush and the Symbolic Presidency." In *Considering the Bush Presidency,* edited by Gary L. Gregg II and Mark J. Rozell, 88–106. New York: Oxford University Press.

Gregory, William H. 1989. *The Defense Procurement Mess*. Lexington, MA: Lexington Books.

Grieco, Joseph M., Christopher Gelpi, Jason Reifler, and Peter D. Feaver. 2011. "Let's Get a Second Opinion: International Institutions and American Public Support for War." *International Studies Quarterly* 55 (2): 563–583.

Grimmett, Richard F. 2001. *The War Powers Resolution: After Twenty-Eight Years*. Washington, DC: Congressional Research Service, November 15.

———. 2004. *Instances of Use of United States Armed Forces Abroad, 1798–2004*. Washington, DC: Congressional Research Service, October 5.

———. 2012a. *Instances of Use of United States Armed Forces Abroad, 1798–2012*. Washington, DC: Congressional Research Service, September 19. http://www.fas.org/sgp/crs/natsec/R42738.pdf.

———. 2012b. *War Powers Resolution: Presidential Compliance*. Washington, DC: Congressional Research Service, September 25. http://www.fas.org/sgp/crs/natsec/RL33532.pdf.

Grimmett, Richard F., and Paul K. Kerr. 2012. *Conventional Arms Transfers to Developing Nations, 2004–2011*. Washington, DC: Congressional Research Service, September 22. http://www.fas.org/sgp/crs/weapons/R42678.pdf.

Grunwald, Henry A. 1993. "The Post–Cold War Press: A New World Needs a New Journalism." *Foreign Affairs* 72 (summer): 12–16.

Haass, Richard N. 2014, November/December. "The Unraveling: How to Respond to a Disordered World." *Foreign Affairs* 93 (6).

———. 2015. "The Future of the Iran Nuclear Deal." *Council on Foreign Relations*, April 3. http://www.cfr.org/iran/future-iran-nuclear-deal/p36400.

Habel, Philip D. 2012. "Following the Opinion Leaders? The Dynamics of Influence among Media Opinion, the Public, and Politicians." *Political Communications* 29 (July): 257–277.

Hafner-Burton, Emilie M. 2008. "Sticks and Stones: The Efficacy of Human Rights 'Naming and Shaming.'" *International Organization* 62, no. 4.

Halchin, L. Elaine, and Frederick M. Kaiser. 2012. *Congressional Oversight of Intelligence: Current Structure and Alternatives*. Washington, DC: Congressional Research Service, May 14. http://www.fas.org/sgp/crs/intel/RL32525.pdf.

Hallin, Daniel C., and Todd Gitlin. 1994. "The Gulf War as Popular Culture and Television Drama." In *Taken by Storm: The Media, Public Opinion, and U.S. Foreign Policy in the Gulf War,* edited by W. Lance Bennett and David L. Paletz, 149–163. Chicago: University of Chicago Press.

Halper, Stefan A. 2010. *The Beijing Consensus: How China's Authoritarian Model Will Dominate the Twenty-First Century.* New York: Basic Books.

Halperin, Morton. 1963. *Limited War in the Nuclear Age.* New York: Wiley.

Hamilton, Alexander, John Jay, James Madison, and Edward Gaylord Bourne. 1937. *The Federalist: A Commentary on the Constitution of the United States,* edited by Edward Mead Earle. Washington, DC: National Home Library.

Hamilton, Alexander, James Madison, and John Jay. 1787–1788. *The Federalist.* The Library of Congress THOMAS/ Project Gutenberg. http://thomas.loc .gov/home/histdox/fedpapers.html.

Hamilton, Lee. 2009. *Strengthening Congress.* Bloomington: Indiana University Press.

Haney, Patrick J. 1997. *Organizing for Foreign Policy Crises: Presidents, Advisers, and the Management of Decision Making.* Ann Arbor: University of Michigan Press.

———. 2005. "Foreign-Policy Advising: Models and Mysteries from the Bush Administration." *Presidential Studies Quarterly* 35 (2): 289–302.

Harding, Luke. 2014. *The Snowden Files: The Inside Story of the World's Most Wanted Man.* New York: Vintage.

Hart, Jeffrey A. 1992. *Rival Capitalists: International Competitiveness in the United States, Japan, and Western Europe.* Ithaca, NY: Cornell University Press.

Hart, John. 1987. *The Presidential Branch.* New York: Pergamon Press.

Hart, Justin. 2013. *Empire of Ideas: The Origins of Public Diplomacy and the Transformation of U.S. Foreign Policy.* New York: Oxford University Press.

Hart, Paul 't. 1994. *Groupthink in Government: A Study of Small Groups and Policy Failure.* Baltimore: Johns Hopkins University Press.

Hart, Paul 't., Eric Stern, and Bengt Sundelius, eds. 1997. *Beyond Groupthink: Political Group Dynamics and Foreign Policy-making.* Ann Arbor: University of Michigan Press.

Hayden, Patrick, and Chamsy el-Ojeili, eds. 2005. *Confronting Globalization: Humanity, Justice, and the Renewal of Politics.* New York: Palgrave Macmillan.

Hayton, Bill. 2014. *The South China Sea: The Struggle for Power in Asia.* New Haven, CT: Yale University Press.

Heclo, Hugh. 1978. "Issue Networks and the Executive Establishment." In *The New American Political System,* edited by Anthony King, 87–124. Washington, DC: American Enterprise Institute.

Heilbroner, Robert L. 1999. *The Worldly Philosophers: The Lives, Times, and Ideas of the Great Economic Thinkers,* Rev. 7th ed. New York: Simon & Schuster.

Henehan, Marie T. 2000. *Foreign Policy and Congress: An International Relations Perspective.* Ann Arbor: University of Michigan Press.

Henkin, Louis. 1996. *Foreign Affairs and the United States Constitution,* 2nd ed. New York: Oxford University Press.

Henry J. Kaiser Family Foundation. 2015. "The U.S. Government and International Family Planning and Reproductive Health." April 23.

Herman, Edward, and Noam Chomsky. 1988. *Manufacturing Consent: The Political Economy of the Mass Media.* New York: Pantheon.

Herman, Susan. 2011. *Taking Liberties: The War on Terror and the Erosion of American Democracy.* New York: Oxford University Press.

Hermann, Margaret G. 1984. "Personality and Foreign Policy Decision Making: A Study of 53 Heads of Government." In *Foreign Policy Decision Making: Perception, Cognition, and Artificial Intelligence,* edited by Donald A. Sylvan and Steve Chan, 53–80. New York: Praeger.

———. 1993. "Leaders and Foreign Policy Decision-Making." In *Diplomacy, Force, and Leadership: Essays in Honor of Alexander L. George,* edited by Dan Caldwell and Timothy J. McKeown, 77–94. Boulder, CO: Westview Press.

Hersh, Seymour M. 1974. "Huge CIA Operation Reported in U.S. against Antiwar Forces, Other Dissidents in Nixon Years." *New York Times,* December 21.

———. 2004. "Torture at Abu Ghraib." *New Yorker,* May 10. http://www.newyorker .com/archive/2004/05/10/040510fa_ fact.

Hess, Gary R. 2009. *Vietnam: Explaining America's Lost War.* Oxford: Blackwell.

Hess, Stephen, and James P. Pfiffner. 2002. *Organizing the Presidency,* 3rd ed. Washington, DC: Brookings Institution Press.

Hetherington, Marc J. 1998. "The Political Relevance of Political Trust." *American Political Science Review* 92 (4): 791–808.

Hewitt, Elizabeth. 2012. "U.N. Scientists: Climate Change behind Recent Freak Weather." *Slate,* August 1.

Higgins, Andrew. 2014. "Oil's Swift Fall Raises Fortunes of U.S. Abroad." *New York Times,* December 24.

Hildreth, Steven A. 2005. *Missile Defense: The Current Debate.* Washington, DC: Congressional Research Service, July 19. http://www.fas.org/sgp/crs/ weapons/RL31111.pdf.

Hill, Christopher. 2003. *The Changing Politics of Foreign Policy.* New York: Palgrave Macmillan.

Hilsman, Roger. 2000. "After the Cold War: The Need for Intelligence." In *National Insecurity: U.S. Intelligence after the Cold War,* edited by Craig Eisendrath, 8–22. Philadelphia: Temple University Press.

Hinckley, Barbara. 1994. *Less than Meets the Eye: Foreign Policy Making and the Myth of the Assertive Congress.* Chicago: University of Chicago Press.

Hirsh, Michael. 2003. *At War with Ourselves: Why America Is Squandering Its Chance to Build a Better World.* New York: Oxford University Press.

Hixson, Walter L. 2008. *The Myth of American Diplomacy: National Identity and U.S. Foreign Policy.* New Haven, CT: Yale University Press.

Hodgson, Godfrey. 2009. *The Myth of American Exceptionalism.* New Haven, CT: Yale University Press.

Hoffman, Bruce. 1998. *Inside Terrorism.* New York: Columbia University Press.

Hofman, Ross J. S., and Paul Levack, eds. 1949. *Burke's Politics: Selected Writings and Speeches on Reform, Revolution and War.* New York: Knopf.

Holmes, Jack E. 1985. *The Mood/Interest Theory of American Foreign Policy.* Lexington: University of Kentucky Press.

Holsti, Kal J. 1970. "National Role Conceptions in the Study of Foreign Policy." *International Studies Quarterly* 14 (3): 233–309.

Holsti, Ole R. 1962. "The Belief System and National Images: A Case Study." *Journal of Conflict Resolution* 6 (3): 244–252.

———. 1984. "Theories of Crisis Decision Making." In *International Conflict and Conflict Management: Readings in World Politics*, edited by Robert O. Matthews, Arthur G. Rubinoff, and Janice Gross Stein, 65–83. New York: Prentice Hall.

———. 1992. "Public Opinion and Foreign Policy: Challenges to the Almond-Lippmann Consensus Mershon Series; Research Programs and Debates." *International Studies Quarterly* 36 (4): 439–466.

———. 1996. *Public Opinion and American Foreign Policy.* Ann Arbor: University of Michigan Press.

———. 2011. *American Public Opinion on the Iraq War.* Ann Arbor: University of Michigan Press.

Holsti, Ole R., and James M. Rosenau. 1979. "Vietnam, Consensus, and the Belief Systems of American Leaders." *World Politics* 32 (1): 1–56.

Hook, Steven W. 1995. *National Interest and Foreign Aid.* Boulder, CO: Lynne Rienner.

———. 1998. "'Building Democracy' through Foreign Aid: The Limitations of United States Political Conditionalities, 1992–96." *Democratization* 5 (3): 156–180.

———. 2003. "Domestic Obstacles to International Affairs: The State Department under Fire at Home." *PS: Political Science and Politics* 36 (1): 23–29.

———. 2008. "Ideas and Change in U.S. Foreign Aid: Inventing the Millennium Challenge Corporation." *Foreign Policy Analysis* 4 (2): 147–167.

Hook, Steven W., and Franklin Barr Lebo. 2010. "Development/Poverty Issues and Foreign Policy Analysis." In *The International Studies Encyclopedia,* edited by Robert A. Denemark. Malden, MA: Blackwell.

———. 2014. "Sino-American Trade Relations: Privatizing Foreign Policy." In *Contemporary Cases in U.S. Foreign Policy: From Terrorism to Trade,* 5th ed., edited by Ralph G. Carter, 305–333. Washington, DC: CQ Press.

Hook, Steven W., and Xiaoyu Pu. 2006. "Framing Sino-American Relations under Stress: A Reexamination of News Coverage of the 2001 Spy Plane Crisis." *Asian Affairs: An American Review* 33 (3): 167–183.

Hook, Steven W., and David Rothstein. 2005. "New Rationales and Old Concerns about U.S. Arms Exports." In *Guns and Butter: The Political Economy of International Security*, edited by Peter Dombrowski, 153–178. Boulder, CO: Lynne Rienner.

Hook, Steven W., and James M. Scott, eds. 2012. *U.S. Foreign Policy Today: American Renewal?* Washington, DC: CQ Press.

Hook, Steven W., and John Spanier. 2013. *American Foreign Policy since World War II*, 19th ed. Washington, DC: CQ Press.

———. 2016. *American Foreign Policy Since World War II*, 20th ed. Washington, DC: CQ Press.

Houghton, David Patrick. 2007. "Reinvigorating the Study of Foreign Policy Decision Making: Toward a Constructivist Approach." *Foreign Policy Analysis* 3 (1): 24–45.

Howell, William G. 2003. *Power without Persuasion: The Politics of Direct Presidential Action*. Princeton, NJ: Princeton University Press.

Howell, William G., and Douglas Kriner. 2008. "Power without Persuasion: Identifying Executive Influence." In *Presidential Leadership: The Vortex of Power*, edited by Bert A. Rockman and Richard W. Waterman, 105–144. New York: Oxford University Press.

Howell, William G., and Jon C. Pevehouse. 2005. "Presidents, Congress, and the Use of Force." *International Organization* 59 (1): 209–232.

Hu, Jane C. 2014. "The Battle for Space." *Slate*, December 23.

Human Security Report Project. 2012. *Human Security Report 2012.* Vancouver: Human Security Report Project, Simon Fraser University. http://www.hsrgroup.org/human-security-reports/2012/overview.aspx.

Hunt, Michael. 1987. *Ideology and U.S. Foreign Policy.* New Haven, CT: Yale University Press.

———. 1970/1971. "Foreign Aid for What and for Whom." *Foreign Policy* 1 (winter): 161–189.

Huntington, Samuel P. 1957. *The Soldier and the State: The Theory and Practice of State-Society Relations.* New York: Vintage Books.

———. 1981. *American Politics: The Promise of Disharmony.* Cambridge, MA: Harvard University Press.

———. 1982. "American Ideals versus American Institutions." *Political Science Quarterly* 97 (1): 1–37.

Ignatieff, Michael. 2005. "Introduction: American Exceptionalism and Human Rights." In *American Exceptionalism and Human Rights,* edited by Michael Ignatieff, 1–26. Princeton, NJ: Princeton University Press.

Ikenberry, G. John. 2001. *After Victory: Institutions, Strategic Restraint, and the Rebuilding of Order after Major Wars.* Princeton, NJ: Princeton University Press.

———. 2011. *Liberal Leviathan: The Origins, Crisis, and Transformation of the American World Order.* Princeton, NJ: Princeton University Press.

Ikenberry, G. John, David A. Lake, and Michael Mastanduno, eds. 1988. *The State and American Foreign Economic Policy.* Ithaca, NY: Cornell University Press.

Independent Task Force on U.S. Immigration Policy. 2009. *U.S. Immigration Policy.* New York: Council on Foreign Relations. http://www.cfr.org/immigration/us-immigration-policy/p20030/.

Inderfurth, Karl F., and Loch K. Johnson. 2004. *Fateful Decisions: Inside the National Security Council.* New York: Oxford University Press.

Indyk, Martin S., Kenneth G. Lieberthal, and Michael E. O'Hanlon. 2012. "Scoring

Obama's Foreign Policy." *Foreign Affairs* 91 (3): 29–43.

Inglehart, Ronald, Miguel Basáñez, and Alejandro Menéndez Moreno. 1998. *Human Values and Beliefs: A Cross-Cultural Sourcebook.* Ann Arbor: University of Michigan Press.

Institute for Economics and Peace. 2012a. 2012 Global Peace Index. Press release. http://www.visionofhumanity .org/wp-content/uploads/2012/06/ GPI-2012-GLOBL-PRESS-RELEASE.pdf.

Institute for Economics and Peace. 2012b. *Global Peace Index.* Sydney: Institute for Economics and Peace. http:// economicsandpeace.org/research/ iep-indices-data/global-peace-index/.

International Committee of the Red Cross (ICRC). 2004. *Guantanamo Bay: Overview of the ICRC's Work for Internees.* Geneva: ICRC. http://www .icrc.org/eng/resources/documents/ misc/5qrc5v.htm.

International Criminal Court (ICC). 2015a. *The State Parties to the Rome Statute.* The Hague, Netherlands: ICC, January 6.

———. 2015b. *Situation and Cases.* The Hague, Netherlands: ICC.

International Monetary Fund. 2011. *Fiscal Monitor: Addressing Fiscal Challenges to Reduce Economic Risks.* Washington, DC: International Monetary Fund.

———. 2014. *Heavily Indebted Poor Countries (HIPC) Initiative and Multilateral Debt Relief Initiative (MDRI)—Statistical Update.* Washington, DC: International Monetary Fund.

———. 2015. "World Economic Outlook Database." April. http://www.imf.org/ external/pubs/ft/weo/2014/02/ weodata/index.aspx.

Internet World Stats. 2012. "Top 20 Internet Countries by Users." http://www .internetworldstats.com/top20.htm.

IPCC (Intergovernmental Panel on Climate Change). 2007. *Climate Change 2007: The Physical Science Basis.* Paris: IPCC.

———. 2012. "Managing the Risks of Extreme Events and Disasters to Advance Climate Change Adaptation (SREX)." http://ipcc-wg2.gov/SREX/.

Isaacson, Walter, and Evan Thomas. 1986. *The Wise Men: Six Friends and the World They Made.* New York: Simon & Schuster.

Iyengar, Shanto. 1991. *Is Anyone Responsible? How Television Frames Political News.* Chicago: University of Chicago Press.

Iyengar, Shanto, Kyu S. Hahn, Heinz Bonfadelli, and Mirko Marr. 2009. "Dark Areas of Ignorance Revisited: Comparing International Affairs Knowledge in Switzerland and the United States." *Communications Research* 36 (3): 341–358.

Iyengar, Shanto, and Adam Simon. 1994. "News Coverage of the Gulf Crisis and Public Opinion: A Study of Agenda-Setting, Priming, and Framing." In *Taken by Storm: The Media, Public Opinion, and U.S. Foreign Policy in the Gulf War,* edited by W. Lance Bennett and David L. Paletz, 167–185. Chicago: University of Chicago Press.

Jacobs, Lawrence R., and Benjamin I. Page. 2005. "Who Influences U.S. Foreign Policy?" *American Political Science Review* 99 (1): 107–123.

Jacobs, Lawrence R., and Robert Y. Shapiro. 1995. "The Rise of Presidential Polling: The Nixon White House in Historical Perspective." *Public Opinion Quarterly* 59 (2): 163–195.

Jacobson, Gary C. 1987. "Running Scared: Elections and Congressional Politics in the 1980s." In *Congress: Structure and Policy,* edited by Mathew McCubbins and Terry Sullivan, 34–81. New York: Cambridge University Press.

———. 2000. "Party Polarization in National Politics: The Electoral Connection." In *Polarized Politics: Congress and the President in a Partisan Era,* edited by Jon R. Bond and Richard Fleisher, 9–30. Washington, DC: CQ Press.

———. 2010a. "George W. Bush, the Iraq War, and the Election of Barack Obama." *Presidential Studies Quarterly* 40 (2): 207–224.

———. 2010b. "A Tale of Two Wars: Public Opinion on the U.S. Military Interventions in Afghanistan and Iraq." *Presidential Studies Quarterly* 40 (4): 585–610.

Jaffe, Greg. 2012. "With Military at 'Turning Point,' Defense Chief Leon Panetta Avoids Bold Moves." *Washington Post,* September 3. http://articles .washingtonpost.com/2012-09-03/ world/35497230_1_bold-moves-andrew-hoehn-defense-secretary/.

Jagger, Suzy. 2008. "Vladimir Putin Blames America for World Economic Crisis." *Times Online,* October 2. http://www .thetimes.co.uk/tto/business/markets/ russia/article2143029.ece.

Janis, Irving L. 1982. *Groupthink: Psychological Studies of Policy Decisions and Fiascoes,* Rev. 2nd ed. Boston: Houghton Mifflin.

Jefferson, Thomas. 1787. Letter to Edward Carrington, January 16. In Philip B. Kurland and Ralph Lerner, eds., *The Founders' Constitution* (Web edition). http://press-pubs.uchicago.edu/found ers/documents/amendl_speechs8.html.

———. 1801. First Inaugural Address, March 4, Washington, D.C. http://www .presidency.ucsb.edu/ws/index .php?pid=25803.

Jehl, Douglas. 2003. "On Environmental Rules, Bush Sees a Balance, Critics a Threat." *New York Times,* February 23, 1A.

Jentleson, Bruce W. 1992. "The Pretty Prudent Public: Post Post–Vietnam American Opinion on the Use of Military Force." *International Studies Quarterly* 36 (1): 49–73.

Jervis, Robert L. 1976. *Perception and Misperception in International Politics.* Princeton, NJ: Princeton University Press.

———. 2010. *Why Intelligence Fails: Lessons from the Iranian Revolution and the Iraq War.* Ithaca, NY: Cornell University Press.

Jess, Kevin. 2009. "IMF: Total Cost of Financial Crisis at $11.9 Trillion." *Digital Journal,* August 9. http://www .digitaljournal.com/article/277282/.

Joffe, Josef. 2009. "The Default Power: The False Prophecy of America's Decline." *Foreign Affairs* 88 (September–October): 21–35.

Johnson, Chalmers. 2000. *Blowback: The Costs and Consequences of American Empire.* New York: Metropolitan Books.

Johnson, Gene. 2015. "In Rough Seas, Greenpeace Gets off Arctic Oil Rig." *Seattle Times,* April 11.

Johnson, James T. 1981. *Just War Tradition and the Restraint of War: A Moral and Historical Inquiry.* Princeton, NJ: Princeton University Press.

Johnson, Richard T. 1974. *Managing the White House: An Intimate Study of the Presidency.* New York: Harper & Row.

Johnson, Robert D. 2001. "Congress and the Cold War." *Journal of Cold War Studies* 3 (2): 76–100.

Johnson, Toni. 2013. *Congress and U.S. Foreign Policy.* New York: Council on Foreign Relations, January 24.

Jones, Alex S. 2009. *Losing the News: The Future of the News That Feeds Democracy.* New York: Oxford University Press.

Jones, Dorothy V. 2002. *Toward a Just World: The Critical Years in the Search for International Justice.* Chicago: University of Chicago Press.

Jones, Gordon S., and John A. Marini, eds. 1988. *The Imperial Congress: Crisis in the Separation of Powers.* New York: Pharos Books.

Jones, Howard. 1988. *The Course of American Diplomacy,* 2nd ed. Chicago: Dorsey Press.

———. 2002. *Crucible of Power: A History of American Foreign Relations to 1913.* Wilmington, DE: SR Books.

Jordan, Amos A., William J. Taylor Jr., and Michael J. Mazarr. 1999. *American National Security,* 5th ed. Baltimore: Johns Hopkins University Press.

Joskow, Paul L. 2002. "United States Energy Policy during the 1990s." *Current History* 101 (March): 105–125.

Joyner, Daniel H. 2011. *Interpreting the Nuclear Non-proliferation Treaty.* New York: Oxford University Press.

Kagan, Robert. 2006. *Dangerous Nation: America's Foreign Policy from Its Earliest Days to the Dawn of the Twentieth Century.* New York: Vintage.

———. 2014. "Superpowers Don't Get to Retire What Our Tired Country Still Owes the World." *New Republic,* May 26.

Kane, John. 2008. *Between Virtue and Power: The Persistent Moral Dilemma of U.S. Foreign Policy.* New Haven, CT: Yale University Press.

Kant, Immanuel. [1795] 1914. *Eternal Peace and Other International Essays.* Boston: World Peace Foundation.

Kaplan, Fred. 2014. "The Realist." *Politico,* February 27.

Karnow, Stanley. 1983. *Vietnam: A History.* New York: Viking Press.

Karns, Margaret P., and Karen A. Mingst. 2004. *International Organizations: The Politics and Processes of Global Governance.* Boulder, CO: Lynne Rienner.

Kastner, Scott L., and Douglas B. Grob. 2009. "Legislative Foundations of U.S.–Taiwan Relations: A New Look at the Congressional Taiwan Caucus." *Foreign Policy Analysis* 5 (1): 57–72.

Katagiri, Noriyuki. 2014. *Adapting to Win: How Insurgents Fight and Defeat Foreign States in Wars.* Philadelphia: University of Pennsylvania Press.

Katovsky, Bill, and Timothy Carlson, eds. 2003. *Embedded: The Media at War in Iraq.* Guilford, CT: Lyons Press.

Katzenstein, Peter J. 1996. *The Culture of National Security: Norms and Identity in World Politics.* New York: Columbia University Press

Katzenstein, Peter J., and Robert O. Keohane, eds. 2007. *Anti-Americanisms in World Politics.* Ithaca, NY: Cornell University Press.

Katzman, Kenneth. 2012. *Iran Sanctions.* Washington, DC: Congressional Research Service, October 15.

Kaufman, Scott. 2008. *Plans Unraveled: The Foreign Policy of the Carter Administration.* DeKalb: Northern Illinois University Press.

Kaufmann, Chaim. 2004. "Threat Inflation and the Failure of the Marketplace of Ideas: The Selling of the Iraq War." *International Security* 29 (1): 5–48.

Kaye, David. 2011. "Who's Afraid of the International Criminal Court?" *Foreign Affairs* 90 (May–June): 118–129.

Keating, Joshua E. 2012. "Who Won the Great Recession? Those 7 Countries." *Foreign Policy* 196 (November): 53–54.

Keck, Margaret E., and Kathryn Sikkink. 1998. *Activists beyond Borders: Advocacy Networks in International Politics.* Ithaca, NY: Cornell University Press.

Keller, Jared. 2010. "Evaluating Iran's Twitter Revolution." *New York Times,* June 18.

Kengor, Paul. 2004. "Cheney and Vice Presidential Power." In *Considering the Bush Presidency,* edited by Gary L. Gregg II and Mark J. Rozell, 177–200. New York: Oxford University Press.

Kennan, George F. 1951. *American Diplomacy, 1900–1950.* Chicago: University of Chicago Press.

———. 1996. *At a Century's Ending: Reflections 1982–1995.* New York: Norton.

———. 1997. "Diplomacy without Diplomats?" *Foreign Affairs* 76 (September–October): 198–212.

Kennedy, Paul M. 1987. *The Rise and Fall of the Great Powers: Economic Change and Military Conflict from 1500 to 2000.* New York: Random House.

Kennedy, Ross A. 2009. *The Will to Believe: Woodrow Wilson, World War I, and America's Strategy for Peace and Security.* Kent, Ohio: Kent State University Press.

Keohane, Robert O., and Joseph S. Nye Jr. 2001. *Power and Interdependence,* 3rd ed. New York: Longman.

Kepel, Gilles. 2002. *Jihad: The Trail of Political Islam.* Cambridge, MA: Harvard University Press.

Kertzer, Joshua D., and Kathleen M. McGraw. 2012. "Folk Realism: Testing the Microfoundations of Realism in Ordinary Citizens." *International Studies Quarterly* 56 (2): 245–258.

Key, V. O. 1961. *Public Opinion and American Democracy.* New York: Knopf.

Keys, Barbara. 2011. "Henry Kissinger: The Emotional Statesman." *Diplomatic History* 35 (4): 587–609.

Khong, Yuen F. 1992. *Analogies at War: Korea, Munich, Dien Bien Phu, and the Vietnam Decisions of 1965.* Princeton, NJ: Princeton University Press.

Kim, Soo Yeon. 2010. *Power and the Governance of Global Trade: From the GATT to the WTO.* Ithaca, NY: Cornell University Press.

Kinder, Donald R., and Lynn M. Sanders. 1996. *Divided by Color: Racial Politics and Democratic Ideals.* Chicago: University of Chicago Press.

Kirshner, Jonathan. 2015. "American Power and the Global Financial Crisis: How About Now?" *Forbes,* March 12.

Kirshner, Orin. 2005. "Triumph of Globalism: American Trade Politics." *Political Science Quarterly* 120 (3): 479–503.

Kissinger, Henry. 1957. *Nuclear Weapons and Foreign Policy.* New York: Harper.

Klaidman, Daniel. 2012. *Kill or Capture: The War on Terror and the Soul of the Obama Presidency.* New York: Houghton Mifflin Harcourt.

Klingberg, Frank L. 1952. "The Historical Alternation of Moods in American Foreign Policy." *World Politics* 4 (2): 239–273.

———. 1983. *Cyclical Trends in American Foreign Policy Moods: The Unfolding of America's World Role.* New York: University Press of America.

Knecht, Thomas. 2009. "A Pragmatic Response to an Unexpected Constraint: Problem Representation in a Complex Humanitarian Emergency." *Foreign Policy Analysis* 5 (2): 135–168.

Kohut, Andrew, and Bruce Stokes. 2006. *America against the World: How We Are Different and Why We Are Disliked.* New York: Times Books.

Kopp, Harry W., and Charles A. Gillespie. 2008. *Career Diplomacy: Life and Work in the U.S. Foreign Service.* Washington, DC: Georgetown University Press.

Korey, William. 1999. "Human Rights NGOs: The Power of Persuasion." *Ethics and International Affairs* 13 (1): 151–174.

Kostadinova, Tatiana. 2000. "East European Public Support for NATO Membership: Fears and Aspirations." *Journal of Peace Research* 37 (2): 235–249.

Krasner, Stephen D. 1972. "Are Bureaucracies Important? (Or Allison Wonderland)." *Foreign Policy* 7 (summer): 159–179.

———. 1978. *Defending the National Interest: Raw Materials Investments and U.S. Foreign Policy.* Princeton, NJ: Princeton University Press.

Kriesberg, Martin. 1949. "Dark Areas of Ignorance." In *Public Opinion and Foreign Policy,* edited by Lester Markel, 49–64. New York: Harper.

Kriner, Douglas L. 2014. "Obama's Authorization Paradox: Syria and Congress's Continued Relevance in Military Affairs." *Presidential Studies Quarterly* 44 (2): 309–327.

Kriner, Douglas L., and Francis X. Shen. 2012. "How Citizens Respond to Combat Casualties: The Differential Impact of Local Casualties on Support for the War in Afghanistan." *Public Opinion Quarterly* 76 (winter): 761–770.

Kris, Ernst, and Nathan Leites. 1947. "Trends in Twentieth Century Propaganda." In *Psychoanalysis and the Social Sciences,* edited by Géza Róheim,

393–409. New York: International University Press.

Krogstad, Jens Manuel, and Jeffrey S. Passel. 2015. *5 Facts about Illegal Immigration in the U.S.* Washington, DC: Pew Research Center.

Krutz, Glen S., and Jeffrey S. Peake. 2009. *Treaty Politics and the Rise of Executive Agreements: International Commitments in a System of Shared Powers.* Ann Arbor: University of Michigan Press.

Kukla, Jon. 2003. *A Wilderness So Immense: The Louisiana Purchase and the Destiny of America.* New York: Knopf.

Kull, Steven, and I. M. Destler. 1999. *Misreading the Public: The Myth of a New Isolationism.* Washington, DC: Brookings Institution Press.

Kull, Steven, and Clay Ramsay. 2001. "The Myth of the Reactive Public: American Public Attitudes on Military Fatalities in the Post–Cold War Period." In *Public Opinion and the International Use of Force,* edited by Philip P. Everts and Pierangelo Isernia, 205–228. New York: Routledge.

Kumar, Priya. 2011. "Foreign Correspondents: Who Covers What." *American Journalism Review,* December/January. http://www.ajr.org/Article.asp?id=4997.

Kurtz, Howard. 1998. *Spin Cycle: How the White House and the Media Manipulate the News.* New York: Simon & Schuster.

Kux, Dennis. 1998. "Pakistan." In *Economic Sanctions and American Diplomacy,* edited by Richard N. Haass, 157–176. New York: Council on Foreign Relations.

LaFeber, Walter. 1989. *The American Age: United States Foreign Policy at Home and Abroad since 1750.* New York: Norton.

———. 2004. *America, Russia, and the Cold War, 1945–2002,* 9th ed. Boston: McGraw-Hill.

Lake, Anthony. 1993. "From Containment to Enlargement." *U.S. Department of State Dispatch* 4 (39): 658–665.

Lake, David A. 2010. "Rightful Rules: Authority, Order, and the Foundations of Global Governance." *International Studies Quarterly* 54 (3): 587–613.

Lal, Deepak. 2006. *Reviving the Invisible Hand: The Case for Classical Liberalism in the Twenty-First Century.* Princeton, NJ: Princeton University Press.

Lancaster, Carol. 2007. *Foreign Aid: Diplomacy, Development, Domestic Politics.* Chicago: University of Chicago Press.

Landler, Mark. 2012. "Obama, on the Trail, Plays for Time on Foreign Policy." *New York Times,* July 19, A8. http://www.nytimes.com/2012/07/20/world/election-trumps-foreign-policy-white-house-memo.html.

———. 2014a. "In the Scripted World of Diplomacy, a Burst of Tweets." *New York Times,* February 4, A8.

———. 2014b. "A Shake-Up Stops at One." *New York Times,* November 24, A12.

Lanoszka, Anna. 2009. *The World Trade Organization: Changing Dynamics in the Global Political Economy.* Boulder, CO: Lynne Rienner.

Lantis, Jeffrey S. 2009. *The Life and Death of International Treaties: Double-Edged Diplomacy and the Politics of Ratification in Comparative Perspective.* New York: Oxford University Press.

LaPira, Timothy M. 2014. "Lobbying after 9/11: Policy Regime Emergence and Interest Group Mobilization." *Policy Studies Journal* 42 (2): 226–251.

Laqueur, Walter. 1977. *Terrorism.* Boston: Little, Brown.

———. 1999. *The New Terrorism: Fanaticism and the Arms of Mass Destruction.* New York: Oxford University Press.

Larson, Deborah Welch. 1985. *Origins of Containment: A Psychological Explanation.* Princeton, NJ: Princeton University Press.

Larson, Eric V. 1996. *Casualties and Consensus: The Historical Role of Casualties in Domestic Support for U.S. Military Operations.* Santa Monica, CA: RAND.

Larson, Eric V., et al. 2009. *Foundations of Effective Influence Operations: A Framework for Enhancing Army Capabilities.* Santa Monica, CA: RAND.

Lavelle, Kathryn C. 2011. *Legislating International Organization: The US Congress, the IMF, and the World Bank.* New York: Oxford University Press.

Layne, Christopher. 2006. *The Peace of Illusions: American Grand Strategy from 1940 to the Present.* Ithaca, NY: Cornell University Press.

Lebow, Richard Ned. 1981. *Between Peace and War: The Nature of International Crisis.* Baltimore: Johns Hopkins University Press.

Lee, Alexander. 2011. "Who Becomes a Terrorist? Poverty, Education, and the Origins of Political Violence." April. *World Politics* 63 (2): 203–215.

Leffler, Melvyn P. 1992. *A Preponderance of Power: National Security, the Truman Administration, and the Cold War.* Stanford, CA: Stanford University Press.

———. 2011. "Politics and National Security." *Diplomatic History* 35 (3): 563–566.

Leggett, Jane A. 2011. *A U.S.-Centric Chronology of the International Climate Change Negotiations.* Washington, DC: Congressional Research Service, February 8.

Lehman, Ingrid. 2005. "Exploring the Transatlantic Media Divide over Iraq." *Harvard International Journal of Press/Politics* 10 (1): 63–89.

Lektzian, David, and Mark Souva. 2003. "The Economic Peace between Democracies: Economic Sanctions and Domestic Institutions." *Journal of Peace Research* 40 (6): 641–660.

LeLoup, Lance T., and Steven A. Shull. 2003. *The President and Congress: Collaboration and Combat in National Policymaking.* New York: Longman.

Lemann, Nicholas. 2001. "The Quiet Man: Dick Cheney's Discreet Rise to Unprecedented Power." *New Yorker,* May 7, 56–71.

Lepore, Jill. 2010. *The Whites of Their Eyes: The Tea Party's Revolution and the Battle over American History.* Princeton, NJ: Princeton University Press.

Lesser, Ian O., Bruce Hoffman, John Arquilla, David Ronfeldt, and Michele Zanini, eds. 1999. *Countering the New Terrorism.* Santa Monica, CA: RAND.

Levy, Jack. 1987. "Declining Power and the Preventive Motivation for War." *World Politics* 40 (1): 82–107.

———. 1989. "The Diversionary Theory of War: A Critique." In *Handbook of War Studies,* edited by Manus Midlarsky, 259–288. London: Unwin Hyman.

Lew, Jacob J. 2014. "Remarks of Secretary Lew at CSIS." Washington, DC: Department of the Treasury, June 2. http://www.treasury.gov/press-center/press-releases/Pages/jl2414.aspx.

Lewis, David A., and Roger P. Rose. 2002. "The President, the Press, and the War-Making Power: An Analysis of Media Coverage Prior to the Persian Gulf War." *Presidential Studies Quarterly* 32 (3): 559–571.

Lewis, David E. 2008. "The Evolution of the Institutional Presidency: Presidential Choices, Institutional Change, and Staff Performance." In *Presidential Leadership: The Vortex of Power,* edited by Bert A. Rockman and Richard W. Waterman, 237–259. New York: Oxford University Press.

Liberman, Peter. 2014. "War and Torture as 'Just Desserts.'" *Public Opinion Quarterly* 78 (spring): 47–70.

Liddell Hart, B. H. 1967. *Strategy,* 2nd rev. ed. New York: Praeger.

Lieber, Keir A., and Gerard Alexander. 2005. "Waiting for Balancing: Why the World Is Not Pushing Back." *International Security* 30 (1): 109–139.

Lieberman, Robert C. 2009. "The 'Israel Lobby' and American Politics." *Perspectives on Politics* 7 (2): 235–257.

Lightman, David. 2015. "Poll: Americans Are Down on Obama's Foreign Policy." Sacramento, CA: McClatchy Newspapers, March 9.

Lindsay, James M. 1994. "Congress, Foreign Policy, and the New Institutionalism." *International Studies Quarterly* 38 (2): 281–304.

———. 2003. "Deference and Defiance: The Shifting Rhythms of Executive-Legislative Relations in Foreign Policy." *Presidential Studies Quarterly* 33 (3): 530–546.

Lippmann, Walter. 1922. *Public Opinion.* New York: Macmillan.

———. 1947. *The Cold War: A Study in U.S. Foreign Policy.* New York: Harper.

———. 1955. *Essays in the Public Philosophy.* Boston: Little, Brown.

Lipset, Seymour Martin. 1966. "The President, the Polls, and Vietnam." *Trans-Action* 3 (6): 19–24.

Lipton, Eric. 2014. "Lawmaker Assails Foreign Donations to Think Tanks." *New York Times,* September 12.

Lipton, Eric, Brooke Williams, and Nicholas Confessore. 2014. "Foreign Powers Buy Influence at Think Tanks." *New York Times,* September 6.

Lohr, Steve. 2000. "Ideas & Trends: Net Americana; Welcome to the Internet, the First Global Colony." *New York Times,* January 9.

Lovins, Amory B. 2012. "A Farewell to Fossil Fuels." *Foreign Affairs* 91 (March–April): 134–146.

Lowrey, Annie. 2014. "Aiming Financial Weapons from Treasury War Room." *New York Times,* June 3.

Lowry v. Reagan, 676 F.Supp. 333 (1987).

Luce, Ed. 2014. "Uncertainty, Not China, Is Replacing U.S. Power." *Financial Times,* May 4.

Lugar, Richard G. 2012. "Overcoming Foreign-Policy Disunity." *The National Interest,* November 20.

Lynch, Edward A. 2011. *The Cold War's Last Battlefield: Reagan, the Soviets, and Central America.* Albany, NY: State University of New York Press.

Lynn, William S. 2014. "The End of the Military-Industrial Complex: How the Pentagon Is Adapting to Globalization." *Foreign Affairs* 93 (November-December): 104–110.

Mabee, Bryan. 2011. "Historical Institutionalism and Foreign Policy Analysis: The Origins of the National Security Council Revisited." *Foreign Policy Analysis* 7 (1): 27–44.

MacGregor, Douglas A. 2003. *Transformation under Fire: Revolutionizing How America Fights.* Westport, CT: Praeger.

Mackinder, Halford J. 1942. *Democratic Ideals and Reality: A Study in the Politics of Reconstruction.* New York: Norton.

Maddow, Rachel. 2012. *Drift: The Unmooring of American Military Power.* New York: Crown.

Mahan, Alfred Thayer. 1897. *The Interest of America in Sea Power: Present and Future.* Boston: Little, Brown.

Malkasian, Carter, and J. Kael Weston. 2012. "War Downsized: How to Accomplish More with Less." *Foreign Affairs* 91 (March-April): 111–121.

Mandelbaum, Michael. 1983. "Vietnam: The Television War." *Daedelus* 111 (4): 157–169.

———. 2010. *The Frugal Superpower: America's Global Leadership in a Cash-Strapped Era*. New York: Public Affairs.

Manila Bulletin. 2012. "M.C.C. Supports More Philippine Projects." October 20. http://www.mb.com.ph/articles/379051/mcc-supports-more-philippine-projects/.

Mann, James. 2009. *The Rebellion of Ronald Reagan: A History of the End of the Cold War*. New York: Viking.

———. 2012. *The Obamians: How a Band of Newcomers Redefined American Power*. New York: Viking.

Mannheim, Karl. 1952. *Essays in the Sociology of Knowledge*. New York: Routledge & Kegan Paul.

Manning, Bayless. 1977. "The Congress, the Executive, and Intermestic Affairs: Three Proposals." *Foreign Affairs* 55 (January): 306–324.

Marbury v. Madison, 5 U.S. 137 (1803).

Maren, Michael. 1997. *The Road to Hell: The Ravaging Effects of Foreign Aid and International Charity*. New York: Free Press.

Margolis, Michael, and David Resnick. 2000. *Politics as Usual: The Cyberspace "Revolution."* Thousand Oaks, CA: Sage.

Margulies, Joseph. 2006. *Guantánamo and the Abuse of Presidential Power*. New York: Simon & Schuster.

Markon, Jerry, Ellen Nakashima, and Alice Crites. 2014. "Top-Level Turnover Makes It Harder for DHS to Stay on Top of Evolving Threats." *Washington Post*, September 21.

Marra, Robin F., and Charles W. Ostrom Jr. 1989. "Explaining Seat Changes in the U.S. House of Representatives, 1950–1986." *American Journal of Political Science* 33 (3): 541–569.

Marsh, Kevin. 2014. "Obama's Surge: A Bureaucratic Politics Analysis of the Decision to Order a Troop Surge in the Afghanistan War." *Foreign Policy Analysis* 10 (3): 265–288.

Marshall, Tyrone C., Jr. 2011. "Panetta Discusses Security Challenges in STRATCOM Visit." American Forces Press Service, August 5.

Martin, William. 1999. "The Christian Right and American Foreign Policy." *Foreign Policy* 114 (spring): 66–80.

Masters, Jonathan. 2015. "What Are Economic Sanctions?" *Council on Foreign Relations*, April 8. http://www.cfr.org/sanctions/economic-sanctions/p36259.

Mathiesen, Karl. 2015. "What Is the Bill and Melinda Gates Foundation?" *The Guardian*, March 16.

Mathews, Jessica T. 1997. "Power Shift." *Foreign Affairs* 76 (January-February): 50–66.

Mayer, Jane. 2009. "The Predator War: What Are the Risks of the C.I.A.'s Covert Drone Program." *New Yorker*, October 26, http://www.newyorker.com/reporting/2009/10/26/091026fa_fact_mayer/.

Mayer, Michael. 2015. *U.S. Missile Defense: Engaging the Debate*. Boulder, CO: First Forum Press.

Mayer, William G. 1992. *The Changing American Mind: How and Why American Public Opinion Changed between 1960 and 1988*. Ann Arbor: University of Michigan Press.

Mayhew, David R. 1974. *Congress: The Electoral Connection*. New Haven, CT: Yale University Press.

Mazzetti, Mark. 2010. "U.S. Expands Role of Diplomats in Spying." *New York Times*, November 28, A1.

———. 2014. *The Way of the Knife: The CIA, a Secret Army, and a War at the Ends of the Earth*. New York: Penguin.

McCombs, Maxwell E., R. Lance Holbert, Spiro Kiousis, and Wayne Wanta. 2011. *The News and Public Opinion: Media Effects on Civic Life*. Cambridge, MA: Polity.

McCormick, James M., and Neil J. Mitchell. 2007. "Commitments, Transnational Interests, and Congress: Who Joins the Congressional Human Rights Caucus?" *Political Research Quarterly* 60 (4): 579–592.

McCormick, James M., Eugene R. Wittkopf, and David M. Danna. 1997. "Politics and Bipartisanship at the Water's Edge: A Note on Bush and Clinton." *Polity* 30 (1): 133–149.

McCormick, Thomas J. 1995. *America's Half Century: United States Foreign Policy in the Cold War and After*, 2nd ed. Baltimore: Johns Hopkins University Press.

McCubbins, Mathew D., Roger G. Noll, and Barry R. Weingast. 1987. "Administrative Procedures as Instruments of Political Control." *Journal of Law, Economics, and Organization* 3 (2): 243–277.

McDermott, Rose. 1998. *Risk-Taking in International Politics: Prospect Theory in American Foreign Policy*. Ann Arbor: University of Michigan Press.

———. 2004. *Political Psychology in International Relations*. Ann Arbor: University of Michigan Press.

———. 2014. "The Biological Bases for Aggressiveness and Nonaggressiveness in Presidents." *Foreign Policy Analysis* 10 (October): 313–327.

McDougall, Walter A. 1997. *Promised Land, Crusader State: The American Encounter with the World since 1776*. Boston: Houghton Mifflin.

McGann, James G. 2014. *2013 Global Go To Think Tank Index Report*. Philadelphia: Think Tanks and Civil Societies Program.

McGann, James G., and Mary Johnstone. 2005. "The Power Shift and the NGO Credibility Crisis." *Brown Journal of World Affairs* 11 (2).

McGann, James G., and Richard Sabatini. 2011. *Global Think Tanks: Policy Networks and Governance*. New York: Routledge.

McMahon, Robert J. 2008. *Dean Acheson and the Creation of an American World Order*. Dulles, VA: Potomac Books.

McMillan, Samuel Lucas. 2008. "Subnational Foreign Policy Actors: How and Why Governors Participate in U.S. Foreign Policy." *Foreign Policy Analysis* 4 (3): 227–253.

McNamara, Robert S., and Brian VanDeMark. 1995. *In Retrospect: The Tragedy and Lessons of Vietnam*. New York: Times Books.

Mead, Walter Russell. 2006. "The Israel Lobby and U.S. Foreign Policy." *Middle East Policy* 13 (3): 29–87.

———. 2011. "The Tea Party and American Foreign Policy." *Foreign Affairs* 90 (March-April): 28–44.

Mearsheimer, John J. 2001. *The Tragedy of Great Power Politics*. New York: Norton.

Mearsheimer, John J., and Stephen M. Walt. 2006. "The Israel Lobby and U.S. Foreign Policy." Faculty Research Working Papers Series. Cambridge, MA: Harvard University.

———. 2007. *The Israel Lobby and U.S. Foreign Policy.* New York: Farrar, Straus, & Giroux.

Merrill, Dennis, and Thomas G. Paterson, eds. 2000. *Major Problems in American Foreign Relations,* 5th ed. Boston: Houghton Mifflin.

Merolla, Jennifer L., and Elizabeth J. Zechmeister. 2009. *Democracy at Risk: How Terrorist Threats Affect the Public.* Chicago: University of Chicago Press.

Meyer, David S., and Catherine Corrigall-Brown. 2005. "Coalitions and Political Context: U.S. Movements against Wars in Iraq." *Mobilization* 10 (3): 327–344. https://webfiles.uci.edu/dmeyer/coalitions.mobe.pdf.

Meyer, Jeffrey. 2015. "Nets Spend 48 Minutes on Jenner's Cover, Skip Obama's Bad News." Reston, VA: Media Research Center, NewsBusters, June 3. http://newsbusters.org/blogs/jeffrey-meyer/2015/06/03/nets-spend-48-minutes-jenners-cover-skip-obamas-bad-news.

Migration Policy Institute. 2014. "U.S. Immigrant Population and Share over Time." Washington, DC: Migration Policy Institute.

Miller, Greg. 2012. "Attack on U.S. Consulate in Libya Determined to Be Terrorism Tied to al Qaeda." *Washington Post,* September 27. http://articles.washingtonpost.com/2012-09-27/world/35494761_1_benghazi-attack-al-qaeda-qaeda/.

Miller, Paul D. 2012. "Five Pillars of American Grand Strategy." *Survival* 54 (5): 7–44.

———. 2013. "The Contemporary Presidency: Organizing the National Security Council: I Like Ike's." *Presidential Studies Quarterly* 43 (3): 592–606.

Mills, C. Wright. 1956. *The Power Elite.* New York: Oxford University Press.

Mingst, Karen, and Ivan M. Arreguín-Toft. 2011. *Essentials of International Relations,* 5th ed. New York: Norton.

Mintz, Alex, and Karl DeRouen Jr. 2010. *Understanding Foreign Policy Decision Making.* New York: Cambridge University Press.

Mitchell, David, and Tansa George Massoud. 2009. "Anatomy of Failure: Bush's Decision-Making Process and the Iraq War." *Foreign Policy Analysis* 5 (3): 265–286.

Modelski, George. 1987. *Long Cycles in World Politics.* Seattle: University of Washington Press.

Moe, Terry M. 1989. "The Politics of Bureaucratic Structure." In *Can the Government Govern?,* edited by John E. Chubb and Paul E. Peterson, 267–330. Washington, DC: Brookings Institution Press.

Moghadam, Assaf. 2008/2009. "Motives for Martyrdom: Al-Qaeda, Salafi Jihad, and the Spread of Suicide Attacks." *International Security* 33 (3): 46–78.

Mondak, Jeffrey J., and Jon Hurwitz. 2012. "Examining the Terror Exception: Terrorism and Commitments to Civil Liberties." *Public Opinion Quarterly* 76 (June): 193–213.

Moniz, Ernest. 2011. "Why We Still Need Nuclear Power." *Foreign Affairs* 90 (November-December): 83–94.

Monroe, James. 1823. Annual Message to Congress (excerpt), December 2, Washington, D.C. http://avalon.law.yale.edu/19th_century/monroe.asp.

Monten, Jonathan. 2005. "The Roots of the Bush Doctrine." *International Security* 29 (4): 112–156.

Monten, Jonathan, and Andrew Bennett. 2010. "Models of Crisis Decision Making and the 1990–91 Gulf War." *Security Studies* 19 (3): 486–520.

Montgomery, Evan Braden. 2014. "Contested Primacy in the Western Pacific: China's Rise and the Future of U.S. Power Projection." *International Security* 38 (4): 115–139.

Montgomery, John D. 1962. *The Politics of Foreign Aid: American Experience in Southeast Asia.* New York: Published for the Council on Foreign Relations by Praeger.

Mooney, Chris. 2004. "The Editorial Pages and the Case for War: Did Our Leading Newspapers Set Too Low a Bar for a Preemptive Attack?" *Columbia Journalism Review* 42 (March-April): 28–34.

Moravcsik, Andrew. 2005. "The Paradox of U.S. Human Rights Policy." In *American Exceptionalism and Human Rights,* edited by Michael Ignatieff, 147–197. Princeton, NJ: Princeton University Press.

Morgenson, Gretchen, and Louise Story. 2011. "Naming Culprits in the Financial Crisis." *New York Times,* April 14, B1.

Morgenthau, Hans J. 1967. *Politics among Nations: The Struggle for Power and Peace,* 4th ed. New York: Knopf.

Morell, Michael. 2015. *The Great War of Our Time: The CIA's Fight against Terrorism from al Qa'ida to ISIS.* New York: Twelve.

Morris, Edmund. 2001. *The Rise of Theodore Roosevelt.* New York: Modern Library.

Morris, Richard. 1966. *Great Presidential Decisions: State Papers That Changed the Course of History.* Greenwich, CT: Fawcett.

Morrison, Wayne M. 2009. *China's Economic Conditions.* Washington, DC: Congressional Research Service, December 11.

Moschella, Manuela. 2010. *Governing Risk: The IMF and Global Financial Crises.* New York: Palgrave Macmillan.

Mowle, Thomas S. 2003. "Worldviews in Foreign Policy: Realism, Liberalism, and External Conflict." *Political Psychology* 24 (3): 561–592.

Mueller, John E. 1970. "Presidential Popularity from Truman to Johnson." *American Political Science Review* 64 (1): 18–34.

———. 1973. *War, Presidents, and Public Opinion.* New York: Wiley.

———. 1994. *Policy and Opinion in the Gulf War.* Chicago: University of Chicago Press.

Mullen, Michael. 2011. Address at the *Government Executive Magazine* Leadership Forum, April 28. National Press Club, Washington, DC: http://www.defense.gov/News/NewsArticle.aspx?ID=63739.

Murdie, Amanda M., and David R. Davis. 2012. "Shaming and Blaming: Using Events Data to Assess the Impact of Human Rights INGOs." *International Studies Quarterly* 56 (1): 1–16.

Murphy, Joe, Craig Hill, and Elizabeth Dean. 2013. "Social Media, Sociality and Survey Research." In *Social Media, Sociality and Survey Research,* edited by Dean Hill and Joe Murphy, 1–34. Hoboken, NJ: Wiley.

Murray, Shoon. 2012. "Broadening the Debate about War: The Inclusion of Foreign Critics in Media Coverage and Its Potential Impact on US Public Opinion." *Foreign Policy Analysis* 10 (4): 329–250.

Myers, Steven Lee. 2012. "Hillary Clinton's Last Tour as a Rock-Star Diplomat." *New York Times Magazine,* June 27, MM18.

Nabers, Dirk. 2009. "Filling the Void of Meaning: Identity Construction in U.S. Foreign Policy after September 11, 2001." *Foreign Policy Analysis* 5 (2): 191–214.

Nacos, Brigitte L., Yaell Bloch-Elkon, and Robert Y. Shapiro. 2011. *Selling Fear: Counterterrorism, the Media, and Public Opinion.* Chicago: University of Chicago Press.

National Center for Education Statistics. 2011a. *The Nation's Report Card: Science.* National Assessment of Education Progress at Grades 4, 8, and 12. Washington, DC: U.S. Department of Education.

———. 2011b. *The Nation's Report Card: Grade 12-Reading and Mathematics 2009.* Washington, DC: U.S. Department of Education National Center for Education Statistics.

———. 2011c. *The Nation's Report Card: Civics 2011.* Washington, DC: U.S. Department of Education. http://nces .ed.gov/pubsearch/pubsinfo .asp?pubid=2011466/.

National Commission on Terrorist Attacks upon the United States. 2004. "The 9/11 Commission Report." http:// www.9-11commission.gov.

National Conference of State Legislatures. 2014. 2013 Immigration Report. January 20. http://www.ncsl.org/ research/immigration/2013- immigration-report.aspx.

National Counterterrorism Center (NCTC). 2009. *2008 Report on Terrorism.* April 30. Washington, DC: NCTC.

National Geographic Education Foundation. 2006. "National Geographic–Roper Public Affairs 2006 Geographic Literacy Study." http://www.national geographic.com/roper2006/.

National Intelligence Council. 2002. "Iraq's Continuing Programs of Weapons of Mass Destruction." National Intelligence Estimate, October. http:// www.gwu.edu/~nsarchiv/NSAEBB/ NSAEBB129/nie.pdf (redacted).

———. 2012. *Global Trends 2030: Alternative Worlds.* December. http:// www.dni.gov/files/documents/ GlobalTrends_2030.pdf.

Neack, Laura. 2014. *The New Foreign Policy: Power Seeking in a Globalized Era,* 3rd ed. Lanham, MD: Rowman & Littlefield.

Nelson, Douglas R. 1996. "The Political Economy of U.S. Automobile Protection." In *The Political Economy of American Trade Policy,* edited by Anne O. Krueger, 133–190. Chicago: University of Chicago Press.

Nelson, Michael. 2004. "George W. Bush and Congress: The Electoral Connection." In *Considering the Bush Presidency,* edited by Gary L. Gregg II and Mark J. Rozell, 141–160. New York: Oxford University Press.

Nephew, Richard. 2015. "The Grand Bargain: What Iran Conceded in the Nuclear Talks." *Brookings Institution,* April 18. http://www.brookings.edu/blogs/ markaz/posts/2015/04/21-nephew- us-iran-nuclear-deal-compromise- diplomacy.

Netcraft. 2014. "November 2012 Web Server Survey." http://news.netcraft.com/ archives/2012/11/01/november-2012- web-server-survey.html.

Neuman, W. Russell. 1986. *The Paradox of Mass Politics: Knowledge and Opinion in the American Electorate.* Cambridge, MA: Harvard University Press.

Neustadt, Richard E. 1960. *Presidential Power: The Politics of Leadership.* New York: Wiley.

New America Foundation. 2013. "The Year of the Drone: An Analysis of U.S. Drone Strikes in Pakistan, 2004–2013." http://counterterrorism.newamerica .net/drones/.

Newhouse, John. 2009. "Diplomacy, Inc." *Foreign Affairs* 88 (May-June): 73–92.

New York Times. 1971. *The Pentagon Papers.* New York: Bantam Books.

———. 1992. "Excerpts from Pentagon's Plan: 'Prevent the Re-emergence of a New Rival.'" March 8, A14.

———. 2004. "Testimony of Condoleezza Rice before 9/11 Commission." April 8.

New York Times Company v. United States, 403 U.S. 713 (1971).

Nexon, Daniel H. 2009. "The Balance of Power in the Balance." *World Politics* 61 (2): 330–359.

Nichols, Thomas M. 2014. *No Use: Nuclear Weapons and U.S. National Security.* Philadelphia: University of Pennsylvania Press.

Nincic, Miroslav. 1988. "The United States, the Soviet Union, and the Politics of Opposites." *World Politics* 40 (4): 452–475.

Nincic, Miroslav, and Donna J. Nincic. 2002. "Race, Gender, and War." *Journal of Peace Research* 39 (5): 547–568.

Nixon, Ron. 2014. "Social Media in Afghanistan Takes On Life of Its Own." *New York Times,* April 29.

Norris, Pippa, Montague Kern, and Marion Just, eds. 2003. *Framing Terrorism: The News Media, the Government, and the Public.* New York: Routledge.

North American Treaty Organization. 2015. Press conference by NATO Secretary General Jens Stoltenberg. Brussels: NATO, February 5.

Nye, Joseph S., Jr. 2002. *The Paradox of American Power: Why the World's Only Superpower Can't Go It Alone.* New York: Oxford University Press.

———. 2004. *Soft Power: The Means to Success in World Politics.* New York: Public Affairs.

Obama, Barack. 2009a. "Remarks by President Barack Obama in Prague." April 5. https://www.whitehouse.gov/ the-press-office/remarks-president- barack-obama-prague-delivered.

———. 2009b. "Remarks by the President in Address to the Nation on the Way Forward in Afghanistan and Pakistan." December 1. http://www.whitehouse .gov/the-press-office/remarks- president-address-nation-way- forward-afghanistan-and-pakistan/.

———. 2010. "National Security Strategy." http://www.whitehouse.gov/sites/ default/files/rss_viewer/national_ security_strategy.pdf.

———. 2012. "Remarks by the President to the United Nations General Assembly." September 25. http://www .whitehouse.gov/the-press- office/2012/09/25/remarks-president- un-general-assembly/.

———. 2013. "State of the Union Address," February 12. https://www.whitehouse .gov/the-press-office/2013/02/12/ remarks-president-state-union- address.

O'Connor, John. 2006. "Sanford in Iraq, Kuwait." *The State,* June 22, B3.

OECD (Organisation for Economic Co-operation and Development). 2010.

Statistical Annex of the 2010 Development Co-operation Report. Paris: OECD. http://www.oecd-ilibrary .org/development/development-co-operation-report-2010/statistical-annex_dcr-2010-40-en/.

———. 2011. "Education at a Glance 2011: Country Note: United States." September 13. Paris: OECD Centre for Educational Research and Innovation. http://www .oecd.org/unitedstates/48678896.pdf.

———. 2012. *Foreign Direct Investment (FDI) Statistics—OECD Data, Analysis and Forecasts*. July 27. Paris: OECD. http://www.oecd.org/investment/ statistics.htm.

———. 2014. *FDI in Figures*. OECD, December.

Office of the U.S. Trade Representative. 2013. "Free Trade Agreements." http:// www.ustr.gov/trade-agreements/ free-trade-agreements.

O'Hanlon, Michael E. 2009. *Budgeting for Hard Power: Defense and Security Spending under Barack Obama*. Washington, DC: Brookings Institution Press.

———. 2012. "Getting Real on Defense Costs." *Politico*, July 22. http://www .politico.com/news/ stories/0712/78816.html.

O'Hanlon, Michael E., Peter R. Orszag, Ivo H. Daalder, I. M. Destler, David L. Gunter, James M. Lindsay, Robert E. Litan, and James B. Steinberg. 2002. *Protecting the American Homeland: One Year On*. Washington, DC: Brookings Institution Press.

Olson, Mancur. 1982. *The Rise and Decline of Nations*. New Haven, CT: Yale University Press.

Onea, Tudor A. 2013. *US Foreign Policy in the Post–Cold War Era: Restraint versus Assertiveness from George H. W. Bush to Barack Obama*. New York: Palgrave Macmillan.

Onuf, Nicholas G. 1989. *World of Our Making: Rules and Rule in Social Theory and International Relations*. Columbia: University of South Carolina Press.

O'Reilly, K. P. 2013. "A Rogue Doctrine? The Role of Strategic Culture on U.S. Foreign Policy Behavior." *Foreign Policy Analysis* 9 (1): 57–77.

Ornstein, Norman J., and Thomas E. Mann. 2006. "When Congress Checks Out."

Foreign Affairs 85 (November-December): 67–82.

O'Rourke, Ronald. 2015. *A Shift in the International Security Environment: Potential Implications for Defense*. Washington, DC: Congressional Research Service, January 21.

Osgood, Robert. 1957. *Limited War: The Challenge to American Strategy*, 2nd ed. Chicago: University of Chicago Press.

Overby, L. Marvin. 1991. "Assessing Constituency Influence: Congressional Voting on the Nuclear Freeze, 1982–1983." *Legislative Studies Quarterly* 16 (2): 297–312.

Overseas Presence Advisory Panel. 1999. *America's Overseas Presence in the 21st Century*. Washington, DC: U.S. Department of State. http://www.fas .org/irp/threat/rpt-9911_opap.pdf.

Owen, John M., IV. 2015. "From Calvin to the Caliphate: What Europe's Wars of Religion Tell Us about the Modern Middle East." *Foreign Affairs* (May-June).

Page, Benjamin I., and Jason Barabas. 2000. "Foreign Policy Gaps between Citizens and Leaders." *International Studies Quarterly* 44 (3): 339–364.

Page, Benjamin I., and Marshall M. Bouton. 2006. *The Foreign Policy Disconnect: What Americans Want from Our Leaders but Don't Get*. With the assistance of Marshall M. Bouton. Chicago: University of Chicago Press.

Page, Benjamin I., and Robert Y. Shapiro. 1992. *The Rational Public: Fifty Years of Trends in Americans' Policy Preferences*. Chicago: University of Chicago Press.

Panetta, Leon E. 2012. "Defending the Nation from Cyber Attack." Address to Business Executives for National Security, October 11. Washington, DC: U.S. Department of Defense. http:// www.defense.gov/speeches/speech .aspx?speechid=1728.

Panetta, Leon, with Jim Newton. 2014. *Worthy Fights*. New York: Penguin.

Pape, Robert. A. 2005. *Dying to Win: The Strategic Logic of Suicide Terrorism*. New York: Random House.

Paterson, Thomas G., J. Garry Clifford, and Kenneth J. Hagan. 2000. *American Foreign Relations, Volume 2: A History since 1895*, 5th ed. Boston: Houghton Mifflin.

Paulson, Michael. 2014. "Jewish Coalition Rejects Lobbying Group's Bid to Join." *New York Times*, April 30.

Peake, Jeffrey S. 2002. "Coalition Building and Overcoming Legislative Gridlock in Foreign Policy." *Presidential Studies Quarterly* 32 (1): 67–83.

Peffley, Mark, and Jon Hurwitz. 1992. "International Events and Foreign Policy Beliefs: Public Response to Changing Soviet-U.S. Relations." *American Journal of Political Science* 36 (2): 431–461.

Peksen, Dursun. 2011. "Economic Sanctions and Human Security: The Public Health Effect of Economic Sanctions." *Foreign Policy Analysis* 7 (3): 237–251.

Perl, Raphael. 2006. *Trends in Terrorism: 2006*. Washington, DC: Congressional Research Service, July 21.

Perlez, Jane. 2015. "Stampede to Join China's Development Bank Stuns Even Its Founder." *New York Times*, April 2.

Peters, Jeremy W. 2015a. "Obama to See War Power Bill from Congress, to Fight ISIS. *New York Times*, February 10, A1.

———. 2015b. "Rand Paul Begins to Make Believers Out of His Father's Supporters." *New York Times*, June 2, A17.

Peterson, Timothy M. 2013. "Sending a Message: The Reputation Effect of US Sanction Threat Behavior." *International Studies Quarterly* 57 (4): 672–692.

Pew Global Attitudes Project. 2005. "American Character Gets Mixed Reviews: U.S. Image Up Slightly, but Still Negative." June 23. Washington, DC: Pew Research Center.

———. 2012. "Global Opinion of Obama Slips, International Policies Faulted." June 13. Washington, DC: Pew Research Center.

Pew Hispanic Center. 2012. "Net Migration from Mexico Falls to Zero—and Perhaps Less." Washington, DC: Pew Research Center. http://www .pewhispanic.org/files/2012/04/ Mexican-migrants-report_final.pdf.

Pew Research Center. 2014a. *Global Attitudes and Trends*. 2014. Washington, DC: Pew Research Center.

———. 2014b. *About Half See Interrogation Methods as Justified*. Washington, DC: Pew Research Center.

Pew Research Center for the People and the Press. 2005. "Opinion Leaders Turn Cautious, Public Looks Homeward." November 17. http://www.people-press.org/2005/11/17/opinion-leaders-turn-cautious-public-looks-homeward/.

———. 2006a. "Many Americans Uneasy with Mix of Religion and Politics." August 24. http://www.pewforum.org/Politics-and-Elections/Many-Americans-Uneasy-with-Mix-of-Religion-and-Politics.aspx.

———. 2006b. "Online Papers Modestly Boost Newspaper Readership: Maturing Internet News Audience Broader than Deep." July 30. http://www.people-press.org/2006/07/30/online-papers-modestly-boost-newspaper-readership/.

———. 2008. "Audience Segments in a Changing News Environment: Key News Audiences Now Blend Online and Traditional Sources." August 17. http://people-press.org/ reports/pdf/444.pdf.

———. 2011a. "Strong on Defense and Israel, Tough on China: Tea Party and Foreign Policy." October 7. http://www.people-press.org/2011/10/07/strong-on-defense-and-israel-tough-on-china/.

———. 2011b. "What the Public Knows—In Words and Pictures." November 7. http://www.people-press.org/2011/11/07/what-the-public-knows-in-words-and-pictures/.

———. 2012a. "In Changing News Landscape, Even Television Is Vulnerable: Trends in News Consumption, 1991–2012." September 27. http://www.people-press.org/2012/09/27/in-changing-news-landscape-even-television-is-vulnerable/.

———. 2012b. "Little Public Support for U.S Intervention In Syrian Conflict." March 15. http://www.people-press.org/2012/03/15/little-support-for-u-s-intervention-in-syrian-conflict/.

———. 2015a. "Views of Western Powers Fall in Russia." June 9. http://www.pewresearch.org/fact-tank/2015/06/10/key-findings-from-our-poll-on-the-russia-ukraine-conflict/ft_15-06-09-russia-west/.

———. 2015b. "Social Media Update 2014." January 9. http://www.pewinternet.org/2015/01/09/social-media-update-2014/.

———. 2015c. "State of the News Media 2015." April 29. http://www.journalism.org/2015/04/29/state-of-the-news-media-2015/.

Pexton, Patrick B. 2012. "Leaks Bill: Bad for Journalism, Bad for the Public." Washington Post, August 3. http://articles.washingtonpost.com/2012-08-03/opinions/35490105_1_plug-leaks-sensitive-information-ships/.

Pfiffner, James P. 2005. "Presidential Decision Making: Rationality, Advisory Systems, and Personality." Presidential Studies Quarterly 35 (2): 217–228.

———. 2011. "Decision Making in the Obama White House." Presidential Studies Quarterly 41 (2): 244–262.

Phillips, Kevin P. 2006. American Theocracy: The Peril and Politics of Radical Religion, Oil, and Borrowed Money in the 21st Century. New York: Viking.

Pierce, Charles P. 2009. Idiot America: How Stupidity Became a Virtue in the Land of the Free. New York: Doubleday.

Pifer, Steven. 2015. "The Limits of Missile Defense." National Interest, March 30.

Pillar, Paul R. 2011. Intelligence and U.S. Foreign Policy: Iraq, 9/11, and Misguided Reform. New York: Columbia University Press.

Pious, Richard M. 2011. "Prerogative Power in the Obama Administration: Continuity and Change in the War on Terrorism." Presidential Studies Quarterly 41 (2): 263–290.

Pitkin, Hanna Fenichel. 1967. The Concept of Representation. Berkeley: University of California Press.

Polsby, Nelson W. 1990. "Congress, National Security, and the Rise of the 'Presidential Branch.'" In The Constitution and National Security: A Bicentennial View, edited by Howard E. Shuman and Walter R. Thomas, 201–210. Washington, DC: National Defense University Press.

Pomper, Miles. 1998. "The New Faces of Foreign Policy." CQ Weekly, November 28, 3203–3208.

Population Reference Bureau. 2014. 2014 World Population Data Sheet. Washington, DC: Population Reference Bureau. http://www.prb.org/Publications/Datasheets/2014/2014-world-population-data-sheet.aspx.

Porter, Gareth. 2015. "The Israel Lobby Shows Its Clout." Consortiumnews.com, February 2. https://consortiumnews.com/2015/02/02/the-israel-lobby-shows-its-clout/.

Posen, Barry R. 2001/2002. "The Struggle against Terrorism: Grand Strategy, Strategy, and Tactics." International Security 26 (3): 39–55.

———. 2003. "Command of the Commons: The Military Foundation of U.S. Hegemony." International Security 28 (1): 5–46.

———. 2013. "The Case for a Less Activist Foreign Policy." Foreign Affairs 92 (January–February): 116–128.

———. 2014. Restraint: A New Foundation for Foreign Policy. Ithaca, NY: Cornell University Press.

Posen, Barry R., and Andrew Ross. 1996/1997. "Competing Visions for U.S. Grand Strategy." International Security 21 (3): 5–53.

Posner, Eric. 2014. The Twilight of Human Rights Law. New York: Oxford University Press.

Potter, Philip B. K. 2013. "Electoral Margins and American Foreign Policy." International Studies Quarterly 57 (3): 505–518.

Powell, Bill. 2014. "A Social Media Storm Descends on Taiji, the Japanese Town at the Center of a Dolphin Slaughter." Newsweek, March 27.

Powell, Colin L. 1992. "Why Generals Get Nervous." New York Times, October 8, A35.

———. 1992/1993. "U.S. Forces: Challenges Ahead." Foreign Affairs 71 (winter): 32–45. http://www.cfr.org/world/us-forces-challenges-ahead/p7508/.

Powell, Jody. 1984. The Other Side of the Story. New York: Morrow.

Prados, John. 1996. Presidents' Secret Wars: CIA and Pentagon Covert Operations from World War II through the Persian Gulf, Rev. and expanded ed. Chicago: I. R. Dee.

Pratt, Julius. 1927. "The Origin of 'Manifest Destiny.'" American Historical Review 32 (4): 795–798.

Pressman, Jeremy. 2009. "Power without Influence: The Bush Administration's

Foreign Policy Failure in the Middle East." *International Security* 33 (4): 149–179.

Preston, Julia. 2012. "Republicans Reconsider Positions on Immigration." *New York Times*, November 10, A12.

Prestowitz, Clyde V. 2003. *Rogue Nation: American Unilateralism and the Failure of Good Intentions*. New York: Basic Books.

Priest, Dana. 2005. "CIA Holds Terror Suspects in Secret Prisons." *Washington Post*, November 2, A1. http://www.washingtonpost.com/wp-dyn/content/article/2005/11/01/AR2005110101644.html.

Priest, Dana, and William M. Arkin. 2011. "'Top Secret America': A Look at the Military's Joint Special Operations Command." *Washington Post*, September 2. http://www.washingtonpost.com/world/national-security/top-secret-america-a-look-at-the-militarys-joint-special-operations-command/2011/09/02/gIQAOILIxJ_gallery.html#photo=1/.

Priest, Dana, and Robin Wright. 2005. "Cheney Fights for Detainee Policy." *Washington Post*, November 7, A01. http://www.washingtonpost.com/wp-dyn/content/article/2005/11/06/AR2005110601281.html.

Prior, Markus. 2005. "News vs. Entertainment: How Increasing Media Choice Widens Gaps in Political Knowledge and Turnout." *American Journal of Political Science* 49 (3): 577–592. http://www.princeton.edu/~mprior/Prior2005.News%20v%20Entertainment.AJPS.pdf.

PRNewswire. 2011. "U.S. Students Score Low Marks in the Nation's Report Card for Civics." May 4. http://www.prnewswire.com/news-releases/us-students-score-low-marks-in-the-nations-report-card-for-civics-121253899.html.

Project for Excellence in Journalism. 2009. *The New Washington Press Corps: A Special Report*. July 16. http://www.journalism.org/print/14678.

———. 2013. *The State of the News Media 2013: An Annual Report on American Journalism*. Washington, DC: Pew Research Center.

Putnam, Robert D. 1988. "Diplomacy and Domestic Politics: The Logic of Two-Level Games." *International Organization* 42 (3): 427–460.

———. 2000. *Bowling Alone: The Collapse and Revival of American Community*. New York: Simon & Schuster.

Puyvelde, Damien. 2012. "Intelligence Accountability and the Role of Public Interest Groups in the United States." *Intelligence and National Security* 28 (2): 139–158.

Randall, Stephen J. 2005. *United States Foreign Oil Policy since World War I: For Profits and Security*, 2nd ed. Montreal: McGill-Queen's University Press.

Rarick, Charles A. 2006. "Destroying a Country in Order to Save It: The Folly of Economic Sanctions against Myanmar." *Economic Affairs* 26 (2): 60–63.

Rasler, Karen A., and William R. Thompson. 2005. *Puzzles of the Democratic Peace: Theory, Geopolitics, and the Transformation of World Politics*. New York: Palgrave Macmillan.

Rasmussen Reports. 2015. *Obama Approval Index History*. Asbury Park, NJ: Rasmussen Reports.

Rathbone, Meredith, Peter Jeydel, and Amy Lentz. 2014. "Sanctions, Sanctions Everywhere: Forging a Path through Complex Transnational Sanctions Law." *Georgetown Journal of International Law* 2013: 1055–1126.

Reagan, Ronald. 1981. First Inaugural Address, January 20, Washington, D.C. http://www.presidency.ucsb.edu/ws/index.php?pid=43130.

———. 1983. Remarks at the Annual Convention of the National Association of Evangelicals in Orlando, Florida, March 8. http://www.reaganfoundation.org/pdf/Remarks_Annual_Convention_National_Association_Evangelicals_030883.pdf.

Redd, Steven B., and Alex Mintz. 2013. "Policy Perspectives on National Security and Foreign Policy Decision Making." *Policy Studies Journal* 41 (S1): S11–S37.

Reddy, Movindri. 2013. "Can Social Media Sustain a Revolution?" *E-International Relations*, August 15.

Reich, Simon, and Richard Ned Lebow. 2014. *Good-Bye Hegemony! Power and Influence in the Global System*. Princeton, NJ: Princeton University Press.

Reiter, Dan. 1995. "Exploding the Powder Keg Myth: Preemptive Wars Almost Never Happen." *International Security* 20 (fall): 5–34.

Renanah, Miles. 2013. "After War: Inside the U.S. Civilian Struggle to Build Peace." *Political Research Quarterly* 128 (3): 489–515.

Renshon, Jonathan, and Stanley A. Renshon. 2008. "The Theory and Practice of Foreign Policy Decision Making." *Political Psychology* 29 (4): 509–536.

Renshon, Stanley Allen. 1996. *High Hopes: The Clinton Presidency and the Politics of Ambition*. New York: New York University Press.

———. 2012. *Barack Obama and the Politics of Redemption*. New York: Routledge.

Renshon, Stanley Allen, and Deborah Welch Larson, eds. 2003. *Good Judgment in Foreign Policy: Theory and Application*. Lanham, MD: Rowman & Littlefield.

Rich, Andrew. 2004. *Think Tanks, Public Policy, and the Politics of Expertise*. New York: Cambridge University Press.

Richelson, Jeffrey T. 1985. *The U.S. Intelligence Community*. Cambridge, MA: Ballinger.

———. 2008. *The U.S. Intelligence Community*, 5th ed. Boulder, CO: Westview Press.

Ricks, Thomas E. 2006. *Fiasco: The American Military Adventure in Iraq*. New York: Penguin Press.

Rieff, David. 2003. "Blueprint for a Mess: How the Bush Administration's Prewar Planners Bungled Postwar Iraq." *New York Times Magazine*, November 2, 28–78.

Rielly, John E. 1999. "Americans and the World: A Survey at Century's End." *Foreign Policy* 114 (spring): 97–114.

———, ed. 2003. *American Public Opinion and U.S. Foreign Policy 2002*. Chicago: Chicago Council on Foreign Relations.

Risen, James. 2014. *Pay Any Price: Greed, Power, and Endless War*. Boston: Houghton Mifflin Harcourt.

Risen, James, and Eric Lichtblau. 2005. "Bush Lets U.S. Spy on Callers without Courts." *New York Times*, December 15.

Risse-Kappen, Thomas. 1996. "Collective Identity in a Democratic Community: The Case of NATO." In *The Culture of National Security: Norms and Identity* in *World Politics,* edited by Peter J. Katzenstein, 357–399. New York: Columbia University Press.

Rivers, Douglas, and Nancy L. Rose. 1985. "Passing the President's Program: Public Opinion and Presidential Influence on Congress." *American Journal of Political Science* 29 (2): 183–196.

Robinson, Donald L. 1996. "Presidential Prerogative and the Spirit of American Constitutionalism." In *The Constitution and the Conduct of American Foreign Policy,* edited by David Gray Adler and Larry Nelson George, 114–132. Lawrence: University Press of Kansas.

Robinson, Piers. 2001. "Operation Restore Hope and the Illusion of a News Media Driven Intervention." *Political Studies* 49 (5): 941–956.

Rockman, Bert A. 1981. "America's *Departments* of State: Irregular and Regular Syndromes of Policy Making." *American Political Science Review* 75 (4): 911–927.

———. 1997. "The Presidency and Bureaucratic Change after the Cold War." In *U.S. Foreign Policy after the Cold War,* edited by Randall B. Ripley and James M. Lindsay, 21–41. Pittsburgh: University of Pittsburgh Press.

Rodman, Peter W. 2009. *Presidential Command: Power, Leadership, and the Making of Foreign Policy from Richard Nixon to George W. Bush.* New York: Knopf.

Rohde, David W. 1994. "Partisanship, Leadership, and Congressional Assertiveness in Foreign and Defense Policy." In *The New Politics of American Foreign Policy,* edited by David E. Deese, 76–101. New York: St. Martin's Press.

Rohter, Larry. 1993. "The Supreme Court: Rights Groups Fault Decision, as Do Haitians." *New York Times,* June 22, A18.

Romano, Andrew. 2011. "How Dumb Are We?" *Newsweek,* March 20, 56–63. http://www.thedailybeast.com/newsweek/2011/03/20/how-dumb-are-we.html.

Roosevelt, Theodore. 1904. Fourth Annual Message to Congress, December 6, Washington, D.C. http://www.presidency.ucsb.edu/ws/index.php?pid=29545.

Rosati, Jerel A. 1987. *The Carter Administration's Quest for Global Community: Beliefs and Their Impact on Behavior.* Columbia: University of South Carolina Press.

Rosenau, James N. 1961. *Public Opinion and Foreign Policy: An Operational Formulation.* New York: Random House.

Rosenson, Beth A., Elizabeth A. Oldmixon, and Kenneth D. Wald. 2009. "U.S. Senators' Support for Israel Examined through Sponsorship/Cosponsorship Decisions, 1993–2002: The Influence of Elite and Constituent Factors." *Foreign Policy Analysis* 5 (1): 73–91.

Roskin, Michael. 1974. "From Pearl Harbor to Vietnam: Shifting Generational Paradigms and Foreign Policy." *Political Science Quarterly* 89 (3): 563–588.

Rosner, Jeremy D. 1995. *The New Tug-of-War: Congress, the Executive Branch, and National Security.* Washington, DC: Carnegie Endowment for International Peace.

Ross, Lial Radcliffe. 2013. "Muslim Interest Groups and Foreign Policy in the United States, Canada, and the United Kingdom." *Foreign Policy Analysis* 9 (3): 287–306.

Rossiter, Clinton, ed. 1999. *The Federalist Papers.* New York: Mentor.

Roth, Kenneth. 2004. "The Law of War in the War on Terror." *Foreign Affairs* 83 (January-February): 2–7.

Rothgeb, John M. Jr. 2001. *U.S. Trade Policy: Balancing Economic Dreams and Political Realities.* Washington, D.C.: CQ Press.

Rothkopf, David. 2012. *Power, Inc.: The Epic Rivalry between Big Business and Government—and the Reckoning That Lies Ahead.* New York: Farrar, Straus, & Giroux.

———. 2013. "Managing the Oval Office." *New York Times,* January 20, SR1, 6–7.

———. 2014a. *National Insecurity: American Leadership in an Age of Fear.* New York: Public Affairs.

———. 2014b. "National Insecurity: Can Obama's Foreign Policy Be Saved?" *Foreign Policy* (September-October): 44–51.

Rubenzer, Trevor. 2011. "Campaign Contributions and U.S. Foreign Policy Outcomes: An Analysis of Cuban American Interests." *American Journal of Political Science* 55 (1): 105–116.

Rubenzer, Trevor, and Steven B. Redd. 2010. "Ethnic Minority Groups and U.S. Foreign Policy: Examining Congressional Decision Making and Economic Sanctions." *International Studies Quarterly* 54 (3): 755–777.

Rubin, Barry M. 1985. *Secrets of State: The State Department and the Struggle over U.S. Foreign Policy.* New York: Oxford University Press.

Rudalevige, Andrew. 2005. *The New Imperial Presidency: Renewing Presidential Power after Watergate.* Ann Arbor: University of Michigan Press.

Rutherford, Kenneth R. 2000. "The Evolving Arms Control Agenda: Implications of the Role of NGOs in Banning Antipersonnel Landmines." *World Politics* 53 (1): 74–114.

Rutledge, Paul E., and Heather A. Larsen-Price. 2014. "The President as Agenda Setter-in-Chief: The Dynamics of Congressional and Presidential Agenda Setting." *Policy Studies Journal* 42 (3): 443–464.

Rytz, Henriette M. 2013. *Ethnic Interest Groups in U.S. Foreign Policy Making.* New York: Palgrave Macmillan.

Sagan, Carl. 1983/1984. "Nuclear War and Climatic Catastrophe: Some Policy Implications." *Foreign Affairs* 62 (2): 257–292.

Sagan, Scott D. 2011. "The Causes of Nuclear Weapons Proliferation." *Annual Review of Political Science* 17 (14): 225–241.

Salam, Reihan. 2012. "The Missing Middle in American Politics: How Moderate Republicans Became Extinct." *Foreign Affairs* 91 (March-April): 147–155.

Salant, Jonathan D. 2013. "Snowden Seen as Whistle-Blower by Majority in New Poll." *Bloomberg News,* July 10.

Salazar, Barbara. 2015. *Instances of Use of United States Armed Forces Abroad, 1798–2015.* Washington, DC: Congressional Research Service, January 15.

Sanger, David E. 2012. *Confront and Conceal: Obama's Secret Wars and Surprising Use of American Power.* New York: Crown.

———. 2013a. "In Cyberspace, New Cold War." *New York Times,* February 24, A1.

———. 2013b. "Pursuing Ambitious Global Goals, but Strategy Is More." *New York Times,* January 20, 10A.

Sanger, David E., and William J. Broad. 2009. "New Missile Shield Strategy Scales Back Reagan's Vision." *New York Times,* September 18, A1.

Savage, Charlie. 2012. "Nine Leak-Related Cases." *New York Times*, June 20, A14.

Savage, Charlie, William Glaberson, and Andrew W. Lehren. 2011. "Classified Files Offer New Insights into Detainees." *New York Times,* April 25, A1.

Schafer, Mark, and Scott Crichlow. 2002. "The Process-Outcome Connection in Foreign Policy Decision Making: A Quantitative Study Building on Groupthink." *International Studies Quarterly* 46 (1): 45–68.

———. 2010. *Groupthink versus High-Quality Decision Making in International Relations.* New York: Columbia University Press.

Schafer, Mark, and Stephen G. Walker, eds. 2006. *Beliefs and Leadership in World Politics: Methods and Applications of Operational Code Analysis.* New York: Palgrave Macmillan.

Scharnberg, Kirsten. 2007. "Governors Say War Has Gutted Guard: States Fear Lack of Disaster Response." *Chicago Tribune,* May 13, 1A.

Schattschneider, E. E. 1960. *The Semisovereign People: A Realist's View of Democracy in America.* New York: Holt, Rinehart & Winston.

Schell, Jonathan. 1983. *The Abolition.* New York: Knopf.

Schelling, Thomas C. 1960. *The Strategy of Conflict.* Cambridge, MA: Harvard University Press.

Schlesinger, Arthur M., Jr. 1973. *The Imperial Presidency.* Boston: Houghton Mifflin.

———. 1978. "Human Rights and the American Tradition." *Foreign Affairs* 57 (3): 503–526.

Schmidt, Michael S., and David E. Sanger. 2015. "Russian Hackers Read Unclassified Emails, Officials Say." *New York Times*, April 25.

Schmitt, Eric. 1999. "Defeat of a Treaty: The Overview; Senate Kills Test Ban Treaty in Crushing Loss for Clinton; Evokes Versailles Pact Defeat." *New York Times,* October 14, A1.

———. 2012. "Defense Department Plans New Intelligence Gathering Service." *New York Times*, April 24, A5.

Schmitt, Michael N., and Peter J. Richards. 2000. "Into Uncharted Waters: The International Criminal Court." *Naval War College Review* 53 (1): 93–136.

Schoultz, Lars. 2009. *That Infernal Little Cuban Republic: The United States and the Cuban Revolution.* Chapel Hill: University of North Carolina Press.

Schulzinger, Robert D. 1994. *American Diplomacy in the Twentieth Century,* 3rd ed. New York: Oxford University Press.

Schwartz, Herman M. 2009. *Subprime Nation: American Power, Global Capital, and the Housing Bubble.* Ithaca, NY: Cornell University Press.

Scott, James M. 1996. "Reagan's Doctrine? The Formulation of an American Foreign Policy Strategy." *Presidential Studies Quarterly* 26 (4): 1047–1061.

Scott, Robert E. 2012. "U.S. Trade Deficit Up in 2011; China Accounted for Three-fourths of Rise in Non-oil Goods Trade Deficit." Washington, DC: Economic Policy Institute, February 10.

Seib, Philip M. 1997. *Headline Diplomacy: How News Coverage Affects Foreign Policy.* Westport, CT: Praeger.

———. 2012. "Conclusion: AJE in the World." In *Al Jazeera English: Global News in a Changing World,* edited by Philip M. Seib, 187–197. New York: Palgrave Macmillan.

Seidman, Harold, and Robert S. Gilmour. 1986. *Politics, Position, and Power: From the Positive to the Regulatory State.* New York: Oxford University Press.

Sengupta, Somini. 2015. "60 Million People Fleeing Chaotic Lands, U.N. Says." *New York Times*, June 18.

Serle, Jack. 2015. "Almost 2,500 Now Killed by Covert US Drone Strikes since Obama Inauguration Six Years Ago." *Bureau of Investigative Journalism,* February 2.

Shane, Scott. 2005. "Behind Power, One Principle as Bush Pushes Prerogatives." *New York Times,* December 17, A1. http://www.nytimes.com/2005/12/17/politics/17legal.html.

———. 2015. "Drone Strikes Reveal Uncomfortable Truth: U.S. Is Often Unsure about Who Will Die." *New York Times,* April 23, A1.

Shane, Scott, and Andrew W. Lehren. 2010. "Leaked Cables Offer Raw Look at U.S. Diplomacy." *New York Times,* November 29, A1.

Shanker, Thom. 2011. "Warning against Wars like Iraq and Afghanistan." *New York Times,* February 25, A7.

Shannon, Vaughn P., and Jonathan W. Keller. 2007. "Leadership Style and International Norm Violation: The Case of the Iraq War." *Foreign Policy Analysis* 3 (1): 79–104.

Shapiro, Robert Y. 2011. "Public Opinion and American Democracy." *Public Opinion Quarterly* 75 (5): 982–1017.

Shapiro, Robert Y., and Lawrence R. Jacobs. 2002. "Public Opinion, Foreign Policy, and Democracy: How Presidents Use Public Opinion." In *Navigating Public Opinion: Polls, Policy, and the Future of American Democracy*, edited by Jeff Manza, Fay Lomax Cook, and Benjamin I. Page, 184–200. New York: Oxford University Press.

Shenkman, Rick. 2008. *Just How Stupid Are We? Facing the Truth about the American Voter.* New York: Basic Books.

Shishkin, Philip, and Joel Schectman. 2014. "West's 'Smart Sanctions' on Russia Can Still Cause Collateral Damage." *Wall Street Journal,* October 19.

Shoon, Murray. 2014. "Broadening the Debate about War: The Inclusion of Foreign Critics in Media Coverage and Its Potential Impact on U.S. Public Opinion." *Foreign Policy Analysis* 10 (4): 329–350.

Shrestha, Laura B., and Elayne J. Heisler. 2011. *The Changing Demographic Profile of the United States.* Washington, DC: Congressional Research Service, March 31.

Shuman, Michael H. 1992. "Dateline Main Street: Courts v. Local Foreign Policies." *Foreign Policy* 86 (spring): 158–177.

Sicker, Martin. 2002. *The Geopolitics of Security in the Americas: Hemispheric Denial from Monroe to Clinton.* Westport, CT: Greenwood.

Silverstein, Gordon. 1997. *Imbalance of Powers: Constitutional Interpretation and the Making of American Foreign Policy.* New York: Oxford University Press.

Simmons, P. J. 1998. "Learning to Live with NGOs." *Foreign Policy* 112 (fall): 82–96. http://carnegieendowment .org/1998/10/01/learning-to-live-with-ngos/4tt8/.

Simon, Herbert A. 1957. *Administrative Behavior*. New York: Macmillan.

Singer, Peter W. 2003. *Corporate Warriors: The Rise of the Privatized Military Industry*. Ithaca, NY: Cornell University Press.

———. 2009. *Wired for War: The Robotics Revolution and Conflict in the 21st Century*. New York: Penguin.

———. 2013. "The Global Swarm." *Foreign Policy*, March 11.

Singh, Robert. 2012. *Barack Obama's Post-American Foreign Policy*. New York: Bloomsbury.

SIPRI (Stockholm International Peace Research Institute). 2011. *SIPRI Yearbook 2011: Armaments, Disarmament and International Security*. Oxford: Oxford University Press.

———. 2015. *SIPRI Arms Transfers Database*. Stockholm: SIPRI.

Sjöstedt, Roxanna. 2007. "The Discursive Origins of a Doctrine: Norms, Identity, and Securitization under Harry S. Truman and George W. Bush." *Foreign Policy Analysis* 3 (3): 233–254.

Skidmore, David. 2005. "Understanding the Unilateralist Turn in U.S. Foreign Policy." *Foreign Policy Analysis* 1 (2): 207–228.

Slaughter, Anne-Marie. 2004. *A New World Order*. Princeton, NJ: Princeton University Press.

———. 2011. "Occupy Wall Street and the Arab Spring." *The Atlantic*, October 7.

Small Arms Survey. 2012. "Weapons and Markets." http://www.smallarms survey.org/weapons-and-markets .html.

Smeltz, Dina, and Craig Kafura. 2015. *Latinos and the Future of American Foreign Policy*. Chicago: Chicago Council on Global Affairs.

Smist, Frank J. 1990. *Congress Oversees the United States Intelligence Community, 1947–1989*. Knoxville: University of Tennessee Press.

Smith, Adam. 2000. *An Inquiry into the Nature and Causes of the Wealth of Nations*. First published in 1776. New York: Modern Library.

Smith, Rupert. 2005. *The Utility of Force: The Art of War in the Modern World*. London: Allen Lane.

Smith, Tony. 1994. *America's Mission: The United States and the Worldwide Struggle for Democracy in the Twentieth Century*. Princeton, NJ: Princeton University Press.

———. 2007. *A Pact with the Devil: Washington's Bid for World Supremacy and the Betrayal of the American Promise*. New York: Routledge.

Snow, Donald M. 2004. *National Security for a New Era: Globalization and Geopolitics*. New York: Pearson/ Longman.

Snyder, Glenn Herald. 1961. *Deterrence and Defense: Toward a Theory of National Security*. Princeton, NJ: Princeton University Press.

Snyder, Jack. 2003. "Imperial Temptations." *National Interest* 71 (Spring): 29–40.

———. 2004. "One World, Rival Theories." *Foreign Policy* 145 (November).

Snyder, Michael. 2014. "Who Owns the Media? The 6 Monolithic Corporations that Control Almost Everything We Watch, Hear, and Read." *D.C. Clothesline*. http://www.dcclothesline .com/2014/10/23/owns-media-6-monolithic-corporations-control-almost-everything-watch-hear-read/.

Snyder, Richard C., Henry W. Bruck, and Burton M. Sapin. 2002. *Foreign Policy Decision-Making: An Approach to the Study of International Politics*, 2nd rev. ed. New York: Palgrave Macmillan.

Sobel, Richard. 2001. *The Impact of Public Opinion on U.S. Foreign Policy since Vietnam: Constraining the Colossus*. New York: Oxford University Press.

Spykman, Nicholas J. 1942. *America's Strategy in World Politics: The United States and the Balance of Power*. New York: Harcourt, Brace.

Stanglin, Doug. 2014. "U.S. Eases Some Economic Sanctions on Iran." *USA Today*, January 20.

Stanton, John J. 2002. "Terror in Cyberspace: Terrorists Will Exploit and Widen the Gap between Governing Structures and the Public." *American Behavioral Scientist* 45 (6): 1017–1032.

Starrs, Sean. 2013. "American Economic Power Hasn't Declined—It Globalized.

Summoning the Data and Taking Globalization Seriously." *International Studies Quarterly* 57 (4): 817–830.

Statista. 2015. *Statista: The Statistics Portal*. New York. www.statista.com

Steele, Ian K. 1994. *Warpaths: Invasions of North America*. New York: Oxford University Press.

Steger, Manfred. 2010. *Globalization: A Brief Insight*. New York: Sterling.

Steil, Benn, and Robert E. Litan. 2006. *Financial Statecraft: The Role of Financial Markets in American Foreign Policy*. New Haven, CT: Yale University Press.

Stein, Jeff. 2006. "Can You Tell a Sunni from a Shiite?" *New York Times*, October 17, A21.

Stern, Jessica, and J. M. Berger. 2015. *ISIS: The State of Terror*. New York: HarperCollins.

Stiglitz, Joseph E. 2002. *Globalization and Its Discontents*. New York: Norton.

Stoessinger, John G. 1985. *Crusaders and Pragmatists: Movers of Modern American Foreign Policy*. New York: Norton.

Stone, Chad, Danilo Trisi, Arloc Sherman, and Brandon Debot. 2015. "A Guide to Statistics on Historical Trends in Income Inequality." Center on Budget and Policy Priorities, February 20.

Stout, David. 2006. "Bush, Signing Bill for Border Fence, Urges Wider Overhaul." *New York Times*, October 27, 16.

Strobel, Warren P. 1997. *Late-Breaking Foreign Policy: The News Media's Influence on Peace Operations*. Washington, DC: U.S. Institute of Peace Press.

Stroud, Natalie J. 2008. "Media Use and Political Predispositions: Revisiting the Concept of Selective Exposure." *Political Behavior* 30 (3): 341–366.

———. 2011. *Niche News: The Politics of News Choice*. New York: Oxford University Press.

Stuart, Douglas T. 2008. *Creating the National Security State: A History of the Law That Transformed America*. Princeton, NJ: Princeton University Press.

Sullivan, Andrew. 2008. "Why I Blog." *Atlantic Monthly* (November): 106–113.

Sutcliffe, Kathleen. 2006. "The Growing Nuclear Club." *Backgrounder*, November 17. New York: Council on

Foreign Relations. http://www.cfr.org/
publication/12050/#2.

Sweig, Julia E. 2006. *Friendly Fire: Losing
Friends and Making Enemies in the
Anti-American Century*. New York:
Public Affairs.

Takeyh, Ray, and Suzanne Maloney. 2011.
"The Self-Limiting Success of Iran
Sanctions." *International Affairs* 87 (6):
1297–1312.

Talbott, Strobe. 2014. "Think Tanks Should
Take Money from Foreign
Governments." *The New Republic*,
September 11.

Tarnoff, Curt. 2007. *Millennium Challenge
Account*. Washington, DC:
Congressional Research Service,
January 3.

Thies, Cameron G., and Marijke Breuning.
2012. "Integrating Foreign Policy
Analysis and International Relations
through Role Theory." *Foreign Policy
Analysis* 8 (1): 1–4.

Thrandardottir, Erla. 2015. "NGO Legitimacy:
Four Models." *Representation* 51 (1):
107–123.

Throntveit, Trygve. 2011. "The Fable of the
Fourteen Points: Woodrow Wilson and
National Self-Determination."
Diplomatic History 35 (3): 445–481.

Thumma, Scott, and Warren Bird. 2009. "Not
Who You Think They Are: A Profile of
the People Who Attend America's
Megachurches." Hartford Institute for
Religious Research. http://hirr.hartsem
.edu/megachurch/megachurch_
attender_report.htm.

Tice, Jim. 2015. "Active Army Drops Below
500,000 Soldiers." *Army Times*,
February 5.

Tocqueville, Alexis de. 1988. *Democracy in
America,* edited by J. P. Mayer.
Originally published in 1835. New York:
Perennial Library.

Todorov, Alexander, and Anesu N. Mandisodza.
2004. "Public Opinion on Foreign
Policy: The Multilateral Public That
Perceives Itself as Unilateral."
Public Opinion Quarterly 68 (fall):
323–348.

Tomei, Lizzy. 2012. "Anti-U.S. Protests and
the Challenges of '21st Century
Statecraft.'" *Global Post*, September 25.

Tomz, Michal R., and Jessica L. P. Weeks.
2013. "Public Opinion and the
Democratic Peace." *American Political
Science Review* 107 (November):
849–865.

Towell, Pat. 2012. "Defense: FY1012 Budget
Request, Authorization and
Appropriations." Washington, DC:
Congressional Research Service,
February 13.

Tower Commission. 1987. *The Tower
Commission Report*. New York:
Bantam/Times Books.

Trubowitz, Peter. 1992. "Sectionalism and
American Foreign Policy: The Political
Geography of Consensus and Conflict."
International Studies Quarterly 36 (2):
173–190.

Truman, David B. 1951. *The Governmental
Process: Political Interests and Public
Opinion*. New York: Knopf.

Truman, Harry S. 1947. Address on Foreign
Economic Policy at Baylor University,
Waco, TX, March 6. http://truman
library.org/publicpapers/index
.php?pid=2193&st=&st1=.

Trumbore, Peter F., and David A. Dulio. 2013.
"Running on Foreign Policy: Examining
the Role of Foreign Policy Issues in the
2000, 2002, and 2004 Congressional
Campaigns." *International Studies
Quarterly* 9 (July): 267–286.

Tuchman, Barbara W. 1962. *The Guns of
August*. New York: Macmillan.

Turchin, Peter. 2003. *Historical Dynamics:
Why States Rise and Fall*. Princeton,
NJ: Princeton University Press.

Turner, Frederick Jackson. 1920. *The
Frontier in American History*.
New York: Holt.

Turner, Susan. 2009. "Russia, China, and a
Multipolar World Order: The Danger in
the Undefined." *Asian Perspective* 33
(1): 159–184.

Twight, Charlotte. 1989. "Institutional
Underpinnings of Parochialism: The
Case of Military Base Closures." *Cato
Journal* 9 (1): 73–105.

Tyler, Patrick E. 1992. "U.S. Strategy Plan
Calls for Insuring No Rivals Develop."
New York Times, March 8, A1.

United Nations. 2015. *The Millennium
Development Goals Report, 2015*. New
York City: United Nations Department
of Public Information. http://www.un
.org/millenniumgoals/.

United Nations Economic and Social Council.
2006. *Situation of Detainees at
Guantánamo Bay*. Report No. E/

CN.4/2006/120. New York: United
Nations.

United Nations Refugee Agency. 2014.
*Concluding Observations on the Fourth
Periodic Report of the United States of
America*. International Covenant on
Civil and Political Rights, Human Rights
Committee. April 23.

———. 2015. *Worldwide Displacements Hit
All-Time High as War and Persecution
Increase*. New York: UN High
Commission of Refugees.

United States v. Curtiss-Wright, 299 U.S. 304
(1936).

U.S. Census Bureau. 2012. "The Foreign-
Born Population in the United States:
2010." http://www.census.gov/
prod/2012pubs/acs-19.pdf.

U.S. Commission on National Security/21st
Century. 2001. *Road Map for National
Security: Imperatives for Change*.
Phase III Report. http://www.nssg.gov/
Reports.html. http://govinfo.library.unt
.edu/nssg/PhaseIIIFR.pdf.

U.S. Congress. 2001. *Authorization for Use of
Military Force*. Pub. L. No. 107-40,
197th Cong., 2nd sess. (September 18).

U.S. Department of Commerce. 2015. *U.S.
Export Fact Sheet*. Washington, DC:
Commerce Department, International
Trade Administration. http://www.trade
.gov/press/press-releases/2015/
export-factsheet-060315.pdf.

U.S. Department of the Army. 2014. *U.S.
Army Field Manual: Counterinsurgency*.
FM 3-24, June. Washington, DC:
Department of the Army. http://www
.fas.org/irp/doddir/army/fm3-24
.pdf.

U.S. Department of Defense. 2008. *National
Defense Strategy*. June. http://www
.defense.gov/news/2008%20
National%20Defense%20Strategy.pdf.

———. 2010. *Nuclear Posture Review
Report*. April.

———. 2011. *Active Duty Military
Personnel Strength by Regional Area
and by Country*. Washington, DC:
Defense Manpower Data Center.
http://siadapp.dmdc.osd.mil/personnel/
MILITARY/history/hst1109.pdf.

———. 2012. *Annual Report to Congress:
Military and Security Developments
Involving the People's Republic of
China*. Washington, DC: Office of the
Secretary of Defense.

————. 2015. *About the Department of Defense.* http://www.defense.gov/about/.

U.S. Department of Homeland Security. 2015. *Budget in Brief, Fiscal Year 2016.* Washington, DC: http://www.dhs.gov/budget-performance.

U.S. Department of Labor. 2015. *Union Members—2014.* January 23. http://www.bls.gov/news.release/union2.nr0.htm.

U.S. Department of State. 2006. *Country Reports on Terrorism 2005.* Washington, DC: Office of the Coordinator for Counterterrorism. http://www.state.gov/documents/organization/65462.pdf.

————. 2010. "International Military Education and Training Account Summary." http://www.state.gov/t/pm/ppa/sat/c14562.htm.

————. 2012. *2011 Agency Financial Report.* Washington, DC: Department of State.

————. 2015a. *2014 Financial Report.* Washington, DC: http://www.state.gov/documents/organization/234331.pdf.

————. 2015b. *Country Reports on Terrorism 2014.* Washington, DC: U.S. Department of State, Bureau of Counterterrorism.

————. 2015c. *International Military Education and Training Account Summary.* Washington, DC: U.S. Department of State.

U.S. Department of the Treasury. 2015. *Sanctions Programs and Country Information.* Washington, DC: Office of Foreign Assets Control. http://www.treasury.gov/resource-center/sanctions/Programs/Pages/Programs.aspx.

U.S. Energy Information Administration. 2014. "Twelve States Produced 80% of U.S. Wind Power in 2013." April 15. http://www.eia.gov/todayinenergy/detail.cfm?id=15851.

U.S. Environmental Protection Agency. 2009. *Endangerment and Cause or Contribute Findings for Greenhouse Gases under Section 202(a) of the Clean Air Act.* December 7. http://www.epa.gov/climatechange/endangerment/.

U.S. Office of Management and Budget. 2002. *Budget of the United States Government: Historical Tables.* Washington, DC: Government Printing Office.

————. 2015. *Budget of the United States Government: Historical Tables.* Washington, DC: Government Printing Office.

U.S. Office of Science and Technology Policy. 2006. *U.S. National Space Policy.* October 6. http://www.fas.org/irp/offdocs/nspd/space.pdf.

U.S. Office of the Director of National Intelligence (UODNI). 2012. *2011 Report on Security Clearance Determinations.* Washington, DC: UODNI. http://www.fas.org/sgp/othergov/intel/clear-2011.pdf.

————. 2015. *The National Intelligence Strategy of the United States of America.* Washington, DC: Office of the Director of National Intelligence.

U.S. Senate. 1976. *Final Report of the Select Committee to Study Governmental Operations with Respect to Intelligence Activities of the United States.* 94th Cong., 2nd sess., April 26. Washington, DC: U.S. Government Printing Office.

————. 2004. Report of the *Select Committee on the U.S. Intelligence Community's Prewar Intelligence Assessments on Iraq Together with Additional Views.* 108th Cong., 2nd sess., July 7. Washington, DC: U.S. Government Printing Office.

————. 2014. *Committee Study of the Central Intelligence Agency's Detention and Interrogation Program,* Executive Summary. 113th Congress, 2nd sess., December 9.

U.S. Senate, Office of Sen. Tom Cotton (R-AR). 2015. Open Letter to the Leaders of the Islamic Republic of Iran, March 9. http://www.cotton.senate.gov/sites/default/files/150309%20Cotton%20Open%20Letter%20to%20Iranian%20Leaders.pdf.

U.S. Senate Permanent Subcommittee on Investigations. 2011. *Wall Street and the Financial Crisis: Anatomy of a Financial Collapse.* New York: Cosimo.

Uslaner, Eric M. 2002. "Cracks in the Armor? Interest Groups and Foreign Policy." In *Interest Group Politics,* 6th ed., edited by Allan J. Cigler and Burdett A. Loomis, 355–377. Washington, DC: CQ Press.

Van Alstyne, Richard W. 1965. *Empire and Independence: The International History of the American Revolution.* New York: Wiley.

Van Belle, Douglas A., and Steven W. Hook. 2000. "Greasing the Squeaky Wheel: News Media Coverage and U.S. Development Aid, 1977–1992." *International Interactions* 26 (3): 321–346.

Van Buren, Peter. 2011. *We Meant Well: How I Helped Lose the Battle for the Hearts and Minds of the Iraqi People.* New York: Metropolitan.

Vanderbush, Walt. 2009. "Exiles and the Marketing of U.S. Policy toward Cuba and Iraq." *Foreign Policy Analysis* 5 (3): 287–306.

Vargas, Jose Antonio. 2012. "Spring Awakening: How an Egyptian Revolution Began on Facebook." *New York Times Book Review,* February 19.

Vaughan, Adam. 2012. "Amazon Deforestation Falls Again." *The Guardian,* August 3.

Vertzberger, Yaacov. 1990. *The World in Their Minds: Information Processing, Cognition, and Perception in Foreign Policy Decisionmaking.* Stanford, CA: Stanford University Press.

Veseth, Michael. 2010. *Globaloney 2.0: The Crash of 2008 and the Future of Globalization.* Lanham, MD: Rowman & Littlefield.

von Clausewitz, Carl. 1982. *On War.* Originally published in 1832. New York: Penguin Books.

von Hippel, Karin. 2000. "Democracy by Force: A Renewed Commitment to Nation Building." *Washington Quarterly* 23 (1): 95–112.

Walcott, Charles E., and Karen M. Hult. 2004. "The Bush Staff and Cabinet System." In *Considering the Bush Presidency,* edited by Gary L. Gregg II and Mark J. Rozell, 52–68. New York: Oxford University Press.

Wald, Kenneth, and Clyde Wilcox. 2006. "Getting Religion: Has Political Science Rediscovered the Faith Factor?" *American Political Science Review* 100 (4): 523–529.

Walker, Stephen G. 1977. "The Interface between Beliefs and Behavior: Henry Kissinger's Operational Code and the

Vietnam War." *Journal of Conflict Resolution* 21 (1): 129–168.

———. 2011. "Quantum Politics and Operational Code Analysis: Theories and Methods." In *Rethinking Foreign Policy Analysis: States, Leaders, and the Microfoundations of Behavioral International Relations*, edited by Stephen G. Walker, Akan Malici, and Mark Schafer, 62–79. New York: Routledge.

Walker, Stephen G., Mark Schafer, and Michael D. Young. 2003. "William Jefferson Clinton: Beliefs and Integrative Complexity; Operational Code Beliefs and Object Appraisal." In *The Psychological Assessment of Political Leaders,* edited by Jerrold M. Post. Ann Arbor: University of Michigan Press.

Walt, Stephen M. 1987. *The Origin of Alliances*. Ithaca, NY: Cornell University Press.

———. 2005. *Taming American Power: The Global Response to U.S. Primacy*. New York: Norton.

———. 2014. "AIPAC Is the Only Explanation for America's Morally Bankrupt Israel Policy." *Huffington Post*, July 22.

Walton, C. Dale. 2007. *Geopolitics and the Great Powers in the Twenty-First Century: Multipolarity and the Revolution in Strategic Perspective*. New York: Routledge.

Waltz, Kenneth N. 1979. *Theory of International Politics*. Reading, MA: Addison-Wesley.

———. 1997. "Evaluating Theories." *American Political Science Review* 91 (4): 913–917.

Walzer, Michael. 1977. *Just and Unjust Wars: A Moral Argument with Historical Illustrations*. New York: Basic Books.

Wanta, Wayne, Guy Golan, and Cheolhan Lee. 2004. "Agenda Setting and International News: Media Influence on Public Perceptions of Foreign Nations." *Journalism & Mass Communication Quarterly* 81 (2): 364–377.

Wardlaw, Grant. 1989. *Political Terrorism: Theory, Tactics, and Counter-Measures,* 2nd rev. ed. New York: Cambridge University Press.

Warner, Carolyn M., and Stephen G. Walker. 2011. "Thinking about the Role of

Religion in Foreign Policy: A Framework for Analysis." *Foreign Policy Analysis* 7 (1): 113–135.

Washington, George. 1796. "The Address of General Washington to the People of the United States on His Declining of the Presidency of the United States" (Farewell Address). Originally published in *American Daily Advertiser*, September 19. http://avalon.law .yale.edu/18th_century/washing .asp.

Washington Times. 2009. "Editorial: Iran's Twitter Revolution." June 16. http:// www.washingtontimes.com/ news/2009/jun/16/irans-twitter-revolution/.

Wawro, Gregory J. 2000. *Legislative Entrepreneurship in the U.S. House of Representatives*. Ann Arbor: University of Michigan Press.

Weber, Max. 1946. *From Max Weber: Essays in Sociology*. Translated, edited, and with an introduction by H. H. Gerth and C. Wright Mills. New York: Oxford University Press.

Weber, Steven, and Bruce W. Jentleson. 2010. *The End of Arrogance: America in the Global Competition of Ideas*. Cambridge, MA: Harvard University Press.

Weed, Matthew C. 2015. "The War Powers Resolution: Concepts and Practice." Washington, DC: Congressional Research Service, April 3.

Weingast, Barry R. 1984. "The Congressional-Bureaucratic System: A Principal-Agent Perspective (with Applications to the SEC)." *Public Choice* 44 (1): 147–191.

Weissman, Stephen R. 1995. *A Culture of Deference: Congress's Failure of Leadership in Foreign Policy*. New York: Basic Books.

Weldes, Jutta. 1999. *Constructing National Interests: The United States and the Cuban Missile Crisis*. Minneapolis: University of Minnesota Press.

Wendt, Alexander. 1992. "Anarchy Is What States Make of It: The Social Construction of World Politics." *International Organization* 46 (2): 391–425.

Western, Jon, and Joshua S. Goldstein. 2011. "Humanitarian Intervention Comes of

Age." *Foreign Affairs* 90 (November-December): 48–59.

Whang, Taehee. 2011. "Playing to the Home Crowd? Symbolic Use of Economic Sanctions in the United States." *International Studies Quarterly* 55 (3): 787–801.

Wheeler, Winslow T., ed. 2008. *America's Defense Meltdown: Pentagon Reform for President Obama and the New Congress*. Washington, DC: Center for Defense Information.

White House. 2001a. "Detention, Treatment, and Trial of Certain Non-Citizens in the War against Terrorism." Press release, November 13, 2001. http:// georgewbush-whitehouse.archives .gov/news/releases/2001/11/ 20011113-27.html.

———. 2002. "The National Security Strategy of the United States of America." September. http://www .state.gov/documents/ organization/63562.pdf.

———. 2010. "National Security Strategy." May. https://www.whitehouse.gov/ sites/default/files/rss_viewer/national_ security_strategy.pdf.

Wiarda, Howard J. 2000. "Beyond the Pale: The Bureaucratic Politics of United States Policy in Mexico." *World Affairs* 162 (4): 174–190.

Widmaier, Wesley W. 2007. "Constructing Foreign Policy Crises: Interpretive Leadership in the Cold War and War on Terrorism." *International Studies Quarterly* 51 (4): 779–794.

Wildavsky, Aaron. 1966. "The Two Presidencies." *Trans-Action* 4 (December): 7–14.

Wildavsky, Aaron, and Naomi Caiden. 1997. *The New Politics of the Budgetary Process,* 3rd ed. New York: Longman.

Wight, Martin. (1946). *Power Politics: Looking Forward Pamphlet n.8* (1st ed.). London: Royal Institute of International Affairs.

Willett, Thomas D. 2001. "Understanding the IMF Debate." *Independent Review* 5 (4): 593–610.

Williams, Brock R. 2015. *African Growth and Opportunity Act (AGOA): Background and Reauthorization*. Washington, DC: Congressional Research Service, April 22.

Williams, William A. 1959. *The Tragedy of American Diplomacy*. Cleveland, OH: World.

Wilson, James Q. 1989. *Bureaucracy: What Government Agencies Do and Why They Do It*. New York: Basic Books.

Wilson, Joseph C. 2004. *The Politics of Truth: Inside the Lies That Led to War and Betrayed My Wife's CIA Identity; A Diplomat's Memoir*. New York: Carroll & Graf.

Winograd, Ben. 2012. *Q&A Guide to Arizona v. United States*. Washington, DC: American Immigration Council. http://www.immigrationpolicy.org/sites/default/files/docs/Winograd%20-%20Supreme%20Court%20Q&A%20Guide%20040212.pdf.

Witkover, Jules. 2014. *The American Vice President: From Irrelevance to Power*. Washington, DC: Smithsonian Books.

Wittes, Benjamin. 2008. *Law and the Long War: The Future of Justice in the Age of Terror*. New York: Penguin Press.

Wittkopf, Eugene R. 1990. *Faces of Internationalism: Public Opinion and U.S. Foreign Policy*. Durham, NC: Duke University Press.

Wittkopf, Eugene R., and James M. McCormick. 1998. "Congress, the President, and the End of the Cold War: Has Anything Changed?" *Journal of Conflict Resolution* 42 (4): 440–466.

Wohlforth, William C. 2012. "How Not to Evaluate Theories." *International Studies Quarterly* 56 (1): 219–222.

Wohlstetter, Albert. 1959. "The Delicate Balance of Terror." *Foreign Affairs* 37 (January): 211–234.

Wong, Wendy H. 2012. *Internal Affairs: How the Structure of NGOs Transforms Human Rights*. Ithaca, NY: Cornell University Press.

Wood, B. Dan. 2009. "Presidential Saber Rattling and the Economy." *American Journal of Political Science* 53 (3): 695–709.

Woods, Ngaire. 2006. *The Globalizers: The IMF, the World Bank, and Their Borrowers*. Ithaca, NY: Cornell University Press.

Woodward, Bob. 2002. *Bush at War*. New York: Simon & Schuster.

———. 2004. *Plan of Attack*. New York: Simon & Schuster.

———. 2006. *State of Denial*. New York: Simon & Schuster.

———. 2008. *The War Within: A Secret White House History, 2006–2008*. New York: Simon & Schuster.

———. 2010. *Obama's Wars*. New York: Simon & Schuster.

Woolf, Amy F. 2013. *U.S. Strategic Nuclear Forces: Background, Developments, and Issues*. Washington, DC: Congressional Research Service, October 22.

World Bank. 2012. *Annual Report*. Washington, DC: The World Bank. http://siteresources.worldbank.org/EXTANNREP2012/Resources/8784408-1346247445238/AnnualReport2012_En.pdf.

———. 2015. "Gross Domestic Product 2014, PPP." World Bank Database, http://databank.worldbank.org/data/download/GDP_PPP.pdf.

World Public Opinion. 2006. "World Public Says Iraq War Has Increased Global Terrorist Threat." Washington, DC: Program on International Policy Attitudes, December 1. http://www.globescan.com/news_archives/bbcpoll06-4.html.

———. 2008. "American Public Says Government Leaders Should Pay Attention to Polls." March 21. http://www.worldpublicopinion.org/pipa/articles/governance_bt/461.php.

Wong, Kristina. 2015. "Pentagon Announces Base Closures in Europe." *The Hill*, January 8.

World Trade Organization. 2006. "Country Profiles: United States." http://stat.wto.org/CountryProfiles/US_e.htm.

———. 2015. *International Trade Statistics 2014*. Geneva, Switzerland: World Trade Organization.

Wright, Benjamin Fletcher, ed. 2004. *The Federalist*. New York: Barnes & Noble.

Yankelovich, Daniel. 2005. "Poll Positions: What Americans Really Think about U.S. Foreign Policy." *Foreign Affairs* 84 (September-October): 2–16.

Yergin, Daniel. 1977. *Shattered Peace: The Origins of the Cold War and the National Security State*. New York: Houghton Mifflin.

———. 1991. *The Prize: The Epic Quest for Oil, Money, and Power*. New York: Simon & Schuster.

———. 2011. *The Quest: Energy, Security and the Remaking of the Modern World*. New York: Penguin Press.

Yetiv, Steven A. 2004. *Explaining Foreign Policy: U.S. Decision Making and the Persian Gulf War*. Baltimore: Johns Hopkins University Press.

———. 2011. *Explaining Foreign Policy: U.S. Decision Making in the Gulf Wars*, 2nd ed. Baltimore: Johns Hopkins University Press.

Yoo, John. 2006. *War by Other Means: An Insider's Account of the War on Terror*. New York: Atlantic Monthly Press.

Yost, David S. 1998. *NATO Transformed: The Alliance's New Roles in International Security*. Washington, DC: U.S. Institute of Peace Press.

Youngstown Sheet and Tube Co. v. Sawyer, 343 U.S. 579 (1952).

Zakaria, Fareed. 2008. *The Post-American World*. New York: Norton.

Zaller, John R. 1992. *The Nature and Origins of Mass Opinion*. New York: Cambridge University Press.

Zaller, John R., and Dennis Chiu. 1996. "Government's Little Helper: U.S. Press Coverage of Foreign Policy Crises, 1945–1991." *Political Communication* 13 (4): 385–405.

Zarate, Juan Carlos. 2013. *Treasury's War: The Unleashing of a New Era of Financial Warfare*. New York: Public Affairs.

Zegart, Amy B. 1999. *Flawed by Design: The Evolution of the CIA, JCS, and NSC*. Stanford, CA: Stanford University Press.

———. 2011. *Eyes on Spies: Congress and the United States Intelligence Community*. Washington, DC: Hoover Institution Press.

Zelizer, Julian E. 2010. *Arsenal of Democracy: The Politics of National Security—From World War II to the War on Terrorism*. New York: Basic Books.

Zenko, Micah. 2013. *Reforming U.S. Drone Strike Policies*. New York: Council on Foreign Relations, January.

Zinn, Howard. 1968. *Disobedience and Democracy: Nine Fallacies on Law and Order*. New York: Vintage.

Naval History and Heritage Command, 341
Naylor, S. D., 213
NBC News/Wall Street Journal Survey, 245
Neack, L., 84
Nelson, M., 115, 154, 324, 427
Nephew, R., 313
Netcraft, 283
Neustadt, R. E., 22, 113, 146
Newhouse, J., 316, 326
New York Times, 94, 312, 339
Nexon, D. H., 80
Nichols, T. M., 354
Nielsen Media Research, 268
Nincic, D. J., 251
Nincic, M., 233, 251
Nixon, R., 284
Noll, Roger G., 184
Norris, P., 275
Norris, R. S., 353
North Atlantic Treaty Organization, 57, 203
Nunn, S., 353
Nye, J. S., Jr., 7, 9, 80, 331, 335, 376

Obama, B., 33, 159, 260, 339
O'Connor, J., 98
Officer of the Director of National
    Intelligence, 208
O'Hanlon, M. E., 133, 174, 241, 361
Oldmixon, E. A., 161
Oleszek, W. J., 148, 162
Olson, M., 171
Onea, T. A., 67
Oneal, J. R., 80, 242
Onuf, N. G., 81
O'Reilly, K. P., 82
Organisation for Economic Co-operation and
    Development (OECD), 8, 24, 391, 393
Organization of American States, 57
Ornstein, N. J., 155
O'Rourke, R., 3
Orszag, P. R., 361
Ortman, J. M., 415
Osgood, R., 352
Ostrom, C. W., Jr., 238
O'Sullivan, J., 39
Overby, L. M., 161
Overseas Presence Advisory Panel, 176
Owen, J. M., IV, 361
Oxley, Z. M., 272

Page, B. I., 232, 233, 237, 251, 253, 254, 255
Paletz, D. L., 267
Panetta, L., 133, 343
Pape, R. A., 361
Passel, J. S., 415
Paterson, T. G., 426

Paulson, M., 307
Peake, J. S., 119, 147
Peffley, M., 233
Peksen, D., 398
Perlez, J., 387
Perry, W. J., 353
Peters, J. W., 303
Peterson, T. M., 395
Pew Global Attitudes Project, 246, 247
Pew Hispanic Center, 417
Pew Research Center, 214, 248, 249,
    282, 283
Pew Research Center for the People and the
    Press, 229, 238, 244, 252, 254, 260,
    261, 263, 265, 303
Pexton, P. B., 278
Pfiffner, J. P., 130, 132
Phillips, K. P., 20
Pierce, C. P., 235
Pifer, S., 355
Pillar, P. R., 211
Pious, R. M., 124
Pitkin, H. F., 228
Poitras, L., 278
Polsby, N. W., 128
Pomper, M., 162
Population Reference Bureau, 406, 407
Porter, G., 306
Posen, B. R., 8, 17, 241, 330, 365
Potter, P. B. K., 127
Powell, B., 284
Powell, J., 274
Prados, J., 207
Pratt, J., 39
Pressman, J., 367
Prestowitz, C. V., 34, 413
Priest, D., 134, 169, 213
Prior, M., 266
PRNewswire, 235
Project for Excellence in Journalism, 268, 269
Pu, X., 275
Public Broadcasting Service, 381
Putnam, R. D., 86, 306, 325, 383
Puyvelde, D., 296

Ramsay, C., 233, 247
Randall, S. J., 412
RAND Corporation, 376
Rarick, C. A., 398
Rasler, K. A., 423
Rasmussen Reports, 246
Rathbone, M., 394
Redd, S. B., 85, 89
Reddy, M., 288
Reifler, J., 227
Reiter, D., 349

Renanah, M., 186
Renshon, J., 105
Renshon, S. A., 101, 105, 132
Resnick, D., 282
Rice, C., 187
Rice, S., 159
Rich, A., 310
Richards, P. J., 424
Richelson, J. T., 122, 207
Ricks, T. E., 69, 288
Rieff, D., 102
Rielly, J. E., 18, 24, 241, 265
Ripsman, N. M., 398
Risen, J., 7, 277, 281, 430
Risse-Kappen, T., 82, 297
Rivers, D., 238
Robinson, D. L., 124
Robinson, L., 105
Robinson, P., 267
Rockman, B. A., 111, 186, 189
Rodman, P. W., 122, 130
Rohde, D. W., 147
Romano, A., 24, 236
Ronfeldt, D., 360, 363
Roosevelt, T., 42, 83
Rosati, J. A., 125
Rose, N. L., 238
Rose, R. P., 275
Rosenau, J. N., 228, 240
Rosenson, B. A., 161
Roskin, M., 251
Ross, A., 17, 241
Ross, L. R., 307
Rossiter, C., 114
Rothenberg, D., 118
Rothgeb, J., 388
Rothkopf, D., 111, 127, 130, 132, 321
Rothstein, D., 91
Rubenzer, T., 89, 307
Rubin, B. M., 190, 193
Rudalevige, A., 22
Rumsfeld, D., 362
Russett, B., 80
Rutherford, K. R., 296, 315
Rutledge, P. E., 124
Rytz, H. M., 306

Sabatini, R., 310
Sagan, C., 61, 352
Saideman, S. M., 201
Salam, R., 148
Salazar, B., 332
Sanders, L., 250
Sanger, D. E., 6, 126, 345, 355, 363, 396
Sapin, B. M., 78
Savage, C., 140, 277

Note: n in page locator refers to footnote number.

Center on Budget and Policy Priorities, 108, 222
Center on Congress, 179
Central Intelligence Agency (CIA), 222
   congressional oversight, 169–170
   covert operations, 212–213, 213n7
   creation of, 52
   domestic spying, 280–281
   interrogation techniques, 140, 141, 169–170
   organizational culture, 186
   and war on terrorism, 210, 215
Centre for Foreign Policy Studies, 108
Cheney, Dick, 69, 134, 169, 173, 230
Chicago Council on Global Affairs, 257
China
   cyberattacks, 345
   economic strength, 377–378, 387
   foreign policies, 7
   human rights violations, 147
   Russia and, 71–72
   Soviet Union and, 55
   state capitalism, 375
   as superpower, 3
   U.S. relations, 59–60, 376 (box)
Chinese Communist Party, 375
Church, Frank, 213
Church Committee, 213
Churchill, Winston, 49
Civil disobedience, 318–319
Civil Rights Act of 1964, 153n4
Civil society, influence on foreign policy,
   88–92, 89 (figure), 91 (figure)
Clean Alternative Energy Act, 98–99
Clientitis, 193
Climate change, 5, 67, 309, 408–412, 409
   (table), 410 (figure)
Clinton, Bill, 18, 19, 63, 101 (table), 121, 167,
   218, 230
Clinton, Hillary, 22, 93n5, 177, 190, 193, 194
   (table), 276, 284
Clinton administration
   congressional relations, 151, 154, 167
   economic policies, 385
   foreign policy of, 17–18, 63–64, 128
   global power strategies, 11
   military interventions, 167
   public opinions, 241–242
Clinton Doctrine, 125 (table)
CNN, 292
CNN effect, 267
CNN Special Coverage and Hot Topics, 74
Codetermination, 114
Coercive diplomacy, 347–349
Cognitive psychology, 101
Cold War, 3
   alliances during, 56, 57 (map)
   economy, global, 53–54, 392–393

European divisions, 50 (map)
   power balances, 49 (figure), 54–56,
      57 (map)
   public opinion, 238–241
   U.S. executive and legislative relations,
      151–153
   U.S. foreign policy strategies, 20, 48
      (table), 49
Cold War Museum, 74–75
Collective security, 44–45
Communism, 49, 55, 374
Comparative advantage, 388
Comprehensive Test Ban Treaty, 67, 352
Congress, U.S.
   Benghazi terrorist attack, handling of,
      159 (box)
   during Bush (G. W.) administration,
      154–155
   characteristics of legislative politics,
      148–149
   during Clinton administration, 151, 154
   during Cold War era, 151–153
   congressional activism, 146, 147
   congressional oversight hearings,
      165 (table)
   constraints on power, 157–158
   defense spending, control of, 171–177,
      173, 176 (figure)
   economic regulatory powers, 216
   foreign policy committees, 162–165, 163
      (figure), 165 (table)
   Iran nuclear agreement and, 156 (box)
   legislative process, 158–160
   military actions, role in, 168 (table)
   during new world order, 153–154
   during Obama administration, 155–157
   polarization, 148, 153
   public discontent, 148, 149 (figure)
   voting behavior of, 160–162, 161 (figure)
   War Powers Resolution of 1973, 166–169
   See also Legislative branch
Congressional activism, 146, 147, 162
Congressional Budget Office, 180
Congressional diplomacy, 151
Congressional dominance model of decision
   making, 96–97
Congressional Research Service Reports and
   Issue Briefs, 109, 188
Congress.org, 180
Constitution. *See* U.S. Constitution
Construction of reality, 82
Conyers v Reagan, 136 (table)
Cooperative internationalism, 232
Core Documents of U.S. Democracy, 75
Corporations. *See* Multinational corporations
Council of Economic Advisers, 217 (table)

Council on Foreign Relations, 28, 310–311
Counterinsurgency, 362
Counterintelligence, 207
Counterterrorism, 361–366
Covert operations, 207
CQ Press Guide to U.S. Foreign Policy
   (McMahon & Zeiler), 31n1
CQPolitics.com, 180
Crockett v. Reagan, 136 (table), 137
Crosby v. National Foreign Trade Council,
   136 (table)
CRS Reports, 222
Cruz, Ted, 303
Cuba, 56, 58, 307, 397
Cuban missile crisis, 56–57, 96, 106,
   106 (photo)
Cultural values
   national style and, 19
   power and, 10
Curtiss-Wright Export Corporation, U.S. v.,
   135, 135n8
Cyberwarfare, 4, 343, 345

The Daily Dish, 285
Decision-making process
   belief systems, influences from, 100–103
   bureaucratic politics and, 93–94
   congressional dominance model, 96–97
   during crisis, 105–106
   groupthink, 104–105
   issue networks, 91–93, 92 (figure)
   personality factors, 103–104
   presidential control model, 96
   rational choice, 86–87, 87 (table)
   standard operating procedures, 94
   See also Policy-making process
Defense contractors, 321–323, 322 (table)
Defense Reorganization Act of 1986, 198
Defense spending
   federal budget, 172–175, 173 (figure),
     176 (figure)
   global, 10 (figure), 331 (table)
   military contractors, 321–323, 322 (table)
Dellums v. Bush, 136 (table)
Democracy
   and human rights, 421–430
   impact of civil society, 88–92, 89 (figure),
     226–228
   as new world order, 63, 153–154
   political divisions, challenges of, 21
   political representation models, 228–230
   threats to, 429–430
   Tocqueville on, 23 (box)
Democracy Arsenal, 285
Democracy in America (Tocqueville), 371
Democratic peace, 80

HIV/AIDS aid programs, 302
Ho Chi Minh, 58
Hobbes, Thomas, 83 (box)
Holbrooke, Richard, 120, 194 (table)
Homeland Security Council, 197
Hoover Institution, 28
House Committee on Foreign Affairs, 162–165
House of Representatives, U.S. *See* Congress, U.S.
Hull, Cordell, 375
Human intelligence (HUMINT), 207
Human rights
    Abu Ghraib abuses, 14
    democracy and, 421–430
    public interest groups, 308–309
    slavery, 13
Hussein, Saddam, 6, 68–69, 34
Hyperpluralism, 297

Idea brokers, 310–312
Identity. *See* Group identity
Idiot America (Pierce), 235
Illegal Immigration Reform and Immigrant Responsibility Act, 417–418
Image Intelligence (IMINT), 207
Immigration policies, 415–418, 415 (photo), 416 (box), 417 (table)
Imperial presidency, 22
Infotainment, 272
Inhofe, Jim, 411
The Innocence of Muslims (film), 259, 277
INS v. Chadha, 136 (table)
Institute for Foreign Policy Analysis, 28
Institute for Global Communications, 433
Intelligence
    counterintelligence activities, 207
    covert operations, 207, 212–213, 213n7
    importance of, 205–206
    intelligence cycle, 207
    intelligence failures and scandals, 209–211, 212 (table)
    organization of intelligence agencies, 207, 208 (figure), 209
    types of, 206–207
    See also Central Intelligence Agency (CIA)
Intelligence gap, 206
Intelligence Oversight Act of 1980, 152
Intergovernmental organizations, global governance and, 80
Intermediate-Range Nuclear Forces Treaty, 194 (table)
International Action Center, 109
International Affairs Resources, 434
International Bank for Reconstruction and Development, 219

International Campaign to Ban Landmines, 296
International Development Association, 219
International Institute for Strategic Studies, 368
International Monetary Fund (IMF), 53, 216, 219–220, 223, 380, 400
International Panel on Climate Change (IPCC), 408
International political economy, 373–375
International relations
    liberal theory, 80–81, 84 (table), 230
    neoliberal institutionalism, 81
    social constructivism theory, 81–82, 84 (table)
    structural realism, theory of, 79–80, 84 (table), 230
International Religious Freedom Act of 1998, 302
International Studies Association, 109
International trade, 8
    congressional policies, 147, 388–389
    domestic trade politics, 387–389
    early history of U.S. exports, 34–35, 384–385
    global trade politics, 384–387
    with Japan, 39
    mercantilism, 374, 375
    top ten world traders, 378 (table)
International Trade Administration, 400
International trust, 232
Internet. *See* Digital technology; Social media
Interrogation techniques, 138, 139, 140, 141, 169–170
Inter-University Consortium for Political and Social Research, 257
Iran
    Iran-Contra scandal, 60, 96
    1979 revolution, 14, 60
    nuclear program, regulation of, 78, 145, 156–157, 156 (box), 313 (box), 396
    U.S. sanctions, 395–396
Iraq
    invasion of Kuwait, 64
    ISIS in, 2
    media coverage of war, 267–268, 268 (table)
    Operation Iraqi Freedom, 68–70
Iron triangle, 90, 91 (figure), 173, 321–323, 322 (table)
ISIS. *See* Islamic State of Iraq and Syria (ISIS)
Islamic State of Iraq and Syria (ISIS), 169, 356 (photo)
    emergence of, 71, 356
    growth of, 358
    in Iraq, 2
    territories under control of, 359 (map)

Ismay, Lord Hastings, 201
Israel, 145, 273 (figure)
Issue networks, 91–93, 92 (figure)

Jackson-Vanik Amendment, 152, 152n3
Japan
    as trade partner, 39
    in World War II, 46
Jasmine Revolution, 288
Jay, John, 114n2
Jefferson, Thomas, 34, 37, 38 (box), 43, 262, 388
Jihadists, 358
Jinping, Xi, 3, 71–72, 412
Johnson, Lyndon B., 58
Joint Chiefs of Staff, 198, 201
Journalism. *See* News media
Judicial interventions, 134–140, 136 (table)
Just How Stupid Are We? (Shenkman), 235
Just-war doctrine, 346

Kant, Immanuel, 80, 83, 230
Karzai, Hamid, 68
Kellogg-Briand Pact, 45
Kennan, George, 20, 49, 51 (box)
Kennedy, Carolyn, 284
Kennedy, John, 56, 106 (photo), 152
Kennedy administration, Cuban missile crisis and, 56–57, 96, 106, 348
Kent State University, 299–300
Kerry, John, 110 (photo), 190, 284
Keystone XL oil pipeline, 157, 316, 316n9
Khrushchev, Nikita, 348
Kissinger, Henry, 59, 60, 194 (table)
Koch, David, 316
Koch, John, 316
Korean War, 55–56, 151
Kosovo, 18, 67, 128, 167, 230, 241
Kroft, Steve, 33
Kyoto Protocol on Climate Change, 67, 410

Labor unions, 323–325
Lake, Anthony, 64
Land mines, 296
Latin America, U.S. territorial expansions in, 39, 41–42
League of Nations, 44–45
Legislative branch
    congressional oversight measures, 152–153
    executive branch relations with, 22, 146–147, 149–157, 166–169, 171, 177–178
    legislative process, 158–160
    political characteristics, 148–149
    See also Congress, U.S.

Lend-lease program, 46
Lew, Jacob J., 394
Libby, Lewis "Scooter," 134n7
Liberal internationalism, 60
Liberal theory, 80–81, 83 (box), 84 (table)
Library of Congress, 75
Library of Congress's THOMAS, 180
Libya, 340, 346n4
Lincoln, Abraham, 223
Living-room war, 266–267
Livingston Group, 316
Lobbying, 316
Locke, John, 83, 230
Louisiana Purchase, 37–38
Lowry v. Reagan, 136 (table), 137

Maddow, Rachel, 258 (photo)
Madison, James, 34, 114, 171
Management styles
    collegial, 131 (figure), 132
    competitive, 130, 131 (figure), 132
    formalistic, 130, 131 (figure)
Manhattan Project, 47
Manifest destiny, 39
Manning, Bradley, 278
Mao Zedong, 55, 59–60
Marbury v. Madison, 135
Marcos, Ferdinand, 14
Marshal, John, 135
Marshall, George, 53
Marshall Plan, 53–54, 151
McCain, John, 144 (photo), 159, 167 (photo)
McKinley, William, 41
Media. *See* News media
Media Research Center, 292
Mercantilism, 374, 375
Merchants of Death (Engelbrecht &
        Hanighen), 45n5
Mexico, 417–418
Mexico City policy, 407
Militant internationalism, 232
Military Commissions Act of 2006, 139
Military contractors, 317–318, 321–323,
        322 (table)
Military force, 345–350
Military spending. *See* Defense spending
Military strategy and tactics, 339–345
Military strength
    geographical distribution of active-duty,
        335 (table)
    national security and, 330–332, 331
        (table), 333 (figure)
    nuclear weapons, 350–354, 353 (table)
    technology and, 4
    U.S. commands, 8–9, 332
    use of force justifications, 345–350

Military-industrial complex, 90, 91 (figure),
        197–198, 321–323, 322 (table),
        324 (box)
Millennium Challenge Corporation, 394
Millennium Development Goals, 390
Miller Center of Public Affairs, 142
Missile defense, 354
Mission creep, 347
Missouri v. Holland, 136 (table)
Mobutu Sese Seko, 14
Mohammad, Khalid Sheikh, 170
Monkey Cage, 285
Monroe, James, 38–39
Monroe Doctrine, 4n1, 38–39, 82
Moore, Michael, 301, 301 (photo)
Morsi, Mohamed, 70–71
MoveOn, 327
Mubarak, Hosni, 70
Mujahidin, 68n12
Mullen, Mike, 201
Multilateral cooperation, 63, 352
Multinational corporations, 319–325,
        320 (table)
Multipolar world order, 8
Murrah Federal Building bombing, 360
Mutual assured destruction (MAD), 61

Nation building, 426
National Center for Policy Analysis, 109
National Center for Public Policy Research, 109
National Council of Churches, 327
National Counterterrorism Center, 215
National Defense Strategy (U.S. DoD), 332
National Economic Council, 217 (table), 218
National interests, 79
National Military Establishment. *See*
        Department of Defense
National Opinion Research Center, 257
National Public Radio (NPR), 266
National security
    economic security, 329
    environmental security, 330
    grand strategy, elements of, 333–339
    military security, 329, 330–332, 331
        (table), 333 (figure), 337 (box),
        366–367
    past strategies of, 338–339
    political security, 329
    societal security, 330
    See also Economic policies; Global
        commons; Military strength
National Security Act of 1947, 52, 151, 184,
        195, 206
National security adviser, 195
National Security Agency, 211
    PRISM program, 280–281, 280 (figure)

Snowden leaks and, 278 (box), 279–281
    WikiLeaks scandal, 18, 278–279
National Security Council, 22, 182 (photo),
        217 (table)
    creation of, 52, 128
    functions of, 111, 195–196
    organization of, 196–197, 196 (table)
National style, 19
Native Americans
    displacement of, 37
    treatment of, 13–14
Natural disasters, 268
Nelson-Bingham Amendment, 152
Neoliberal institutionalism, 81
Netanyahu, Benjamin, 145
Netcraft, 292
New world order, 62–64, 153–154
New York Times, 278–279
*New York Times v. United States (Pentagon
        Papers),* 136 (table), 137
News media
    cable television news, 267
    domestic issues, focus on, 261, 262 (figure)
    embedded journalism, 275
    foreign policy coverage, characteristics of,
        269–272
    foreign-based sources, 288–290,
        289 (table)
    functions of, 262–264
    future of, 290–291
    government controls, 273–277
    interactive technology, 268
    international news coverage, 24–25, 261,
        261n2, 262 (figure), 265–273
    media outlets, 268–269
    press leaks, 277–281
    propaganda, 274
    public attention, 261, 266, 261 (table)
    public diplomacy, 276–277
    roles in foreign policy process, 263–264
    selective exposure, 265
    soft news, 272–273
    sources of, 271 (figure)
    spin control, 273–274
    war coverage, 266, 267
    See also Social media
Nicaragua, 14, 60
Nixon, Richard M., 58, 59, 60, 121
Nixon Doctrine, 125 (table)
Nongovernmental organizations (NGOs)
    civil disobedience, 318–319
    consciousness raising, 314–315
    environmental protections, 308–309
    ethnic groups, 207n4, 306–308
    group activism, 297–298
    human rights, 308

international development, 309–310
multinational corporations, 319–325,
320 (table)
policy and program implementation,
316–318
policy influences, 89–90
political pressure and lobbying, 315–316
private foundations, 314
private interest groups, 308–310
religious and ethnic groups, 306–308
strengths, 305
think tanks, 310–312, 311 (figure), 312
(table), 313 (box)
weaknesses, 304–305
North American Free Trade Agreement
(NAFTA), 133, 325, 385
North Atlantic Treaty Organization (NATO), 53,
201–202, 203 (map), 369
North Korea, 350, 355, 418
Nuclear Non-Proliferation Treaty, 419
Nuclear Posture Review (U.S. DoD), 419
Nuclear weapons
deterrence, 350–354, 351 (map)
Iran's nuclear program, 78
mutual assured destruction (MAD), 61, 352
proliferation of, 418–421
U.S. arsenal of, 353 (table)
in World War II, 47
Nunn-Lugar Cooperate Threat Reduction
Program, 134n6

Obama, Barack, 33 (box), 70, 78, 110 (photo),
120, 121, 177, 182 (photo), 229, 260,
272, 353, 358, 363 (photo)
Obama administration
congressional relations, 155–157
drone warfare, 214 (box), 215
environmental regulations of, 412,
413–414
foreign policy of, 6, 128, 133 (box)
global power strategies, 11
Guantánamo Bay detention facility,
handling of, 140, 140n10
on Iran nuclear program, 78, 145,
156–157, 313 (box)
ISIS, handling of, 71, 358, 360
Middle East uprisings, 70–71
nonproliferation goals, 420
public diplomacy during, 276
public opinion, 244–246, 245 (table)
U.S. economy during, 6, 380–383
and war in Afghanistan, 70
war powers, 168–169
Obama Doctrine, 6, 125 (table)
Occupy Wall Street movement, 303–304
O'Connor Sandra Day, 138, 235

Office of Foreign Assets Control, 394
Office of International Information
Programs, 276
Office of Management and Budget, 217 (table)
Office of the United States Trade
Representative, 223, 400
Office of the U.S. Trade Representative,
217 (table)
Omnibus Trade and Competitiveness Act of
1988, 388
ONE, 327
Open Door policy, 41
Operation Desert Storm, 64
Operation Iraqi Freedom, 68–70, 340
O'Reilly, Bill, 258
Organisation for Economic Co-operation and
Development, 401
Organization for European Economic
Coorperation (OEEC), 54
Organization of the Petroleum Exporting
Countries (OPEC), 385, 412
Organizational behaviors, 95–97, 186, 188
Organizational culture, 94, 186, 188
Organizational process in decision making, 94

Pakistan, 397
Panama Canal, 30 (photo)
Path dependency, 184–185
Patton Boggs, 316
Paul, Rand, 303
PBS, 75
Pearl Harbor, 206
Pentagon, 186, 188, 198, 201, 209
Pentagon Papers, 136 (table), 137
Perestroika, 61
Persian Gulf War, 340, 347
Personality dimensions, 103–104
Peterson Institute for International
Economics, 400
Pew Research Center for the People and the
Press, 257
Pew Research Center's Journalism Project, 292
Plame, Valerie, 277
Podesta Group, 316
Policy Section, American Political Science
Association, 109
Policy-making process
civilian influences on, 88–90
within executive branch, 22
iron triangles and, 90, 91 (figure)
levels of analysis, 85–86, 86 (table)
lobbying efforts, 23–24
politics and, 20–21, 93–94, 95 (box)
public opinion, role of, 24
rational choice and, 86–87, 87 (table)
See also Decision-making process

Political action committees (PACs), 315–316
Political economy, 373–375
Political process
bureaucratic politics, 93–94, 95 (box)
domestic politics, 84–88
legislative, 148–149
policy-making process and, 20–21, 93–94,
95 (box)
power politics, 71–72
Political psychology, 99
belief systems, 100–101, 101 (table)
cognitive processes, 101–103
crisis decision making, 105–106
groupthink, 104–105
personality factors, 103–104
Political representation
delegate model, 228–230
trustee model, 228–230
Polk, James K., 39
Polling Report, 257
Population growth, 406–408, 407 (figure)
POTUS website, 142
Powell, Colin, 69, 76 (photo), 96, 193, 347
Powell, Jody, 274
Powell doctrine, 347
Power
balances of, 8, 12–13, 48–49, 49 (figure),
62 (figure), 79–80
political, 21
soft balancing, 80
See also World power
Power politics, 71–72
Pravda, 292
Preemptive war, 349–350
President, U.S.
appointment process, 120
chain of command, 126–127
congressional obstacles, 112–113
doctrines and agendas, 124–127,
125 (table)
executive agreements, 112–113,
118–120, 119 (figure)
Executive Office of the President,
organization of, 128–134, 129
(figure), 131 (figure)
foreign policy sources and influences, 113,
113 (figure)
formal powers in foreign policy, 115–121
informal powers, 121–122
limitations of power, 122–123
management styles, 130–132, 131
(figure)
national security adviser relations,
195–196
personality dimensions, 103–104
stewardship theory, 114–115, 115 (box)

World Summit on Sustainable Development, 309
World Trade Organization, 15, 217, 220, 298,
    385, 387, 401
World War I, 42–45
World War II, 46–47

Xi Jinping, 3, 71, 72, 412

Yeltsin, Boris, 61
Yom Kippur War, 194 (table)
Yoo, John, 22

Youngstown Sheet and Tube Co. v. Sawyer,
    21, 123, 136 (table), 137
Yugoslavia, 67

Zone of twilight, 123